Stockholm

timeout.com/stockholm

Penguin Books

PENGUIN BOOKS

Published by the Penguin Group
Penguin Books Ltd, 80 Strand, London WC2R ORL, England
Penguin Books USA Inc., 375 Hudson Street, New York, New York 10014, USA
Penguin Books Australia Ltd, 250 Camberwell Road, Camberwell, Victoria 3124, Australia
Penguin Books Canada Ltd, 10 Alcorn Avenue, Toronto, Ontario, Canada M4V 3B2
Penguin Books (NZ) Ltd, cnr Rosedale and Airborne Roads, Albany, Auckland, New Zealand

Penguin Books Ltd, Registered Offices: Harmondsworth, Middlesex, England

First published 2003
10 9 8 7 6 5 4 3 2 1

Colour reprographics by Icon, Crowne House, 56-58 Southwark Street, London SE1 1UN
Printed and bound by Cayfosa-Quebecor, Ctra. de Caldes, Km 3, 08 130 Sta. Perpètua de Mogoda, Barcelona, Spain

Edited and designed by
Time Out Guides Limited
Universal House
251 Tottenham Court Road
London W1T 7AB
Tel + 44 (0)20 7813 3000
Fax + 44 (0)20 7813 6001
Email guides@timeout.com
www.timeout.com

Editorial
Editor Cath Phillips
Deputy Editor Claudia Martin
Consultant Editor Chad Henderson
Listings Editors Victoria Hesselius, Jenny Egeland
Proofreader Tamsin Shelton
Indexer Selena Cox

Editorial Director Peter Fiennes
Series Editor Ruth Jarvis
Deputy Series Editor Jonathan Cox
Guides Co-ordinator Anna Norman

Design
Group Art Director John Oakey
Art Director Mandy Martin
Art Editor Scott Moore
Senior Designer Lucy Grant
Designer Sarah Edwards
Picture Editor Kerri Littlefield
Deputy Picture Editor Kit Burnet
Picture Desk Trainee Bella Wood
Scanning & Imaging Dan Conway
Ad make-up Glen Impey

Advertising
Group Commercial Director Lesley Gill
Sales Director Mark Phillips
Advertisement Sales (Stockholm) AdCityMedia
International Sales Co-ordinator Ross Canadé
Advertising Assistant Sabrina Ancilleri

Administration
Chairman Tony Elliott
Chief Operating Officer Kevin Ellis
Managing Director Mike Hardwick
Chief Financial Officer Richard Waterlow
Group Marketing Director Christine Cort
Marketing Manager Mandy Martinez
US Publicity & Marketing Associate Rosella Albanese
Group General Manager Nichola Coulthard
Guides Production Director Mark Lamond
Production Controller Samantha Furniss
Accountant Sarah Bostock

Features in this guide were written and researched by:
Introduction Cath Phillips, Claudia Martin. **History** Lars Ericson, Tanis Bestland Malminen. **Stockholm Today** Chad Henderson. **Architecture** Tanis Bestland Malminen. **Design** Tanis Bestland Malminen. **Accommodation** Amy Brown, Cath Phillips. **Sightseeing** Chad Henderson (*Introduction* Cath Phillips; *The Stockholm Bloodbath* Lars Ericson; *Walk 1: Gamla Stan* Maria Lindberg Howard; *Breaking the mould* Frida Cornell; *Super Swedes: August Strindberg* Claudia Martin; *Where to swim outdoors* Tobias Nielsén; *Walk 2: The heights of Söder* Maria Lindberg Howard). **Restaurants** Jonas Malmborg, Petter Oloffson. **Bars** Jonas Leijonhufvud. **Cafés** Robert Börjesson. **Shops & Services** Ulrika K Engström (*Fashion & Fashion accessories* Kicki Norman). **Festivals & Events** Amy Brown. **Children** Lisa Del Papa. **Clubs** Kristoffer Poppius. **Film** Anna Boreson. **Galleries** Frida Cornell (*Street art* Felix Mannheimer). **Gay & Lesbian** Kristoffer Poppius. **Music** *Rock, Pop & Jazz* Kristoffer Poppius. *Classical Music & Opera* Martin Olofsson. **Sport & Fitness** Tobias Nielsén. **Theatre & Dance** Danjel Andersson. **Trips Out of Town** Chad Henderson (*Introduction, Utö* Cath Phillips; *The big chill* Claudia Martin). **Directory** Victoria Hesselius (*Vocabulary, Further Reference* Claudia Martin).

The Editor would like to thank:
Sylvie Kjellin at Stockholm Information Service, Ann-Charlotte Carlsson at Swedish Travel & Tourism Council, Anders Malm from Utö Värdshus, Lotta Wästberg from Berns Hotel, Vibeke Linse from Birger Jarl, Åsa Karlsson from Nordic Hotels, Mats Bengtsson from Victory Hotel, Jacob von Arndt from Hotell Tre Små Rum, Sunniva Fallan Röd from Lydmar Hotel, Ola Nyman from Långholmen Hotel, Maria Hessedahl from Hotel J, Viveca Carlsson, Dag Hermelin, Lisa Förare Winbladh, Johan Croneman, Daniel Sparr, Viggo Cavling, Marika Jarislowsky, Ingrid Larsson, Andy White, Gareth Evans, Guy Dimond, Sarah Guy, Peterjon Cresswell, Mike, and Chad, Vicki and Jen for services above and beyond.

Maps on pages 236-237, 301-315 JS Graphics (john@jsgraphics.co.uk).
Map on page 316 supplied by Connex, Stockholm.

Photography by Elan Fleisher except: pages 6 and 12 Art Archive; pages 5, 13 and 14 AKG London; pages iii, 16, 107, 242, 254, 267, 268, 269 Corbis; page 9 Stockholms Stadsmuseum; page 76 top The National Museum of Fine Arts; page 79 Strindbergsmuseet; pages 194 and 197 British Film Institute; pages 221 and 227 Allsport; pages 20, 224 Associated Press; page 231 Bengt Wanselius; page 232 Petra Hellberg.

The following images were supplied by the featured establishments/artists: pages 11, 34, 35, 36, 46, 61, 97 top, 97 right, 106, 111, 112, 115, 195, 199, 201, 203, 204, 235, 240, 247.

Contents

Introduction 2

In Context 5

History 6
Stockholm Today 20
Architecture 23
Design 32

Accommodation 39

Accommodation 40

Sightseeing 55

Introduction 56
Gamla Stan & Riddarholmen 58
Norrmalm & Vasastaden 70
Djurgården & Skeppsholmen 80
Södermalm & Långholmen 88
Östermalm & Gärdet 94
Kungsholmen 101
Further Afield 105

Eat, Drink, Shop 109

Restaurants 110
Bars 130
Cafés 140
Shops & Services 149

Arts & Entertainment 177

Festivals & Events 178
Children 184
Clubs 189
Film 194
Galleries 199
Gay & Lesbian 205
Music 210
Sport & Fitness 218
Theatre & Dance 229

Trips Out of Town 235

Map: Trips Out of Town 236
Introduction 238
Day Trips 239
Central Archipelago 251
Southern Archipelago 259
Northern Archipelago 265
The Baltic & Beyond 267

Directory 271

Getting Around 272
Resources A-Z 276
Vocabulary 289
Further Reference 290
Index 292
Advertisers' Index 298

Maps 299

Stockholm Overview 300
Stockholm street maps 301
Street Index 312
Tunnelbana 316

Introduction

The Swedes are very proud of their capital – and deservedly so. For a start, its setting is fantastic: perched on a series of islands at the edge of the Baltic, the overwhelming impression on first arrival is of light, space and water, especially water. As is often said, Stockholm is made up of one-third water, one-third parkland, one-third buildings – surely the best formula if you want to create a city that values human scale and quality of life above show-off skyscrapers and urban grit. It's true that you'll find little grit – Stockholm must be one of the cleanest cities in the world – but that doesn't mean that it's lacking in urban thrills.

In fact, Stockholm offers the best of both worlds: the size of a small town and the buzz of the big city. The city centre is compact enough to walk around – perfect for visitors who don't want to waste precious time journeying from one sight to the next (though the efficient metro system and bus network is always there if your feet begin to feel the strain). And walking is the best way to enjoy the distinct character of each island. Start with the winding alleyways and royal attractions of Gamla Stan (everyone does), the site of the original 13th-century city, then move on. The choices are many. For grand boulevards that rival Paris and designer boutiques to match, visit swanky Östermalm. For more everyday shopping and a big-city buzz, join the throngs in modern-looking Norrmalm. Or get lost among the green open spaces of Djurgården, the royal island and home to some of Stockholm's best museums. For a funkier, bohemian feel, the bars and nightclubs of Södermalm await.

Stockholmers are a trend-conscious lot (some would say overly so) and determined that their position on the edge of Europe doesn't mean they're on the edge in cultural terms too. Swedish design has been a byword for cool for years, feted in design and lifestyle magazines around the world, and it would be hard to find a more fashionable set of clubs, restaurants, bars and shops in such a small space anywhere.

It's cool in other ways too – but don't let the northern climate put you off. The shortness of the Swedish summer makes it that much sweeter; and Stockholm in winter has its own distinct charms. Snow is rare but the city is probably at its most beautiful under a white blanket. Whenever you visit, you won't be disappointed.

ABOUT THE TIME OUT CITY GUIDES

The *Time Out Stockholm Guide* is one of an expanding series of Time Out City Guides, now numbering over 40, produced by the people behind London and New York's successful listings magazines. Our guides are all written by resident experts who have striven to provide you with all the most up-to-date information you'll need to explore the city or read up on its background, whether you're a local or a first-time visitor.

THE LOWDOWN ON THE LISTINGS

Above all, we've tried to make this book as useful as possible. Addresses, telephone numbers, websites, transport information, opening times, admission prices and credit card details have all been included in the listings. And, as far as possible, we've given details of facilities, services and events, all checked and correct as we went to press. However, owners and managers can change their arrangements at any time, and often do so. Also, particularly in Stockholm's archipelago, restaurants, cafés, shops and other facilities often do not keep precise opening hours, and may close earlier or later than stated according to the level of trade. Before you go out of your way, we'd advise you to phone and check opening times, ticket prices and other particulars. While every effort has been made to ensure the accuracy of the information contained in this guide, the publishers cannot accept responsibility for any errors it may contain.

THE LIE OF THE LAND

The centre of Stockholm is small and easy to get around on foot, but we've also given details of the nearest T-bana (metro) station and bus routes for everywhere included in the guide. The city centre is made up of clearly defined islands and neighbourhoods – in our **Sightseeing** chapters we've concentrated on 12 main areas (for an introduction to central Stockholm, *see p56*). Postal addresses in Stockholm include a five-digit postcode

(which is written before the name of the city, as in 111 30 Stockholm), and we've provided these codes for organisations or venues you might need to write to, such as hotels. For all places listed in the city centre we also give a map reference, which indicates the page and square on which the venue will be found on our **street maps** at the back of the book (starting on page 301).

PRICES AND PAYMENT

We have noted where shops, hotels, restaurants, museums and the like accept the following credit cards: American Express (**AmEx**), Diners Club (**DC**), MasterCard (**MC**) and Visa (**V**). Some may also accept other credit cards (including JCB or Carte Blanche).

The prices we've supplied should be treated as guidelines, not gospel. If they vary wildly from those we've quoted, please write and let us know. We aim to give the best and most up-to-date advice, so we always want to know if you've been badly treated or overcharged.

ESSENTIAL INFORMATION

For all the practical information you might need for visiting the city – including visa and customs information, advice on facilities and access for the disabled, emergency telephone numbers, health services, the local and national media, a lowdown on the local transport network and information on studying and working in the city, as well as tips on books, films and websites for further reference – turn to the **Directory** chapter, starting on page 272.

There is an online version of this guide, as well as weekly events listings for over 35 international cities, at www.timeout.com.

TELEPHONE NUMBERS

The area code for Stockholm is 08, but you don't need to use it when phoning from within the city. Throughout the guide we've listed all phone numbers as you need to dial them from within the city. If you're calling Stockholm from abroad, you must first dial 46 (the code for Sweden) then 8 then the number.

MAPS

The map section at the back of the guide includes an overview map of Stockholm, detailed street maps of the whole of the city centre with a comprehensive street index, and a map of the Tunnelbana metro system. The map section begins on page 299. For a map of the surrounding area to help with planning trips outside Stockholm, see pages 236-7.

LET US KNOW WHAT YOU THINK

We hope that you enjoy the *Time Out Stockholm Guide*, and we'd like to know what you think of it. We welcome tips for places that you think we should include in future editions of the guide and take note of your criticism of our choices. There's a reader's reply card at the back of this book for your feedback, or you can email us at guides@timeout.com.

Advertisers

We would like to stress that no establishment has been included in this guide because it has advertised in any of our publications and no payment of any kind has influenced any review. The opinions given in this book are those of *Time Out* writers and entirely independent.

In Context

History 6
Stockholm Today 20
Architecture 23
Design 32

Features

Gustav Vasa & the Vasaloppet 11
Two murders 14
Key events 19
Ordning och reda 22
The pastel city 27
Super Swedes: Gunnar Asplund 28
A million homes 31
Top ten designers 33
The story of IKEA 34

History

The eventful journey from Viking raids to neutrality.

EARLY BEGINNINGS TO THE VIKINGS

The history of the city of Stockholm stretches back 750 years, but the region that surrounds Stockholm, geographically defined by Lake Mälaren, has been a hotbed of human activity for several millennia.

The earliest evidence of human habitation in Sweden is of nomadic reindeer hunters from continental Europe, who appear to have followed the receding glaciers north into Scandinavia at the end of the last Ice Age in approximately 11,000 BC. By about 7,500 BC Mesolithic hunter-gatherers had migrated to the coastal areas of central and northern Sweden. Between 4,000 and 2,800 BC, villages dotted the southern half of the country, their inhabitants eking out a living as farmers. Sweden's inhabitants began establishing trading links with the wider world during the Bronze Age (1,500 to 500 BC). They had access to abundant supplies of fur and amber, which they traded for raw metals, weapons and decorative objects.

► Many of the places and buildings mentioned here are covered in more detail in other chapters, including **Sightseeing**, **Day Trips** and **Architecture**.

Shortly after the birth of Christ, Scandinavia was 'discovered' by the classical world, the historians of the Roman Empire writing about its geographical location and the fact that its populace was well armed and well equipped with ships. Between AD 550 and 1,000 two main rival groups emerged in Sweden – the Svear, who were based in the Lake Mälaren region, and the Götar, who controlled a swathe of territory to the west and south of the Svear. (Although the Svear eventually defeated and assimilated the Götar, the geographical terms Svealand and Götaland are still in use today.) Sverige, Sweden's modern name in Swedish, comes from *Svea rike* – the Svea kingdom.

The Viking culture emerged in various parts of Scandinavia in the early ninth century. It is believed that the word Viking comes from the *viks* (Old Norse for 'inlets') in which they harboured their long ships. The 'Thing', an assembly of powerful men who advised the ruler, was at the centre of Viking law-making and politics. Vikings were committed pagans, devoutly worshipping the many gods of Norse mythology. Odin was the supreme deity, the god of war and founder of art and culture. Human sacrifice was an important aspect of Viking worship; every nine years nine people were offered to the gods at Uppsala's temple.

'The Vikings effectively dominated the political and economic life of the whole of Europe until the mid 11th century.'

There is evidence that the Lake Mälaren Vikings were among the first to set sail in search of new lands. They were probably motivated by rapid population growth at home, as well as persistent domestic unrest. By the mid ninth century they had reached both the Black and Caspian Seas, where they launched attacks on Byzantium and north-east Iran. While often still violent, the Vikings of Sweden were somewhat more business-minded than those of Denmark and Norway, and in time they successfully developed lucrative trading contacts with Byzantium.

Taken as a group, the Vikings effectively dominated the political and economic life of the whole of Europe until the mid 11th century. Remnants of their civilisation have been uncovered at a number of sites not far from Stockholm's city limits, most notably at Birka, a town founded in about AD 700 that was Sweden's leading trading centre during the early tenth century. A little further afield, Gamla Uppsala is even older than Birka, with some of its royal graves dating back to the sixth century. Stockholm's Historiska Museet has an excellent exhibition that introduces visitors to a wealth of information and artefacts that cast light on Viking culture.

MEDIEVAL POWER STRUGGLES

The Swedes were among the last Europeans to abandon paganism. In spite of the efforts of a number of crusading monks and priests, and the baptism of King Olof Skötkonung in 1008 (and all his successors after him), many Swedes stubbornly remained true to the old gods until the end of the 11th century. Finally, by the middle of the 12th century, Uppsala had fully shed its bloody pagan history and Sweden's archbishopric was established there, atop the remains of the old temple. The first Swedish archbishop appointed, in 1164, was an English monk called Stephen.

From the end of the Viking period in the mid 11th century, Swedish history was characterised for several centuries by one deadly power struggle after the other. While there was always one king or another in place, power and influence remained spread widely among an array of local chiefs and noblemen. A few of Sweden's leaders of this period are worth mention, however, such as Erik Jedvardsson (1156-60), the king who, a century after his death, was chosen to become Sweden's patron saint (so chosen for the crusade he undertook to christianise Finland). His memory is kept alive today in place names such as St Eriksplan and St Eriksgatan; his remains are entombed at Uppsala cathedral.

Another big name of the medieval period is that of Birger Jarl. *Jarl* indicates that he was one of the king's chief administrators. The king in question was a weak one by the name of Erik Eriksson. When he was deposed in 1229, Birger Jarl was well placed to assume power quickly. Birger Jarl is remembered for two main accomplishments: the long and turbulent process he initiated to centralise political power in Sweden, and the founding of the city of Stockholm. In 1247-51 he made

Vikings remains: a rune stone and treasure.

significant progress toward achieving his first goal by using German money and soldiers to successfully defeat a rebellion led by noblemen in the area around Lake Mälaren. Shortly after his victory he offered good trading terms to German merchants, especially those from Lübeck, which led to Sweden's long-lasting and strong ties to the Hanseatic League.

The 13th-century Swedish kingdom consisted of the area around Lake Mälaren, the Stockholm and Åland archipelagos, and the Gulf of Finland all the way to Viborg (now part of Russia). At this point in time the sea level had dropped in Stockholm's archipelago to such an extent that it was only possible to pass from the Baltic Sea into Lake Mälaren via a narrow channel now known as Norrström, just north of Gamla Stan. This passage became a vital trade route and a key defensive position – both in the middle of the waterways that held Sweden together and blocking any foreign attacks against the Swedish heartland. It is for this reason that in 1252 Birger Jarl chose precisely that spot to erect a mighty fortress, Tre Kronor (on the site of the present-day Kungliga Slottet), thereby founding a settlement that would grow to become the city of Stockholm.

Archaeological evidence suggests that there had already been a trading post at this location for some time, as well as a small fortification,

Birger Jarl, Stockholm's legendary founder.

but Birger Jarl was the first Swedish leader to fully recognise the island's strategic significance. In the summer of 1252 he wrote two letters in which the name 'Stockholm' was mentioned for the first time. The origin of the name is unclear, but one of the most convincing suggestions is that it comes from the fact that logs (*stockar*) were used to build up the small island (*holme*) upon which the fortress was built. The city was to be besieged numerous times in the succeeding centuries, by both rebellious peasants and foreign armies, because anyone who wanted to control Sweden knew he had to win control of Stockholm's castle.

The new fortress quickly mushroomed into one of Sweden's most important trading centres, where iron products, fur and grain from inland Sweden could be traded with salt from Lüneburg in Germany, cloth from Flanders and wine from Germany, France and Spain. Ships from Lübeck and other Hanseatic towns traded enthusiastically with the expatriate Germans who were setting up copper and iron-ore mines in Bergslagen and Dalarna, north of Mälaren.

Birger Jarl's son Magnus rose to power in 1275, after a nasty power struggle with his brothers. Magnus cracked down hard on the raucous nobility and in so doing became one of the most powerful kings in Swedish history. One of his key contributions to Swedish society was his decree that forbid *våldgästning*. This deprived the nobility of its right to collect taxes and make other financial, territorial or material demands upon the lower classes in rural society, and is credited with preventing feudalism from taking root in Sweden. (Magnus's nickname, Ladulås, which means 'barn lock', is also linked with this decree.) To tighten his hold on power, he decreed that certain key groups of society should have tax-free status, mainly those who were in the service of the Church or the state (particularly knights in the king's service). The early Gothic cathedral at Uppsala was also erected at this time.

Magnus Ladulås was a keen supporter of the new city of Stockholm and eager to promote its growth. Among many measures, he donated to monasteries land north of the city in what is today the area around the Central Station. Stockholm seems to have been well established as a town by about 1300, and a few decades later it had grown to be the largest and most important town in the country. (It was not considered as the capital until at least 1436, however.) The city centre sprouted several churches and monasteries, including that of St Nicholas, now known as Storkyrkan (completed in 1306), and the church in the monastery of the Order of St Francis (founded in 1270), now called Riddarholmskyrkan.

The **Parhelion Painting** and Sten Sture's statue of **St George and the Dragon**. *See p10.*

After Magnus's death in 1290, power shifted to a faction of nobles led by Torgil Knutsson. In 1302 Magnus's son Birger reached adulthood and assumed the throne. His brothers Erik and Valdemar made it very difficult for him to rule effectively, however: they wanted him to split the kingdom three ways rather than rule it alone. After they murdered Knutsson, Birger was forced to do as his brothers demanded, but in 1317 he had them arrested, thrown in prison and starved to death. The nobility, horrified by his bout of fratricide, promptly deposed him, forcing him to flee the country.

The nobility then set out to find a new king. They settled on Magnus, the child of a Swedish duke and, at the age of three, already king of Norway. Upon reaching adulthood Magnus assumed the throne and set about making some important changes to the Swedish social order. He abolished *trälldom*, a form of slavery, in 1335, and established Sweden's first national legal code in 1350. His dual kingdom was huge – after the signing of the treaty of Novgorod in 1323 Finland had officially become part of the Swedish realm – but the vast majority of his subjects lived in abject poverty. In the mid 14th century his kingdom was hit by the bubonic plague and approximately one-third of his subjects wiped out. Sweden's nobility fell on hard times – there were too few workers to support the lifestyles to which they had become accustomed. Seeing that Sweden was weak, Hanseatic merchants seized their chance to push Swedish traders off the best Baltic trade routes.

By the mid 1300s King Magnus was in serious trouble, and it was about this time that the construction of a thick ring wall around Stockholm was initiated. Long-running disputes about the then Danish provinces of Skåne and Blekinge resulted in devastating Danish attacks on Swedish targets. In the early 1360s Sweden's nobility lost all patience with Magnus and enlisted the help of Duke Albrecht of Mecklenburg (1364-88) to unseat him. The ring wall not yet complete, Albrecht and his forces quickly conquered Stockholm and assumed nominal control over the kingdom, but the nobles held the real power and divided up the country between themselves.

THE KALMAR UNION AND DISSENT

Upon the death in 1386 of Bo Jonsson Grip – chief of Sweden's ruling nobles – the nobility turned to Margaret, daughter of Danish King Valdemar and wife of Magnus's son King Håkon of Norway. Since the deaths of her father and husband she had already been made regent in both Denmark and Norway for her son Olof. Though Olof died in 1387, she retained her hold on power in the three kingdoms. In 1389 she was proclaimed ruler of Sweden and in return she confirmed all the privileges of the Swedish nobility. When they asked her to choose a king she nominated 14-year-old Erik VII of Pomerania; he was elected to the post in 1397. Since he was already king of Norway and Denmark, Scandinavia now had just one ruler. However, Margaret was the real power behind the throne, and remained so until her death in 1412.

In 1397 she formalised a Nordic alliance called the Kalmar Union, whose purpose was to limit both the commercial and political influence of the Hanseatic League. By the start of the 15th century the union encompassed Norway, Sweden, Finland, Iceland and the immensity of Greenland, making it the largest kingdom in Europe. The union was threatened many times, however, over the next 125 years, by Swedish rebellion against Danish forces.

Christopher of Bavaria ruled the union from 1439 to 1448, after being elected by the nobility. Upon his death, the noble families of Norway, Sweden and Denmark could not agree on a single candidate to fill the kingships. Sweden's nationalists, led by the Sture family, seized this opportunity to attempt to free Sweden from the union. This led to vicious fighting with Sweden's unionist faction, which was led by the Oxenstierna family. Finally, in 1470, the nationalists had the upper hand and Sten Sture the Elder (1471-97, 1501-3) was appointed the 'Guardian of the Realm'. A year later the Battle of Brunkeberg broke out in the middle of modern Stockholm, resulting in the decimation of the unionist forces. The *St George and the Dragon* statue in Storkyrkan was donated by Sture to commemorate the victory.

Aside from his crucial military victories, Sten Sture the Elder is remembered for the many technological, cultural and educational steps forward that Sweden made under his leadership. He established Sweden's first university in Uppsala in 1477, and in 1483 Sweden's first printing press was set up. Decorative arts became more sophisticated, as shown by the many fine German- and Dutch-style paintings that adorn Swedish churches of this period.

The city of Stockholm continued to grow throughout the 15th century, and by the early 16th century Stockholm had between 6,000 and 7,000 inhabitants, most of them living in present-day Gamla Stan. Poorer people, such as fishermen and artisans, had begun to build shacks to the north of the city centre, as well as on Södermalm. By Swedish standards it was a large town – the country's largest, in fact – but by continental standards it was tiny. By 1500 Bremen and Hamburg both had about 20,000 inhabitants, while Lübeck had 25,000 and Paris more than 100,000. The *Parhelion Painting* in Storkyrkan gives an idea of how the city looked around this time; it depicts an unusual light phenomemon seen in 1535.

From the start, the population of Stockholm was a mix of people from different parts of Sweden and other areas of Europe. The largest 'foreign' contingent – between 10 and 20 per cent of the population – was made up of Finns, largely a result of the fact that between the mid 12th and early 19th centuries Finland was a Swedish province. The Germans comprised a somewhat smaller, but much more powerful, proportion; since the city had been founded with Hanseatic support, wealthy German merchants had been living in Stockholm from its earliest beginnings. Records show that by the 1580s at least 12 per cent of the city's population was of German extraction. In fact, many German historians regarded Stockholm as a German town in the period before the anti-German rebellion of 1434. Germans continued to dominate Stockholm's city council until 1471, when a decision was made at a national level that Germans would be banned from participating in city politics. Dutch, Scottish, French, English, Italian, Danish, Russian and Polish merchants and traders also became increasingly significant in Stockholm during the 15th century.

'Gustav Vasa is best remembered as the king who turned Sweden into a nation.'

By the late 15th century, most Swedes thought the Kalmar Union was a thing of the past, but the alliance was still popular in Denmark and Sweden's rulers had to deal with numerous Danish attacks. When Christian II assumed the Danish throne in 1513, the unionist movement rejoiced, thinking it had now finally found a leader who would be able to crush the Swedish nationalists. Sure enough, Christian attacked Sweden and killed the then ruler Sten Sture the Younger (1512-20). After Sture's death, Christian gathered leading members of the Swedish nobility together at Stortorget under the guise of granting them amnesty for their opposition to the union. Instead, he found an excuse to execute 80-100 of the city's nobles and burghers. The event came to be known as the Stockholm Bloodbath (*see p66* **The Stockholm Bloodbath**), while Christian II came to be known (in Sweden, at least) as Christian the Tyrant.

Following the bloodbath, Sture's followers were endlessly persecuted by King Christian – which proved to be a mistake since it provoked widespread opposition to Danish rule and finally resulted in the complete breakdown of the union in 1521-3. Sweden then became a totally independent country under the strong leadership of Gustav Eriksson, who was crowned King Gustav Vasa (1523-60; *see p11* **Gustav Vasa & the Vasaloppet**).

Gustav Vasa & the Vasaloppet

Born in 1496 just north of Stockholm, Gustav Eriksson Vasa belonged to one of Sweden's highest-ranking noble families. Most importantly, he was a vocal opponent of the Kalmar Union tying Sweden to Denmark. In 1518 he was taken prisoner of war by the Danes and taken to Denmark, from where he managed to escape and travel to Lübeck.

He then returned to Sweden, where his father was one of the victims of the famous **Stockholm Bloodbath** (*see p66*) perpetrated by King Christian II of Denmark. He headed straight to the province of Dalarna and tried, unsuccessfully, to convince the farmers to rise against King Christian. Disappointed, Gustav set off on skis for the Norwegian border in an attempt to escape the Danish troops who were hot on his heels. By then news of the Bloodbath had reached Dalarna, and skiers set out to tell him they were now ready for rebellion. The two fastest skiers caught up with Gustav in Sälen, and he returned with them to Mora in Dalarna, and put together a small army of peasants. The army grew as it marched southwards and in 1521 besieged Stockholm, which finally surrendered in 1523. On 6 June 1523 Gustav Vasa was crowned king of Sweden – an event still celebrated as Sweden's **National Day** (*see p179*). Gustav Vasa came to be regarded as the founding father of the Swedish nation, a country independent of Danish kings.

Popular stories all about Gustav Vasa's exploits in Dalarna flourished almost immediately after they had happened, and continued down the years. In 1922 the first **Vasaloppet** ski race took place. It was an attempt to follow in Gustav's footsteps (or rather ski steps) as he fled from the Danish soldiers – though in fact it followed a slightly different route and went in the opposite direction, from Sälen to Mora.

From 119 competitors in 1922, the 90-kilometre (56-mile) race has grown steadily in popularity and profile. Held annually on the first Sunday in March, it's now one of the biggest sporting events in Scandinavia, with around 15,000 participants and numerous side events. The fastest skier along the route is Peter Göransson, who won the 1998 race in three hours, 38 minutes and 57 seconds. For more info on the race, visit www.vasaloppet.se.

Statue by Milles in the Nordiska Museet.

THE VASA DYNASTY AND THE RISE OF EMPIRE

Under Gustav Vasa's long leadership Sweden was changed in two fundamental ways: it was unified under a strong hereditary monarch and it became a Protestant country. Never a particularly religious man, Gustav Vasa's Reformation had much more to do with politics and economics than it did with theology. He was an ambitious king, but cash-strapped, so the handover of Church lands to the Crown and the subordination of the Church, which had become a rival power base, suited his purposes perfectly. Shortly after taking power, he set out on a propaganda campaign in which he stressed the negative role the Church's leadership had often played in the past – in particular, the unsavoury role Archbishop Gustav Trolle had played in the lead-up to the Stockholm Bloodbath. In the end, he got his way and the Lutheran faith was established as the state religion.

The Reformation led to the state-sanctioned destruction of scores of Swedish monasteries, convents and churches, their riches going directly to an increasingly wealthy and powerful king. Gustav Vasa even had plans to tear down Storkyrkan because he felt it was situated too close to the royal residence at Tre Kronor

The Battle of Björko in 1790, part of Gustav III's war against Russia. *See p15.*

castle, thereby complicating its defence. But public opinion was strongly opposed to the outright destruction of Stockholm's spiritual heart, however, so the king relented and decided only to move one of the church's walls slightly. (Gustav Vasa's son Johan was more interested in both architecture and religion than his father: in the 1580s he had a number of Stockholm's demolished churches rebuilt.)

His larder full and his domestic goals largely accomplished, Gustav Vasa launched a campaign to weaken Russia, Poland and Denmark and thereby make Sweden the dominant Baltic power, beginning with a modestly successful war against Russia in 1555-7. After his death in 1560, his sons, King Erik XIV, King Johan III and King Karl IX, took up the quest. Gustav Vasa (along with his sons) is seen as the monarch who was most responsible for turning Sweden into a nation. He created a modern army, navy and civil service. He and his sons imported men of learning to fill their royal court and introduced the Renaissance style of architecture, painting and sculpture to Swedish high society.

In 1570-95 Sweden fought another war against Russia, with some success. But Denmark was harder to beat – in spite of the break-up of the Kalmar Union, it had remained the most powerful country in the region, as Sweden learned to its cost in the expensive wars of 1563-70 and 1611-13. It was during the reign of Gustav Vasa's grandson, Gustav II Adolf (1611-32), that Sweden began to make some significant progress in its efforts to expand around the Baltic Sea, helped largely by that king's extensive reforms of the armed forces and civil service. By 1617 Sweden had pushed Russia back from the Baltic coastline, and in 1621 it succeeded in taking Riga from Poland. The Thirty Years War, which started in Germany in 1618, finally turned the tide decisively in Sweden's favour in its rivalry with Denmark. After suffering a devastating defeat at the hands of the Swedes in the battle of Lutter-am-Barenburg in 1626, Denmark was forced to pull out of the war. In 1630 Sweden officially entered the war on the side of the Protestants. The resulting peace treaty of 1648 gave Sweden new provinces in northern Germany, and by 1658 a severely weakened Denmark had been forced to surrender parts of Norway plus all Danish provinces east of Öresund to Sweden. As a result, by the end of the 17th century Sweden had become the most powerful nation in northern Europe.

'Gustav III was a man of culture who imported French opera, theatre and literature to Sweden.'

Gustav II Adolf and his chancellor Axel Oxenstierna were eager to develop Stockholm and make it the political and administrative centre of the growing Swedish empire. They issued numerous regulations that strengthened Stockholm's position as a centre of foreign trade, and also founded Sweden's Supreme Court in the city. In 1626 they reorganised the national assembly into four estates – nobility, clergy, burghers and farmers – and based it in Stockholm. The capital's medieval wall was torn down in this period so that the city could expand to the north and south. The old wooden buildings that dominated Södermalm and Norrmalm were razed and replaced by new, straight streets lined with stone buildings.

After Gustav II Adolf's death his young daughter Christina became queen, with Oxenstierna as regent until 1644. In 1654

Christina converted to Catholicism, renounced the throne and moved to Rome, where she lived out her life building up one of the finest art and book collections in Europe. She left the throne to Karl X Gustav (1654-60), who is remembered best for his invasion and defeat of Denmark in 1657, thereby creating the largest Swedish empire ever. He was succeeded by his son, Karl XI (1660-97), who in 1682 pronounced himself to be Sweden's first absolute monarch, answerable only to God.

Stockholm's population grew rapidly during Sweden's age of empire; by the 1670s it had between 50,000 and 55,000 citizens. Literacy had now become important, leading to the establishment of many grammar schools, and creativity flourished under the likes of George Stiernhielm (1598-1672), the father of modern Swedish poetry. Architecturally, this was the age of the Tessins, who completed the fabulous Drottningholms Slott in 1686. It was truly a golden age for Swedish history, in military, cultural, economic and social terms.

AN EMPIRE IN DECLINE AND A CITY IN FLUX

It was during the reign of Karl XII (1697-1718) – who assumed the throne at the tender age of 15 – that Sweden lost her empire. Between 1700 and 1721 Sweden fought the Great Northern War against a number of opponents, notably the defensive alliance of Saxony-Poland, Russia and Denmark. The young king fought valiantly against the odds to hold on to all of Sweden's far-flung possessions, but suffered a terrible loss to Russia's Peter the Great at the Battle of Poltava in 1709. His bravery in battle is still revered in Sweden's far-right circles to this day. He was finally killed in Norway by a sniper's bullet in 1718. Since he had no heir, the period after Karl's death was marked by a weakening of the monarchy (the end of absolutism) and the rise of the aristocracy. In 1719 the role of the monarch was reduced to that of nominal head of state; it was the chancellor who exercised real power, with the support of shifting aristocratic factions. With the government dominated by cabals of squabbling noblemen, the economy was left to stagnate, and political and social reforms were slow in coming.

Art-loving and ill-fated **Gustav III**. *See p14.*

By the end of the Great Northern War in 1721, Sweden had lost parts of Pomerania in Germany, as well as its strongholds in modern-day Estonia, Latvia, north-west Russia and Finland. Sweden made disastrous attempts to reconquer at least some of these territories by fighting wars with Russia in 1741-3 and 1788-90. Participation in the Seven Years War (1756-63) resulted in the loss of Swedish territory to Prussia. It was clear that Sweden was no longer a great power in Europe, but it took a very long time for the country's political and military establishment to accept the fact.

This was also a trying time for the citizens of Stockholm – on top of coping with their country's political and military difficulties, the city was repeatedly ravaged by fire and disease. In 1697 the city was devastated by a fire that completely destroyed Tre Kronor, the royal palace and pride of Stockholm. In 1710 plague swept through the city and in just a few months killed approximately 20,000 people, about a third of the population. Later in the century the city suffered three more devastating fires, which resulted in a municipal ban on wood as a building material for new houses. Over the course of the 18th century the population of the city stayed static at about 70,000 inhabitants; it would probably have declined had there not been a fresh supply of men and women from the countryside every year. Unsanitary conditions, overcrowding, cold and disease contributed significantly to the fact that Stockholm's death rate was among the highest of all European cities.

But there was a brighter side. In the decades leading up to 1754, Stockholm buzzed with the building of the new Kungliga Slottet to replace Tre Kronor. The construction work was a huge stimulus for the city's artisans, and for Stockholm's economy overall. Foreign painters, furniture makers and craftsmen initially came to work temporarily on the palace, but many decided to stay permanently, opening small businesses and teaching their trades to others. They made a good living, as many noblemen and burghers were quick to order paintings, furniture and wallpaper similar to those in the new royal palace. New industries also began to grow up in Stockholm, such as textile manufacturing, and the city's foreign trade was developing rapidly – not only with Europe but also with the Far East and the Americas.

Many of Stockholm's burghers used their increasing wealth to build larger and larger houses, especially along Skeppsbron in Gamla Stan. The reconstruction of the city led to the old town hall at Stortorget being torn down in 1768 and replaced with Börsen, a stock exchange. New residential neighbourhoods sprang up on Södermalm and Norrmalm, and many of the old houses on Gamla Stan were renovated.

The 18th century was also an age of scientific and intellectual advance in Stockholm, and throughout Sweden. Key figures included the famous botanist Carl von Linné (aka Linnaeus; 1707-78); Anders Celsius (1701-44), inventor of the centigrade temperature scale; and mystical philosopher Emanuel Swedenborg (1688-1772). Sweden's best-loved poet, Carl Michael Bellman (1740-95), did much to encourage Swedish nationalism. Free religious groups also began to form and to challenge the iron-fisted monopoly of the state church; Jews were allowed to settle in Sweden in 1744, and in 1781 Catholics were permitted to establish a church in Stockholm for the first time since the Reformation.

The monarchy regained some of its old power under Gustav III (1771-92). Seeing that the Riksdag (Parliament) was divided, the king seized the opportunity to force through a new constitution that would make the nobility share power with the Crown. Gustav III was initially popular with his subjects because he built hospitals, allowed freedom of worship and lessened economic controls. He was also a man of culture who imported French opera, theatre and literature to Sweden, and in 1782 he founded Stockholm's first opera house, the Kungliga Operan. During his reign, several newspapers were established, and political and cultural debate flourished. The nobility were not so happy with his increasingly tyrannical behaviour, however, especially after the start of the French Revolution. In 1792 an assassin shot Gustav III at a masked ball at the Kungliga Operan; he died two weeks later (*see above* **Two murders**).

In 1805 Gustav III's successor, Gustav IV Adolf (1792-1809), was drawn into the Napoleonic Wars on the British side. This resulted in a number of gains and losses; most significantly, Sweden lost Finland to Russia and gained Norway from Denmark. All this upheaval resulted in a variety of political changes, notably the constitution of 1809, which established a system in which a liberal monarchy would be responsible to an elected Riksdag.

Two murders

For several hundred years Sweden has carried out its political affairs peacefully. Rebellions by armed farmers were fairly commonplace in the 15th and 16th centuries, with a final but limited rebellion in 1743, but Sweden's last open civil war occurred as long ago as 1598. Since then, some violent demonstrations back in 1838 and 1848 are about as heavy as it's got. Except for two notorious political assassinations – both in Stockholm – a couple of hundred years apart.

Gustav IV Adolf was followed by Karl XIII. He died in 1818, and one of Napoleon's generals, Marshal Bernadotte, was invited to assume the Swedish throne. He accepted the offer and took the name Karl XIV Johan (1818-44). In spite of the fact that he spoke no Swedish and had never even visited Scandinavia prior to accepting the kingship, Sweden prospered under his rule. He was a strong liberalising influence, both socially and economically. In 1832 he presided over the opening of the Göta Canal, an important transportation corridor that still links Stockholm to Sweden's west coast.

His successor, Oscar I (1844-59), gave women inheritance rights equal to those of their brothers in 1845, passed an Education Act (1842) and a Poor Care law (1855), and then reformed the restrictive craftsmen's guilds. The reign of his son, Karl XV (1859-72), is remembered for

For much of the 18th century, during the so-called Age of Freedom, the nobility and burghers in the Riksdag (Parliament) controlled the nation's affairs and limited the power of the king. In 1771 **Gustav III** came to power; in August 1772 he mounted a coup d'état and declared his own absolute power. The move was unpopular and, after a costly war against Russia in 1788-90, opposition to the king grew. At a masked ball on 16 March 1792 at the Kungliga Operan, a nobleman and former army officer, Johan Jacob Anckarström, shot the king with a pistol (*pictured*). Although the king was wearing a mask, like everyone else, his killer picked him out by his telltale medals. The event inspired Verdi's 1859 opera *Un Ballo in Maschera* ('A Masked Ball'). Anckarström escaped but was arrested the following morning; the king died from his wounds a couple of weeks later. Anckarström was whipped on four different squares in Stockholm before being beheaded. A statue of Gustav III, sculpted by JT Sergel in 1799, stands on Skeppsbron, at the foot of Slottsbacken.

Almost 200 years later, just after 11pm on 28 February 1986, Social Democrat prime minister **Olof Palme** was walking home from the cinema with his wife Lisbeth. As they strolled along Sveavägen in the city centre, Palme was shot by a man in an overcoat and died instantly. The murderer vanished without trace. The huge police operation that followed was badly bungled: no roadblocks were set up during the night and, bizarrely, a civil servant rather than a policeman was put in charge of the investigation. In 1988 an alchoholic petty criminal, Christer Pettersson (who presumably had 'patsy' stamped on his forehead) was convicted of the crime and sentenced to life in prison. But he was almost immediately released on appeal due to the circumstantial nature of the evidence against him, and was awarded huge compensation. To date, the killer has not been found.

Over the years several nations, criminals and terrorist groups have figured in press discussions about the murder. Palme was in favour of disarmament and a vocal opponent of apartheid, which led to rumours about the involvement of the South African security forces. Conspiracy theories, almost on the scale of those surrounding the murder of JFK, are still rife. A brass memorial plaque on the pavement (*pictured*), at the corner of Sveavägen and Tunnelgatan, marks the spot where Palme died.

introducing a very limited franchise, and reforming the Riksdag in 1866 – the old four estates were replaced with a dual-chamber representative parliament along continental lines. This act marked the beginning of the end for the monarch's role in the country's politics – all Sweden's kings since then have been little more than figureheads.

INDUSTRIALISATION AND THE GROWTH OF STOCKHOLM

Industrialisation arrived late to Sweden, and the mechanisation of what little industry did exist (mining, forestry and the like) was half-hearted – hardly what you would call a revolution. Meanwhile, the rural population had grown steadily through the first half of the 19th century. There was neither enough land, nor jobs in the cities, to support everyone. The poor got used to going hungry, but in 1867-8 the situation became critical when a terrible famine broke out. As a result, over one million Swedes emigrated to North America between 1860 and 1910 – a cataclysmic event for a country whose population in 1860 was only four million.

In the 1860s, Sweden's first railway lines finally opened reliable communications between Stockholm and the country's southern regions; by 1871 the railway to the north was complete. The railways were a boon for nascent industry. The two most notable Swedish manufactured products were to become its high-quality, efficiently made steel and its safety matches (a Swedish invention). By the late 19th century a number of large industries had been established in Stockholm; for example, a shoe factory on Södermalm employed 300 to 400 people, and a huge Bolinders factory (800 employees) on

Kungsholmen produced steam engines, cast-iron stoves, pans, furniture and other household items. In 1876, engineer Lars Magnus Ericsson opened his Ericsson telephone company in Stockholm, and soon the city had more phones per capita than any other city in Europe (a trend that has continued to this day).

By 1900 almost one in four Swedes lived in a city, and industrialisation (based primarily on timber, precision machinery and hardware) was finally in full swing. Stockholm's factories attracted workers from all over the country, causing the capital's population to balloon from 100,000 in 1856 to 300,000 in 1900. Conditions in many of these factories were appalling, and trade unions emerged to fight for the rights of workers. The unions formed a confederation in 1898 but found it difficult to make progress – under Swedish laws at the time, even peaceful picketing carried a two-year prison sentence.

Living conditions in the city were nearly as bad as working conditions. In response to Stockholm's growing housing crisis, the city planners – led by Claes Albert Lindhagen – put forward a proposal in 1866 to build wide boulevards and esplanades similar to those in Paris, which would create some green space within the city as well as allowing traffic to move freely. The plan resulted in the construction of some of the city's key arteries, such as Birger Jarlsgatan, Valhallavägen, Karlaplan, Ringvägen, Karlavägen, Narvavägen, Karlbergsvägen and, perhaps most impressive of all, Strandvägen. In just one decade alone, the 1880s, Stockholm's population increased by 46 per cent – which is why more buildings were constructed in the 1880s than in all of the previous seven decades together. Neighbourhoods such as Östermalm, Vasastaden, Kungsholmen, Hornstull and Skanstull were created at this time.

The late 19th century also saw the arrival of Stockholm's first continental-style hotels, cafés, restaurants, shopping galleries and department stores, to serve the city's upper classes and the beginnings of a tourist industry. Classic hotels and restaurants such as the Grand Hôtel, Berns and Hasselbacken were either opened or entirely remodelled. Foreign circuses and theatre groups became popular, which led to the construction of many new theatres. International exhibitions promoting industry and art were held in Stockholm in 1866 and 1897.

During the same period Swedish dramatist August Strindberg (*see p78* **Super Swedes: August Strindberg**) achieved critical success across Europe, and folk historian Artur Hazelius (*see p83* **The man behind Skansen**) founded the Nordiska Museet and open-air museum Skansen to preserve Sweden's rich cultural heritage. The Academy of Stockholm (now the University of Stockholm) was founded in 1878, and in 1896 Alfred Nobel donated his fortune to fund the Nobel Prizes (*see p104* **Alfred Nobel & the Nobel Prizes**).

Swedish soldiers in **World War II**. *See p17.*

NEUTRALITY AND DEMOCRACY

In 1901 the Swedish government introduced conscription in reaction to the rising militarism in Europe and, more specifically, because of its fears about a potential conflict with Russia. At the outbreak of World War I Sweden declared itself neutral in spite of its German sympathies. The British demanded that Sweden enforce a blockade against Germany. When Sweden refused to co-operate, the British blacklisted Swedish goods and interfered with Swedish commercial shipping as much as they could, going so far as to seize ships' cargoes. The economy suffered terribly and inflation shot through the roof. The British tactics led to rationing as well as food shortages so severe that demonstrations broke out in 1917-18, inspired by the Russian Revolution.

In 1907 the government had granted all men the right to vote. In 1920 Hjalmar Branting became Sweden's first Social Democratic prime minister. Reforms quickly followed, including voting rights for women – the very first in the world – the establishment of a state-controlled alcohol-selling system and the introduction of the eight-hour working day. The Social Democrats' dominance of political affairs in the 1930s made it possible to take the first steps towards Sweden's famous welfare state. The first components of the welfare system were unemployment benefits, paid holidays, family allowances and a substantial increase in old-age pensions. The Social Democrats also managed to talk the country's trade unions and major employers into meeting at Saltsjöbaden in 1938 to come to an agreement about how to regulate labour disputes, such as strikes and lock-outs. Known as the Saltsjöbaden Agreement, it marked the start of what was to become Sweden's hallmark corporative capitalism.

At the outbreak of World War II there was little sympathy in Sweden for the Germans – unlike in 1914. Sweden declared neutrality but was in a difficult position. Germany was allied with Finland against the Soviet Union, and the relationship between Sweden and Finland was traditionally close – with Russia the age-old enemy. But when the Soviets invaded Finland in 1939, Sweden was only drawn in to a certain degree, providing weapons, volunteers and refuge to the Finns, but refusing to send regular troops. Sweden's position became even more uncomfortable in 1940, when Germany invaded Denmark and Norway, thereby isolating Sweden and compelling it to supply the Nazis with iron ore and to allow them to transport their troops across Swedish territory and in Swedish waters. In 1942 the Swedish navy fought an undeclared war against Soviet submarines.

'The main goal for the government in World War II was not strict neutrality but rather to avoid being dragged into it.'

On the other hand, western Allied airmen were rescued in Sweden and often sent back to Britain, and Danish and Norwegian armed resistance groups were organised on Swedish soil in 1942-3. Jewish lives were also saved, notably by Swedish businessman Raoul Wallenberg, who managed to prevent about 100,000 Hungarian Jews from being deported by the SS. After the Soviet conquest of Budapest in January 1945, Wallenberg was arrested, as a suspected spy, and disappeared. For years, no one knew what had happened to him and rumours flew about whether or not he had died in a Moscow prison in 1947; Soviet documents unearthed in 1989 indicated this was most likely what had happened.

The main goal for the Swedish government during the war was not strict neutrality but rather to avoid Sweden's being dragged into the war – this was accomplished at high diplomatic and moral cost. Rather than suffering as it had during World War I, Sweden weathered World War II relatively well, since it was now less dependent on foreign imports.

During the first emergence of the Cold War, in 1948-9, Sweden tried to form a defensive alliance with Denmark and Norway, but her plans failed partly because the other two countries wanted close links with the Western allies. When the Danes and Norwegians became members of NATO in 1949, Sweden remained outside. One semi-official reason given for this was Sweden's not wanting to leave her friend Finland too isolated and at risk of being pressed by the Soviet Union. But in recent years it has emerged that Sweden was, in fact, in secret co-operation with NATO from as far back as the early 1950s.

TO THE PRESENT

After the end of World War II, a large-scale transformation of Stockholm's city centre began, despite the fact that – other than the minimal damage caused by Soviet aeroplanes that bombed the southern parts of the city one night in early 1944 – Stockholm was one of the few European capitals to survive the war completely unscathed. But once the rebuilding process on the Continent was in full swing, with American-style skyscrapers rising from the ashes of all the bombed-out cities, Sweden felt left out. The city government began to tear down many of its decaying old buildings and construct anew, leading to the construction of such areas as Sergels Torg.

Opposition grew over the years, however, and in 1971 a large-scale demonstration in Kungsträdgården successfully prevented the destruction of parts of the park to build a new Tunnelbana station – an event that marked the end of the 'modernisation' of central Stockholm. In 1974 writer Jan Olof Olsson expressed the popular sentiment: 'An ignorant American tourist this summer asked whether it was the Russians or Germans who destroyed Stockholm. He got the proud answer that we have done this all by ourselves.'

As more and more people moved to Stockholm in the post-war period (in the 20th century the capital's population grew from a mere 300,000 to 800,000), the city once again developed a severe housing crisis. To help ease the problem, Stockholm's Tunnelbana metro system was inaugurated in 1950 and a number of new suburbs were built along it, out to the south and north-west of the city centre.

Under the leadership of Tage Erlander (1946-69), the Social Democrats introduced models for industrial bargaining and full employment that were successful in spurring the economy. At the same time, the country created a national health service and a disability benefits system, improved the quality of its schools and instituted free university education. Sweden established itself as a leading industrial country and was proud of its 'Third Way', a blending of corporative capitalism with a cradle-to-grave social safety net for all.

In 1953 Swedish diplomat Dag Hammarskjöld was appointed secretary-general of the United Nations. A controversial figure who tried to use his position to broker peace in the conflicts of the period, he became a thorn in the side of the superpowers. He died in 1961 in a mysterious plane crash over Northern Rhodesia while on a mission to try to solve the Congo crisis. News of his death caused profound sadness across Sweden as he personified the Swedes' perception of themselves as the world's conscience.

Sweden's booming post-war economy produced a great demand for labour that the national workforce could not meet. From about 1950, Sweden began to import skilled labour, primarily from the Nordic countries but also from Italy, Greece and Yugoslavia. This immigration increased gradually and continued unrestricted until the mid 1960s, reaching its peak in 1969-70, when more than 75,000 immigrants were entering Sweden each year. Thereafter numbers fell significantly, although Sweden continued to welcome political refugees, primarily from Latin America (in the 1970s), the Middle East, Asia and Africa (in the 1980s) and the Balkans (in the 1990s), as well as granting residence permits to the relatives of earlier immigrants. By the mid 1990s, more than one million people – 11 per cent of Sweden's population – were foreign-born.

In the 1970s international economic pressures began to put the squeeze on Sweden's social goals, and it was under Prime Minister Olof Palme's leadership (1982-6) that the Third Way first began to falter. Palme spent a lot of time and energy on building up Sweden's international image and trying to influence world affairs – while Sweden's high-tax economy was sliding slowly into stagnation. When an unknown assailant murdered Palme on a Stockholm street in 1986 (*see p14* **Two murders**) it created a national trauma equivalent to that surrounding the murder of JFK, despite the fact that many Swedes had come to dislike his politics.

The end of the Cold War in the late 1980s led to a serious re-evaluation of Sweden's position in international politics. In 1990 the Social Democrats considered signing up to the European Union (although joining NATO was still totally out of the question). In the early 1990s, long-term economic stagnation and budgetary problems provoked frenzied speculation against the Swedish *krona*, forcing a massive devaluation of the currency. A harsh programme of austerity measures was then implemented, but it was not enough to stem the tide. Sweden suffered its worst recession since the 1930s and unemployment soared to a record 14 per cent. With both its economy and national confidence severely shaken, Sweden voted (by a very narrow margin) to join the EU, its membership taking effect on 1 January 1995. In the same year, gay couples were given virtually the same rights as married couples, in line with legislation already existing in both Norway and Denmark.

'Sweden was proud of its "Third Way": a blending of capitalism with a cradle-to-grave social safety net for all.'

Since then, Sweden's welfare state has undergone major reforms and the economy has improved considerably, with both unemployment and inflation falling greatly, particularly during the IT boom of the 1990s. However, when the IT bubble burst, Sweden slipped into another recession as its industrial giants, such as Ericsson, as well as the flashy IT start-ups, suffered the consequences of the bust. Widespread redundancies raised the unemployment rate and the stock market took a nosedive. Sweden has remained half-hearted about a common European currency, and opted (along with Britain, Denmark and Finland) not to adopt the euro in January 1999. It's likely that a referendum will be held before a decision one way or the other is finally made.

In September 2002 the country's national election bucked the continental right-wing trend by delivering a parliament very similar to the previous one, with the Social Democrats receiving enough votes to build a minority government with the support of Vänsterpartiet (the Left Party) and Miljöpartiet (the Greens). Within the right and left blocks, support shifted towards the parties nearest the centre, but the balance between the blocks stayed the same. At the time of going to press, the results of the Stockholm city election were as yet unclear, though it seems that power will shift from a right-wing coalition to a left-wing one led by the Social Democrats.

Key events

800-1050 The Viking age.
1008 King Olof Skötkonung is the first Swedish king to convert to Christianity.
1150s First invasion of Finland, which later becomes an integrated part of Sweden.
1252 Birger Jarl, Sweden's de facto ruler, founds Stockholm and starts to build Tre Kronor fortress.
1275 Magnus Ladulås becomes king and starts to develop Stockholm.
1350 The Black Death wipes out as much as one-third of Sweden's population.
1397 The Kalmar Union is formed by Denmark–Norway and Sweden–Finland, ruled by Queen Margaret in Copenhagen. For the next 125 years there are numerous Swedish rebellions against the union.
1477 Sweden's first university is established in Uppsala.
1520 The Stockholm Bloodbath. Between 80 and 100 political opponents of the Danish king, Christian II, are beheaded on Stortorget.
1523 Gustav Vasa defeats the Danes and is elected king. A long line of Swedish–Danish wars begins.
1524-5 Parliament confiscates Church property, and the Lutheran Reformation unfolds.
1544 Parliament makes the monarchy hereditary.
Early 1500s Stockholm's population is between 6,000 and 7,000.
1628-41 Stockholm's medieval city wall is torn down so that the city can expand.
1630-48 Sweden participates in the Thirty Years War on the side of the Protestants.
1630-50s Planning regulations mean that Stockholm expands on to Södermalm and Norrmalm with straight streets and stone houses.
1686 Drottningholms Slott is completed to designs by Nicodemus Tessin the Elder and Younger.
1700-21 The Great Northern War, during which Sweden fights an alliance of Denmark, Russia and Poland–Saxony, and loses much of her territory.
1719 A new constitution transfers power from the king to Parliament, and the Age of Liberty begins.
1740 The poet Carl Michael Bellman is born; his work encourages Swedish nationalism.
1754 Kungliga Slottet is completed to designs by Nicodemus Tessin the Younger.
1781 Catholics are allowed to establish a church in Stockholm for the first time since the Reformation.
1792 King Gustav III, who had restored the absolute power of the monarchy, is shot; the power of parliament is subsequently restored.
1814 Sweden forces Norway into a union, which is to last until 1905.
1860s The first railway line gives Stockholm increased contact with the rest of the country. Widespread emigration to North America begins.
1872 August Strindberg writes his first major play, *Master Olof*.
1878 The Academy of Stockholm is founded, today the University of Stockholm.
1891 Artur Hazelius opens the folk museum Skansen, as part of a revival of Swedish culture.
1897 A large international exhibition is held on Djurgården.
1900 Stockholm's population reaches 300,000 after tripling in size during the previous 50 years.
1902 Extensive demonstrations for universal suffrage take place.
1907 Men are given the right to vote.
1914-18 Sweden remains neutral during World War I.
1917-18 Stockholm sees political riots inspired by the Russian Revolution.
1921 Women are given the right to vote.
1930s The first steps are taken towards the creation of the welfare state.
1939-45 Sweden remains neutral during World War II.
1950-70 Large parts of the city centre are rebuilt and many historic buildings are lost. The first underground train line is opened.
1955 Compulsory national health insurance is initiated.
1973 Carl XVI Gustav inherits the title of king.
1974 The monarchy loses all political power.
1986 Prime Minister Olof Palme is shot dead.
Early 1990s The *krona* is devalued. Sweden is gripped by recession and unemployment soars to 14 per cent.
1995 Sweden joins the European Union, and gay couples are effectively allowed to marry.
2000 The Church is separated from the state.
September 2002 In the general election the Social Democrats gain enough votes to form a coalition government with the Left Party and the Greens.

Prime Minister Göran Persson after the general election in September 2002.

Stockholm Today

The problems of maintaining an egalitarian society.

Stockholm celebrated its 750th anniversary in June 2002 with week-long festivities all over town. From a fortress on a hill protecting a few hundred people, the city has grown into the capital of a nation attempting to ensure a high quality of life for all its citizens. The question of how to maintain that quality of life is at the core of the never-ending political debate between Sweden's left- and right-wing parties. During the general election in September 2002, Prime Minister Göran Persson of the Social Democratic Party (Socialdemokratiska Partiet) – who won the election – stressed the importance of building a society together. His party's campaign was unique within western Europe since it did not promise lower taxes – in fact, quite the opposite. The Social Democrats' main opponent, the Moderate Party (Moderaterna), called for large tax cuts that, it claimed, would stimulate the economy and free people from social welfare.

Although the majority of voters opted for the Social Democrats' higher taxes, Sweden's political and economic future is hardly secure. For most of the 20th century, the domestic policies of the ruling Social Democrats have been based on creating a society of economic equality. This means that social welfare in Sweden is much more than helping those in poverty. Most Swedes receive some kind of direct government assistance, ranging from housing aid to monthly payments for those with children – which has enabled Sweden to develop into one of the most egalitarian countries in the world. Critics argue, however, that high taxes are inhibiting the business growth upon which everyone is ultimately dependent. Long after the government spending sprees of the 1960s and '70s, Sweden is now facing a weak global market for its exports, upon which its economy heavily relies. As an indication of changing times, the clear victors of the 2002 election – the left-wing Social Democrats and the right-wing Liberal Party (Folkpartiet) – have both moved closer to the centre.

NEIGHBOURS AND ALLIANCES

Stockholm has a population of roughly 755,000, making it the largest city in Scandinavia, while Stockholm County has a population of 1.8 million. Stockholm is the financial centre of the

Baltic region and home to the nation's telecoms, service and pharmaceutical industries. Half of Sweden's new businesses start in Stockholm County, which also contains more IT and telecoms firms than any area in Scandinavia. Mobile phone penetration in Sweden is 70 per cent (just behind Finland and Norway), and 79 per cent of Stockholmers aged between 16 and 79 use the internet. In contrast to the sprawl of other large metropolitan areas, carefully managed development combined with a well-developed public transport system have allowed the region's towns to develop in relatively green environments. Around 46 per cent of the county's land is covered with forests (compared with 59 per cent for all of Sweden).

Although Sweden is slightly larger than the state of California, it has only a quarter of its population: nearly nine million people. The bulk of Swedes live in the country's central and southern sections – 20 per cent in the Stockholm area – leaving the thickly forested north-west to moose, reintroduced wolf packs and smaller coastal towns. The port city of Göteborg, on the west coast, ranks second in size with 471,000 residents; it is Sweden's major car manufacturing centre, with large Volvo and Saab factories. Malmö is the third largest city, with 265,000 inhabitants, and is already benefiting from its connection to Denmark via the Öresund bridge. Paper, pulp and metals form the basis of the economy in the north, while agriculture is the primary industry of the flatter, sunnier section of southern Sweden.

No nation is complete without regional and international animosities based on tiny cultural differences, odd dialects and vague memories of the past. People living outside the capital sometimes stereotype Stockholmers as being trendy and arrogant. Behind their backs they're called *08-ors* ('08-ers'), in reference to the capital's area code – often with a swear word before the nickname. Stockholmers, on the other hand, say that people from Skåne, in the south, talk like they have porridge in their mouths.

Swedes have been called the Americans of Scandinavia, partly for their economic dominance, partly for insisting that their way is best and for their relative ignorance of the neighbouring countries they once controlled. While Norway prospers from oil discovered in the North Sea 30 years ago, Swedes can't help but turn a jealous eye toward their former 'little brother'. Mention Norway to a Swede and they will tell you that it is very, very expensive. Although the Nordic countries feel a common bond against the rest of the world, relations between Sweden and Denmark have cooled recently as the latter has moved to the right politically. To make matters trickier, Danes can understand Swedish better than the Swedes can understand Danish, which leads to some rather odd television interviews.

As a country with a history of avoiding international alliances, Sweden was less eager than most to join the European Union. The issue was extensively debated in the mid 1990s, with the referendum in November 1994 voting for joining by a narrow margin: 52.3 per cent in favour, 46.8 per cent against. Anti-EU sentiment subsequently grew, with the bizarre outcome that more than half of the Swedish politicians elected to the European parliament actually opposed EU membership. Sweden has been similarly reluctant to embrace membership of the European Monetary Union – although opinion polls since the 2002 election suggest that a slight majority of Swedes are ready for the euro, so perhaps its adoption is not as far away as previously supposed.

HOUSING AND IMMIGRATION

The powerhouse of the Swedish economy has suffered some setbacks in the past decade, with massive state debts leading to the *krona* falling to new lows in the early 1990s. The global downturn in the IT sector has had a particularly negative effect on Stockholm. Telecoms giant Ericsson – which employs roughly 9,000 people in the Stockholm region and 85,000 across the world – has recently laid off thousands of workers, and even its top managers are openly pessimistic about its future.

> **'Since World War II more than a million people have emigrated to Sweden, mainly to work or as refugees.'**

The city is also facing a severe housing shortage, made worse by the influx of nearly 7,000 people a year. Property development has not kept up with population growth, and such buildings as have been constructed are usually sold privately rather than rented. Apartments in Stockholm are not rented on the open market, but distributed through queues run by various government and private agencies. The system was designed to avoid high prices, and to keep society egalitarian – as the Swedes like it. Some argue that the conservative city government has complicated matters by allowing renters to group together to buy their buildings from the government at below-market prices. This has reduced the number of available apartments, which were already scarce – it's common to have to wait ten years to be offered an apartment within the city. Black-market deals abound, with people illegally selling their first-hand contracts at obscene prices.

Immigration is also an issue. Since World War II more than a million people have emigrated to Sweden, mainly to work or as refugees. About 20 per cent of the population of Stockholm County were born abroad or have an immigrant background. Finns are the largest group of immigrants, while recent refugees have come mainly from the Middle East. Although the amount of state aid for refugees has declined over the years, the government provides housing, monthly allowances and courses in Swedish – far more than most countries. The integration of refugees into the larger society has been less successful, however. Thanks to Stockholm's housing shortage and high cost of living, many immigrants and refugees have become grouped in the suburbs, notably Rinkeby and Tensta.

Although most Swedes reject the anti-immigrant attitudes of other European countries, an undercurrent of prejudice still exists. Immigrants and discrimination became a hot topic a few days before the 2002 election, when a popular TV documentary programme showed an undercover reporter posing as a voter with anti-immigrant opinions at party information booths. Several leading members of the Moderate Party were forced to resign when their racist comments and jokes were caught on film. In another alarming development, the nationalistic and overtly anti-immigrant Sweden's Democrats party (Sverigedemokraterna) received more than eight per cent of the votes in district elections in Skåne. The Social Democrats have promised to redouble their efforts aimed at integration and tolerance.

The Green Party (Miljöpartiet) – which claims to belong to neither the left or right political blocks – gained an unusual bargaining position after the recent election. Without the Green Party's four per cent of the vote, neither block could form governments in either the Riksdag or Stockholm city council. After several days of negotiations, a national government was finally formed between the Green Party, the Social Democrats and the Left Party (Vänsterpartiet). At the time of writing, control of Stockholm city was still undecided.

In the past four years, the right-wing coalition that ran Stockholm from the Stadshuset has privatised hospitals, schools and public transport, in addition to selling off government-run apartment buildings. If the Green Party does team up with the left-wing parties, Stockholmers can expect a new era of raised taxes and government spending on road projects, apartment buildings, education and the police. At a national level, the newly formed government has already promised to extend parental leave and to ban all cod fishing in the Baltic Sea. Whether business will thrive remains to be seen, but at least in the near future fish, parents and tourists should all flourish.

Ordning och reda

The name of a well-known Swedish stationery chain, *ordning och reda* is also a common expression meaning orderliness, something the Swedes are great admirers of – particularly when it's their own orderly behaviour. A classic example is Sweden's switch from driving on the left-hand side of the road to the right in 1967. In preparation for the change, the government distributed a 30-page booklet to every household in the country and created a special right-handed-driving traffic commission. Soldiers stood ready by the road on Sunday morning, 3 September, to rearrange the traffic signs at the exact moment of the change. At 5am when the switch was made, all the Swedes on the road drove over to the correct lane and not one accident was reported.

Or consider the omnipresent queuing-by-number system. Instead of standing around in a shop in a messy huddle, each newcomer collects a numbered ticket from a machine, then patiently waits their turn. The system is used not just at supermarket deli counters, but at post offices, banks, bakeries, alcohol shops – basically anywhere where disorder might possibly occur.

This love of efficiency also extends into the social realm. Swedes generally do not like saying more than is required, and small talk is often referred to as *kall prat* ('cold talk'). Supermarket cashiers greet each customer with the same monotone *hej*, like a machine stamping packages on a conveyor belt. At parties, it is a tradition for each new guest to methodically introduce themselves with a handshake to each person in the room. Don't worry if they don't remember your name: when the drinks start flowing you'll soon be their best friend – another very Swedish trait.

Architecture

From fortresses to functionalism via rococo.

Undeniably one of Europe's most beautiful cities, Stockholm has a dramatic skyline that has changed surprisingly little with each passing century. For hundreds of years the same church spires have dominated a watery landscape punctuated by rocky-shored islands packed neatly with brightly painted low-rise buildings and prim green parks. Swedish neutrality in both World Wars meant that, unlike most of Europe's other major cities, Stockholm has never been bombed. As a result, visitors can experience an unbroken history of architectural development that began in about 1100 and continues right up to the present day. Stockholm boasts buildings that range dramatically in style from ancient churches of early Nordic Christianity, through the quaint Renaissance and baroque townhouses of Gamla Stan, to Kafkaesque high-rises in some of the city's suburbs. If you want to find out more, **Stockholms Stadsmuseum** (*see p90*) tells the story of the building of the city through plans and models.

► Many of the buildings mentioned here are described in more detail in the **Sightseeing** chapters.

ORIGINS TO RENAISSANCE

In 1252 Birger Jarl began constructing **Tre Kronor** castle (only the foundation remains), on the site of several earlier wooden fortresses, in the part of Gamla Stan where the Royal Palace now stands; a town, Stockholm, quickly sprang up within its ring wall. The Medeltidsmuseet (underneath the parliament building) and Museet Tre Kronor (underneath the Royal Palace) exhibit excavations that give an indication of what Stockholm was like during this period.

Riddarholmskyrkan, on Riddarholmen, was begun in the late 13th century and is considered to be one of the first Gothic buildings constructed in Sweden (though much of it has been rebuilt since then; the oldest section is the north aisle). **Storkyrkan** in Gamla Stan was founded in 1306, but it gained its present shape in the late 1400s and underwent a baroque makeover in the 1730s. Even older than these buildings are the suburban churches of **Bromma Kyrka** and **Solna Kyrka**, erected in the 1100s even before the official founding of Stockholm.

Birger Jarl's town on Gamla Stan grew steadily and by the 15th century had developed the maze of narrow lanes that still defines its structure today. If you look at a map you will

Riddarholmskyrkan. *See p23.*

see that the lane structure is almost that of a wheel, with spokes radiating out from the centre. The reason for this is that Stockholm suffered from a number of devastating fires in its early centuries, and the wheel structure was an innovation that allowed townspeople to rapidly reach the shore and fetch water to extinguish fires. Without it the medieval town visible today would probably not have survived to see the 21st century.

In the late 15th century the Church was still the key protagonist in Sweden's architectural development, as it had been since the end of the Viking period. But in the 16th century the balance of power began to change. By 1523 King Gustav Vasa had united Sweden and he was determined to turn it into a modern nation-state and hereditary monarchy. He knew success depended on limiting the influence of the Church and intimidating all potential rivals, and that architecture had an important role to play.

Since by the mid 1500s Stockholm had become Sweden's most important town, he decided to centralise his power base at Tre Kronor and make it his permanent royal residence. He began importing foreign architects and craftsmen to build a series of defensive castles at strategic locations across his realm to ward off Danish attacks. In the late 1500s he commissioned these architects and craftsmen to convert Tre Kronor into a classical Italian Renaissance palace fit for a king of his stature. Unfortunately, Tre Kronor and all its splendour burned to the ground in 1697.

During the 17th century three different Renaissance styles came to be widely popular, as the aristocracy began to build townhouses in the capital to be able to spend more time at court. The castles in Vadstena and Kalmar (both a few hours' drive south of Stockholm) are the best remaining examples of the early classicism that defined Tre Kronor. The second style to become popular, German-Dutch Renaissance, gained precedence in the 1620s – you can recognise it by its highly decorated gables adorned with imaginative ornamental forms. Gamla Stan contains a number of fine examples, including Christian Julius Döteber's **Petersenska Huset** at Munkbron 11-13, as well as **Grillska Huset** and **Schantzska Huset** on Stortorget. Dutch Palladianism was the third Renaissance style to be all the rage; it's characterised by columns that stretch across at least two storeys. The best example in Stockholm is the palace of **Riddarhuset** (1674), which was designed by the man who is considered Sweden's first professional architect, Simon de la Vallée. His son Jean was responsible for the building's distinctive *säteri* roof (a roof with a small vertical rise halfway up) – the first of many buildings to be crowned with this entirely Swedish architectural invention.

'The Swedish royal court hired Nicodemus Tessin as court architect in 1646 and he became Stockholm's first official city architect in 1661.'

Jean (1620-96) became one of the leading architects of the Carolinian period, along with a German architect named Nicodemus Tessin (1615-81). The Swedish royal court hired Tessin as court architect in 1646. In 1661, he became Stockholm's first official city architect.

BAROQUE AND THE TESSINS

By the mid 17th century Sweden was a great power and King Karl XI wanted to construct grand buildings that would show off his wealth and status. He sent Tessin and Jean de la Vallée to Italy and France for new ideas, and they came back with baroque. Most of the buildings constructed in Stockholm between 1650 and 1730 reflected one of three baroque styles: French, Roman or 'Swedish' (a French-Roman hybrid). The French style is the most fanciful, often created by linking a group of structures together under an imposing copper roof. In creating **Bondeska Palatset** (1662-73) at Riddarhustorget 8, Tessin and de la Vallée worked together, carefully copying French examples. The grand palaces of Rome were clearly the inspiration for de la Vallée's designs for **Oxenstiernska Palatset** (1653) at Storkyrkobrinken 2. Greatly admired, this palace inspired the faintly Roman look of the new Kungliga Slottet built shortly thereafter.

The greatest example of truly Swedish baroque is Tessin's **Drottningholms Slott** – where the royal family now lives – just to the west of Stockholm, a World Heritage Site often referred to as Sweden's own mini-Versailles. The palace is a majestic blend of Roman and French styles crowned with a *säteri* roof. Church builders leaped on the baroque style too. **Tyska Kyrkan** on Gamla Stan received a lovely baroque makeover in 1638-42, while **Katarina Kyrka** on Södermalm (1656-95), designed by de la Vallée, is a breathtaking example of an entirely baroque construction.

After his father's death, Nicodemus Tessin the Younger (1654-1728) put the finishing touches to Drottningholms Slott, his father's masterwork, and designed the impressive gardens. Following the fire at Tre Kronor palace, King Karl XII chose Tessin the Younger to draw up plans for a new palace on the site; he is also well known for his work at the Amalienborg Palace in Copenhagen and the Louvre in Paris. When he died, his son Carl Gustav Tessin (1695-1770) became superintendent of all the royal palaces and it was under his leadership that the new **Kungliga Slottet** (Royal Palace) was completed in 1754.

ROCOCO AND BEYOND

By the end of the 1720s Sweden's upper classes had tired of the ostentation of baroque styles; they wanted more simplicity and rationality in their homes. As if on cue, Carl Gustav Tessin and Carl Hårleman introduced French rococo architecture to Sweden. The style quickly became popular and is responsible for many of Stockholm's most beautiful buildings. Rounded window frames and a low foundation are typical features of this style; a new type of roof called mansard (a four-sided roof with a double slope on all sides) replaced the *säteri*. Hårleman's **Observatoriet** (observatory; 1748-53) at Observatoriekullen gives a good sense of the simplicity of the style, while Erik Palmstedt's **Börsen** (1773-6) – the former Stock Exchange, now the Nobelmuseet – on Stortorget, and the 1727-9 exterior and interior remodelling of **Ulriksdals Slott** in Solna by Hårleman and Göran Josuae Adelcrantz, give a sense of how elegant Swedish rococo could be.

Mid to late 18th-century architecture in Stockholm is characterised by a light-heartedness not seen in earlier periods. For example, Carl Fredrik Adelcrantz was commissioned to erect **Kina Slott** (Chinese Pavilion) in Drottningholm's park as an exotic gift from King Adolf Fredrik to his queen. Soon after its unveiling in 1763 the fanciful pseudo-Asian pavilion became a popular rural retreat for members of the royal family. Fredrik Magnus Piper's design of **Hagaparken** illustrates the ideals of King Gustav III's reign (1771-92); it is also the foremost example of an English park in Sweden. It contains many buildings of interest, including the peculiar Pavilion, the sublime Ekotemplet, the playful Koppartälten and the dainty Haga Slott.

As the 18th century reached its end, a more austere classicism came to rule the day again. In 1793 the lakefront side of **Karlbergs Slott** in north-west Stockholm (home of the Swedish military academy) underwent renovation in neo-classical style under the guidance of Louis Jean Desprez and Carl Christopher Gjörwell. Fredrik Blom based his plans for **Rosendals Slott** – a pleasure palace for King Karl XIV Johan on Djurgården – on

Drottningholms Slott.

Uncompromising modernism at **Sergels Torg**. *See p29.*

the tenets of French classicism. The building, finished in 1827, is easily distinguishable by its light imperial style and delicately ornamented façade.

By the 1830s Swedish architects had tired of all this restraint and turned back to the 'romance' of the Italian and French Renaissance for inspiration, resulting in a revival in the building of highly ornamental exteriors. The **National Museum** (1846-66), designed by the German architect Friedrich August Stüler, is a prime example of Italian Renaissance, while Adolf Wilhelm Edelsvärd's **Central Station** (1867-71) was clearly inspired by the French Renaissance. Later in the century many architects became fascinated by Sweden's medieval architecture. Fredrik Blom was one of the first; his medieval-inspired **Kastellet** (citadel), a key landmark when approaching the city by sea, was erected in 1846-8. Stockholm's **Synagogan** (synagogue; 1870) by Fredrik Wilhelm Scholander is a one-of-a-kind house of worship in 'ancient Eastern style'.

In the mid 1800s materials such as glass and cast iron became cheaper and more accessible, inspiring architects to create spacious rooms with abundant natural light and to mix styles with abandon. Another great change was that architects began to work for companies and municipalities rather than exclusively for the royal court or wealthy individuals. New factories, office buildings, hospitals, schools and prisons were put up at lightning speed. The monumental **Konradsberg Sjukhus** (1855-75) that Albert Törnqvist built at Gjörwellsgatan 16 offers an insight into the key principles of health care at the time; its many windows give the building a bright and airy interior, while its strict form and clean lines suggest order and hygiene.

Architect Aron Johansson constructed the bold, baroque-inspired **Riksdagshuset** (Parliament) in 1892-1905. In so doing he raised the ire of the young architects of the nascent National Romantic movement. They argued passionately that its busy exterior was entirely inappropriate – altogether too showy and pretentious for a country whose architectural tradition had always (in their romantic view, at least) been centred on simplicity.

NATIONAL ROMANTICISM AND ART NOUVEAU

In the late 19th century, nationalism was on the rise across Europe. Sweden's National Romantic style emerged in response to the national confidence generated by its rapidly expanding industrial might. Rather than looking for inspiration abroad, Swedish architects rediscovered their country's own rich architectural tradition. The Scandinavian Renaissance style that had been popular in the 17th century was the main focus.

In the 1880s the long-neglected area of Gamla Stan (and its unique 17th-century portals, in particular) began to attract the attention of architects such as Isak Gustav Clason (1856-1930). Curious about medieval building techniques, he designed a new building at **Österlånggatan 14** (1888-9) that quite successfully mimicked the look of the medieval originals that surround it. Clason's enormous **Nordiska Museet** is a fine example of the National Romantic style, with its cupolas, towers and richly adorned portal. When it opened in 1907 it was hailed as a masterpiece, 'the likes of which have not been created since the days of the great Tessin'. The grand indoor market, **Östermalms Saluhall** (1888), is another of Clason's creations.

His later work on **Timmermansordern** (the Order of Carpenters building; 1927), at Eriksbergsparken 1, marks the end of the National Romantic movement.

A drive to preserve Sweden's architectural heritage began at about the same time. In 1891 Artur Hazelius opened **Skansen**, an open-air museum that displays an authentic collection of traditional buildings from all over Sweden. It includes a Stockholm neighbourhood from the 1700s made up of apartments and small workshops of different kinds. The National Romantic architects visited the park frequently for inspiration.

'Swedish classicism of the 1920s was known as "Swedish Grace" because it charmed everyone with its simplicity and elegance.'

Art nouveau (known as Jugendstil in Sweden) came briefly into fashion in parallel with National Romanticism, but its influence is easier to see in privately owned apartment buildings than in public works of the time. Fredrik Liljekvist's **Kungliga Dramatiska Teatern** (Royal Dramatic Theatre; 1901-8), with its exquisitely sculpted white marble exterior, bright gold detailing and magnificent approach ramp, and **Centralbadet** (1902-5), a huge art nouveau bath house built by Wilhelm Klemming, are the two major exceptions. Klemming's visionary concepts about urban design, architecture and city-park planning came together perfectly in the Centralbadet project. (It is also of note for being the first building in Sweden constructed using Hennebique's reinforced concrete technique.) Ferdinand Boberg's **Thielska Galleriet** (1904-5) on Djurgården offers another example of art nouveau influence.

National Romanticism reached its peak in the 1910s. Architects had now turned for inspiration to the time of the 16th-century Vasa kings, and were designing buildings with clean façades displaying little if any decor, and steep roofs. The best example of this style is Stockholm's **Rådhuset** (Courthouse; 1908-15), which was designed by Carl Westman to look like the Renaissance classicist Vadstena castle.

At the turn of the 20th century Stockholm's city architect Per Olof Hallman (1869-1941) oversaw some ground-breaking residential neighbourhoods. He is best remembered for the artistic flair that he brought to urban planning and his ability to smoothly integrate new residential complexes within the

The pastel city

Many visitors find it striking that a large proportion of Stockholm's buildings are painted in complementary shades of pink, yellow, orange and red. (In more recent years blue and green have been added to the mix too.) It's a distinctive feature of the cityscape, and one of the reasons why Stockholm is so visually appealing.

In the 20th century the city government made an effort to find out the original colour of buildings, and to repaint them in those colours. In fact, all buildings in the city, even private homes in the suburbs, require permission (given by the city planning department) to be painted another colour. If the applicant wishes to use a colour that is not in line with the styles of the time at which the building was constructed, their application will almost certainly be rejected. Buildings listed as being of special cultural or historical value (such as those in Gamla Stan and other older parts of the city) require the approval of the experts who work at the Stockholms Stadsmuseum.

Thus, to a certain extent one can judge the age of a building by the colour and shade in which it is painted. In Gamla Stan, for instance, many 17th-century buildings are red, while most of the 18th-century ones are yellow. In newer parts of the city, such as Kungsholmen, there are many green buildings. And in Gärdet, built in the 1930s, there are plenty of light-coloured buildings: shades of off-white, grey and pale yellow.

surrounding natural environment. Fine examples of his skills can be seen in Östermalm in **Lärkstaden** (around Friggagatan and Baldersgatan), **Danderydsgatan** and **Diplomatstaden** (around Dag Hammarskjölds Väg), and in Vasastaden in **Rödabergsområdet** (Falugatan and around).

Ragnar Östberg (1866-1945) is one of the best-known architects of this period. His most famous creation is Stockholm's **Stadshuset** (City Hall; 1923), which was influenced by both Gothic and Italian Renaissance styles. He also designed **Östermalms Läroverket** (now a secondary school called Östra Real; 1906-10) and **Patent och Registreringsverket** (1911-21), the patent and licensing authority's building on Valhallavägen in Östermalm.

During the 1910s classicism slowly became fashionable yet again, and by the 1920s it was in full flow. The construction of the Stadshuset and the Göteberg Exhibition of 1923 were the start of a period of international acclaim for Swedish architecture – a heady time, since no one outside the country had paid much attention to its architects since Tessin the Younger. Swedish classicism of the 1920s was known as 'Swedish Grace' because it charmed everyone with its lightness, simplicity and elegance – especially when compared with the bombastic works that were being constructed in other parts of the world at the time. The best example of Swedish Grace in Stockholm is the **Stadsbiblioteket** (1920-28) built by Gunnar Asplund (*see below* **Super Swedes: Gunnar Asplund**), who was without doubt the most influential Swedish architect of the 20th century.

MODERNISM AND FUNCTIONALISM

As leading architect of the Stockholm Fair in 1930, Asplund is credited as the man who introduced modernism to Sweden in the form

Super Swedes: Gunnar Asplund

More than 60 years after his death, Erik Gunnar Asplund (1885-1940) is as influential in Scandinavian architectural circles as he ever was. He is perhaps best remembered as being the only Swedish architect who fully succeeded in humanising the strict utilitarian underpinnings of functionalism. He rose to prominence in the interwar years and went on to have a huge impact on the development of 20th-century architecture. He was especially masterful in his delicate balancing of the relationships between light and dark, natural landscapes and human construction, and architecture and people.

In his role as lead architect for the 1930 Stockholm Fair, Asplund introduced functionalism to Sweden. The fair was a huge international success and Asplund won praise for its open airy buildings and the arty advertising used to promote it. The clean-lined, rational buildings Asplund designed in the following decade (such as Bredenbergs department store at Drottninggatan 54 in 1935, his Stennäs summer house on Lis island in 1936 and the National Bacteriological Laboratory in Solna in 1937) all demonstrated his incomparable talent for managing light, as well as showcasing his love of fine architectural detailing. His magical work on Göteborg's law courts (1913-37) brought natural light down into the great hall from high above in a way that made it impossible to judge the distance to the ceiling.

More than anything else, though, it's the 'humanist' aspect of Asplund's work that has made him such an enduring inspiration. This was achieved largely through the materials he used in his interiors – glass cases, wood panelling, mouldings, elegant railings and soft-edged columns, for example. He is best known for three works in Stockholm: the **Skandia** cinema (1923 – *see p196*), the **Stadsbiblioteket** (1920-28 – *pictured; see p77*) and the **Skogskyrkogården** (1914-40).

Many of the central themes of Asplund's work can be seen at Skandia. For example, he often shaped buildings around the experience of the interior or innermost room. At Skandia, the grand yet intimate auditorium resembles a public square surrounded by festively decorated buildings with canopied balconies. To enter the upper balcony visitors must pass through one of a series of classically decorated and starkly painted doorways, set at a slight angle from the wall. The lobby ceiling seems to disappear into nowhere, courtesy of an unlit cupola.

The Stadsbiblioteket (City Library), with its distinctive artwork and finely worked interior designs, is one of the country's most internationally celebrated buildings. It is the perfect representation of the ideals of the Swedish Grace period – though some say its simplified volumes also show the influence of utopian French neo-classicism. A monumental stone propylaeum guards the of functionalism (*Funkis*). It was a radical new approach to architecture that rejected tradition and focused sharply on the ideals of utilitarianism, rationality, economics and health. A building boom ensued and scores of sober *Funkis* apartment buildings painted in a palette of light pastels sprouted up in a variety of patterns across the city. The best examples can be seen in the Gärdet area of Stockholm, particularly around **Tessinparken** (1932-7), north of Östermalm.

In the early 1950s many Swedes felt a little left out – across Europe bombed-out cities were being rebuilt in a modernist style, and tall, proud, American-style skyscrapers were springing up all over. And yet there was Stockholm with its embarrassingly old city centre dominated by crumbling, tiny houses. In an effort to 'be modern', the area to the north of Gamla Stan, known as the old Klara district, was brutally demolished and later replaced with **Sergels Torg** (1960) and the **Kulturhuset** (1968-73). Shortly after the deed was done, many Stockholmers regretted it, and Peter Celsing, the architect of the Kulturhuset, became a scapegoat for the destruction. While the Kulturhuset has succeeded in becoming a well-loved Stockholm institution, the rest of the area has long been considered an eyesore, the sunken square itself fast becoming a magnet for drug dealers. (Yet, ironically, there were many who opposed recent plans to revamp Sergels Torg and pull down its discoloured glass tower, arguing that it has now become an important part of Stockholm's architectural history.) The city's first skyscrapers were also built nearby: **Hötorgshusen** (1952-6), the five towers that line Sveavägen from Sergels Torg to Hötorget.

Not content with the destruction of the old Klara district, there was even discussion of levelling the whole of Gamla Stan, which was

entrance; passing under it, the visitor ascends a staircase to reach the centre – a broad, cylindrical hall lined with books.

Asplund worked with fellow architect Sigurd Lewerentz on the Skogskyrkogården (Woodland Cemetery) project, based on the prize-winning plan they submitted to an international competition in 1914. The harmony they achieved in unifying the surrounding landscape with the buildings attracted international attention: the cemetery is one of the few works of 20th-century architecture selected for UNESCO's World Heritage List. The project took 26 years to complete, so it also provides an overview of Swedish architecture from National Romanticism to mature functionalism.

Asplund mainly designed the cemetery's buildings. His **Skogskapellet** (chapel; 1918), set in a small, walled churchyard, is most admired for its unexpectedly sunny and warm interior. The **Skogskrematoriet** (crematorium; 1934-40) shows his total mastery of the building style of the '30s and is recognised as one of the most noteworthy buildings of the 20th century anywhere.

Globen: a whole different ball game.

at that time a neglected slum rather than the bustling tourist attraction it is today. Luckily, city leaders decided to let Gamla Stan stand; they did, however, knock down a number of buildings in the area in order to build an unsightly transportation corridor that virtually cuts Gamla Stan off from Riddarholmen.

It was also in the 1950s that Swedish architects tired of traditional functionalism and its strict reliance on straight lines. They began to design buildings in unusual geometric patterns – with a star-shaped foundation, for example, rather than a square or rectangular one. They also reconsidered how buildings in a neighbourhood should be grouped in relation to one another. These ideas are best represented in the internationally acclaimed suburban neighbourhood of **Vällingby**, the first of Sweden's many A-B-C neighbourhoods. A stands for *arbete* (work), B for *bostad* (home) and C for *centrum* (shopping centre) – the concept was an attempt to decentralise the city that ultimately failed.

In the 1960s and '70s Stockholm and many other Swedish cities suffered an acute housing shortage, and an increase in the number of cars. The government pledged to build a million new homes in ten years, a project that was known as the 'Million Programme' (*see p31* **A million homes**). During the years of the programme, Sweden's builders erected new apartment buildings faster than any other country in the world. However, these buildings were for the most part Eastern Bloc-inspired, prefabricated high-rises of little architectural note.

At the same time that new suburbs were popping up around the city, the **Tunnelbana** metro system expanded dramatically; the blue line opened in the mid 1970s. The 1970s were a tumultuous period for Swedish architecture, and significant ideological shifts took place before the decade was out. This is well illustrated by writer Olof Hultin's comparison of two buildings designed by the firm Coordinator Arkitekter just a decade apart: the **Garnisonen** office building (1965-71) at Karlavägen 100, and the **Salénhuset** office block (1975-8) at Norrlandsgatan 15.

At Garnisonen the architects followed the functionalist approach to the letter, and as a result the exterior suffers from a kind of terminal dreariness – it stands out like a sore thumb, but there isn't anything particularly interesting about it. By the time they designed Salénhuset, however, the firm had discovered that by breaking a structure down into its component parts and varying the materials used it was possible to create a building that both had its own personality and broadly fitted in with its neighbours. Based loosely on the tenets of 'variation ideology', this approach has been called 'functionalism in traditional garb'.

'Now some architects and politicians would like to see green space in the centre sacrificed to build skyscrapers.'

Probably the most visible postmodern building in Stockholm is the indoor arena of **Globen** (1989), the world's largest spherical structure, whose 'geometrical precision has a curiously disruptive effect on the scale of the townscape', as Hultin has written. Another good example of postmodernism is Ricardo Bofill's **Båge** (part of Södra Stationsområdet), a colossal residential development on Söder in the shape of a semicircle that was completed in 1992. Part of the same housing development, Henning Larsen's stubby apartment towerblock at **Medborgarplatsen** was controversial from the moment he submitted the blueprints. It ended up half the height it was meant to be, which has thrown the look of the whole neighbourhood off-kilter.

From 1995 to '98 Spanish architect Rafael Moneo worked on the **Moderna Museet** and **Arkitekturmuseet** on Skeppsholmen, both of which are admired for their boxy interiors. Despite the substantial size of the maze-like complex, Moneo won the praise of Stockholmers for designing it in such a way that it did not overwhelm the historical look and feel of Skeppsholmen. Both buildings recently developed mould problems and are currently closed (until 2004) for repairs.

THE PRESENT AND THE FUTURE

Stockholm currently finds itself with a serious housing crisis and is having a hard time deciding how to deal with it. Some architects, politicians and citizens would like to see densification of the city centre – sacrificing some green space to build skyscrapers that could house thousands. Traditionalists strongly resist such proposals, believing they have a duty to protect Stockholm's unique skyline and historic parks from fast-talking developers. Some progress is being made with new housing developments – in Hammarby Sjöstad and Gåshaga, for example – but these are luxury condo developments out of the reach of most of those waiting in the city's housing queues. Some downtown office buildings are having residential units built on their roofs.

Today's famous Swedish architects – such as Thomas Sandell, Gert Wingårdh and Anders Wilhelmson – are almost exclusively known for what they have built outside Stockholm. Disappointingly, one of the most talked-about new buildings in the city in the past few years is the striking new **Finnish Embassy**, designed by a non-Swede, the Finnish architect Kristian Gullichsen. For the most part, leading Swedish architects' ideas for new buildings in Stockholm are considered altogether too radical by municipal city planners. But who's to say what the future might hold?

A million homes

'The Million Programme' is the unofficial name given to a loosely defined housing policy undertaken by the Swedish government between 1964 and 1974. It was taken from the Social Democrats' 1964 election slogan 'A million homes in ten years'. By this time Sweden's housing shortage was so acute – approximately 400,000 people were queuing for apartments – that it had become a key political issue. The problem was rooted in the fact that strict rent controls had been in place since 1942 and little new housing had been built after World War II because capital and labour had been invested in export industries instead.

In its effort to tackle the housing shortage, the government offered loans to private companies to build massive apartment complexes surrounded by greenery in the suburbs of cities and towns across Sweden. The complexes were mostly made up of tall building slabs and endless concrete, the vast majority revealing little or no imagination on the part of their architects. A side effect of the huge building boom was a delay in follow-up investment and in the development of retail and service centres. Many commentators criticised the new areas sharply, calling them monotonous, grim and inhuman. Some of the most monumental, all-concrete edifices were even condemned as Stalinist. The most characteristic Million Programme examples in Stockholm are the suburban communities of Brandbergen, Hallonbergen, Hallunda and Tensta-Rinkeby.

In the late 1960s the government decided to partially liberalise the housing market and offer tax breaks for homeowners, which made it easier for Swedes to buy their own homes instead of renting. As a result the production of new apartment complexes started to slow down in 1970. By the end of 1972 more and more housing companies were suffering from liquidity problems due to difficulties finding tenants, and by 1974 the Million Programme era was over.

In total, 1,006,000 apartments were built in Sweden during this period, significantly improving the standard of living for a sizeable proportion of the Swedish population. Most of these apartments remain in use today. In fact, in Stockholm some Million Programme developments have become much sought after because the apartments are roomy and well planned – and because the city is once again facing a severe housing shortage.

Svenskt Tenn. See p35.

Design

String shelves, concrete chairs and inside-out houses.

Think of Swedish design and the first things to come to mind are probably blond wood and IKEA. But Swedish design includes so much more than that, with materials ranging from fine glass to porcelain, and products including clothing, shoes, textiles and furniture, as well as home electronics from Electrolux and Husqvarna, telephones from Ericsson and cars from Volvo and Saab. Swedish design ranges across virtually all fields and a veritable kaleidoscope of styles, and has been in a state of constant and often rapid development since the Industrial Revolution.

Most Stockholmers – possibly even Swedes in general – have a keen interest in design. They tend to be passionate about the look of their homes and are willing to spend significant amounts of time and money finding exactly the right furniture and accessories. As a result, Stockholm has myriad specialised design shops; its newsstands are always packed with numerous Swedish-language design, architecture and home-decorating magazines; and the culture pages of the major daily newspapers generally include a design story or two. Then, of course, there's the **Stockholm Furniture Fair** (*see p183*) every winter – a major event on the international design calendar. In short, Stockholm is a city on the cutting edge of contemporary design and it offers interested visitors both a rich past and a vital present to explore.

The relationship between design from Sweden and design from other Scandinavian countries is somewhat blurred. The great 20th-century designers of Sweden, Denmark, Finland and Norway have all impacted on each other and on other less famous designers in the region, so the styles of the four countries are similar in many ways – but there are some general differences. Finnish design, for instance, is best known for its elegance and sophistication; the Danes are regarded as having the strongest sense of tradition; and Swedish design is considered most pertinent. The simplicity, craftsmanship and choice of materials of Nordic designers are, however, strikingly similar.

BEGINNINGS

The roots of modern Swedish design lie in the late 1800s, when the Swedish elite was first exposed to German art nouveau. The new style dramatically changed the way well-to-do Swedes thought about their homes. Rooms that had previously been heavily draped and crowded with overstuffed furniture were carefully remade according to an interior design concept defined by elegance and openness. Rooms became bright and airy, with loosely grouped furniture. Nature inspired the design of new furniture and household accessories – straight lines were abandoned in favour of curvy, organic forms. And the communal 'living room' became the centre of the house, replacing separate drawing rooms for men and women.

'Fresh air, natural light and access to greenery became the defining characteristics of Swedish home design.'

The celebrated artist **Carl Larsson** (1853-1919) and his wife Karin played a significant role in changing the understanding of what a home should be, and in making interior design a subject of interest for the average Swede. In 1899 Larsson published his bestselling book *Ett hem* ('A Home'), which contained beautiful illustrations of his home in Sundborn in the province of Dalarna. The house showed wide-ranging influences (Swedish 'rustic', Gustavian, rococo, art nouveau and the English Arts and Crafts movement, among others), but despite its mishmash of styles it was remarkable in its simplicity – a soothing place to live, work and raise a family. The style was a huge hit with all social classes and spread rapidly into both urban and rural homes across the country.

In 1925 Le Corbusier's pavilion at the Paris International Exhibition introduced a new design

Top ten Designers

As well as **Jonas Bohlin** and **Bruno Mathsson**, here are some legendary Swedish names to watch out for as you hit Stockholm's design shops.

Astrid Sampe (1909-2002). Famous textile designer.
Sixten Sason (1912-67). Industrial designer for Electrolux and Husqvarna. His design principles are still seen in products designed today.
Yngve Ekström (1913-88). Famous furniture designer, most well known for his Lamino chair.
Sigurd Persson (born 1914). Celebrated modernist silversmith.
Stig Lindberg (1916-82). Designer of fine porcelain.
Katja Hallberg (born 1920). Sweden's most famous clothing and shoe designer, founder of Katja of Sweden.
John Kandell (1925-91). Designer of chairs and cabinets inspired by architectural and sculptural principles.
Erik Höglund (1932-98). Internationally renowned glass designer.

10 Swedish Designers: the fabric of Swedish design. *See p36*.

The story of IKEA

'A long time ago a boy was born in a poor country called Small-land.' That's how IKEA – a company that has its humble beginnings in the sleepy town of Älmhult in the southern Swedish province of Småland – introduces its story in its employee handbook. That same little boy, Ingvar Kamprad (born 1926), went on to revolutionise furniture retailing and interior decorating worldwide and, in so doing, single-handedly built the world's largest furniture empire. He is now the 17th richest person in the world, with a personal fortune of $13.4 billion. His company currently operates 175 superstores in 31 countries, employing 70,000 people to supply approximately 200 million customers a year with IKEA classics such as the Billy bookcase, Klippan sofa and Poäng chair, generating annual revenues in excess of €7.7 billion. The IKEA catalogue has a circulation of 100 million, making it 'the second most read publication in the world', as one of the company's ads proclaims.

Kamprad got an early start in business, selling ballpoint pens, fish, matches and watches. At 17 he registered his company under the name IKEA, from the initials of his name and those of the farm (Elmtaryd) and village (Aggunaryd) of his birth. In a brief

idea to the Swedish consciousness: modernism. The movement made its true breakthrough in Sweden at the Stockholm Fair organised by architect **Gunnar Asplund** (1885-1940) in 1930, and the Swedish offshoot came to be known as functionalism (*see p28* **Super Swedes: Gunnar Asplund**). The key to functionalism's success in Sweden may well have been the fact that it was well suited to the *folkhemmet* ('home of the people') socio-political concept introduced by the Social Democrats in 1928.The fresh air, natural light and access to greenery extolled by Asplund's functionalism quickly became the defining characteristics of Swedish home design and urban planning. Architects and designers in Sweden and other Nordic countries were spurred to make the function of the building or object their main focus.

The modernism and functionalism that were so celebrated at the Stockholm Fair did generate some opposition, however – particularly among traditionalist designers such as **Elsa Gullberg** (1886-1984) and **Carl Malmsten** (1888-1972). They reacted strongly against the industrial design ideals of functionalism and fought for the survival of traditional Swedish methods, styles and materials. Ironically, although Sweden is famous for functionalism, it is Malmsten, more than any other 20th-century designer, who best represents a truly Swedish interior design style. He was responsible for furnishing a number of important buildings in Stockholm, including the Stadshuset (1916) and Konserthuset (1926). He strove to create a new Swedish furniture style with roots in both rustic traditions and 18th-century classicism. The

departure from the fairy story, it has since been revealed that at this time Kamprad attended a few meetings of the pro-Nazi New Swedish Movement – a brief, naive flirtation that he has wholeheartedly apologised for and calls 'the greatest mistake of [his] life'.

By the 1950s Kamprad was selling locally made furniture by mail order. He opened his first furniture showroom in Älmhult in 1953, offering his now famous 'factory prices' – often deeply undercutting his rivals. Delighted Swedish consumers flocked to the store, but it didn't take long for IKEA's competitors to react, threatening its suppliers and banning it from trade fairs. As a result, IKEA was forced to start designing its own furniture and to move its production to Poland.

Kamprad and his team soon introduced the winning concepts of self-assembly and flat-packaging. At a furniture fair in Milan in the mid 1950s, Kamprad came up with the basis of his 'democratic design' concept. The stark contrast between the sleek, exclusive designer furniture at the fair and the drab, unsightly homes of Italian workers struck Kamprad deeply. 'Why do poor people have to put up with ugly things?' he pondered. He left the fair more determined than ever to offer attractive, functional products at low prices.

In 1965 IKEA opened its first store in Stockholm in the suburb of Kungens Kurva. The building, modelled on Frank Lloyd Wright's Guggenheim Museum in New York, had plenty of showroom space as well as a self-service warehouse – a then unheard-of idea. The firm launched a series of catchy ads in the 'Why pay more?' vein and, before you could say 'My, that's cheap', nearly every home in Sweden was furnished with at least a few of his products. Even today, nearly 40 years later, you would be hard pressed to find a Swedish home that doesn't boast something from IKEA – and this is also increasingly true in the rest of Europe and in North America.

In spring 2002 IKEA unveiled its largest store in the world when it completed its lengthy renovation and expansion project at Kungens Kurva (*see p170; pictured*). With the addition of a huge new rectangular warehouse, the size of the outlet has now increased to 58,000 square metres (69,000 square yards). The old, round 'Guggenheim' section has been converted into complete show homes of various sizes.

What's next? The company has plans for vast expansion in the USA, Russia and China. After all, the IKEA experience has always been: 'If you build it, they will come.'

fusion of the two styles is best seen in his work of the 1920s, with its signature intarsia decor. In the 1940s and '50s he developed a variety of home furnishings, including armchairs and sofas. In 1955 he began to manufacture his own furniture, and in 1960 he founded Capellagården, a school of craft and design – still going strong – in Vickelby on the island of Öland. Today, his furniture and other products are sold at **Carl Malmsten Inredning** (*see p170*).

Another important influence on design in Sweden in the first half of the 20th century was the company **Svenskt Tenn** (*see p171*) and the celebrated Austrian-Swedish furniture designer and architect **Josef Frank** (1885-1967). Svenskt Tenn was founded by artist and pewter designer Estrid Ericson in 1924. In 1930 the shop began to sell classic Bodafors and Gemla furniture as well as custom-designed pieces by Uno Åhrén and Björn Trädgårdh. Josef Frank joined in 1934, and went on to design most of the company's signature products.

Frank started out as an architect in Austria, where he made a name for himself as an early proponent of modernism. After moving to Sweden, he spent more than 30 years working for Svenskt Tenn, where he blended Chinese and English influences to create printed fabrics, furniture, lamps and glassware that reflected his relaxed, graceful approach to design. Never an orthodox modernist, Frank anchored his work in tradition, symbolism and comfort; he harboured a lifelong scepticism about those who took refinement too seriously. By the end of his life, his work had made a huge contribution to the Swedish interior design tradition.

Svenskt Tenn's products have always been marked by quality, comfort and strong visual appeal, while at the same time embodying a modernism that is free and non-dogmatic. Over the decades the shop has become synonymous with Swedish good taste, and often hosts exhibitions of products by young designers.

SCANDINAVIAN DESIGN AND BEYOND

The term 'Scandinavian design' was coined in the 1950s when the exhibition 'Design in Scandinavia' toured across the USA and Canada. The style quickly became a symbol of life in the Nordic welfare states, and was more internationally influential than any other design movement of the time. Sweden's new industrial design ethic centred on high-level functionality, universal accessibility and a clean-lined yet elegant aesthetic. A radical modernisation was undertaken in homes across Sweden – low coffee tables, teakwood furniture, String shelves and **Viola Gråsten**'s two-toned abstract patterns were all the rage. Also, the experience of nature became fundamental to the experience of the room. Intrigued by traditional Japanese building techniques, the renowned furniture designer and architect **Bruno Mathsson** (1907-88) mixed them with American modernism to create a series of glass-walled and concrete-floored houses in the 1950s.

Mathsson had first made a name for himself years earlier, in 1936, when he exhibited a range of laminated, bentwood chairs at Röhsska Konstslöjdmuseet in Göteborg. Graceful and refined, his work somehow gave the impression of weightlessness; he went on to attract a great deal of attention at the World Fairs in Paris in 1937 and New York in 1939. (In fact, New York's newly opened Museum of Modern Art bought his chairs for its café.) Aside from his famous chairs, Mathsson is probably best known for the Superellipse table he designed with the Dane Piet Hein in the 1960s (its form is based on the peculiar 'round rectangle' shape first used for Sergels Torg and invented by Hein). You can see Mathsson's collection at Dux stores, including **Duxiana Home** at Götgatan 59 (702 78 22); his office furniture is on show at **Bruno Mathsson International** (Studio B3, Barnhusgatan 3; 21 42 31/www.bruno-mathsson-int.com).

In the 1960s an 'anti-functional' movement took root and Swedish designers looked to their Italian counterparts for inspiration. Free from the rules of functionalism, they began to produce chairs, lamps and sofas in all sizes, shapes and colours, and in a variety of new and/or unusual materials, notably plastic. Classic '60s Swedish design can be seen in the stations that make up the Midsommarkransen–Ropsten stretch of the red line in Stockholm's Tunnelbana system. Of special note are Östermalmstorg station, by Siri Derkert, and Mariatorget, designed by Karin Björkquist.

In 1970, ten young textile artists and designers made names for themselves shortly after forming **10-Gruppen** ('the group of ten'). The purpose of creating the group was for the designers to gain full control over their work, from sketch to finished fabric to shop. The group's members, among them Birgitta Hahn, Tom Hedqvist and Ingela Håkansson, produced hundreds of lively, colourful fabrics that remain widely recognisable and can be found in many Swedish homes and public spaces. The group has exhibited in museums across Sweden and around the world. You can buy some of its most popular textiles at the **10 Swedish Designers** shop (*see p166*) in Södermalm.

In 1976 Svenska Slöjdföreningen (the Swedish Handicraft Association) changed its name to **Svensk Form** (Swedish Society of Crafts and Design), and reconstituted itself as an organisation whose purpose would be to 'promote good design of Swedish products, support improvement in the design of homes and public environments, and spread knowledge about good design principles'.

Loungechair model 36 by **Bruno Mathsson**.

Bedtime at the **Birger Jarl** hotel. *See p38.*

Its magazine, *Form*, has been published since 1932, and since 1983 the society has presented the annual Utmärkt Svensk Form awards to the creators of the best-designed new Swedish products of the year. You can visit the society's design centre on the island of Skeppsholmen (Holmamiralens Väg 2; 463 31 30/www.svenskform.se; admission 20kr), which contains a gallery, café, library and photo archive. Established by Nils Månsson Mandelgren in 1845, Svensk Form claims to be the oldest organisation of its kind in the world.

'Suddenly, every bar and restaurant in Stockholm was painted white, with unobtrusive furniture and almost no decoration.'

In tandem with the economic boom of the 1980s, eclecticism and postmodernism became the dominant design trends. Designers such as **Jonas Bohlin** (born 1953) and **Mats Theselius** (born 1956) began creating 'work of art' furniture in limited editions for sale to collectors. Bohlin's breakthrough came in 1980 with Concrete, a monumental chair made out of – you guessed it – concrete. He's also a well-known interior designer and was responsible for the late 1990s redesign of the Sturehof restaurant (*see p127*). Bohlin has always been fascinated by boats: after rowing from Stockholm to Paris as part of the Life project, he created a new range of furniture to express what he had experienced. You can see it at his showroom at Södermalmstorg 4 (615 23 90).

Mats Theselius, also considered one of Sweden's leading contemporary designers, is best known for his round aluminium chairs and the bright yellow bookcase he specially designed to hold *National Geographic* magazines. You can see his designs for furniture company **Källemo** at its shop in Östermalm (Skeppargatan 4, 665 19 89).

Thomas Sandell (born 1959) is another world-famous Swedish designer, known for his unusual chairs, outlandish skyscraper proposals and the inside-out house he designed for *Wallpaper** magazine and exhibited at the 1999 Milan Furniture Fair. In 1998 he decorated Kantin Moneo, the restaurant in the Moderna Museet (currently closed for renovation).

The past came into vogue in Swedish design in the early 1990s. Stockholmers became intrigued by their city's architectural legacy and there was a movement to restore both public and private old buildings to their former glory. Antique furniture became popular, as did reproductions, such as Mats Theselius's 1700 Collection, his take on 18th-century furniture. This phase passed rather quickly, however, and by the late '90s a kind of neo-functionalist minimalism was the dominant trend. Suddenly, every bar and restaurant in the city, it seemed, was painted white, with unobtrusive furniture and almost no decoration on the walls or tables. This Scandinavian ultra-simplicity quickly spread to the rest of the world, in no small part due to the praise it earned from international style magazines such as *Wallpaper**.

After the turn of the millennium a few interior designers started adding a little more colour to their work (usually with furniture in stark solids such as orange, green, yellow and red), while others have turned to America and Asia for ideas. Simplicity is still the order of the day, though, and while a little colour and clutter have led to a loosening up of the minimalist dogma, no one new trend has yet emerged to displace it.

WHERE TO SEE IT

The **National Museum** (*see p75*) has a permanent exhibition of Scandinavian design from 1900 to 2000, while at the **Nordiska Museet** (*see p82*) furniture, photographs and room reconstructions show Swedish interior design from 1870 until 2000 (the second part of the exhibition will cover the period 1520-1870). For contemporary design, the **Birger Jarl** hotel (*see p45*) contains 17 one-off rooms by Swedish designers such as Thomas Sandell and Jonas Bohlin. Website **www.scandinavian design.com** is packed with the products and personalities of Nordic design, plus information on museums, magazines and design schools. For the best of Stockholm's numerous design shops, *see p169* **Interiors**.

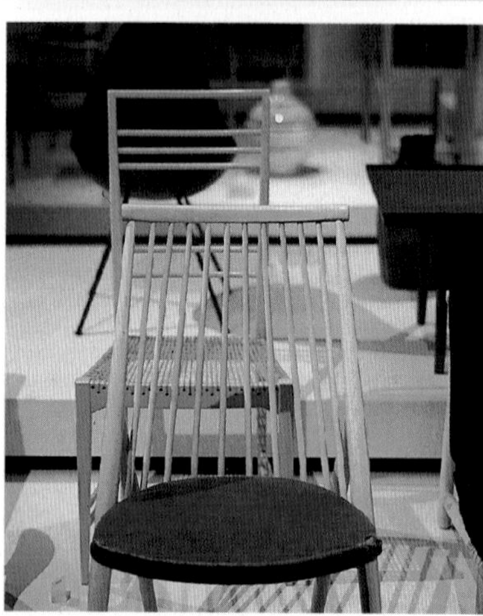

The 'Design 19002000' exhibition at the **National Museum**.

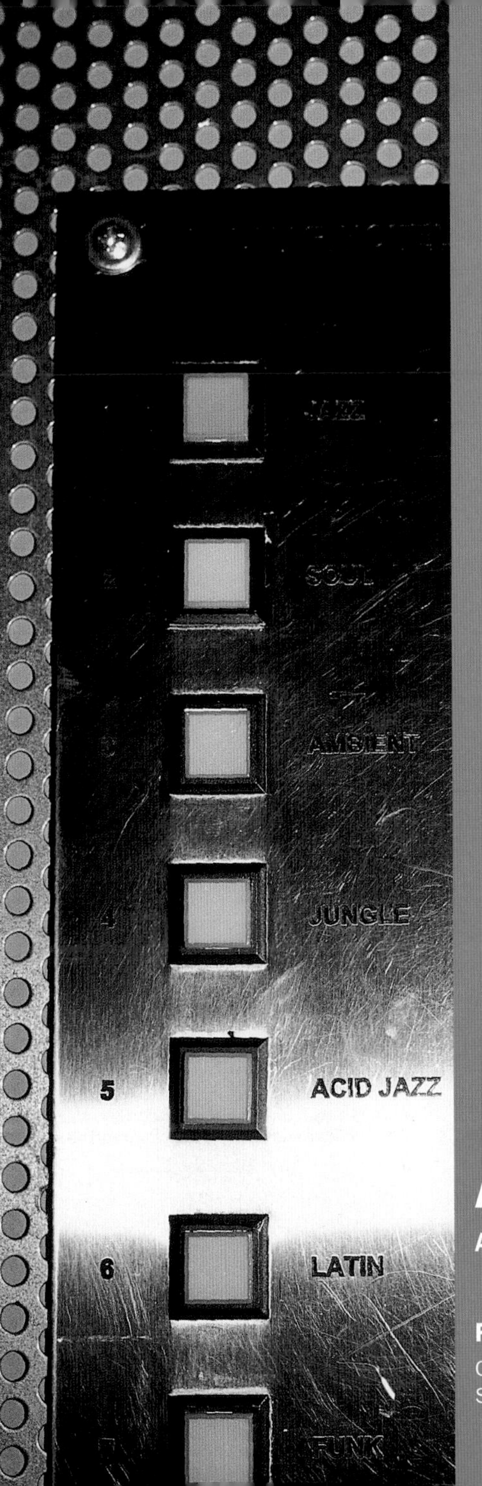

Accommodation

Accommodation 40

Features

Chain hotels 47
Staying on a boat 50

Accommodation

Sleeping options galore – and cheaper rates for weekend and summer visitors.

Where would you like to sleep tonight? In a quirky historic inn stuffed with antiques amid the narrow alleyways of Gamla Stan? Or in an ultra-modern, clean-lined designer hotel near the shops, bars and restaurants of Norrmalm? Stockholm has a wealth of accommodation options, to suit all tastes and budgets, including a handful of floating boat-hotels in lovely watery locations – not something you find in most cities, and surely the most romantic, if somewhat cramped, option.

Where you choose to stay in isn't as crucial as in more sprawling metropolises; the compactness of Stockholm means that it's usually only a walk or short hop on the Tunnelbana to the next sight, or back to your hotel in the evening. If you're after a historic, characterful experience, then Gamla Stan is the best place to stay – but be aware that there are only five hotels on the island (including an eccentric nautical trio), all of which are popular and pretty expensive.

Stockholm is a very busy business and conference city, so there's a glut of rather dull chain hotels servicing the business traveller, but also a growing number of design-driven boutique hotels, mainly in and around Norrmalm. These include **Berns** (*see p42*), **Birger Jarl** (*see p45*), the **Nordic Light** and **Nordic Sea** duo (*see p43*) and the eternally hip **Lydmar Hotel** (*see p53*). Old-fashioned glamour is available along the waterfront at the likes of the **Grand** (*see p43*), Stockholm's only five-star hotel, and the four-star **Hotel Diplomat** (*see p52*). Vasastaden, slightly further out from the action, has the greatest choice in the moderate price range, while Södermalm is best for budget travellers. There are also some picturesque hotels a boat ride away from the city centre.

Although Stockholm is not a cheap city, it has a surprising number of youth hostels – many on boats, and one, on leafy Långholmen, inside the unusual location of a former prison (*see p51*). They aren't scuzzy pads suitable only for unwashed students and backpackers but clean, fresh, Scandinavian hostels ideal for families. And you don't have to sleep in a dorm with a bunch of strangers; many double as cheap hotels, offering single and double rooms at slightly higher rates. Note that you may have to buy membership if you're not already a member of a recognised hostelling association, and you'll pay extra for bedlinen, towels and breakfast.

As you might expect, standards in Stockholm's hotels are generally high (and everyone will speak English). And most places offer fantastic breakfast buffets – an eye-popping spread of cereals, fruit, meat, fish, cheese, hot dishes, crispbreads, juices, teas and coffee – easily enough to set you up for a morning of sightseeing. Cultural note: double beds tend to come with two single duvets rather than one large duvet.

PRICES AND RESERVATIONS

Stockholm's position as a business capital – seven out of ten visitors are in the city on business or for a conference – means that rates are higher during the week (usually Sunday to Thursday) and can drop considerably at the weekend – sometimes by as much as half. So it's often possible to stay in deluxe surroundings for much less than you'd expect. Always ask about packages and special deals (you may have to book for two nights at the weekend to get a discounted rate). Summer rates, especially in July, when the city goes on holiday, are also cheaper, usually the same as weekend rates.

We've divided the hotels by area and then according to the price of a standard double room. The categories are: deluxe (from 1,900kr); expensive (1,500kr-1,900kr); moderate (750kr-1,500kr); and budget (under 750kr), which also includes youth hostels. Breakfast is included in the price unless stated otherwise.

The sheer number of business travellers means that hotels can and do get booked up, especially during the major trade fairs (*see p276* for dates of the main annual events) – it's always a good idea to book ahead. The tourist office produces a free hotel brochure and also runs a very good hotel reservations service: you can book online (www.stockholmtown.com), by phone (789 24 56), email (hotels@stoinfo.se) or in person at the small **Hotellcentrallen** office on the concourse of Central Station (*see p285*). If you visit the office in person, a 50kr fee applies for a hotel, 20kr for a hostel (same-day hostel bookings only). It also sells the useful Stockholm Card (*see p56* **Pick a card**). Also try **Destination Stockholm** (663 00 80), which offers hotel/sightseeing packages in the off-season (for details, *see p291*)

Enjoy old-fashioned comfort and nautical knick-knacks at the **Victory Hotel**. *See p42.*

Gamla Stan

Deluxe

First Hotel Reisen

Skeppsbron 12, 111 30 Stockholm (22 32 60/ fax 20 15 59/www.firsthotels.com). T-bana Gamla Stan/bus 43, 46, 55, 59, 76. **Rates** *Mon-Fri* single 1,893kr-2,993kr; double 2,543kr-3,193kr; suite 3,993kr-5,493kr. *Sat, Sun* single 1,153kr-2,093kr; double 1,403kr-2,093kr; suite 2,593kr-4,093kr. **Credit** AmEx, DC, MC, V. **Map** p303 H8.

This former 18th-century coffeehouse, facing one of Stockholm's most spectacular waterfront views, is the oldest hotel in the city. Once frequented by sailors who came here to drink their java because their ships had no coffee-making facilities, it became a hotel in 1819. It's now run by the First Hotel chain, which fully exploits the view by having trick mirrors in every room (144 in all), so that, even if you can't afford one of the superior rooms that overlook the water, you'll still have a water-tinged view. There's a sauna in a vaulted cellar, and the deluxe rooms have a sauna and/or jacuzzi en suite. An excellent restaurant adjoins the lobby.

Hotel services *Babysitting. Bar. Bike rental. Business services. Conference facilities. Laundry. No-smoking rooms. Parking. Pool. Restaurant. Sauna.* **Room services** *Dataport. Hairdryer. Iron. Minibar. Room service (7-11am, 2-10.30pm Mon-Fri; 8am-noon, 4-10pm Sat, Sun). Telephone. TV: cable/pay movies/VCR.*

Lady Hamilton Hotel

Storkyrkobrinken 5, 111 28 Stockholm (50 64 01 00/ fax 50 64 01 10/www.lady-hamilton.se). T-bana Gamla Stan/bus 3, 43, 53, 55, 59. **Rates** *Mon-Thur* single 1,990kr-2,190kr; double 2,350kr-2,560kr; triple 2,750kr-2,950kr. *Fri-Sun* single 1,050kr-1,250kr; double 1,650kr-1,950kr; triple 2,050kr-2,350kr. **Credit** AmEx, DC, MC, V. **Map** p303 H7.

One of a trio of small hotels owned by the Bengtsson family – the others are the Lord Nelson (*see below*) and Victory (*see p42*). As you might have guessed, all have some connection with the one-eyed, one-armed British naval hero and nautical goings-on. A ship's figurehead and a portrait (by the English painter George Romney) of Nelson's famous mistress dominates the lobby, but the rest of this warren-like building (dating from 1470) is stuffed with Swedish folk art antiques. The 34 rooms – each named after a regional wild flower – provide a veritable tour of Sweden, from the northernmost counties (Lapland, Jämtland) on the top floor down to the southern counties of Dalarna and Skåne. All the beds are by the very famous and terribly expensive Hästens.The mix of colourful painted cupboards, wall paintings, grandfather clocks and old-fashioned fabrics is utterly charming; this is probably the nicest of the three hotels. A 14th-century well in the basement is now a plunge pool for the sauna.

Hotel services *Bar. Business services. No-smoking rooms. Parking. Sauna. Snack bar.* **Room services** *Dataport. Hairdryer. Minibar. Telephone. TV: cable/ pay movies.*

Lord Nelson Hotel

Västerlånggatan 22, 111 29 Stockholm (50 64 01 20/fax 50 44 01 30/www.lord-nelson.se). T-bana Gamla Stan/bus 3, 43, 53, 55, 59. **Rates** *Mon-Thur* single 1,590kr-1,790kr; double 1,990kr-2,190kr. *Fri-Sun* 850kr-1,050kr; double 1,350kr-1,550kr. **Credit** AmEx, DC, MC, V. **Map** p303 J7.

The smallest (and cheapest) of the Bengtsson family's hotels, the recently renovated Nelson must also be Sweden's narrowest hotel, only 5m (16ft) wide. Located on Gamla Stan's tourist strip, the tall 17th-century building with its glass and brass entrance is pretty ship-like itself. Add in the long mahogany reception desk, the portraits of Nelson and assorted naval antiques, the names of the floors (Gun Deck, Quarter Deck, Poop Deck et al) – and you could be

forgiven for thinking you were riding the ocean wave. The 29 rooms are pleasant but smallish; 18 are singles, ideal for lone or business travellers. Each room is named after an antique model ship, which is on display inside. There's no restaurant, but a small seating area in the lobby is used for breakfast, and the rooftop terrace has views across medieval Gamla Stan.
Hotel services *Business services. No-smoking rooms. Parking. Sauna. Terrace.* **Room services** *Dataport. Hairdryer. Telephone. TV: cable/pay movies.*

Rica City Hotel Gamla Stan

Lilla Nygatan 25, 111 28 Stockholm (723 72 50/ fax 723 72 59/www.rica.se). T-bana Gamla Stan/ bus 3, 43, 53, 55, 59. **Rates** *Mon-Thur, Sun* single 1,640kr-1,840kr; double 1,890kr. *Fri, Sat* single 950kr-1,050kr; double 1,390kr-1,590kr. **Credit** AmEx, DC, MC, V. **Map** p303 J7.
Just down the street from the Nelson (*see p41*), this 51-room hotel is a few steps from the waterfront (although none of the rooms has a view). For 65 years this 17th-century building, with its simple façade, was owned by the Salvation Army, who used it for good works and, later, as a hostel. Norwegian chain Rica City Hotels bought it in 1998, and transformed it into a first-class hotel. The decor of the rooms is elegant, in an understated 18th-century Gustavian style, but they're not particularly large. If you want to steep yourself in the city's history – and location matters more than having lots of space – this is the place.
Hotel services *Conference facilities. No-smoking rooms. Parking. Sauna. Terrace.* **Room services** *Dataport. Hairdryer. Minibar. Telephone. TV: cable/ pay movies.*

Victory Hotel

Lilla Nygatan 5, 111 28 Stockholm (50 64 00 00/ fax 50 64 00 10/www.victory-hotel.se). T-bana Gamla Stan/bus 3, 43, 53, 55, 59. **Rates** *Mon-Thur* single 2,190kr-2,390kr; double 2,490kr-3,490kr; suite 3,890kr-5,190kr. *Fri-Sun* single 1,190kr-1,390kr; double 1,790kr-2,090kr; suite 2,690-4,190kr. **Credit** AmEx, DC, MC, V. **Map** p303 J7.
Named after Admiral Lord Nelson's flagship, the characterful Victory is also the flagship of this three-hotel chain. You can't move for nautical knick-knacks, both British and Swedish: colourful ship's figureheads, shiny brass instruments, embroidered pictures of ships, carved whalebone and model boats; an 1801 letter from Nelson to Lady Hamilton is proudly displayed in the lobby. There's also plenty of Swedish folk art, another passion of the owners. The 45 rooms (all different in size and decor – including 22 doubles and four suites) are named after Swedish sea captains. Downstairs are a sauna, meeting rooms and the Leijontornet restaurant, where part of a medieval city tower was unearthed in the 1980s. A hoard of 18,000 silver coins (Sweden's largest silver discovery) was also dug up here in 1937. The hotel offers an apartment for rent as well, for periods of two weeks or longer.

Grand Hôtel: Stockholm's only five-star.

Hotel services *Babysitting. Bar. Business services. Conference facilities. Garden. Laundry. No-smoking rooms. Parking. Pool. Restaurant. Sauna.* **Room services** *Dataport. Hairdryer. Minibar. Room service (7-10am, 6-10pm Mon-Fri; 8-11am, 6-10pm Sat, Sun). Telephone. TV: cable/pay movies.*

Norrmalm

Deluxe

Berns Hotel

Näckströmsgatan 8, 111 47 Stockholm (56 63 20 00/ fax 56 63 22 01/www.berns.se). T-bana Kungsträdgården or Östermalmstorg/bus 46, 47, 62, 69, 76. **Rates** single 2,050kr; double 2,350kr-3,650kr; suite 4,250kr-5,950kr. **Credit** AmEx, DC, MC, V. **Map** p303 G8.
This boutique hotel on the edge of Berzelii Park near Kungsträdgården is popular with visiting pop-stars and business types. It adjoins Berns Salonger with its marvellous historic decor and pulsing bars (*see p131*) and restaurants (*see p113*), but is more modern in design. Don't expect Scandinavian stereotypes, though; the 65 rooms, all different sizes, are quite masculine in design, decorated in cherry wood and marble in rich dark colours. Each contains a nifty cylindrical console containing the TV,

CD player and minibar that you can swivel 360°. The top-floor rooms, accessed by a separate lift, have big windows overlooking the park, and there's an idiosyncratic suite, once a dressing room for the performers in the salon. Service is first class, and guests get to use some of the facilities at Berns' sister hotel, the peerless Grand (*see below*). Ask about special deals and weekend rates.
Hotel services *Air-conditioning. Babysitting. Bars. Business services. Conference facilities. Disabled: adapted room (1). No-smoking rooms. Parking. Restaurant.* **Room services** *CD player. Dataport. Hairdryer. Iron. Minibar. Room service (24hrs). Telephone. TV: cable/pay movies/VCR.*

Grand Hôtel

Blasieholmshamnen 8, PO Box 16424, 103 27 Stockholm (679 35 00/fax 611 86 86/www.grandhotel.se). T-bana Kungsträdgården/bus 46, 55, 59, 62, 65. **Rates** single 2,095kr-2,895kr; double 3,295kr-4,095kr; suite 5,295kr-12,995kr. **Credit** AmEx, DC, MC, V. **Map** p303 G8.
This truly sumptuous five-star hotel is where you'll find visiting royals, rock stars and Nobel Prize winners, who traditionally stay here after the ceremony. Built in 1874, the imposing orange pile is located right on the waterfront, with great views across to the Kungliga Slottet. Each of the 310 rooms is decorated differently and thoughtfully, in a range of styles. It's the suites that have the real wow factor, though – the Flag Suite has its very own tower (at 12,995kr a night you might well expect it to have its own minor principality). The public areas are decorated in a rather heavy classical style, but you'll find all the facilities you would expect from a world-class hotel. There are two restaurants, the Verandan, which serves a traditional smörgåsbord, and the renowned Franska Matsalen (*see p113*).
Hotel services *Air-conditioning. Babysitting. Bar. Beauty salon. Business services. Conference facilities. Disabled: adapted rooms. Gym. No-smoking rooms. Parking. Patio. Restaurants. Sauna.* **Room services** *Dataport. Hairdryer. Minibar. Room service (24hrs). Telephone. TV: cable/pay movies/VCR.*

Radisson SAS Strand Hotel

Nybrokajen 9, PO Box 16396, 103 27 Stockholm (50 66 40 00/fax 50 66 40 01/www.radissonsas.com). T-bana Kungsträdgården or Östermalmstorg/bus 46, 47, 62, 69, 76. **Rates** *Mon-Thur, Sun* single 1,850kr; double 2,300kr; suite 3,000-6,500kr. Breakfast 165kr. *Fri, Sat* single 1,390kr; double 1,595kr; suite 3,000-6,500kr. **Credit** AmEx, DC, MC, V. **Map** p303 G8.
The Radisson SAS delivers everything you would expect from a business hotel of this price: comfort, luxury and efficiency – and in a setting that fully captures the beauty of Stockholm's waterfront. The superior rooms offer a fantastic view of the boats and ferries moored at Nybrokajen and the majestic buildings of Strandvagen across the water. All the 152 rooms are tastefully furnished in classic 18th-century Swedish style. Built in 1912 for the Stockholm Olympics, the hotel has undergone many renovations since then. The large and comfortable lobby has sofas and armchairs that you can sink right into and a wall full of books to borrow. A real splurge is the Tower Suite, a two-floor apartment with a rooftop terrace, with dining room and sitting room on one level, and a spiral staircase leading up to the bedroom. There is surely no better view in Stockholm, but – no surprise – it doesn't come cheap.
Hotel services *Babysitting. Bar. Conference facilities. Disabled: adapted rooms. Gym/pool/spa (Sturebadet). Laundry. No-smoking rooms. Restaurant. Sauna.* **Room services** *Dataport. Hairdryer. Iron. Minibar. Room service (24hrs). Telephone. TV: cable/pay movies.*

Expensive

Nordic Light & Nordic Sea

Vasaplan, PO Box 884, 101 37 Stockholm (50 56 30 00/fax 50 56 30 60/www.nordichotels.se). T-bana T-Centralen/bus 1, 47, 53, 59, 69. **Rates** (for 1 person; extra person in M, L, and XL rooms 200kr) *Mon-Thur, Sun* S 2,200kr; M 2,400kr; L 2,700kr; XL 3,200kr. *Fri, Sat* S 890kr-1,090kr; M 1,190kr-1,390kr; L 1,490kr-1,690kr; XL 3,200kr. **Credit** AmEx, DC, MC, V. **Map** p303-4 G6.

The stylish designer duo of **Nordic Light** (left) and **Nordic Sea**.

Restaurant, Terrace, Lounge bar, Cocktail bar, Wine bar, Nightclub, Conference, Private dining and H

This designer hotel duo couldn't be more convenient, located next door to the Arlanda Express train station. Nordic Light is the nicer and more upmarket of the two; its spacious and airy lobby/bar/restaurant area has floor-to-ceiling windows, white walls and sophisticated lighting effects – watch the huge 'icicle' chandelier slowly change colour. The attractive rooms (classified by size from S to XL) are cool and minimalist: they're predominantly black, white and grey with splashes of colour, and patterns of light rather than paintings decorate the walls. Its wine cellar specialises in US wines. Nordic Sea is larger – 367 rooms to Nordic Light's 175 – cheaper (by about about 200kr per room) and less exclusive in feel. An aquarium dominates the lobby, and the hotel also houses the recently opened Icebar (*see p132*), sculpted completely out of ice. The two hotels are joined by an underground passage (useful in winter). Both are full of business types during the week, but offer a variety of enticing weekend packages.

Hotel services *Bars. Conference facilities. Disabled: adapted rooms. Gym. No-smoking rooms. Parking. Restaurant. Sauna. Spa.* **Room services** *Hairdryer. Iron. Minibar. Room service (8am-11pm). Telephone. TV: cable/VCR.*

Scandic Hotel Sergel Plaza

Brunkebergstorgs 9, PO Box 16411, 103 27 Stockholm (51 72 63 00/fax 51 72 63 11/ www.scandic-hotels. com). T-bana T-Centralen/ bus 43, 47, 52, 56, 65. **Rates** *Mon-Thur, Sun* single 1,980kr-2,580kr; double 2,413kr-3,013kr; suite 4,780kr. *Fri, Sat* single 1,550kr; double 1,895kr; suite 4,780kr. **Credit** Amex, DC, MC, V. **Map** p303 E7.

The central location is this hotel's biggest lure, and it's so popular with Japanese tourists that a Japanese breakfast is now served. Located next to the Kulturhuset and the famous fountain of Sergels Torg, it's just a credit card's throw from the main shopping streets of Hamngatan and Drottninggatan. The rooms (405 in all) are furnished with bright fabrics and a hint of classic Swedish design. There's a popular Swedish *smörgåsbord* buffet in the restaurant. Families are welcomed, with surprises for children at check-in and a babysitting service. Room prices drop substantially at Easter, Christmas and during the summer, so it's worth enquiring about special deals.

Hotel services *Babysitting. Bars. Conference facilities. Disabled: adapted rooms. No-smoking rooms. Parking. Restaurant. Sauna. Spa/gym/pool (225kr).* **Room services** *Hairdryer. Minibar. Room service (24hrs). Telephone. TV: cable/pay movies.*

Moderate

Friendly **Pensionat Oden** (*see p206*) attracts a mainly gay crowd, especially at the weekend, but is more mixed during the week. It has three branches, in Norrmalm, Södermalm and Vasastaden.

Queen's Hotel

Drottninggatan 71A, 111 36 Stockholm (24 94 60/ fax 21 76 20/www.queenshotel.se). T-bana Hötorget/ bus 1, 47, 52, 53, 69. **Rates** *Mon-Thur, Sun* single 650kr-1,390kr; double 750kr-1,490kr; suite 1,150kr-1,490kr. *Fri, Sat* single 650kr-1,250kr; double 750kr-1,350kr; suite 1,150kr-1,350kr. **Credit** AmEx, DC, MC, V. **Map** p303 F6.

Situated on the main pedestrian shopping street in the heart of the shopping district, and a couple of blocks from Hötorget, this is a good bet if you like hustle and bustle and the convenience of a central location. It's a family-owned place, with friendly and chatty staff. The 32 rooms are clean and plainly furnished, with hardwood floors and tiled showers (some en suite). Only one room has a bath tub. Most doubles are large enough to accommodate an extra bed or sofa bed, and some have an adjoining sitting room. The furniture in the big sitting room and adjoining TV room is rather haphazard, but a large piano beckons in the corner for any guest with the urge to strike up a tune.

Hotel services *Garden. No smoking. TV room.* **Room services** *Minibar. Telephone. TV: cable/ pay movies.*

Budget/youth hostels

City Backpackers Inn

Norra Bantorget, Upplandsgatan 2A, 111 23 Stockholm (20 69 20/fax 10 04 64/www.cityback packer.se). T-bana T-Centralen or Hötorget/bus 47, 53, 69. **Rates** 170kr-245kr per person; 6-bed apartment 1,500kr. **Credit** MC, V. **Map** p302 F5.

Located in a 19th-century building on Norra Bantorget square, this 51-bed hostel is certainly convenient, a ten-minute walk from Central Station and near Hötorget and the shopping district. There are two-, four- and eight-bed rooms, as well as an apartment with a private kitchen, shower and toilet, sleeping up to seven. Facilities include a comfy lounge with a TV, books and games, a kitchen, laundry room and – this is Sweden – a sauna. You can park on the street outside, and there's no curfew. Breakfast is not provided.

Hotel services *Computer with internet access. Garden. Kitchen. Laundry room. No smoking. Payphones. Sauna. TV room: cable.*

Vasastaden

Expensive

Birger Jarl

Tulegatan 8, PO Box 190 16, 104 32 Stockholm (674 18 00/fax 673 73 66/www.birgerjarl.se). T-bana Rådmansgatan/bus 42, 43, 46, 52. **Rates** *Mon-Thur, Sun in winter* single 1,520kr-2,250kr; double 1,835kr-2,181kr; suite 2,750kr-4,500kr. *Fri, Sat & summer* single 940kr-1,475kr; double 1,150kr-1,745kr; suite 2,750kr-4,500kr. **Credit** AmEx, DC, MC, V. **Map** p307 D6.

Once a pretty standard business hotel, the four-star Birger Jarl has repositioned itself as a showcase for Swedish design. In a prime location near Stureplan and Hötorget, it's still popular with business types, but 17 of the 235 rooms are one-off creations, the work of some of the nation's hottest designers (including Jonas Bohlin, Thomas Sandell, Tom Hedqvist and Svenskt Tenn). Although the rooms vary widely, playfulness and idiosyncrasy are the name of the game; expect unconventional materials, oversized furniture and special lighting effects. More are in the pipeline. Five other rooms have been given a Feng Shui makeover; the rest are more conventional, but still distinctly Swedish. The lobby (used for art shows) and restaurant are also modern in style but use traditional elements (pale birch wood, copper-red paint). The small gym has views over Norrmalm's rooftops – use it to work up an appetite so you can do justice to the fab buffet breakfast.
Hotel services *Bar. Business services. Conference facilities. Gym. No-smoking rooms. Parking. Restaurant. Sauna.* **Room services** *Dataport. Hairdryer. Iron. Minibar. Room service (8am-1am). Telephone. TV: cable/pay movies.*

Moderate

Clas på Hörnet

Surbrunnsgatan 20, 113 48 Stockholm (16 51 30/ fax 612 53 15/www.claspahornet.com). T-bana Tekniska Högskolan/bus 4, 42, 46, 53, 72. **Rates** *Mid Aug-June Mon-Thur, Sun* single 1,545kr; double 1,745kr; suite 1,845kr. *Fri, Sat* single 1,345kr; double 1,545kr; suite 1,745kr. *July-mid Aug* 900kr per room. **Credit** AmEx, DC, MC, V. **Map** p307 C6.

Lie back in a canopied, antique four-poster bed and imagine yourself in another century. That's the feeling Clas på Hörnet ('Clas on the corner') tries to give its guests – quite successfully, as many have become regulars, much like the 18th-century poet Carl Michael Bellman, who frequently stayed here. Each of the ten rooms is named after a famous person associated with the inn, including Clas Browall (the Clas of the name), who opened it in 1731. A general sprucing up is in progress (due to be completed by January 2003), during which the carpeting will be removed to reveal the original hardwood floors. The restaurant is highly recommended for its excellent Swedish food. The hotel is situated on a quiet tree-lined corner, a ten-minute walk from both Odenplan and Stureplan.
Hotel services *Bar. Business services. Conference facilities. Disabled: adapted rooms. No-smoking rooms. Parking. Patio. Restaurant.* **Room services** *Dataport. Hairdryer. Minibar. Room service (7am-midnight). Telephone. TV: pay movies.*

Hotel Gustav Vasa

Västmannagatan 61, 113 25 Stockholm (34 38 01/ fax 30 73 72/www.hotel.wineasy.se/gustav.vasa). T-bana Odenplan/bus 4, 40, 46, 47, 53. **Rates** single 725kr-850kr; 900kr-1,100kr; family 1,225kr-1,460kr. **Credit** AmEx, DC, MC, V. **Map** p306 D4.

Birger Jarl: for one-off rooms. *See p45.*

Across from the majestic Gustav Vasa Kyrka at Odenplan, the hotel that bears the name of the former king is a quiet, entirely no-smoking place. The 37 good-value rooms (some with shared bathroom) are clean and comfortable, if a bit stuffy. The family rooms are big enough for four or five people. There's a cheerful, sunny breakfast room, with 19th-century touches such as the *kakelugn* (tiled stove), which looks out over the church.
Hotel services *Business services. Garden. No smoking. Refrigerator.* **Room services** *Dataport. Room service (8am-noon). Telephone. TV: cable.*

Hotell August Strindberg

Tegnérgatan 38, 113 59 Stockholm (32 50 06/ fax 20 90 85/www.hotellstrindberg.se). T-bana Hötorget/bus 40, 47, 53, 69. **Rates** *Mon-Thur, Sun* single 800kr-1,200kr; double 1,200kr-1,450kr. *Fri, Sat* single 600kr-800kr; double 800kr-900kr. **Credit** MC, V. **Map** p307 E5.

Just across from Tegnérlunden, a pretty park containing a rather imposing statue of the Swedish dramatist August Strindberg, is the hotel that bears his name. He never lived in this particular building, though the Strindbergsmuseet (where he did live – *see p76*) is nearby. The 21 rooms in this privately owned hotel are plain, but clean and pleasant; as might be expected, the walls are decorated with portraits of a mean and moody Strindberg. There's a tranquil garden with a few tables and a trickling birdbath, and the breakfast room often has the aroma of freshly baked bread and pastries. A fine choice in a quiet and central neighbourhood.
Hotel services *Garden. Laundry. No smoking.* **Room services** *Dataport. Minibar. Telephone. TV: cable/VCR.*

Hotell Bema

Upplandsgatan 13, 111 23 Stockholm (23 26 75/ fax 20 53 38). T-bana Hötorget/bus 40, 47, 53, 69. **Rates** *Mon-Thur, Sun* single 820kr-890kr; double

990kr; triple 1,200kr; quad 1,400kr. *Fri, Sat* single 590kr-600kr; double 790kr; triple 990kr; quad 1,200kr. **Credit** AmEx, MC, V. **Map** p307 E5.

Round the corner from Hotell August Strindberg (*see p46*), facing Tegnérlunden park, is this small 12-room hotel. Despite being on street level, the rooms are relatively quiet, and fresh and clean. The corner double room is particularly spacious, with a fold-out couch for a third bed. Continental breakfast is served in the rooms. If you're seeking no-fuss lodgings in a central spot, this is a good deal.

Hotel services *No-smoking rooms. Parking.* **Room services** *Room service (24hrs). Telephone. TV: satellite.*

Hotel Tegnérlunden

Tegnérlunden 8, 113 59 Stockholm (54 54 55 50/ fax 54 54 55 51/www.hoteltegnerlunden.se). T-bana Hötorget/bus 40, 47, 53, 69. **Rates** *Mon-Thur, Sun* single 1,300kr-1,435kr; double 1,400kr-1,560kr; suite 1,895kr. *Fri, Sat* single 800kr-900kr; double 900kr-990kr; suite 1,395kr. **Credit** AmEx, DC, MC, V. **Map** p307 E5.

Yet another moderately priced hotel situated near Tegnérlunden. Guests are often members of the police force or the military – so you don't need to worry about noise or rowdiness. The rooms are plainly furnished but clean. The best feature is the light-filled breakfast room with a terrace overlooking the rooftops of Vasastaden.

Hotel services *Bar. Business services. Conference facilities. Disabled: adapted room (1). No-smoking rooms. Sauna.* **Room services** *Dataport. Hairdryer. Iron. Telephone. TV: cable/pay movies.*

Hotel Oden

Karlbergsvägen 24, PO Box 6246, 102 34 Stockholm (457 97 00/fax 457 97 10/www.hoteloden.se). T-bana Odenplan/bus 4, 40, 42, 46, 47. **Rates** *Mon-Thur, Sun* single 1,020kr-1,585kr; double 1,270kr-1,585kr. *Fri, Sat* single 710kr-1,140kr; double 880kr-1,140kr. **Credit** AmEx, DC, MC, V. **Map** p306 D4.

This nondescript hotel is remarkable only for its low prices. The smell of cigarette smoke is evident in the lobby as well as a number of the rooms, even though some are supposed to be no-smoking. For budget travellers looking to save money on meals, the double rooms have a cooler box and a stove (no frying allowed), while singles just have a cooler. Garage parking costs just 100kr per night. A rather sad-looking solarium, sauna and exercise room in the basement complete the list of amenities. Not the best choice in the area, but it could serve as a standby.

Hotel services *Business services. Conference facilities. No-smoking rooms. Parking. Sauna.* **Room services** *Dataport. Hairdryer. Iron. Telephone. TV: cable.*

Budget/youth hostels

Hostel Bed & Breakfast

Rehnsgatan 21, 113 57 Stockholm (15 28 38/ fax 15 28 38/www.hostelbedandbreakfast.com). T-bana Rådmansgatan/bus 4, 42, 43, 46, 52. **Rates** dormitory 165kr per person; four-bed room 185kr per person; single 350kr; double 450kr. Breakfast 25kr. **Credit** MC, V. **Map** p307 D6.

This is your basic youth hostel – with the advantage of being located in the heart of the capital, just across the street from the Stockholm School of Economics. There are 40 beds in all, in three dorms (with four, eight or ten beds) and the rest in double rooms. All showers and toilets are shared. It's open all year and offers some handy services such as a kitchen and laundry room.

Hotel services *Computer with internet access. Kitchen. Laundry room. No smoking. Payphone. TV room: VCR.*

Chain hotels

If you're having trouble finding a hotel, there's always the chain option. They'll probably be rather corporate in feel and full of business people, but you'll be assured of high standards and services. All websites are in English.

Choice Hotels Scandinavia

www.choicehotels.se.

Has around 135 hotels in the Nordic countries, including four in the middle of Stockholm and two near Arlanda Airport.

First Hotels

www.firsthotels.com.

This 60-hotel chain has two in the city centre: the **Reisen** (*see p41*) on Gamla Stan and the **Amarenten** on Kungsholmen.

Rica City Hotels

www.rica.se.

Rica's 80 or so hotels in Scandinavia include three in Stockholm: two near Hörtorget and one on **Gamla Stan** (*see p42*).

Scandic Hotels

www.scandic-hotels.com.

Sweden's largest hotel chain, now part of the Hilton group. It has seven hotels in the centre of Stockholm, including the **Sergel Plaza** (*see p45*) and **Hasselbacken** (*see p49*), as well as the **Scandic Hotel Continental** by T-Centralen and the **Scandic Hotel Anglais** by Stureplan. It's also has nine hotels in the suburbs.

Radisson SAS

www.radisson.com.

Two large hotels in the city centre – the **Strand** (*see p43*) and the **Royal Viking** in Vasastaden – plus two at Arlanda Airport.

Djurgården

Deluxe

Scandic Hotel Hasselbacken

Hazeliusbacken 20, 100 55 Stockholm (51 73 43 00/ fax 51 73 43 11/www.scandic-hotels.se). Bus 44, 47. **Rates** *Mon-Thur, Sun* single 1,729kr-2,169kr; double 2,162kr-2,601kr; suite 2,995kr. *Fri, Sat* single 1,098kr-1,698kr; double 1,398kr-1,798kr; suite 2,995kr. **Credit** AmEx, DC, MC, V. **Map** p304 J11.

On a hill overlooking the carnival rides and stilt walkers of Gröna Lund stands the elegant Scandic Hotel Hasselbacken, built in 1925. Leafy green trees and a wooden picket fence surround the property, which is just a few minutes' walk from Djurgården's main attractions. Its 122 rooms have hardwood floors and were completely remodelled in 1992 to their original style. People have been gathering on the hill since a tavern was built here in the 1740s. Today, as part of one of Scandinavia's largest hotel chains, the hotel has nearly everything the spoiled traveller might need, including a sauna, satellite TV and an attractive lobby bar. The classic Restaurang Hasselbacken on the ground floor is popular with wedding parties and serves an excellent breakfast buffet with live music on the weekends.

Hotel services *Bars. Business services. Conference facilities. Disabled: adapted rooms. No-smoking rooms. Parking. Patio. Restaurants. Sauna.* **Room services** *Dataport. Hairdryer. Minibar. Room service (24hrs). Telephone. TV: cable/pay movies/VCR.*

Södermalm

Expensive

Hilton Stockholm Slussen

Guldgränd 8, PO Box 15270, 104 65 Stockholm (51 73 53 00/fax 51 73 53 11/www.hilton.com). T-bana Slussen/bus 3, 43, 46, 53, 76. **Rates** *Mon-Thur, Sun* single 2,600kr-2,900kr; double 2,800kr-3,100kr; suite 3,800kr-4,000kr. *Fri, Sat* single 1,500kr-1,650kr; double 1,700kr-1,850kr; suite 2,100kr-2,300kr. Breakfast 120kr. **Credit** AmEx, DC, MC, V. **Map** p310 K7.

This former Scandic Hotel was extensively spruced up when it reopened as Sweden's first Hilton in February 2002. The marble floor of the huge lobby now gleams, and two executive floors, with a separate reception, bar and breakfast room for weary business travellers, opened in September 2002. The most striking aspect of the new Hilton, however, has always been there: a panoramic view of the city across Riddarfjarden towards Gamla Stan. It can be yours for the price of an executive double room, but – if your budget is more modest – you can still enjoy the view from the dining room of Ekens Bar & Matsal (a few tables are even perched on the window ledge). The outdoor terrace is packed at the weekends; there's also a quieter bar off the lobby.

Hotel services *Air-conditioning. Babysitting. Bars. Business services. Chiropractic clinic. Conference facilities. Disabled: adapted rooms. Gym. Laundry. No-smoking rooms. Parking. Patio. Pool. Restaurants. Sauna.* **Room services** *Dataport. Hairdryer. Iron. Minibar. Room service (24hrs). Telephone. TV: cable/ pay movies.*

Moderate

Columbus Hotell

Tjärhovsgatan 11, 116 21 Stockholm (50 31 12 00/fax 50 31 12 01/www.columbus.se). T-bana Medborgarplatsen/bus 55, 59, 66. **Rates** *Mon-Thur, Sun* single 595kr-1,195kr; double 795kr-1,495kr; suite 2,295kr. *Fri, Sat* single 595kr-895kr; double 795kr-1,195kr; suite 1,995kr. **Credit** AmEx, DC, MC, V. **Map** p311 L9.

This 18th-century building on a quiet side street near Medborgarplatsen has a colourful history, having been at various times a brewery, a barracks for beggars and thieves, and a hospital during the 1834 cholera epidemic. Since 1976 it's been a hotel, and its present owners have carefully restored the three-storey building, with polished original wood floors and tasteful Gustavian-style furnishings. Room 120 is often booked by honeymooners, as it's slightly larger and overlooks pretty Katarina Kyrka, a popular wedding venue. Almost every room has a view of the green park around the church. The 70 rooms come in three price categories; even the

Serve time at **Långholmen**. *See p51.*

cheapest, with shared shower and toilet facilities, are clean and comfortable. The courtyard is a pleasant place to eat breakfast or enjoy a glass of wine.
Hotel services *Bar. Garden. No smoking. Parking.* **Room services** *Dataport. Telephone. TV: pay movies.*

Ersta Konferens & Hotell

Erstagatan 1K, PO Box 4619, 116 91 Stockholm (714 63 41/fax 714 63 51/www.ersta.se/konferens). Bus 3, 46, 53, 66, 76. **Rates** *Mid Aug-mid June* single 550kr-950kr; double 750kr-1,250kr. *Mid June-mid Aug* single 380kr-600kr; double 520kr-870kr. **Credit** MC, V. **Map** p311 L10.

This 22-room hotel is a quiet oasis perched at the tip of Södermalm near Fjällgatan, where the tour buses deposit visitors for one of Stockholm's most phenomenal views. Constructed for the Deacons' Society in the early 19th century, the building is in a square amid beautifully landscaped gardens and across from the Ersta Café, with its large veranda overlooking the city. Many of the brightly decorated rooms offer a view of the water. There are small guest kitchens on each floor, and you can enjoy breakfast in the garden when the weather's good. There's also a bookshop, church and museum on the premises, as well as a hospital, hospice and senior citizens' home in the building across the street – all vestiges of the deacons' good works.
Hotel services *Business services. Café. Conference facilities. Disabled: adapted rooms. Garden. No smoking. Parking.* **Room services** *Dataport. Telephone. TV.*

Budget/youth hostels

Hotel Tre Små Rum

Högbergsgatan 81, 118 54 Stockholm (641 23 71/fax 642 88 08/www.tresmarum.se). T-bana Mariatorget/bus 4, 43, 55, 66, 74. **Rates** single/double 695kr. **Credit** AmEx, MC, V. **Map** p310 L6.

This basement hotel in Söder had 'three small rooms' when it opened in 1993; now there are seven (six doubles, one single, all with shared showers). Clean and simple, with pale yellow walls, limestone floors and furniture provided by the Grand Hôtel (in return for a donation to the Swedish Red Cross), it's ideal for budget travellers who are planning to spend most of their time out and about. The only communal room is the breakfast room, where you can help yourself to pastries, muesli, fruit, bread and drinks. Run by the very friendly Jakob and Christian, it's a few minutes' walk from Mariatorget T-bana station.
Hotel services *Bike rental. No smoking. Payphone.* **Room services** *TV.*

Zinkensdamm Vandrarhem & Hotel

Zinkens Väg 20, 117 41 Stockholm (616 81 10/fax 616 81 00/www.zinkensdamm.com). T-bana Hornstull or Zinkensdamm/bus 4, 40, 66, 74. **Rates** *Hostel* 155kr-200kr over-15s; 75kr-100kr 3-15s;

Staying on a boat

Stockholm has often been called the 'Venice of the North', mainly because its 14 islands offer a glimpse of the water from nearly every part of town. But to make the most of Stockholm's watery location, nothing beats staying on a boat. Being lulled to sleep by the waves slapping against the hull, and waking to a spectacular view of the city – even if you have to crawl from your tiny cabin to the deck above – make Stockholm's boat hotels a popular option for many visitors.

Most are youth hostels or budget hotels, but a moderately priced boat hotel, the **Log Inn Hotel**, just opened in 2002. And for really tasteful shipside living, there's the upmarket option of **Mälardrottningen**.

Af Chapman

Flaggmansvägen 8, Skeppsholmen, 111 49 Stockholm (463 22 66/fax 611 71 55/www.stf chapman.com). T-bana Kungsträdgården/bus 46, 55, 62, 65, 76.

Small and sweet **Tre Små Rum**. *See p50.*

breakfast 25kr-55kr. *Hotel* 200kr-245kr over-15s; 100kr-125kr 3-15s. **Credit** AmEx, DC, MC, V. **Map** p301 L4.

This youth hostel and hotel is tucked away in the green oasis of Tantolunden just a few minutes' walk from the busy main street of Horngatan. Nearby are the *koloniträdgårdar* with their charming small houses where, for decades, city-dwellers have cultivated a bit of countryside in the middle of the city. The hostel itself, a yellow wooden building, has a large courtyard where young travellers congregate to chat or strum guitars. The rooms are clean and the bedding and furnishings in good shape. Reasonably priced hotel rooms, all non-smoking, are also available, and come with a buffet breakfast.

Hotel services *Baggage storage. Bar. Bike rental. Garden. Kitchen. Laundry room. No smoking. Parking. Payphone. Sauna.* **Room services (hotel only)** *Dataport. Telephone. TV: cable.*

Långholmen

Budget/youth hostels

Långholmen Hotel

Långholmsmuren 20, PO Box 9116, 102 72 Stockholm (720 85 00/fax 720 85 75/www.langholmen.com). T-bana Hornstull/bus 4, 40, 66, 74. **Rates** *Hostel Mon-Thur, Sun* 175kr-225kr over-15s; 90kr-115kr 3-15s. *Fri, Sat* 200kr-245kr over-15s; 100kr-125kr 3-15s. Breakfast 35kr-65kr. *Hotel Mon-Thur, Sun* single 1,095kr; double 1,395kr. *Fri, Sat* single 795kr; double 1,095kr. **Credit** AmEx, DC, MC, V. **Map** p301 K2.

Fans of prison dramas will get a perverse thrill out of staying in this unusual youth hostel/hotel in the former 19th-century Kronohäktet jail. The large yellow building is still very prison-like, with cells

Rates *Members* 120kr-180kr; children 70kr. *Non-members* 165kr-225kr; children 95kr. Breakfast 55kr. *Annual membership* 275kr; 100kr under-25s; free under-15s. **Credit** AmEx, MC, V. **Map** p304 J9.

Probably the most beautiful youth hostel in the world, this three-masted, fully rigged schooner off Skeppsholmen (*pictured*) is a treasured Stockholm landmark. Named after a 17th-century Stockholm master shipbuilder, it took its maiden voyage in 1888 and later served as a training ship for the Swedish Navy. It has been a youth hostel since 1949. The 140 beds (in two- to 15-bed rooms), along with the shower and toilet facilities, are located on the ship, while a building on the shore houses a kitchen, small grocery store, recreation room and a dining room. The café on deck has an unbeatable view.

Hotel services *Café. Disabled: adapted rooms. Kitchen. Laundry. No smoking. Parking. Payphone. Shop. TV room.*

Den Röda Båten Mälaren

Södermälarstrand, kajplats 6, Södermalm, 117 20 Stockholm (644 43 85/fax 641 37 33/www.rodabaten.nu). T-bana Slussen/ bus 3, 43, 46, 55, 76. **Rates** *Hostel* (per person) dormitory 185kr; single 400kr; double 225kr; triple/quad 215kr. Breakfast 55kr. *Hotel* single 665kr-775kr; double 915kr-1,150kr. **Credit** MC, V. **Map** p310 K7.

You can't miss this cosy riverside hotel, because it's painted bright red – hence its name, 'the Red Boat'. It's located in a perfect spot for strolling down the small alleys of Gamla Stan, having a beer in the pubs of Södermalm or simply watching the boats pass by. In summer the floating restaurant Ludvigshafen is open too. *Den Röda Båten* is an old Göta Canal steamer, built in 1914. She carried lumber until 1950 and was on the verge of being destroyed at the end of the 1960s when a German boat enthusiast, Peter Vogel, found her and turned her into a youth hostel. There are 182 hostel beds and a few tiny cabins; the furnishings are rather shabby, but she sure is sweet.

Hotel services *Café. No smoking. Payphones. TV room.*

(yep, that's where you sleep) arranged around a two-storey central atrium. The single cells with their tiny windows will give travellers a feeling for life inside; other rooms are larger and lighter. A ghoulish sense of humour prevails: the mirrors are guillotine-shaped, and the clocks in reception tell the time in penitentiaries around the world. Långholmen is run mainly as a hotel in winter and as a youth hostel in summer. Facilities are good; as well as a pub, a café (open in summer, in the pie-shaped former exercise yard), there's the 17th-century Wärdshus, which serves fine Swedish cuisine and has a charming summer garden. The place is a ten-minute walk from the Hornstull T-bana station.
Hotel services *Bar. Business services. Café. Conference facilities. Disabled: adapted rooms. Garden. Kitchen. Laundry room. No-smoking rooms. Parking. Payphone. Restaurant.* **Room services** *(hotel only) Dataport. Hairdryer. Room service (noon-9pm). Telephone. TV: cable.*

Östermalm

Deluxe

Hotel Diplomat

Strandvägen 7C, 104 40 Stockholm (459 68 00/ fax 459 68 20/www.diplomathotel.com). T-bana Östermalmstorg/bus 47, 62, 69, 76. **Rates** *Mon-Thur, Sun* single 1,895kr; double 2,495kr-2,795kr; suite 3,295kr-3,695kr; Stockholm Suite 6,290kr. *Fri, Sat* single 1,095kr-1,295kr; double 1,495kr-1,795kr. **Credit** AmEx, DC, MC, V. **Map** p304 G9.
One of Stockholm's best-preserved art nouveau buildings, the six-storey Diplomat, built in 1911, occupies a fabulous site on grand Strandvägen, looking out across Nybroviken to Blasieholmen. Formerly an apartment building, it was turned into a hotel in the 1960s – it's still family-run. Its 128 rooms (30 of which have views of the water) are gradually being renovated in an updated classical style in beige, blue and green pastel colours. It's a tad stuffy but very classy. Lottery winners should head for the Stockholm Suite with its domed ceiling covered in murals. The cage lift is marvellously old-fashioned, and stained-glass windows line the staircase. More modern touches appear in the serene first-floor lounge and the airy T/Bar restaurant on the ground floor; take a pavement seat outside and enjoy some fine Swedish and Mediterranean food. If you're planning a trip to the archipelago, you're in luck; boats leave from the quay outside the front door.
Hotel services *Babysitting. Bars. Business services. Conference facilities. Gym (at SATS Sports Club). No-smoking rooms. Parking. Restaurant. Sauna.* **Room services** *Dataport. Hairdryer. Minibar. Room service (7am-midnight). Telephone. TV: pay movies/satellite.*

Staying on a boat (continued)

Gustaf Af Klint

Stadsgårdskajen 153, Södermalm, 116 45 Stockholm (640 40 77/78/fax 640 64 16/http://hem.fyristorg.com/ gustafafklint). T-bana Slussen/bus 3, 43, 46, 55, 76. **Rates** *Hostel* (per person) dormitory 120k; double 170kr; quad 150kr per person. Breakfast 55kr. *Hotel* single 395kr; double 595kr-650kr. **Credit** MC, V. **Map** p310 K8.
One of Stockholm's most popular youth hostels, this boat moored along Stadsgårdskajen – just a step away from Slussen – offers a spectacular view from its onboard café, although not, alas, from the tiny rooms or dorms, which give only a glimpse of the water. It offers both hotel and youth hostel accommodation, but don't expect much. The furnishings are a bit shabby and run-down – but the price is right if you're on a tight budget and the idea of a nautical lifestyle appeals.
Hotel services *No smoking. Parking. Payphones. Restaurant. TV room.*

Lighthouse Hotel

Årstaänsvägen 11B, Liljeholmen, 150 98 Stockholm (640 40 08/fax 640 48 45/ www.shiphotel.nu). T-bana Liljeholmen. **Rates** single 550kr; double 650kr; family 750kr. **Credit** MC, V.
This cosy boat hotel lies anchored off Liljeholmen, rather far from the city centre (though it's only ten minutes by T-bana to Central Station). From the big sundeck you can gaze at the passing boats on Årstaviken, beautiful Tantolunden park on Södermalm and the Roman arches of the railway bridge. Recently renovated, the ship now offers 16 spacious, colourfully designed cabins, all with room for up to three people. None is en suite, but all are non-smoking. After serving breakfast (included in the price), the reception area becomes an all-day café.
Hotel services *Café. No smoking. TV room.*

Log Inn Hotel

Södermälarstrand, kajplats 16, Södermalm (442 44 20/www.loginn.se). T-bana Slussen/ bus 3, 43, 46, 55, 76. **Rates** *Mon-Thur, Sun*

The lobby bar of the ultra-hip **Lydmar Hotel**.

Expensive

Lydmar Hotel

Sturegatan 10, 114 36 Stockholm (56 61 13 00/ fax 56 61 13 01/www.lydmar.se). T-bana Östermalmstorg/bus 1, 46, 55, 56, 62. **Rates** *Mon-Thur, Sun* S 1,900kr; M 2,250kr; L 2,500kr; XL 3,500kr; XXL 4,950kr. *Fri, Sat* S 1,280kr; M 1,520kr; L 1,790kr; XL 2,950kr; XXL 4,100kr. **Credit** AmEx, DC, MC, V. **Map** p303 E8.

Don't wear black at the uber-cool Lydmar (though everyone does, of course) or you'll disappear into the decor. Overlooking green Humlegården and a few steps from the heaving nightclubs of Stureplan, this is Stockholm's hippest hotel.The lobby doubles as a very popular bar (*see p138*), known for its DJs, beautiful clientele and general all-round coolness. Music is the predominant theme: live gigs happen weekly (*see p214*), there's an annual soul/funk festival, bands on tour often stay here (and occasionally play impromptu sets) – and you can even change the music in the lift (ten choices, from acid jazz to jungle). The rooms – 62 in total, categorised from S to XXL – vary from sexy designer mimimalism (all marble, wood and satin in black, white and grey) to classic-with-a-modern-twist (carpets, opulent fabrics and funky chandeliers).

Hotel services *Babysitting. Bar. Gym (Sturebadet). No-smoking rooms. Parking. Restaurants.* **Room**

single 595kr-795kr; double 895kr-1,195kr; triple 1,095kr; family 1,395kr. *Fri, Sat* 495kr-695kr; double 695kr-895kr; triple 795kr; family 1,195kr. **Credit** MC, V. **Map** p310 K7.

Opened in June 2002, this boat hotel is now the largest on Södermälarstrand, with 22 rooms offering everything from bunk beds to family rooms. Originally built in 1928, the *Kronprinsesse Märtha* is named after the Swedish princess who married Norway's Prince Olav V. She's had a rather eventful history, having served as a cargo ship on Norwegian routes in the 1930s, a dive ship in the West Indies in the late '70s and even as a floating casino in the '80s. Now she's in the process of being fully renovated by her new owners, who have created clean, comfortably furnished en suite rooms that are bigger than your average boat-hotel cabin. Some of the single rooms share a bathroom. An onboard restaurant opened in autumn 2002.

Hotel services *No smoking. Restaurant. TV room.*

Mälardrottningen

Riddarholmen, 111 28 Stockholm (54 51 87 80/fax 24 36 76/www.malardrottningen.se). T-bana Gamla Stan/bus 3, 53. **Rates** *Mon-Thur, Sun* single 1,050kr-2,100kr; double 1,180kr-2,100kr. *Sat, Sun* single 870kr-2,100kr; double 980kr-2,100kr. **Credit** AmEx, DC, MC, V. **Map** p303 J6.

This luxury yacht once belonged to Barbara Hutton, the Woolworth's heiress, and is the classiest of Stockholm's hotel boats. It sits regally on its own perch at Riddarholmen, just a quick walk from Gamla Stan. The 60 cabins are elegant and well equipped, but opt for a more spacious double instead of a single even if you're travelling solo – the price difference is modest. There's an onboard sauna, which will be appreciated if you visit Stockholm in the cooler months.

Hotel services *Business services. Café (summer only). Conference facilities. No-smoking rooms. Parking. Restaurants. Sauna.* **Room services** *Dataport. Hairdryer. Telephone. TV: pay movies/satellite.*

services *Dataport. DVD player. Hairdryer. Minibar. Room service (6.30-10.30am, 1-11pm). Telephone. TV: cable/pay movies.*

Gårdet

Deluxe

Villa Källhagen

Djurgårdsbrunnsvägen 10, 115 27 Stockholm (665 03 00/fax 665 03 99/www.kallhagen.se). Bus 69. **Rates** *Mon-Thur, Sun* single 1,900kr-2,500kr; double 2,400kr-2,700kr; suite 3,000kr. *Fri, Sat* single 1,100kr-1,600kr; double 1,300kr-1,600kr; suite 2,000kr. **Credit** AmEx, DC, MC, V. **Map** p305 F13.

Taking full advantage of its waterside location, Villa Källhagen is a tranquil retreat just minutes from the city's busy streets. The original inn, the Red Cottage, dating from 1810, is now situated in the garden behind the new hotel, built in 1990. The sunny rooms (all facing the water) feature the best of Scandinavian design, with bright fabrics on the sofas and armchairs, and light fittings designed by Josef Frank of Svenskt Tenn fame. Suites have separate sitting rooms and small patios. The hotel is often used by guests of the nearby US Embassy. The excellent restaurant serves classic Swedish food with continental influences, prepared by award-winning chef Fredrik Eriksson. There are just 20 rooms, so you'll need to book well in advance.

Hotel services *Bar. Business services. Conference facilities. No-smoking rooms. Parking. Patio. Restaurant. Sauna.* **Room services** *Dataport. Hairdryer. Minibar. Telephone. TV: free movies.*

Further afield

Expensive

Hotel J

Ellensviksvägen 1, 131 27 Nacka Strand (601 30 00/ fax 601 30 09/www.hotelj.com). Boat from Nybrokajen or Slussen/T-bana to Slussen then bus 404, 443. **Rates** *Mon-Fri* single 1,195kr-2,995kr; double 1,595kr-3,495kr; suite 2,995kr-3,395kr. *Sat, Sun* single 950kr-1,350kr; double 1,350kr-1,750kr; suite 2,900kr. **Credit** AmEx, DC, MC, V.

A 20-minute bus, boat or taxi ride from the city, Hotel J is beautifully sited, on the edge of the water overlooking Djurgården. Named after the famous J boats of the America Cup, it's all very New England boathouse in feel, decorated in blue and white and flooded with light. A 1912 summer house and two modern extensions house 44 rooms; rooms 216 and 218 are probably the best. The rooms in the old building are smaller (shower, no bath) and don't have balconies. An excellent buffet breakfast is provided in the lobby-cum-dining room, which later turns into a self-service bar. Full of business types in the week (Ericsson has offices just up the hill), at weekends Hotel J is popular with Stockholmers wanting a break from the city. You can rent mini catamarans and the hotel has its own motorboat. The hotel restaurant is a short walk away, at Nacka Strand harbour, where boats to the archipelago stop in the summer.

Hotel services *Air-conditioning. Boat moorings. Business services. Conference facilities. Disabled: adapted room (1). Garden. Gym. Laundry. No smoking. Parking. Restaurants. Sauna.* **Room services** *Dataport. Hairdryer. Minibar. Room service (24hrs). Telephone. TV: pay movies.*

Moderate

Hasseludden Konferens & Yasuragi

Hamndalsvägen 6, 132 81 Saltsjö-Boo (747 61 00/ fax 747 61 01/www.hasseludden.com). Boat from Strömkajen/bus 444 to Orminge Centrum then bus 417 to Hamndalsvägen then 5-10mins walk. **Rates** *Room only* single 1,350kr-1,550kr; double 2,300kr-2,500kr; suite 3,300kr. *Yasuragi Package Fri, Sat* single 1,550kr-1,850kr; double 1,450kr-1,650kr per person; suite 2,050kr-2,350kr per person. *Mon-Thur, Sun* single 1,800kr-2,100kr; double 1,600kr-1,700kr per person. **Credit** AmEx, DC, MC, V.

For something unusual, try Hasseludden, Sweden's only Japanese spa, or *yasuragi*, where you can ease travel-weary muscles with a traditional Japanese bath, a swim or a soak in a steaming outdoor jacuzzi overlooking the sea. Guests are pampered with a *yukata* (robe), swimsuit and slippers. You can refresh yourself at the fruit and juice buffet, and try a session of *qi gong*, *do in* or Zen meditation – or go to the sushi school. All sorts of massages and treatments are available too. All the rooms and suites (162 in total) have calming views overlooking the sea, but are sparely furnished – designed for sleeping and not much else. The suites (*ryokan*) include a separate Japanese bath, full service and an invigorating massage. The hotel is a 30-minute boat ride from the centre of Stockholm. You can also just visit the spa (*see p168*).

Hotel services *Business services. No-smoking rooms. Parking. Pool. Restaurant. Sauna. Spa.* **Room services** *Dataport. Hairdryer. Minibar. Room service (7am-9pm). Telephone. TV: pay movies.*

Camping

Camping is a pleasant and cheap option – but only during Sweden's short-lived summer. Stockholm's most central campsite is **Östermalms Citycamping**, located at the Östermalm sports ground behind Stockholms Stadion (Fiskartorpsvägen 2; 10 29 03). Near woodland, it's got 150 camping places and is open from the end of June to mid August. There's also a site for camper vans (not tents) on **Långholmen** (669 18 90/772 96 00; open end June-end Aug). The tourist office (*see p285*) also produces a handy guide to campsites in Stockholm and the archipelago. To camp in Sweden, you need a validated Camping Card, which you can buy (90kr) at any campsite.

Sightseeing

Introduction **56**
Gamla Stan & Riddarholmen **58**
Norrmalm & Vasastaden **70**
Djurgården & Skeppsholmen **80**
Södermalm & Långholmen **88**
Östermalm & Gärdet **94**
Kungsholmen **101**
Further Afield **105**

Features

Pick a card 56
Don't miss sights 57
The Stockholm Bloodbath 66
Walk 1: Gamla Stan 68
Breaking the mould 73
Super Swedes: August Strindberg 78
The man behind Skansen 83
Raising the *Vasa* 85
Where to swim outdoors 91
Walk 2: The heights of Söder 92
The best viewpoints 99
Alfred Nobel & the Nobel Prizes 104

Introduction

Get your bearings here.

Stockholm is a remarkably easy city to be a tourist in. For a start, the city centre is very compact and it's never more than a couple of metro stops from one sight to another – though often the best, and most pleasant, way to get around is to walk, especially in summer when the sun is sparkling on the water and the views stretch for miles. It takes about 30 minutes to cross the city, from Norrmalm to Södermalm, but many places are only a few minutes' walk apart. The streets are spotless, of course, and – except on crowded medieval Gamla Stan – wide, often verging on the grand.

If you'd prefer to take public transport, the Tunnelbana metro system with its three lines – red, green and blue – is fast, clean and efficient. Alternatively, a network of buses criss-crosses the capital and these are equally well run and frequent. Some places – notably the royal park of Djurgården – are not on the T-bana and are accessible only by bus or foot. Or ferry. Ferries run between Södermalm, Djurgården and Norrmalm – though not all year round (*see p272* **Getting Around** for detailed information on all the public transport options).

Navigation is also very straightforward. The city breaks down into quickly recognisable, well-defined areas. There's none of this lurching from one overlapping neighbourhood to another, never quite knowing where you are. This is mainly because most of the city's districts are on self-contained islands: the main islands of **Gamla Stan**, **Södermalm**, **Djurgården** and **Kungsholmen**, and the smaller ones of **Skeppsholmen**, **Långholmen**, **Riddarholmen** and tiny **Helgeandsholmen**. Only **Norrmalm**, **Vasastaden**, **Östermalm** and **Gärdet** overlap each other.

One of your first stops should be the **Stockholm Information Service** (*see p285*), the very good tourist office located in the centre of Norrmalm directly opposite NK department store. It offers excellent info on all subjects; maps; an exchange bureau; tickets to concerts, theatre and other events; and a small gift shop.

Pick a card

If you're planning on doing a lot of sightseeing while in town, consider buying a **Stockholm Card** (Stockholmskortet). It provides free admission to more than 70 museums and attractions, plus free travel on the Tunnelbana, city buses, commuter trains and sightseeing boats (but not the city or archipelago ferries), and free street parking at official parking spots. Available for 24, 48 or 72 hours (the time starts from its first use), it costs 220kr, 380kr or 540kr for adults; 60kr, 120kr or 180kr for 7-17s. In the Sightseeing chapters, **Free with SC** indicates which museums provide free entry for Stockholm Card holders.

The less useful **Tourist Card** also provides free travel, and free admission to Kaknästornet and Gröna Lund, plus 50 per cent off Skansen, but no other discounts. It costs 80kr for 24 hours, 150kr for 72 hours (45kr and 90kr for children).

You can purchase both cards at the **tourist office** and **Hotellcentrallen** (for both, *see p285*) and also at **SL information centres** (*see p273*).

THE AREAS

Arranged by area, our Sightseeing chapters start with **Gamla Stan**, the Old Town: the site of the original city. Its historic buildings and narrow, twisting streets make it the most atmospheric part of the capital, and it also contains some of the main tourist attractions – notably the Kungliga Slottet (Royal Palace). Two small islands lie next to Gamla Stan: **Riddarholmen** and **Helgeandsholmen**, the latter the home of the Swedish parliament.

Just north of Gamla Stan is **Norrmalm**. The pulsing modern heart of Stockholm, it contains the main business and shopping district, some leading hotels, important cultural institutions including the opera house, and various museums. It's also the transport hub: the central railway station is here – joined to T-Centralen, the T-bana station where all three lines converge – as is the Arlanda Express station, for trains to the airport.

Norrmalm is bordered by water to the south and west. To the north (on the other side of Tegnérgatan, though the exact dividing line is

Don't miss Sights

Kungliga Slottet
Discover royal life down the ages, then stroll around the rest of Gamla Stan. *See p58.*

Skansen
An outdoor cultural and historical tour of Sweden. And bears too. *See p84.*

Stadshuset
Stockholm's finest National Romantic building, and the setting of the Nobel Prize banquet. *See p103.*

Vasamuseet
You'll be overwhelmed by this perfectly preserved 300-year-old warship. *See p86.*

Take a guided boat tour
The best way to get a feeling for the capital's islands and waterways. *See p57.*

a bit vague) lies **Vasastaden**. A bit further from the action, the streets are wider and grander and the attractions more spread out – though it's also got some bucolic parks, fine bars and most of the city's moderately priced hotels.

From Norrmalm it's a leap across the water to **Djurgården** and **Skeppsholmen**. The latter, connected by a bridge to the south-eastern tip of Norrmalm, houses a cluster of museums (some currently closed). Green and leafy Djurgården is one of Stockhom's treasures. On its western edge are some of the city's most popular and highly rated museums and sights, including the awe-inspiring Vasamuseet and the famous open-air museum Skansen.

South from Gamla Stan, and connected to it by a busy network of roads, is extensive **Södermalm**. Formerly a working-class district, with an edgier feel than the rest of the city, its numerous bars, clubs and shops offer a renegade alternative to the norm. Attached to its north-western edge are **Långholmen**, formerly a prison island, now a tranquil wooded haven, and little **Reimersholme**.

Back north across the water lies the upper-class enclave of **Östermalm**, to the east of Norrmalm. It's bordered on the west by the broad thoroughfare of Birger Jarlsgatan, to the south by Strandvägen and the water, and to the north by the wide boulevard of Vallhallavägen. Its lower reaches, around Stureplan, contain some of the city's most exclusive and trendy clubs, bars and restaurants, as well as some of its most upmarket and expensive shops. North of Vallhallavägen is residential **Gärdet**, while to the east stretch the open fields and woodland of **Ladugårdsgärdet**. Finally, there's middle-class **Kungsholmen**, separated by a narrow channel from the western edge of Normalm. Its must-see attraction is the Stadshuset, but it also has a number of decent restaurants and cafés.

It's also worth heading just outside the city centre, north to the green expanses of **Hagaparken** and a couple of fascinating museums, and west to **Lidingö** and a sculpture garden devoted to Carl Milles.

Guided tours

Authorised Guides of Stockholm

789 24 96/www.guidestockholm.com.
This association has been around for 50 years and all its guides must complete a two-term programme. You can join the walking tour of Gamla Stan (1hr, 50kr) at 1.30pm on Sat and Sun, or book a taxi tour for up to four people (500kr for the first hour).

City Sightseeing & Stockholm Sightseeing

587 140 30/www.citysightseeing.com/ www.stockholmsightseeing.com.
Tours by bus (City Sightseeing) or boat (Stockholm Sightseeing). The Stockholm Panorama bus tour (1.5hrs, 170kr) is very popular, but the boat tours are probably the nicest way to see the city. These include the Royal Canal Tour (1hr, 90kr) around Djurgården and the Under the Bridges Tour (2hrs, 150kr). Tours run all year round (except there are no boat tours from January to March, because the water is too frozen), but are most frequent from May to September. For more information, visit the City Sightseeing ticket booth on Gustav Adolfs Torg by the opera house, or the Stockholm Sightseeing booth on Strömkajen in front of the Grand Hotel.

Hot-air balloon flights

Unlike most capital cities, Stockholm allows hot-air balloons to fly over its centre. The season is May to September, and flights are generally in the early evening. Book at least two weeks in advance, and note that bad weather can result in changes or cancellations. Try **Scandinavia Balloons** (55 64 04 65/ www.balloons-sweden.se) – 1,495kr per person for a 1hr flight – or **City Ballong** (34 54 64/www.city ballong.se) – 1,695kr for a 1-1.5hr flight and a champagne picnic on the ground afterwards.

Stockholm Stories

0708 85 05 28/www.stockholmstories.com.
For guided walks with a personal touch, join native Stockholmer Maria Lindberg Howard on her 1-2hr tours of Gamla Stan and Söder. Discover the stories, past and present, behind the city's streets, buildings and personalities. Tours are held year round, in English and/or Swedish. Call or check the website for details and up-to-date rates. You'll need to book.

Gamla Stan & Riddarholmen

The site of the original city is crammed with unmissable sights.

Gamla Stan

Long before Stockholm stretched itself out into the countryside, the entire city was once limited to the small island of Gamla Stan. Some clever people built a fortress on the island's north-eastern shore around the 11th century, which enabled them to control the trade and traffic into Lake Mälaren, but there's no record of an actual city on Gamla Stan – which means 'the Old Town' – until Birger Jarl's famous letter of 1252. The island city grew into a horrible mess of winding streets and ramshackle houses until most of the western half burned down in 1625. The city planners finally crafted a few right angles (today the streets surrounding Stora Nygatan and Lilla Nygatan) and tore down the crumbling defensive wall around the island to make room for waterfront properties for the city council. The island's been the home of the Swedish monarchy for hundreds of years, and the immense and splendiferous **Kungliga Slottet** (Royal Palace) is still the main sight.

Nowadays, walking around Gamla Stan's charming tangle of narrow streets and alleyways lined with yellow, orange and red buildings is like taking an open-air history lesson. It can get very packed, but you can avoid the bus-tour clusters by keeping off the main drags or ducking down a side street when the crowds get too much. The best approach is to just wander at will, soaking up the atmosphere.

Kungliga Slottet

The **Kungliga Slottet** (*see p60*) sits on a hill at the highest point in Gamla Stan where the old fortress of Tre Kronor once stood. The fortress was almost completely destroyed – except for the north wing – by a fire in 1697. Royal architect Nicodemus Tessin the Younger designed the new palace with an Italianate exterior and a French interior with Swedish influences; it was completed in 1754.

The low, yellowy-brown building is imposing rather than beautiful; its monolithic northern façade looms menacingly as you approach Gamla Stan over the bridges from Norrmalm. The square central building around an open courtyard is flanked by two wings extending to the west and two more to the east – rather

Gamla Stan, with the spire of Tyska Kyrkan.

The grand **Kungliga Slottet** where...

as if the palace were stretching out its front and hind legs. Between its eastern wings lie the gardens of Logården and between the curved western wings is an outer courtyard; the ticket/information office and gift shop are in the south-western curve.

The southern façade with its triumphal central arch is the most attractive, along **Slottsbacken**, the steep hill that leads up from Skeppsbron and the water to the back of **Storkyrkan** (*see p64*). This large space was kept open to make it easier to defend the palace. The obelisk in front of the church, designed by Louis Jean Desprez, was put up in 1799 as a memorial to Gustav III's war against Russia in 1788-90.

Although the palace is the official residence of the royal family, they actually live on the island of Drottningholm (itself well worth a visit – *see p239*), so visitors are welcome to explore its sumptuous **Royal Apartments** (Representationsvåningarna) and museums. The **Museet Tre Kronor** presents the history of the palace, while the **Skattkammaren** (Treasury), **Livrustkammaren** (Royal Armoury) and **Gustav III's Antikmuseum** (Museum of Antiquities) show off its prized possessions. A good bargain, if you plan on seeing most of the palace, is to buy the combination ticket (rather than individual tickets for each attraction), which provides admission to everything except the Livrustkammaren. But the limited opening hours and sheer size of the place mean that you'll probably have to visit a couple of times if you want to see it all.

Another royal museum, the **Kungliga Myntkabinettet** (*see below*) is located at the bottom of Slottsbacken, opposite the entrance to the Royal Armoury.

The **Högvakten** (Royal Guard; 402 63 17/ www.hogvakten.mil.se) has been stationed at the palace since 1523, and is a popular tourist attraction. The guard changes posts, every day in summer but less frequently in winter (June-Aug 12.15pm Mon-Sat; 1.15pm Sun; Sept-May 12.15pm Wed, Sat; 1.15pm Sun), to the sound of a marching brass band. Around 20 soldiers dressed in blue uniforms with silver spiked helmets walk with stiff legs and straight faces in the palace's outer western courtyard. The ceremony can be wonderful free entertainment depending on the size of the crowd and the weather. The whole thing lasts about 35 minutes and schedules are listed in *Svenska Dagbladet* and *Dagens Nyheter*. For a guaranteed good view of the guard and band, catch them on their parade route from the **Armémuseum** (*see p96*), from where they leave about 30 minutes before the change.

Kungliga Myntkabinettet

Slottsbacken 6 (51 95 53 04/www.myntkabinettet.se). T-bana Gamla Stan/bus 43, 46, 55, 59, 76. **Open** 10am-4pm daily. **Admission** 45kr; 35kr concessions; 12kr 7-17s; free under-7s. Free Sun. **Free with SC. Credit** MC, V. **Map** p303 H8.

The Royal Coin Cabinet, a museum of rare coins and monetary history, is surprisingly large, filling three floors in a building directly south of the palace. The darkened ground floor displays numerous coins in different contexts, from the first coin made in Greece in 625 BC to what is claimed to be the world's biggest coin, weighing a hefty 19.7kg (43lb). The first and second floors house displays on hoards

... you can see the **Changing of the Guard**.

Sightseeing

and treasures, savings banks and medals. The museum is cleverly designed, with motion-triggered sounds and lights, multimedia displays and a special exhibition and playroom for kids. Nevertheless, unless you are especially fond of the filthy lucre, or an economist, it's probably best to save this museum for a Sunday when admission is free.

Kungliga Slottet

Bordered by Slottsbacken, Skeppsbron, Lejonbacken & Högvaksterrasen (402 61 30/www.royalcourt.se). T-bana Gamla Stan/bus 43, 46, 55, 59, 76.
Open *Representationsvåningarna, Museet Tre Kronor, Skattkammaren Mid May-Aug* 10am-4pm daily. *Sept-early Jan, Feb-mid May* noon-3pm Tue-Sun. Closed 3wks Jan. *Gustav III's Antikmuseum Mid May-Aug* 10am-4pm daily. Closed Sept-mid May. **Admission** *Combination ticket* 110kr; 65kr concessions. *Individual tickets* 70kr; 35kr 7-18s. Free under-7s. **Free with SC. Credit** AmEx, DC, MC, V. **Map** p303 H8.

Representationsvåningarna

Entrance in western courtyard.
The Royal Apartments occupy two floors of the palace and are entered by a grand staircase in the western wing. King Adolf Fredrik and Queen Lovisa Ulrika moved into the new palace in 1754, after five decades of construction and delays following the 1697 fire. The apartments are still used for official ceremonies, although over the years the function of individual rooms has changed repeatedly, from bedroom to audience chamber to roped-off curiosity. The furnishings, tapestries and paintings range in style from the ornate rococo to the more reserved neo-classical Gustavian. Banquets are held several times a year in Karl XI's Gallery in the **State Apartments** on the second floor. This long hall seats up to 150 guests and was modelled after the Hall of Mirrors in Versailles. The ballroom at the end of the gallery is often used as a salon during banquets, with the king and queen standing in the entrance to greet guests. Heads of state stay in the **Guest Apartments** during their visits to the capital, and for this reason parts or all of the palace may be occasionally closed. Downstairs in the **Bernadotte Apartments**, portraits of the current dynasty's ancestors hang in the Bernadotte Gallery, including a large portrait of the former French marshal Karl XIV Johan who became king in 1818. Medals and orders of various kinds are awarded in the **Apartments of the Orders of Chivalry**, and paintings of coats of arms decorate its walls. Until 1975, the monarch opened parliament each year in the impressive **Hall of State**, and directly across from this lies the **Royal Chapel** with pew ends made in the 1690s for the Tre Kronor castle. Services are held every Sunday, and all are welcome to attend. Since it's the stories behind the rooms and decorations that make the palace especially interesting – such as Gustav III's invitation to aristocrats to watch him wake up in the morning – taking a guided tour is highly recommended.

Museet Tre Kronor

Entrance on Lejonbacken.
A boardwalk built through the palace cellars, along with several models, enables visitors to see how war, fire and wealth have shaped the palace seen today. An old well from the former courtyard, a 13th-century defensive wall and the arched brick ceilings are evidence of how the palace was built up around the fortress it once was. Panels describe life in the castle, archaeological discoveries and building techniques. After the fire of 1697, rumours flew about architect Tessin the Younger's involvement in the fire, since he had hated the castle's former tower and produced his plans for the new palace rather fast. With its artefacts clustered in groups along the walls, the museum is more informative than dazzling.

Gustav III's Antikmuseum

Entrance on Lejonbacken.
This museum of Roman statues, in two halls in the north-east wing of the palace, has been laid out to look exactly as it did in the 1790s when King Gustav III returned from Italy with the collection, which includes *Apollo and His Nine Muses* and the sleeping *Endymion*. The repairs and additions made to the statues at the time have been left intact, as well as the odd combinations of pieces, such as table legs on fountains. It's worth a look if you already have the combined ticket, or an interest in Roman art. Nothing is labelled, in accordance with the period, so take the 20-minute tour or borrow a pamphlet.

Skattkammaren

Entrance on Slottsbacken.
If you're a fan of jewel-encrusted crowns and gaudy, gold geegaws, the small Treasury in the basement of the palace is worth a peek. The regalia of past Swedish royal families sparkles behind glass, with orbs, sceptres and crowns in both adult's and children's sizes. The museum also contains Gustav Vasa's etched sword of state from 1541, the coronation cloak of Oscar II and the ornate silver baptismal font of Karl XI.

Livrustkammaren

Entrance on Slottsbacken (51 95 55 44/www.lsh.se/livrustkammaren). T-bana Gamla Stan/bus 43, 46, 55, 59, 76. **Open** *May-Aug* 11am-5pm daily. *Sept-Apr* 11am-5pm Tue, Wed, Fri-Sun; 11am-8pm Thur. **Guided tours** *English July-Aug* 1pm Mon-Fri; noon Sat, Sun. *Swedish* 2pm daily. **Admission** 65kr; 50kr concessions; 20kr 7-18s; free under-7s. **Free with SC. Credit** AmEx, DC, MC, V. **Map** p303 H8.
The Royal Armoury – Sweden's oldest museum, founded in 1633 – is stuffed with armour, weapons and clothes from the 16th century onwards. With wonderfully descriptive texts, the museum's first room resembles a gruesome forensic lab, showing what a bloody and dangerous business being a king once was. It contains the masked costume King Gustav III wore when he was assassinated in 1792, and the stuffed body of Streiff, the horse that Gustav

Stuffed Streiff in the **Livrustkammaren**. *See p60.*

II Adolf was riding when he was killed in battle in 1632. Don't overlook the glass jar preserving the stomach contents of one of the conspirators to Gustav III's murder. Other rooms display splendid mounted knights, suits of armour, swords and muskets. Two rooms of clothes and toys – including a miniature carriage and suit of armour – describe the lost childhoods and early responsibilities of the royal children. The ceremonial coaches of the nobility lie beneath the main floor, in another dimly lit hall. It's one of the palace's best museums – don't miss it.

Other sights

There are plenty of other sights on Gamla Stan apart from the Royal Palace. At the top of Slottsbacken stands the imposing yellow bulk of Stockholm's de facto cathedral, **Storkyrkan** (*see p64*), scene of royal weddings and coronations. Trångsund, the street at the front of the church, leads down to Gamla Stan's main square, **Stortorget**. A former marketplace, it's surrounded by handsome, colourful 18th-century buildings, some containing cafés: the two next door to each other at the western end of the square, **Chokladkoppen** and **Kaffekoppen** (for both, *see p142*), are the best.

The large white building is the former Stock Exchange, designed by Erik Lallerstedt; it now houses the high-tech **Nobelmuseet** (*see p63*), telling the history of the esteemed Nobel Prizes. Lallerstedt also designed the 1778 well in the centre of the square. Due to the land rising, the well dried up in the 19th century and was moved to Brunkebergstorg in Norrmalm, but it was then moved back again in the 20th century.

The notorious **Stockholm Bloodbath** (*see p66* **The Stockholm Bloodbath**) occurred in Stortorget in 1520. You can see a cannon ball in the façade of the building at Stortorget 7, on the corner with Skomakargatan. It is said to have been fired at the Danish king at the time of the Bloodbath, but in fact was placed much later, as a joke, probably in 1795 by a furniture dealer named Grevesmühl. Every time the building has been restored the ball has been removed and then carefully replaced – even myths have to be nurtured.

Round the corner from Stortorget is the **Cornelis Vreeswijkmuseet** (Transgund 8; 667 73 65/www.cornelis.nu; open mid June-mid Aug noon-4pm Wed-Sun; mid Aug-mid June noon-4pm Sat, Sun; admission 20kr). The museum is devoted to Cornelis Vreeswijk, a famous radical folk singer of ballads and blues in the mid 1960s. Displaying his photos, letters and shoes, the museum is probably mainly of interest to fans of his music and the Dutch, since he was born in Holland.

Gamla Stan's main square, **Stortorget**, with the **Nobelmuseet** on the right.

Gamla Stan's four main thoroughfares – **Västerlånggatan**, **Österlånggatan**, **Stora Nygatan** and **Lilla Nygatan** – run north–south along the island. Crowded and noisy, Västerlånggatan acts as a giant sluice, gently sifting out the notes and coins from the pockets of tourists. The parallel street – narrow, curving **Prästgatan** – is a quiet alternative to the hubbub and far more atmospheric, giving you a much better idea of life in the crowded medieval city. The shops on Österlånggatan are also less touristy than those on Västerlånggatan. At the southern end of Västerlånggatan is **Mårten Trotzigs Gränd**, the city's narrowest street at only 90 centimetres (three feet) wide.

There are only five hotels on Galma Stan; two of them – the **Victory Hotel** and **Rica City Hotel Gamla Stan** (for both, *see p42*) – are on Lilla Nygatan, as is the surprisingly interesting **Postmuseum** (*see p64*).

Other churches include the **Tyska Kyrkan** (German Church; *see p64*) and the **Finska Kyrkan** (Finnish Church) – proof of Sweden's long connections with its European neighbours. The latter is housed in a 1640s building opposite the Kungliga Slottet; originally a ball games court for the palace, it has been the religious centre of the Finnish community since 1725.

Gamla Stan also contains a number of beautiful palaces, former homes of the aristocracy. On the island's north-western tip on Riddarhustorget is **Bondeska Palatset**, designed by Tessin the Elder and the seat of the Supreme Court since 1949, and the lovely **Riddarhuset** (723 39 90/www.riddarhuset.se). The latter is a superb example of Dutch Palladianism, with a typically Swedish *säteri* roof, completed in 1674. The architects were Simon de Vallée and his son Jean (who were responsible for many of Stockholm's finest 17th-century buildings), Heinrich Wilhelm and Justus Vingboons. The nobility governed from here until parliamentary reforms in 1866 knocked them down a notch or two. They still own the place and will let you in during the lunch hour (11.30am-12.30pm Mon-Fri; admission 40kr) to admire their coats of arms (more than 2,000) and the wonderful double staircase. Another way to see inside is to attend a concert by the **Stockholm Sinfonietta** (*see p216*).

Nobelmuseet

Börshuset, Stortorget (23 25 06/www.nobel.se/nobelmuseum). T-bana Gamla Stan/bus 3, 43, 46, 53, 55, 59, 76. **Open** *Mid May-mid Sept* 10am-6pm Mon, Wed-Sun; 10am-8pm Tue. *Mid Sept-mid May* 11am-8pm Tue; 11am-5pm Wed-Sun. **Guided tours** *English Mid May-mid Sept* 11am, 2pm, 4pm Mon, Wed-Sun; 11am, 2pm, 4pm, 5pm Tue. *Mid Sept-mid May* 11am, 4pm Tue-Sun. **Admission** 50kr; 40kr concessions; 20kr 7-18s; 100kr family ticket; free under-7s. **Free with SC. Credit** AmEx, MC, V. **Map** p303 J7.

The Nobel Museum opened in 2001 to commemorate the centenary of the Nobel Prizes. Although the museum is not that large, its two theatres showing captivating short films about the laureates, television clips about the prizes and a computer room with an 'e-museum' bombard you with enough information to keep you entertained for a while. A track on the ceiling moves 734 white placards (one for each prizewinner) around the main hall, each with a description and photo. Alfred Nobel's books, lab equipment and two packs of dynamite are displayed at the back of the hall, along with an enlarged copy of his one-page will, which called for the creation of the prizes. Some of the chairs in the café were signed underneath by Nobel laureates during the centennial celebrations, and one was sat in by – ooh – Bill Clinton. *See also p104* **Alfred Nobel & the Nobel Prizes**.

Sightseeing

Postmuseum

Lilla Nygatan 6 (781 17 55/www.posten.se/museum). T-bana Gamla Stan/bus 3, 53. **Open** *June-Aug* 11am-4pm Tue-Sun. *Sept-May* 11am-4pm Tue, Thur-Sun; 11am-7pm Wed. **Admission** 50kr; 40kr concessions; 25kr 13-18s; free under-13s. **Free with SC. Credit** MC, V. **Map** p303 J7.

Life-size action scenes depicting more than 360 years of the Swedish postal service make this an unexpectedly enjoyable museum. A carriage on a rough road, a farmer running with the mail, and a postal train wagon, among other tableaux, illustrate the effect of the postal service on people's lives over the centuries. From 1720 until 1869, the city's only post office was housed on this spot. The museum opened in 1906, underwent extensive renovations in 1999 and now occupies the entire building. The collection also includes the first post bus, which was used in northern Sweden in the 1920s, and no fewer than four million stamps. The Little Post Office is popular with kids, and the gift shop sells an assortment of stationery, pens and, of course, stamps.

Storkyrkan

Storkyrkobrinken, Trångsund 1 (723 30 16). T-bana Gamla Stan/bus 3, 43, 46, 53, 55, 59, 76. **Open** *June-Aug* 9am-6pm daily. *Sept-May* 9am-4pm daily. **Admission** 20kr; free under-16s. Free Sept-May. **Map** p303 H7.

Dating from the mid 13th century, 'the Great Church' is the oldest congregational church in Stockholm and the site of past coronations and royal weddings. A huge brick church with a rectangular plan, it's been added on to and rebuilt numerous times. Between 1736 and 1742, its exterior was renovated from medieval to baroque to match the neighbouring palace, and in 1743 the tower was raised to its current height of 66m (216ft). In the early 1900s, the red bricks of the church were exposed to achieve a medieval appearance. Inside, the style is primarily Gothic with baroque additions – such as the extravagant golden booths designed for the royal family by the palace architect Tessin the Younger. The main attraction is Bernt Notke's intricately carved wooden statue, *St George and the Dragon*, which is decorated with authentic elk antlers. The statue symbolises Sten Sture's victory over the Danes in a battle in 1471, and was given to the church by Sture himself in 1489. (A bronze copy of the statue can also be found in Köpmantorget not far from the church.) Don't miss the famous *Parhelion Painting*, which shows an unusual light phenomenon – six sparkling halos – that appeared over Stockholm on 20 April 1535. It's one of the oldest depictions of the capital, though the painting is a 1630s copy of the earlier original.

Tyska Kyrkan

Svartmangatan 16A (10 12 63). T-bana Gamla Stan/bus 3, 53. **Open** *May-mid Sept* noon-4pm daily. *Mid Sept-Apr* noon-4pm Sat, Sun. **Admission** free. **Map** p303 J8.

Narrow streets and historic buildings – all part of Gamla Stan's charm.

Monumental **Storkyrkan**. *See p64.*

At the height of the Hanseatic League when Stockholm had strong trade links with Germany, many German merchants settled in this area of Gamla Stan. They originally worshipped at the monastery on what is now Riddarholmen, but moved to St Gertrude's guildhouse after its expansion in the 1580s. Baroque renovations in 1638-42 gave the German Church its present appearance; its tower was rebuilt after a fire in 1878. Nicodemus Tessin the Elder designed the royal pews, and Jost Henner created the richly decorated ornaments and figures on the portal. The church is best viewed from Tyska Brinken, where the tower rises up 96m (315ft) from the narrow street. About 2,000 Swedes of German origin belong to the congregation, and services are held in German at 11am on Sundays.

Riddarholmen

Separated from Gamla Stan by several lanes of traffic and a narrow canal, the tiny island of Riddarholmen is a quiet sanctuary of cobblestone streets, 17th-century palaces and spectacular watery views. Most of the buildings now house government offices, and no one actually lives permanently on the island.

The main attraction is the medieval brick church, **Riddarholmskyrkan** (*see p66*), which was built in the late 13th century as a monastery for Franciscan monks. In 1527, following the Reformation, the monks were kicked off the island; the church is now the burial site of Swedish monarchs. Riddarholmen was originally called 'Grey Friars' Island' after the colour of the monks' clothing. In the 17th century, Sweden's Age of Greatness, Gustav II Adolf rewarded noblemen who served in the Thirty Years War with palaces on the island – this is when Riddarholmen received its current name, 'the Island of Knights'.

Next to the church is **Birger Jarls Torg**, the site of an 1854 statue of Stockholm's founder, Birger Jarl, dressed in a helmet and coat of mail. Beneath the stones of the square lie the graves of the former church cemetery. The huge white **Wrangelska Palatset** stands to the west of the statue. Constructed as a nobleman's residence in the mid 17th century, it was extensively rebuilt a few decades later by Tessin the Elder, under its new owner, Field Marshal Carl Gustaf Wrangel. The palace became the home of the royal family for several years after the Tre Kronor fire of 1697. In 1792 the murderer of Gustav III was kept in dungeons here during his trial.

On the other side of the square is the well-preserved **Stenbockska Palatset**, built in the 1640s by state councillor Fredrik Stenbock, and extended and renovated in succeeding centuries. The palaces of Riddarholmen are today used by the Swedish courts and government authorities and are seldom open to the public, but taking a walk around them is highly recommended.

Down by the water on **Evert Taubes Terrass**, you'll find one of the best views in Stockholm, looking out across the choppy water of Riddarfjärden and towards the northern and southern shores of Lake Mälaren. The terrace is named after the much-loved Swedish poet and troubadour Evert Taube (who died in 1976) and there's a bronze sculpture of him, lute in hand, near the water. It's also a prime spot to celebrate the arrival of spring on **Walpurgis Night** (*see p178*), with a bonfire by the water and communal singing. Swedish author and

Evert Taube sings on.

The Stockholm Bloodbath

Stortorget might be a pleasant place today, with its colourful buildings, outdoor café tables in summer and the Nobelmuseet, but it was the scene of one of the most gruesome events in Swedish history.

Between the late 1300s and 1521, the Nordic countries – Sweden (which then included Finland), Denmark and Norway – formed a political union, the Kalmar Union, led by the monarch in Copenhagen. The alliance was often unpopular in Sweden, there were frequent armed rebellions and for many years Sweden was ruled by opponents to the Danish king.

In 1517 a Danish army led by King Christian II invaded Sweden and landed on Södermalm, but was beaten back by Sten Sture the Younger. The troops returned in 1520 and Sten Sture was killed in battle, but they again failed to conquer Stockholm. So King Christian decided to negotiate, promising an amnesty and political influence for his Swedish adversaries if they surrendered. He invited the most important political personalities to a banquet at Tre Kronor castle. After three days of feasting and celebrations, the doors were suddenly locked and the guests arrested.

King Christian and his supporter, the Swedish archbishop Gustav Trolle, held a trial, accusing the high-ranking priests, noblemen and burghers of having had the archbishop removed from office, in 1517 – a crime of heresy, for which the sentence was death. In their defence the nobles said their decision had been fair and impartial and no one could be singled out. To prove this, Kristina Gyllenstierna (widow of Sten Sture the Younger) produced a document with all their signatures and personal seals. But one of the accused, Bishop Hans Brask, claimed he had been against removing the archbishop. He told the court to break his seal. Inside they found a note that read, 'To this I was forced and compelled.' This inspired a popular term, still used in Sweden: if you want to cover yourself from a promise, you give a *brasklapp* – a 'Brask note'.

Brask avoided punishment, but around 90 men were sentenced to death. On 8 and 9 November, the victims were dragged out to Stortorget, where the town hall was situated, and decapitated or hanged one by one. Witnesses spoke gorily of streams of blood running from the square along Kåkbrinken and other streets to lower-lying parts of the

dramatist August Strindberg was born here in 1849 in a building – which no longer exists – that housed the steamboat commission's office (for more on Sweden's most famous playwright, *see p78* **Super Swedes: August Strindberg**). Riddarholmen was then a busy port for unloading and selling goods, and a point of departure for steamboat excursions. An outdoor café is open in the summer, and there's also a restaurant and hotel on the permanently anchored luxury yacht **Mälardrottningen** (*see p53* **Staying on a boat**).

North along the waterfront, on Norra Riddarholmshamnen, is the distinctive circular **Birger Jarls Torn**. The only remnant of the defensive fortifications built by Gustav Vasa around 1530 (along with part of the Wrangelska Palatset), it was given its name in the 19th century when it was mistakenly thought to have been built under Birger Jarl 600 years earlier. It's not open to the public.

Riddarholmskyrkan

Birger Jarls Torg (402 61 30). T-bana Gamla Stan/ bus 3, 53. **Open** *Mid May-Aug* 10am-4pm daily. *Sept* noon-3pm Sat, Sun. Closed Oct-mid May. **Admission** 20kr; 10kr concessions, 7-18s; free under-7s. **Free with SC. No credit cards. Map** p303 J7.

The black, lattice-work spire of Riddarholmskyrkan is one of Stockholm's most distinctive sights, visible from all over the city. Construction on the church started in the late 13th century as a monastery for Franciscan monks. The church's benefactor, King Magnus Ladulås, is buried in the church along with 16 other monarchs, including Gustav III, Gustav II Adolf and, the last to be buried here in 1950, Gustav V. Only two Swedish monarchs have not been buried here since the 17th century. Additions have been made to the church over time, in part to make room for more graves, since an estimated 500-1,000 people are buried in its floors and vaults. The southern wall was moved back in the 15th century, the tower was added in the late 16th century, and work began in 1838 on the current cast-iron spire after lightning struck the original. Colourful plaques of the Serafim order, which are awarded to Swedish nobility and visiting heads of state, decorate the northern wall of the church. The helpful tour guides describe the history of the church, burial ceremonies and what the monarchs look like now in their coffins – whether you want to hear it or not.

Old Town. On 10 November the bodies were taken to where Katarina Kyrka is now located and burned.

Not surprisingly, the bloodbath reinvigorated the rebellion and in 1523 the son of one of the dead, Gustav Eriksson Vasa, was crowned king of Sweden (*see p11* **Gustav Vasa & the Vasaloppet**). Sweden had definitely left the Nordic Union – and instead embarked on three centuries of costly war and rivalry with Denmark.

Helgeandsholmen

This tiny oval-shaped island is connected to Norrmalm and Gamla Stan by two bridges: a pedestrian one on the western end, which connects to Norrmalm's shopping street of Drottninggatan, and a car/pedestrian bridge on the eastern end. The **Riksdagshuset** (Parliament Building; *see below*) dominates the western half of the island. Walking north, the new parliament building is to your left and the old one to your right, joined by two stone arches. The older section, completed in 1905, was designed by Aron Johansson, with two chambers for a bicameral parliament, baroque motifs and a grand staircase. At the same time he also designed a curved stone building across the street for the Bank of Sweden. After the country changed to a unicameral system in 1971, the bank moved out, the roof was flattened and the parliament's new glass-fronted debating chamber built on top.

This being Sweden, it's a pretty open system of government. There's a very detailed website (in Swedish and English), an information centre (at Västerlånggatan 1) and the parliament building is open for guided tours year round. You can also visit the public gallery when parliament is in session and listen to debates. Of the 349 members of parliament, an impressive 43 per cent are currently women – the highest ratio in the world. MPs sit in rows grouped by constituency rather than by party.

Beneath the lawns at the other end of the island, the **Stockholms Medeltidsmuseum** (*see below*) provides a fascinating insight into life in medieval Stockholm.

Riksdagshuset

Riksgatan 3A (786 48 62/www.riksdagen.se). T-bana Kungsträdgården/bus 43, 62. **Open** (guided tours only) *Mid June-Aug* 11am (Swedish), 12.30pm, 2pm, 3.30pm (Swedish & English) Mon-Fri. *Sept-mid June* noon (Swedish), 1.30pm (Swedish & English) Sat, Sun. **Admission** free. **Map** p303 H7.

Free 50-minute guided tours of the Riksdagshuset are given in Swedish, English and German. The guides are exceptionally well informed and the tour is pretty interesting – if you don't mind a little education. You'll see the modern semicircular main chamber, lined with rows of birch tables and chairs. At the front is a large tapestry, *Memory of a Landscape* by Elisabet Hasselberg Olsson, woven in 200 shades of grey. In the old building visitors are shown the grand former main entrance with its marble columns and busts of prime ministers, as well as the old dual chambers that are now used as meeting rooms. The tour ends in the main hall of the former bank, which has been converted into a lobby for the parliamentarians. Increased security requires all visitors to check in at the entrance near Riksbron and have ID with them.

Stockholms Medeltidsmuseum

Strömparterren, Norrbro (50 83 18 08/www.medel tidsmuseet.stockholm.se). T-bana Gamla Stan/bus 43, 62, 65. **Open** *July-Aug* 11am-4pm Mon, Fri-Sun; 11am-6pm Tue-Thur. *Sept-June* 11am-4pm Tue, Thur-Sun; 11am-6pm Wed. **Guided tours** *English July-Aug* 2pm daily. *Swedish* 1pm daily (not Mon, Sept-June). **Admission** 40kr; 20kr concessions; 5kr 7-17s; free under-7s. **Free with SC. Credit** AmEx, MC, V. **Map** p303 H7.

During an excavation of Helgeandsholmen in the late 1970s, for the construction of a new parking garage for MPs, archaeologists discovered thousands of artefacts from medieval Stockholm. So, instead of the garage, parliament decided to build this underground museum, containing more than 850 medieval objects, a hidden passage to the castle and a 14th-century cemetery wall. Dimly lit, with spooky sound effects, it's an atmospheric place. The old harbour has been re-created, with a quayside, warehouses and fishing huts smelling of tar, to show the living standards and building techniques of the time. A 20m-long (66ft) wooden ship from the 1520s (discovered off Riddarholmen in 1930) lies next to an exhibit about archaeology with uncovered skeletons.

Walk 1: Gamla Stan

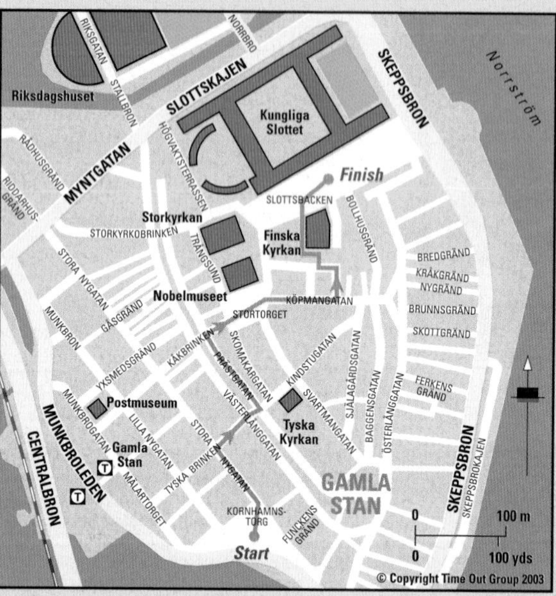

The city's recorded history began in Gamla Stan back in 1252, when Birger Jarl had a fortress built on the site of the present Kungliga Slottet. This walk – about 1.5km (one mile) – through Gamla Stan's winding streets and alleyways offers glimpses of layer upon layer of the city's history, from medieval days to modern times.

Start at Kornhamnstorg by the statue of the archer.

The **lock** (Slussen) that connects Gamla Stan and Söder is where Lake Mälaren meets the Baltic Sea. Since the Ice Age the land has continued to rise, which has caused the island upon which Gamla Stan is situated to slowly grow. Every 100 years the land rises by about 40 centimetres (16 inches). By 1642 it had become necessary to construct a lock due to the difference in water level between the lake and the sea. Since then the lock has been rebuilt on several occasions; the current one dates from 1935. Every year thousands of pleasure boats pass through the lock, which is often called the 'Divorce Ditch' because of the quarrels that are heard on board the boats, especially on Sunday afternoons after a trip to sea.

A king should always ride into his city, but the nearby equestrian statue of Karl XIV Johan is facing the wrong way – out of town (though this was the sculptor's original intention). The statue was moved when the lock was rebuilt in the 1930s and turned around when it was put back in position.

Turn around and walk along Stora Nygatan to the next street, Tyska Brinken.

In 1625 a fire broke out in a brewery and a large area in the south-west part of Gamla Stan was destroyed. Afterwards a city plan was decided on and two new streets were created – **Stora Nygatan** ('Big New Street') and **Lilla Nygatan** ('Small New Street'). Today they are two of the main thoroughfares on Gamla Stan.

Turn right on Tyska Brinken, walk to the corner of Prästgatan and turn left.

As the name suggests, **Prästgatan** ('Priest Street' – *pictured*) is where the city's priests used to live. While unaware tourists crowd Västerlånggatan below, this narrow street has retained much of its medieval look and charm, making it one of the best-kept secrets of Gamla Stan. In the Middle Ages this street ran just inside the first city wall.

Continue along Prästgatan to the corner of Kåkbrinken, then stop.

Kåkbrinken leads up to Stortorget ('Big Square'), the very heart of the city. The name Kåkbrinken dates from 1477 – '*kåk*' means 'pillory' and '*brink*' means 'steep hill', referring to the fact that this hill once led up to the city's pillory on Stortorget. Traffic on these narrow streets was a problem. At this junction you can see examples of different ways people tried to protect the corners of buildings from horses and carts – a cannon, an iron grate and a Viking rune stone. The inscription on the stone reads, 'Torsten and Frögunn had this stone erected over their son...', but the rest of the stone is gone so who knows what happened to him.

Turn right down Kåkbrinken and stop in the centre of Stortorget.

An important meeting place since the Middle Ages, **Stortorget** – the site of the infamous **Stockholm Bloodbath** in 1520 (*see p66*) – used to house a thriving market. The largest building on the square is the Börsen (Stock Exchange), built in 1768 on the site of the former town hall; it's now the home of the **Nobelmuseet** (*see p63*). In the Middle Ages new laws and regulations were read to the public twice a year from an upstairs window of the hall. These laws concerned everyday life, covering such weighty matters as how to dress, how to speak to virgins and during what hours you were allowed to drink beer. The death penalty was common and was often carried out in the square straight after the trial.

The **Schantz house** (Stortorget 20) is a stately gabled house in the German-Dutch style. Its windows are adorned with 90 decorative white limestone tiles, said to symbolise the victims of the Bloodbath. It's more likely just a coincidence as the house was built 130 years after the massacre. Also, estimates of the number of dead range from 80 to 100.

Take Köpmangatan east from Stortorget to the corner of Skeppar Olofs Gränd.

Named in 1323, **Köpmangatan** ('Merchant Street') is one of the city's oldest streets. During the Middle Ages it was a through street for traffic, which is why it is a little wider than most of the other streets around here. A walkway made out of wooden planks was placed in the middle of the street so that pedestrians would escape the chamber-pot contents and rubbish being thrown out of the windows.

Turn down Skeppar Olofs Gränd, then turn left and walk through the open gate on your right.

This is one of Stockholm's least-known public spots, watched over by *Järnpojken* ('the iron boy'), the city's smallest statue. Created by Liss Eriksson, he was placed here in 1967. In recent years an urban myth has grown up claiming that rubbing the statue's head and leaving some money brings good luck. The **Finska Kyrkan** (Finnish Church) next door collects the money for its charity work.

Walk past the statue, turn to the right and continue to the large open space, Slottsbacken, in front of the Kungliga Slottet.

In 1697 the original royal residence, Tre Kronor castle, burned down; the current **Kungliga Slottet** (*see p58*) was completed in 1754. During the construction work, architect Nicodemus Tessin the Younger ran into one of the old castle ghosts, the Grey Man. He told Tessin that he would never live to see the palace finished, that his family line would end and that one day no one would be living in the palace. In an attempt to protect himself and the building from the curse, Tessin had '*Stet fortuna domus avorum numeret avus*' inscribed in the stonework – which means 'May the building's prosperity remain, may it count generation after generation.' But the ghost's prophecy was realised: Tessin died in 1728 before the palace was finished, his family line petered out in 1770 with the death of his son, and in 1981 the royal family moved out to **Drottningholms Slott** (*see p239*) – but that's another walk for another day.

Norrmalm & Vasastaden

Cultural institutions jostle with shops and offices in Stockholm's modern centre.

Norrmalm

The downtown Norrmalm district – also known as City – is a tightly packed mixture of office buildings, shopping centres and historical landmarks and museums. Most of the city's larger and finer hotels are located here, as well as many highly rated restaurants and popular nightclubs. During the 1960s and '70s the entire lower section of Norrmalm was bulldozed in a plan – much criticised today – aimed at moving out residents, creating office space and making the area more accessible to automobile traffic. You can shop, eat and sleep here, but don't expect any medieval splendour.

In the early years of Stockholm, the city authorities discouraged construction on Norrmalm for military reasons, fearing that an enemy attacking Gamla Stan would take shelter in the buildings. There must be something about the area that cries for destruction, since even in the early 16th century Gustav Vasa tore down many of Norrmalm's structures. By 1602, however, the district had grown to the extent that it was declared a separate city, and operated as such for three decades. When competition between the two cities became ridiculous, Norrmalm lost its independence, and in 1637 the district's first street plan was laid down.

Norrmalm is where most visitors arrive in Stockholm. Trains from the airport zoom to the **Arlanda Express** station, located next to **Central Station** on busy Vasagatan, where you can catch trains for destinations all over Sweden, and also link up with **T-Centralen**, the main Tunnelbana station, where all three lines of the metro network converge. Stepping out from Central Station you immediately see across the street the kind of functionalist concrete and steel buildings that dominate the area. Behind them peeks the brick tower of the late 16th-century **St Clara Kyrka** (*see p76*), one of the area's oldest churches.

Heading south on Vasagatan, manoeuvre your way through a horrible tangle of highways and viaducts to the water near Vasabron, one of the five northern bridges that lead to Gamla Stan. The **Konstakademien** (Royal Academy of Art; www.konstakademien.se) at Fredsgatan 12 occupies a renovated palace designed by Tessin the Elder in the 1670s. The academy was founded by King Gustav III in 1773, and moved into its current premises in 1780. In 1978 it was separated from the Royal University College of Fine Arts, which is today situated on Skeppsholmen. As well as its own exhibition space, the academy currently houses temporary shows for the Arkitekturmuseet (*see p87*),

Park life at **Kungsträdgården**. *See p71.*

while its permanent home is being repaired. The academy's terrace bar, **Fredsgatan 12** (*see p132*), is very popular in summer, as is the highly recommended restaurant of the same name (*see p113*).

Many of Sweden's government departments are located nearby, such as the light orange building called **Rosenbad**, which houses the offices of the prime minister. East on Fredsgatan is Gustav Adolfs Torg, named after King Gustav II Adolf, who greatly expanded the city during his reign in the early 17th century; an equestrian statue of the king stands in the centre of the square. You'll find Mediterranean antiquities inside the **Medelhavsmuseet** (*see p75*) and dance costumes from around the world in the **Dansmuseet** (*see p73*), both housed in converted early 20th-century banks.

On the square's eastern flank is the grand **Kungliga Operan** (*see p217*), styled after the Royal Palace in the late 19th century, with a splendid 28-metre long (92-foot) gold foyer full of mirrors and chandeliers. The original opera building, where King Gustav III was assassinated in 1792, looked exactly like **Arvfurstens Palats**, the building directly across from it, constructed in the 1780s and now used by the Ministry for Foreign Affairs. The opera house contains a trio of restaurants, varying in splendour and price; the fanciest is the famous **Operakällaren** (*see p113*). From the front of the opera house you get a beautiful view across the water towards the Kungliga Slottet; behind it is the earthy red Gothic structure of **St Jacobs Kyrka** (*see p76*).

Next to the opera house is Karl XIIs Torg and north from here stretches the long rectangular park of **Kungsträdgården** (King's Garden), a popular venue for free concerts, open-air events and kids' fairground rides. Originally used as a vegetable garden for the royal castle in the 15th century, the park later developed into a pleasure garden and opened to the public in the 18th century. A hundred years later, French-born King Karl XIV Johan tore out the trees, erected a statue of his adoptive father, Karl XIII, and converted the garden into a field for military exercises. After his death, the area was turned into the park you see today. The statue of Karl XII – his finger pointing east to his old battlegrounds in Russia – was added in 1868 near the waters of Norrström. Two tree-lined avenues shade the restaurants and kiosks along the park's western and eastern edges. At the top end, in front of a shallow pool with three fountains, is tourist haven Friday's American Bar; Volvo's newest and oldest cars are displayed in a showroom nearby. At the **Systembolagets Museet** (*see p77*), hidden away in a basement, you can learn all about

NK department store: first among equals.

Sweden's peculiar attitude to alcohol, and in winter you can join kids skating on the park's small temporary ice rink.

The crowded thoroughfare of **Hamngatan** crosses the top of the park. On the park's north-western edge, at No.27, is Sverige Huset, home to the Swedish Institute and its informative little bookshop, **Sverigebokhandeln** (*see p151*), and the main **tourist office** (*see p285*), on the ground floor. Bang opposite is **NK** (*see p152*), Sweden's first and most exclusive department store. For people who need to keep track of how much they spend, the cheaper **Gallerian** shopping mall (*see p152*) lies just up the street.

A couple of blocks west along from NK is **Sergels Torg**, a two-level area – traffic above, pedestrians below – of glass, concrete and underground shops that was built after the bulldozer extravaganza of the 1960s. The sunken square of black and white triangles is a popular spot for both political speeches and demonstrations; the rather grubby tall glass tower surrounded by fountains in the middle of the traffic island was designed by sculptor Edvin Öhrström in 1972.

Architect Peter Celsing was responsible for **Kulturhuset** (www.kulturhuset.stockholm.se; *see p230*), the seven-storey structure that stands behind Sergels Torg like a great glass wall. He won a design competition in 1966 to develop a cultural centre for the area, which was rapidly becoming overdeveloped with commercial buildings and traffic. Swedish egalitarianism saw to it that the Kulturhuset – which opened in 1974 – should have something

Culture vultures should head to the **Kulturhuset** at Sergels Torg. *See p71.*

for everybody. It's home to Sweden's one and only comic book library, Serieteket, and next door is one of Stockholm's biggest theatres, **Stadsteatern** (*see p231*). You can play chess on the ground floor or take the escalators up to one of the three art galleries on the floors above. There is also a library, workshops for young adults and children, an internet café and a branch of **DesignTorget** (*see p165*). Step in, check the programme and see if something appeals. If nothing else, a window seat in **Café Panorama** (*see p142*) on the top floor gives you a great view of the square below.

Several main streets converge on Sergels Torg, including Klarabergsgatan and Sveavägen. The block-long, red-brick, windowless **Åhléns** department store (*see p152*) occupies the north-west corner of the former, and is just one of scores of options for visitors looking for retail therapy. The packed pedestrian street of **Drottninggatan** is lined with shops from its start at the water's edge all the way north to Tegnérgatan.

North from Sergels Torg five 18-storey glass office buildings stand in a row like playing cards towards the open space of Hötorget; built in the 1950s, they're city landmarks – whether people want them to be or not. **Hötorget** is home to the **PUB** department store (*see p152*) and an outdoor market selling fruit, flowers and a bit of everything. On one side of the square is an indoor international food hall, **Hötorgshallen** (*see p163* **Food markets**), beneath the **Filmstaden** cinema (*see p198*). On another side stands the **Konserthuset** (*see p215*), Stockholm's main concert hall and a prime example of the Swedish neo-classical style. To the untrained eye, however, the 1926 building looks suspiciously like a bright blue box with ten grey pillars attached to its front.

Ivar Tengbom modelled the hall on the temples of ancient Greece, and the artworks inside – created by the country's leading artists of the 1920s – depict figures and scenes from Greek mythology. Tengbom's son, Anders, renovated the building in 1972 to improve the acoustics. Einar Forseth (who also decorated the Golden Hall at the Stadshuset) created the floor mosaics in the entrance hall and main foyer, and famous Swedish artist Carl Milles sculpted the bronze statue of *Orpheus* near the front steps. There are guided tours most Saturdays (12.30pm; 40kr), but you'll have more fun if you attend a performance. The Kungliga Filharmonikerna has played here since the building's completion. It also performs every year on 10 December when the Nobel Prizes are awarded in the main hall (*see p104* **Alfred Nobel & the Nobel Prizes**).

Further north on Drottninggatan you'll find **Centralbadet** (*see p168*), a lovely art nouveau bath house built in 1905, with café tables in its pretty front courtyard. Nearby is **Dansens Hus** (*see p234*), the capital's main venue for modern dance and, just to the east, on Sveavägen, stands classical **Adolf Fredriks Kyrka**. It has a Greek cross plan and a beautifully painted ceiling; famous 18th-century sculptor Johan Tobias Sergel is buried in its cemetery, as is the assassinated prime minister Olof Palme. On the corner of Drottninggatan and Tengnérgatan is the building in which August Strindberg spent the last four years of his life. His apartment is now the sweet **Strindbergsmuseet** (*see p76*) – a must for fans of Sweden's greatest author.

Down at the southern tip of Norrmalm the Blasieholmen peninsula pokes out into the water towards Skeppsholmen. At the end of this spur of land stands the imposing limestone façade of the **National Museum** (*see p75*) – Sweden's

Breaking the mould

Visitors wanting to check out Stockholm's modern art museum, the **Moderna Museet**, will find it trickier than usual. Its avant-garde home on the island of Skeppsholmen, designed by world-famous Spanish architect Rafael Moneo, is currently closed thanks to an ongoing damp problem. The building is due to be reopened (mould-free) in January 2004.

During its 'homeless' period, temporary exhibitions and selected works are on show at the old post office building near the Central Station, on **Klarabergsviadukten**. The sudden flexibility caused by the problems at Skeppsholmen has its advantages: it's allowed a variety of other projects, under the umbrella title Moderna Museet c/o, to happen in various spaces around the city, including **Magasin 3** (*see p204*), **Skulpturens Hus** (Vinterviksvägen 60; 19 62 00/www.skulpturenshus.se) and **Prins Eugens Waldemarsudde** on Djurgården (*see p83*). The projects have been so popular that they're likely to continue even after the reopening of the main museum. Check the website or ask staff for the latest info on what's happening where.

Opened in 1958, the Moderna Museet gained a reputation as one of the world's most interesting and groundbreaking contemporary art venues under its first director, Pontus Hultén. Housed originally in an old, disused naval exercise building on Skeppsholmen, the museum's heyday came in the 1960s and 1970s, when the legendary Hultén introduced the likes of Andy Warhol, Claes Oldenburg, Joseph Beuys, Robert Rauschenberg, Jasper Johns, Naum Gabo, Yves Klein, Niki de Saint Phalle, Jean Tinguely, Donald Judd, Frank Stella, Emil Nolde, Edward Kienholz and many more to an astonished Swedish audience. It also became a centre for contemporary film, dance and music – drawing in avant-garde artists and performers such as Merce Cunningham, Robert Morris, David Tudor and John Cage – and a vibrant meeting place where all kinds of artistic and experimental actions regularly took place.

By the end of the '80s, the museum's invaluable collection of modern and contemporary art had grown too big for its space. In 1993 it closed, reopening in Moneo's new building in 1998, with its first foreign director, Englishman David Elliott. Plagued with technical problems, even before the current mould crisis, Moneo's creation has always aroused controversy. Many have criticised it for being dark and maze-like, while others have defended it, saying the building is only the container of what is important – the art. The current renovations are also addressing some of these problems, with – among other visitor-friendly alterations – a new, more imposing entrance overlooking the water being constructed.

Since November 2001 the museum has had a new director, Swede Lars Nittve. He's back on home turf: he grew up in Stockholm and started his career as a curator at the Moderna Museet in the 1980s before moving to Malmö, then Denmark, and ending up as the inaugural director of the very high-profile, and hugely successful, Tate Modern in London. Happy to be back, despite the temporary closure, Nittve's long-term plan is to make the Moderna Museet a powerhouse in the art world once again.

Moderna Museet

Klarabergsviadukten 61 (51 95 52 00/www.modernamuseet.se). T-bana T-Centralen/bus 47, 52, 53, 59, 91. **Open** 10am-8pm Tue-Thur; 10am-6pm Fri-Sun. **Admission** free. **Map** p302 G6.

largest art museum. North along the waterfront, on Strömkajen, in front of Sweden's only five-star hotel, the aptly named **Grand Hôtel** (*see p43*), is the boarding point for sightseeing boats and ferries heading to the archipelago.

There's another wharf for ferries (nipping to Djurgården and Slussen) on the other side of the peninsula, at the small harbour of Nybroviken. Overlooking the green lawns of Berzelii Park is **Berns Salonger**, a legendary entertainment venue since the 1860s. It is still a nightlife favourite, its magnificent salons, all gilt decor and crystal chandeliers, now housing one of Stockholm's largest restaurants (*see p113*) and numerous bars (*see p131*). The adjoining boutique hotel (*see p42*) is charming.

Dansmuseet

Gustav Adolfs Torg 22-4 (441 76 50/www.dansmuseet.nu). T-bana Kungsträdgården/bus 3, 43, 62, 65. **Open** *June-Aug* 11am-4pm Mon-Fri; noon-4pm Sat, Sun. *Sept-May* 11am-4pm Tue-Fri; noon-4pm Sat, Sun. **Admission** 50kr; 30kr concessions; free under-12s. **Free with SC. Credit** AmEx, MC, V. **Map** p303 G7.

Hötorget's popular street market, with the Konserthuset behind. *See p72.*

The Dance Museum is situated in the sombre, pillared main hall of a former bank built in 1918. It displays costumes and scenery sketches from Swedish ballets, plus traditional masks and costumes from Africa, Thailand, China, Japan and Tibet. A brightly coloured cubist backdrop, recreated from the 1923 Swedish production of *La Création du Monde* by the composer Darius Milhaud, is opposite the hall's entrance. There's also a bronze bust of the museum's founder, Rolf de Maré, who managed the Swedish Ballet in Paris between 1920 and 1925, and opened this museum in the French capital in 1933. The temporary exhibitions downstairs can be worth a look sometimes, but otherwise you're better off spending your money on an actual performance at the Kungliga Operan (*see p217*) just across the street.

Medelhavsmuseet

Fredsgatan 2 (51 95 53 80/www.medelhavsmuseet.se). T-bana Kungsträdgården/bus 3, 43, 62, 65.
Open 11am-8pm Tue; 11am-4pm Wed-Fri; noon-5pm Sat, Sun. **Admission** 50kr; free under-20s.
Free with SC. **Map** p303 G7.

Artefacts from Greece, Rome, Egypt and Cyprus are housed in the Museum of Mediterranean Antiquities, in a building that was a field marshal's palace back in the 1640s and later remodelled as a bank in the 1910s. Note the marble columns and a beautiful glass ceiling that was designed to look like that of a Renaissance *palazzo*. Displayed in the main hall are Roman busts and statues, as well as 18th-century cork models of ancient structures. A side room features clay figures and pottery from Cyprus; another contains medical instruments from AD 300. One floor below you'll find a six-ton Egyptian basalt sarcophagus and wrapped mummies, including two cats and a small crocodile. If you like shiny things, plan your visit here between 12.30pm and 1pm or 2.30pm and 3pm, when the Goldrummet is open. The museum is definitely worth a visit once you've seen the city's major attractions; there are guided tours in English in summer. The café on the second floor is decorated with colourful rugs and has an excellent view of Gustav Adolfs Torg and Kungliga Slottet. Reproductions of Greek and Egyptian jewellery are on sale in the gift shop.

National Museum

Södra Blasieholmen (51 95 43 00/www.national museum.se). T-bana Kungsträdgården/bus 46, 55, 59, 62, 65, 76. **Open** *Sept-May* 11am-8pm Tue, Thur; 11am-5pm Wed, Fri-Sun. *June-Aug* 11am-8pm Tue; 11am-5pm Wed-Sun. **Admission** 75kr (60kr Wed); 60kr concessions; free under-16s. **Free with SC**. **Credit** AmEx, MC, V. **Map** p303 H8.

Tens of thousands of paintings, sculptures, drawings and decorative arts, dating from the Middle Ages to the present, are stored in Sweden's largest art museum. Two benefactors in particular are responsible for the collections: Carl Gustaf Tessin, avid art buyer and Swedish ambassador to France in the 1740s, and the art-loving king, Gustav III, who left the royal collections to the state in his will. The National Museum is not as impressive as some of Europe's big art museums, but there are works by the likes of Rembrandt, Rubens, Goya and Degas, and substantial collections of 17th-century Dutch, 18th-century French and 18th- and 19th-century Swedish art. The building, designed by the German architect Friedrich August Stüler to look like a

See *Midsommardans* by Anders Zorn...

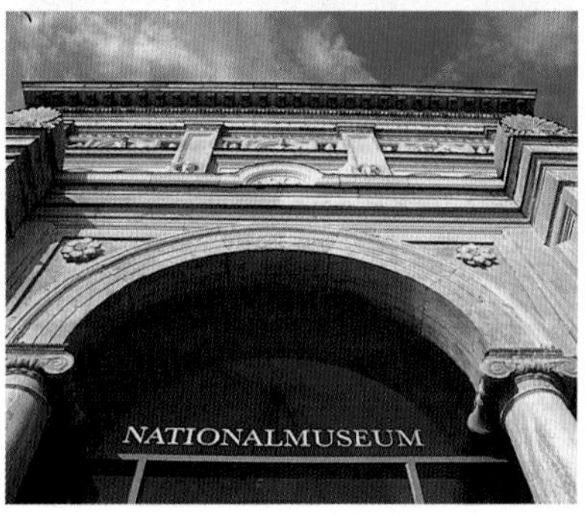

... at the **National Museum**. *See p75.*

northern Italian Renaissance palace, and completed in 1866, is suitably grand and awe-inspiring. The central staircase is adorned with colourful frescoes by famous Swedish artist Carl Larsson, including two large and wonderful works at the top: *Gustav Vasa's Entry into Stockholm 1523* and *Midwinter Sacrifice*. About ten temporary exhibitions are organised each year, based around historical and national perspectives, and there are guided tours in English in summer. Don't miss the permanent exhibition on the first floor, 'Design 19002000', which showcases 20th-century Scandinavian design, including porcelain, glassware and chairs made of every material known to man. The Atrium café/restaurant (*see p142*), inside the high-ceilinged atrium on the ground floor, is a lovely spot for lunch.

St Clara Kyrka

Klara Östra Kyrkogata 7 (723 30 31/www.sthdomkyrko.com). T-bana T-Centralen/bus 47, 52, 56, 59, 91. **Open** 10am-5pm daily. **Admission** free. **Map** p303 G6.

The copper spire of this brick 16th-century church, across from Central Station, rises from the midst of a cluster of dull, box-like 1960s buildings. It was one of many churches built in the late 16th century during the reign of Johan III, who had a Catholic wife and a love of architecture. He decided to build St Clara's here in the 1570s since it was the site of a former convent, torn down in the Reformation. Dutch architect Willem Boy designed the church, and Carl Hårleman – who also completed the interior of the Kungliga Slottet – redesigned its roof and spire after a fire in the mid 18th century. The four turrets of the spire were restored to their original appearance in 1965. Inside the sunlit church you'll find a large wooden balcony with an organ, and a ceiling painted with biblical scenes. The congregation gives out meals to those in need, so the graveyard and steps are a sanctuary for local homeless people. Services are held in Swedish and, curiously enough, Swahili, and there are classical concerts at lunchtime.

St Jacobs Kyrka

Västra Trädgårdsgatan 2 (723 30 38/www.sthdomkyrko.com). T-bana Kungsträdgården/ bus 43, 46, 55, 59, 65. **Open** 24hrs daily (but may change). **Admission** free. **Map** p303 G7.

St Jacobs Kyrka was commissioned in 1588 by King Johan III. The project was abandoned after Johan's death four years later, but was resumed in 1630 under Karl IX and completed in 1643. The church is named after the patron saint of pilgrims, who is depicted carrying a walking staff in the sandstone sculpture above the southern entrance. GJ Adelcrantz and Carl Hårleman redesigned the copper roof and spires after a fire in 1723. The church underwent several interior renovations in the 19th century, including the addition of five stained-glass panels behind the altar, showing scenes from the New Testament. (One panel can only be seen from outside because the wooden altarpiece blocks the view.) Coats of arms decorate the church's walls, and its renovated organ has a whopping 83 stops. You could take a quick look in the church on your way somewhere else, but there's no need to go out of your way. Sunday services are held in English at 6pm.

Strindbergsmuseet

Drottninggatan 85 (411 53 54/www.strindbergsmuseet.se). T-bana Rådmansgatan/bus 52, 69. **Open** *Sept-May* noon-7pm Tue; noon-4pm Wed-Sun. *June-Aug* noon-4pm Tue-Sun. **Admission** 40kr; 25kr concessions; free under-14s. **Free with SC**. **No credit cards**. **Map** p307 E6.

August Strindberg moved into an apartment in the Blå Tornet (Blue Tower) in 1908; it was his last home and is now a museum. Much of it is taken up with temporary exhibits (with labelling in Swedish) on Strindberg as a writer, dramatist, photographer and painter, but it's his tiny apartment that's the reason for visiting. An air of reverence dominates: you have to put on little white slippers over your shoes to protect the floor, and his bedroom, study and sitting room (no kitchen; a family upstairs sent down food) are preserved as they were at the time of his death, his pens still neatly lined up in rows on his writing desk. It's an atmospheric and moving place: you can imagine the ailing playwright standing on the balcony to greet a torchlit procession of well-wishers on his last birthday, on 22 January 1912. He died in bed a few months later, on 14 May. *See also p78* **Super Swedes: August Strindberg**.

Systembolagets Museet

Kungsträdgårdsgatan 14 (789 36 42/www.systembolaget.se/svenska/om/historia/xindex.htm). T-bana Kungsträdgården/bus 46, 55, 59, 62, 76. **Open** (guided tours only) 2pm Tue, Wed; call in advance for tours in English. Closed Christmas-Epiphany. **Admission** 20kr. **No credit cards**. **Map** p303 G8.

Tucked into the basement of Systembolaget's headquarters (from where the state-owned company conducts its monopoly of alcohol sales), this museum presents the history of the company and the sale of alcohol in Sweden. The guided tour – which is the only way visitors can see the museum – walks you through some reconstructed sections of stores, from a worn wooden counter from 1907 to a self-service boutique from 1991. The real story of the museum is how Systembolaget has tried to limit or discourage alcohol consumption with ration books, blacklists and anti-alcohol marketing campaigns. Although its policies are changing, only 15 years ago one of its cashiers was reprimanded for saying to a customer, 'Welcome back.' For information on actually purchasing booze in Systembolaget's retail outlets, *see p166* **How to buy alcohol**.

Vasastaden

The wide residential streets of Vasastaden – commonly known as Vasastan – spread out northwards from comparatively congested Norrmalm. It's probably most visited for its restaurants and budget hotels, but there are also some worthwhile sights. The street blocks can be rather long, so you might want to jump on the T-bana between certain destinations.

In the south-west corner of the district lies the small rectangular park of **Tegnérlunden**. On one side a man-made stream flows out of a gazebo; at the other there's a statue of a very beefy, naked August Strindberg sitting on a rock. Eastwards on Tegnérgatan, past the **Strindbergsmuseet** situated on Drottninggatan, you'll come to an array of pubs, restaurants and antique shops. Turn left on **Sveavägen**, one of Vasastan's main thoroughfares, and walk two blocks north along this broad, tree-lined boulevard.

The south-east corner of the hillside park of **Observatorielunden** is dominated by the magnificent **Handelshögskolan** (Stockholm School of Economics), which was designed by Ivar Tengbom, architect of the Konserthuset. Up the steep steps on top of the hill is the **Observatorie Museet** (*see p78*), overlooking a fountain/skateboard park. Gunnar Asplund's orange **Stadsbiblioteket** (Stockholm Public Library), instantly identifiable by its round central building, and one of Sweden's most famous architectural works, stands at the park's north-east corner. Several blocks north on Sveavägen is the kid-friendly indoor water adventure park, **Vilda Vanadis** (*see p188*), in the quiet, hilly park of Vanadislunden.

If you head west from the library along busy **Odengatan**, which cuts east–west through Vasastaden, you'll reach the triangle-shaped square of **Odenplan**, bordered by the beautiful baroque **Gustaf Vasa Kyrka** (*see below*) and surrounded by the rumble of buses. Several budget hotels are located in this area, as well as the unusual **Leksaks Palatset** (*see below*).

Two blocks further west is the green retreat of **Vasaparken**, ever popular with energetic dogs and Frisbee throwers. The small **Judiska Museet** (*see p78*) – the only Jewish museum in Scandinavia – is just across the street, and at the end of the park there's the bustling intersection of **St Eriksplan**. The charming early 20th-century buildings, cafés and shops of Birkastan are located around **Rörstrandsgatan**, west of St Eriksplan. If you take St Eriksgatan south, you'll end up on Kungsholmen; if you head north, you'll arrive at the warehouse of the **Vin & Sprithistoriska Museet** (*see p79*).

Gustaf Vasa Kyrka

Odenplan (50 88 86 00/www.gustafvasa.nu). T-bana Odenplan/bus 4, 40, 42, 47, 53. **Open** *June-Aug* 11am-7pm daily. *Sept-May* 11am-6pm Mon-Thur; 11am-3pm Fri-Sun. **Admission** free. **Map** p306 D4.

The striking 60m-high (200ft) dome of Gustaf Vasa Kyrka rises far above Odenplan and its decidedly less impressive neighbouring buildings. Architect Agi Lindegren designed this nearly all-white church in the Italian baroque style with a Greek-cross plan, and it's without doubt Vasastaden's most beautiful building. Completed in 1906, it stands on a triangular island near the intersection of two busy streets. There's room for 1,200 people inside. The altarpiece from 1731, in fact Sweden's largest baroque sculpture, was originally created for the Uppsala cathedral. It depicts Jesus on the cross in front of a relief of Jerusalem. The ceiling paintings, by Vicke Andrén, show scenes from the New Testament.

Leksaks Palatset

Hagagränd 2 (30 34 03/www.leksakspalatset.se). T-bana Odenplan/bus 4, 42, 46, 52, 72. **Open** 11am-3pm Wed, Thur; noon-3pm Sat, Sun. **Admission** 40kr; 30kr concessions; 20kr 3-16s; free under-3s. **No credit cards**. **Map** p307 C5.

Formerly the Stockholm Miniature Museum, the privately operated Toy Palace is run by a couple who are obviously obsessed with toys. Nearly all

Sightseeing

the toys are arranged in a variety of bizarrely kitsch scenes. Barbie is hopping on to the diving board while grimacing plastic soldiers engage in hand-to-hand combat; train sets, Smurf villages, dolls and doll's houses all appear, as well as *Star Wars* and *Harry Potter* action figures. They really must have had a lot of fun making this museum, and you should have a lot of fun visiting it.There's also a small café and a gift shop (no admission required) that sells low-price new and used toys.

Judiska Museet

Hälsingegatan 2 (31 01 43/www.judiska-museet.a.se). T-bana Odenplan/bus 4, 42, 47, 72. **Open** noon-4pm Mon-Fri, Sun. **Admission** 50kr; 20kr-40kr concessions; free under-12s. **Guided tours** 1.30pm Wed, Sun. **Credit** AmEx. **Map** p306 D4.

Half of Sweden's Jewish population of about 22,000 live in or near Stockholm, so it's fitting that the city should contain a Jewish museum. Located across the street from Vasaparken, it contains religious objects and works of art. The permanent exhibition in the first room focuses on Jewish holidays and traditions. A Torah, Sabbath candlesticks and *yarmulkes* (skull-caps) are displayed, as well as a wooden piece of the first synagogue in Stockholm, dating from 1795. Temporary exhibitions usually deal with some aspect of Jewish life in Sweden. This is a small museum and probably only for those who are particularly interested in Judaism, or want to learn more about it. In the lobby you can buy books, shawls and menorahs.

Observatorie Museet

Drottninggatan 120 (54 54 83 90/www.observatoriet. kva.se). T-bana Rådmansgatan/bus 40, 52, 53, 69. **Open** (guided tours only) *Apr-Sept* noon, 1pm, 2pm Sat, Sun. *Oct-Mar* 6-8pm Tue; noon, 1pm, 2pm Sat, Sun. **Admission** 40kr; 20kr 7-18s; free under-7s. **No credit cards**. **Map** p307 D6.

The Royal Swedish Academy of Sciences built this hilltop observatory in the late 1740s. Now a museum, it's open for half-hour guided tours of the observation rooms and the 18th-century instruments of Pehr

Super Swedes: August Strindberg

The prolific dramatist, author, poet and sometime painter and photographer August Strindberg managed to provoke controversy and outrage throughout his life, and long after his death. His ideas were so ahead of their time that his works were alternately censored, banned and panned. Perhaps not surprising for a man who wanted to 'blow up the entire bastion of culture'.

Born in Stockholm in 1849, Strindberg was the son of a shipping merchant, Carl Oscar Strindberg, and his former servant, Ulrika Norling. Strindberg wrote later about his unhappy childhood – his cold and authoritarian father and his mother's early death, both of which cast a long shadow over his life and work. He studied at Uppsala University but left without gaining a degree and then found work as a librarian, teacher, journalist and critic. At the time Scandinavia was at the forefront of world culture, with the widespread fame of Ibsen in theatre and Munch in painting, both of whom deeply influenced the young Strindberg. In 1872 he wrote his first major play, *Master Olof*, a historical drama with a difference. It was a total revolt against both social and theatrical conventions, using naturalistic language and psychology, and stark scenery.

In 1877 Strindberg married Baroness Siri von Essen, who was seven months pregnant at the time, and together they had three children. His breakthrough as a novelist came two years later with *The Red Room* – using a then unknown colloquial style and laying bare contemporary society. One of the private dining rooms in the **Berns Salonger** (*see p73*) is the room immortalised in the title.

In 1883, feeling unappreciated in Sweden and hoping to gain world literary domination by travel, Strindberg moved abroad. He was to wander fairly aimlessly through bohemian Europe for the next 15 years, often longing for and writing about his homeland. During this time he wrote some of the works that were to gain him not only fame but also his perhaps undeserved reputation as a misogynist, such as *Miss Julie* and *The Father*, exploring – well ahead of their time – the psychology of gender roles.

In 1888 he wrote succinctly in a letter, 'If I had to define my present standpoint it would be: Atheist, Christhater, Anarchist... PS. Woman, being small and foolish and therefore evil, should be supressed.' With friends like Zola and Nietzsche, it's hardly surprising that he felt that way.

However, Strindberg had a penchant for unconventional relationships with independent and talented young women. After his divorce in 1892, he had a brief and unhappy marriage to Austrian journalist Frieda Uhl, and later married, not particularly third time lucky, actress Harriet Bosse, whom he divorced in 1904. In the 1890s Strindberg also began to gain the international success that

Wargentin, an astronomer and statistician who lived and worked here for 30 years. The guide (phone first if you want a tour in English) describes how scientists tried to solve the problems of their day, from calculating the distances between planets to determining longitude at sea. A narrow staircase leads to the observatory's dome, where you get a wonderful and unobstructed view of the surrounding park, Vasastaden and downtown Stockholm. Although this is one of the city's lesser-known museums, it's pretty entertaining. On Tuesday evenings in autumn and winter, you can stargaze through the museum's early 20th-century telescope.

Vin & Sprithistoriska Museet

Dalagatan 100 (744 70 70/www.vinosprithistoriska.se). Bus 69, 73. **Open** 10am-7pm Tue; 10am-4pm Wed-Fri; noon-4pm Sat, Sun. **Guided tours** *Summer* 2pm Tue, Fri; 12.30pm (English) Sun. *Winter* 2pm Wed; 12.30pm, 2pm Sun. **Admission** 40kr; 20kr-30kr concessions; free under-12s. **Free with SC. Credit** MC, V. **Map** p306 B3.

Between the 1920s and 1960s, all the imported wine and alcohol consumed in Sweden was processed through this brick warehouse situated in northern Vasastaden. The Historical Museum of Wines & Spirits, on the fourth floor, contains bottling equipment and barrels from the warehouse as well as machinery and distilling tanks from a Stockholm vodka factory founded in 1869. You can press buttons to activate some of the machinery, and pump a 'spice organ' to test your sense of smell. The museum was originally operated by Vin & Sprit AB – the company that produces Absolut Vodka – and contains its tasting room from the 1920s. The subject might not appeal to everyone, but the educational exhibits are certainly well made and comprehensive. There are also temporary exhibitions, covering such weighty matters as whisky or punsch production. You can book schnapps- or wine-tastings, in case you get thirsty. Most of the exhibits are labelled in Swedish, so make sure you borrow the English guidebook from the front desk.

he longed for, with his works being translated into numerous languages.

In 1894 some sort of emotional crisis provoked the onset of his famous 'inferno period', which was to gain him the reputation, again perhaps rather unfairly, of a madman. Influenced by the 18th-century Swedish mystic Emanuel Swedenborg, he became increasingly fascinated by the occult and alchemy. At the same time he was also very involved in painting and photography, experimenting with symbolism and even prefiguring the surrealists. The largest collection of his remarkable paintings can be found at the **Nordiska Museet** (*see p82*).

Recovering from his crisis, in 1897 Strindberg returned to Stockholm, where he was to stay until his death. His flirtation with the occult had caused a creative sea change, and he began to write dozens of expressionistic plays – works that no one knew how to stage, let alone understand. Dramas such as *A Dream Play* and *Ghost Sonata* were to inspire the later development of absurdist theatre. In 1907 he founded his own theatre in Stockholm, the Intima, no doubt in an attempt to have his plays presented sensitively. In 1908, he moved to what was to be his last home, 'the Blue Tower', at Drottninggatan 85, which is now the **Strindbergsmuseet** (*see p76*). A rather imposing statue of the dramatist stands in nearby Tegnérlunden park.

On his last birthday, in 1912, Strindberg was finally hailed as writer of the people and the working class when he was awarded the Anti-Nobel Prize with money raised by national subscription to compensate him for not winning the Nobel Prize itself. He died later that year on 14 May.

Djurgården & Skeppsholmen

A green and pleasant land, packed with unmissable sights.

Djurgården

Many of Stockholm's best museums and attractions are located on the long, green island of Djurgården. The famous Vasamuseet, the open-air museum of Skansen and Gröna Lund amusement park on the island's western half draw hundreds of thousands of visitors each year. Walking and cycling paths and quiet roads wind through the leafy trees of the rest of the island, which is part of Ekoparken, the National City Park. Closed to traffic (except for buses) at the weekend, its acres of undeveloped land are a green retreat from the bustle of the rest of the city. Whether you're looking for a shady lawn, historical artefacts, a waterfront rollercoaster or Nordic wildlife, Djurgården is the place. Expect to spend some time here.

Swedish monarchs have owned the island since it was acquired by King Karl Knutsson in 1452. First developed for agriculture, it later became the private hunting grounds of royalty. King Karl XI established a series of manned gates in the 1680s to protect the park from wolves, bears and poverty-stricken peasants looking for food. The Stockholm Exhibition was held here in 1897; many of its buildings are still standing. A branch of the royal court continues to administer the island and uses all the rents and fees it collects for Djurgården's preservation.

Crossing to the island from Strandvägen, over Djurgårdsbron – where you can rent bicycles and paddleboats – you'll see the magnificent **Nordiska Museet** (*see p82*) directly in front of you. This city landmark was designed in the style of a Nordic Renaissance palace and holds historical and cultural objects from all over Scandinavia. The path on the right of the museum leads to **Junibacken** (*see p185*), a children's fantasyland with a train ride through the stories of Astrid Lindgren's books.

Further on lies the fabulous **Vasamuseet** (*see p86*), home of the vast warship *Vasa*, which sank just off the island of Beckholmen on her maiden voyage in 1628. The ship remained lost on the seabed for over three centuries, until she was discovered in the 1950s (*see p85* **Raising the *Vasa***). Fittingly, the purpose-built museum – one of the most popular in Scandinavia, with around 800,000 visitors a year – occupies the site of the former naval dockyard. If you're only going to visit one museum in Stockholm – and there are plenty – make it this one. The area near the waterfront, **Galärparken**, popular with picnickers and sunbathers, was used by royalty in the 18th century to stage fights between lions and bears. The lions were kept near what is now the Nordiska Museet, hence the name Lejonslätten ('Lions' Den'). East of the Vasamuseet stands the triangular memorial to the 852 people who died when the *Estonia* ferry sunk in the Baltic en route from Tallinn to Stockholm in 1994.

Djurgårdsvägen, the main route into and around the island, passes by the Nordiska Museet, the western entrance to Skansen and the quaint, old-fashioned **Biologiska Museet** (*see p82*), devoted to Scandinavian wildlife. Further south, the beautiful **Liljevalchs Konsthall** (*see p200*) stands on the corner of Djurgården's most developed area. It was set up by an unspecified donation of 500,000 kronor in the will of the enormously rich industrialist Carl Fredrik Liljevalch. After the artist Prince Eugen persuaded the state to donate the land, the gallery opened in 1916, with sculptures by Carl Milles over the door and on top of the tall black pillar nearby. It's now one of the best exhibition spaces in Sweden, with contemporary shows that change every three months. Next to the building is the lovely restaurant-café **Blå Porten** (*see p144*).

Next door is the fascinating **Aquaria Vattenmuseum** (*see p82*), situated on the water next to the depot for the island's old-fashioned trams. Its waterfront café has a spectacular view towards Skeppsholmen. Screams, laughter and live music can be heard coming from the summer-only **Gröna Lund** amusement park (*see p185*), one block to the south. There are several hamburger and pizza places here, as well as the 1920s Hasselbacken restaurant on the hill across the street, next to the **Cirkus** concert/theatre venue (*see p212*), originally a riding school in the 1820s.

Centuries-old wooden houses line the narrow streets of nearby **Djurgårdsstaden**, the island's only real residential area. About 200 people live here and apartments are much sought after; a one-bedroom flat was recently put on the market for $800,000. Whipping posts like the one in the district's tiny square once stood in public places all over the city.

Continuing along Djurgårdsvägen, you arrive at the main entrance for **Skansen** (*see p84*). Stockholm's number one attraction (and deservedly so), with close on 1.4 million visitors a year, it's a mix of open-air history museum, amusement park and zoo, covering almost the entire width of Djurgården. The museum is as popular with locals as it is with visitors, and you should not leave Stockholm without seeing it. It includes the **Skansen Akvariet** (*see p84*), which houses monkeys, crocodiles and bats – you have to pay a separate entrance fee.

The 47 bus route ends at the cove of Ryssviken, from where you can walk south to the palatial mansion of **Prins Eugens Waldemarsudde** (*see p83*) or north for about ten minutes to the café at **Rosendals Trädgård** (*see p144*). It's a great spot for lunch, and nearby is **Rosendals Slott** (*see p83*), the summer retreat of Karl XIV Johan, the French marshal elected as Sweden's crown prince in 1810 and later crowned king.

To explore the area of the island further east be prepared to walk, cycle or drive. To reach the eastern half of Djurgården by bus, you'll need to plan ahead and take line 69 from the northern side of Djurgårdsbron. The bus takes you to the south-eastern tip of the island where a Nordic art collection is displayed at swanky **Thielska Galleriet** (*see p85*). The southern shore of this area of Djurgården is lined with the homes and estates of the extremely wealthy, including Princess Lilian (aunt by marriage to the present king).

With the exception of the Manilla school for the deaf, the rest of eastern Djurgården is a nature reserve with a marsh, old oak trees and paths for horses, bikes and hikers. The narrow canal, **Djurgårdsbrunnskanalen**, which opened in 1834, is a pleasant place for a stroll, with its charming cottages and small footbridge near the sea.

Transport note: there's no Tunnelbana station on or near Djurgården. Bus 44 runs along Djurgårdsvägen as far as Skansen; bus 47 goes further to Ryssviken, as does the historic tram line 7 (which operates daily from June to August, weekends only the rest of the year). Alternatively, you can catch a ferry from Slussen, which stops at a jetty near Gröna Lund and then on Skeppsholmen. Between May and August, it also stops at the Vasamuseet and at Nybroplan on Norrmalm.

All the fun of the fair at **Gröna Lund** amusement park. *See p80.*

Aquaria Vattenmuseum

Falkenbergsgatan 2 (660 49 40/www.aquaria.se). Bus 44, 47/tram 7/ferry from Slussen or Nybroplan. **Open** *Mid June-mid Aug* 10am-6pm daily. *Mid Aug-mid June* 10am-4.30pm Tue-Sun. **Admission** 60kr; 50kr concessions; 30kr 6-15s; free under-6s. **Free with SC. Credit** MC, V. **Map** p304 J11.

A waterfall cascades over the entrance of this unusual aquarium next to the Vasamuseet. In the amazing rainforest exhibit, you get an underwater view and can go eyeball to eyeball with 1.5m-long (5ft) catfish, then step into a realistic jungle environment, with dripping plants, chirping insects and rain showers every ten minutes. Elsewhere, sharks and tropical fish swim in a long blue aquarium, and a mountain waterfall splashes down on a pool of trout. Environmental concerns are also highlighted; a sign next to an open manhole encourages you to climb down for a 'sewer adventure', where you see the effects of pollution and acid rain. On the deck outside there's an exhibit on the Baltic Sea. The aquarium is a definite winner with both adults and kids – though the gift shop is clearly stocked for ten year olds alone – goofy pencils, trinkets and fish-shaped soaps abound.

Biologiska Museet

Hazeliusporten (442 82 15/www.skansen.se/besok/biologiskamuseet.asp). Bus 44, 47/tram 7/ferry from Slussen or Nybroplan. **Open** *Apr-Sept* 10am-4pm daily. *Oct-Mar* 10am-3pm Tue-Sun. **Admission** 20kr; 10kr 6-15s; free under-6s. **Free with SC. No credit cards. Map** p304 H11.

Before or after you see the live animals at Skansen's zoo, see the stuffed version at this small museum devoted to Scandinavian wildlife. The A-frame building styled after a medieval Norwegian church was designed by Agi Lindegren, the architect of Gustav Vasa Kyrka. Except for replacing a few of its stuffed animals, the museum has remained unchanged since it opened in 1893. On the ground floor old-fashioned dioramas depict a valley in east Greenland and an Arctic cave. Check out the box containing a '*skvader*' – a fantasy hybrid of a hare and a grouse. The double spiral staircase leads to the first floor, where a fabulous 360° diorama wraps around a wooden viewing platform. In this incredibly life-like display, animals of the coast and forest are shown behind trees, in the water and sitting on cliffs. Swedish artist Bruno Liljefors (whose depictions of nature hang in the National Museet) painted the detailed backdrop. Another platform on the second floor gives a better view of the birds and their nests. Admission to Skansen gets you in here too; alternatively, if you save the museum ticket receipt, it will be deducted from the fee for Skansen.

Nordiska Museet: it's big and full of stuff.

Museifartygen

Galärvarvet (51 95 48 91/www.vasamuseet.se). **Open** *July-mid Aug* noon-7pm daily. *Early June-end June, mid Aug-end Aug* noon-5pm daily. *1wk late Feb* noon-5pm daily. **Admission** 35kr; 20kr concessions; 10kr 7-16s; free under-7s. **Free with SC. No credit cards. Map** p304 H10.

The entrance fee to the Vasamuseet (*see p86*) also lets you on to two ships docked nearby. The lightship *Finngrundet* was built in 1903 and anchored in the ice-free part of Sweden's Gulf of Bothnia. It was decommissioned in the late 1960s when lightships were replaced by fixed, unmanned lighthouses. The other ship, the *St Erik*, was Sweden's first ice-breaker. Built in 1915 to help keep the archipelago channels clear, it later assisted shipping in southern Sweden. Hop on board for 15 minutes if you're not already worn out by the *Vasa*.

Nordiska Museet

Djurgårdsvägen 6-16 (51 95 60 00/457 06 60/www.nordm.se). Bus 44, 47/tram 7/ferry from Slussen or Nybroplan. **Open** *July, Aug* 10am-5pm daily. *Sept-June* 10am-5pm Tue-Sun. **Admission** 60kr; free under-18s. **Free with SC. Credit** AmEx, MC. **Map** p304 G11.

The Nordiska Museet, Sweden's national museum of cultural history, was the brainchild of Artur Hazelius, who also created Skansen. Everything about the place is big. The building itself, designed by Isak Clason and completed in 1907, is massive – though only a quarter of the originally intended size. On entering the aptly named Great Hall visitors are greeted by Carl Milles' wonderful – and colossal – pink statue of a seated Gustav Vasa. (In his forehead is a chunk of oak from, legend claims, a tree planted

The man behind Skansen

Two of Stockholm's most popular sights – **Skansen** (*see p84*) and the **Nordiska Museet** (*see p82*) – wouldn't exist if it wasn't for the inspiration, dedication and sheer bloodymindedness of one man.

As a student **Artur Hazelius** (1833-1901) was fired up by the student movement for Scandinavianism, which promoted the common past and present of the Nordic countries. In his late thirties, he quit his job as a linguistics lecturer and began to travel around Sweden collecting tools, clothing and anything else of cultural interest. This period, at the end of the 19th century, was a time of rapid change in Sweden. New railways had opened up previously isolated communities, and hordes of people were moving into the cities. Hazelius wanted to find a way to preserve the country's rapidly disappearing agrarian heritage. He acquired his first items – a folk costume, several music sheets of folk songs and even a cottage – on a trip through Dalarna in 1872. A year later he opened a museum on Drottninggatan to exhibit the objects that he had assembled.

Hazelius was an aggressive fundraiser and determined to educated the Swedes about their history. In 1888 he convinced the government to give him land on Djurgården where he could construct a new, much larger museum. Even though the Nordiska Museet's main hall is today the biggest secular room in Sweden – a humongous 126.5 metres long and 24 metres high (about 400 by 80 feet) – the original plan called for a building four times that size.

Only three years after construction began (it wasn't finished until 1907) Hazelius had raised enough money to purchase another piece of land on Djurgården – where he planned to create a park where Scandinavian houses, animals and plants could be displayed in realistic environments. Skansen opened in 1891 as the world's first open-air museum, with cottages that had been moved whole or piece by piece from all over Sweden.

The museum became a popular excursion for Stockholmers, who also came to see its Nordic and exotic animals. Life-size dolls wearing folk costumes originally inhabited the cottages, but these were soon replaced by real people demonstrating traditional crafts. Middle-class homes, shops, schools and churches were eventually added, and the collection continues to grow today. Hazelius's idea of a living, open-air museum inspired others to create similar museums all over the world. He lived in Skansen's Gula Huset until his death in 1901.

by the king himself.) And the museum's collections of cultural artefacts from the early 16th century to the present are immense. Permanent exhibitions include fashion and folk costumes, recreated table settings from the 16th to the 20th centuries, the Sami people, and Swedish traditions, manners and customs. There are also marvellously detailed doll's houses, and a collection of doom-laden paintings and photos by Strindberg that do nothing to dispel his madman image. The museum is quite old-fashioned in presentation, but no less fascinating for that. Lekstugan, the special play area aimed at kids aged five to 12, is always popular.

Prins Eugens Waldemarsudde

Prins Eugens Väg 6 (54 58 37 00/ www.waldemarsudde.com). Bus 47/tram 7. **Open** *Mansion & gallery* 11am-5pm Tue, Wed, Fri-Sun; 11-8pm Thur. *Gamla Huset* 11am-5pm Tue-Sun. **Admission** 70kr; 50kr concessions; free under-18s. **Credit** MC, V. **Map** p305 K13.

A grand three-storey mansion and an art gallery stand on this beautiful waterfront property, owned by Prince Eugen from 1899 until his death in 1947. The prince, a well-known Swedish landscape painter and the brother of King Gustav V, moved into the mansion upon its completion in 1904. The house's architect, Ferdinand Boberg, later designed the NK department store (*see p152*). The light, simply decorated rooms on the ground floor are furnished as the prince left them. Temporary art exhibitions and the prince's paintings are displayed upstairs and in the art gallery next door; he even designed the classical white flowerpots for sale in the gift shop. The artwork and mansion are impressive, but you can skip them and just enjoy the grounds and views outside. The estate includes the original manor house, Gamla Huset, and an old linseed mill, both dating from the 1780s. Sculptures by Auguste Rodin and Carl Milles adorn the park, and a path leads to an 18th-century windmill. You can fill up on fresh waffles at the nearby Ektorpet cottage.

Rosendals Slott

Rosendalsvägen (402 61 30/www.royalcourt.se). Bus 47, 69 or tram 7 then walk. **Open** (guided tours only) *June-Aug* noon, 1pm (English), 2pm, 3pm Tue-Sun. Closed Sept-May. **Admission** 50kr; 25kr concessions; free under-7s. **Free with SC. No credit cards**. **Map** p305 H14.

King Karl XIV Johan's summer retreat, this light yellow building with grey pillars is designed in the empire style, its wall paintings and decorative scheme reflecting the king's military background. The cotton fabric around the dining room is pleated to resemble an officer's tent, and the frieze in the Red Salon shows the Norse god Odin's victory over the frost giants. The fable of Eros and Psyche is told on the beautifully painted domed ceiling in the Lantern Room. The palace was designed by Fredrik Blom, who also created the Historiska Museet (*see p96*) and Skeppsholm church; it was prefabricated in Norrmalm then shipped out to Djurgården in pieces. Karl Johan always remained a Frenchman at heart: he never ate Swedish food and sometimes forced his less fragrant guests to wash their hands in cologne. The 45-minute tour offered in summer is the only way to see the inside of the palace.

Skansen

Djurgårdsslätten 49-51 (442 80 00/www.skansen.se). Bus 44, 47/tram 7/ferry from Slussen or Nybroplan. **Open** *June-Aug* 10am-10pm daily. *May* 10am-8pm daily. *Sept* 10am-5pm daily. *Jan-Apr, Oct-Dec* 10am-4pm daily. **Admission** *May-Aug* 30kr-70kr; free-30kr 6-15s. *Sept-Dec* 30kr-60kr; 20kr 6-15s. Free under-6s. **Free with SC**. **Credit** AmEx, DC, MC, V. **Map** p305 H-J12.

Founded in 1891 by Artur Hazelius (*see p83* **The man behind Skansen**), Skansen is a one-stop cultural tour of Sweden. The 150-plus traditional buildings – homes, shops, churches, barns, workshops – are organised as a miniature Sweden, with buildings from the north of the country at the north, those from the middle in the middle, and so on. Most of the structures, situated along paths lined with elm, oak and maple trees, date from the 18th and 19th centuries. The striking 14th-century Norwegian storage hut overlooking Djurgårdsbrunnsviken is the oldest; newest are the small garden cottages from the 1920s. Most complete is the 1850s town quarter, with its cobblestone streets and artisans' workshops, including a baker, glassblower and potter. Watch them work, then buy the proceeds. Skansen's staff – dressed in folk costumes – spin wool, tend fires and perform other traditional tasks inside some of the buildings (open 11am-3/5pm).

Animals from all over Scandinavia, including brown bears, moose and wolves, are kept along the northern cliff in natural habitats (with the exception of the reindeers' wooden shed and sawdust floor). There's also a petting zoo containing pigs, hedgehogs and kittens, and an aquarium/zoo, Skansen Akvariet (*see below*) near the southern entrance. An old-fashioned marketplace sits at the centre of the park, and folk-dancing demonstrations – with lots of boisterous foot-stamping and fiddle-playing – take place in summer on the Tingsvallen stage. Hunger pangs can be satisfied at a variety of eating places; the café in the red, octagonal Bredablick tower has a super view of the grounds. The 19th-century Gubbhyllan building to the left of the main entrance houses a Tobacco and Match Museum and an old-fashioned café that serves simple dishes. Skansen is a popular destination on Sweden's national holidays since most of them, including Midsummer and Lucia, are celebrated here in traditional style – for more info, *see chapter* **Festivals**. The Christmas market is a big draw too. And don't miss the shop (*see p174*) by the main gate, which is packed with well-made traditional arts and crafts.

You can grin and bear it at **Skansen**.

Skansen Akvariet

Djurgårdsslätten 49-51 (660 10 82/www.skansen-akvariet.se). Bus 44, 47/tram 7/ferry from Slussen or Nybroplan. **Open** *Midsummer-early Aug* 10am-8pm daily. *Early Aug-Midsummer* 10am-4pm Mon-Fri; 10am-5pm Sat, Sun. **Admission** 60kr; 30kr 6-15s; free under-6s. **Free with SC**. **Credit** AmEx, MC, V. **Map** p305 J12.

Some of the smallest monkeys you've ever seen are on show in this zoo and aquarium located inside Skansen. Bright orange tamarins and pygmy marmosets hang from trees behind glass, and you can walk up the steps of a giant tree house where more than three dozen striped lemurs hop around while chewing on fresh vegetables. The less friendly looking baboons crawl around a steep hill in another exhibit, complete with a crashed jungle jeep hanging from a branch. There's lots to see – snakes, a nocturnal room full of bats, tanks containing stingrays

Raising the *Vasa*

After sinking on her maiden voyage in 1628, the *Vasa* warship lay on the seabed 30 metres (100 feet) below the surface, relatively intact, for more than 330 years. Her main mast originally stuck up above the water, but after it broke off the location of the ship was forgotten. She was eventually rediscovered thanks to the efforts of one man in a rowing boat using a home-made device.

For five years in the 1950s amateur naval historian Anders Franzén studied archives and searched the waters around Beckholmen, repeatedly sending a small core sampler down to the sea's muddy bottom. In 1956 the sampler finally pulled up a chunk of blackened oak. A diver went down and confirmed that he'd found the *Vasa*.

But how to raise the huge ship? Such an operation had never been done before. One of the more outlandish suggestions was to freeze the *Vasa* in a massive block of ice, let her float to the surface and then melt in the sun. Another was to fill the ship with enough tennis balls to make her rise to the surface of her own accord. A more conventional (and saner) method was finally decided upon.

Six tunnels were dug beneath the wreck and threaded with steel cables attached to two water-filled pontoons. When the water was pumped out of the pontoons, they lifted, stretching the cables and rising the *Vasa* from the seabed. The first nerve-wracking lift took place in 1959. Fortunately, the hull held and the *Vasa* was gradually lifted in 16 stages over the next two years. More than 5,000 holes had to be patched before she finally breached the surface on 24 April 1961. It was a huge news story, and the televised image of the *Vasa* emerging after three centuries on the seabed captivated people around the world.

The *Vasa*'s magnificent stern.

The ship was floated on to a dry dock and the black oak sprayed with polyethylene glycol, to prevent the timbers from shrinking and cracking apart after the water dried out. Archaeologists eventually removed and cleaned more than 2,000 items from the ship. A temporary museum opened in 1962 on the western shore of Djurgården; the current purpose-built museum opened in 1990. It's deliberately low-lit and climate-controlled to help preserve the fragile vessel. Recently a new problem has appeared: sulphur absorbed on the sea bed has reacted with the air to form sulphuric acid, which has started to eat away at the wood. Steps are underway to save the *Vasa* once again.

and two crocodiles – and it's always a hit with kids. You can even pet a boa constrictor and a tarantula. If you don't want to pay the separate entrance fee, you can glimpse the baboons and lemurs from the path outside.

Thielska Galleriet

Sjötullsbacken 6 (662 58 84/www.thielska-galleriet.a.se). Bus 69. **Open** noon-4pm Mon-Sat; 1-4pm Sun. Closed 1wk before Christmas. **Admission** 50kr; 30kr concessions; free under-16s. **No credit cards**.

Wealthy banker and art collector Ernest Thiel built this palatial home on the eastern tip of Djurgården in the early 1900s. The eclectically styled building, with influences from the Italian Renaissance and the Orient, was designed by Ferdinand Boberg, who built Prins Eugens Waldemarsudde (*see p83*) at roughly the same time. Thiel lost most of his fortune after World War I, and the state acquired the property in 1924. Two years later this museum opened, displaying his collection of turn-of-the-20th-century Nordic art – including works by Carl Larsson, Bruno Liljefors and Edvard Munch. Thiel's bathroom has been turned into a small café, and his urn lies beneath a statue by Auguste Rodin in the park. If you haven't seen enough Scandinavian art at the National Museet, perhaps this will satisfy you.

After 300 years underwater, the *Vasa* warship now has its very own museum.

Vasamuseet

Galärvarvsvägen 14 (51 95 48 00/www.vasa museet.se). Bus 44, 47/tram 7/ferry from Slussen or Nybroplan. **Open** *Mid June-late Aug* 9.30am-7pm daily. *Late Aug-mid June* 10am-5pm Mon, Tue, Thur-Sun; 10am-8pm Wed. **Guided tours** (Swedish, English) *Mid June-late Aug* on the hr 10.30am-6.30pm. *Late Aug-mid June* 12.30pm, 2.30pm Mon-Fri; 10.30am, 12.30pm, 2.30pm, 4.30pm Sat, Sun. **Admission** 70kr (5-8pm Wed 50kr); 40kr concessions; 10kr 7-15s; free under-7s. **Credit** AmEx, MC, V. **Map** p304 H10.

Entering the Vasa Museum for the first time is a jaw-dropping experience, as your eyes adjust to the gloom and you realise the monstrous size of the *Vasa* – the largest and best-preserved ship of its kind in the world. In the 1620s Sweden was at war with Poland and King Gustav II Adolf needed several new ships as soon as possible. With two gun decks and 64 cannons, the *Vasa* was to be the mightiest ship in his fleet, possibly the world. Unfortunately, the gun decks and heavy cannon made the ship top heavy. During a stability test, in which 30 men ran back and forth across the deck, she nearly toppled over. Still, the king needed his ship and the maiden voyage went ahead. But only a few minutes after the *Vasa* set sail from near present-day Slussen on 10 August 1628, she began to lean to one side. The gun ports soon filled with water and the ship sank – after a voyage of only 1,300m (1,400yds). Of the 150 people on board 30-50 died – the number would have been higher if the ship had reached Älvsnabben in the archipelago, where 300 soldiers were waiting to board. The reason the *Vasa* is so well preserved – 95% of the ship is original – is because the Baltic Sea is insufficiently saline to contain the tiny shipworm, which destroys wood in saltier seas.

Head first for the theatre to watch a short film about the *Vasa* and her discovery. On your own or with a tour you can walk around the exterior of the 69m-long (225ft) warship and view the upper deck and keel from above and below. The fantastically ornate stern is covered with sculptures intended to express the glory of the Swedish king and frighten enemies. The recreated masts sticking out from the museum's slanting roof show the original height of the *Vasa*: 52.5m (170ft) from keel to mast. No one's allowed on board, but you can walk through a re-creation of one of the gun decks, learn about the crew's life and view the sails carefully preserved behind glass. Down by the keel, computers enable you to experiment with the design of ships and test their seaworthiness. Restoration of the *Vasa* continues today. Of the ship's 500 sculptures of warriors, naked women, Swedish symbols and scenes from Greek mythology and the Bible, 17 have been repainted in their original bright colours of gold, green, blue and red.

The gift shop is stocked with everything the *Vasa* lover might need. Most interesting are the replicas of cooking pots, glasses and candlesticks found on board. The fridge magnets were designed in more recent times.

Skeppsholmen

Once an important naval base and shipyard, the small island of Skeppsholmen is now known for its museums and schools, many housed in ex-naval buildings. It's also a pleasant place for an amble; the shoreline provides some beautiful views of the city. If you cross the narrow bridge from Blasieholmen you'll see on your left the **Östasiatiska Museet** (*see below*) in a long, low yellow building, originally designed by Kungliga Slottet architect Nicodemus Tessin the Younger in 1700. To your right is the three-masted schooner **Af Chapman**, now an unusual youth hostel (*see p50* **Staying on a boat**). The round, white, empire-style **Skeppsholmskyrkan** lies straight ahead; designed for the navy by Fredrik Blom, it was completed in 1842. It's now deconsecrated.

Behind the church the **Moderna Museet** occupies a large red building designed by Spanish architect Rafael Moneo and opened in 1998; the adjoining **Arkitekturmuseet** (*see below*) is housed in a former naval drill hall. Unfortunately, both museums are currently closed because of damp problems, and won't reopen until the end of 2003 at the earliest. The Moderna Museet's collections have moved to temporary homes around Stockholm; for details, *see p73* **Breaking the mould**. The quirky multicoloured creatures in front of the museum site were created by Niki de Saint Phalle and Jean Tinguely, and have been located here since 1972.

The stage on the north-western shore is used for the annual **Stockholm Jazz Festival** (*see p181*).

Other cultural buildings include the **Kungliga Konsthögskolan** (Royal University College of Fine Arts), which stands on the south-west corner in beautifully restored 18th-century naval barracks. Nearby is the headquarters of the Swedish Society of Crafts and Design, **Svensk Form** (*see p36*).

South of Skeppsholmen, and connected to it by a bridge, is the tiny granite island of **Kastellholmen**, named after a castle built here in the 1660s. The castle blew up in 1845 after an accident in a cartridge-manufacturing laboratory. A year later, Fredrik Blom designed a new, medieval-style castle with two red towers (not open to the public); whenever a visiting naval boat arrives, a salute is fired from the castle's four cannons.

Arkitekturmuseet

58 72 70 00/www.arkitekturmuseet.se. Bus 65.
Open *Skeppsholmskyrkan* 1-5pm Tue-Sun. *Konstakademien* 11am-8pm Tue-Thur; 11am-6pm Fri-Sun. **Admission** free. **Map** p304 H9.
While the museum is closed, a permanent exhibition looking at 1,000 years of building is housed in Skeppsholmen church, and temporary exhibitions and a bookshop are housed at the Royal Academy of Art in Norrmalm (*see p70*).

Östasiatiska Museet

51 95 57 50/www.mfea.se. Bus 65. **Map** p304 H9.
The Museum of Far Eastern Antiquities opened in 1963 and has one of the finest collections in Europe of stoneware and porcelain from the Song, Ming and Qing dynasties. Artwork from Japan, Korea and India is also displayed. The excellent gift shop sells calligraphy material, teas and antique porcelain. The state requires lifts to be installed, so the museum is undertaking more widespread renovations at the same time; the building is closed until summer 2003.

Lively art at the **Moderna Museet**.

Sightseeing

Södermalm & Långholmen

Take a walk on the wild side – on bohemian Söder and a leafy ex-prison island.

Södermalm

Södermalm (usually known as Söder) is Stockholm's hippest and most alternative district, better known for its bars, clubs and restaurants than its museums. It's a student hangout, so prices are often cheaper than elsewhere, and there are some good budget accommodation options. The district's two main focal points, Slussen and Medborgarplatsen, lie along Götgatan, a heavily trafficked street that runs up the middle of the island.

The first place you'll arrive at from Gamla Stan is the transport interchange of **Slussen** – a busy Tunnelbana and bus station surrounded by a confusing complex of roads. Pleasure boats manouevre around the lock (*slussen*) that separates Lake Mälaren from the Baltic Sea and is named after Karl XIV Johan, whose equestrian statue stands above it. Slussen is not the most attractive introduction to Söder's charms, but it does contain two of the island's main sights: the **Stockholm Stadsmuseum** (*see p90*), where you can learn about the 750-year history of the city, and **Katarinahissen** (*see p90*), the lift that offers one of the best views in the capital. Make a meal (or a drink) of it at **Eriks Gondolen** restaurant (*see p123*) and bar (*see p135*) at the top of the lift.

Wonderful panoramic views of the water are also available from the cliffs along the island's northern edge, particularly on **Monteliusvägen** and **Fjällgatan**, the latter a picturesque parade of 18th-century houses and cottages. Beneath the former, a string of vessels is docked along Söder Malarstrand, including a couple of boat hotels (*see p50* **Staying on a boat**).

Head south from Slussen along Gotgätan, past some funky little shops and bars – including late-night beer hall **Kvarnen** (*see p136*) – to **Medborgarplatsen**, where there's an indoor shopping mall with two cinemas, and a civic centre. This large square is filled with cafés in summer, and skate rats practise their moves on the skateboard ramp across the street. Numerous bars, restaurants and music venues are located nearby, as is the brand-new cultural centre **Mondo** (*see p213*).

Although the residents of Södermalm are today as well off as many other Stockholmers, the district has traditionally been a working-class one. Functionalist apartment buildings have replaced nearly all of the small wooden houses that once covered the island. If you walk west up the hill on Bastugatan near Slussen, you'll see a few of these 17th- and 18th-century houses on **Lilla Skinnarviksgränd** overlooking Riddarfjärden. Heading west on the main thoroughfare of Hornsgatan you arrive at **Maria Magdalena Kyrka** (*see p90*), the oldest church on Söder.

Heading east from Götgatan, walk up Urvädersgränd past the rarely open **Bellmanhuset** (*see p89*), former home of 18th-century balladeer Carl Michael Bellman, to **Mosebacke Torg**. This busy cobblestone square has been Söder's entertainment centre since the mid 19th-century, and is bordered by two of Stockholm's most popular and lively nightlife venues, **Södra Teatern** and the

Götgatan, with Globen in the distance.

Katarina Kyrka looming over the Söder cliffs.

adjoining **Mosebacke Etablissement** (for both, *see p213*). Together they'll cover all your nightlife needs, from clubbing to drinking, cutting-edge performance to live music; Mosebacke's outdoor terrace also provides a fabulous view of Stockholm's harbour.

Further south is **Katarina Kyrka** (*see p90*), masterfully restored in the 1990s to its original baroque splendour, and a preserved early 18th-century neighbourhood on **Mäster Mikaels Gata** (*see p92* **Walk 2: The heights of Söder**).

Since Södermalm is one of Stockholm's largest islands, and the noise and exhaust from its main thoroughfares can be unpleasant, taking a bus or T-bana is often the best way to get to your destination. Devotees of more old-fashioned forms of transport should head to the **Spårvägsmuseet** (*see p90*) on the eastern edge of the island, near nothing but apartments and the steep hillside park of Vita Bergen.

The wide street of Ringvägen curves around the southern border of Södermalm, passing through a shopping centre at Götgatan. The island's biggest and best park, **Tantolunden**, sits near the south-western shore, while the large red-brick church of **Högalidskyrkan**, designed by Ivar Tengbom in the National Romantic style and completed in 1923, stands on a hill to the north. Its octagonal twin towers are a striking landmark visible from many parts of the city. South of Södermalm is another of the city's best-known landmarks, the huge white sphere of sports arena **Globen** (*see p225*).

Bellmanhuset

Urvädersgränd 3 (640 22 29/www.par-bricole.a.se/historia/bellhus.htm). T-bana Slussen/bus 3, 46, 53, 59, 76. **Open** (guided tours only) 1pm 1st Sun of the mth. **Admission** 60kr. **No credit cards**. **Map** p310 K8.

Famous Swedish songwriter Carl Michael Bellman lived in this small orange house near Götgatan between 1770 and 1774. He wrote much of his *Fredmans Epistlar* here, a book of 82 songs about Stockholm's drunks and prostitutes that parodies the letters of the apostle Paul in the New Testament. If the monthly tour (in Swedish) fits into your sightseeing schedule, it can be quite entertaining. During it you hear about Bellman's life and the history of the building, and a troubadour or choir performs his songs.

KA Almgren Sideväveri Museum

Repslagargatan 15 (642 56 16/www.kasiden.se). T-bana Slussen/bus 59. **Open** *Jan-Midsummer* 9am-5pm Mon-Thur; 10am-4pm Fri; 11am-3pm Sat; guided tour 1pm Sun. *Midsummer-Dec* 2-5pm Mon-Thur; 9am-5pm Fri; 10am-2pm Sat. **Admission** 55kr-65kr. **50% discount with SC**. **No credit cards**. **Map** p310 L7.

Knut August Almgren stole the technology for this former silk-weaving factory in the late 1820s. While recovering from tuberculosis in France, he posed as a German-speaking Frenchman and gained access to factories where the innovative Jacquard looms with their punch-card system were being used. He took notes, smuggled machinery out of the country and opened a factory in Sweden in 1833. The factory here closed in 1974, but was reopened as a working museum in 1991 by a fifth-generation Almgren. It reproduces silk fabrics for stately homes around Scandinavia, including the Chinese pavilion at Drottningholms Slott (*see p239*). The museum displays silk portraits, landscapes and fabrics, as well as several 160-year-old looms. Once you've watched a slide show, followed by a 1940s documentary on silk weaving, you can see a demonstration of the looms in the main room. Silk scarves, ties and other hand-woven fabrics are for sale in the gift shop. While the museum should not be at the top of your must-see list, its quirky operators and ramshackle approach can make for a fun visit.

Katarinahissen

Stadsgården 6, Slussen. T-bana Slussen/bus 3, 46, 53, 76. **Open** 7.30am-10pm Mon-Sat; 10am-10pm Sun. **Rate** 5kr; free under-7s. **Free with SC. No credit cards. Map** p310 K8.

The 38m-tall (125ft) black steel Katarina Lift rises beside the busy intersection near Södermalmstorg. Its observation platform and walkway connects pedestrians to the Katarinaberget district above the square, although it's mainly just a tourist attraction and used as the entrance to the Eriks Gondolen restaurant housed beneath the walkway. The platform offers a beautiful view of Riddarfjärden, Gamla Stan and Djurgården. The original 1883 steam lift was demolished in 1933, and rebuilt two years later – this time running on electricity. The giant black box at the top of the elevator is used as advertising space. If you're the thrifty (and fit) type, you can also reach the platform by climbing the wooden hillside staircase.

Katarina Kyrka

Högbergsgatan 15 (743 68 00/www.svkyrkan katarina.com). T-bana Medborgarplatsen or Slussen/ bus 3, 46, 53, 59, 76. **Open** *Apr-Sept* 11am-5pm daily. *Oct-Mar* 11am-4pm daily. **Guided tours** *Swedish June-Aug* 12.30pm Tue, Thur. **Admission** free. **Map** p311 L8.

As Södermalm's population grew, it was agreed in the mid 17th century to split Maria Magdalena parish and build a new church. Katarina Kyrka, completed in 1695, was designed by Jean de la Vallé in the baroque style with a central plan. A huge fire in 1723 destroyed the church's cupola and half the buildings in the parish. A more recent fire in 1990, probably caused by a faulty electrical cable, burned down all but the church's walls and side vaults. Architect Ove Hildemark reconstructed the church (based on photos and drawings) using 17th-century building techniques. The yellow church with flat white pillars now looks much as it did before, although with a distinctly modern interior. Many victims of the Stockholm Bloodbath of 1520 were buried in the church's large cemetery. Organ music is played at noon on Tuesdays and Thursdays.

Maria Magdalena Kyrka

St Paulsgatan 10 (462 29 40/51). T-bana Slussen/ bus 4, 43, 55, 59, 66. **Open** 11am-5pm Mon-Sun. **Admission** free. **Map** p310 K7.

During his church-destroying spree after the Reformation in 1527, Gustav Vasa tore down the chapel that had stood on this site since the 1300s. His son, Johan III, methodically rebuilt most of the churches in the late 1500s. Construction on this yellowish-orange church with white corners began in 1580, but was not completed for 40 or so years. It's Söder's oldest church, and the first in Stockholm to be built with a central plan rather than a cross plan. Tessin the Elder designed the transept in the late 17th century, and his son created the French-inspired stonework of the entrance portal in 1716. The church's rococo interior – with its depiction of Maria Magdalena on the golden pulpit and Carl Fredrik Adelcrantz's elaborate organ screen – was created after a fire in 1759. Several of the cemetery's graves were moved when Hornsgatan was built to the north in 1900. Stop by for the organ music on Thursdays at 12.15pm.

Spårvägsmuseet

Tegelviksgatan 22 (462 55 31/www.sparvagsmuseet. sl.se). Bus 46, 55, 66. **Open** 10am-5pm Mon-Fri; 11am-4pm Sat, Sun. **Admission** 20kr; 10kr 7-18s, concessions; free under-7s. **Free with SC. Credit** AmEx, MC, V. **Map** p311 M11.

What the Transport Museum lacks in descriptive texts and focused exhibits it makes up for in quantity – more than 60 vehicles are stored in this former bus station in eastern Söder. Rows of carriages, trams and buses from the late 1800s to the present cover the development of Stockholm's public transport system. For 1kr you can sit behind the wheel of an old red bus and pretend to drive as a grainy film of city streets flashes in front of you. Children can try on a ticket collector's uniform and, in summer, ride a miniature Tunnelbana train. There's also a self-service café and a shop selling transport-related paraphernalia. Although a sign by the front desk apologises for the museum's lack of funds, a new exhibit on travel in Stockholm County from 1100 to 1800 is scheduled to open soon. The museum's nostalgic, forlorn feel makes it perfect for a rainy-day visit. Borrow a guidebook in English from the cashier since everything is labelled in Swedish.

Stockholms Stadsmuseum

Ryssgården, Slussen (50 83 16 00/www.stads museum.stockholm.se). T-bana Slussen/bus 3, 4, 46, 53, 55, 59. **Open** *Sept-May* 11am-5pm Tue, Wed, Fri-Sun; 11am-9pm Thur. *June-Aug* 11am-5pm Tue, Wed, Fri-Sun; 11am-7pm Thur. **Admission** 50kr; 10kr-40kr concessions, 7-18s; free under-7s. **Free with SC. Credit** AmEx, DC, MC, V. **Map** p310 K8.

Nicodemus Tessin the Elder, who also made additions to Tyska Kyrkan and Riddarholmskyrkan, designed this building in the 1670s. After a fire in 1680, the renovations were supervised by his son, Tessin the Younger – architect of the Kungliga Slottet. You'll find temporary exhibitions on the ground floor, along with a charming café decorated with objects from an early 20th-century bakery. A series of rooms on the floor above covers Stockholm's development from 1252 to the present day. One room contains an intricate model of the city's layout in the 1650s; another recreates the atmosphere and sounds of an 18th-century pub. The government's solution to the 1960s' housing shortage – the 'Million Programme' (*see p31* **A million homes**) – is the focus of the exhibition on the second floor. You can walk through an eerily realistic apartment from the 1940s and view architectural models of the buildings later constructed in the suburbs. This is Söder's best museum and a great place to learn more about the city.

Where to swim outdoors

Finish your night out with a dip by the Stadshuset. Start your day with a refreshing swim in the middle of the city. Use bridges as diving boards. Stockholm's lifeblood is its surrounding water – not for nothing is the city called 'the Nordic Venice'. Yes, the water adds beauty to the cityscape, but the extraordinary thing is that it can actually be used (compared with the Seine, the Thames, the Hudson) – thanks to a successful purification treatment since the 1960s.

Although you can swim almost everywhere, avoid dirty Karlbergskanalen (between Kungsholmen and Vasastaden) and leave the waves and the strong current in Strömmen (east of Gamla Stan) to the fishermen. July and August are the best months for swimming, though the water is also warm enough for a dip in June and September.

Djurgården

Bus 47, then walk. **Map** p305 K13.
The island of Djurgården is big, but more suited to land activities than swimming. Nevertheless, the small spit **Waldemarsudde** on the southern edge is great for a bathe. Get off bus 47 or tram 7 at Ryssviken and follow the path south along the water's edge; the swimming area is next to the museum and garden.

Långholmen

T-bana Hornstull/bus 4, 40, 66, 74. **Map** p301 J1-K3.
This green island offers plenty of swimming opportunities. For some privacy, head to the west side of the island and jump from the small rocks. For people-watching, go to the overcrowded little beach near the former prison (now a youth hostel/hotel). From there, continue east on the path and very soon you'll find a wharf, the wild kids' favourite diving place, or further on, a handful of spots just waiting to be cornered for a day's sunbathing before anybody else gets there.

Kungsholmen

Smedsuddsbadet: T-bana Thorildsplan/ bus 1, 4, 40, 57, 62, 74, 91.
Fredhäll: T-bana Kristineberg/bus 62.
Two options here, both on the southern side of Kungsholmen. **Smedsuddsbadet**, off Smedsuddsvägen opposite Långholmen, is a small sandy beach that attracts families with young kids. Further along the shore, on the south-western tip at **Fredhäll**, climb down from Snoilskyvägen or Atterbomsvägen to the rocks. If you're peckish, visit unpretentious restaurant Solstugan (Snoilskyvägen 37-9; 656 80 85) and continue to enjoy the view of the water from there.

Stadshuset

T-bana T-Centralen/bus 3, 62. **Map** p302 H5.
Of course, the purpose of this beautiful architectural creation was not to function as a bathing spot, but – and promise not to tell anyone – this makes it even more attractive.

Långholmen

Just off the north-west tip of Södermalm lies the long, narrow former prison island of **Långholmen** ('Long Island'). For 250 years this beautiful green island, 1.4 kilometres (almost one mile) long, was best known for the prison that stood at its centre from 1724 to 1975. Thanks to the jail, Långholmen has remained largely undeveloped and its small beach, shaded walking paths and waterfront cliffs feel much further away from the city than they actually are. Today, the remaining part of the prison is run as a budget hotel-cum-youth hostel (*see p51*), restaurant and prison museum (**Långholmens Fängelsemuseum**; *see p93*).

A walking/bicycle path leads from the south of the island to the sloping cliffs and beach in the north. The **Bellmanmuseet** (*see p92*) and the former prison complex lie behind the beach – one of the most popular places to swim in the city – and to the west there's a community gardening area. Karlshäll, the previous residence of the director of prison buildings, stands in the island's north-west corner and is now a conference centre and restaurant. The path curves around and follows the southern shore where small, private boats are docked.

You can walk to the island across Långholmsbron (which leads to the back of the former prison) or via Pålsundsbron to the east, near a shipyard established in the 1680s. To land yourself smack in the middle of the island, walk across the enormous Västerbron bridge and take the stairs down on either side into the tree canopy.

Prisoners used to walk across a bridge to work at factories on **Reimersholme**, the tiny island next to Långholmen. It's now residential and there's really nothing of interest to visitors.

Bellmanmuseet

Stora Henriksvik (669 69 69). T-bana Hornstull/ bus 4, 40, 66, 74. **Open** *June-Aug* noon-6pm daily. *May, Sept* noon-4pm Sat, Sun. Closed Oct-Apr. **Admission** 30kr; free under-15s. **No credit cards**. **Map** p301 J2.

The oldest part of this attractive two-storey house was built in the late 17th century as the toll office for boats travelling into Stockholm. The ground floor is now divided between a café and a museum about the songwriter Carl Michael Bellman. In the late 18th century Bellman would visit Långholmen to see an opera singer friend who worked at the prison. Aside from a few copies of portraits and Bellman's handwriting there's not much to see. The café and gardens are popular with bathers using the beach in front of the house (*see p91* **Where to swim outdoors**). There are concerts in summer.

Walk 2: The heights of Söder

This short walk – about 1.5km (one mile) long – provides a brief introduction to the history of Söder, from public execution sites to 18th-century working-class homes. En route you get a great view of the city.

Start the walk on Högbergsgatan, in front of Katarina Kyrka. Walk through the churchyard to the left of the church.

The baroque masterpiece of **Katarina Kyrka** (*see p90*) was completed in 1695. It has suffered two devastating fires, in 1723 and 1990: after the last fire it was completely restored, and reopened in 1995. The church has been the scene of some grim events over the years. In 1520 victims of the Stockholm Bloodbath (*see p66*) were burned alive in the churchyard. During the witch hunts of the late 1600s, trials were held in a room above the vestry. The death penalty for witchcraft was abolished in 1778.

Exit the churchyard by the open gate Mäster Mikaels Gata, and walk down Mäster Mikaels Gata, across Nytorgsgatan, and stop in front of the wooden cottages.

Mäster Mikaels Gata is named after one of the city's executioners. Condemned convicts were reprieved if they accepted the position, but often relapsed into their old criminal ways and had to be executed and replaced. So, in 1635, the city decided to make the executioner a paid position, and Mikael Reissur, an impoverished shopkeeper from a small provincial town, applied for the job. The pay was good, and included housing, clothing and firewood; he also received a monetary tip for each execution. Master Mikael was skilled at his new job and remained executioner until 1650, when he unintentionally killed a man in a fight and was subsequently executed himself.

The wooden cottages (*pictured*) were built after the 1723 fire, which destroyed some 500 buildings in the area as well as Katarina Kyrka. They may look quaint today, but in the 1880s as many as 45 people were crammed into No.10. Poor families often had to take in lodgers to pay the rent, and even the kitchen was used as sleeping quarters.

Continue to the end of the street; walk down the stairs and across Renstiernas Gata on to Fjällgatan. Stop in front of the wooden steps called Sista Styverns Trappor.

Fjällgatan was connected to Mäster Mikaels Gata before the hill was blasted away to create Renstiernas Gata at the turn of the 20th century. The buildings on Fjällgatan were also built after the fire of 1723. To prevent new conflagrations, wooden houses were prohibited, but the rule was overlooked in poorer quarters of the city. The house to the right of the stairs is painted with typical Swedish *Falu rödfärg* paint; a by-product of copper mining, the paint has been manufactured in Falun in northern Sweden since the 16th century. From Fjällgatan there's a great view over the sea approach to Stockholm as well as towards Gamla Stan and Djurgården.

Långholmens Fängelsemuseum

Långholmen Hotell, Långholmsmuren 20 (668 05 00/www.langholmen.com). T-bana Hornstull/ bus 4, 66. **Open** 11am-4pm daily. **Guided tours** *Swedish June-Aug* 2pm Sun; for other languages, call 720 85 81. **Admission** 25kr; 10kr under-14s. **Credit** AmEx, DC, MC, V. **Map** p301 K2.

This small museum describes the history of the Swedish penal system and life inside Kronohäktet prison before it was turned into a hotel/youth hostel. You can visit typical cells used from 1845 to 1930, read about Sweden's last executioner, Anders Gustaf Dalman, and view an assortment of prison paraphernalia, including the sinister hoods worn during sentencing (used until 1935). Nowadays, the Swedish government tries to avoid incarceration and a quarter of the 12, 000 criminals dealt with each year are electronically tagged rather than imprisoned.

Walk up the steepish stairs to Stigbergsgatan and stop at the top.

Sista Styverns Trappor means 'Stairs of the Last Penny', after the name of a pub located in the harbour below in the 18th century. Humorous pub names were common; another was called 'Pain in the Pocket'. After a long day's work dockworkers often spent their hard-earned money on drink before climbing the steps on their way home. The green area to the right of the stairs is a public park, sometimes referred to as the 'Hanging Gardens of Söder'. Both flowers and herbs grow in the park.

Across the street at the top of the stairs is a tall building with a tower. Built in 1907, it once housed a navigation school. On top is a mast with a time ball, which was hoisted and lowered at 1pm to indicate noon Greenwich Mean Time. Unfortunately, it's been out of order for some time and the ball is now stuck at the bottom.

From the early 1500s to 1654, this hilltop was a public execution site; Master Mikael lived further down the street. The hill was remote but still clearly visible from the city – a highly desirable location as the gallows were to serve as a warning to both residents and visiting ships. (The small hill above Björns Trädgård by the mosque was also used as an execution site, in the 1300s.) In the Middle Ages, stealing was considered a felony while murder was just a misdemeanour: murderers were beheaded while thieves were hanged. Being hanged was a more serious punishment since it also brought shame to the offender and his family. The larger the theft, the higher up the gallows on which you were hanged. The last public exection in Sweden took place in 1862.

Turn to the right and walk down Stigbergsgatan to No.27.

In the 1920s there was a plan to replace the small 18th-century wooden cottages lining **Stigbergsgatan** with more modern residences, but No.27 – designed by Ragnar Östberg, the architect of the Stadshuset – was the only one constructed, in 1927. Instead, the cottages were kept as a typical example of working-class dwellings. No.21 is known as the **Blockmakarens House** (Block Maker's House) after Gustaf Andersson, who made pulleys for the navy and owned the house in the early 1900s. Looking over the fence you can see two small windows on the bottom floor at the far end of the cottage. This tiny, unheated one-room apartment with a small kitchen was rented by Emilia Gustafsson and her five children from 1916 to '23 (they left because of rats attacking the children). Today it's a museum and occasionally open to the public.

Continue down Stigbergsgatan and stop in front of the fence at the end, before you take the wooden steps to the left leading down to Renstiernas Gata.

Here the street comes to an abrupt stop; before the mountain was blasted away, the street continued on the other side. Stockholm is situated on 14 hilly islands and **Renstiernas Gata** is one example of how Alfred Nobel's invention, dynamite, was put to great use in remodelling the city from a slumbering small town to the bustling modern capital of today.

Östermalm & Gärdet

Head east for glamorous nightlife haunts and a cluster of museums.

Östermalm

The main focus of activity in affluent and largely residential Östermalm is the busy square of **Stureplan**. At its centre stands a concrete rain shelter called Svampen ('the mushroom'). The odd-shaped sculpture, with four public telephones attached to its base, is a popular meeting place for people on their way to one of the district's trendy nightspots. Formerly a rather run-down area, Stureplan was revamped at the end of the 1980s and is now party central for glamour-seeking, fashion-conscious Stockholmers.

Nearby are nightclubs **Spy Bar** (*see p192*) and **Sturecompagniet** (*see p192*); bars **East** (*see p138*), **Halv Trappa Plus Gård** (*see p138*) and **Laroy** (*see p138*); and restaurants **Sturehof** (*see p127*), **PA & Co** (*see p125*) and **Brasserie Godot** (*see p127*). Just north from the square, on Sturegatan, is the hip, music-oriented **Lydmar Hotel** (*see p53*), whose lobby bar (*see p138*) pulses with the young and beautiful. The clubs close at around 5am at the weekend – later than the capital's other party spots – so you'll often see hordes of clubbers queuing in the small hours, in all weathers, to get into the most fashionable places.

This is also the city's most upmarket shopping area. The ultra-posh shopping mall **Sturegallerian** (*see p152*) borders the square; among its designer boutiques is the exclusive art nouveau bath house **Sturebadet** (*see p168*). Shopaholics can spend a few happy hours trawling the surrounding streets, notably the lower end of **Birger Jarlsgatan** (which extends from the north of the city all the way to the water of Nybroviken), **Biblioteksgatan**, **Grev Turegatan** and **Mäster Samuelsgatan**. This is where you'll find international designer fashion boutiques, classy jewellery, fancy cosmetics and posh chocolates. But don't expect cutting-edge anything in conventional Östermalm – the upper classes, both young and old, come here to reconfirm their status in that time-honoured way of spending lots of money.

At the bottom end of Birger Jarlsgatan is **Nybroviken**, where the Cinderella and Strömma Kanalbolaget ferries depart for destinations in Lake Mälaren and the archipelago. Classics

Stureplan, the epicentre of fashionable Stockholm.

by Strindberg and Shakespeare – sometimes directed by Ingmar Bergman – are performed in the ornate white marble building facing Nybroplan square, the **Kungliga Dramatiska Teatern** (*see p96*) – one of Stockholm's leading theatres. Nearby is idiosyncratic museum **Hallwylska Palatset** (*see p96*).

If you walk up Sibyllegatan to the right of the theatre, you'll pass three buildings constructed under the authority of the Crown. Bread for the Royal Army was baked at the Kronobageriet, which today houses the charming and child-friendly **Musikmuseet** (*see p97*). The royal family's horses and cars are still kept in the **Kungliga Hovstallet** (*see p97*), the huge brick building to the right of the bakery. Further up is the unusual **Armémuseum** (*see p96*), where the royal arsenal used to be stored. Behind this lies 17th-century **Hedvig Eleonora Kyrka**, the former place of worship for the Royal Navy, which holds regular classical music concerts.

To catch a glimpse of the Östermalm upper classes, head to **Östermalms Torg** opposite the church. When the first plans for Östermalm were drawn up back in the 1640s, sailors and craftsmen lived around this square. Nowadays, expensive boutiques sell clothes and home accessories, and the pavements are teaming with mink-clad elderly women walking small dogs. On the corner of the square is **Östermalms Saluhall**, a dark red-brick building constructed in 1888 and the flagship of the city's market halls (*see p163* **Food markets**). You can buy all sorts of gourmet delicacies, from fresh Baltic fish to wild rabbit – but it's pricey, so you could just stroll around the magnificent interior with its swooping ceiling.

Östermalm's main green space is the **Humlegården**, the site of the king's hop gardens back in the 16th century and today a pleasant and very popular park with the **Kungliga Bibliotek** (Royal Library) at its southern end. Theatre performances are held in the park in summer. Further up Karlavägen,

The quay at **Nybroviken**. *See p94.*

on a hill overlooking the city, looms the tall brick tower of **Engelbrektskyrkan**. Designed by the leading Jugendstil architect Lars Israel Wahlman and opened in 1914, the church has an amazingly high nave – supposedly the tallest in Scandinavia.

For another kind of high life, follow the water's edge from Nybroplan along grand **Strandvägen**, lined with luxurious late 19th-century residences and still among the city's most prestigious addresses. There are also a couple of deluxe hotels and one of Stockholm's most celebrated interior design shops, **Svenskt Tenn** (*see p171*). Until the 1940s sailing boats carrying firewood from the archipelago islands used to dock on the quayside at Strandvägen; some of these vintage boats – with labels by each one – are now docked on its southern edge.

At the end of Strandvägen is the bridge leading over to leafy Djurgården, and north from there, on Narvavägen, is the imposing **Historiska Museet** (*see p96*), Sweden's largest archaeological museum. Its collection of Viking artefacts is exceptional.

Strandvägen is part of an esplanade system mapped out for Östermalm in the late 1800s by city planner Albert Lindhagen. The project was only partially implemented, but includes the broad boulevards of **Valhallavägen**, **Narvavägen** and **Karlavägen** – the latter two radiating out from the fountain and round

Isak Gustav Clason's **Östermalms Saluhall**: the Harrods of food markets.

pond (added in 1929) at **Karlaplan**. The central section of Karlavägen is dotted with sculptures by various international artists, and at its eastern end – on the site of a former military training ground – are the headquarters of Swedish radio and television. The buildings were designed by Erik Ahnborg and Sune Lindström, who were also responsible for the next-door concert hall **Berwaldhallen** (*see p215*), home of the Swedish Radio Symphony Orchestra and Radio Choir.

Beyond the TV and radio buildings, on the border with Gärdet, is **Diplomatstaden**, a complex of grand mansions that houses most of the city's foreign embassies, including those of the UK and US. The adjoining park next to the water is named after Alfred Nobel, scientist, inventor and founder of the famous prizes.

Sightseeing

Armémuseum

Riddargatan 13 (788 95 60/www.armemuseum.org). T-bana Östermalmstorg/bus 46, 47, 55, 62, 69, 76, 91. **Open** 11am-8pm Tue; 11am-4pm Wed-Sun. **Guided tours** *English July, Aug* noon Tue-Sun. *Swedish July, Aug* 1pm daily. *Sept-June* 1pm Sat, Sun. **Admission** 60kr; 40kr concessions; 30kr 7-18s; free under-7s. Free 4-8pm Tue June-Aug. **Free with SC. Credit** MC, V. **Map** p304 F9.

When the first thing you see in an exhibition about war is three chimpanzees tearing one another apart, you realise this is not your typical military museum. The Army Museum – housed since 1879 in the former arsenal, an impressive white pile built in the 18th century – reopened in May 2000 after seven years of renovation. It presents about 1,000 years of Swedish military history – and it's not all pretty uniforms and gleaming weaponry. Life-size (and life-like) tableaux, such as a woman scavenging meat from a dead horse and doctors performing an amputation, show the gruesome and brutal effects of war on both soldiers and civilians. The main exhibition begins on the third floor with the late Viking age and the Thirty Years War, and continues on the second floor with the 20th century. The ground floor houses an artillery exhibit and a restaurant. Nominated for the European Museum of the Year Award in 2001, this is one of Stockholm's most fascinating museums. Most of the labelling is in Swedish, but the front desk provides a detailed pamphlet in English. The Royal Guard marches off from the museum, usually at 11.45am (summer only), for the changing of the guard (*see p59*) at the Kungliga Slottet.

Hallwylska Museet

Hamngatan 4 (51 95 55 99/www.lsh.se/hallwyl). T-bana Östermalmstorg/bus 47, 62, 69, 91. **Open** (guided tours only) *English End June-mid Aug* 1pm daily. *Mid Aug-end June* 1pm Sun. *Swedish End June-Aug* on the hr 11am-4pm Tue, Thur-Sun; on the hr 11am-4pm, 6pm Wed. *Sept-end June* on the hr noon-3pm Tue, Thur-Sun; on the hr noon-3pm, 6pm Wed. **Admission** 65kr; 30kr 7-18s; free under-7s. **Free with SC. Credit** AmEx, MC, V. **Map** p303 F8.

One of Stockholm's most eccentric and engaging museums, this palatial residence was built as a home for the immensely rich Count and Countess Walther and Wilhelmina von Hallwyl in 1898. Designed by Isak Gustav Clason (architect of the Nordiska Museet), it was very modern for its time, with electricity, central heating, bathrooms and phones. The countess was an avid collector – of pretty much everything, from paintings and furniture to silverware – and always planned that the house should become a museum (which it did in 1938). The tour takes you through an assortment of incredibly lavish rooms, decorated in a mix of historical styles and packed with objets d'art. Highlights include the green and gold skittle alley and the Steinway grand piano with its ornate, custom-made baroque casing. If you end up on a Swedish tour but don't speak Swedish, you can always borrow a pamphlet in English.

Historiska Museet

Narvavägen 13-17 (51 95 56 00/www.historiska.se). T-bana Karlaplan/bus 44, 47, 56, 69, 76. **Open** *Mid May-mid Sept* 11am-5pm daily. *Mid Sept-mid May* 11am-5pm Tue, Wed, Fri-Sun; 11am-8pm Thur. **Guided tours** *Summer* usually daily. *Winter* Sat, Sun. **Admission** 60kr; 50kr concessions; 35kr 13-16s; 140kr family; free under-13s. **Free with SC. Credit** AmEx, DC, MC, V. **Map** p304 F10.

Objects from the Stone Age to the 16th century are displayed in the Museum of National Antiquities, Sweden's largest archaeological museum. The plain design of this 1940 building – the façade looks like a tall brick wall with a door – gives no indication of the treasures within. To see the best exhibit, enter the darkened hall on the ground floor, where an impressive collection of Viking rune stones, swords, skeletons and jewellery is displayed. Detailed texts (in English) and maps describe the Vikings' economy, class structure, travels and methods of punishment. The remaining displays on the ground floor, covering earlier periods, are rather dull. In the large halls upstairs, you'll find beautiful wooden church altarpieces, textiles and other medieval ecclesiastical artworks. And don't miss the basement, where the circular Guldrummet (Gold Room) displays more than 3,000 artefacts in gold and silver, from the Bronze to the Middle Ages. This collection was made possible by a unique Swedish law, more than 300 years old, which entitles the finders of such treasures to payment equal to their market value. In the foyer there's a copy of an Athenian marble lion statue – check out the Viking graffiti on its side.

Kungliga Dramatiska Teatern

Nybrogatan 2 (tour information 665 61 15/667 84 00/www.dramaten.se). T-bana Kungsträdgården or Östermalmstorg/bus 46, 47, 55, 62, 69, 76, 91. **Guided tours** *June, July* 3pm daily. *Sept-May* 3pm Sat. Closed Aug. **Tickets** 40kr. **Free with SC. Credit** (Sept-May) AmEx, DC, MC, V. **Map** p303 F8.

The lavish Royal Dramatic Theatre, or Dramaten, was built between 1902 and 1908 in Jugendstil style, with a white marble façade and gilded bronzework.

The **Armémuseum** pulls no punches in showing the brutality of warfare. *See p96.*

Paintings and sculptures by Sweden's most famous artists decorate the building: Theodor Lundberg created the golden statues of *Poetry* and *Drama* at the front; Carl Milles was responsible for the large sculptural group below the raised central section of the façade; and Carl Larsson painted the foyer ceiling. The theatre's architect, Fredrik Liljekvist, wanted to create a grand and imposing structure, and added the domed attic to give the building more prominence. It worked – it's one of Stockholm's most striking structures, particularly when the setting sun hits the golden lampposts and statues. The auditorium is equally stunning. Ingmar Bergman still directs plays here, as he has for the past 40 years. A guided tour (phone first if you want it in English) covers the main stage, smaller stages and rehearsal rooms (July tours only happen if there's a show on). For a wonderful view over Nybroviken, visit the outdoor café on the second-floor balcony. *See also p230.*

Kungliga Hovstallet

Väpnargatan 1 (402 61 06/www.royalcourt.se). T-bana Östermalmstorg/bus 46, 47, 55, 62, 69, 76, 91. **Open** (guided tours only) *Mid Aug-mid June* 2pm Mon-Fri. *Mid June-mid Aug* 2pm Sat, Sun. **Tickets** 30kr; 10kr under-10s. **Free with SC. No credit cards. Map** p304 F9.

The royal family's own horses, carriages and cars are still taken care of in this late 19th-century striped brick building designed by architect Fritz Eckert. The building's so vast that it occupies almost the entire block next to Dramaten. A collection of 40 carriages from the 19th and 20th centuries (some still used for ceremonial occasions) stands in a long hall above the garage. Inside the garage are 11 cars, including a 1950 Daimler and a 1969 Cadillac Fleetwood. The stalls and riding arena may be empty if you visit in the summer, as this is when the horses are 'on vacation'. The tour (guides speak English) is not particularly thrilling.

Musikmuseet

Sibyllegatan 2 (51 95 54 90/www.musikmuseet.se). T-bana Östermalmstorg/bus 46, 47, 55, 62, 69, 76, 91. **Open** 11am-4pm Tue-Fri; noon-4pm Sat, Sun. **Admission** 40kr; 20kr concessions; free under-7s. **Free with SC. Credit** MC, V. **Map** p303 F8.

This fun, child-friendly museum teaches visitors about music and instruments through hands-on exhibits and recordings. With its stucco walls, wood-beamed ceilings and narrow window shutters, the building still looks much like the Crown Bakery it was from the 1640s to 1958, when it was supplying bread to the Swedish armed forces. On the entrance floor, the nature of sound is described and you can get your hands on several instruments, including the distinctly Swedish stringed *hommel.* On the floor below, 16 types of Swedish musical ensembles of the past 500 years are presented, among them a violin maker's workshop, a string quartet, a jazz band and, of course, ABBA. The Music Museum also has the largest collection of Swedish folk instruments in the world, plus folk instruments from Africa, Asia and elsewhere in Europe. Concerts are often held on Sundays (call for a programme), and the upper floor is reserved for temporary exhibitions, always worth a look. *See also p186.*

Sightseeing

Gärdet

The whole area to the east of Norrmalm was previously called Ladugårdsgärdet, which roughly translates as 'the field of barns'. As more affluent people moved into the district and the association with cattle became less desirable, the city voted in 1885 to change the name to Östermalm. Today, the residential area north of Valhallavägen is known as **Gärdet**, and the open field and forests to its south-east are once again referred to as **Ladugårdsgärdet**.

Functionalist apartment complexes were built for working people in Gärdet and its northern neighbour, **Hjorthagen**, in the 1930s. The apartments are now mainly inhabited by middle-class residents and students. The stately complexes of the **Försvarshögskolan** (Swedish National Defence College) and the **Kungliga Musikhögskolan** (Royal College of Music) are located next to each other on the northern side of Valhallavägen. Just across Lidingövägen (the main road that heads north to the island of Lidingö) stands the historic **Stockholms Stadion** (*see p226*), built for the 1912 Olympic Games. It was designed by architect Torben Grut in National Romantic style to resemble the walls surrounding a medieval city. Its twin brick towers are a striking landmark, and numerous sculptures of athletes dot the complex. Today, it's the home ground of Djurgården IF's football team.

Ladugårdsgärdet is part of Ekoparken, the world's first national city park, which also includes Djurgården, Norra Djurgården and the Fjäderholmarna islands. Mainly open grassland and woods, with a few scattered buildings, it stretches for about two-and-a-half kilometres (four miles) to the waters of Lilla Värtan, on the other side of which lies the island of Lidingö. Stockholmers come here to picnic, jog, ride horses or just get a taste of the countryside.

Nearer Östermalm, along the shoreline, there is also 'Museum Park', a convenient cluster of four museums: the **Sjöhistoriska Museet** (*see p100*), **Etnografiska Museet** (*see below*), **Tekniska Museet** (*see p100*) and the **Telemuseum** (*see p100*). Ultra-keen sightseers with a lot of stamina could try to visit the lot in one day. Bus 69 passes the museums, along Djurgårdsbrunnsvägen. Alternatively, follow the path next to the water. The view is stunning.

Further east – and also on the 69 bus route – is the **Kaknästornet** broadcasting tower (*see below*), rising up from the forest like a giant concrete spear chucked into the ground. Ascend to the observation deck at the top of the tower for a stunning view right across the city; high-altitude refreshments are available in the tower's restaurant and café.

If you follow Ladugårdsgärdet, the road that runs past the Kaknäs tower, north-east towards the water you will come to a dirt trail in the forest to your right that winds around the scenic shoreline of **Lilla Värtan**. A 100-year-old pet cemetery with dogs, cats and a circus horse lies to the right of the trail.

Etnografiska Museet

Djurgårdsbrunnsvägen 34 (51 95 50 00/www.etnografiska.se). Bus 69. **Open** 11am-5pm Tue, Thur-Sun; 11am-8pm Wed. **Guided tours** *Museum* children 1pm Sun; adults 2pm Sun. *Tea house* 5.30pm Wed. **Admission** 50kr; free under-21s. **Free with SC. Credit** MC, V. **Map** p305 F14.

Cultures from all over the world (except Europe) are presented in the exotic-looking National Museum of Ethnography. The dimly lit ground floor features masks, musical instruments and religious objects from seven holy cities (Auroville, Benin, Benares, Jerusalem, Yogyakarta, Beijing and Teotihuacan). The high ceiling of the second floor was specifically created for the Haisla totem pole, which is part of an exhibition on Native American culture. Near the stairs stands a Mongolian nomad tent that was brought back from an expedition to Central Asia in the 1920s. The wide variety of artefacts and colourful displays are worth seeing, but more explanations in English wouldn't hurt. When you're tired of feeling thoughtful, beers and teas of the world are served at the museum's mellow Babjan restaurant. In summer, the restaurant lends bamboo mats for sitting outside. You can also reserve a place for a tea ceremony in the Japanese tea house in the garden. The small shop sells ethnic toys, trinkets and books.

Kaknästornet

Mörka Kroken (789 24 35/restaurant 667 21 80). Bus 69. **Open** *Tower May-Aug* 9am-10pm daily. *Sept-Apr* 10am-9pm daily. *Restaurant* 10.30am-10pm daily. **Admission** 25kr; 15kr 7-15s; free under-7s. **Free with SC. Credit** AmEx, DC, MC, V.

For an utterly spectacular view of Stockholm and its surroundings, visit this 155m-high (510ft) tower – one of Scandinavia's tallest buildings. On a clear day you can see up to 60km (37 miles) from its observation points up on the 30th and 31st floors. Nearer to hand are the island of Djurgården to the south, Gamla

The best Viewpoints

Stockholm is a city of views. The open water and low-rise skyline mean there are numerous opportunities to catch a breathtaking vista, but certain vantage points should not be missed. Not in order of height…

Kaknästornet

One of Scandinavia's tallest buildings, in the centre of Ladugårdsgärdet. *See p98.*

Gondolen

Don't miss out on having dinner or cocktails at this bar/restaurant/viewing gallery at Slussen. *See p135.*

Söder cliffs

From the long steep cliffs of Södermalm the whole of the city is spreadeagled before you. Head for **Monteliusvägen**, the small path that winds along the front of the Maria cliffs, or to **Fjällgatan**, on the other side of Slussen, where there's an open terrace above the Katarina cliffs.

Stadshuset tower

A 360° view across Norrmalm, Kungsholmen and Gamla Stan (*pictured*). It's only open from May to September, though. *See p103.*

Skansen

It's hilly, so there are some good views across the city – to the north across Djurgårdsbrunnsviken from near the bear pit, and to the south across Saltsjön from the restaurant near Solliden, above the entrance gate. *See p84.*

Café Panorama

Spy on shoppers and skyscrapers while having a coffee break at the top-floor café of the Kulturhuset. *See p142.*

Gröna Lund

If you're quick and not made nauseous by funfair rides, you can grab a view on the move from the top of the Ferris wheel or the 80-metre-high (264 feet) free-fall 'power tower'. *See p185.*

Sky Bar

The panoramic windows of the ninth-storey bar at the Radisson SAS Royal Viking Hotel next to the Central Station, at the corner of Vasagatan and Klarabergsgatan, provide a unique view of the downtown area. It's open 5pm-2am Mon-Sat.

Kaknästornet: spectacular views. *See p98.*

Stan and downtown to the west, and the beginning of the archipelago to the east. Designed by Bengt Lindroos and Hans Borgström, the rather ugly concrete structure (itself visible from all over the city) was completed in 1967 and still transmits radio and TV broadcasts. On the ground floor, the Stockholm Information Service operates a busy visitor centre and gift shop. Lunch and dinner are served in the restaurant and café on floor 28. The tower was due to change hands at the end of 2002, so ring to check that the opening hours are the same.

Sjöhistoriska Museet

Djurgårdsbrunnsvägen 24 (51 95 49 00/www.sjohistoriska.nu). Bus 69. **Open** 10am-5pm daily. **Guided tours** adults 1pm, 3pm Sun; children 2pm Sun. **Admission** 50kr; 40kr concessions; 20kr 7-16s; free under-7s. Free Mon. **Free with SC. Credit** MC, V. **Map** p305 F13.

Hundreds of model ships – from Viking longboats to sailing ships, oil tankers and submarines – are displayed within the long, curved National Maritime Museum, designed in 1936 by Ragnar Östberg, the architect behind Stockholm's famous Stadshuset (*see p103*). Occupying a suitably watery setting, on the bank overlooking Djurgårdsbrunnsviken, it's an extensive and thorough survey – as it should be, considering Sweden's long and dramatic maritime history. Two floors of minutely detailed models are grouped in permanent exhibitions on merchant shipping, battleships and ocean liners. Ship figureheads depicting monsters and bare-breasted women decorate the museum walls, and the upper floor displays two ship's cabins from the 1870s and 1970s. But unless you're a nautical or miniatures enthusiast, it can all be a bit too much, and the temporary exhibitions are probably the main reason for coming here; Arctic expeditions and archaeological finds from the Baltic Sea have featured recently. In the basement, the children's room Saltkråkan offers ships and a lighthouse to play in, and a kids' workshop is run every Sunday (noon-4pm).

Tekniska Museet

Museivägen 7 (450 56 00/www.tekniskamuseet.se). Bus 69. **Open** 10am-5pm Mon, Tue, Thur, Fri; 10am-8pm Wed; 11am-5pm Sat, Sun. **Guided tours** *Engine Hall* adults 1pm Sat, Sun. *Mine* children 1pm Sat, Sun. *Miniature railway* 3pm Mon-Fri; noon, 3pm Sat, Sun. **Admission** (incl Telemuseum) 60kr; 40kr concessions; 30kr 6-19s; 120kr family; free under-6s. Free 5-8pm Wed. **Free with SC. Credit** MC, V. **Map** p305 G14.

The Museum of Science and Technology fills about 18,000sq m (20,000sq yds) with exhibits and activities intended to entertain and educate children and adults – and they do. Sweden's biggest and oldest steam engine, built in 1832, dominates the large Engine Hall, where aeroplanes – including one of Sweden's first commercial aircraft, a Junkers from 1924 – hang from the ceiling above bicycles, engines and cars. Among the cars are early automobiles from Volvo and Saab. A dark stairwell leads down from here into an exceptional re-creation of a mine. In the History of Electric Power, a recreated street from 1915 comes complete with a trolley car, workshop and streetlamps. Kids get their own special rooms: in the Teknorama, children can conduct scientific experiments with trick mirrors, pulleys and levers, and operate the cameras in a TV studio. For smaller children there are the slides and tunnels of the Minirama. The museum is a fun place to spend a couple of hours, and no one is going to notice if you skip a few hundred square metres. You can also take a break in the cafeteria, and pick up a *Star Trek* uniform in the gift shop on your way out.

Telemuseum

Museivägen 7 (670 81 00/www.telemuseum.se). Bus 69. **Open** 10am-5pm Mon, Tue, Thur, Fri; 10am-8pm Wed; 11am-5pm Sat, Sun. **Admission** (incl Tekniska Museet) 60kr; 40kr concessions; 30kr 6-19s; 120kr family; free under-6s. Free 5-8pm Wed. **Free with SC. Credit** MC, V. **Map** p305 G14.

The Telemuseum's two floors display telephones, radios and TVs behind glass, described by Swedish text. There's also a two-storey room commemorating LM Ericsson, the founder of the Swedish telecommunications industry; an original 1903 meeting room from the Ericsson phone company, it was moved inside the museum in 1976. Peek through the windows to see the opulent mahogany furnishings and the cupids in the ceiling corners talking on phones. Another point of interest in the otherwise lacklustre museum is its new high-tech exhibition on mobile phones with interactive computers and displays. Entrance is via the Tekniska Museet (*see above*) and one fee covers both museums.

Kungsholmen

Home of the monumental Stadshuset, shoreside walks and good restaurants.

Separated from Norrmalm and Vasastaden by a narrow channel, Barnhusviken, the island of Kungsholmen is a bounty of offices, apartment complexes and government agencies. It has little in the way of major sights – the magnificent and not-to-be-missed **Stadshuset** (City Hall; *see p103*), on the island's eastern tip, is the main attraction for visitors – but the island's wide residential streets and quiet parks make a pleasant alternative to the hustle and bustle of the city centre.

It's a predominantly middle-class area – but with a younger and less snobbish population than posh Östermalm on the other side of Norrmalm – and has all the comforts associated with a middle-class lifestyle: good neighbourhood restaurants, popular but not achingly trendy bars, individual shops – all catering for locals rather than tourists.

During the 1640s, craftsmen and factory owners were lured to Kungsholmen, which was then still mostly covered in fields, by the promise of a ten-year tax break. The island rapidly became a home to the smelly, fire-prone and dangerous businesses that no one else wanted. Its cheery reputation didn't improve when Sweden's first hospital, the Serafimerlasarettet, was built here in the 1750s and several more followed. At the time of the Industrial Revolution, the conditions were so dismal on Kungsholmen that it was nicknamed 'Starvation Island'. The factories finally left the island in the early 1900s, to be replaced by the city's government agencies and numerous apartment buildings.

The quickest way to get to the **Stadshuset** is to walk across Stadshusbron bridge from Norrmalm – though navigating the roads and railway lines leading from the Central Station can be a bit of a nightmare. The Stadshuset is on your left – its gigantic structure is hard to miss – and the former Serafimerlasarettet hospital on your right. If you continue on down Hantverkargatan, you'll soon reach **Kungsholms Kyrka**, a 17th-century church with a Greek-cross plan and a park-like cemetery. Two blocks further on, a right on to **Scheelegatan** will leave you on one of Kungsholmen's major thoroughfares, packed with restaurants and bars.

Further along Scheelegatan, on the corner of Bergsgatan, squats the city's gigantic, majestic **Rådhuset** (courthouse), designed by Carl Westman (1866-1936), a leading architect of the National Romantic School. Completed in 1915, it was designed to look like 16th-century Vadstena castle in southern Sweden, but there are also touches of art nouveau. There are no guided tours, but you can wander around the public areas, which include a very pleasant cloister-like garden with a sundial.

Behind the courthouse lies the police headquarters; you might want to time your visit so you can tour its macabre **Polishistoriska Museet** (Police History Museum; *see p103*). Continuing west on Bergsgatan, you arrive at **Kronobergsparken**, a pleasant hillside park with a cemetery for Stockholm's first Jewish inhabitants in its north-west corner. To the north of the island is the **Tullmuseet** (Customs Museum; *see p103*), situated within the Customs Office on Alströmergatan. Nearby is one of Stockholm's trendiest interior design shops, **R.O.O.M.** (*see p171*).

Kungsholmen's main shopping streets are **St Eriksgatan** and **Fleminggatan**, particularly around the Fridhemsplan Tunnelbana station. The former is a godsend for music lovers, containing a huge number of second-hand CD and vinyl shops, lined up one after the other. Stop for coffee and cakes at **Thelins** (*see p148*), one of the city's best traditional *konditori*. A brand-new shopping mall, **Västermalmsgallerian** (*see p153*), opened in August 2002 on the corner of St Eriksgatan and Fleminggatan.

The huge but oddly elegant double-spanned **Västerbron** bridge connects Kungsholmen, across the blue expanse of Lake Mälaren, with Södermalm. Built in 1935, it's often crowded with traffic, but if you can face the noise and fumes you'll get a spectacular view of Stockholm from the centre of the bridge. **Marieberg**, the area on Kungsholmen just to the north of the bridge, once contained military installations and a porcelain factory, but has been the city's main newspaper district since the 1960s.

Two of the four Stockholm dailies – *Dagens Nyheter* and *Expressen* – have their offices in Marieberg (*Svenksa Dagbladet* was there too, but moved to Norrmalm in 2001). The *DN/ Expressen* building, which was designed by Paul Hedqvist in the early 1960s, is pretty

Sightseeing

The landmark 1923 **Stadshuset**, home of the annual Nobel Prize banquet. *See p103.*

prominent, soaring to 82 metres (270 feet), and is one of the city's landmarks; its neon sign is visible for miles at night.

The flat green lawns of adjoining **Rålambshovparken** were created in 1935, at the same time as Västerbron; it's popular with runners, sunbathers and picnickers, and there's a small sandy beach just along the shore at **Smedsuddsbadet** (*see p91* **Where to swim outdoors**). Look out also for various interesting sculptures in the park. There is not much to see west of St Görans Sjukhus (hospital), near the middle of Kungsholmen, except for apartment buildings, two athletic fields and the E4/E20 highway that cuts right across the island.

Walking and bicycle paths line both the northern and southern shores of Kungsholmen. For a beautiful view across the water, stroll from the Stadshuset along **Mälarpromenaden**, which is lined with willow, birch, poplar and alder trees. Vintage boats and yachts are moored here too, and there are a couple of well-placed cafés en route. **Norr Mälarstrand**, the road that runs alongside the promenade, is lined with grand apartment blocks, built in the early 20th century when the factories had finally departed. Look out particularly for No.76, designed by Ragnar Östberg, who was also the architect of the Stadshuset.

Stadshuset

Hantverkargatan 1 (50 82 90 59/www.stockholm.se/stadshuset). T-bana T-Centralen/bus 3, 62. **Open** *Stadshuset* (guided tours only) *May-Aug* 10am, 11am, noon, 2pm, 3pm daily. *Sept-Apr* 10am, noon, 2pm daily. *Tower May-Sept* 10am-4.30pm daily. Tower closed Oct-Mar. **Admission** Guided tour 50kr; tower 15kr; free under-12s. **Free with SC. Credit** AmEx, DC, MC, V. **Map** p302 H5.

The City Hall (1923), Stockholm's most prominent landmark, stands imposingly on the northern shore of Riddarfjärden. A massive red-brick building, it was designed by Ragnar Östberg (1866-1945) in the National Romantic style, with two inner courtyards and a 106m (348ft) tower. It's most famous for hosting the annual Nobel Prize banquet, held in the Blue Hall on 10 December and attended by 1,300 guests, after the prizes have been awarded at the Konserthuset (*see p104* **Alfred Nobel & the Nobel Prizes**). The hall – designed to look like an Italian Renaissance piazza – was supposed to be painted blue, but Östberg liked the way the sun hit the red bricks and changed his mind. The hall is also the home of an immense organ, with over 10,000 pipes and 138 stops. In the truly gobsmacking Golden Hall upstairs, scenes from Swedish history are depicted on the walls in 18 million mosaic pieces. The artist, Einar Forseth, covered the northern wall with a mosaic known as 'Queen of Lake Mälaren', representing Stockholm being honoured from all sides.The beamed ceiling of the Council Chamber, where the city council meets every other Monday, resembles the open roof of a Viking longhouse; the furniture was designed by Swede Carl Malmsten.

You can only visit the interior of the Stadshuset by guided tour, but you can climb the tower on your own. Follow a series of winding red-brick slopes then wooden stairs for a fantastic view over Gamla Stan. Three gold crowns – the Tre Kronor, Sweden's heraldic symbol – top the tower. At the edge of the outdoor terrace below the tower, by the waters of Riddarfjärden, are two statues by famous Swedish sculptor Carl Eldh (1873-1954): the female *Dansen* (Dance) and the male *Sången* (Song). For refreshments, a cafeteria-style restaurant, entered from the outdoor courtyard, serves classic Swedish dishes at lunchtime, while the Stadshuskällaren cellar restaurant offers the previous year's menu from the Nobel banquet (cooked fresh, presumably).

Polishistoriska Museet

Polhemsgatan 30 (401 90 63/64/www.police.se). T-bana Rådhuset/bus 40, 52, 62. **Open** (guided tours only) 2.30pm Tue-Fri. **Admission** 60kr; 40kr concessions. **Free with SC. No credit cards. Map** p302 G3.

The Museum of Police History, in the basement of the city's police headquarters, presents confiscated items from some of the most sensational crimes in Swedish history. Despite the museum's name, the collection of police badges and uniforms occupies only a small section of the long room. The rest of the exhibits consist of punishment devices from the past 300 years, drug paraphernalia, equipment from a terrorist organisation and a gallery of counterfeit paintings. The final section is certainly not for the squeamish – it contains murder weapons, horribly gruesome black and white photos, and stained suitcases that were not used for carrying clothes. The bank vault at Norrmalmstorg, where hostages were taken during a famous robbery in 1973, has also been re-created. If you're the type of person who slows down to look at automobile accidents, you will probably enjoy this museum. It's only open for guided tours – in Swedish – but you can show up at the time of the tour and read the descriptive texts in English. Not a museum for kids.

Tullmuseet

Alströmergatan 39 (653 05 03/www.tullverket.se/museum). T-bana Fridhemsplan/bus 1, 3, 4, 57. **Open** 11am-4pm Tue-Sun. **Admission** free.

The most interesting part of the Customs Museum is its section on smuggling. Here you see the loaves of bread, teddy bears and sofas in which people have tried to sneak drugs across the borders of Sweden. In 1622 a fence and toll (*tull*) booths were built around the edge of Stockholm to raise money for the wars of King Gustav II Adolf, and the museum also displays a copy of one of these toll booths, as well as an early 20th-century customs office and laboratory. The text in English is minimal, but the museum is free so you might want to take a quick peek if you're in the neighbourhood.

Alfred Nobel & the Nobel Prizes

Popular myth has it that after Alfred Nobel invented dynamite he felt so guilty about how it was used in warfare that he left most of his fortune to the Nobel Prizes. Reality suggests otherwise, however – Nobel never actually expressed remorse about his invention, and continued to develop weapons technology throughout his life.

Born in Stockholm in 1833, Nobel was nine when his family moved to St Petersburg, where his father manufactured naval mines for the tsar. Nobel received a first-rate education and was fluent in five languages. During his studies abroad, he met the inventor of nitroglycerine, Ascanio Sobrero, and on his return to Russia in 1852 he and his father investigated ways to make the explosive liquid less volatile.

In 1863 Nobel moved to Sweden and soon began mass-producing nitroglycerine. When a year later his brother and four others were killed in an explosion, Nobel was prohibited from experimenting within the city limits. Nobel eventually discovered that by mixing nitroglycerine with silica a stable paste was formed that could be shaped into rods. He patented his dynamite in 1867, taking the name from *dunamis*, the Greek for power.

A dynamic scientist, inventor and industrialist, at the time of his death Nobel held 355 patents and owned 90 companies in 20 countries. He had also written several poems, drafted three novels and even published his own play. He may have been inspired to leave his wealth to a good cause by his long friendship with the Austrian peace activist Bertha von Suttner, who wrote the book *Lay Down Your Arms* in 1889. Expressing not quite the same sentiment, Nobel believed that one of the best deterrents to war was the production of weapons so ghastly that no nation would dare to use them.

When Nobel died alone in his home in Italy in 1896, his one-page will stated that his estate should be used for 'prizes to those who, during the preceding year, shall have conferred the greatest benefit on mankind'. Nobel specified in the will the categories of physics, chemistry, physiology or medicine, literature and peace. In 1969 the Swedish National Bank contributed money for the creation of an economics prize.

The cash amount awarded varies; in 2000 the Nobel Prize laureates each received about US$1,000,000. The Swedish king hands out the prizes at the Konserthuset on 10 December, the anniversary of Nobel's death, followed by a lavish banquet in the Stadshuset's **Blue Hall** (*pictured*). Sweden and Norway were a political union when Nobel died, and it is perhaps for this reason that Nobel selected Norway to award the peace prize, which it does, on the same day, in Oslo City Hall.

For more information on Nobel, the prizes and previous laureates, visit the **Nobelmuseet** (*see p63*) or check www.nobel.se.

Further Afield

Attractions natural and man-made await a few miles from the city.

Haga & around

If you like parks, you'll definitely want to explore the rolling green lawns and 18th-century architecture of **Hagaparken**, located north-west of Vasastaden on the edge of the Brunnsviken inlet. King Gustav III bought the land in the 1770s and transformed it, with the help of architect Fredrik Magnus Piper, into a romantic English-style park with wandering paths, scenic views and assorted pavilions. It's now part of Ekoparken, the world's first national city park.

In Haga's northern section stand the lush greenhouses of **Fjärilshuset** (*see p184*), full of exotic butterflies and tropical rainforest vegetation. To the south two colourful copper tents, **Koppartälten** – built as Gustav III's stables and guards' quarters – house a restaurant and café. The 'ruins' of a palace left incomplete after Gustav III's assassination in 1792 are situated just to the east of the tents. Sweden's current king, Carl XVI Gustaf, was born in nearby **Haga Slott**, now run as a hotel and conference centre. Other buildings include the waterfront **Gustav III's Paviljong**, with Pompeian style interiors by Louis Masreliéz. It's open for guided tours in summer (June-Aug noon, 1pm, 2pm, 3pm Tue-Sun; 50kr). You can also test the acoustics in the outdoor **Ekotemplet**, originally used as a summer dining room. The 18th-century's obsession with the exotic is evident in the Chinese pagoda and Turkish pavilion in the south of the park. A small island nearby (May 1-3pm Sun; June-Aug 9am-3pm Thur) has been the burial place of Swedish royalty since the 1910s.

On the southern tip of Hagaparken, enjoy a meal or weekend brunch at **Haga Forum**, a bus-terminal-turned-restaurant with a terrace that overlooks the park and water. The nearby **Carl Eldhs Ateljémuseum** (*see below*), located south of Bellevueparken, contains sculptures by this famous 20th-century Swedish artist (1873-1954).

Across the E4 highway to the west stands the **Medicinhistoriska Museet** (*see below*) – which hopefully will be your only reason for visiting the hospital grounds of Karolinska Sjukhuset. Sculptures by some of Sweden's best-known artists stand in **Solna Kyrkogard**, an elaborate late 19th-century cemetery to the north of the hospital. Amid its hedges and landscaped hills you can find the graves of Alfred Nobel, August Strindberg and Ingrid Bergman.

Bus 3 or 52 will take you to Karolinska Sjukhuset from where you can walk to southern Hagaparken. For northern Haga, take the T-bana to Odenplan then catch bus 515; get off at the Haga Norra stop. A good way to explore Brunnsviken is by vintage steamboat operated by Ekoparken (58 71 40 14; 40kr). It runs daily from July to mid August, with stops at Frescati, Fjärilshuset, Haga Slott and Haga Forum.

Carl Eldhs Ateljémuseum

Lögebodavägen 10, Bellevueparken (612 65 60/ http://hotel.telemuseum.se/carleldhsatelje/). Bus 40, 46, 52, 73. **Open** (guided tours only) *Swedish* on the hr noon-3pm, *English* 1.30pm *June-Aug* Tue-Sun. *May, Sept* Sat, Sun. *Apr, Oct* Sun. *Nov-Mar* tours by appointment. **Admission** 40kr; 30kr concessions; 20kr 7-18s; free under-7s. **No credit cards. Map** p307 A5.

Eldh's former studio, built by his friend, architect Ragnar Östberg, who's better known for having designed the Stadshuset, is now a museum containing more than 400 of the artist's works in plaster, clay, bronze and marble. Several of his more famous monuments that you can see around Stockholm are here, including the Olympic runners outside Stadion, the male and female figures by the Stadshuset waterfront and the Strindberg statue in Tegnérlunden.

Medicinhistoriska Museet

Eugeniahemmet, Karolinska Sjukhuset, Solna (54 54 51 50/www.medhm.se). Bus 3, 52, 73. **Open** 11am-4pm Tue, Thur-Sun; 11am-7pm Wed. **Admission** 40kr; 30kr concessions; 10kr 8-16s; free under-8s. **No credit cards. Map** p306 B3.

Objects reflecting more than two centuries of medical development are displayed in this intriguing museum. Situated in Eugeniahemmet, a former home for incurably sick children, each room focuses on a different field of medicine. Early prosthetic devices feature in the orthopaedics room, while the psychiatry room contains a large tub covered with canvas used for 'calming' baths and a model of a spinning chair that made troublemakers nauseous. There's also a pre-electricity dentist's office, a late 19th-century birthing room and a new display on disease, with disgusting wax models of infected body parts. It will all make you very glad you're alive now, not then. Almost everything is labelled in Swedish, so borrow an English booklet from the front desk. The gift shop sells plastic skeletons.

It's a jungle out there: lush **Fjärilshuset** in **Hagaparken**. *See p105.*

Northern Frescati

Stockholm's main scientific and academic institutions are clustered one kilometre north of the city on the eastern shore of Brunnsviken. The Royal Swedish Academy of Sciences and the **Naturhistoriska Riksmuseet** (*see p107*) are situated on either side of the noisy thoroughfare of Roslagsvägen, which connects to the E18 to the north. Further west stand the lovely gardens and greenhouses of **Bergianska Trädgården** (*see below*). The sprawling **Stockholm University** campus to the south, in Frescati, was built in the 1970s and is one of Sweden's largest, with 34,000 students. From the campus you can head east to **Norra Djurgården** for hiking, horse riding or birdwatching, or west to swim or rent canoes at **Brunnsviksbadet**.

You can get to northern Frescati on the T-bana to Universitetet station, then walk for about seven minutes. Alternatively, take the Roslagsbanan commuter train, which leaves from Stockholm's Östra station near the Tekniska Högskolan. Get off at Frescati station: the gardens and museum are directly to the west and east, respectively. If you continue on the Roslagsbanan for 15 minutes, you'll arrive in **Djursholm**, one of Sweden's wealthiest neighbourhoods and the home of ABBA's Björn Ulvaeus.

Bergianska Trädgården

Frescati (15 65 45/www.bergianska.se). T-bana Universitetet/bus 40, 540. **Open** *Gardens* 9am-8pm daily. *Edvard Andersons Växthus* 11am-5pm daily. *Victoriahuset May-Sept* 11am-4pm Mon-Fri; 11am-5pm Sat, Sun. Closed Oct-Apr. **Admission** *Gardens* free. *Edvard Andersons Växthus* 40kr. *Victoriahuset* 15kr. Free under-15s. **Free with SC**. **Credit** MC, V.

Amateur botanists and picnickers will love this idyllic park and botanical garden situated on a hilly peninsula by Brunnsviken. The Royal Swedish Academy of Sciences, which still conducts research here, moved the garden from Vasastaden to its current waterfront location in 1885. Orchids and clinging vines fill Victoriahuset, a small greenhouse from 1900; its pond contains giant water lilies measuring up to 2.5m (8ft) across. The more recent Edvard Andersons Växthus, an all-glass greenhouse with slanted walls, contains Mediterranean plants and trees in its central room and flora from Australia, South Africa, the Californian coast and a rainforest in four corner rooms. Its restaurant is a popular spot to thaw out in winter. The paths outside curve around the shore and hills, giving you beautiful views of Haga Park across the water, and a chance to check out the 9,000 species of plants growing nearby. You can also take a meditative stroll across the little island in the middle of the Japanese pond, or enjoy the pastries in the Gamla Orangeriet's summer café. If all this gets your green fingers itching, stop by the Plantagen nursery and garden supply shop on your way out.

Naturhistoriska Riksmuseet

Frescativägen 40 (51 95 40 00/www.nrm.se). T-bana Universitetet/bus 40, 540. **Open** *May, Midsummer-Aug* 10am-7pm Mon-Wed, Fri-Sun; 10am-8pm Thur. *Sept-Apr, June* 10am-7pm Tue, Wed, Fri-Sun; 10am-8pm Thur. **Admission** *Museum* 65kr; 50kr concessions; 40kr 6-18s; free under-6s. *IMAX* 75kr; 50kr 5-18s. *Museum & IMAX* 120kr; 105kr concessions; 80kr 6-18s. **Museum free with SC. Credit** AmEx, MC, V.

Founded in 1739, the National Museum of Natural History is today the largest museum complex in Sweden. More than nine million biological and mineral samples are stored in this monolithic brick building designed in 1907 by Axel Anderberg, architect of the Royal Opera. Beneath the black-shingled roof and light-filled cupola you'll find exceptionally well-made tableaux of extinct creatures, prehistoric man and Swedish wildlife. Visitors enter the dinosaur exhibit through a dark volcano environment to see sharp-toothed birds sitting in trees above a skeletal T-Rex and life-like Plateosaurus. The hands-on exhibits about space and the human body include a red Martian landscape, a spaceship's cockpit and a gigantic walk-through mouth. The older exhibits are labelled in Swedish only, so borrow a booklet in English from the information desk. Sweden's only IMAX theatre, the Cosmonova (*see p198*), opened in 1993 and shows movies about the natural world on its 11m-high (36ft) dome-shaped screen – which also functions as a planetarium. To hear the soundtrack in English, rent a headset for 10kr; under-5s are not admitted. The gift shop sells a wide assortment of popular science books, plastic animals and polished rocks, and there's also a cafeteria-style restaurant downstairs.

Lidingö

On the residential island of Lidingö, one kilometre north-east of the city centre, green parks and forests surround the apartment complexes and houses of the middle and upper-middle classes. The main attraction is **Millesgården** (*see below*), the former home and studio of the sculptor Carl Milles, which sits on a hill in the south-west of the island above the waters of Lilla Värtan.

The island is also popular with outdoor enthusiasts. There's an 18-hole golf course near Sticklinge, and cycling and jogging paths around Stockby Motionsgård, which are converted into cross-country ski trails during the winter. Lidingö also offers one of the nearest downhill ski slopes to Stockholm at the 70-metre high (230-foot) **Ekholmsnäsbacken**, situated south of the Hustegafjärden inlet that cuts into the middle of the island. At **Fågelöuddebadet** in Lidingö's north-east corner, there's a popular beach, café and miniature golf course.

Millesgården

Heserudsvagen 30 (446 75 90/www.millesgarden.se). T-bana Ropsten then bus 207 or bus 201, 202, 204, 205, 206, 207, 212 to Torsvik then walk. **Open** *Mid May-Aug* 10am-5pm daily. *Sept-mid May* noon-4pm Tue-Fri; 11am-5pm Sat, Sun. **Admission** 75kr; 60kr concessions; 20kr 7-16s; free under-7s. **Free with SC. Credit** AmEx, DC, MC, V.

Works by Sweden's most famous sculptor, Carl Milles (1875-1955), are displayed at his home and studio, which he donated to the state in 1936. Wide stone terraces with views of the water hold copies of his bronze statues, as well as work by other artists. The house, built in 1908, is decorated with paintings, drawings and antiques purchased by Milles on his travels. He also amassed the largest private collection of Greek and Roman statues in Sweden. The studio was not as tranquil as it appears today during three days in 1917, when Milles decided to destroy all his work and start again from scratch. After emigrating to the US in 1931, he became a professor at Cranbrook Academy of Art in Michigan, where he created more than 70 sculptures – the nude ones often had to be fitted with fig leaves. The museum's café serves nice cakes and pastries, as well as beer and wine, and outdoor concerts are held in summer.

Millesgården: Milles' *Hand of God.*

Eat, Drink, Shop

Restaurants **110**
Bars **130**
Cafés **140**
Shops & Services **149**

Features

The best restaurants 116
Husmanskost 118
Super Swedes: Mathias Dahlgren 121
The best bars 130
The best cafés 143
Food markets 163
How to buy alcohol 166
Glass with class 172

Restaurants

Fashion, fusion and fish – the key ingredients of Stockholm's dining scene.

Over the past decade the number of restaurants in Stockholm has more than doubled, and a lot has happened on the previously rather dull dining scene. Nowadays you'll find reducing, souffléing and caramelising not only in the affluent business district around Stureplan but just about all over the city. The city's restaurants are constantly getting more ambitious, more experimental and even trendier – which is a bit of a double-edged sword. The interest in new places is vast, which makes it easy for a brand-new venture to attract a crowd of eager diners – but difficult to turn them into regular customers. And many new restaurants concentrate, to their cost, on the decor and concept, which at times leads to trendiness with a clear expiry date.

The area around Stureplan has the greatest concentration of restaurants, and it's here that you'll find the city's most exclusive, fashionable – and most expensive – places. On Södermalm, the restaurant scene has exploded over the past ten years. The area's numerous new bars and restaurants attract a young and price-sensitive crowd – a particularly good area for cheap eating options is around Medborgarplatsen. Another neighbourhood that's seen major changes in recent years is Vasastaden, especially the streets around Odenplan. Stockholm's attempt at a Chinatown is Luntmakargatan, parallel to Sveavägen.

Crossover or fusion cuisine – where oriental cooking techniques or flavourings are used to jazz up European ingredients – still reigns pretty much supreme in Stockholm (as it does everywhere else). But you'll also find plenty of traditional Swedish cooking, known as *husmanskost* ('house food') – both old-fashioned places that seemingly haven't changed recipes or decor for years as well as modernised and poshed-up versions of classic dishes. For more information on key ingredients and dishes, *see p118* **Husmanskost.**

French and Mediterranean influences are just about everywhere, and more and more restaurateurs are finding their way back to the classic brasserie in terms of concept and cookery; you'll find an increasing number of capacious premises attracting a wide audience with unpretentious service and menus that cater for every wallet. From being somewhat culturally isolated as late as the 1980s, Stockholm is increasingly cosmopolitan. Inevitably, it doesn't offer the same range of international cuisines as larger cities, but there are quite a few places offering Thai, Vietnamese, Malaysian, Kurdish, Lebanese or Cantonese food.

The restaurants of the moment are always packed, so it can sometimes be a battle to find a free table, even on weekdays. For the most popular places, you should book in advance, especially for Fridays and Saturdays. Stockholmers are also driven by pay day, the 25th of every month. In the preceding days the restaurants are deserted, only to be filled by a starving crowd when pay day comes. Some places don't take bookings, but it's still wise to give your chosen restaurant a call a couple of hours before you go. Note that many of the better restaurants close down in July – not the best month for gourmands to visit Stockholm.

Children are welcome everywhere, even in the smartest restaurants, and many places provide high chairs and kids' menus. Very few restaurants are completely no-smoking, but most have a no-smoking section.

If you're after fast food on the run, burgers, kebabs, hot dogs and paninis can be bought in most neighbourhoods. More traditional but rarer are the Swedish *strömming* stands, which serve delicious fried fish on a piece of bread.

PRICES, TIMING AND TIPPING

Unfortunately, it is still expensive to eat out in Sweden's capital. Stockholmers tend to go to a restaurant in order to have a whole new food experience rather than just a simple well-cooked meal in an informal environment. This, of course, has an effect on the atmosphere as well as the prices – places can often be more pretentious than cosy. Don't expect restaurants serving Swedish food to be automatically cheaper; Swedish cuisine appears at the upper end of the price scale, together with French and Italian. There are restaurants that serve simple and straightforward Swedish food, but they're rare. If you're looking for a budget meal, your best bet is Indian, Thai or Turkish.

For something fairly fancy at a reasonable price, it's a good idea to have your main meal at lunchtime rather than in the evening. Most Stockholmers eat a proper meal between noon and 1pm (this was once subsidised by the government, which claimed that citizens worked better if they ate a healthy lunch),

Classy **Pontus in the Green House.**

when many restaurants swap their à la carte menu for a fixed-price menu at a considerably lower price – look out for signs offering 'Dagens Lunch' or 'Dagens Rätt'. In the evening, people tend to eat early, around 7-8pm. Most kitchens close around 11pm, even if the restaurant's bar stays open later.

Service charge is included in the bill, but it's still common to tip ten to 20 per cent, unless you're unhappy with the food or service.

Gamla Stan

American/French

Bistro Ruby & Grill Ruby

Österlånggatan 14 (20 60 15/57 76/www.bistroruby.com). T-bana Gamla Stan/bus 43, 46, 55, 59, 76. **Open** *Restaurant* 5-11pm daily. *Bar* 5pm-1am daily. Closed 2wks from Midsummer. **Main courses** Bistro Ruby 170kr-279kr; Grill Ruby 129kr-255kr. **Credit** AmEx, DC, MC, V. **Map** p309 J8.

These two sister restaurants set out to combine Paris and Texas. Bistro Ruby offers European formality in a classically pleasant environment ideal for a quiet chat. The menu goes from classic French to more modern Mediterranean influences, and it's all well cooked, tasty and not overworked. Grill Ruby next door is noisier and more fun. And it's all about meat – grilled with love and served in huge quantities – so vegetarians should steer clear. With each piece of meat you get a wide choice of tapas, salsas, sauces and other accompaniments. The weekend brunch is recommended.

Contemporary

Mandus

Österlånggatan 7 (20 60 55). T-bana Gamla Stan/bus 43, 46, 55, 59, 76. **Open** 5pm-midnight daily. **Main courses** 128kr-200kr. **Credit** AmEx, DC, MC, V. **Map** p303 H8.

This tiny, lively gay bar offers simple plain food – nourishing soups, tender beef dishes – at reasonable prices. The atmosphere is frolicsome, bordering on the insane, with personal service and loud music. The place for a nibble, drink and buzz before the drag show and the wild party begins. *See also p206.*

Pontus in the Green House

Österlånggatan 17 (23 85 00/www.pontusfrithiof.com). T-bana Gamla Stan/bus 43, 46, 55, 59, 76. **Open** *Mid Aug-June* 11.30am-3pm, 6-11pm Mon-Fri; 5-11pm Sat. *July-mid Aug* 6-11pm Mon-Fri; 5-11pm Sat. **Main courses** 325kr-450kr. **Set menus** 895kr; 1,100kr. **Credit** AmEx, DC, MC, V. **Map** p303 J8.

If you close a business deal, launch a successful takeover bid or just win the lottery while in Stockholm, this is the place to burn a substantial share of the profits. It's a luxury restaurant in the true sense of the word, watched over by star chef Pontus Frithiof. Truffles, foie gras, Iranian caviar and plenty of other exclusive ingredients are given the full works. Most exciting are the two Pontus Temptation menus, entitled Classique Rustique and Moderne Innovatif. There are also reliable vegetarian dishes and the odd traditional Swedish creation. The wine list is filled with collectors' wines, so don't automatically go for the second most expensive.

Traditional Swedish

Den Gyldene Freden

Österlånggatan 51 (24 97 60/www.gyldenefreden.se). T-bana Gamla Stan/bus 43, 46, 55, 59, 76. **Open** *Restaurant* 6-11pm Mon-Fri. *Bar* 6pm-midnight Mon-Fri; 1-11pm Sat. **Main courses** 98kr-445kr. **Set menu** 468kr. **Credit** AmEx, DC, MC, V. **Map** p303 J8.

This first-class restaurant is housed in an 18th-century building owned by the Swedish Academy, and there is certainly something reverently grandiose about the gloomy interior. Head chef Ulf Kappen focuses on heavy Swedish ingredients (pike-perch, reindeer, duck) and methods, but does it with an obvious creative joy and brilliance. Kappen's stuffed pigs' trotters is as elegant a classic as it is unconventional. As is the crayfish sausage. As well as such artistic creations requiring platinum credit cards, there are ambitious vegetarian dishes and more traditional Swedish dishes.

BELLINI
MEHUL
GADE
SCHUBERT

Norrmalm

Contemporary

Berns Salonger

Berzelii Park (56 63 22 22/www.berns.se). T-bana Kungsträdgården/bus 46, 47, 55, 69, 76. **Open** *Mid Aug-June* 11.30am-3pm Mon, Sun; 11.30am-3pm, 5-11pm Tue-Thur; 11.30am-3pm, 5-11.30pm Fri, Sat. *July-mid Aug* 11.30am-3pm Mon, Sun; 11.30am-3pm, 5-11pm Tue-Thur; 11.30am-11.30pm Fri; 1-11.30pm Sat. **Main courses** 245kr. **Set menu** 345 kr. **Credit** AmEx, DC, MC, V. **Map** p303 G8.

When Sir Terence Conran took over this palace-like restaurant with its jaw-dropping decor and grand traditions a few years back, many were suspicious. And, indeed, some of the original charm has been lost, but it's also far more exciting now. The big busy kitchen is trying its best to be industrial and innovative at the same time. The result is crossover cuisine based in the Mediterranean; ambitious but not always that creative. The clientele consists mainly of well-dressed tourists and business people from the nearby financial district. One of the private dining rooms at Berns was the inspiration for Strindberg's *The Red Room*. The various bars (*see p131*) are always packed.

Bon Lloc

Regeringsgatan 111 (660 60 60/10 76 35). T-bana Rådmansgatan/bus 42, 43, 44, 46, 52. **Open** *Aug-June Restaurant* 5-11pm Mon-Sat. *Bar* 5pm-midnight Mon-Sat. Closed July. **Main courses** *Restaurant* 250kr-325kr. *Bar* 105kr-235kr. **Set menus** 635kr; 1,050kr. **Credit** AmEx, DC, MC, V. **Map** p307 D7.

Bon Lloc ('Good Place' in Catalan) is definitely the most avant-garde restaurant in town. Chef Mathias Dahlgren (*see p121* **Super Swedes: Mathias Dahlgren**) has been perfecting his own special 'Estilo Nuevo Euro-Latino' cuisine for some years. He started out in a small cornershop restaurant in Kungsholmen (today's worthy successor being Perssons – *see p129*), then moved to this old theatre. Here food is indeed an art form. The terminology might be Spanish, but Bon Lloc's tapas are nothing like their Spanish counterparts. The chef and staff seem to have a good time in the kitchen – how else could the creativity and perfection be explained? Bon Lloc won *Gourmet* magazine's prestigious best restaurant in Sweden award in 2002. Such quality doesn't come cheap, of course, and you'll have to reserve your table well in advance.

Franska Matsalen

Grand Hôtel, Blasieholmshamnen 8 (679 35 84/611 86 86/www.franskamatsalen.com). T-bana Kungsträdgården/bus 46, 55, 59, 62, 65. **Open** 6-11pm Mon-Fri. **Main courses** 195kr-465kr. **Set menus** 925kr; 1,300kr. **Credit** AmEx, DC, MC, V. **Map** p303 G8.

The very definition of a luxury restaurant. Grand surroundings in the Grand Hôtel overlooking the Kungliga Slottet, discreet and super-professional service, and all sorts of people-watching to be done, from rock stars to blue-haired American ladies seeking their Swedish roots. Oh, did we mention the food? It's good, of course. Some even say it's the best. The finest ingredients money can buy, with an added touch of truffle or caviar. Try the roasted sweetbreads with beetroot and sage ravioli, or the oven-baked sole with langoustines and tomato and olive linguini. Dress up.

Berns: modern Conran-inspired food in a fantastic historic setting.

Fredsgatan 12

Konstakademien, Fredsgatan 12 (24 80 52/23 76 05/www.fredsgatan12.com). T-bana T-Centralen/bus 3, 53, 62, 65. **Open** *Aug-June* 11.30am-2pm, 5-11pm Mon-Fri; 5-11pm Sat. Closed July. **Main courses** 260kr-325kr. **Set menus** lunch 295kr; dinner 500kr, 650kr, 700kr, 850kr. **Credit** AmEx, DC, MC, V. **Map** p303 H7.

One of the most stylish of Stockholm's restaurants, in terms of both food and decor. Melker Andersson became the first of a series of talented young chefs producing their own crossover cuisine in the 1990s, creating food sculptures just like their counterparts from Chicago to Lyon. If you're part of the crowd that never checks the bill before handing over the plastic, a high-level international food treat awaits – with inspiration from Morocco to Japan, and the best of Swedish ingredients. It's not always worth the money, but even the lows are still pretty good. And the setting, in the Royal Academy of Art, just across the water from the parliament building and Gamla Stan, is spectacular. The terrace bar (open only in summer) is very popular; *see p132*.

Operakällaren

Kungliga Operan, Karl XIIs Torg (676 58 01/www.operakallaren.se). T-bana Kungsträdgården/bus 46, 55, 59, 62, 76. **Open** *Aug-June* 6-10pm daily. Closed July. **Main courses** 370kr-420kr. **Set menus** 550kr; 950kr; 1,250kr. **Credit** AmEx, DC, MC, V. **Map** p303 G7.

Without doubt one of Sweden's best restaurants, and with the history and setting to match it. As the name implies, it's located in the opera house, which has been open for business since 1787 – although the present building was erected in 1895, from which time the dining room's interior dates. The present restaurant was created in the 1960s by legendary Swedish chef Tore Wretman, who more than any other person is responsible for turning the Swedes into foodies. Today, Stefano Catenacci is in charge of the pots and pans, offering exciting modern cuisine. The desserts are the pride and joy, created by pâtissier Magnus Johansson. This is a luxury establishment in terms of food, service and wine. And make no mistake, the prices are equally spectacular, with main courses starting at 400kr.

Restaurangen™

Oxtorgsgatan 14 (22 09 52/www.restaurangentm.com). T-bana Hötorget/bus 1, 43, 52, 56. **Open** *Early Aug-June* 11.30am-2pm, 5pm-1am Mon-Fri; 5pm-1am Sat (kitchen closes 11pm). Closed July-early Aug. **Set menus** 250kr; 350kr; 450kr. **Credit** AmEx, DC, MC, V. **Map** p303 F7.

Chef Melker Andersson had a key role in the resurgence of Swedish gastronomy in the mid '90s. This is his ambitious venture, a dining concept unlike any other. The menu is divided into 15 different tastes, exhibited in 15 different dishes, all created in ingenious style. Bitter, sour, soy, juniper berry, ginger – each diner creates their own spectrum of tastes. Three, five or seven small dishes make up a whole meal; it's up to you to decide how many you need. Then choose your wines, preferably a small glass for each course. The gourmets queue up – and for anyone genuinely interested in food it's pretty unmissable. Those who prefer cosiness and tradition will find it all rather pretentious.

Mediterranean

Glenn Miller Café

Brunnsgatan 21A (10 03 22). T-bana Hötorget/bus 1, 43, 52, 56. **Open** *Restaurant* 5-10.30pm Mon-Sat. *Bar* 5pm-midnight Mon-Thur; 5pm-1am Fri, Sat. **Main courses** 90kr-175kr. **Credit** MC, V. **Map** p303 E7.

This tiny place is a sympathetic bistro for anyone looking for cheapish food in a relaxed environment. There are only a few seats and it doesn't take much to pack the place – but who cares when the service is personal and the food well cooked? The blackboard lists ten or so starters and main courses, most of them rustic French. *Moules frites* and fillet of beef cooked in one way or another have become compulsory. Jazz bands jam themselves into a corner to perform some nights (*see p210*).

Letizia

Hamngatan 17 (611 25 22/www.letiziastockholm.com). T-bana Kungsträdgården/bus 46, 55, 59, 62, 76. **Open** 11.30am-midnight Mon-Fri; 1pm-midnight Sat; 5-11pm Sun. **Main courses** 98kr-239kr. **Set menu** 290kr. **Credit** AmEx, DC, MC, V. **Map** p303 G8.

The location is phenomenal for anyone who wants to watch the fashion-conscious Stockholm crowds pass by the window. And the restaurant itself is anxious about its appearance. The concept is New York Italian; the menu has no ambitions to be up to date, but is reliable in its approach to ravioli, bresaola, saltimbocca and other Italian classics.

Traditional Swedish

Bakfickan

Kungliga Operan, Karl XIIs Torg (676 58 09/20 95 92/www.operakallaren.se/bakfickan.cfm). T-bana Kungsträdgården/bus 46, 55, 59, 62, 65. **Open** 11.30am-11.30pm Mon-Fri; noon-11.30pm Sat. **Main courses** 100kr-170kr. **Credit** AmEx, DC, MC, V. **Map** p303 G7.

Cheapest of the opera trio: **Bakfickan.**

In the opera house, alongside Operakällaren (*see p113*) and Operabaren (*see below*), you'll find Bakfickan ('the hip pocket'), the little brother of the trio that shares the same giant kitchen. Sit at the large counter stretching around the tiny room to eat a late supper of *köttbullar* (meatballs) with a beer, listening to the opera singers talk about the evening's performance, or some less inspiring financial market gossip from workers from the bank headquarters lining Kungsträdgården.

Grand National

Regeringsgatan 74 (56 63 98 00/www.grandnational.aos.se). T-bana Hötorget/bus 1, 43, 56. **Open** *Aug-June* 11.30am-11pm Mon-Wed; 11.30am-midnight Thur-Sat; 5-11pm Sun. Closed July. **Main courses** 135kr-245kr. **Set menus** vegetarian 200kr; fish or meat 410kr. **Credit** AmEx, DC, MC, V. **Map** p303 E7.

This restaurant (in the same building as old jazz haunt Nalen – *see p212*) serves classic *husmanskost* with a refined finish. Sometimes Mediterranean influences find their way on to the menu, but classic Swedish fish is the star turn. Head chef Jesper Taube once worked as a sailor, and it's when he knocks up something with halibut, turbot or perch that the real culinary heights are reached.

Operabaren

Kungliga Operan, Karl XIIs Torg (676 58 08/20 95 92/www.operakallaren.se). T-bana Kungsträdgården/ bus 46, 55, 59, 62, 65. **Open** *Aug-June* 11.30am-3pm, 5pm-1am Mon-Wed; 11.30am-3pm, 5pm-2am Thur, Fri; 1pm-2am Sat. Closed July. **Main courses** 100kr-170kr. **Credit** AmEx, DC, MC, V. **Map** p303 G7.

If you're visiting the opera house but can't stretch to Operakällaren's prices, there is always this place, which is particularly good for Saturday lunch. To walk in and sit in the old leather sofas is to turn back time, and many of the customers seem to have been here since just after the master carpenters created the magnificent Jugendstil interior. This is the place to enjoy some excellent Swedish *husmanskost* and a schnapps. The indoor restaurant closes for lunch whenever the weather is warm enough to sit outdoors – it then shares an outside dining area with Bakfickan (*see p115*).

Vasastaden

Asian

Koreana

Luntmakargatan 76 (15 77 08). T-bana Rådmansgatan/bus 4, 42, 43, 46, 52, 72. **Open** 11am-9pm Mon-Fri; 1-9pm Sat. **Main courses** 65kr-140kr. **No credit cards**. **Map** p307 D6.

This is one of many excellent Asian restaurants on Luntmakargatan. Come here for cheap, fast and genuine Korean street food, including *bibimbab* (seasoned vegetables and egg on rice) or *bulgogi* (barbecued beef). More mainstream is the selection of ordinary but good sushi. Lunchtime is busy and very affordable; in the evening you'll see a growing number of Asian tourists digging in – always a reassuring indicator of quality.

Lao Wai

Luntmakargatan 74 (673 78 00). T-bana Rådmansgatan/bus 4, 42, 43, 46, 52, 72. **Open** *Mid Jan-June, mid Aug-23 Dec* 11.30am-2pm, 5.30-9pm Tue-Fri; 5.30-9pm Sat. Closed July-mid Aug, 24 Dec-mid Jan. **Main courses** 100kr-175kr. **Credit** AmEx, DC, MC, V. **Map** p307 D6.

Stockholm's best vegetarian restaurant is a bit hidden away, but it's worth seeking out. The base is Chinese, but with influences from several other Asian cuisines. You won't find any meat or animal products; tofu, soya and loads of fresh vegetables take their place. Anyone thinking that veggie restaurants are boring is soon set straight – try the Jian Chang tofu (smoked tofu with shiitake mushrooms, sugar peas and fresh spices). At lunchtime, the menu is reduced to only one option and the pressure on the kitchen is heavy. This is when the customer can get a bit of a mouthful from the slightly choleric owner. Well, it's certainly colourful.

Lilla Pakistan

St Eriksgatan 66 (30 56 46). T-bana St Eriksplan/bus 3, 4, 72. **Open** 5-10pm Mon-Thur; 5-11pm Sat. **Main courses** 165kr-285kr. **Credit** AmEx, DC, MC, V. **Map** p306 E3.

Unlike most Indian restaurants in Stockholm, Little Pakistan offers authentic Pakistani and northern Indian dishes. Everything is delicious and well prepared, and the kitchen even serves nice *amuse-bouches*. The slightly stuffy staff are certainly well aware that their restaurant is no ordinary curry house. Unfortunately, quality comes at a price, and quite a heavy one.

Malaysia

Luntmakargatan 98 (673 56 69). T-bana Rådmansgatan/bus 4, 42, 43, 46, 52, 72. **Open** 10am-10pm Mon-Thur; 10am-11pm Fri; 1-11pm Sat; 1-10pm Sun. Closed 2wks July. **Main courses** 125kr-380kr. **Credit** AmEx, DC, MC, V. **Map** p307 C6.

Malaysia looks a bit lonely amid Stockholm's remnainder of a Chinatown. Malaysian cuisine is not as renowned as its spicy cousins from Southeast Asia, but this place is reliable, fresh and good value for money. Fiery spices and citrus fruits get the menu going, and the choice of chicken, duck, beef, tiger prawns, lamb or noodles is impressive. There are plenty of vegetarian options too.

Mooncake

Luntmakargatan 95 (16 99 28/www.mooncake.se). T-bana Rådmansgatan/bus 4, 42, 43, 46, 52, 72. **Open** 5-11pm Tue-Sat. Closed 3wks July, 2wks from Christmas. **Main courses** 191kr-275kr. **Set menus** 420kr. **Credit** AmEx, DC, MC, V. **Map** p307 C6.

The decor and ambience at Mooncake are carefully composed – it's a bit like being on a film set. And the same goes for what's on the plates. The chefs

The best Restaurants

For celebrated chefs

Sweden's top chefs work their magic at **Bon Lloc** (*see p113*), **Franska Matsalen** (*see p113*), **Fredsgatan 12** (*see p113*), **Pontus in the Green House** (*see p111*), **Restaurangen™** (*see p115*) and **Vassa Eggen** (*see p127*). Or **Edsbacka Krog** (*see p129*) outside the city.

Inside landmark buildings

Step back in time at **Berns** (*see p113*), **Den Gyldene Freden** (*see p111*), **Operakällaren** (*see p113*) and **Pelikan** (*see p124*).

For cheap eats

You can dine well on a budget at **Babs Kök & Bar** (*see p125*), **Broncos Bar** (*see p119*), **Koreana** (*see p116*), **Mandus** (*see p111*) and **Glenn Miller Café** (*see p115*).

For vegetarians

Asian restaurants tend to be a good choice if you want to avoid meat – **Lao Wai** (*see p116*) is completely veggie. Places serving Swedish cuisine are also a good bet. Or try soup supremo **Papphanssons Soppor** (*see p128*).

Tranan: simple look, fab food. *See p118.*

combine dishes from Sichuan, Beijing, Vietnam and Thailand in new ways. The Peking duck takes pride of place, but the Vietnamese spring rolls and soy-caramelised chicken are equally impressive. Where other Asian restaurants lean towards conservative solutions, Mooncake doesn't compromise with ambition and style. And it works. The place is usually packed with a young and beautiful crowd.

Narknoi

Odengatan 94 (30 70 70/www.narknoi.nu). T-bana St Eriksplan/bus 3, 4, 47, 72. **Open** 11am-3pm, 5-11pm Mon-Fri; 4-11pm Sat, Sun. Closed 1wk from Christmas. **Main courses** 93kr-139kr. **Set menus** 215kr; 255kr. **Credit** AmEx, DC, MC, V. **Map** p306 D4.

A reliable Thai located between Odenplan and St Eriksplan. It's got lime-coloured walls and a fairly trendy interior without being pretentious. The menu has all the compulsory favourites: green curry, lemongrass dishes, noodles. It may seem traditional, but it's not boring – Narknoi knows its stuff without falling into the trap of clichés. The crowd is diverse, and includes locals and visitors.

Contemporary

Rolfs Kök

Tegnérgatan 41 (10 16 96/www.rolfskok.se). T-bana Rådmansgatan/bus 40, 47, 53, 69. **Open** *Restaurant* 11am-11.15pm Mon-Fri; 5-11.45pm Sat, Sun. *Bar* 11am-1pm Mon-Fri; 5pm-1am Sat, Sun. **Main courses** 160kr-250kr. **Credit** AmEx, DC, MC, V. **Map** p307 E5.

A favourite haunt for nearby publishers and advertising executives, this is a Swedish modern design classic and well worth a visit, for both the food and decor. Designers Thomas Sandell and Jonas Bohlin have created an environment that's functional yet intimate. Chairs hang on the grey concrete walls, to be quickly taken down if more diners arrive – on some nights, it often becomes one long table. Solo eaters are lined up by the long bar, which gives a perfect view into the open kitchen. Enjoy fresh fish lined up with tender meat, East Asian ideas combined with southern European tricks. The creative somersaults usually succeed, though sometimes aim too high. Even so, a visit to Rolfs Kök is always a highly pleasurable experience.

South of Siberia

Luntmakargatan 99 (15 44 70/www.southofsiberia.com). T-bana Rådmansgatan/bus 4, 43, 46, 52, 53, 72. **Open** *Restaurant* 5-11pm Tue-Sat. *Bar* 5pm-1am Tue-Sat. Closed July, 24 Dec-2 Jan. **Main courses** 172kr-249kr. **Set menus** 595kr. **Credit** AmEx, DC, MC, V. **Map** p307 C6.

South of Siberia is one of the newest additions to the category of high-profile contemporary restaurants. Anyone looking for a casual neighbourhood joint has come to the wrong place – this is a luxury restaurant that aims high. Diners can take their pick from a wide range of champagnes before digging into the fascinating menu – everything from Swedish fish (char, pike-perch) to Asiatic tastes. The concept is crossover, but with a solid Mediterranean base. The name refers to the restaurant's position just south of the dull grey neighbourhood on the other side of Odengatan.

Storstad

Odengatan 41 (673 38 00). T-bana Rådmansgatan/bus 4, 42, 46, 53, 72. **Open** *June-Aug* 4pm-1am Mon-Fri; 4pm-3am Sat. *Sept-May* 5pm-1am Mon-Thur; 4pm-3am Fri; 6pm-3am Sat. **Main courses** 125kr-235kr. **Credit** AmEx, DC, MC, V. **Map** p307 C6.

At first sight Storstad looks like a spacious living room, strictly and typically furnished according to the Swedish less-is-more principle. The long bar (*see p133*) and lounge area are very busy, even chaotic, especially at the weekend. But if you manage to elbow your way through, you'll find a laid-back and stylish restaurant. Storstad stands on the border of being a star restaurant, with one foot in the heat of the Stockholm night, and the other in a top-class kitchen, serving sensual creations with contributions from all over Europe, particularly Sweden,

France and Italy. Most of all, Storstad is proof that exquisite gastronomy doesn't have to be accompanied by stifling formality.

Tranan

Karlbergsvägen 14 (52 72 81 00/30 07 65). T-bana Odenplan/bus 4, 40, 46, 69, 72. **Open** *Restaurant* 5-11.45pm daily. *Bar* 5pm-1am daily. **Credit** AmEx, DC, MC, V. **Map** p307 D5.

On the surface, this is a well-worn, Parisian-style bistro with red and white checked tablecloths, creaking wooden chairs and fading film posters adorning the walls. The atmosphere is lively and loud and the clientele on the young side. But the truth is that Tranan is a little gastronomic treasure with high culinary ambitions. Classic *husmanskost* such as lard sausage and meatballs are always on the menu, but climbing the price ladder means a real treat for the palate. The kitchen is international in its approach, but based in France and Sweden; the shellfish, glazed flatfish and braised meats are impressive. After you've finished your meal, it's strongly recommended that you slink down to the buzzing basement bar (*see p133*) – one of the coolest in town, with a host of good DJs.

Mediterranean

Le Bistro de Wasahof

Dalagatan 46 (32 34 40/www.wasahof.se). T-bana Odenplan or St Eriksplan/bus 3, 4, 40, 47, 72. **Open** *Restaurant* 5-11pm Mon-Sat. *Bar* 5pm-1am Mon-Sat. **Main courses** 139kr-220kr. **Set menus** 327kr; 342kr; 509kr; 1,116kr. **Credit** AmEx, DC, MC, V. **Map** p306 D4.

This classic French restaurant near Odenplan is the second home of many a writer, actor, singer or just well-dressed wannabe. Wasahof functions as a bar as well as a bistro, and its main contribution to the culinary scene is its seafood. It imports its own oysters from France and the Swedish west coast. Next door the hipper little sister Musslan ('the clam') serves a younger crowd with the same menu.

Middle Eastern

Eyubi

Döbelnsgatan 45 (673 52 36/www.eyubi.com). T-bana Rådmansgatan/bus 4, 42, 43, 46, 52, 72. **Open** *Sept-Midsummer* 5pm-midnight Tue-Thur;

Husmanskost

Traditional Swedish cuisine is known as *husmanskost*. Some restaurants specialise in traditional dishes, but many places simply offer a separate *husmanskost* section on the menu. Look out for the following specialities. For other traditional food and drink, *see p180* **A food for all seasons**. For more food terms, see p289 **Vocabulary.**

FISH

Herring – called ***sill*** on the west coast and ***strömming*** in Stockholm – used to be the staple food of the Swedish diet. Today, this little fish is still much loved and always on the menu, in the cheapest lunch restaurant and the poshest luxury establishment. For lunch it's often blackened (*sotare*) and served with mashed potatoes, melted butter and perhaps lingonberry sauce. Don't be put off by the sweet lingonberries: all the savoury traditional foods are served with sweet preserves and sauces – and it tastes good.

Inlagd strömming (pickled herring) is prepared in as many different ways as there are Swedes. If you manage to find a traditional Swedish smörgåsbord (available in every single restaurant around Christmas), this is what you should start with, before moving on to the meats. A plate of pickled herring and fresh new potatoes with special soured cream (*gräddfil*) will make any

Swede foggy-eyed, while ***gravad strömming*** (pickled herring cured with a mustard sauce) is indispensable for celebrating Midsummer. Served, of course, with some beer and aquavit, a strong liqueur distilled from potato or grain mash and flavoured with caraway seeds (*kalled snaps*). For the ultimate smörgåsbord, visit **Operakällaren** (*see p113*). In summer, head to the archipelago or **Värdshuset Ulla Winbladh** (*see p120*).

Happy red ***kräftor*** (crayfish) are eaten everywhere when the season starts in August. Cooked with huge amounts of dill, they're an unmissable special treat. Ask the waiter for instructions on how to eat them as they require some training. Beer and schnapps are also the crayfish's two compulsory companions.

5pm-1am Fri, Sat. Closed Midsummer-Aug. **Main courses** 60kr-190kr. **Credit** AmEx, MC, V. **Map** p307 C6.
In a short time Eyubi has become one of the most talked-about places on the Stockholm dining scene. People come on a pilgrimage to the pleasant open dining room in a converted garage, to eat innovative and well-cooked Kurdish food. The pride of Kurdish cuisine, bulgar wheat, is joined by Persian meatballs and Mediterranean sauces. For anyone keen to set out on a mini culinary odyssey, the Oriental platter (160kr) is recommended. Museum executives and other cultural types pop by for family dinners and are well looked after by the friendly staff.

Traditional Swedish

Broncos Bar

Tegnérgatan 16 (16 02 15). T-bana Rådmansgatan/ bus 43, 52. **Open** 11am-11.30pm Mon-Fri; 1-11.30pm Sat, Sun. **Main courses** lunch 62kr-72kr; dinner 64kr-199kr. **Credit** AmEx, MC, V. **Map** p307 E6.
Mr Bronco himself, Lennart 'Hoa Hoa' Dahlgren, was a successful weightlifter who grew tired of the ridiculously small portions that restaurants were serving – and did something about it. Expect honest hamburgers, heavy Swedish *husmanskost* and large beers – as well as modest prices and no frills. It's a good place to start a night of bar-hopping up and down Tegnérgatan.

Rabarber

Torsgatan 55 (31 17 75). T-bana St Eriksplan/ bus 3, 42, 47, 507. **Open** 11am-1am Mon-Fri; 4pm-1am Sat; from 4pm Sun. **Main courses** 75kr-225kr. **Set menu** 285kr. **Credit** AmEx, MC, V. **Map** p306 D3.
If you're tired of artfully arranged asparagus and menus that need translation from the fashionable food argot, this is a good alternative. Rabarber (which translates as 'Rhubarb') is a reliable, over-sized neighbourhood restaurant with smiling staff. On the walls, photographs of old film stars jostle with kitsch oil paintings. The well-priced menu is not ashamed to offer plain Swedish grub. You can stuff yourself with meatballs, *pytt i panna*, herring and salmon; especially good value is the three-course set menu. Some nights the atmosphere is turned up with poetry readings or live music.

Lax (salmon) needs no introduction: just remember that ***gravlax*** means cured with sugar and salt, not to be confused with the smoked variety. Fish from inland lakes and the Baltic are relatively rare, the most delicious being the ***gös*** (pike-perch). However, plenty of fish from the west coast lands on the plates of Stockholm's restaurants, and ***torsk*** (cod), although more and more scarce, is a vital part of Swedish culinary tradition and is served in many different ways. The most interesting is ***lutfisk***, which is only served around Christmas. The cod is salted and air-dried, then soaked in lye, which transforms it into something that looks and tastes nothing like fish. It's served with peas, butter and a béchamel sauce.

MEAT

Swedish ***köttbullar*** (meatballs) are, of course, a speciality, immortalised not least by the Swedish chef in *The Muppet Show*. They're eaten with pickled cucumber, a cream sauce and lingonberries. Bar-restaurant **Kvarnen** (*see p136*) is the right place to go for this most Swedish of dishes. A schnapps (or two) is best drunk with it.

Pytt i panna is regularly found in most restaurants: it consists of diced and fried meat and potatoes, adorned with a fried egg and pickled beetroots. ***Rimmad oxbringa*** (lightly salted brisket of beef) is simply delicious. Anything with '*rimmad*' attached to it means that it is first salted and then boiled. The meat is made amazingly tender by the long cooking.

Kåldolmar (stuffed cabbage rolls), relatives of the eastern Mediterranean *dolmas* and very popular, are made Swedish by wrapping cabbage leaves rather than vine leaves around minced pork. The concept was introduced to Sweden when King Karl XII was stranded in Turkey after attempting, and failing, to invade Russia in 1708.

Game, such as ***älg*** (elk) and ***rådjur*** (roe deer), are popular in the autumn. They are mainly roasted and served with potatoes, lingonberries and a cream sauce.

DESSERTS

Swedish desserts are highly seasonal. There are always fruits and berries in pies and cakes in summer and autumn. Favourite fruits include wild strawberries, blueberries, cloudberries and lingonberries, although the latter are usually used in savoury dishes. The heavy Swedish cheesecake ***ostkaka*** should be reserved for the darker months. But miniature pancakes, ***plättar***, with jam and cream, are delicious all year round.

Djurgården

Traditional Swedish

Värdshuset Ulla Winbladh

Rosendalsvägen 8 (663 05 71/73/www.ulla winbladh.se). Bus 44, 47. **Open** 11.30am-10pm Mon; 11.30am-11pm Tue-Fri; 1-11pm Sat; 1-10pm Sun. **Main courses** 210kr-275kr. **Credit** AmEx, DC, MC, V. **Map** p305 H11.

This is about as picturesque as it gets: a small old house surrounded by flowers, on the green retreat of Djurgården – and not far from the island's main attractions. In summer, people eat outdoors in the green yard; otherwise, the tiny but cosy dining rooms will do the trick. It's a place to eat traditional Swedish food and relax. Don't expect a culinary adventure, though it's good enough to make you leave with a smile. Try the pickled herring smörgåsbord if it's on the menu – it usually is.

Södermalm

Asian

For a reliable local Thai, try **Tamrab Thai** (Hornsgatan 126; 668 55 20). Located in the uninspiring no-man's-land between Hornstull and Zinkensdamm, it serves tasty curries and stir-fries as well as more exotic dishes: boar in red curry, steamed pig's ears, stir-fried frog's legs and dried fish intestines.

Ho's

Hornsgatan 151 (84 44 20/www.restauranghos.com). T-bana Hornstull/bus 4, 74. **Open** 11am-2.30pm, 5-10pm Tue-Thur; 11am-2.30pm, 5-10.30pm Fri; 2-10.30pm Sat; 2-10pm Sun. Closed 2wks Mar. **Main courses** 90kr-235kr. **Credit** AmEx, DC, MC, V. **Map** p301 L3.

Long a well-kept secret for a small crowd of Chinese and sussed locals, nowadays Ho's is well known all over town for its personal service and exquisite stir-fries. The room is simply decorated, without attempting to be either trendy or exotic. The menu has the standard selections of chicken, pork, beef, duck, fish and shellfish. It's a no-fuss joint – the deal is straightforward wok-frying with fresh ingredients. The chicken dishes with black beans and ginger are classic. It takes a real effort to leave Ho's without being satisfied, and it's pretty good value for money.

Koh Phangan

Skånegatan 57 (642 50 40/www.kohphangan.nu). T-bana Medborgarplatsen or Skanstull/bus 59. **Open** 11am-2pm, 4pm-1am Mon-Fri; 2pm-1am Sat, Sun. **Main courses** 120kr-255kr. **Credit** AmEx, DC, MC, V. **Map** p311 M9.

Fancy a trip to Thailand? You can spend a night there with dinner at Koh Phangan. The interior is an imaginative and humorous pastiche of Thailand: you eat perched on an imported rickshaw or lounging on a bamboo sofa, accompanied by the sound of waves and crickets. You'll find all the usual standards: red or green curries, prawns with coconut milk and lemongrass. It's fresh, well cooked and at times extremely spicy. The service is sometimes overly unconventional, but the Thai chefs know just what they're doing. It's very popular with the Söder types, so expect long queues.

Sushi Bar Sone

Ringvägen 8 (668 29 88). T-bana Zinkensdamm/ bus 4, 43, 55, 66, 74. **Open** 11am-2pm, 4-9pm Mon-Fri; 3-9pm Sat. **Main courses** 60kr-140kr. **No credit cards**. **Map** p301 K5.

Welcome to one of the best sushi restaurants in town – and there are plenty of them. It's not really a restauant, though; merely a hole in the wall with a couple of seats, but ingredients are always fresh, and prepared by the convivial owner, Mr Sone himself. Don't miss the 'Sone special', a selection of fresh nigiri sushi (pieces of fish served on a pad of rice) that will satisfy the hungriest diner, with the special 'spicy' (a cone of seaweed with salmon and the Korean soya bean paste *kochujang*).

Central European

Humlehof

Folkungagatan 128 (641 03 02). Bus 3, 46, 53, 66, 76. **Open** 5-10pm daily. **Main courses** 89kr-160kr. **Credit** AmEx, MC, V. **Map** p311 L10.

A plain and unaffected Central European restaurant offering sturdy food at humane prices. The clientele is made up of typical Söder bohemians; chefs on their night off munch bratwurst, lefty journalists sit drinking over a schnitzel, and everyone else enjoys the exquisite *kåldolmar* (cabbage parcels). Classics such as sauerkraut are varied with lighter Swedish dishes such as fried salmon and pickled herring. The reliable staff guarantee a friendly atmosphere, and keep your tall beer glass filled with an extensive range of German and Czech beers.

Moldau

Bergsunds Strand 33 (84 75 48). T-bana Hornstull/bus 4, 40, 66, 74. **Open** 5-10.30pm Mon-Fri; 2-10.30pm Sat. **Main courses** 95kr-185kr. **Credit** AmEx, MC, V. **Map** p301 L2.

The rough wooden tables and seats send out an immediate signal that the food at Moldau is going to be no-nonsense. Expect hearty and traditional Austrian and Hungarian cooking, served in generous portions and not too many vegetables. Schnitzels of different kinds are a speciality, but don't forget the desserts, which include some old favourites such as *sachertorte* and *kaiserschmarrn* (crumbled pancakes served with fruit). On summer evenings people fill the outdoor tables to refresh themselves with a selection of Czech draught beers. Moldau is the ideal starting point for a walk along the green northern shore of Södermalm or to the small island of Långholmen.

Super Swedes: Mathias Dahlgren

Over the past 20 years, Sweden has transformed itself from a country of meat- and potato-eaters to a nation of fanatic foodies. Upmarket food magazines such as *Gourmet* abound and more cookbooks are published and bought per capita in Sweden than in any other country. And then there are the chefs. The Swedish national team (yes, chefs compete in cooking in a number of different disciplines) is more successful than any of its athletic counterparts. One of the most decorated young chefs is Mathias Dahlgren, owner and founder of celebrated restaurant **Bon Lloc** (*see p113*). On his white chef's jacket a small 'Bocuse d'Or' is embroidered over his name – a reminder of the first Swedish gold medal in the cooking 'world championships'.

'Nowadays, being interested in food is more like being interested in pop music, art or fashion: it's part of our everyday life,' says Dahlgren. Opened in 1996, Bon Lloc is his first restaurant, merging Mediterranean tastes with Swedish ingredients and craftsmanship. He calls his cuisine 'Estilo Nuevo Euro-Latino' and takes inspiration from France, Italy and Spain.

Dahlgren's approach comes from his questioning of what a national culinary tradition really is in today's world of international fusion cuisine. He reckons that not one of Stockholm's major restaurants serves unadulterated traditional Swedish food. Pizza and pasta are, after all, the most common dishes in Sweden, as in many other European countries. He believes that the only possible innovation is to borrow and learn from the cuisines of other countries, since, he says, 'nothing has really happened in the past 50 years in terms of the techniques used by the cooks. All good restaurants in the Western world, be it New York or Stockholm, are based on French thinking.' In order to continually develop his cooking, Dahlgren travels extensively to see what's on the menu abroad.

His advice to a food tourist is to sample Stockholm's great variety of mid-range restaurants, where you'll find ambitious food at affordable prices – other capital cities just don't offer as much choice in that price range. But he warns: 'In Stockholm you won't find good, cheap, low-end eating places – they're all pizzerias.' Another word of advice is not to visit Stockholm in July, when most of the good restaurants are closed.

Contemporary

Folkhemmet

Renstiernas Gata 30 (640 55 95/www.users.wineasy.se/folkhemmet). Bus 46, 53, 59, 66, 76. **Open** *Restaurant* 5-11pm daily. *Bar* 5pm-1am daily. **Credit** AmEx, DC, MC, V. **Map** p311 M9.

Rockers and music journos from Södermalm flock to this place. The noisy bar (*see p135*) is not for the shy, but Folkhemmet still holds sway as one of the most relaxed and enjoyable restaurants in Stockholm. Whereas many restaurants have adopted minimalist decor and serve strictly contemporary Swedish food, Folkhemmet has kept its unforced atmosphere and crossover philosophy. And why change anything? The service is cheerful, and the chefs really know their stuff. Classic ingredients are mixed with innovative techniques and exotic extras to create cutting-edge pasta, beautiful fish and unconventional but classic meat dishes. It's good, at times even sensational.

Matkultur

Erstagatan 21 (642 03 53). Bus 3, 46, 53, 66, 76. **Open** 5-10pm Mon, Tue; 5-11pm Wed-Sat. **Main courses** 130kr-200kr. **Credit** AmEx, DC, MC, V. **Map** p311 L10.

After a stroll on Stockholm's panoramic Fjällgatan, you might want to end up in this crowded and

For the ultimate restaurant with a view, it's got to be **Eriks Gondolen**.

friendly place. The kitchen is proud of its culinary crossover: mainly Turkish and Lebanese specialities with a hint of Sweden – there's lots of lamb and rice. Prices are moderate and the clientele young and arty. If you still have strength after dinner, it's also close to the bars on Skånegatan.

Mediterranean

Crêperie Fyra Knop

Svartensgatan 4 (640 77 27). T-bana Slussen/ bus 3, 43, 46, 55, 59. **Open** 5-11pm Mon-Fri; noon-11pm Sat, Sun. **Main courses** 44kr-74kr. **Credit** AmEx, MC, V. **Map** p310 L8.

If you're homesick and French, or looking for an inexpensive but romantic meal, this is a good choice. The decor is ultra-kitsch, complete with old fishing nets and lifebelts, in two dark and cosy little rooms. The savoury and sweet crêpes are delicious and cheap enough that you can go on to dance at nearby Mosebacke (*see p191*) afterwards.

Lo Scudetto

Åsögatan 163 (640 42 15). Bus 46, 59, 66, 76, 53. **Open** 5pm-midnight Mon-Sat; kitchen closes 10pm. Closed 4wks from Midsummer. **Main courses** 95kr-220kr. **Credit** AmEx, MC, V. **Map** p311 M9.

This local Italian (named after the Italian football league trophy) is not what it seems. It's rustically styled down, the walls sparsely decorated with portraits of Swedish footballers in the promised land of the Parmesan, and the space between the tables is sometimes too small. But don't expect simple spaghetti here – there's an almost religious relationship with the subtleties of the Italian kitchen, and the bresaola, pecorino and ravioli are prepared with a cautious and skilful hand. This is one of the city's few Italians in the absolute top class.

Middle Eastern

Merhaba

Ringvägen 110 (644 20 60). T-bana Skanstull/ bus 3, 4, 55, 59, 76. **Open** 5pm-midnight Mon-Thur; 3pm-1am Fri, Sat; 3-11pm Sun. **Main courses** 139kr-198kr. **Credit** AmEx, MC, V. **Map** p310 N8.

One of the few genuine Turkish restaurants in the city centre. Situated off the beaten track near Skanstull, it's worth the detour if you want meat in generous portions, or just a plate of meze. The food is simple but well prepared, and prices moderate.

Sahara

Folkungagatan 126 (641 33 87). Bus 3, 46, 53, 66. **Open** 5-11pm Mon-Thur; 5pm-midnight Fri; 4pm-midnight Sat; 4-11pm Sun. **Main courses** 38kr (meze)-185kr. **Credit** AmEx, DC, MC, V. **Map** p311 L10.

This small Lebanese is decorated in a stunning combination of kitsch and exotica. But it's the meze that you really come for: there's a choice of around 30, all highly accomplished. The main courses are delicious too, but feel traditional and a bit too hefty in comparison. Staff will recommend a couple of tasting menus and it's a good idea to follow their advice. Having feasted on tabouleh, houmous and an array of skewers from the grill, round it all off in the time-honoured manner with honey-dripping baklavas, cardamom coffee and a strong hookah.

Traditional Swedish

Eriks Gondolen

Stadsgården 6 (641 70 90/40/www.eriks.se). T-bana Slussen/bus 3, 43, 46, 53, 76. **Open** *Restaurant* 11.30am-2pm, 5-11pm Mon-Fri; 1-11pm Sat. *Bar*

11.30am-1am Mon-Fri; 1pm-1am Sat. **Main courses** lunch 95kr-295kr; dinner 255kr-450kr. **Set menus** 320kr; 395kr. **Credit** AmEx, DC, MC, V. **Map** p310 K8.
It's hard to imagine a restaurant with a more spectacular view anywhere in Europe. The name means gondola, and the bar is actually suspended over Slussen, underneath the Katarinahissen walkway, overlooking Gamla Stan and the water. As well as the bar (*see p135*), there is an exclusive dining room and a simpler restaurant (both in the adjoining building, but also with a good view) – which gives you the choice to make an evening here anything from merely expensive to extremely expensive. The menu takes in French dishes as well as traditional Swedish. The owner, Erik, is jovial and will probably drop by your table. This is where Stockholmers bring their foreign friends or business associates to impress them with the city, summer and winter. You can enter via the bridge from Mosebacke Torg or the lift from the waterfront.

Pelikan

Blekingegatan 40 (55 60 90 90/www.pelikan.se). T-bana Skanstull/bus 3, 55, 59, 74. **Open** *Mid Aug-Midsummer* 11.30am-1am Mon-Fri; 1pm-1am Sat, Sun. *Midsummer-mid Aug* 4pm-1am daily. **Main courses** 69kr-220kr. **Credit** AmEx, MC, V. **Map** p311 M8.
Not many restaurants feel as genuinely Swedish as this beer hall located in southern Södermalm. With its elegant painted ceilings and wood-panelled walls, it hasn't changed since Söder was exclusively working class and restaurants served only *husmanskost*. Classics available include *pytt i panna*, SOS (*smör, ost och sill* – butter, cheese and herring) and meatballs with lingonberries and pickled cucumber. Check the dishes listed on the blackboard to find the real bargains (under 100kr), such as knuckle of pork with root vegetable mash, or fried salted herring with onion sauce. Accompanying the food with an ice-cold schnapps is close to compulsory. In the afternoon and early evening the dining room is dominated by lonely old men in worn suits drinking beer; later on it gets younger and louder. The staff are of the hearty old-fashioned sort, and handle with panache even the oddest customers.

Östgötakällaren

Östgötagatan 41 (643 22 40/www.matsedel.com). T-bana Medborgarplatsen/bus 59, 66. **Open** 5pm-midnight daily. **Main courses** 80kr-175kr. **Credit** AmEx, DC, MC, V. **Map** p311 M8.
You'll enjoy a good night out at this faithful old restaurant in the heart of Söder. It's not the place for snobby waitresses or foodie trends. Here, straightforward ladies serve substantial portions of hearty, well-priced, plain fare. Not that it's old-fashioned or stodgy. Tuck in to classic *husmanskost*, jazzed-up meats and fried fish, preferably washed down with beer. It's as cosy and homely as an old living room where everyone knows each other.

Visit **PA & Co** for that plush, pricey Östermalm experience. *See p125.*

Östermalm

Asian

Miyako

Kommendörsgatan 23 (662 25 06/663 35 10/ www.miyako.se). T-bana Östermalmstorg or Stadion/ bus 42, 44, 55, 56, 62. **Open** 5-10pm Mon-Sat. **Main courses** 150kr-225kr. **Set menus** 330kr-500kr. **Credit** AmEx, DC, MC, V. **Map** p308 E9.

Stockholm's best Japanese restaurant offers the whole experience. Borrow slippers and try to sit on the floor gracefully in the shoe-free section, or sit in 'normal' chairs if you'd prefer. Take hours over a full Japanese meal or, if you're not in the mood for something so advanced, try the excellent well-prepared sushi. The friendly staff make it even more enjoyable. Miyako is always filled with posh locals, including plenty of Japanese diners.

Contemporary

Babs Kök & Bar

Birger Jarlsgatan 37 (23 61 01). T-bana Östermalmstorg/bus 1, 46, 55, 56. **Open** 5pm-midnight Mon-Tue; 5pm-1am Wed-Sat; 4-10pm Sun. **Main courses** 130kr-170kr. **Credit** AmEx, DC, MC, V. **Map** p307 E7.

You have to walk through the foyer of art-house cinema Zita (*see p196*) to find this down-to-earth bar and restaurant. Have a drink, eat a simple dish from the open kitchen or drink a coffee before the film starts. It's also one of few places around Stureplan where it's possible to eat and drink without ending up skint. The chicken sandwich is always a reliable choice. Ageing cultural revolutionaries and radical twentysomethings are among the clientele.

Elverket

Linnégatan 69 (661 25 62/www.castrull.se/elverket). T-bana Karlaplan/bus 44, 56, 62. **Open** *Restaurant* 11am-2pm, 5.30-10pm Mon-Fri; noon-4pm, 6-10pm Sat; noon-4pm, 6-9pm Sun. *Bar* 11am-midnight Mon-Thur; 11am-1am Fri; noon-1am Sat; noon-10pm Sun. **Main courses** lunch 80kr-120kr; dinner 98kr-210kr. **Credit** AmEx, DC, MC, V. **Map** p304 F10.

This busy bar and restaurant is in an old electricity plant, together with the more experimental stage of the Dramaten theatre. It's a favourite place for both young suits and black-dressed intellectuals. The atmosphere is friendly, with a big lounge area with low sofas where you can just hang out with a drink. Food is modern crossover, with dishes such as a delicate mushroom risotto or a purée of jerusalem arthichoke in cardamom sauce. Prices are moderate to expensive and the drinks well shaken.

Lydmar Hotel

Sturegatan 10 (56 61 13 00/01/www.lydmar.se). T-bana Östermalmstorg/bus 1, 46, 55, 56, 91. **Open** *Restaurant* 11.30am-2pm, 5-11pm Mon-Fri; 6-11pm Sat, Sun. *Bar* 11.30am-1am Mon-Thur; 11.30am-2am Fri; 6pm-2am Sat; 6pm-1am Sun. **Main courses** lunch 95kr-155kr; dinner 150kr-265kr. **Credit** AmEx, DC, MC, V. **Map** p303 E8.

This popular watering hole for the glitterati, well-paid consultants and the occasional jazz singer or movie star is actually a hotel restaurant. Then again, this is the eternally hip Lydmar Hotel (*see p53*), so perhaps it's not surprising. Situated near Stureplan, this is a place with a pulse. Dining here can sometimes be a bit hysterical, but the modern Swedish food is actually good, sometimes great and always trendy. Main dishes are surprisingly simple: order something as everyday as a grilled pork chop and it will arrive perfect and virtually 'naked' – garnishes come on the side. The bartenders take pride in their work, to the degree that asking for a beer could be sneered at. If you can overlook that, this is a good place to start an evening out at Stureplan, or to just watch the in-crowd do their thing; *see p138*.

PA & Co

Riddargatan 8 (611 08 45). T-bana Östermalmstorg/ bus 46, 55, 91, 96. **Open** 5pm-midnight daily. **Main courses** 95kr-250kr. **Credit** AmEx, DC, MC, V. **Map** p303 F8.

This restaurant – which a couple of years ago got a much discussed novel dedicated to it – exists mainly for a small mutual admiration society. Photos of the rock stars of yesteryear look down on advertising execs, celebrated writers and famous journos. The air of exclusiveness, and the feeling of sitting smack in the middle of the celebs' colony, are the main draw. The food – Swedish classics and international fare –is up to it, but prices are high. Some dishes are treated well, some are really interesting, but others are pretty dull: it's best to stick with the simple and well-tried options.

Riche

Birger Jarlsgatan 4 (54 50 35 60). T-bana Östermalmstorg/bus 46, 47, 55, 62. **Open** 11.30am-2am Mon-Fri; noon-midnight Sat. **Main courses** 120kr-345kr. **Credit** AmEx, DC, MC, V. **Map** p303 F8.

Yet another Stureplan restaurant overhauled with a new design and a brasserie concept. With huge windows on to the street, the spacious dining room is perfect for people-watching. The menu – a mix of the odd refined trad Swedish dish with international classics – is fairly ambitious, but what you get on your plate is neither that creative nor particularly good value. There's a lot of cheek-kissing and drinking of expensive wines. For a more intimate experience, the adjacent Teatergrillen (Nybrogaten 3; 54 50 36 65) is a far better alternative. The room is decorated with old theatre costumes, and the menu covers oysters, champagne and classic French cuisine.

Undici

Sturegatan 22 (661 66 17/www.undici.org). T-bana Östermalmstorg/bus 1, 46, 55, 56. **Open** *Mid Aug-June* 5pm-1am Tue-Thur; 5pm-3am Fri, Sat. Closed July-mid Aug. **Main courses** 160kr-260kr. **Set menu** 695kr. **Credit** AmEx, DC, MC, V. **Map** p308 E8.

Owner, footballer Tomas Brolin, grew up in the north of Sweden and played professionally in the north of Italy. Undici (11 in Italian), named after his shirt number, is a tribute to both regions. The space is bare, almost sterile, but the menu is more interesting. Plain Swedish classics mingle with swish Italian dishes and the odd truly luxurious creation. If you're eager to explore the two cuisines in more depth, try the tasting menu (695kr).

Vassa Eggen

Birger Jarlsgatan 29 (21 61 69/20 34 46/ www.restaurangguiden.com/sth/city/eggen). T-bana Östermalmstorg/bus 1, 43, 46, 55, 56. **Open** *Restaurant* 11.30am-2pm, 5-11pm Mon-Fri; 5-11pm Sat. *Bar* 11.30am-1am Mon-Fri; 5pm-1am Sat; 4pm-midnight Sun. **Main courses** lunch 95kr-200kr; dinner 255kr-385kr. **Set menus** 605kr; 795kr. **Credit** AmEx, DC, MC, V. **Map** p308 E7.

The name of this place ('Sharp Edge') is no joke: under the leadership of Christian Olsson, the kitchen produces super-modern food with a twist, such as red wine-glazed duck with sauerkraut and foie gras. It may be experimental, but it's always great. Not far from Stureplan, it's the number one choice for a culinary experience in the area. Expensive, though. The crowd is young and quite informal, many of them consultants from nearby offices.

Mediterranean

Brasserie Godot

Grev Turegatan 36 (660 06 14/www.godot.se). T-bana Östermalmstorg/bus 1, 56. **Open** 5pm-1am Mon-Sat. Closed 3wks July, 2wks from Christmas. **Main courses** 180kr-295kr. **Credit** AmEx, DC, MC, V. **Map** p308 E8.

Another Östermalm restaurant at the forefront of the new brasserie trend. The decor is fairly simple, but the attention to detail of the owners is noticeable. Classics such as snails, oysters, steak frites and crème caramel endure, but there are also more creative dishes that show both Swedish and French influences. The food is rarely outstanding, but it is beautifully presented and very good, and the staff are exemplary. The clientele is typically Östermalm, and the bar in particular is invaded by the Ralph Lauren-shirt crowd.

Divino

Karlavägen 28 (611 02 69/611 12 04/www.divino.se). Bus 1, 42, 44, 55, 56. **Open** *Aug-June* 6-11pm Mon-Sat. Closed July. **Main courses** 155kr-295kr. **Set menu** 685kr. **Credit** AmEx, DC, MC, V. **Map** p308 D7-8.

An Italian restaurant with ambitions. American chef Jodi Cohen prepares sumptuous risottos with Swedish ingredients. It's multicultural, but very Mediterranean. With a truffle on top. The minimalist interior (like nine out of ten restaurants in Stockholm) makes a good background for the colourful, well-heeled guests.

Sturehof

Stureplan 2 (440 57 30/www.sturehof.com). T-bana Östermalmstorg/bus 1, 46, 55, 56, 91. **Open** *Restaurant* 5pm-1am daily. *Bar* 5pm-2am daily. **Credit** AmEx, DC, MC, V. **Map** p303 F8.

This classic brasserie offers a choice of several different environments. Those who want to be seen sip white wine at the outdoor tables; the tiled bar is a popular after-work meeting place for local suits; the upper lounge bars are more laid-back and perfect for chilling out with a cocktail; and the massive dining room is full of diners of all shapes and sizes. The setting is elegant, with white linen tablecloths, uniformed waiters and nicely designed furniture, but the atmosphere stays lively and cheerful. The lengthy menu follows the classic French bistro tradition, from simple traditional food (around 100kr) to more decadent shellfish platters. It's best to stay with the simpler Swedish and French dishes, such as a rare steak minute, butter-fried perch fillets or the sturdy *isterband* with creamed potatoes. Among the starters the Dalarö sandwich with smoked Baltic herring, vendace roe and egg yolk is worth mentioning. After dinner, step into the lively O-baren (*see p139*).

Middle Eastern

Halv Grek Plus Turk

Jungfrugatan 30 (665 94 22/www.halvgrekplus turk.com). T-bana Stadion/bus 1, 44, 62. **Open** 5.30pm-midnight Mon-Sat; 5.30-11pm Sun. **Main courses** 45kr-225kr. **Credit** AmEx, DC, MC, V. **Map** p308 E9.

A friendship between Greek and Turkish restaurateurs resulted in a restaurant that for a long time was one of Stockholm's famous celebrity hotspots. And you can still spot a famous film director in one corner, a fashion photographer in another. Lounge on an elegant sofa, enjoying one of the most congenial restaurant interiors in town, and be astonished by just how good meze can be. Aside from classics (tzatziki, baba ghanoush, dolmades, lamb meatballs), the menu includes some sparkling new compositions, such as feta cheese cigars, Caucasian chicken and chicken liver terrine with Metaxa. Better Middle Eastern food than this is hard to find.

Traditional Swedish

Prinsen

Mäster Samuelsgatan 4 (611 13 31/www.restaurang prinsen.se). T-bana Östermalmstorg/bus 55, 59, 69. **Open** 11.30am-11.30pm Mon-Fri; 1-11.30pm Sat; 5-10pm Sun. **Main courses** 129kr-295kr. **Credit** AmEx, DC, MC, V. **Map** p303 F8.

This legendary writers' haunt has become something of an institution – in one corner there's a poet dressed in black; in another a patron of the arts holds court. 'The Prince' can be relied upon to offer atmosphere and an excellent range of classic *husmanskost*. The herring platter and 'Biff Rydberg' are part of

Sturehof: a classic brasserie in the middle of fashionable Stureplan. *See p127*.

Stockholm's cultural heritage. But amid the beef and halibut, you'll find more contemporary dishes, with European and especially Italian influences – all served in the same exquisite manner.

Kungsholmen

Asian

Hong Kong

Kungsbro Strand 23 (653 77 20). Bus 1, 40, 59. **Open** 11am-10pm Mon-Fri; 1-10pm Sat, Sun. **Main courses** 60kr-200kr. **Credit** AmEx, DC, MC, V. **Map** p302 G5.

One of the few places serving truly authentic and well-cooked Chinese food. The decor is fairly standard, but the cuisine is excellent – as you'd expect with over 30 years' experience. The owner, Sonny Li, delivers spicy Cantonese and Sichuanese dishes from the giant gas stove. Apart from the standard stir-fry dishes, there's an ambitious array of steam-cooked choices that varies with the season. But the speciality is the Peking duck (1,580kr for four people) – Chinese business folk and His Majesty the King, no less, all come here to enjoy the red-glazed bird, which has to be ordered two days in advance.

Roppongi

Hantverkargatan 76 (650 17 72). T-bana Fridhemsplan/bus 3, 40, 52, 62, 74. **Open** 11am-10pm Mon-Fri; 5-10pm Sat; 5-9pm Sun. **Main courses** lunch 70kr-90kr; dinner 120kr-170kr. **Credit** AmEx, DC, MC, V.

Roppongi serves the best sushi in this part of town, plus decent tempura and *gyoza* (pockets of fried dough stuffed with minced pork or shrimp), among other things. It's always crowded, especially the few tables that appear outside in summer. You can always take the fish back to where it belongs by ordering takeaway sushi in a box and walking down to the water at nearby Rålambshovsparken.

Contemporary

Papphanssons Soppor

Wargentinsgatan 3 (654 56 10/www.papphanssons soppor.com). T-bana Rådhuset/bus 1, 59, 91. **Open** 11am-8pm Mon-Thur; 11am-6pm Fri. **Main courses** 55kr-59kr. **Credit** MC, V. **Map** p302 G4.

A stylish yet cosy soup café, this is one of the best-kept food secrets on Kungsholmen. Head here for a lunch that is as tasty and filling as it is nutritious and inexpensive. Specialities include African peanut soup, Caribbean fish soup, tomato soup with feta cheese, and authentic Hungarian goulash. Generous portions are served in fine Mita Lundin ceramic bowls, and there's as much freshly baked bread as you can eat. The regularly changing menu always includes some vegetarian and lactose/gluten-free soups, as well as a few dishes for those who aren't in the mood for soup. It might be about to change hands, so best to call first before you visit.

Salzer

John Ericssonsgatan 6 (650 30 28/www.salzer.nu). T-bana Rådhuset/bus 3, 40, 52, 62. **Open** 5pm-midnight Mon-Sat. **Main courses** 109kr-230kr. **Credit** AmEx, DC, MC, V. **Map** p302 H3.

An intimate restaurant situated on the ground floor of one of Stockholm's most beautiful functionalist houses. The atmosphere is calm and the buzz of the city seems far away. Swedish dishes are elegantly mixed with inspiration from France and Italy. You'll find traditional offerings such as *kåldolmar* (stuffed cabbage leaves) and *isterband* (lard sausage), as well as sole and fillet of lamb. Few other places can offer such a pleasing combination of good old Swedish cosiness with conscious style, perfect for a quiet intimate dinner. In the tiny streetfront bar, Propellern, there's room to pose quietly with a drink.

Spisa Hos Helena

Scheelegatan 18 (654 49 26/50 26/www.spisahos helena.se). T-bana Rådhuset/bus 1, 3, 40, 52, 62. **Open** *Aug-June Restaurant* 11am-2pm, 5-11pm Mon-Fri; 5-11pm Sat. *Bar* 11am-11pm Mon-Thur; 11am-midnight Fri; 5pm-midnight Sat. Closed July. **Main courses** lunch 69kr; dinner 125kr-275kr. **Set menus** 255kr; 265kr. **Credit** AmEx, DC, MC, V. **Map** p302 G4.

A friendly neighbourhood restaurant with a welcoming atmosphere, cosy red walls and only female staff. People from the block drop in for dinner, to mingle with workers from the nearby law courts and radio stations. You'll find straightforward, sometimes even delicious, modern European cuisine such as lime-marinated salmon, and a large bar. It's the first in a row of bars and restaurants on this party street on Kungsholmen.

Traditional Swedish

Perssons

Bergsgatan 33 (652 50 30). T-bana Rådhuset/bus 1, 3, 40, 52, 62. **Open** *Aug-June* 11am-1.30pm Mon; 11am-1.30pm, 5-11pm Tue-Fri; 5-11pm Sat. Closed July. **Main courses** lunch 90kr-120kr; dinner 100kr-240kr. **Credit** AmEx, DC, MC, V. **Map** p302 G3.

This tucked-away little place is not somewhere you'll stumble into without meaning to. Situated in a small street next to the police headquarters, this friendly restaurant has a very ambitious kitchen crew. They produce unusual creations with the usual ingredients: fish, meat and vegetables from around Stockholm. There are no strange crossover creations, as in so many other restaurants in this mid-range bracket, and it's not fancy, but it's definitely above average. If you're looking for a good price-to-performance ratio, this is the place. Round the corner on Scheelegatan you'll find a couple of bars to move on to afterwards.

Further afield

Contemporary

Edsbacka Krog

Sollentunavägen 220, Sollentuna (96 33 00/ 40 19/www.edsbackakrog.se). Commuter train to Sollentuna Centrum then bus 525, 527, 607 to Edsbacka. **Open** *Aug-June* 11.30am-2.30pm, 5.30pm-midnight Mon-Fri (Jan-Apr, Aug-Nov closed Mon); 2pm-midnight Sat. Closed July. **Main courses** lunch 170kr-395kr; dinner 295kr-425kr. **Set menus** lunch 335kr; dinner 720kr. **Credit** AmEx, DC, MC, V.

This temple to the great food god – with a distinctly French bent – has been run by chef Christer Lingström for 20 years. It's the only restaurant in Sweden to receive two Michelin stars. Situated in Sollentuna just outside Stockholm, the easiest way to get here is by cab. A small price to pay, compared with what your dinner will cost. But you'll get food at the highest international level, although it's sometimes on the verge of being overworked. The menu is French-cum-Swedish and follows the seasons, with mainly the *crème de la crème* of Swedish fish, game and vegetables. You might come across Swedish duck served with sea buckthorn, truffle sauce and ravioli, and desserts such as a soufflé of wild strawberries. And the interior, surroundings and service are all exquisite too. There's been a restaurant here since 1626.

Middle Eastern

Cave de Roi

Storgatan 70, Huvudsta Centrum (27 13 54). T-bana Huvudsta Centrum/bus 113, 196, 198, 396. **Open** *Restaurant* 3pm-midnight Mon-Sat. *Bar* 3pm-1am Mon-Thur; 3pm-3am Fri, Sat. **Main courses** 109kr-149kr. **Set menu** 275kr. **Credit** AmEx, DC, MC, V.

One of the unlikeliest places to find an excellent restaurant, but it's one worth finding. Situated in an ordinary boring suburban mall on top of a T-bana station, Cave de Roi is one of very few restaurants that will make the city-centre crowd leave town. It serves Lebanese cuisine, and is filled with hip ad-agency types and happy Lebanese families. The food is good, but the ambience is even better. When they start playing (loud) Middle Eastern hits, people dance around the tables – and so should you. Just remember to give yourself time for some coffee and a go on the *nargileh* (water pipe). You can order à la carte Monday to Wednesday, but it's the set menu only during the rest of the week. There's belly dancing from Thursday to Saturday.

Traditional Swedish

Fjäderholmarnas Krog

Stora Fjäderholmen (718 33 55/716 39 89/ www.fjaderholmarna.com). Ferry from Nybrokajen or Slussen. **Open** *May-Sept* 11.30am-11pm daily. *Oct-Nov, Jan-Apr* 6-11pm Mon-Sat. *Dec* (Julbord) noon-11pm Mon-Sat; 1-8pm Sun. **Main courses** lunch 70kr-150kr; dinner 100kr-300kr; Julbord 445kr-545kr. **Credit** AmEx, DC, MC, V.

A once-celebrated restaurant on Stockholm's closest archipelago island, a 25-minute boat ride from the city. The view of passing boats on summer evenings is fabulous. Focusing on traditional Swedish and archipelago dishes, it manages to attract both tourists and corporate diners. The performance doesn't match the prices, however, and it's probably better to instead take a picnic to the island or settle for a glass of wine in the bar.

Bars

Stockholm's bars are frighteningly fashionable, and often double as clubs.

Far from the clubbing scene of London or the café culture of Paris, Stockholm's nightlife is centred on the *krog* – basically, a bar-cum-restaurant (all bars have to serve food, by law). The *krog* may also take on elements of the club, sporting DJs, bouncers at the door and late-night dancing on whatever floorspace is available; in fact, many of Stockholm's best bars also house its best clubs (*see chapter* **Clubs** for details). Opening hours can vary greatly, though most bars open on Friday and Saturday nights until either 1am or 3am. A small number of places around Stureplan shut at 5am, which is the latest closing time allowed by law.

Although the drinking age in Sweden is 18, bars are free to set their own age limits – the most common being 20 or 23. But the rules are by no means set in stone and, of course, exceptions are made constantly, particularly for attractive young women. In the following listings we've mentioned the age restriction only when it's 19 or over.

Although *krogar* come in many shapes and sizes, the distinction between a trendy *krog* and an untrendy one (aka *B-krog*) is usually quite clear. While happy to queue for 30 minutes to get into a popular bar, most Stockholm twentysomethings, in their desperation to be seen in only the hippest bar, shun local pubs, unwilling to stop in even for a single beer.

Stockholm's trendiest bars (and clubs) are located in the business district around Stureplan in Östermalm. Recognisable by their stylish, minimalist interiors (birch wood, white walls, frosted glass), these venues set out to convey an air of luxury. The doormen are notoriously fussy, often rejecting would-be patrons solely on appearance. To enjoy this part of town at the weekend, dress fashionably and arrive before the queues start building at around 10pm or 10.30pm. In other parts of town, notably the former workers' district of Södermalm, where there are plenty of great bars, the doormen are more egalitarian. Although long queues occur in other areas too, only the truly inebriated risk being rejected.

Untrendy *B-krogar* are easily recognised by their total lack of class and attention to detail. Many have nondescript interiors or are remnants of Stockholm's faux-Irish/London pub phase of the 1980s. Some offer rowdy fun, while others have advantages such as cheap beer, pool tables and jukeboxes. Generally, the clientele is either too young to get into the trendier bars (18 to 20 or younger) or too old to want to (35 and up).

Stiff taxes make alcohol expensive in Sweden. A 40cl glass of beer will usually cost between 38kr and 45kr at a hip bar, while cocktails start off at around 70kr. As far as choice goes, most pubs offer only a few rather tasteless Swedish lagers on tap. None of these stands out and you're not expected to order by brand – the usual request is *stor stark* ('large strong') – but common names are Pripps, Spendrups and Färsköl (from local brewery Gamla Stans Bryggeri). This bleak selection is, however, usually complemented by a range of international bottled beers priced only slightly

The best Bars

In summer

Head for the outdoor terraces at **Halv Trappa Plus Gård** (*see p138*), **Berns Salonger** (*see p131*), **Mosebacke** (*see p136*) or **Fredsgatan 12** (*see p132*).

In winter

For a warm and cosy feeling, try **Tranan** (*see p133*), **Kvarnen** (*see p136*) or **Pelikan** (*see p137*). Alternatively, if you want a shiver with your schnapps, head for the **Icebar** (*see p132*).

For a view

It's gotta be **Gondolen** (*see p135*) or, in summer, the outside terrace at **Mosebacke** (*see p136*).

If you're on a budget

If you like grimy bars with beer at giveaway prices, try **Dovas** (*see p139*) or **Johnny's** (*see p139*).

For hanging with the hipsters

Stockholm specialises in trendy bars. For starters, try **Storstad** (*see p133*), **O-baren** (*see p139*), **East** (*see p138*), **Laroy** (*see p138*) or the infamous **Spy Bar** (*see p192*).

Café Opera: still stylish. *See p132.*

higher. Irish and British pubs have a wider choice of beers on tap, including Guinness.

To counterbalance the high cost of alcohol, a typical Stockholmer's weekend will start with a few drinks with friends at home. This tradition, called *värma* ('warming'), is particularly common among students and the underpaid. As a result, the bars don't begin to fill up until around 9.30pm to 11pm. The popular places fill up quickly, however, so arrive before 10.30pm to avoid queuing. Bars tend to be quieter during the week, when you'll have a better chance of getting into the trendier places without standing in line first.

Although notorious drinkers in any country where booze is cheap, Swedes, particularly Stockholmers, don't like to be seen puking in their own capital. Public drunkenness may be more common in Stockholm than in other major European cities, but pissed youths rolling around in the gutter are a frequent sight only during the weeks following school graduation.

A particular quirk of Stockholm nightlife are the ubiquitous cloakrooms manned by authoritarian attendants who, it seems, will stop at nothing to get you to hand over your coat. Accept this drawback with a smile. Although the 10kr to 15kr fee is annoying, it will at least prevent your jacket from being stolen. Huge, dripping, winter coats are to blame for this mildly menacing culture.

Gamla Stan

If you're a jazz fan, you could also try the bar at **Stampen Jazzpub** (*see p211*), which is usually pretty lively.

Engelen

Kornhamnstorg 59 (20 10 92/611 62 00). T-bana Gamla Stan/bus 3, 53, 55, 59, 76. **Open** *Bar* 4pm-3am daily. *Kitchen* 4-11pm daily. **Minimum age** 23. **Admission** Mon-Thur 40kr; Fri, Sat 60kr. **Credit** AmEx, DC, MC, V. **Map** p303 J7.

Posing as a rustic tavern, Engelen (both bar and restaurant) caters to tourists and middle-aged locals looking to get down and party. The main room has a stage where live bands play covers from 8.30pm to midnight most days. When that's over, guests move downstairs to the vaulted nightclub in the cellar where top 40 music is mixed with popular faves.

Medusa

Kornhamnstorg 61 (21 87 00/www.medusabar.com). T-bana Gamla Stan/bus 3, 53, 55, 59, 76. **Open** *Bar* 2pm-3am daily. *Kitchen* 2-10pm daily. **Minimum age** Mon-Thur, Sun women 18, men 20; Fri, Sat women 21, men 23. **Credit** AmEx, MC, V. **Map** p303 J7.

A small bar with a cavernous basement, Medusa is Gamla Stan's heavy metal hangout. The upstairs bar, painted in plain orange, plays basic rock music to a mixed crowd of tourists and headbangers. Downstairs, in the twisty blue catacombs, the music is louder and harder. A small bar serves beer to guests whooping it up on the two tiny dancefloors. Mind your head.

Norrmalm

Berns Salonger

Berzelii Park (56 63 20 00/www.berns.se). T-bana Kungsträdgården/bus 46, 47, 55, 69, 76. **Open** *Bar Mid Aug-June* 11.30am-1am Mon, Tue; 11.30am-3am Wed, Thur; 11.30am-4am Fri, Sat; 11.30am-midnight Sun (*July-mid Aug* from 1pm Sat, Sun). *Kitchen Mid Aug-June* 11.30am-3pm Mon, Sun; 11.30am-3pm, 5-11pm Tue-Thur; 11.30am-3pm,

The day the heating broke at the **Icebar**.

5-11.30pm Fri, Sat (*July-mid Aug* 11.30am-11.30pm Fri; 1-11.30pm Sat). **Minimum age** 23. **Credit** AmEx, DC, MC, V. **Map** p303 G8.

Built in 1863, Berns was once Stockholm's foremost venue for exclusive, cabaret-style entertainment. Since reopening in 1989, the baroque mansion has once again emerged as the city's number one late-night party palace. Sporting no fewer than five bars on three levels, Berns combines a hip club in the basement with a ballroom bar and various balcony-area hideaways. In summer, the outside terrace bar is packed with Stockholmers. Watch out for the notoriously fickle bouncers. The queue varies in size through the evening: arrive before 11pm to be on the safe side or chance it just before 1am, when the neighbouring bars close. Attached is the upmarket Berns Hotel (*see p42*).

Café Opera

Operahuset, Karl XIIs Torg (676 58 07/ www.cafeopera.se). T-bana Kungsträdgården/ bus 46, 55, 59, 62, 76. **Open** *Bar* 5pm-3am daily. *Kitchen* 5pm-2.30am daily. **Minimum age** 23. **Admission** *after 11pm* 100kr. **Credit** AmEx, DC, MC, V. **Map** p303 G7.

Located in the back of the Stockholm Opera House, Café Opera remains one of the most elegant and exclusive venues in town. A restaurant by day, in the evening 'the Café' turns into an extravagant party bar with a sizeable dancefloor. The interior is a luxurious mix of Scandinavian chic and remodelled baroque. Visitors here range from twentysomething hipsters to some scantily dressed women and older businessmen in suits.

Fredsgatan 12

Fredsgatan 12 (411 73 48). T-bana Kungsträdgården/ bus 3, 53, 62, 65. **Open** *Terrace bar & kitchen May-Aug* 9pm-3am Tue-Sun. **Minimum age** 20. **Credit** AmEx, DC, MC, V. **Map** p303 H7.

Located in the historic Royal Academy of Arts building, trendy Fredsgatan 12 is best known for its outside terrace, which is open only in the summer. This consists of two level platforms on either side of the wide set of steps leading up to the building's main entrance. Hip twentysomethings rub elbows, groove to the music and occasionally take in the view towards Gamla Stan and the Riksdag. Watch out for the odd broken beer glass rolling down the steps. The restaurant inside is highly rated (*see p113*).

Icebar

Nordic Sea Hotel, Vasaplan 4 (50 56 30 00/ www.nordichotels.se). T-bana T-Centralen/bus 1, 47, 53, 59, 69. **Open** 3pm-midnight Mon-Sat; 3-9pm Sun. **Admission** 125kr. **Credit** AmEx, DC, MC, V. **Map** p303 G6.

Branded as the world's first permanent bar built entirely out of ice, the Icebar in the Nordic Sea Hotel is a unique experience. For 125kr you are equipped with a silvery high-tech poncho, guided into a room built from ice bricks and, at the ice bar itself, treated to a frosty vodka drink in a glass made from – you guessed it – ice. (Refills cost 70kr.) Although cool in more ways than one, the -4°C (23°F) bar is essentially a tourist attraction. Expect large groups and picture-taking. The Icebar is designed by the people behind the well-known Icehotel in Jukkasjärvi in the far north of Sweden.

The Loft

Regeringsgatan 66 (411 19 91). T-bana Hötorget/ bus 1, 52, 56. **Open** *Bar* 3pm-1am Mon-Thur; 3pm-2am Fri, Sat; 3pm-midnight Sun. *Kitchen* 3-10.30pm daily. **Minimum age** 23. **Credit** AmEx, MC, V. **Map** p303 F7.

One of the few Irish pubs in Stockholm actually staffed by Irishmen, the Loft bar-restaurant has become home to expats from all corners of the English-speaking world. Although the interior is irritatingly reminiscent of a medieval tavern, the Loft doesn't try as hard as some of its more commercial competitors. Sports are shown on two TVs and one projector screen in the bar area. Priority is given to good ol' Anglo-Saxon events such as Gaelic football, rugby and hurling.

Vasastaden

The Bagpipers Inn

Rörstrandsgatan 21 (31 18 55). T-bana St Eriksplan/ bus 3, 4, 42, 72. **Open** *Bar* 4pm-midnight Mon; 4pm-1am Tue-Thur; 3pm-1am Fri; 2pm-1am Sat; 2-11pm Sun. *Kitchen* 4-11pm Mon-Thur; 3-11pm Fri; 2-11pm Sat, Sun. **Minimum age** 23. **Credit** AmEx, MC, V. **Map** p306 D2.

The bartenders wear kilts at this Scottish-themed pub decorated with dark wood, green walls and knick-knacks from the Highlands. The beer is not cheap (46kr-49kr for a pint), but there's a good selection of around a dozen brews on tap, mainly from the UK and Ireland. The crowd consists of thirtysomethings and out-of-towners drawn in by the cosy atmosphere. The Bagpipers Inn is usually packed at the weekends and in the summer, when outside seating is available.

Cliff Barnes

Norrtullsgatan 45 (31 80 70). T-bana Odenplan/ bus 40, 46, 52, 69. **Open** *Bar* 11am-midnight Mon; 11-1am Tue-Fri; 5pm-1am Sat. *Kitchen* 11am-11pm Mon-Fri; 5-11pm Sat. **Minimum age** 23. **Credit** AmEx, MC, V. **Map** p306 C4.

Located on the outskirts of town in what was once a home for widowed women, Cliff Barnes is a down-to-earth party bar. The worn wooden floors, high ceilings and large vaulted windows make it ideal for enthusiastic beer drinking and loud conversation. At 11pm on Fridays and Saturdays the lights are turned down and the music (popular faves from the 1960s and '70s) is turned up. Although several large signs clearly forbid it, dancing on the tables is not uncommon. Cliff Barnes takes its name from JR's unlucky arch rival in *Dallas*, and a framed portrait of Ken Kercheval (the actor who portrayed Cliff Barnes) decorates the bar's main wall.

Gotchå

Gästrikegatan 3 (34 15 15). T-Bana St Eriksplan/ bus 3, 4, 42, 72. **Open** *Bar* 5pm-midnight Tue-Sat. *Kitchen* 5-11pm Tue-Sat. **Minimum age** 20. **Credit** AmEx, MC, V. **Map** p306 D3.

Tastefully decorated and furnished in the style of the 1960s, Gotchå is the perfect place to bring either a date or a small group of friends. You'll be mixing mainly with hip twentysomethings there to enjoy the laid-back atmosphere and hip hop or soul music playing on the sound system. The downstairs cocktail bar is even cooler: it's decorated in a lush '70s style, with a long orange couch winding its way round the far wall; there are red-tinted lights, a disco ball and a projector continually playing kung fu and blaxploitation films.

La Habana

Sveavägen 108 (16 64 65/www.lahabana.nu). T-bana Rådmansgatan/bus 42, 46, 52, 53, 72. **Open** *Bar* 5pm-1am daily. *Kitchen* 5-10pm Mon-Wed, Sun; 5-10.30pm Thur-Sat. **Minimum age** 20. **Credit** AmEx, DC, MC, V. **Map** p307 D6.

As one of only two Cuban bars in Stockholm, La Habana is a refreshing alternative to the largely mainstream bars in the area. The interior consists mainly of dark wood and white walls, but the crowd, the drinks and the music are all more colourful. Latin-Americans and Swedes meet and mix. The small basement bar (open Wed-Sat) serves great Mojitos, and the floor comes alive with spurts of salsa dancing in the late hours.

Musslan Bar

Dalagatan 46 (34 64 10). T-bana Odenplan/bus 4, 40, 47, 53, 72. **Open** *Bar* 8pm-1am Mon; 6pm-1am Tue-Sat. *Kitchen* 8-11pm Mon; 6-11pm Tue-Sat. **Minimum age** 20. **Credit** AmEx, DC, MC, V. **Map** p306 D4.

Trendy young things frequent this tiny, dimly lit bar. Lush sofas, stainless-steel tables and a blue ceiling with tiny starry lights set Musslan apart from the competition. It's a place to chill out and have a cocktail while the DJ (Wed-Sat) spins soul or ambient techno.

Paus

Rörstrandsgatan 18 (34 44 05). T-bana St Eriksplan/ bus 3, 4, 42, 72. **Open** *Bar* 5pm-1am Mon-Sat. *Kitchen* 5-11pm Mon-Sat. **Minimum age** 23. **Credit** AmEx, DC, MC, V. **Map** p306 E3.

Located on a quiet residential street filled with cafés and bars, Paus has a cream-coloured interior with large monochrome paintings and a giant mirror wall. The bar specialises in quality cocktails but doesn't take itself too seriously, with a laid-back, neighbourhood feel. Shunning the guest DJs of similarly decorated places, the soft music seems to be whatever CDs the bartender decided to bring to work that day.

Storstad

Odengatan 41 (673 38 00). T-bana Rådmansgatan/ bus 4, 42, 46, 53, 72. **Open** *Bar* 5pm-1am Mon, Tue; 5pm-3am Wed, Thur; 4pm-3am Fri; 6pm-3am Sat. *Kitchen* 5-11pm Mon-Fri; 6-11pm Sat. **Minimum age** 23. **Credit** AmEx, DC, MC, V. **Map** p307 C6.

Hipsters mix with the suit-and-tie brigade at the hottest bar in Vasastaden. Storstad (literally 'Big Town') sports a Stockholm-chic white interior, huge windows and a large L-shaped bar that allows for a great deal of person-to-person interaction. Storstad is undoubtedly a trendy spot, and features the usual guest DJs playing all the right tunes. But it is not as reserved as similar venues – some may even call it a classy pick-up bar. For a darker version of the same thing, check out its sister bar, Olssons Skor, which is just next door.

Tranan

Karlbergsvägen 14 (52 72 81 00). T-bana Odenplan/ bus 4, 40, 46, 69, 72. **Open** *Bar* 5pm-1am daily. *Kitchen* 5-11.45pm daily. **Minimum age** 23. **Credit** AmEx, DC, MC, V. **Map** p307 D5.

Described as a 'modern classic' in the local entertainment guides, Tranan is surely the quintessential Stockholm bar. Situated in the basement of the

well-respected Tranan restaurant, the bar combines minimalist chic with the cosy feel of a cellar. A DJ spins records as hip professionals in their late twenties congregate around sturdy wooden tables. Never too surprising, Tranan holds its own as one of the most enduring grade-A bars in Stockholm.

Södermalm

Also worth checking out is **Patricia** (*see p208*): a bar/club/restaurant on a boat permanently moored at Slussen. Most famous for its gay nights (Sundays), it draws a more mixed crowd the rest of the week.

Akkurat

Hornsgatan 18 (644 00 15/www.akkurat.se). T-bana Mariatorget/bus 43, 55, 66, 74. **Open** *Bar* 11am-1am Mon-Fri; noon-1am Sat. *Kitchen* 11am-11pm Mon-Fri; noon-11pm Sat. **Minimum age** 23. **Credit** AmEx, DC, MC, V. **Map** p310 K7.

Beer lovers should head for Akkurat, which offers a huge selection of bottled Belgian beers, plus regularly changing draught beers, 280 kinds of whisky, live music and a kitchen serving mussels and the like. Don't be deterred by its unappealing looks.

Fenix

Götgatan 40 (640 45 06). T-bana Slussen or Medborgarplatsen/bus 59, 66. **Open** *Bar & kitchen* 11am-1am Mon-Fri; noon-1am Sat; noon-midnight Sun. **Minimum age** 23. **Credit** AmEx, DC, MC, V. **Map** p310 L8.

This gaudy party bar offers a refreshing alternative to the tasteful minimalism of many Stockholm drinking places. Fenix sports red walls, crazy artwork and mosaic decorations. The crowd is a mix of twenty- and thirtysomethings dressed for a night out. The cavernous basement features a dancefloor and winding lounge area.

Folkhemmet

Renstiernas Gata 30 (640 55 95/www.users.wineasy.se/folkhemmet). Bus 46, 53, 59, 66, 76. **Open** *Bar* 5pm-1am daily. *Kitchen* 5-11pm daily. **Credit** AmEx, DC, MC, V. **Map** p311 M9.

One of the most enduring bars in the Nytorget area, Folkhemmet is a favourite watering hole for artists, musicians and media folk in their late twenties and early thirties. It gets jam-packed at the weekends. The minimalist interior combines a dining area (*see p121*) with a bar and DJ stand. A tiny adjoining bar (closed Mon), decorated in bright red, doubles as a dancefloor as the night progresses. Folkhemmet takes its name from the 1930s political ideal of the 'people's home' or welfare state. When staying out late on Söder, be sure to leave Folkhemmet at 12.30am to avoid the second rush at Snaps (*see p137*), Kvarnen (*see p136*) and the other 3am bars.

Gondolen

Stadsgården 6 (641 70 90/www.eriks.se). T-bana Slussen/bus 3, 46, 53, 76. **Open** *Bar Aug-June* 11.30am-1am Mon-Fri; 1pm-1am Sat. *July* 5.30pm-1am

Gondolen: unmissable views of the city.

Eat, Drink, Shop

Mon-Sat. *Kitchen Aug-June* 11.30am-2.30pm Mon-Fri; 5-11pm Sat. *July* 5.30-11pm Mon-Sat. **Credit** AmEx, DC, MC, V. **Map** p310 K8.
Located at the top of the historic Katarina lift, Gondolen is an ideal place for a tall drink and a wide view of the city. The bar sits under the walkway that connects the lift with Mosebacke, and provides a panoramic view of Djurgården to the east and Riddarfjärden to the west. Drinks are reasonably priced, despite the feeling of international luxury. You can get to the bar either from Mosebacke in the Katarinahissen (5kr) or via the restaurant's own lift at Stadsgården 6.

Guldapan

Åsögatan 140 (640 97 71/www.guldapan.rgsth.com). T-bana Medborgarplatsen/bus 46, 59, 66, 76.
Open *Bar* 5pm-1am daily. *Kitchen* 5-11pm daily. **Credit** AmEx, MC, V. **Map** p311 M9.
At this chic, out-of-the-way, hole-in-the-wall bar and restaurant two bartenders take turns serving beer and flipping records. Though packed at the weekends, 'the Golden Ape' is free from both bouncers and queues. Its popularity is partly due to its impressive faux-gold ceiling. The music is edgy, mainly hip hop, soul and reggae.

Kvarnen

Tjärhovsgatan 4 (643 03 80/www.kvarnen.com). T-bana Medborgarplatsen/bus 55, 59, 66. **Open** *Kvarnen* 11am-3am Mon-Fri; 5pm-3am Sat, Sun. *H2O* 5pm-3am Mon-Fri; 7pm-3am Sat. *Eld* 10pm-3am Tue-Sun. *Kitchen* 11am-11pm Mon-Fri; 5-11pm Sat, Sun. **Minimum age** 23. **Credit** AmEx, MC, V. **Map** p311 L8.
Originally a beer hall, Kvarnen ('the Windmill') has evolved into one of the most popular late-night pubs on Söder. The lofty main room, filled with rows of tables and loud chatter, plays no music and retains the traditional look and feel of a beer hall. It is flanked by two more recent additions: the small Mediterranean-themed H20 bar in what used to be a kitchen area, and the flame-inspired Eld ('Hell') bar in the basement. Eld heats up in the wee hours when dancing truly erupts on the black and white chequered floor. Kvarnen is also the pub of choice for Hammarby supporters before matches (*see p226* **The big three**). Show up early at the weekend, preferably before 10pm, to avoid the horrific line that winds down the block. Bouncers are strict but fair: everyone gets in – sooner or later.

London New York

Götgatan 54 (644 50 93). T-bana Medborgarplatsen/bus 55, 59, 66. **Open** *Bar* 4pm-3am daily. *Kitchen* 4-11pm daily. **Minimum age** women 23, men 25. **Admission** after 10pm 50kr-60kr. **Credit** AmEx, DC, MC, V. **Map** p310 M8.
This loud bar fuses a British pub-style interior with American flags and a Europop dancefloor. The punters are typically aged 25 to 35, and dressed to kill. Although most sophisticated Stockholmers consider London New York something of a tourist trap, the place throws a good party and is packed from Thursday to Saturday. Its 3am closing time makes it a last resort for those unwilling (or unable) to stand in line at nearby Kvarnen (*see above*) and Snaps (*see p137*).

Mosebacke Etablissement

Mosebacketorg 3 (55 60 98 90/www.mosebacke.se). T-bana Slussen/bus 3, 46, 53, 76. **Open** *Bar Summer* 11am-1am daily. *Winter* 4pm-1am Mon-Thur, Sun; 4pm-2am Fri, Sat. *Kitchen Summer*

Late-night stalwart **Kvarnen.**

A drink with a view at **Mosebacke**.

11am-midnight daily. *Winter* 4-9pm daily. **Minimum age** varies. **Admission** 60kr-80kr. **Credit** AmEx, DC, MC, V. **Map** p310 K8.

A definite winner among musicians and underground types, Mosebacke is Stockholm's hottest venue for cutting-edge performance acts and live music (*see p213*). The historic building, part of Södra Teatern (*see p213*), features two bars and a dancefloor/stage area – check local papers for details or drop by for a surprise show. In the summer, two additional bars open on the large outdoor terrace, which offers a fantastic view of the Stockholm harbour. It also hosts some great clubs; *see p191*.

O'Learys

Götgatan 11 (644 69 01/www.olearys.se). T-bana Slussen/bus 3, 46, 53, 59, 76. **Open** *Bar* 5pm-midnight Mon-Thur; 4pm-1am Fri; 1pm-1am Sat; 1pm-midnight Sun. *Kitchen* 5-10pm Mon-Thur; 4-10pm Fri; 1-10pm Sat, Sun. **Minimum age** 21. **Credit** AmEx, DC, MC, V. **Map** p310 K8.

This Boston-Irish sports bar is home to Anglophiles, expats and die-hard sports fans mainly in their thirties and forties. The green interior is covered with framed sports posters, neon beer signs and, above all, televisions: it's got three big-screen TVs and 35 regular units – including one in the loo. There are 45 beers to choose from, most from England, Ireland and the USA. Aside from the obligatory slot machines, O'Learys also has a 'pop-a-shot' basketball game. Call in advance to reserve tables during major sporting events.

Branch: Kungsholmsgatan 31, Kungsholmen (654 52 10).

Pelikan

Blekingegatan 40 (55 60 90 90). T-bana Skanstull/bus 3, 55, 59, 74. **Open** *Pelikan* noon-1am daily. *Kristallen* 5pm-1am daily. *Kitchen* noon-11pm daily. **Credit** AmEx, MC, V. **Map** p311 M8.

This charming beer hall is located well away from the action in a mainly residential area in southern Södermalm. The clientele ranges from ageing regulars to young Southside hipsters in designer clothes. Drop in for a beer at one of the many tables or visit the adjoining bar, Kristallen, adorned with oriental rugs and ornate chandeliers.

Snaps

Götgatan 48 (640 28 68/www.snaps.org). T-bana Medborgarplatsen/bus 55, 59, 66. **Open** *Bar* 5pm-1am Mon-Wed; 5pm-3am Fri, Sat. *Kitchen* 5-11pm Mon-Sat. **Minimum age** 23. **Credit** AmEx, DC, MC, V. **Map** p310 L8.

Located in the vaulted basement of a 17th-century mansion, Snaps is one of Söder's most popular party bars, second only to Kvarnen and Mosebacke (for both, *see p136*). The main room features a dining area, bar and blackjack table. For more action, venture yet further downstairs to the Rangus Tangus club (*see p191*), a dance/lounge area in tones of deep red. In summer, you can eat outside in a large courtyard. Show up before 11pm to avoid queuing.

Tonic

Hornsgatan 66B (668 85 00). T-bana Mariatorget/bus 43, 55, 66, 74. **Open** *Bar* 5pm-1am Mon, Tue; 5pm-3am Wed-Sat. *Kitchen* 5pm-midnight Mon-Sat. **Minimum age** 23. **Admission** after 10pm 70kr. **Credit** AmEx, DC, MC, V. **Map** p310 K6.

This large, semi-trendy party bar attracts a mixed crowd of twentysomethings. The ground-floor bar gives a somewhat swanky impression, while the basement features the more folksy set-up of a bar, a small dancefloor, pool tables and darts.

WC

Skånegatan 51 (644 19 81). T-bana Medborgarplatsen/bus 59. **Open** *Bar* 5pm-1am daily. *Kitchen* 5-11pm daily. *Brunch served* 11.30am-

Expat alert at sports bar **O'Learys**. *See p137.*

3.30pm Sat, Sun. **Minimum age** 20. **Credit** AmEx, MC, V. **Map** p311 M8.
A small, rectangular, basement venue, WC is one of the more popular of the many bars on Skånegatan. The colourful interior, funky lighting and bar stools with holes in the seat (to look like potties) are not without charm. On the downside, WC can get hopelessly crowded at the weekends as the cramped quarters don't allow much room for movement. Claustrophobic people, beware.

Östermalm

If you're looking for glamour, in both decor and clientele, don't miss the myriad bars at famous Stureplan nightclub **Spy Bar** (*see p192*).

East

Stureplan 13 (611 49 59/www.east-restaurang.se). T-bana Östermalstorg/bus 1, 46, 55, 56, 91.
Open *Bar* 11.30am-3am Mon-Sat; 5pm-3am Sun. *Kitchen* 11.30am-11pm Mon-Sat; 5-11pm Sun. **Minimum age** 23. **Credit** AmEx, DC, MC, V. **Map** p303 F8.
A sushi restaurant by day, East turns into Stockholm's foremost hip hop hangout by night. Two bars serve beer and drinks while a DJ plays hard-hitting beats for one of the most ethnically diverse crowds in the city. A small section of the first bar doubles as a dancefloor later. It's a young, hip, bling-bling kind of place. It's also somewhat difficult to get past the bouncers. Dress jiggy and arrive before 10.30pm to avoid the hassle and the wait.

Halv Trappa Plus Gård

Lästmakargatan 3 (611 02 75). T-bana Östermalmstorg/bus 1, 43, 46, 55, 56. **Open** *Bar* 5pm-1am Mon, Tue; 5pm-3am Wed-Sat. *Kitchen* 5-11pm Mon-Sat. **Minimum age** 23. **Credit** AmEx, DC, MC, V. **Map** p303 F8.
With its stylish creamy interior, Halv Trappa remains a favourite among trendy, professional twentysomethings looking for a hint of glamour. The large, winding bar is ideal for impromptu meetings, while the two lounge areas are a great place to kick back, sip drinks and enjoy the tunes, which are largely hip hop and soul. In summer, the backyard patio – complete with a bar, heaters and Chinese lanterns – is a definite Stureplan favourite. The bouncers are notoriously difficult. At the weekend, dress fashionably and arrive before 10pm to be sure of getting in. If all else fails, ask the doorman nonchalantly, 'Excuse me, have my colleagues from Warner Music arrived yet?'

Laroy

Birger Jarlsgatan 20 (54 50 37 00). T-bana Östermalmstorg/bus 1, 46, 55, 56, 91. **Open** *Bar* 5pm-1am Tue, Wed; 5pm-2am Thur; 5pm-3am Fri; 7pm-3am Sat. *Kitchen* 5-10pm Tue-Fri; 7-10pm Sat. **Minimum age** 25. **Credit** AmEx, DC, MC, V. **Map** p303 E8.
Rich kids in designer shirts flash platinum cards and order bottles of champagne at this posh, two-storey bar and restaurant with a view over Stureplan. Although the air is thick with glamour and extravagance, Laroy is also a place for hopeful posers, particularly young girls looking for a hint of the high life and a few free drinks. Although there's no dancefloor, people let loose on all available floorspace as top 40 music pumps through the speakers. Dress posh and arrive before 10pm to ensure admittance.

Lydmar Hotel

Sturegatan 10 (56 61 13 00/www.lydmar.se). T-bana Östermalmstorg/bus 1, 46, 55, 56, 91.
Open *Bar* 11.30am-1am Mon-Thur; 11.30am-2am Fri; 1pm-2am Sat; 1pm-1am Sun. *Kitchen* 11.30am-11pm Mon-Fri; 1-11pm Sat, Sun. **Minimum age** 25. **Credit** AmEx, DC, MC, V. **Map** p303 E8.
As far as hotel bars are concerned, the Lydmar goes way beyond the call of duty. The main room, visible through the large wraparound windows, is spacious and furnished with linear black leather couches and easy chairs. Popular with the after-work crowd and for late-night cocktails, it also features sporadic live

events a few times a week. The bands are usually lesser-known jazz acts, but reputable underground groups such as the Roots have also been known to make unannounced appearances. Dress fashionably: the doorman can be picky when the place is crowded. Guests of the hotel (*see p53*) are automatically let in. *See also p214*.

O-baren

Stureplan 2 (440 57 30/www.sturehof.com). T-bana Östermalmstorg/bus 1, 46, 55, 56, 91. **Open** *Bar* 5pm-2am daily. *Sturehof* 5pm-1am daily. **Minimum age** 23. **Credit** AmEx, DC, MC, V. **Map** p303 F8.

A dark hip hop and soul den, O-baren is located in a back room of the exclusive Sturehof restaurant (*see p127*). Comprising a bar, a large square dancefloor and a bleacher-like seating area with a view of the floor, it's a place to be seen. Although glances and spontaneous dancing are commonplace, O-baren's clientele never lose their cool completely. Dress to kill and arrive before 10.30pm.

Kungsholmen

Dovas

St Eriksgatan 53A (650 80 49). T-bana Fridhemsplan/bus 3, 4, 57, 59. **Open** *Bar* 11am-1am daily. *Kitchen* 11am-11.30pm daily. **Minimum age** 20. **Credit** AmEx, MC, V.

Dovas is easily one of the most unsettling dives in the Fridhemsplan area. Its darkened interior with wooden booths houses a bizarre mix of local drunks, would-be criminals and innocent-eyed teenagers too young-looking to get in anywhere else. Tattoos and shaved heads are commonplace. As are random conversations that start with an accusation and end with some inebriated person putting their arm round your shoulder. The beer is dirt cheap at 23kr for a half-litre glass.

Johnny's

St Eriksgatan 22 (653 50 50). T-bana Fridhemsplan/bus 3, 4, 40, 57, 62. **Open** *Bar* 4pm-1am daily. *Kitchen* 4-11pm daily. **Credit** AmEx, MC, V.

One of the best-known bars around Fridhemsplan, Johnny's offers three pool tables, slot machines, table football, blackjack and a jukebox. If you don't mind colourless walls decorated with charity-shop art, the low beer prices (28kr for a 40cl glass or 99kr for a metal bucket with four 33cl bottles) make Johnny's a great place to start the evening. It heats up at the weekends, when the 18- to 20-year-old crowd form a long queue outside. There's karaoke on Wednesday nights.

Lokal

Scheelegatan 8 (650 98 09). T-bana Rådhuset/bus 3, 40, 52, 59, 62. **Open** *Bar* 4pm-1am Mon, Tue, Sun; 4pm-2am Wed, Thur; 4pm-3am Fri, Sat. *Kitchen* 4-11pm daily. **Minimum age** 23. **Credit** AmEx, DC, MC, V. **Map** p302 G4.

When Lokal first opened, everyone compared it to Storstad (*see p133*) in Vasastaden. Both sport a similarly stylish white interior, enormous shopfront windows, an L-shaped bar and guest DJs spinning soul or house music. However, Lokal is (as the name implies) more of a local venue. This means more suit-and-tie yuppies and fewer downtown hipsters.

Halv Trappa Plus Gård: I won't have what he's having. *See p138*.

Cafés

Stockholmers are addicted to coffee and cookies – and you will be too.

Swedes drink more coffee than any other nation, apart from the Finns. While an Italian drinks only 1.9 cups a day (and Brits no more than one), a Swede stops only after 4.5 cups. In a year, your average Swede consumes a mammoth ten kilos (22 pounds) of coffee. And they are not the least afraid of the side effects: caffeine rules, and even in a big capital like Stockholm you'll have problems finding decaff.

If there's one word you need to know before visiting Stockholm it's *fika*. While Brits meet at the pub, Swedes go to cafés. And *fika* is the verb used to describe having coffee. But it's not just a quick stop for caffeine: *fika* is something you do for hours, preferably while gossiping with friends. And most cafés (also called *fik*) offer endless refills (*påtår*) for free or a token charge. *Fika* is almost an art form, something deeply rooted even in those who don't like coffee and instead drink the classic Swedish fruit punch, *saft*. Traditional times for *fika*, especially at work, are at 10am and 3pm.

It was King Karl XII who brought coffee back to Sweden from Turkey in 1714. And when making your own liquor was forbidden in 1855, many Swedes indulged in caffeine instead. Throughout the 19th century, when sexuality was a taboo subject and spicy food was thought to arouse the desires of the Devil, coffee and biscuits were one of life's few permitted pleasures. Especially biscuits. Housewives would compete in making as many kinds as possible – all with romantic names such as *drömmar* ('dreams') or *hallongrottor* ('caves of raspberry'). An affluent housewife had to serve at least seven kinds of biscuit, and politeness demanded that her guests tried one of each. In some homes this is still a tradition. At the beginning of the 20th century it was considered indecent for a woman to visit a restaurant unless she was accompanied by a man. So, instead, women met up at cafés or organised coffee parties; today you will still sometimes hear the term *kaffekärring* ('coffeelady') for a scandalmonger.

You'll find a great variety of cafés in Stockholm, all worth a visit: old-fashioned *konditori* selling traditional cakes; Italian-run joints, which are the best places for espresso; trapped-in-time places that haven't changed their decor (or staff) since the 1950s; and chilled-out modern cafés with comfy sofas and spaced-out sounds. Nowadays, even chains like 7-Eleven offer a quick *fika* (coffee and a cinnamon bun for 12kr), but most Swedes still prefer a proper *fik*. The American coffee chains such as Starbucks that have invaded the rest of Europe have found it almost impossible to start up in Sweden – perhaps because they don't understand the *fika* tradition and how seriously Swedes take their coffee. However, there are a number of successful home-grown chains based more or less on the American model, such as Wayne's Coffee (*see p148*), Robert's Coffee and Coffee Cup.

Most cafés offer an extensive range of espresso-based coffee drinks, though at the traditional places you'll sometimes have to settle for plain coffee – which is a lot stronger in Sweden than in the UK or USA. You'll also find tea (black and fruit teas, not always herbal ones) and numerous biscuits, cakes and sandwiches. Some of the pastries are seasonal. *Semla* (a bun with whipped cream, sugar and almond paste), sometimes eaten with warm milk, is only served until Easter. And you will only find the Christmas cake *lussekatt* (a saffron bun with raisins) in December. Other popular sweets are gingerbread biscuits and *dammsugare* ('vacuum cleaner'), which is made with green marzipan and chocolate. Some places serve full-blown meals.

Most cafés are not allowed to sell alcohol (although some do have a permit but choose not to). Unless you're being served at a table, drinks should be paid for at the till when you order. If you're at a table, the waiter will bring the bill with your drinks. You may be expected to pay immediately; it is not customary (but appreciated) to tip. And table prices will almost always be the same as bar prices.

But most importantly: as long as you have just a sip of coffee left in your cup, nobody expects you to leave. You're supposed to be there for hours – that's what *fika* is all about.

Gamla Stan

In addition to the Stortorget cafés listed below, there's **Grillska Husets Konditori** (787 86 05). It's not as atmospheric, but it has three large rooms with a front window overlooking the square, and good pastries. It's run by Stockholms Stadsmissions, a charity that

Chokladkoppen: Gamla Stan's finest. *See p142.*

works with the homeless. **Café Kåkbrinken** (Västerlånggatan 41; 411 61 74) has ice-cream and fresh waffles.

Chokladkoppen

Stortorget 20 (20 31 70). T-bana Gamla Stan/bus 3, 53, 55, 59, 76. **Open** 9am-11pm Mon-Thur, Sun; 9am-midnight Fri, Sat. **No credit cards. Map** p303 J7.

Skip Gamla Stan's tourist traps and try this place or its sister café next door, Kaffekoppen (*see below*), on Stortorget, the charming square in the centre of Gamla Stan. Chokladkoppen, on the left in the orange building, has trendy furniture and loud music, and is popular with Stockholm's gay crowd (*see p207*). The service is laid-back and friendly. In summer, there are tables outside in the square. Both cafés have the same menu.

Kaffekoppen

Stortorget 18 (20 31 70). T-bana Gamla Stan/bus 3, 53, 55, 59, 76. **Open** 8am-11pm Mon-Thur, Sun; 8am-midnight Fri, Sat. **No credit cards. Map** p303 J7.

One of two sister cafés on Stortorget, Kaffekoppen has rickety old wooden tables and chairs in a tiny 13th-century interior, and good home-made food.

Sundberg's Konditori

Järntorget 83 (10 67 35). T-bana Gamla Stan/bus 3, 53, 55, 59, 76. **Open** *Summer* 7.30am-10pm Mon-Fri; 9am-10pm Sat, Sun. *Winter* 7.30am-8pm Mon-Fri; 9am-8pm Sat, Sun. **Credit** DC, MC, V. **Map** p303 J8.

On Järntorget, the centre for iron export until 1662, Sundberg's has served hot coffee from the copper samovar for more than 200 years. It was founded in 1785 by Johan Ludvig Sundberg and, according to local lore, King Gustav III had a secret passageway from the Kungliga Slottet straight to the bakery. Don't expect to order frappuccinos and smoothies here: you come to Sundberg's for traditional cakes and the atmosphere. In the same square as the café, in front of Södra Bankohuset (the First Swedish National Bank), you'll find a statue of the popular poet-songwriter Evert Taube.

Norrmalm

Lovely, old-fashioned **Vete-Katten** (*see p162*) near Hötorget is also worth a visit for its outstanding pastries and chocolates.

Atrium

Nationalmuseet, Södra Blasieholmshamnen (611 34 30/www.restaurangatrium.se). T-bana Kungsträdgården/bus 65. **Open** *Summer* 11am-8pm Tue; 11am-5pm Wed-Sun. *Winter* 11am-5pm Mon-Wed, Fri-Sun; 11am-8pm Thur. **Credit** AmEx, DC, MC, V. **Map** p303 H8.

Many museums have excellent cafés, especially the Dansmuseet (*see p73*) and Aquaria Vattenmuseum (*see p82*), but by far the best place to spend a rainy day is without doubt Atrium at the Nationalmuseet. Though the museum itself, which is beautifully located opposite the Royal Palace, is a bit dark and moody, visiting the glass-roofed courtyard café is like having coffee in Renaissance Florence. And the salad buffet is excellent. You don't need to pay the museum entrance fee to go to the café: just tell the guards you're there for *fika*.

Café Panorama

5th floor, Kulturhuset, Sergels Torg 3 (21 10 35/www.kulturhuset.stockholm.se). T-bana T-Centralen/bus 47, 52, 56, 65, 91. **Open** *Summer* 11am-6pm Mon-Sat; 11am-5pm Sun. *Winter* 11am-7pm Tue-Sat; 11am-5pm Sun. **Credit** MC, V. **Map** p303 G7.

If you're looking to discuss art, theatre or literature, this café on the top floor of the Kulturhuset is the place. It's got a reputation for sensational *skorpor* (crisp rolls, usually eaten with jam or cheese) and a good lunch menu. It's also very near the big shopping streets of Hamngatan and Drottninggatan and offers an amazing view of Stockholm's busiest square, Sergels Torg – especially in summer when the *utomhusterassen* (outdoor terrace) is open. If it's full, try the café two floors below, which also offers a fine view. Or the café inside Åhlens on the opposite side of the street: the coffee and atmosphere are not nearly as nice, but it's a decent substitute.

Piccolino

Kungsträdgården (611 88 48). T-bana Kungsträdgården/bus 46, 47, 55, 59, 62. **Open** *Summer* 8am-10pm Mon-Fri; 10am-10pm Sat, Sun. *Winter* 10am-9pm daily. **Credit** DC, MC, V. **Map** p303 G8.

Some older Swedes will remember the first time they tasted a banana; others the day Piccolino brought espresso to Stockholm. Built out of glass, next to Kungsträdgården's ice rink and outdoor stage, this small café is popular with popstars and models, and a perfect people-watching spot. The elms surrounding the café are important for many Stockholmers: 30 years ago they were saved after a sit-down protest against the decision to build a Tunnelbana station next door to Café Opera.

Spårvagn

From Norrmalmstorg to Bellmansro and back (operating company Djurgårdslinjen: 660 77 00/www.ss.se/djurgardslinjen/rollingcafe.php). **Runs** from Norrmalmstorg approx every 30mins 11am-4pm Sat, Sun. **Tickets** (round trip or one way with change of tram) 45kr. **No credit cards. Map** p303 F8.

Not a café as such, but a *fika*-serving old tram travelling between Norrmalmstorg and Djurgården. Not the kind of place to meet locals, but a nice way to reach open-air museum Skansen (*see p84*) past the old sailboats at Nybroviken. And the ticket collectors know enough about the places en route to answer any questions. The price includes a drink and a pastry, but don't fill your cup with too much coffee – it's a bumpy ride.

Tintarella di Luna

Drottninggatan 102 (10 79 55). T-bana Rådmansgatan/bus 4, 42, 46, 52, 72. **Open** 8am-7pm Mon-Fri; 9am-5pm Sat. **No credit cards. Map** p307 E6.

One of the city's more laid-back Italian cafés, but it's really small – so be prepared to wait for a table. The *macchiato* is amazing, although cornetto and *cantuccini* are the only desserts. Don't miss the quotes of world-famous Swedish author/playwright August Strindberg that fill Drottninggatan's pavement – if they wet your appetite, the Strindberg Museum (*see p76*) is just across the street.

Vasastaden

Creem

Karlbergsvägen 23 (32 52 65). T-bana Odenplan/bus 4, 42, 47. **Open** 10am-10pm Mon-Thur; 10am-7pm Fri; 11am-7pm Sat; 11am-10pm Sun. **Credit** DC, MC, V. **Map** p307 D5.

With the simple, stark kind of furniture used in old Swedish schools, Creem might at first sight look a bit too trendy, but it's actually one of Sweden's cosiest cafés. The salads and salami sandwiches are truly excellent, the staff are friendly, and there are international magazines to browse through. The sofas in the inner room are the kind you'll have to try hard not to fall asleep in after a long day of shopping. The only mystery is why on earth some of the fittings in the toilet are upside down.

Branches: Flemminggatan 22, Kungsholmen (651 53 00); Folkungagatan 57, Södermalm (640 28 38).

Kafe Kompott

Karlbergsvägen 52 (31 51 77). T-bana St Eriksplan/bus 3, 42, 47, 507. **Open** *Summer* 8am-8pm Mon-Fri; 9.30am-7pm Sat, Sun. *Winter* 8am-7pm Mon-Thur; 9.30am-6pm Fri-Sun. Closed mid July-mid Aug. **Credit** MC, V. **Map** p307 D4.

A café designed for parents: this is probably the only place in Stockholm where you'll feel odd if you don't have a couple of kids in tow. Kompott offers a microwave for mums and dads who need to heat up bottles, and every door is wide enough for push-chairs to pass through easily. On weekdays it serves a good but too expensive breakfast buffet, and on Sundays there's brunch.

113 50 Café & Deli

Sveavägen 98 (15 74 45). T-bana Rådmansgatan/bus 52. **Open** 9am-9pm Mon-Fri; 11am-5pm Sat; noon-6pm Sun. **No credit cards**. **Map** p307 D6.

Students and travellers on a budget will love the low-priced but enormous salads and sandwiches served here. The service is friendly and efficient, and if anything other than Marvin Gaye is played it will probably be for the first time ever. Named after its postcode, this is mainly a hangout for students from Handelshögskolan, the nearby school of economics, looking for a quick caffeine fix. But on Sundays there's a queue all the way out on to the street.

Ritorno

Odengatan 80-82 (32 01 06). T-bana Odenplan/bus 4, 40, 53, 69, 72. **Open** 7am-10pm Mon-Fri; 8am-6pm Sat; 10am-6pm Sun. Closed usually July. **Credit** AmEx, DC, MC, V. **Map** p306 D4.

A 1950s café with beautiful old jukeboxes. Close to child-friendly Vasaparken, Ritorno offers everything from traditional shrimp sandwiches (shrimp, egg, mayonnaise, lemon and cucumber on rye) to calorie-dripping Danish pastries. The pastries tend to have funny names, such as 'One of those' and 'Sumthin' sweet'. The café's popular with Odengaten's many record- and antique-dealers.

Sirap

Surbrunnsgatan 31A (612 94 19). T-bana Rådmansgatan/bus 4, 42, 46, 72, 96. **Open** 9am-7pm Mon-Fri; 11am-6pm Sat, Sun. Closed 3wks July, 1wk Christmas. **No credit cards**. **Map** p307 C6.

Painted all in yellow, this brunch specialist is busy over the weekend serving American pancakes, club sandwiches, scrambled eggs, toast, bacon and everything else you might crave after a long night out. There's a veggie option too. The rest of the time it's a quiet café and the staff take it extra slow to save strength for the chaotic weekend.

Sosta

Sveavägen 84 (612 13 49). T-bana Rådmansgatan/bus 52. **Open** 8am-7pm Mon-Fri; 10am-5pm Sat; 11am-4pm Sun. **No credit cards**. **Map** p307 D6.

Sosta is a very stylish Italian espresso bar known all over Sweden for its extraordinary coffee and low prices. Although some may say it's as famous for

The best Cafés

In summer

Rosendals Trädgård. *See p144.*

In winter

Saturnus. *See p146.*

For cakes

Gateau. *See p146.*

For brunch

Sirap. *See p143.*

For a quick espresso

Sosta. *See p143.*

For a view

Café Panorama. *See p142.*

For meeting models

Piccolino. *See p142.*

To take the kids

Kafe Kompott. *See p143.*

To travel back in time

Valand. *See p144.*

For the best *semla* in town

Thelins. *See p148.*

Italian-style espresso at **Sosta**. *See p143.*

the well-dressed *baristas* making the *doppios* and serving the cornetto right at the counter (there are no tables). Try the focaccias or the great home-made strawberry sorbet and you'll realise that Sosta is the closest you'll get to Italy in Scandinavia. And, as in Italy, don't expect the bar staff to ask what you want or you could wait all day.
Branch: Jakobsbergsgatan 7, Norrmalm (611 71 07).

Valand

Surbrunnsgatan 48H (30 04 76). T-bana Odenplan or Rådmansgatan/bus 4, 42, 46, 72, 96. **Open** 8am-7pm Mon-Fri; 9am-7pm Sat. **No credit cards. Map** p307 C5.
Most places in Stockholm spend a fortune on looking retro, but the cranky old couple who run this café just haven't changed the place since the '50s. The service is fairly grouchy, but then again this isn't where you come looking for a quick coffee buzz. You head to Valand's vinyl couches for traditional cakes (try the vanilla and almond bun) and to feel like you're an extra in an old black and white movie. Note that you and everyone in your party must order something to be allowed a seat. Or as the lady with the German accent behind the counter will say: 'We sell pastries, not seats!'

Djurgården

Blå Porten

Djurgårdsvägen 64 (663 87 59). Bus 44, 47/tram 7/ferry from Slussen or Nybrokajen. **Open** *Summer* 11am-10pm Mon-Fri; 11am-7pm Sat, Sun. *Winter* 11am-7pm Mon, Wed, Fri-Sun; 11am-9pm Tue, Thur. **Credit** AmEx, MC, V. **Map** p304 H11.
The Blue Door is, without doubt, Stockholm's most romantic café. In a beautiful, well-hidden piazza-like garden close to prominent art gallery Liljevalchs (*see p200*) you can spend hours choosing between German breads, Swedish meringue and Italian pastries. The interior is nice too, but not as amazing, so you should probably choose somewhere else on a rainy day. But if you're making a day of visiting the Vasamuseet, Skansen and Gröna Lund, then Blå Porten is the nearby retreat you need.

Rosendals Trädgård

Rosendalsterrassen 12 (54 58 12 70/www.rosendals tradgard.com). Bus 47/tram 7. **Open** *Mid Jan-Mar, Oct-mid Nov* 11am-4pm Tue-Sun. *Apr* 11am-5pm Tue-Sun. *May-Sept* 11am-5pm daily. Closed mid Nov-mid Jan. **Credit** MC, V. **Map** p305 H13.
The gardens of Rosendal are so well known for their seasonal desserts that the recipes have become the bestselling cookbook *Rosendals trädgårdscafé*. In summer, people eat fruit pie under the apple trees, while in winter you can keep warm with a mug of *glögg* in the greenhouses. There is also a small shop selling jam, bread and flowers. To get there, take bus 47 to the last stop, then continue a few feet in the same direction and you'll see a sign – be prepared to walk for about 15 minutes from Djurgårdsbron. Cars are not allowed into the park at the weekend.

Södermalm

Blooms Bageri

St Paulsgatan 24 (640 90 36). T-bana Mariatorget/ bus 43, 55, 66. **Open** 8am-7pm Mon-Fri; 10am-4pm Sat, Sun. **Credit** MC, V. **Map** p310 L6.
This small café close to Södermalm's beautiful viewpoint Mariaberget knows that there's nothing more relaxing than seeing other people work – only a window divides Blooms Bakery from its café. The bread and the buns are as fresh as can be, and often warm from the oven. Watch out for the porcelain dog in the middle of the café: to the joy of regulars many newcomers bump into it.

Café dello Sport

Pålsundsgatan 8 (669 23 22). T-bana Hornstull/ bus 4, 66. **Open** *Summer* 8am-6pm daily. *Winter* 10am-6pm daily. **Credit** DC, MC, V. **Map** p301 K3.
You might want to stay away from this friendly football-obsessed café during big championships since it's customary to wear the same pair of underpants for as long as Italy is doing well. But the focaccias, cappuccinos and Italian sodas are well worth the trip to otherwise seedy Hornstull.

Cinnamon

Verkstadsgatan 9 (669 22 24). T-bana Hornstull/ bus 4, 40, 66. **Open** 7am-8pm Mon-Thur; 7am-6pm Fri; 8am-6pm Sat; 9am-6pm Sun. **No credit cards. Map** p301 L2.
People who live in Hornstull, on the far western edge of Söder, love their neighbourhood. So it's no surprise that a T-shirt with the logo 'People's Republic of Hornstull' is a bestseller at this cosy bakery and coffeeshop. While Stockholmers from other areas tend to gather at nearby Lasse i Parken (*see below*), the locals prefer this place. Try the pâté sandwiches and the frosted chocolate cake with coconut flakes.

Glasbruket Café & Galleri

Katarinavägen 19 (462 00 17). T-bana Slussen/ bus 3, 46, 53, 76, 96. **Open** 11am-5pm daily. **No credit cards. Map** p311 K8.
The street with the most breathtaking view of the city also has a gallery-cum-café that serves the city's healthiest breakfast. The fresh fruit, yoghurt with nuts and organic coffee are reason enough to visit, but the Greek almond cake is also very good. This is where women in their 50s come to discuss art and weight-loss over a plate of African coconut cake. It closes earlier than 5pm if it's raining.

Lasse i Parken

Högalidsgatan 56 (658 33 95). T-bana Hornstull/ bus 4, 66. **Open** *Summer* usually 11am-4.30pm Tue-Sat. *Winter* 11am-5pm Sat, Sun. **No credit cards. Map** p301 K2.
Ever dreamed of visiting Pippi Longstocking's home Villa Villerkulla? The hackneyed tourist guides will tell you to head for children's theme park Junibacken, but the closest you'll really get to Astrid Lindgren's creation is here, just above the beaches of gloomy Reimersholme. In a Pippi-style wooden house surrounded by a garden, you'll find everything from home-made blueberry pie and cheddar sandwiches to a small outdoor theatre. Be warned: the outdoor toilets are the kind you normally find at rock festivals. To get there, take bus 4 over Västerbron to Högalidsgatan for an amazing view of Långholmen.

Lisas Café & Hembageri

Skånegatan 68 (640 36 36). T-bana Medborgarplatsen/bus 59. **Open** 6.30am-3am Mon-Fri. **No credit cards. Map** p311 M9.
This place is called a *taxifik* because taxi drivers have their *fika* here. To be a *taxifik* you need to have certain standards: you must serve extremely large portions of egg, bacon and oatmeal. And you must be open all hours. Lisas, managed by motherly Lisa herself, might close during some hours of the night, but it's the closest you'll get to a *taxifik* without feeling awkward being the only one not in a cabbie's uniform. The meatball sandwiches are amazing.

Soda

Bellmansgatan 26 (462 00 75). T-bana Slussen or Mariatorget/bus 43, 55, 66. **Open** 8am-8pm Mon-Fri; 10am-7pm Sat, Sun. **No credit cards. Map** p310 K7.
'I wear black on the outside because black is how I feel on the inside.' Such gloomy lyrics and angst-ridden teenage musings are the reason to *fika* here. Smoke-filled Soda offers diaries for its crowd of aspiring authors and intellectuals – if your companions aren't entertaining enough just borrow one of the books. Sadly, the pastries and the service are no better than the amateur paintings on the walls. But if you've forgotten how it feels to be 17, Soda is your place.

String

Nytorgsgatan 38 (714 85 14). T-bana Medborgarplatsen/bus 3, 59, 66. **Open** *Summer* 9.30am-8pm daily. *Winter* 9.30am-9pm Mon-Thur; 9.30am-7pm Fri; 10.30am-6pm Sat, Sun. **No credit cards. Map** p311 M9.

Rosendals Trädgård: gorgeous gardens and delicious desserts. *See p144.*

Eat, Drink, Shop

Like the spotlight? Then try one of String's many window seats: it's surely the closest you'll ever get to having coffee in a shop window. In an area that could be described as Stockholm's attempt at Soho, full of small record shops and independent movie-makers, this picturesque coffeehouse is where the city's young rock scenesters order String's special pots of coffee and sandwiches with goat's cheese and honey. Named after a classic shelf from the 1950s, String is packed with teens smoking Gauloises. All the furniture is for sale.

Viva Espresso

Björns Trägård (640 80 83). T-bana Medborgarplatsen/bus 59, 66. **Open** *Apr/May-mid Oct* 11am-10pm Mon-Fri; noon-10pm Sat, Sun; call for winter hours. **No credit cards. Map** p310 L8.

The surroundings are amazing: opposite a popular skateboarding ramp, below Södermalm's beautiful mosque, and just next to the square where fans of Söder's premier league football team Hammarby meet up for beer before games. But don't go on an empty stomach: the desserts are disappointing.

Östermalm

Café Restaurant Austria

Strandvägen 1 (667 76 24). T-bana Östermalmstorg or Kungsträdgården/bus 47, 62, 69, 76. **Open** 9am-8pm Mon, Sun; 9am-9pm Tue-Sat. **Credit** AmEx, DC, MC, V. **Map** p303 F8.

If you have a craving for *sachertorte* and other Austrian delights, this is the right place. Otherwise, come here for the view of boats leaving Nybroviken for the archipelago. Strandvägen is definitely one of Stockholm's most luxurious streets, and you might just see members of the royal family out for a stroll. Café Austria is definitely a place for cake lovers, but not those on a tight budget.

Gateau

Sturegallerian, Stureplan (611 75 64/www.gateau.se). T-bana Östermalmstorg/bus 1, 46, 55, 56, 91. **Open** *Summer* 8am-6pm Mon-Fri; 10am-4pm Sat; noon-4pm Sun. *Winter* 8am-7pm Mon-Fri; 10am-5pm Sat; noon-5pm Sun. **Credit** AmEx, DC, MC, V. **Map** p303 F8.

If you find yourself in the middle of luxurious shopping centre Sturegallerian, you'll need superpowers not to stop at Gateau's great cookie buffet. *Konditormästare* Tony Olsson is in Sweden's national chef team, and several members of the kitchen have won awards for their skills. Prices are deservedly high, especially for the marzipan, but if you're looking for something extra special during your shopping break, try the *tryffel* (truffle chocolates). Gateau also has a small shop in the mall, on the floor below, that sells cakes and bread.

Saturnus

Eriksbergsgatan 6 (611 77 00). T-bana Östermalmstorg/bus 42, 44, 46. **Open** 9am-8pm Mon-Fri; 10am-6pm Sat, Sun. **Credit** AmEx, DC, MC, V. **Map** p307 E7.

You might have problems finding this café – there isn't a proper sign, just a model of the planet hanging above the entrance – but the mosaic floor in itself is worth the visit. When it comes to the food, the chicken and spinach sandwich is excellent, as is the

Muffin Bakery: so many cakes, so little time... *See p148.*

Eat, Drink, Shop

Traditional cakes at **Thelins**. *See p148.*

dark brown potato bread. And if you order a cinnamon bun, be warned that they're large enough for at least three people. Saturnus is close to independent cinema Zita (*see p198*), so it's packed with cineastes during evenings and weekends.

Stockholms Glass & Pastahus

Vallhallavägen 155 (662 65 24/www.glass-pasta.com). T-bana Karlaplan/bus 4, 72, 91. **Open** *Summer* 9am-10pm daily. *Winter* 9am-9pm daily. **Credit** AmEx, MC, V. **Map** p309 D10.

This white-painted gem serves Italian ice-cream in flavours you never knew existed. Do try the really Swedish ones, such as peppermint and the truly amazing gingerbread dough. As the name suggests, you'll also find pasta dishes (the seafood one is recommended), but it's the ice-cream you'll have to queue for. If all the outdoor seats are taken, try the benches at nearby Tessinparken.

Branches: Birkagatan 8, Vasastaden (30 32 37); Götgatan 58, Södermalm (644 71 20).

Sturekatten

Riddargatan 4 (611 16 12). T-bana Östermalmstorg/bus 46, 55, 91. **Open** *Summer* 9am-6pm Mon-Fri; 10am-5pm Sat. *Winter* 8am-8pm Mon-Fri; 9am-6pm Sat, Sun. **No credit cards**. **Map** p303 F8.

If you want to know what it would be like to live in a doll's house, visit Sturekatten's two floors of lace and antiques, housed in an old townhouse on a hill. The speciality is apple pie with meringue, and it also serves delicious *semlor*. Smoking is forbidden and it may be hard to find a table, especially in the courtyard. You might think this is a place for grandmothers, but it's just as popular with teenagers. In the guestbook you can discover just how passionately people love their doll's house. One man says that he's had *fika* at the same table 3,000 times.

Tilt

Grev Turegatan 8 (678 04 24/www.tilt.se). T-bana Östermalmstorg/bus 46, 55, 91. **Open** 10.30am-11pm Mon-Thur; 10.30am-midnight Fri; 1pm-midnight Sat; 1-9pm Sun. **No credit cards**. **Map** p303 F8.

Cafés don't get much more eclectic than Tilt. Where else can you find supreme health food, a coffee bar, internet workstations and a variety of old and new pinball machines? In the evening, the two rooms are filled with schoolkids fighting for high scores, but the rest of the day you'll see everyone from pinball-crazed businessmen to aerobic instructors craving low-fat foodstuffs. Hungry pinball wizards should go for the salads with feta cheese and potatoes. If it's too packed, try Mono (Tilt without the pinball machines) on the same street.

Wienerkonditoriet

Biblioteksgatan 6-8 (611 21 16). T-bana Östermalmstorg/bus 46, 55, 91, 96. **Open** 7am-10pm Mon-Thur; 7am-11pm Fri; 8am-11pm Sat; 10am-10pm Sun. **Credit** AmEx, MC, V. **Map** p303 F8.

Wienerkonditoriet is a good hangout for an *Ab Fab* scene. The media types might not *fika* here, but you will see them passing by between department store NK and the bars and restaurants on Stureplan or Grev Turegatan. Many Stockholmers have breakfast here, though the main attractions are the shrimp sandwich and the wide variety of fine pastries. You will have to fight for the good seats.

Kungsholmen

Café Julia

St Eriksgatan 15 (651 45 15). T-bana Fridhemsplan/bus 3, 52, 94. **Open** *Summer* 10.30am-10pm Mon-Thur; 10.30am-7pm Fri-Sun. *Winter* 10.30am-9pm Mon-Thur; 10.30am-7pm Fri-Sun. **No credit cards**.

This haven for home-made soft cheese started out, believe it or not, in a one-room apartment with a young couple making cheese in their bathtub. It may sound gross, but now the bathroom has expanded to become one of young Kungsholmen's most popular cafés for lazy Sunday breakfasts. The soft cheese comes in eight different flavours (try the horseradish), and any questions about the recipe are regarded as industrial espionage. It's perhaps the only place in the world where a salad contains more cheese than vegetables. It also sells nice picnic baskets filled with goodies.

Café Kanel

Hantverkargatan 76A (653 90 23). T-bana Fridhemsplan/bus 3, 40, 62. **Open** 11am-8pm Mon-Thur; 11am-6pm Fri-Sun. **No credit cards**.

A young and trendy café serving *limpsmörgås* (sandwiches you'll find only in Sweden). Try the egg, spring onion and Kalles caviar (low-budget caviar) on rye. And for dessert, go for a cinnamon bun. The service may be a bit slow and dopey, but you never end up eating a pre-made sandwich. And if you want slightly less egg, staff are happy to make them exactly as you order. If the walls decorated with tubes of caviar are a bit too much for your taste, try the outdoor benches. But beware of noise – the next-door neighbour is a fire station.

Gli Angelini

Bergsgatan 17 (652 30 04). T-bana Rådhuset/bus 40, 52. **Open** 10am-6pm Mon-Fri; 11am-6pm Sat, Sun. **No credit cards**. **Map** p302 G4.

Wayne's Coffee: for smoothies, cookies, sarnies or just putting your feet up.

It might look like any other small Italian café, but this is the place to *fika* if you want to know where to go later in the evening. And you might have to wait for your cappuccino while the staff discuss a new club, the latest DJ scandal or a record needed for the café's collection. Close to the local police station and law court, it is also popular with the city's crime-fighting world. The bizarre mix of mozzarella-munching judges and a hungover club crowd is entertaining in itself.

Muffin Bakery

Fridhemsgatan 3 (651 88 00/www.muffin specialisten.se). T-bana Fridhemsplan/bus 49, 52, 57, 74. **Open** 9am-8pm Mon-Thur; 9am-6pm Fri-Sun. **Credit** DC, MC, V.

The Muffin Bakery's American-style, supersized muffins are so famous that they even have their own cookbook. The café itself is tiny – you are literally sitting in the bakery. It's very popular with young parents on their way to the playgrounds and beaches of Rålambshovsparken, and during the day it can be hard to find a seat. Stick to the sweet options: the savoury muffins can be a bit too cheesy. Anyway, who needs to consider the other options when there are chocolate cheesecake muffins?

R.O.O.M.

Alströmergatan 20 (692 50 00/www.room.se). T-bana Fridhemsplan/bus 3, 4, 94. **Open** *Summer* 10am-6pm Mon-Fri; 10am-4pm Sat. *Winter* 10am-6pm Mon-Fri; 10am-5pm Sat; noon-5pm Sun. **Credit** AmEx, DC, MC, V.

You might not be able to afford to buy the tables and chairs at this exclusive and trendy furniture store (*see p171*), but you can at least try them out at the in-house café. The variety of coffee is a bit disappointing for a shop selling espresso makers, but the sandwiches and buns are truly delicious. The café is particularly good fun if you find it amusing to watch couples and newlyweds argue over the colour of lampshades.

Thelins

St Eriksgatan 43 (651 19 00/www.thelinskonditori.se). T-bana Fridhemsplan/bus 3, 4, 57, 59. **Open** 7.30am-7pm Mon-Fri; 9am-5pm Sat, Sun. **Credit** AmEx, DC, MC, V.

A traditional *konditori* – the kind of place where you'll find old ladies gossiping over their 'seven kinds of cookies'. Blend in with the locals and order a traditional Swedish plate of *drömmar, schackrutor, finska pinnar, hallongrottor, pepparkakor, havreflan* and *bondkakor* (the legendary seven kinds). And if you don't drink coffee, try the apple soda Pommac, which nowadays you almost only find in these old-fashioned cafés. Don't be afraid to ask the staff for advice on what to order – they might look bored but they are passionate about cookies and cakes.

Branch: Karlaplan 13, Östermalm (663 62 89).

Wayne's Coffee

Kungsholms Strand 175 (653 52 40/www.waynes coffee.se). T-bana Fridhemsplan/bus 59. **Open** 9am-3pm Mon-Fri; 10am-5pm Sat, Sun. **Credit** MC, V.

With its concept of always having an international newsstand next door, Wayne's is one of the reasons why American coffee chains such as Starbucks have found it almost impossible to start up in Sweden. Trying to be more homely than other US-inspired cafés and changing its menu on a regular basis, Wayne's is deservedly popular among Stockholmers. You'll find branches all over the city (including a nice one at Götgatan 31 with a DesignTorget in the same complex), but the most charming one is at Kungsholms Strand's harbour for small boats. During mushroom season (August and September), try the toast with chanterelles. But everything – from the smoothies and chocolate-chip cookies to the pitta bread rolls – is delicious.

Branches: Drottninggatan 31, Norrmalm (20 17 80); Götgatan 31, Södermalm (644 45 90); Kungsgatan 14, Kungsholmen (791 00 86); Odengatan 52, Vasastaden (34 56 88); Vasagatan 7, Norrmalm (24 59 70); Västerlånggatan 54, Gamla Stan (442 22 68).

Shops & Services

Seen enough museums to last a lifetime? It's time to hit the shops.

Stockholm is a city of contrasts, especially when it comes to shopping. There are old-fashioned stores that haven't changed in 50 or 100 years, taking pride in their untouched interiors, traditional values and conservative approach. There are also local chains known internationally for their distinctive 'Scandi-feeling', as well as newly opened boutiques with an edgy attitude. International brands and chains also make an appearance.

Norrmalm, especially around Stureplan and T-Centralen, is the main shopping area. Here you'll find the usual European chains, but also a wide variety of home-grown shops. The main department stores and malls are in this area too: NK and Gallerian on Hamngatan, Sturegallerian on Stureplan, PUB on Hötorget, and Åhléns next to T-Centralen. In Stockholm you can forget all your department-store prejudices: NK and (to some extent) Åhléns and PUB have succeeded in retaining their personal atmosphere, good service and high quality. The district around **Drottninggatan** and **Sergels Torg** is excellent for all kinds of discount stores: shoes, clothes, electronics and souvenirs. Drottninggatan – pedestrianised from the water all the way to Radmansgatan – used to be the royal street, leading straight from Kungliga Slottet to Observatorielunden; now it's the main street for everyday shopping.

Busy **Drottninggatan**.

Biblioteksgatan and **Stureplan** are Stockholm's equivalent of Fifth Avenue: the place for designer clothes, watches, furs, chocolate and jewellery. In recent years, Louis Vuitton, Versace, Mulberry, MaxMara, Emporio Armani, Gucci and Cerrutti have all stationed their flagship boutiques around Stureplan. In doing so, they didn't just add to the flair of the area, but also helped Stockholm develop into a small but proud European shopping metropolis.

But don't think that shopping is limited to the city centre. To find quirky local shops, head for Gamla Stan, Södermalm, Kungsholmen and Vasastaden. In these areas it's worth knowing where to go, since the distances between the shopping goodies might be uncomfortably far.

Unlike in other cities, similar shops don't tend to congregate in one area. However, there are some exceptions. **Gamla Stan** is an undoubted tourist trap, but elegant home-furnishings boutiques and old-fashioned delicatessens are squeezed in between the tacky souvenir shops; get into the narrow alleys and explore. The lively street of **Götgatan** in **Södermalm** has a varied range of intimate and friendly shops offering designed products (10 Swedish Designers, Filippa K, Ordning & Reda, DesignTorget and Granit among others). **Vasastaden** around **Upplandsgatan** and **Odengatan** is good for antiques and home furnishings. **St Eriksgatan** in **Kungsholmen** is the place for second-hand records and CDs.

It might be costly to live in Sweden, but shopping in Stockholm can be good value for visitors (helped by the fact that the Swedish kronor has been pretty weak since the early '90s). What most makes shops stand out is the quality of the products and service. Highly developed consumer-protection rights allow purchasing on a sale-or-return basis (keep the receipt) and lengthy guarantees.

OPENING HOURS AND TAX REFUNDS

Small retailers are usually open 10am to 6pm on weekdays, 11am to 2pm on Saturdays and closed on Sundays. Some aren't even open on Saturdays. Bigger or more tourist-oriented

Glorious **NK**. *See p152.*

shops are also open on Sundays. Department stores are usually open 10am to 7pm weekdays and 10/11am to 5/6pm at the weekend.

In many shops, non-EU residents can ask for a Tax-Free Cheque when purchasing items costing more than 200kr (plus taxes). The cheque can be cashed at customs when leaving the country (with a refund of 10 to 12 per cent). Look for the 'Tax-Free Shopping' sticker on shop doors, and be sure to get only one cheque for all your purchases in the department stores. For further information, call Global Refund on 0410 48 450 or visit www.globalrefund.com.

Auctions

As well as the auctioneers listed below, the world-famous auction houses of **Christie's** (Sturegatan 26; 662 01 31/www.christies.com) and **Sotheby's** (Arsenalsgatan 6; 679 54 78/ www.sothebys.com) have offices in Stockholm open for valuations and advice.

Bukowskis

Arsenalsgatan 4, Norrmalm (614 08 00/ www.bukowskis.se). T-bana Kungsträdgården or Östermalmstorg/bus 46, 47, 55, 59, 76. **Open** 9am-5pm Mon-Fri. **Credit** AmEx, MC, V. **Map** p303 G8.

Bukowskis is probably Scandinavia's biggest and best auction house specialising in art and design. Four times a year it holds auctions of rare pieces of art, furniture, porcelain and jewellery dating from the 16th to the 19th centuries. For less rare (and cheaper) items, visit Lilla Bukowskis for antiques and art that did not make it into to the main house. Alternatively, try the Auktionskompaniet auctions of second-hand bargains, held every other week on Sundays at noon.

Branches: Lilla Bukowskis Strandvägen 7A, Östermalm (614 08 70/www.lillabukowskis.se); Auktionskompaniet Regeringsgatan 47, Norrmalm (23 57 00/www.auktionskompaniet.se).

Books

The book section at department store **NK** (*see p152*) has a good selection of fiction titles in English, as well as guidebooks and maps.

Akademibokhandeln

Mäster Samuelsgatan 32, Norrmalm (613 61 00/ www.akademibokhandeln.se). T-bana T-Centralen or Hötorget/bus 43, 47, 52, 59, 69. **Open** 10am-7pm Mon-Fri; 10am-4pm Sat; noon-4pm Sun. **Credit** AmEx, DC, MC, V. **Map** p303 F7.

Akademibokhandeln has seven branches in the city and offers probably the best range of English paperbacks in Stockholm. Despite the sterile surroundings and sometimes unfriendly service, the flagship store on Mäster Samuelsgatan is an excellent source of fiction, as well as dictionaries and CD-Roms.

Branches: throughout the city.

Hedengrens

Sturegallerian, Stureplan 4, Östermalm (611 51 28/ www.hedengrens.se). T-bana Östermalmstorg/ bus 1, 46, 55, 56. **Open** 10am-7pm Mon-Fri; 10am-5pm Sat; noon-5pm Sun (*June, July* noon-4pm Sun). **Credit** AmEx, DC, MC, V. **Map** p303 F8.

Opened in 1898, Hedengrens is one of Stockholm's most famous bookshops. It specialises in novels and the arts, and 50% of the stock is in English. The fiction section includes titles in Spanish, Italian, German, French, Danish, Norwegian and English (check out the English versions of Swedish authors such as Selma Lagerlöf, Torgny Lindgren and Astrid Lindgren). Ideal for browsing during a rainy afternoon.

Pocketshop

Gallerian, Hamngatan 37, Norrmalm (406 08 18/ www.pocketshop.se). T-bana Kungsträdgården or T-Centralen/bus 46, 47, 55, 59, 69. **Open** 10am-7pm Mon-Fri; 10am-5pm Sat; noon-4pm Sun. **Credit** AmEx, DC, MC, V. **Map** p303 G7.

Pocketshop has around 400 contemporary fiction titles in English. The two branches in the Central Station (one in the main hall, the other downstairs by the commuter trains) are a great place to pick up a book if you're off on a long train ride.

Branches: Central Station, Vasagatan, Norrmalm (24 27 05/24 74 40); Götgatan 40, Södermalm (640 94 05); Kulturhuset, Sergels Torg, Norrmalm (22 05 15).

Sverigebokhandeln

Sverigehuset, Hamngatan 27, Norrmalm (789 21 31/www.si.se). T-bana Kungsträdgården, Östermalmstorg or T-Centralen/bus 43, 47, 55, 59, 69. **Open** 10am-6pm Mon-Fri; 10am-5pm Sat. **Credit** AmEx, DC, MC, V. **Map** p303 G7.

This well-stocked little shop sells books in English about Sweden – its history, architecture, customs, cookery, language, landscapes – plus translations of Swedish classics (Astrid Lindgren et al). You can also buy numerous fact sheets in various languages on all aspects of Swedish society, produced by the impressive Swedish Institute. The shop is located in the same building as the tourist office (*see p285*), on the floor above.

Specialist

For newsstands specialising in international newspapers and magazines, *see p281*.

Alvglans

Folkungagatan 84, Södermalm (642 69 98/ www.alvglans.se). T-bana Medborgarplatsen/ bus 46, 53, 59, 66. **Open** 11am-6pm Mon-Fri; 11am-3pm Sat. **Credit** MC, V. **Map** p311 L9.

The Spawn action figures alone are worth the trip to Södermalm and the comics heaven of Alvglans. They stock bestsellers such as *X-Men* and *Spiderman*, as well as rare animé movies and manga DVDs. Check out the instruction manual on 'how to draw manga'.

Sverigebokhandeln for classics. *See p151.*

Kartcentrum

Vasagatan 16, Norrmalm (411 16 97/www.kartcentrum.se). T-bana T-Centralen/bus 3, 47, 53, 62, 69. **Open** 9.30am-6pm Mon-Fri; 9.30am-3pm Sat. **Credit** AmEx, DC, MC, V. **Map** p303 G6.

Conveniently located opposite Central Station, this travel specialist has a good range of maps, guidebooks and atlases, as well as CD-Rom maps and marine charts for the more intrepid traveller.

Konst-ig

Basement, Kulturhuset, Sergels Torg, Norrmalm (50 83 15 18/ www.konstig.se). T-bana T-Centralen/bus 47, 52, 56, 59, 65. **Open** 11am-7pm Mon; 10am-7pm Tue-Sat; noon-4pm Sun. **Credit** AmEx, MC, V. **Map** p303 G7.

Stockholm's leading art bookshop, covering design, art, architecture, photography and more. It's in the basement of Kulthurhuset, next to DesignTorget (*see p165*) and an internet café.

Rönnells Antikvariat

Birger Jarlsgatan 32, Östermalm (545 05 60). T-bana Östermalmstorg/bus 1, 46, 55, 56. **Open** 10am-6pm Mon-Fri; 11am-3pm Sat. **Credit** AmEx, DC, MC, V. **Map** p308 E7.

This three-storey antiquarian bookshop offers many titles in English. Rönnells is also a publishing company specialising in Swedish experimental art and poetry from the 1960s.

Department stores & malls

Åhléns

Klarabergsgatan 50, Norrmalm (767 60 00/ www.ahlens.se). T-bana T-Centralen/bus 47, 52, 56, 59, 65. **Open** 10am-7pm Mon-Sat; 11am-6pm Sun. **Credit** AmEx, DC, MC, V. **Map** p303 G6.

You can't get much more central than Åhléns, next to Sergels Torg. It's an excellent mid-range department store with a good cosmetics/perfume section, a well-stocked housewares department and a decent music shop. The clothing department was updated a few years ago and Swedish designers now share space with international designer names. You can also get a luxurious facial in the Åhléns Spa on the top floor. There's a big supermarket in the basement.

Gallerian

Hamngatan 37, Norrmalm (www.gallerian.se). T-bana Kungsträdgården/bus 46, 47, 55, 59, 69. **Open** 10am-7pm Mon-Fri; 10am-5pm Sat; noon-4pm Sun. **Map** p303 G7.

Located just next to Sergels Torg, Stockholm's first shopping mall – now looking rather run-down – is the place for everyday items rather than luxury goods. Among its 60 shops and cafés you'll find Foot Locker, Vero Moda, a Body Shop and the Swedish DIY specialist Clas Ohlson.

NK

Hamngatan 18-20, Norrmalm (762 80 00/www.nk.se). T-bana Kungsträdgården or Östermalmstorg/bus 43, 47, 55, 59, 69. **Open** 10am-7pm Mon-Fri; 10am-5pm Sat; noon-5pm Sun (*June, July* noon-4pm Sun). **Credit** AmEx, DC, MC, V. **Map** p303 F7.

Eternally elegant Nordiska Kompaniet celebrated its 100th birthday in 2002. The Selfridges of Stockholm, it's a top-class store, and great value. Located opposite the tourist office, it's now really more of a mall than a department store, with 100 franchises responsible for NK's quality concept. It's particularly good for designer clothes, Swedish souvenirs (crafts and glassware – in the basement), new design, deli foods and books, and it holds fashion shows and other events in its grand entrance hall. The famous revolving clock on the roof – formed from the letters NK – is visible from all over town.

PUB

Hötorget 13-15, Norrmalm (402 16 15/www.pub.se). T-bana Hötorget/bus 1, 52, 56. **Open** 10am-7pm Mon-Fri; 10am-5pm Sat; noon-5pm Sun. **Credit** AmEx, DC, MC, V. **Map** p303 F6.

Facing the chaotic outdoor fruit and veg market of Hötorget, PUB is order itself. Nowadays more of a mall than a department store, it's pretty boring – avoid the clothing department. Greta Garbo once worked in the millinery department, and modelled hats for the store's catalogue.

Sturegallerian

Entrances at Grev Turegatan 9 & Stureplan, Östermalm (www.sturegallerian.se). T-bana Östermalmstorg/bus 1, 46, 55, 56. **Open** 10am-7pm Mon-Fri; 10am-5pm Sat; noon-5pm Sun (*June, July* noon-4pm Sun). **Map** p303 F8.

If Sergels Torg is the people's centre of Stockholm, Sturegallerian and its environs are the centre for the jet set. As the city's glamo mall, it's got plenty of upmarket boutiques for picky customers, as well as super-spa Sturebadet (*see p168*) and the kind of ambience *de luxe* that comes only with a glass roof and marble floors. Café Pluto and Tures are excellent hangouts for post-retail refreshments.

Västermalmsgallerian

St Eriksgatan & Fleminggatan, Kungsholmen (737 20 00). T-bana Fridhemsplan/bus 1, 3, 4, 57, 59. **Open** 10am-7pm Mon-Fri; 10am-5pm Sat; 11am-5pm Sun.

This brand-new shopping mall is exactly what the people of Kungsholmen have been waiting for. This area used to be a hangout place for Fridhemsplan's shady types; now it's been transformed into a small but nice and clean mall, with the likes of H&M, Granit, DesignTorget and Studio.

Electronic goods & cameras

Fotoquick

Sergels Torg 12, Norrmalm (21 30 40/www.fotoquick.se). T-bana T-Centralen/bus 47, 52, 53, 56, 69. **Open** 9am-6.30pm Mon-Fri; 10am-4pm Sat. **Credit** AmEx, MC, V. **Map** p303 G7.

The cost of film developing can vary a great deal, sometimes by as much as 100kr. Fotoquick is the cheapest option in the city centre: processing a 36-print colour film in one hour costs about 154kr.

Branches: Central Station, Norrmalm (21 29 55); Drottninggatan 19, Norrmalm (20 24 25); Götgatan 100, Södermalm (640 98 10).

Onoff

Kungsgatan 29, Norrmalm (701 07 10/www.onoff.se). T-bana Hötorget/bus 1, 43, 52, 56. **Open** 10am-7pm Mon-Fri; 10am-4pm Sat; noon-4pm Sun. **Credit** AmEx, MC, V. **Map** p303 F7.

Sweden's biggest retailer of electronic goods, including computers, cameras, audio-visual equipment and mobile phones. The shops are always clean and the prices are certainly friendly. The only 'but' is that it is understaffed – so you could save some valuable queuing time by calling in advance to check if what you're looking for is in stock.

Branches: Sveavägen 13-15, Norrmalm (54 51 12 00); Fältöversten, Karlavägen 19, Östermalm (701 06 20).

Fashion

Budget

Dressmann

Drottninggatan 30, Norrmalm (53 48 26 26/www.dressmann.com). T-bana T-Centralen/bus 47, 52, 59, 62, 65. **Open** 10am-7pm Mon-Fri; 10am-5pm Sat; noon-5pm Sun. **Credit** AmEx, DC, MC, V. **Map** p303 G6.

Dressmann dresses the man looking for something to wear rather than high design or quality. This is where to find ordinary shirts, plain suits or perhaps a pair of sometimes ill-fitting trousers. But if the seams break within a fortnight, you can easily afford to get a new shirt. The staff are too busy to really be helpful.

Branches: Kungsgatan 5, Norrmalm (679 66 20); Kungsgatan 54, Norrmalm (440 24 10); Flemminggatan 40, Kungsholmen (21 89 20).

H&M

Hamngatan 22, Norrmalm (796 54 32/www.hm.com). T-bana Kungsträdgården or T-Centralen/bus 43, 46, 47, 59, 62. **Open** 10am-7pm Mon-Fri; 10am-5pm Sat; noon-5pm Sun. **Credit** AmEx, DC, MC, V. **Map** p303 G7.

If you haven't heard the Swedish success story of H&M, you must be blind, deaf or dead – or all of the above. By quickly designing copies of each new season's catwalk fashions, H&M has made itself almost as well known worldwide as IKEA. Clothes, for both him and her, are trendy but cheap, while the staff are friendly but often quite busy. The numerous branches around the city include three on Sergelgatan and two on Drottninggatan.

Branches: throughout the city.

Indiska Magasinet

Västerlånggatan 50, Gamla Stan (21 29 34/www.indiska.se). T-bana Gamla Stan/bus 3, 53. **Open** 10am-6pm Mon-Fri; 10am-4pm Sat; noon-4pm Sun. **Credit** AmEx, DC, MC, V. **Map** p303 J7.

Just a few years ago, Indiska was associated with poor quality and crappy design. It dressed only the backpacker coming home from eight months in Asia and missing the tie-dye scarves from those somewhat blurry nights in Goa. But today Indiska has redesigned itself and now sells fashionable but still orientally influenced clothes, bags, scarves and even furniture, to women, at nearly Asian prices.

Branches: throughout the city.

Lindex

Kungsgatan 48, Norrmalm (21 77 80/www.lindex.se). T-bana Hötorget/bus 3, 52, 56. **Open** 10am-6.30pm Mon-Fri; 10am-4pm Sat; noon-4pm Sun. **Credit** AmEx, DC, MC, V. **Map** p303 F6.

As one of the great, very reasonably priced Swedish chains, Lindex is mostly known for its underwear, but you can also find clothes for women and children. Aimed mainly at the middle-aged, but worth a visit for T-shirts and other basic items.

Branches: Sergels Torg 14, Norrmalm (545 177 10); Gallerian, Hamngatan/Regeringsgatan, Norrmalm (21 59 20); PK-Huset, Hamngatan 10-14, Norrmalm (545 242 30); Ringen, Götgatan/Ringvägen, Södermalm (642 33 32).

Studio Clothes

Odengatan 77, Vasastaden (30 70 65/www.studioclothes.nu). T-bana Odenplan/bus 4, 40, 46, 53, 72. **Open** 10am-6.30pm Mon-Fri; 10am-4pm Sat. **Credit** AmEx, DC, MC, V. **Map** p307 D5.

This is where women aged about 20 to 35 get floaty dresses and flowery tops from cheap (and small-sized) Spanish labels. You may end up looking like something from *Little House on the Prairie*.

Branches: Sturegallerian, Stureplan, Östermalm (678 44 47); Götgatan 46, Södermalm (462 96 90).

VeroModa

Hamngatan 37, Norrmalm (14 10 41/www.vero moda.com). T-bana Kungsträdgården or T-Centralen/bus 43, 46, 47, 59, 62. **Open** 10am-7pm Mon-Fri; 10am-5pm Sat; noon-4pm Sun. **Credit** AmEx, DC, MC, V. **Map** p303 G7.

VeroModa is really the only chain of clothes shops that can compete with H&M when it comes to cheap but trendy items. It's slightly funkier than H&M, but has a smaller selection. Womenswear only.

Branches: Drottninggatan 66, Norrmalm (21 52 20); Adam & Eva, Drottninggatan 68, Norrmalm (21 48 11).

Mid-range

If you can't find what you're looking for in any of the following, **Diesel** has a spacious shop on Kungsgatan 3 (678 07 09), near Stureplan.

Bric-a-brac

Swedensborgsgatan 5A, Södermalm (640 02 41/ www.bric-a-brac.se). T-bana Mariatorget/bus 43, 55, 66. **Open** 11am-6pm Mon-Fri; 11am-4pm Sat. **Credit** AmEx, DC, MC, V. **Map** p310 L7.

The Scandinavian minimalist cuts of Bric-a-brac celebrated their tenth anniversary in 2001. The label serves Sweden (as well as the Netherlands) with its classic-but-still-a-bit-funky designs. Colours could be seen as either dull or discreet, depending on your preference. The menswear is just slightly more edgy than the skirts and tops for women.

Brothers

Drottninggatan 53, Norrmalm (411 12 01/www. brothers.se). T-bana T-Centralen/bus 47, 52, 56, 59, 62. **Open** 10am-7pm Mon-Fri; 10am-5pm Sat; noon-4pm Sun. **Credit** AmEx, DC, MC, V. **Map** p303 F6.

This nationwide chain provides Swedish men with everything from suits to socks. The shop is spacious and the staff friendly and happy to sort you out with own label Life of Riley or something slightly more costly from Swedish designer J Lindeberg.

Branches: Fältöversten, Karlavägen 13, Östermalm (664 71 60); Ringen, Götgatan/Ringvägen, Södermalm (642 41 61).

Champagne

PK-Huset, Hamngatan 10-14, Norrmalm (10 75 64). T-bana Kungsträdgården or Östermalmstorg/ bus 43, 46, 47, 55, 59. **Open** 10am-7pm Mon-Fri; 10am-5pm Sat; noon-4pm Sun. **Credit** AmEx, DC, MC, V. **Map** p303 F8.

At this two-floor shop, women can find everything from mid-range label Replay to exclusive designers such as Dolce & Gabbana. Women who are slightly more into fashion than the average lady come here to seek out cleverly cut see-through tops, devilishly high heels or just a pair of plain denim jeans. Don't miss out on own label Do Rose, the low-cut trousers in basic colours (perfectly cut for small, Kylie-esque bums) or the chic shoe selection. Unfortunately for those of us who don't look like Kylie, the fitting rooms are small with unflattering lighting.

Hugo Kläder

St Eriksgatan 39, Kungsholmen (652 49 90/ www.hugo-sthlm.com). T-bana Fridhemsplan/ bus 3, 4, 40, 57, 62. **Open** 10.30am-7pm Mon-Fri; 10am-4pm Sat. **Credit** AmEx, DC, MC, V.

Men who don't worry about paying a little extra to look a little extra expensive – fashion-conscious but strict – get everything from underwear to suits at Hugo Kläder. Both Filippa K and J Lindeberg are sold here, as well as leather specialist Kbayashi and great Italian designer Lubiam.

Monroe

Sturegallerian, Stureplan, Östermalm (611 80 15). T-bana Östermalmstorg/bus 1, 46, 55, 56, 91. **Open** 10am-7pm Mon-Fri; 10am-5pm Sat; noon-5pm (June, July noon-4pm) Sun. **Credit** AmEx, DC, MC, V. **Map** p303 F8.

Really cool, young, trendy clothes – mostly French labels that no one's heard of – in one of the smallest clothes shops in Stockholm. The quality isn't nearly as good as the variety of girly tops, though.

Peak Performance

Biblioteksgatan 18, Östermalm (611 34 00/www. peakperformance.com). T-bana Östermalmstorg/ bus 46, 47, 62, 69, 76. **Open** 10am-6.30pm Mon-Fri; 10am-5pm Sat; noon-4pm Sun. **Credit** AmEx, DC, MC, V. **Map** p303 F8.

Originally designed for hikers, mountain climbers, skiers and other people preferring fresh air to smoky bars, Peak Performance has now turned more mainstream. Today the label makes practical everyday wear for, well, people preferring fresh air to smoky bars. For both men and women.

Plagg

Odengatan 75, Vasastaden (31 90 04/www.plagg.se). T-bana Odenplan/bus 4, 40, 46, 53, 72. **Open** 10am-6.30pm Mon-Fri; 10am-4pm Sat. **Credit** AmEx, DC, MC, V. **Map** p307 D5.

At Plagg, the smart-looking 21st-century woman gets classy clothing and shoes from designers such as Denmark's Lise Jacobsen, Iceland's Reykjavik Collection and Sweden's designer success Tiger. The selection is larger than you think when you see the size of the shop. If you have company, there's even a coffee machine for those hangers-on enduring your lengthy fitting-room sessions.

Branches: St Eriksgatan 37, Kungsholmen (650 31 58); Rörstrandsgatan 8, Vasastaden (30 58 01).

The Shirt Factory

Sturegallerian, Stureplan, Östermalm (678 14 24/ www.shirtfactory.se). T-bana Östermalmstorg/bus 1, 46, 55, 56, 91. **Open** 10am-7pm Mon-Fri; 10am-5pm Sat; noon-5pm (June, July noon-4pm) Sun. **Credit** AmEx, DC, MC, V. **Map** p303 F8.

The place to get new shirts, for both him and her. Linnéa Braun started up with a wide range of plain shirts for men, but has now added a women's collection. Nothing out of the ordinary, but it's high quality and there's lots to choose from. There are also ties, socks and accessories.

Pretty tops for pretty girls at **Monroe**. *See p154*.

Branches: Gallerian, Hamngatan/Regeringsgatan, Norrmalm (22 91 20); Götgatan 9, Södermalm (702 07 10); NK, Hamngatan 18-20, Norrmalm (762 83 33); Sturegallerian, Stureplan, Östermalm (678 14 24).

Solo

Smålandsgatan 20, Östermalm (611 64 41/www.solo.se). T-bana Östermalmstorg/bus 46, 47, 62, 69, 76. **Open** 10am-7pm Mon-Fri; 10am-5pm Sat; noon-5pm Sun. **Credit** AmEx, DC, MC, V. **Map** p303 F8.

Previously a unisex shop but now for women only, Solo has one of the greatest selections of jeans in Stockholm. Here you'll find international labels such as Lee, Evisu and Diesel and also the Swedish jeans specialists Acne and Nudie. Also, keep an eye on Swedish label Whyred – comfortable cool designs in comfortable cool fabrics.

Solo Man

Sturegallerian, Stureplan, Östermalm (678 41 41/www.solo.se). T-bana Östermalmstorg/bus 1, 46, 55, 56, 91. **Open** 10am-7pm Mon-Fri; 10am-5pm Sat; noon-5pm (June, July noon-4pm) Sun. **Credit** AmEx, DC, MC, V. **Map** p303 F8.

The male version of Solo, and the obvious choice if you want some of the top Swedish designers collected under one roof. Here you'll find J Lindeberg (great for shirts, trousers, jeans and accessories), Tiger (suits for the young and trendy) and Björn Borg (best known for underwear), as well as some slightly pricier international labels. The staff are friendly and the service is great too.

Branches: Hornsgatan 41, Södermalm (84 28 079); Biblioteksgatan 2-4, Östermalm (678 45 50).

Star People Design

Katarina Bangata 17, Södermalm (640 88 95/www.starpeopledesign.nu). T-bana Medborgarplatsen/bus 59, 66. **Open** 11am-6pm Mon-Fri; 11am-4pm Sat. **Credit** AmEx, MC, V. **Map** p311 M8.

Star People Design dresses the hair-dyed, possibly pierced youth of Stockholm up until the minute they stop reclaiming the streets and get a job. Funky tops with noisy prints and underwear with a message.

Designer

Most of the designer shops are clustered around hotspot Stureplan: on the lower end of Birger Jarlsgatan and along swanky Biblioteksgatan. Women tend to be better catered for than men. On Birger Jarlsgatan you'll find plenty of top-end international designers, including **Gucci** (No.1; 54 50 05 44), **Cerruti** (No.5; 678 45 00), **Hugo Boss** (No.6; 611 07 50), **Max Mara** (No.12; 611 14 66), **Versace** (Nos.21-3; 611 91 90/678 14 00). **Emporio Armani** can be found at Bilblioteksgatan 3 (678 79 80).

Götgatsbacken on Södermalm had a facelift ten years ago and now houses some fashion boutiques, including **Filippa K** (*see p156*). The department stores (*see p152*) **NK** and **Åhlens** also have a good collection of brands.

Anna Holtblad

Grev Turegatan 13, Östermalm (54 50 22 20/www.annaholtblad.se). T-bana Östermalmstorg/bus 3, 46, 55, 56. **Open** 10.30am-6.30pm Mon-Fri; 10.30am-4pm Sat. **Credit** AmEx, DC, MC, V. **Map** p303 F8.

Anna Holtblad is one of Sweden's top designers, dressing the trendy and financially stable 30-plus woman in classic clothing. The choice of both fabrics and designs is exquisite. If you want to pick up a few staples for your 'capsule wardrobe', let Holtblad sort you out. Get the perfect black turtleneck or an ever-so-soft white T-shirt. The high quality makes her clothes last longer than most.

Visit **Filippa K** for understated Swedish style.

DesignTorget Mode

Götgatan 31, Södermalm (442 09 40). T-bana Slussen or Medborgarplatsen/bus 59. **Open** 10am-7pm Mon-Fri; 10am-5pm Sat; noon-4pm Sun. **Credit** AmEx, DC, MC, V. **Map** p310 L8.

The fashion version of DesignTorget (*see p165*). As it's situated in the same complex as trendy coffee-shop Wayne's Coffee (*see p148*) and a handy Press Stop magazine shop, a visit to DesignTorget Mode is usually followed by a frothy *latte* and a quick flick through some international fashion mag. Collecting small designers, mostly from Swedish design schools such as Beckman's, DesignTorget Mode appeals for the most part to young fashion wannabes. Someone who truly knows fashion wouldn't be seen dead in the spacious boutique (nor reading a copy of *I-D* at a table at Wayne's Coffee), but it is an interesting garden of young budding designers offering wearable everyday clothes with a twist, for both men and women. Jewellery too.

Filippa K

Götgatan 23, Södermalm (55 69 85 85/www.filippak.com). T-bana Slussen/bus 59. **Open** 11am-7pm Mon-Fri; 11am-4pm Sat; noon-4pm Sun. **Credit** AmEx, DC, MC, V. **Map** p310 L8.

With Scandinavian clean lines and not overly imaginative designs, Filippa K has created the uniform for Swedish men and women wanting to dress like everybody else. The label favours colours without colour, such as beige, chocolate, denim blue, navy and black. Prices are semi-expensive.

Branch: Grev Turegatan 18, Östermalm (54 58 88 88).

Götrich

Mäster Samuelsgatan 3, Östermalm (611 23 05/www.gotrich.se). T-bana Östermalmstorg/bus 3, 46, 47, 59, 69. **Open** 10am-6pm Mon-Fri. **Credit** AmEx, DC, MC, V. **Map** p303 F8.

For 30 years, gents wearing shirts and ties that wouldn't look out of place at a funeral have bought their suits here, both made to measure and off the peg. Götrich stocks international labels Armani and Burberry, as well as Swedish label Stenströms. Located in the same area as some of the most expensive designer shops, including Gucci and Cerruti.

J Lindeberg

Grev Turegatan 9, Östermalm (678 61 65/www.jlindeberg.com). T-bana Östermalmstorg/bus 3, 46, 55, 56. **Open** 10am-7pm Mon-Fri; 10am-5pm Sat; noon-5pm (June, July noon-4pm) Sun. **Credit** AmEx, DC, MC, V. **Map** p303 F8.

With his clean designs with a flamboyant twist, Johan Lindeberg has become a household name for all the capital's media, fashion and PR men in their 20s and 30s. Show me a man in Stockholm who does not have a black, sleek-cut Lindeberg shirt in his closet and I will show you a liar. The staff are playful but still professional, the designs impeccable and the quality is certainly high.

Maria Westerlind

Drottninggatan 81A, Norrmalm (23 45 45/www.westerlind.com). T-bana Hötorget or Rådmansgatan/bus 52, 69. **Open** 11am-6pm Mon-Fri; 11am-3pm Sat. **Credit** AmEx, DC, MC, V. **Map** p307 E6.

Traditional lines, mild colours and simple fabrics are what make Maria Westerlind one of Sweden's up-and-coming young designers. The many twenty-something women getting striped dresses and floral tops here are aware of style and quality, but prefer not to be too eye-catching.

Natalie Schuterman

Grev Turegatan 1, Östermalm (611 62 01). T-bana Östermalmstorg/bus 1, 46, 55, 56, 62. **Open** 10.30am-6.30pm Mon-Fri; 11am-4pm Sat. **Credit** AmEx, DC, MC, V. **Map** p303 F8.

If you have a lot of money and nothing to spend it on, do get a Balenciaga sheer top, a miniskirt or a pair of Marc Jacob's Mary Janes at this upmarket boutique. The snotty staff are more than happy to find you a new outfit for around the price of a nurse's monthly salary, or at least make you look as if you just jetted back from a lovely weekend in St Tropez. Make sure your nail polish goes with your shoes in order to get decent service.

Paul & Friends

Grev Turegatan 7, Östermalm (54 50 26 50). T-bana Östermalmstorg/bus 3, 46, 55, 56. **Open** 10am-7pm Mon-Fri; 10am-5pm Sat; noon-5pm (June, July noon-4pm) Sun. **Credit** AmEx, DC, MC, V. **Map** p303 F8.

Clothes, both smart and casual, for the modern man and woman, by Paul Smith and some other expensive labels, such as the Italian Miu Miu. You'll find a similar selection in the NK branch (*see p152*). The Birger Jarlsgatan branch sells shoes only.

Branch: Birger Jarlsgatan 17B, Östermalm (54 50 26 25).

Prêt à porter

Humlegårdsgatan 4, Östermalm (662 60 60). T-bana Östermalmstorg/bus 1, 55, 56, 62. **Open** 11am-6pm Mon-Fri. **Credit** AmEx, DC, MC, V. **Map** p303 F8.

If you need a fresh pair of Tod's while on holiday in Stockholm, this small women's shop is the spot. Classic, expensive labels such as Moschino and Armani are sold too.

Schalin

Bergsgatan 9, Kungsholmen (653 16 25/www.schalin.com). T-bana Rådhuset/bus 3, 40, 52, 62. **Open** *Aug-June* noon-6pm Mon-Fri; noon-4pm Sat. Closed July. **Credit** DC, MC, V. **Map** p302 G4.

Designer couple Johan and Moa Schalin produce very relaxed and easy-to-wear but still utterly modish Swedish fashions. Get your name – or someone else's – embroidered on anything from denim jeans to off-the-shoulder tops in striped tricot. Both men's and women's fashions are available, as well as some cutting-edge accessories.

Skindeep

Humlegårdsgatan 5, Östermalm (662 82 70). T-bana Östermalmstorg/bus 1, 55, 56, 62. **Open** 11am-6pm Mon-Fri; noon-4pm Sat. **Credit** AmEx, DC, MC, V. **Map** p303 F8.

The young, hip and very rich come to Skindeep for designs from Isabel Marant, Matthew Williamson and Sportmax, or a pair of kitten heels from unsentimental designer Dries van Noten. The selection is small – as are the young and trendy sales girls, who look as if they've never ever seen mayonnaise or butter. It's sad to have to say it, but you should be thin and lovely yourself in order to be comfortable trying on tiny clothes in their presence.

Tiger Dam

PK-Huset, Hamngatan 10-14, Norrmalm (20 20 55/www.tigerofsweden.com). T-bana Kungsträdgården or Östermalmstorg/bus 43, 46, 47, 55, 59. **Open** 10am-7pm Mon-Fri; 10am-5pm Sat; noon-4pm Sun. **Credit** AmEx, DC, MC, V. **Map** p303 F8.

Tiger first became known for sponsoring Swedish pop group Kent with suits, and were suddenly dressing a whole generation of young males. Their suits are still their trademark, dressing men aged up to about 35 or so, but now Tiger also makes clothes for women, and is constantly first with the very latest designs. Their look is classic but fashionable, and they also sell some quality shoes and accessories, including cool belts and cufflinks.

Tjalla Malla

Bondegatan 46, Södermalm (640 78 47/www.tjallamalla.com). Bus 46, 53, 59, 66, 76. **Open** noon-6pm Mon-Fri; noon-4pm Sat. **Credit** AmEx, MC, V. **Map** p311 M9.

Situated in bohemian, *caffè latte*-drinking Söder, Tjalla Malla sells young Swedish fashion to young Swedish fashionistas. Clicking away in their straight-out-of-*Elle* shoes, the customers are more NYC than Sarah Jessica Parker herself. They stock plenty of local designers such as Rodebjer, Åsa Westlund and jeans specialist Nudie.

Children

H&M (*see p153*) is the most successful clothes shop for teenagers in Sweden. And when the youngsters mature into parenthood, H&M is still the place to go. You'll find kids' clothes at the larger H&M stores, such as Hamngatan 22 (796 54 34), Sergelgatan 1 (796 54 41) and Drottninggatan 56 (796 54 57), all in Norrmalm.

Guppi

PUB, Hötorget 13-15, Norrmalm (20 78 50/www.guppi.se). T-bana Hötorget/bus 1, 52, 56. **Open** 10am-7pm Mon-Fri; 10am-5pm Sat; noon-5pm Sun. **Credit** AmEx, DC, MC, V. **Map** p303 F6.

This chainstore sells brightly coloured, comfortable cotton clothes for kids aged between playpen and 14. It's the place for parents who care about the price tag rather than the designer, but still want their child to dress reasonably trendily.

Kalikå

Österlånggatan 18, Gamla Stan (20 52 19/www.kalika.se). T-bana Gamla Stan/bus 43, 46, 55, 59, 76. **Open** 10am-6pm Mon-Fri; 10am-4pm Sat; noon-4pm Sun. **Credit** AmEx, DC, MC, V. **Map** p303 J8.

Only the absence of incense reveals that this is not a time machine with the dial set to the 1970s. With clothes, hats, finger puppets and stuffed toys all in brightly coloured velour, you can reincarnate your youngster as a hippie kid. Or get the decade's back-to-the-roots feeling by buying a DIY kit and putting the clothes and products together yourself in the famous Swedish/IKEA way.

NK Kids

1st floor, NK, Hamngatan 18-20, Norrmalm (762 80 00/www.nk.se). T-bana Kungsträdgården or T-Centralen/bus 43, 46, 47, 59, 62. **Open** 10am-7pm Mon-Fri; 10am-5pm Sat; noon-5pm (June, July noon-4pm) Sun. **Credit** AmEx, DC, MC, V. **Map** p303 F7.

If your two-year-old wants to be the best-dressed toddler at kindergarten, the famous NK department store is the place to pick up babies' and children's clothes from the likes of Kenzo, Burberry, Diesel, Gant, Timberland and Donna Karan. Designer shoes for kids are just across the aisle.

Polarn o Pyret

Hamngatan 10, Norrmalm (411 41 40/www.polarnopyret.se). T-bana Kungsträdgården or Östermalmstorg/ bus 43, 46, 47, 55, 59. **Open** 10am-7pm Mon-Fri; 10am-5pm Sat; noon-4pm Sun. **Credit** AmEx, DC, MC, V. **Map** p303 F8.

Polarn o Pyret ('the Pal & the Tot') became famous in the 1970s when its striped, long-sleeved T-shirt, not unsuitable for a mutineer on the *Bounty*, dressed a whole generation of kids of the post-hippie era. With a revival in the new millennium, today both grown-ups and children can be seen in Polarn o Pyret's characteristic soft fabrics, simple styles and easy-to-wear colours. And, of course, stripes.

Branches: Gallerian, Hamngatan/Regeringsgatan, Norrmalm (411 22 47); Sveavägen 9, Norrmalm (23 34 00); Fältöversten, Karlavägen 13, Östermalm (660 62 75); Ringen, Götgatan/Ringvägen, Södermalm (642 03 62).

Fetish

Blue Fox

Gamla Brogatan 27, Norrmalm (20 32 41/www.bluefox.nu). T-bana T-Centralen/bus 1, 47, 53, 69. **Open** 11am-6pm Mon-Fri; 11am-4pm Sat. **Credit** MC, V. **Map** p303 F6.

Feel like dying your hair the same shade of green as Kermit the frog? Is your nose feeling empty without an iron ring that makes you look like Disney's Ferdinand the Bull? Would a little black latex number take Saturday night to wuthering heights for you and your significant other? Blue Fox specialises in tattoos, piercings and heavy metal and Goth clothing. Get everything from glossy trousers, kick-ass boots and Sid Vicious-style tartan trousers to jewellery with lots of attitude.

Cum

Klara Norra Kyrkogata 21-3, Norrmalm (10 40 18/ www.cum-clubwear.nu). T-bana T-Centralen/bus 47, 53, 69. **Open** 11am-6pm Mon-Fri; noon-4pm Sat. **Credit** AmEx, MC, V. **Map** p303 F6.

All the furry, see-through, neon-coloured clothes you can imagine. You can also choose from a wide selection of glittery killer heels. The clubwear is obviously influenced by the fetish scene, though in most outfits you're still just supposed to dance your ass off.

Eve Collection

St Eriksgatan 19, Kungsholmen (650 92 15/ www.evecollection.nu). T-bana Fridhemsplan/bus 3, 4, 40, 62. **Open** 11am-6pm Mon-Fri; noon-4pm Sat. **Credit** MC, V.

Love toys and great underwear in PVC and latex for the bold and beautiful. High-heeled shoes and boots even in size 42 and larger, for those who don't put comfort first and can afford to take a taxi to the party. A treasure island for the kinks and queens of Stockholm's nightlife.

Larger sizes

Big and Trendy

Jakobsbergsgatan 6N, Norrmalm (611 23 23/ www.bigandtrendy.aos.se). T-bana Östermalmstorg/ bus 43, 47, 56, 59. **Open** 10am-6.30pm Mon-Fri; 10am-5pm Sat; noon-4pm Sun. **Credit** AmEx, DC, MC, V. **Map** p303 F8.

Selling Finnish label Almia as well as the English Proforma, Big and Trendy brings traditional ladies' fashion (including suits and blouses) to traditional larger ladies. They stock all sorts of nicely designed and practical gear in sizes from continental 42 (UK 16/US 14) to 54. The branch in PUB has sizes 38-50.

Branch: Almia, PUB, Hötorget 13-15, Norrmalm (21 39 93).

Maritza

Götgatan 42, Södermalm (641 88 91). T-bana Medborgarplatsen/bus 59, 66. **Open** 10am-6.30pm Mon-Fri; 10am-4pm Sat. **Credit** AmEx, DC, MC, V. **Map** p310 L8.

Maritza keeps mid-range fashion labels such as Turnover and Annette Görtz in standard sizes, plus a small selection of larger clothes.

Lingerie

Also try **Lindex** (*see p153*).

Ajas Damunderkläder

Sturegallerian, Stureplan, Östermalm (611 99 69). T-bana Östermalmstorg/bus 1, 46, 55, 56, 91. **Open** 10am-7pm Mon-Fri; 10am-5pm Sat; noon-5pm (June, July noon-4pm) Sun. **Credit** AmEx, DC, MC, V. **Map** p303 F8.

The heavy, pale green curtains at the door give this shop, no larger than a shoebox, the feeling of an intimate boudoir – a boudoir with a large stock of seductive underwear that would fit right into the Moulin Rouge. Well-paid businessmen can often be seen here just before the weekend, picking up a little lacy goodie for the wifey, or someone else. It's not for the claustrophobic.

Gustaf Mellbin

Västerlånggatan 47, Gamla Stan (20 21 93). T-bana Gamla Stan/bus 3, 43, 53, 55, 76. **Open** 10.30am-6pm Mon-Fri; 10.30am-2pm Sat. **Credit** AmEx, DC, MC, V. **Map** p303 J7.

If God gave you maracas larger than a handful, the shop assistants at lingerie shop Gustaf Mellbin could become your new best friends. Here you get good service and cups up to F, G and even H. Better still, they are not beige and decent like something your big-bosomed grandmother would wear. A bit on the pricey side, however.

NK

1st floor, NK, Hamngatan 18-20, Norrmalm (762 80 00/www.nk.se). T-bana Kungsträdgården or T-Centralen/bus 43, 46, 47, 59, 62. **Open** 10am-7pm Mon-Fri; 10am-5pm Sat; noon-5pm (June, July noon-4pm) Sun. **Credit** AmEx, DC, MC, V. **Map** p303 F7.

NK is the best place to buy women's underwear in Stockholm. You'll find expensive, colourful designer lingerie from the likes of DKNY and Calvin Klein, as well as NK's own label of less eye-catching stuff. And the fitting rooms are spacious, with flattering lighting, and include a sitting area for accompanying friends and family. The men's section stocks almost as large a variety of high-quality but rather expensive underwear.

Victor & Victoria

Grev Turegatan 18, Östermalm (667 14 00). T-bana Östermalmstorg/bus 1, 46, 55, 56, 62. **Open** *Aug-June* 11am-6pm Mon-Fri; 11am-3pm Sat. *July* 11am-6pm Mon-Fri. **Credit** AmEx, DC, MC, V. **Map** p303 F8.

A calm and quiet lingerie shop for those who get stressed out by shop assistants constantly asking the fitting-room curtain if you're all right in there. Here, the nobility as well as just plain rich people get their intimate parts covered in La Perla, Dolce & Gabbana or exclusive men's Swiss label Hanro (to order). But lingerie with these kinds of buyers obviously doesn't come cheap.

Second-hand & vintage

Lisa Larssons Second Hand

Bondegatan 48, Södermalm (643 61 53). Bus 46, 53, 59, 66, 76. **Open** 1-5pm Tue-Fri; 11am-3pm Sat (limited opening hours in summer; call to check). **No credit cards**. **Map** p311 M9.

If you want to find the perfect little leather jacket, this is the place. In the crammed and crowded shop, Lisa keeps an entire wall full of second-hand leather jackets and coats. There are also more dressy things for both men and women, but be ready to fight for what you find since this is a popular excursion on Saturdays for Stockholm's trendy and pop-music-listening young ones.

Smalls for all at **NK**. *See p158.*

Mormors Skattkista

Bondegatan 56, Södermalm (643 61 09). Bus 46, 53, 59, 66, 76. **Open** 3-7pm Mon-Fri. **No credit cards**. **Map** p311 M9.

Vintage clothes, bags and jewellery from as far back as the 1920s. The quality is OK since the owner has pre-selected the stock, not letting just any old thing into her shop. For the man in your life how about a pair of '60s cufflinks or a coat from Yves St Laurent? Don't wear a backpack, though: the shop is tiny.

Myrorna

Götgatan 79, Södermalm (55 60 33 68/www.myrorna.se). T-bana Skanstull/bus 3, 4, 55, 74. **Open** 10am-6pm Mon-Fri; 10am-4pm Sat. **Credit** AmEx, DC, MC, V. **Map** p311 M8.

The Swedish Salvation Army's charity shops were originally just charity shops, but have now become the place for teenagers to get everything from costume party outfits to a pair of slightly worn denims. Furniture and household items too.

Branches: Adolf Fredriks Kyrkogata 5-7, Norrmalm (545 208 91); Tomtebogatan 5, Vasastaden (54 54 36 66); Hornsgatan 96, Södermalm (55 60 59 82).

Små Smulor

Skånegatan 75, Södermalm (642 53 34/www.stads missionen.se). Bus 46, 59, 66, 76. **Open** 9.30am-6pm Mon-Fri; 11am-4pm Sat. **Credit** MC, V. **Map** p311 M9.

With its location next to trendy Nytorget, where most residents work in fashion or the media, you would think that this charity shop would be a) exclusively stocked and b) very expensive. But Små Smulor is neither. Discover a dress Farrah Fawcett could have worn in *Charlie's Angels*, as well as 1970s crockery in vibrant colours. Buy them and give the city's homeless a meal.

Branch: Hantverkargatan 78, Kungsholmen (652 74 75).

Fashion accessories

Bags, gloves & hats

Handskmakar'n

PUB, Hötorget 13-15, Norrmalm (54 52 31 83). T-bana Hötorget/bus 1, 52, 56. **Open** 10am-7pm Mon-Fri; 10am-5pm Sat; noon-5pm Sun. **Credit** AmEx, DC, MC, V. **Map** p303 F6.

Looking for soft suede gloves, large bags, a silk scarf or maybe a new leather wallet? Handskmakar'n has it all, with price tags that would suit the yuppie as well as the hippie.

Branches: Drottninggatan 66, Norrmalm (54 52 32 63); Sergelgatan 11-15, Norrmalm (54 51 79 53).

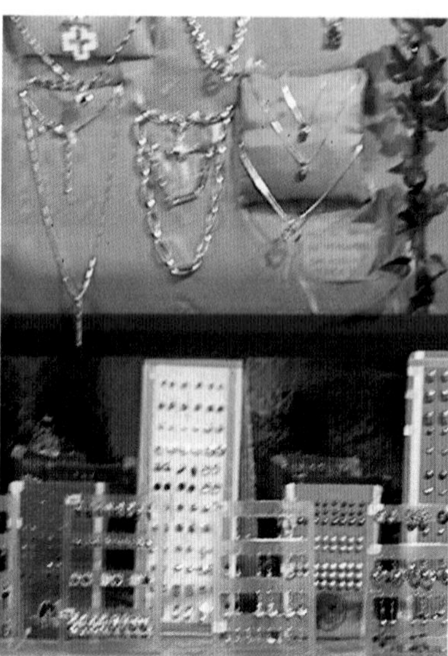

Go glamour at **Zanzlöza Zmycken**.

Mrs H Stockholm

Drottninggatan 110, Vasastaden (30 01 02). T-bana Rådmansgatan/bus 52, 69. **Open** 11am-6.30pm Mon-Fri; 11am-4pm Sat. **Credit** AmEx, DC, MC, V. **Map** p307 E6.

The award-winning accessory expert Mrs H stocks belts, bags, hats, shoes, clothes and some jewellery and make-up, by both Swedish and international designers (such as Sonia Rykiel). For the true fashionista, and quite expensive.

Jewellery

Antikt, Gammalt & Nytt

Mäster Samuelsgatan 11, Norrmalm (678 35 30). T-bana Östermalmstorg/bus 3, 46, 47, 59, 69. **Open** 11am-6pm Mon-Fri. **Credit** AmEx, MC, V. **Map** p303 F8.

The place to go when you need an antique rhinestone tiara or a glass brooch in any colour in any size in any price range. The shop was dreamt up by Tore and Mats Grundström when they discovered a warehouse full of long-forgotten 1940s gear. Be warned: you will have to fight over all the best pieces with stylists and other dedicated followers of fashion. The shop assistants (and owners) are not too interested in assisting, and quality is not what comes first. Great fun, though.

Efva Attlings Studio

Hornsgatan 42, Södermalm (642 99 49/www.efvaattlingstockholm.com). T-bana Mariatorget/bus 43, 55, 59, 66. **Open** 10am-1pm, 2-6pm Mon-Fri; 11am-3pm Sat. **Credit** AmEx, DC, MC, V. **Map** p310 K7.

Efva Attling is the glamorous lady silversmith who first made it as an Eileen Ford model and popstar (with the band X-models) and then hit the headlines for marrying the gorgeous female musician Eva Dahlgren. She makes simply beautiful silver and gold jewellery with names such as 'Homo Sapiens' and 'Divorced with Children'. And who wouldn't want to wear the same ornaments as the likes of Madonna, Jennifer Aniston, Britney Spears or Nina Persson from the Cardigans? As you can no doubt imagine, it doesn't come cheap.

Guldfynd

Ringen, Götgatan/Ringvägen, Södermalm (642 88 10/www.guldfynd.se). T-bana Skanstull/bus 3, 4, 55, 74. **Open** 10am-7pm Mon-Fri; 10am-5pm Sat; noon-4pm Sun. **Credit** AmEx, DC, MC, V. **Map** p311 N8.

Guldfynd is the largest jewellery retailer in Sweden, and they sell a wide selection of basic jewellery in gold and silver rather than diamonds and pearls, as well as watches and the like.

Branches: Adam & Eva, Drottninggatan 68, Norrmalm (54 51 01 10); Gallerian, Hamngatan/Regeringsgatan, Norrmalm (21 49 43); Sergelgatan 11-15, Norrmalm (54 51 04 88); St Eriksgatan 34, Kungsholmen (650 11 36).

WA Bolin

Stureplan 5, Östermalm (611 40 05). T-bana Östermalmstorg/bus 1, 46, 55, 56. **Open** *Sept-mid June* 10am-6pm Mon-Fri; 11am-3pm Sat. *Mid June-Aug* 10am-6pm Mon-Fri. **Credit** AmEx, DC, MC, V. **Map** p303 F8.

Bolin provides the royal family with antique jewellery and – surprise – most of the objects in this shop are rather expensive. But it's possible to find pieces at lower prices.

Zanzlöza Zmycken

Storkyrkobrinken 8, Gamla Stan (411 36 65/www.zanzlozazmycken.se). T-bana Gamla Stan/bus 3, 53. **Open** 11am-6.15pm Mon-Fri; 10.30am-4pm Sat. **Credit** AmEx, DC, MC, V. **Map** p303 H7.

Situated in the Old Town, this shop stands out from the dull surrounding brick walls with its glittery and glamorous selection of necklaces, rings and earrings. The designs are generally more reliable than the quality, unless you can stretch to the really pricey Christan Dior necklaces.

Branch: Jakobsbergsgatan 9, Norrmalm (678 40 55).

Shoes

CC Skor

Sturegallerian, Stureplan, Östermalm (611 09 30). T-bana Östermalmstorg/bus 1, 46, 55, 56, 91. **Open** 10am-7pm Mon-Fri; 10am-5pm Sat; noon-5pm (June, July noon-4pm) Sun. **Credit** AmEx, DC, MC, V. **Map** p303 F8.

Fabulous Italian shoes: smart, dapper, leisure and girlish designs – everything from black pumps for work to snakeskin stilettos for those posh parties. Expensive, but still the finest shoe shop in town for both men and women.

Don & Donna

Biblioteksgatan 9, Östermalm (611 01 32). T-bana Östermalmstorg/bus 1, 46, 55, 56, 76. **Open** 10am-6.30pm Mon-Fri; 10am-5pm Sat; noon-4pm Sun. **Credit** AmEx, DC, MC, V. **Map** p303 F8.

The twentysomething buying his or her shoes from Don & Donna is looking for footwear a bit out of the ordinary. Killer heels, denim boots and strappy sandals, but also sensible things like Hush Puppies.

Jerns Skor

Nybrogatan 9, Östermalm (611 20 32). T-bana Östermalmstorg/bus 46, 47, 62, 69, 76. **Open** 10am-6pm Mon-Fri; 10am-3pm Sat. **Credit** AmEx, DC, MC, V. **Map** p303 F8.

Chainstore Jerns puts the emphasis on elegance when it comes to footwear, although you can still find some beaded thongs. It's the place for Bigfoots to find smart designs in larger sizes. Unfortunately, the shop assistants are a bit too stressed.

Branches: Sveavägen 44, Norrmalm (10 15 33); Drottninggatan 37 (women's shoes only), Norrmalm (40 20 72 09); Gallerian, Hamngatan/Regeringsgatan, Norrmalm (20 97 50); Drottninggatan 33 (men's shoes only), Norrmalm (402 07 21).

Nilson Skobutik

Biblioteksgatan 3, Östermalm (611 94 56). T-bana Östermalmstorg/bus 46, 47, 62, 69, 76. **Open** 10am-6.30pm Mon-Fri; 10am-5pm Sat; noon-4pm Sun. **Credit** AmEx, DC, MC, V. **Map** p303 F8.

Upmarket chainstore Nilsons can fit you out with a pair of high-quality leather boots, dangerously high-heeled slingbacks or smart loafers. Trendy styles, but still very good prices. For women and men.

Branches: Kungsgatan 7, Norrmalm (20 62 25); Gallerian, Hamngatan/Regeringsgatan (men's shoes only), Norrmalm (411 71 75); Sergelgatan 27, Norrmalm (406 04 40); Sergelarkaden 1, Norrmalm (24 99 80).

Rizzo

Biblioteksgatan 10, Östermalm (611 28 08/ www.rizzo.se). T-bana Östermalmstorg/bus 46, 47, 62, 69, 76. **Open** 10am-6.30pm Mon-Fri; 10am-5pm Sat; noon-4pm Sun. **Credit** AmEx, DC, MC, V. **Map** p303 F8.

At Rizzo the section for men is the more creative, including cool labels such as Debut, Paul Smith and Boss, as well as their own label. However, if you're a lucky lady you can find a pair of red suede stilettos, even if most heels are on the sensible side. The staff are all very helpful.

Branches: Kungsgatan 26 (women's shoes only), Norrmalm (781 04 96); Gallerian, Hamngatan/ Regeringsgatan, Norrmalm (21 85 21).

SkoUno

Gamla Brogatan 34, Norrmalm (20 64 58). T-bana Hötorget or T-Centralen/bus 3, 47, 53, 69. **Open** 10am-6pm Mon-Fri; 10am-4pm Sat. **Credit** AmEx, DC, MC, V. **Map** p303 F6.

The assistants at SkoUno have apparently never been to charm school. And given the shop's commercial success, they probably never will. With its punk-influenced selection of Dr Martens and Spice Girls-style platform Buffalos, SkoUno is definitely one of Stockholm's most vibrant boutiques, despite the slightly sniffy staff.

Branches: Drottninggatan 70, Norrmalm (21 98 89); Gamla Brogatan 23, Norrmalm (21 34 61).

Sneakersnstuff

Åsögatan 136, Södermalm (743 03 22/www.sneakersnstuff.com). T-bana Medborgarplatsen/bus 59, 66. **Open** 11am-6pm Mon-Fri; noon-4pm Sat. **Credit** AmEx, MC, V. **Map** p311 M9.

A great variety of sneakers and trainers that you would usually only manage to find in New York, Paris or London. Opting for the cool rather than the sporty, twentysomethings of both sexes, in baggy jeans and brightly coloured T-shirts, come here to pick up the latest release from Nike or a pair from US basketball label And 1.

Florists

For modern-style bouquets, try the ground floor of department store **NK** (*see p152*). You'll also find excellent flower stalls in the city's open spaces, such as **Östermalmstorg**, **Norrmalmstorg**, **Hötorget**, **Odenplan**, **Medborgarplatsen** and **Södermalmstorg**.

Melanders Blommor

Hamngatan 2, Norrmalm (611 28 59/www.melandersblommor.se). T-bana Östermalstorg/bus 46, 47, 62, 69, 76. **Open** 9am-6pm Mon-Fri; 10am-4pm Sat. **Credit** AmEx, DC, MC, V. **Map** p303 F8.

Established in 1894, this is probably the best and most traditional florist in Stockholm, purveyor to HM the King and co. You can also send chocolates or flowers through the website (it's easy to use and in English) via Interflora.

CC Skor. *See p160.*

Food & drink

For information on Sweden's idiosyncratic attitude to the purchase of booze, *see p166* **How to buy alcohol**.

Bakeries & pâtisseries

Tjärhovsbagaren

Tjärhovsgatan 1, Södermalm (642 88 52). T-bana Medborgarplatsen/bus 55, 59, 66. **Open** 24hrs daily. **No credit cards. Map** p310 L8.

If you get the munchies in the wee hours while walking home from the bar district of Medborgarplatsen, knock on the anonymous door of Tjärhovsbagaren. For 5kr you'll get a warm cinnamon roll straight from the oven. It's open 24 hours – as long as they're not too busy baking.

Vete-Katten

Kungsgatan 55, Norrmalm (20 84 05). T-bana Hötorget or T-Centralen/bus 1, 47, 53, 69. **Open** 7.30am-8pm Mon-Fri; 10am-5pm Sat. **Credit** AmEx, DC, MC, V. **Map** p303 F6.

The old-fashioned tearoom of Vete-Katten (established 1928) serves classic Swedish pâtisseries such as *prinsesstårta* ('princess tart' – a cream-filled cake topped with green marzipan), but it's the marvellous mousse gâteaux and delicious fruitcakes that are really outstanding. You can also buy biscuits; bread; cinnamon, vanilla and cardamom rolls; and home-made ice-cream in mandarin, rhubarb and passion-fruit flavours. Yummy.

Chocolate

Ejes Chokladfabrik

Erik Dahlbergsgatan 25, Gärdet (664 27 09/ www.ejeschoklad.se). T-bana Karlaplan/bus 1, 4, 62, 72. **Open** *Late Aug-late July* 10am-6pm Mon-Fri; 10am-3pm Sat. Closed late July-late Aug. **Credit** MC, V. **Map** p308 D10.

The mocha nougat and Irish coffee truffles alone are worth the trip to this traditional chocolate maker, which was established in 1923. Everything is made by hand, without preservatives. Just going into the shop, crammed with chocolates, is an experience. You can even take part in a chocolate tasting; to book call 664 27 09.

Godiva

Grev Turegatan 10, Östermalm (440 34 00). T-bana Östermalmstorg/bus 46, 47, 55, 62, 69. **Open** 10am-6pm Mon-Fri; 11am-4pm Sat; noon-4pm Sun. **Credit** AmEx, DC, MC, V. **Map** p303 F8.

The newly opened Godiva Chocolatier, part of the famous Belgian chain (founded 1926), is well liked here for its golden interior and, above all, for its delicious chocolates. The truffles, ganaches, nut clusters or fruit centres are the perfect nourishment for that broken heart, as well as an excellent gift for somebody you don't know too well.

Coffee & tea

Gamla Stans Te & Kaffehandel

Stora Nygatan 14, Gamla Stan (20 70 47/www.teokaffe.com). T-bana Gamla Stan/bus 3, 53. **Open** 11am-6pm Mon-Fri; noon-4pm Sat. **Credit** AmEx, DC, MC, V on purchases over 100kr. **Map** p303 J7.

Here in Gamla Stan you can buy raw Ethiopian *yirga* coffee, healthy red *rooibos* tea scented with lemongrass and bergamot or organic green Sencha tea. For connoisseurs there's Jamaica Blue Mountain, supposedly the world's most exclusive coffee (330kr for 300g/10oz). Assorted equipment on sale includes a milk skimmer for your latte (229kr) and a tea samovar with golden trim (4,500kr).

Sibyllans Kaffe & Tehandel

Sibyllegatan 35, Östermalm (662 06 63/www.sibyllanskaffetehandel.com). T-bana Östermalmstorg/bus 1, 42, 44, 56, 62. **Open** 9.30am-6pm Mon-Fri. **No credit cards. Map** p304 E9.

When the wind comes from the south you can smell the heady fragrance of Sibyllans ten blocks away. This family-run shop dates back to World War I, and the interior, with its old-fashioned tea- and coffee-jars, hasn't changed since then. There's a vast range of teas – black, green, fruit, herbal, from all over the world; Sibyllans' own blend, Sir Williams, is a mix of Chinese green teas.

Delicatessens

Androuët Ostaffär

Sibyllegatan 19, Östermalm (660 58 33/www.androuet.nu). T-bana Östermalmstorg/bus 46, 47, 62, 69, 76. **Open** 10.30am-6pm Mon-Fri; 10.30am-3pm Sat. **Credit** AmEx, DC, MC, V. **Map** p304 F9.

In 1909 Henri Androuët set up his first cheese (*ost*) store in Paris; in 1997 the first shop in Stockholm opened. You'll find just over 100 different quality cheeses from all over France, many of them fairly obscure but unmissable for cheese addicts.

Cajsa Warg

Renstiernas Gata 20, Södermalm (642 23 50/ www.cajsawarg.aos.se). Bus 3, 46, 55, 66, 76. **Open** 11am-8pm Mon-Fri; 10am-7pm Sat; noon-7pm Sun. **Credit** AmEx, DC, MC, V. **Map** p311 L9.

There's a Swedish proverb that goes, '"You use what you have," said Cajsa Warg.' A famous Swedish chef at the start of the 20th century, Cajsa Warg was known for her creative cooking. This shop uses her name to sell everyday groceries and delicatessen items (Swedish, Mediterranean and Asian), and a large takeaway menu. Perfect for a spontaneous picnic.

Vasastans Ost

St Eriksgatan 90, Vasastaden (32 54 85/www.vasastansost.com). T-bana St Eriksplan/bus 3, 4, 42, 47, 72. **Open** *Sept-July* 10am-6.30pm Mon-Thur; 10am-7pm Fri; 11am-3pm Sat. *Aug* 10am-6.30pm Mon-Thur; 10am-7pm Fri. **Credit** AmEx, MC, V. **Map** p306 D3.

Food markets

There are three indoor markets in Stockholm offering excellent fresh food and deli items: the international stalls of **Hötorgshallen**, the exclusive gourmet haven of **Östermalms Saluhall** and the everyday groceries of **Söderhallarna**. If you think they're a bit overpriced, head for the suburban outdoor markets of **Skärhomen**, **Tensta** and **Rinkeby**, where you can find excellent produce at ridiculously low prices.

Hötorgshallen

Hötorget, Norrmalm (www.hotorgshallen.se). T-bana Hötorget/bus 1, 52, 56. **Open** *Indoor market Sept-Apr* 10am-6pm Mon-Thur; 10am-6.30pm Fri; 10am-4pm Sat. *May-Aug* 10am-6pm Mon-Fri; 10am-3pm Sat. *Outdoor market* usually 10am-7pm Mon-Fri; 10am-5pm Sat; noon-5pm Sun. **Map** p303 F6.

A visit to Hötorgshallen (*pictured*), located below the Filmstaden multiplex, is a culinary trip around the world. Built in the 1950s, the hall was renovated in the '90s, and its international character has grown along with immigration to Stockholm. You can buy Middle Eastern falafel and Indian spices, as well as fantastic fish and meat. There's also a lively daily trade in fresh veg, fruit and flowers on Hötorget outside, which first opened as a market in the 1640s. On Sundays, temporary vendors also sell books and household gadgets.

Östermalms Saluhall

Östermalmstorg, Östermalm (www.ostermalmshallen.se). T-bana Östermalmstorg/bus 47, 55, 56, 62, 76. **Open** 9.30am-6pm Mon-Thur; 9.30am-6.30pm Fri; 9.30am-4pm (June-Aug 9.30am-2pm) Sat. **Map** p303 F8.

The flagship of market halls in Stockholm, this gastronomic temple has been serving the city's gourmets since 1888. Designed by Isak Gustav Clason, the 28m-high (93ft) ceiling and beautifully crafted interiors are magnificent – as are the prices. Get tempted by a wide variety of fresh bread from Amandas Brödbod, delicious chocolate from Betsy Sandbergs Choklad, excellent fish and seafood from Melanders Fisk, vegetables from Lisa Janssons and ready-to-eat foods from Depå Sushi or Tysta Mari. The numerous well-reputed restaurants and cafés are filled with well-heeled Östermalm ladies who lunch. The square outside has a flower stall and an open-air café (Lisapåtorget) with a pleasant atmosphere.

Söderhallarna

Medborgarplatsen 3, Södermalm (714 09 84/ 442 09 80/www.soderhallarna.aos.se). T-bana Medborgarplatsen/bus 55, 59, 66. **Open** 10am-6pm Mon-Wed; 10am-7pm Thur, Fri; 10am-4pm Sat. **Map** p310 L8.

Only ten years old and a rather unsightly glass and chrome building, Söderhallarna is Stockholm's youngest indoor market. In the main hall you'll find coffee, tea, vegetables, meat, fish and takeaway food. Don't sit down, though – the only seats are in unfriendly cafés and smelly kebab or hamburger restaurants. Medborgarplatsen itself has changed in the past few years, from deserted square to lively after-work meeting place.

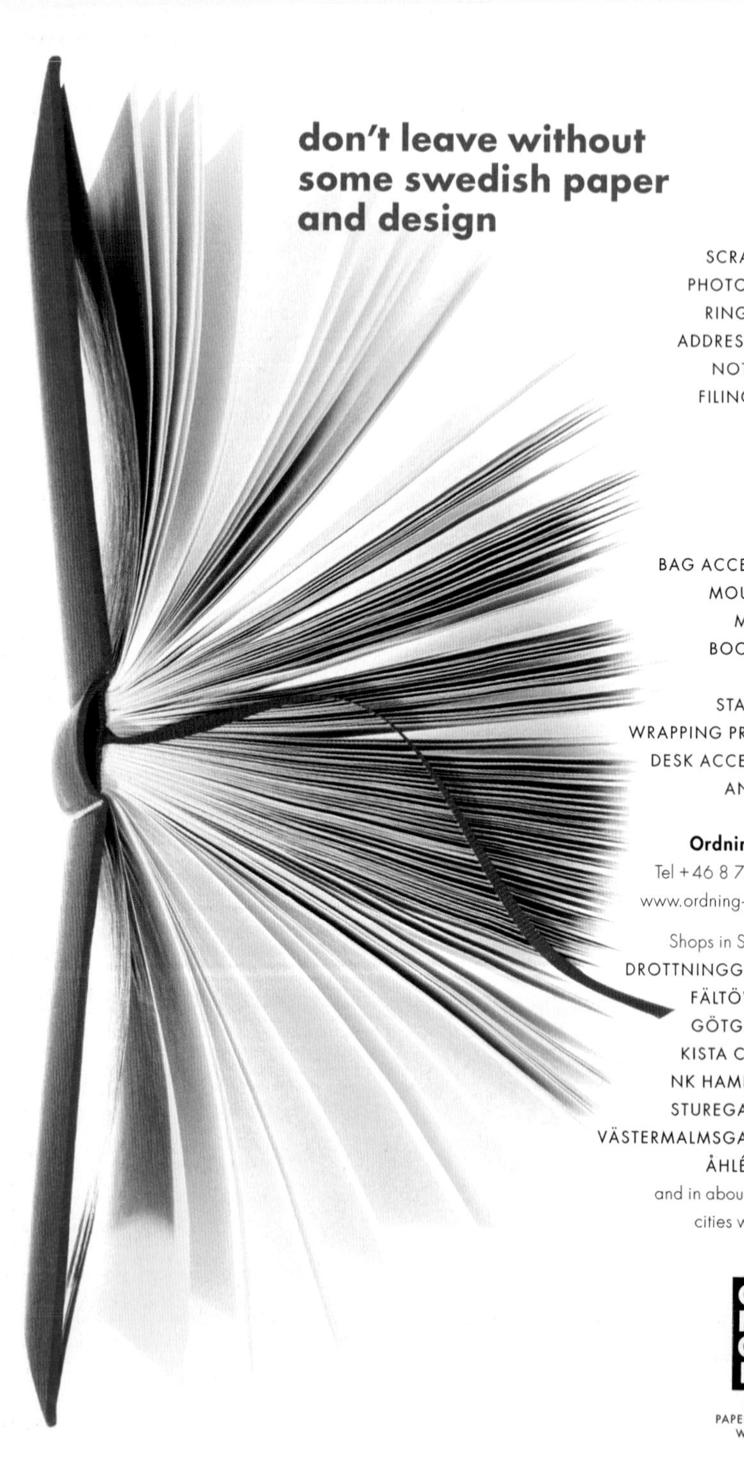
don't leave without
some swedish paper
and design
SCRAPBOC
PHOTO ALBU
RINGBIND
ADDRESS BOC
NOTEBOC
FILING BOC
DIAR
FOLDE
PE
PENC
BA
BAG ACCESSOR
MOUSE PA
MAGNE
BOOKMAR
CAR
STATIONE
WRAPPING PRODUC
DESK ACCESSOR
AND MO
Ordning&Re
Tel +46 8 728 20
www.ordning-reda.c
Shops in Stockho
DROTTNINGGATAN
FÄLTÖVERST
GÖTGATAN
KISTA CENTR
NK HAMNGAT
STUREGALLERI
VÄSTERMALMSGALLERI
ÅHLÉNS CI
and in about 30 ot
cities worldwi
SWEDIS
PAPER AND D
WORLDWI

The place for Italian cheese, cured meats and other Mediterranean specialities. It's packed at lunchtime with people from all over the city on a pilgrimage to seek out their pasta salads and nut breads.

Health food

Herbamin Hälsokost

Ringvägen 106, Södermalm (641 52 79). T-bana Skanstull/bus 3, 4, 55, 74. **Open** 10am-6pm Mon-Fri; 10am-1pm Sat. **Credit** MC, V. **Map** p311 N8.

Organic vegetables, aromatherapy oils and vitamin pills, plus homeopathic medications. Zone therapy and homeopathy are also available.

International

Gray's American Foodstore

Odengatan 39, Vasastaden (612 30 40/www.grays.se). T-bana Rådmansgatan/bus 4, 42, 46, 53, 72. **Open** 10.30am-7pm Mon-Fri; 11am-7pm Sat; noon-6pm Sun. **Credit** AmEx, DC, MC, V. **Map** p307 C6.

Although some supermarkets sell a limited range of American food on special shelves, you can't count on finding pre-packaged macaroni cheese or marshmallow cereal in Ica or Konsum. Gray's has the best range of US snacks and BBQ sauces in Stockholm. It also sells some *South Park* and *Simpsons* figures. Perfect for homesick Yanks.

Branch: Västerlånggatan 14, Gamla Stan (21 95 00).

Hong Kong Trading

Kungsgatan 74, Norrmalm (21 79 76). T-bana T-Centralen/bus 1, 47, 53, 59, 69. **Open** 10am-6.30pm Mon-Fri; 10am-3.30pm Sat. **Credit** AmEx, MC, V. **Map** p302 F5.

There are quite a few Asian food shops around Hötorget, and friendly Hong Kong Trading is one of the biggest. It has a well-assorted stock of noodles and herbs and a great range of fresh Asian vegetables and fruits. Staff are helpful.

Rinkeby Orientlivs

Hinderstorpsgränd 24, Rinkeby (761 36 61). T-bana Rinkeby. **Open** 9am-7pm Mon-Fri; 10am-6pm Sat, Sun. **Credit** MC, V.

It's a common saying that you don't need to travel far to go abroad in Stockholm – just take the T-bana to Rinkeby. Rinkeby Orientlivs stocks food from all over the world, including Middle Eastern baklava, South American *mate*, Greek olives, African coffee, large trunks of exotic nuts and all sorts of canned foods. The shop also has a good butcher, and for fresh and really cheap vegetables there's a great outdoor market just outside the door.

Taj Mahal Livs

Kammakargatan 40, Norrmalm (21 22 81). T-bana Rådmansgatan/bus 43, 46, 52. **Open** 10am-6pm Mon-Fri; 10am-4pm Sat. **No credit cards**. **Map** p307 E6.

Asian, Indian and African foodstuffs are sold in this kitschy shop. There's everything from huge sacks of rice and lentils to shelves stacked with African hairstyling products and Asian herbs and spices. It's a family-run place and will sometimes close for family events and holidays.

Supermarkets

Food is expensive in Sweden in general and in Stockholm in particular. **Ica** is probably the most expensive supermarket chain, while **Konsum** has more reasonable prices and a 'greener' profile, with organic alternatives in most categories. Go to **Prisxtra City** or **Vivo Daglivs Klippet** for cheap bargains and more family sizes. In the fancy area of Östermalm (around Östermalmstorg) you will find more delicatessen-style supermarkets. You'll find small branches all over the city.

Gifts

Coctail

Skånegatan 71, Södermalm (642 07 40/www.coctail.nu). Bus 46, 53, 59, 66, 76. **Open** 11am-6pm Mon-Fri; 11am-4pm Sat. **Credit** MC, V. **Map** p311 M9.

This colourful haven of kitsch is a classic, selling Jesus statues and sacred candles to the secularised IT generation. Plus some Russian tea glasses, 1970s lamps, funky household items, bags and underwear.

DesignTorget

Kulturhuset, Sergels Torg, Norrmalm (50 83 15 20/www.designtorget.se). T-bana T-Centralen/bus 47, 52, 56, 59, 65. **Open** 11am-7pm Mon; 10am-7pm Tue-Fri; 10am-5pm Sat; 11am-5pm Sun. **Credit** AmEx, MC, V. **Map** p303 G7.

The concept of DesignTorget is that promising new designers and art students can sell their work on a commission basis alongside established companies. You'll find a varied assortment of jewellery, household goods, ceramics, textiles and furniture, as well as some original gifts and amusing gadgets. The stock changes regularly.

Branches: Götgatan 31, Södermalm (462 35 20); Sturegallerian, Stureplan, Östermalm (611 53 03); Västermalmsgallerian, St Eriksgatan 45, Kungsholmen (33 11 53).

Gifts and gadgets galore at **DesignTorget**.

Eat, Drink, Shop

Ordning & Reda

Götgatan 32, Södermalm (714 96 01/www.ordning-reda.com). T-bana Medborgarplatsen or Slussen/bus 3, 43, 55, 59, 66. **Open** 10am-6.30pm Mon-Fri; 10am-4pm Sat; noon-4pm Sun. **Credit** AmEx, DC, MC, V. **Map** p310 L8.

Heaver for stationery fans. You'll swoon over these super-slick address books, notebooks, rulers, scissors, paperclips and much more – all in lipsmackingly bright colours. The shop interiors are as beautifully designed as the products.

Branches: Drottninggatan 82, Norrmalm (10 84 96); NK, Hamngatan 18-20, Norrmalm (762 84 62); Åhléns, Klarabergsgatan 50, Norrmalm (676 60 00); Sturegallerian, Stureplan, Östermalm (611 12 00); Fältöversten, Karlaplan 13, Östermalm (667 84 40).

Popcorn

Odengatan 72, Vasastaden (33 04 90/www.popcorn.se). T-bana Odenplan/bus 4, 46, 47, 53, 72. **Open** 10am-6pm Mon-Fri; 11am-2pm Sat. **Credit** AmEx, MC, V. **Map** p306 D4.

The place for small, kitschy gifts. Things you don't really need but somehow can't resist.

Branch: Hornsgatan 3, Södermalm (34 86 96).

10 Swedish Designers

Götgatan 25, Södermalm (643 25 04/www.tiogruppen.com). T-bana Slussen/bus 3, 46, 53, 59, 76. **Open** 10am-6pm Mon-Fri; 11am-4pm Sun. **Credit** MC, V. **Map** p310 L8.

Tiogruppen was set up by ten young textile artists in 1970; since then their creations have become classics of Swedish design. The colourful, bold geometric designs – available in the form of bags, cushions, oven gloves, trays, ironing board covers or just as fabric – are a must-have. The striking black and white plates would make any dinner table a style icon. A retrospective of the group's work was held at the National Museum in 2001. *See also p36.*

Health & beauty

Complementary health

Inspira Handelsbod

Rörstrandsgatan 42, Vasastaden (34 54 23/www.inspira.cc). T-bana St Eriksplan/bus 3, 4, 47, 72. **Open** noon-6.30pm Mon-Fri. Closed 4wks in summer. **No credit cards. Map** p306 D2.

How to buy alcohol

You'll realise pretty quick that Sweden has a fairly tight-assed attitude towards alcohol and its consumption. One result of this is that the only place you can buy strong beer, wine and spirits is at a shop run by the state-owned alcohol-retailing monopoly, **Systembolaget**. The downsides are that prices are high and opening hours limited. Until a few years ago it was only possible to buy alcohol in office hours, but nowadays the 23 Systembolaget shops in the city centre are open 10am-6pm on weekdays (some close at 7pm) and 10am-2pm on Saturdays.

In most shops, the bottles are displayed in glass cabinets – like perfume bottles in a fancy beauty boutique – and you have to take a numbered ticket and wait for your turn. You then tell the cashier the number or name of the item(s) you want (we're told that certain brands are bestsellers just because they're easy to pronounce). The shop at **Klarabergsgatan 62** (*see below*) and five others have become self-service outlets, leaving the annoying queuing system and pronunciation failures behind. The plan is to make all shops self-service in the future.

It's best to bring ID (you must be 20 to buy alcohol, but stories abound of people in their 30s being refused because they couldn't prove their age), and note that only Swedish debit cards are accepted. Avoid Friday afternoons and Saturday mornings unless your idea of fun is standing in a queue for an hour or more.

When you've passed the obstacles the Swedish parliament has imposed to reduce alcohol-related illnesses, you'll find there are some advantages to the monopoly. The shops are spotless, the staff professional and ready to give advice, and there's an impressive selection of both Swedish and imported brands – some 2,500 in total – a far cry from your average off-licence. There are fine wines from around the world, unusual beers, a huge range of spirits from *brännvin* to tequila – and you can always order items not in stock at the particular shop you visit. Systembolaget's new consumer magazine, launched in 2002, aims to increase people's appreciation of drink, especially wine – so it's not all po-faced puritanism.

Systembolaget stocks beer containing 3.5 to 4.5 per cent alcohol by volume (*mellanöl*) and over 4.5 per cent (*starköl*). Weaker beer, called *lättöl* (under 2.5 per cent) or *folköl* (2.25 to 3.5 per cent), is sold in supermarkets.

In 2003 the future of Systembolaget will be decided by parliament. With input from the more relaxed EU trading regulations, it's likely that things will change.

Fresh herbs, natural cough mixtures and other handmade herbal medicines and hygiene products are sold in Inspira. You can browse through the books in the cosy reading chair, or why not try some 'heart wine' or 'nerve cookies'?

Robygge

Grev Turegatan 20, Östermalm (667 79 69/ www.robygge.se). T-bana Östermalmstorg/bus 1, 46, 55, 56, 62. **Open** 10am-6pm Mon-Fri; 11am-4pm Sat. **Credit** AmEx, MC, V. **Map** p303 F8.

Natural make-up and hygiene products, wool underwear, massage oils, oil lamps and glassware. All Robygge's products are made at Järna, the biggest Nordic anthroposophist centre, situated about 50km (30 miles) from Stockholm, where everything is made according to the theories of German philosopher and educator Rudolf Steiner (1861-1925), who believed that creative activities are invaluable to the spirit.

Cosmetics & perfume

As well as the following specialist shops, try the cosmetics counters of the various department stores (*see p152*).

c/o Stockholm

Götgatan 30, Södermalm (442 05 80/www.co stockholm.se). T-bana Medborgarplatsen or Slussen/ bus 43, 55, 59, 66. **Open** 11am-8pm Mon-Fri; 11am-5pm Sat. **Credit** AmEx, DC, MC, V. **Map** p310 L8.

In this light and spacious temple of beauty, traditional names such as Chanel, Helena Rubenstein, Yves St Laurent and Clinique share space with newcomers like Chinese brand Wu. You'll also find the latest accessories (one staff member constantly travels the world to look for trendy gadgets), as well as men's underwear. Extra credits for the long opening hours, well-designed displays and layout and, above all, the warm-hearted staff.

Branch: NK, Regeringsgatan 38, Östermalm (762 80 00).

Cow Parfymeri

Mäster Samuelsgatan 9, Östermalm (611 15 04). T-bana Östermalmstorg/bus 43, 46, 55, 59, 69. **Open** 11am-6pm Mon-Fri; 11am-3.30pm Sat. **Credit** AmEx, DC, MC, V. **Map** p303 F8.

This futuristic boutique claims to be the only one in Scandinavia selling top-line cosmetics brands like Urban Decay, Philosophy and Vincent Longo. The

Systembolaget

Klarabergsgatan 62, Norrmalm (21 47 44/ www.systembolaget.se). T-bana T-Centralen/ bus 47, 52, 56, 59, 65. **Open** 10am-8pm Mon-Fri; 10am-3pm Sat. **No credit cards. Map** p303 G6.

This is the largest Systembolaget shop in Stockholm; it also has longer opening hours than most shops. The branch at Grev Turegatan 3 specialises in wine. You'll find a complete listing of all shops in the back of the Systembolaget catalogue.

Stationer **Ordning & Reda**. *See p166.*

staff are professional make-up artists and although it's all a bit elitist, the products and service are well worth the extra pennies.

Face Stockholm

Biblioteksgatan 1, Östermalm (611 00 74/www.facestockholm.com). T-bana Östermalmstorg/bus 46, 55, 59, 62, 69. **Open** 10am-7pm Mon-Fri; 10am-5pm Sat. **Credit** AmEx, DC, MC, V. **Map** p303 F8.

A combination of high-quality, no-nonsense cosmetics, streamlined packaging, clean interiors and impeccable service have resulted in the success story of Face Stockholm. Mother-and-daughter team Gun Nowak and Martina Arfwidson have now exported the concept to London, New York and Hong Kong, but there's nothing like visiting the original. There are eight branches across the city, including two on Drottninggatan and one in Sturegallerian (*see p152*).

Hair salons

Stockholm has loads of hairdressers. In the simpler drop-in salons, prices for a haircut vary from 150kr to 300kr.

Klippoteket

Riddargatan 6, Östermalm (679 56 50). T-bana Östermalmstorg/bus 46, 47, 62, 69, 76. **Open** 8am-8pm Mon-Wed; 8am-7pm Thur, Fri; 9am-3pm Sat. **Credit** AmEx, DC, MC, V. **Map** p303 F8.

Young, friendly staff offer trendy as well as classic cuts (prices 400kr-450kr). It's usually possible to get an appointment with a few days' notice. The branch on Riddargatan contains a café, solarium and shop. **Branches**: Riddargatan 3, Östermalm (611 40 66).

Toni&Guy

Götgatan 10, Södermalm (714 56 56/www.toniandguy.se). T-bana Slussen/bus 3, 46, 53, 55, 66. **Open** 9am-6pm Mon-Wed, Fri; 9am-7pm Thur; 9am-5pm Sat. **Credit** AmEx, MC, V. **Map** p310 K7.

Toni&Guy, the queen bee of British high-street hairdressing, has its very largest European branch here. Although the salon, on trendy Götgatsbacken, has 50 stations, a large retail area and a make-up section, it might be hard to get an appointment. A cut costs 430kr-700kr depending on the experience of the hairdresser. Full-head highlights cost 950kr-1,050kr.

Pharmacies

Access to medication is strictly controlled in Sweden and in most cases you will need a doctor's prescription (only prescriptions from the Nordic countries are allowed). However, you can buy painkillers and other simple medicines in pharmacies (*apotek*), of which there are many in Stockholm. For information on prescription medicines, call **Läkemedelsupplysningen** (medicine information office) toll-free on 020 66 77 66. English is spoken.

Apoteket CW Scheele

Klarabergsgatan 64, Norrmalm (454 81 30/www.apoteket.se). T-bana T-Centralen/bus 47, 52, 56, 59, 69. **Open** 24hrs daily. **Credit** AmEx, MC, V. **Map** p303 G6.

Apotek Enhörningen

Krukmakargatan 13, Södermalm (669 51 00). T-bana Mariatorget/bus 43, 55, 66, 74. **Open** 8.30am-10pm daily. **Credit** AmEx, DC, MC, V. **Map** p310 L6.

Spas

Centralbadet

Drottninggatan 88, Norrmalm (24 24 02/www.centralbadet.se). T-bana Hötorget/1, 47, 52, 53. **Open** 6am-9pm Mon-Fri; 8am-9pm Sat, Sun (changing rooms close 10pm daily). **Admission** 90kr-110kr. **Minimum age** women 18; men 23. **Credit** AmEx, DC, MC, V. **Map** p303 F6.

In 1904 Jugendstil architect Wilhelm Klemming realised a dream about an 'open window to nature' when he designed Centralbadet. Set back from the street in a pretty garden, it has beautiful art nouveau interiors and an inexpensive café. Take a dip in the pool or jacuzzi, experience different types of sauna, have a massage (one-hour Swedish massage 550kr) or a treatment (herbal bath 300kr). Friendly staff and a slightly shabby air make it more appealing than snobbish Sturebadet (*see below*).

Hasseludden Yasuragi

Hamndalsvägen 6, Saltsjö-boo (747 61 00/www.hasseludden.com). Bus 417 to Hamndalsvägen then 10mins walk/Vaxholmsbolaget boat from Strömkajen. **Open** 8am-10pm daily. **Admission** 8am-4pm Mon-Thur 650kr; 4-10pm Mon-Thur from 850kr; Fri-Sun 950kr. **Credit** AmEx, DC, MC, V.

The renovation of the run-down 1970s premises of Hasseludden into a Japanese spa hotel, including a pool, outdoor hot bath, sauna and restaurant, was a masterstroke. Massages and beauty treatments are also available. Located on the edge of the Stockholm archipelago, it makes for a brilliant day trip. Best to book in advance. For details of the hotel, *see p54*.

Sturebadet

Sturegallerian, Stureplan, Östermalm (54 50 15 00/www.sturebadet.se). T-bana Östermalmstorg/bus 1, 46, 55, 56, 62. **Open** *Sept-June* 6.30am-10pm

Mon-Fri; 9am-7pm Sat, Sun. *July, Aug* 6.30am-9pm Mon-Fri; 9am-6pm Sat, Sun. **Admission** annual membership 11,900kr; day membership 295kr. **Minimum age** 18. **Credit** AmEx, DC, MC, V. **Map** p303 F8.
Dating from 1885, swanky Sturebadet is the traditional upper-class and celeb favourite, next to the hub of their universe, Stureplan. It offers high-class physical and mental training at the gym, different kinds of massages, treatments and cures, as well as an extraordinary Turkish bath for up to 20 people (3,500kr for two hours). In the mornings the members of 'the breakfast club' (ie Swedish celebs and artists) can be seen in the lovely art nouveau pool. Too bad membership is so expensive.

Tattoos & piercing

See also **Blue Fox** (*see p158*).

East Street Tattoo

Östgötagatan 77, Södermalm (702 06 54/www.east-street.com). T-bana Skanstull/bus 3, 55, 59, 74. **Open** noon-7pm Mon-Fri; noon-4pm Sat. **No credit cards**. **Map** p311 N9.
In bohemian Södermalm lies one of Sweden's best-known tattoo studios. Every month a guest tattoo artist comes to the premises. The resident tattooists name some eclectic influences, from Bruno Liljefors to Pink Floyd. Next door is a piercing studio.

Interiors

Antiques & second-hand

For cheap junk, there are several second-hand shops run by charitable organisations, including **Emmaus** (Götgatan 14, Södermalm; 644 85 86), **Myrorna** (*see p159*) and **Små Smulor** (*see p159*). There is also a huge **flea market** in the car park of the Skärholmen centre (710 00 60/www.loppmarknaden.se; open 11am-6pm Mon-Fri; 9am-3pm Sat; 10am-3pm Sun; admission 10kr). Upplandsgatan in Vasastaden specialises in antiques shops.

Afrodite Antik

Odengatan 92, Vasastaden (31 75 00). T-bana St Eriksplan/bus 3, 4, 47, 53, 72. **Open** 10am-2pm, 3-6pm Mon-Fri; 11am-2pm Sat. **Credit** AmEx, MC, V. **Map** p306 D4.
Silverware, porcelain and cut-glass chandeliers.

Jackson

Tyska Brinken 20, Gamla Stan (411 95 87/www.jacksons.se). T-bana Gamla Stan/bus 3, 53, 55, 59 76. **Open & credit** call for details. **Map** p303 J7.
An extensive range of exclusive international and Scandinavian design and decorative arts from the 1880s to the 1980s. Well worth a visit.

Super spa **Centralbadet**. *See p168.*

IKEA.

Furniture & home accessories

Design junkies will be in heaven: Stockholm is heaving with shops devoted to all aspects of interior design. Also check out **DesignTorget** (*see p165*) and **10 Swedish Designers** (*see p166*). For more information on the history, movements and personalities of Swedish design, *see chapter* **Design**.

Carl Malmsten Inredning

Strandvägen 5B, Östermalm (23 33 80/www.c.malmsten.se). T-bana Östermalmstorg/bus 47, 55, 62, 69, 76. **Open** 10am-6pm Mon-Fri; 10am-2/4pm Sat. **Credit** MC, V. **Map** p304 G9.

High-quality furniture, textiles and light fittings by the talented Swedish designer Carl Malmsten (*see p34*) and his successors. The shop sells classics from the 1950s and '60s, as well as rugs and books.

David Design

Nybrogatan 7, Östermalm (611 91 55/www.david.se). T-bana Östermalmstorg/bus 47, 55, 62, 69, 76. **Open** 10am-6pm Mon-Fri; 11am-4pm Sat. **Credit** AmEx, MC, V. **Map** p303 F8.

The latest in contemporary Swedish (and international) design, from the likes of Mats Theselius (*see p37*). Clean lines and bright colours characterise the products, from sofas, chairs and tables to hooks and mirrors. Plus books, clothes, CDs and an espressso bar – in fact, you can get a whole new lifestyle here. Possibly too hip for its own good.

Elviras Värld

Renstiernas Gata 24, Södermalm (640 09 00/www.elvirasvarld.com). Bus 3, 46, 53, 66, 76. **Open** *Mid Aug-June* 11am-6pm Mon-Sat; 11am-3pm Sat. *July-mid Aug* noon-6pm Mon-Fri; noon-3pm Sat. **Credit** AmEx, DC, MC, V. **Map** p311 L9.

Elviras Värld has both new furniture and restored antiques. Much of the furniture is beautiful and well selected, and the textiles are particularly nice.

Granit

Götgatan 31, Södermalm (642 10 68/www.granit.com). T-bana Medborgarplatsen or Slussen/bus 43, 55, 59, 66. **Open** 10am-7pm Mon-Fri; 10am-5pm Sat; noon-4pm Sun. **Credit** AmEx, DC, MC, V. **Map** p310 L8.

This is supposed to be a shop for people without wardrobes (the concept is smart storage), but it's actually the Asian-inspired ceramics, clean glassware, smart bathroom items and plain but nice photo albums and notebooks that make Granit a must-see. The super-low prices don't make things worse.

Branch: Kungsgatan 42, Kungsholmen (21 92 85).

House

Drottninggatan 81, Norrmalm (406 06 81). T-bana Hötorget/bus 1, 47, 52, 53, 69. **Open** 10.30am-6.30pm Mon-Fri; 10.30am-5pm Sat; noon-4pm Sun. **Credit** AmEx, DC, MC, V. **Map** p307 E6.

Furniture, accessories, textiles and all sorts of practical items for the home. Everything's got that clean-lined Scandinavian feeling.

Branch: Humlegårdsgatan 14, Östermalm (54 58 53 40).

IKEA

Kungens Kurva, Skärholmen (744 83 00/www.ikea.se). Bus 173, 707, 710, 748/free IKEA bus from Regeringsgatan 13 on the hr 11am-5pm daily and from IKEA on the half-hr 11.30am-5.30pm daily. **Open** 10am-9pm Mon-Fri; 10am-6pm Sat, Sun. **Credit** AmEx, DC, MC, V.

In Sweden, IKEA is more than just a furniture store – it's a way of life. IKEA is the Sunday excursion, a field trip where dreams come true (or not, as the case may be). Recently renovated and expanded, this is now the world's largest IKEA store. Avoid the weekend if you want to stay away from frustrated families and stroller obstacle courses. *See also p34* **The story of IKEA**.

Branch: Barkarby, Barkarby Handelsplats, Järfälla (020 43 90 50).

Klara
Nytorgsgatan 36, Södermalm (694 92 40). Bus 3, 46, 59, 66, 76. **Open** 11am-6pm Mon-Fri; 11am-4pm Sat. **Credit** AmEx, DC, MC, V. **Map** p311 M9.
A shop that's all about Scandinavian minimalism, free from knick-knacks and unnecessary decoration. You'll find a small but well-selected range of furniture, cutlery and kitchenware. Bestsellers are lamps from Le Klint, ceramics and glassware from Finnish designer Kaj Franck, and furniture from Sweden-based David Design.
Branch: Birger Jarlsgatan 34, Östermalm (611 52 52).

Lagerhaus
Drottninggatan 31-7, Norrmalm (23 72 00/www.lagerhaus.se). T-bana T-Centralen/bus 47, 52, 56, 59, 69. **Open** 10am-7pm Mon-Fri; 10am-5pm Sat; noon-4pm Sun. **Credit** AmEx, MC, V. **Map** p303 G7.
Huge smelly candles, absurd kitchen implements, cheap minimalist porcelain and paperback fiction – all under the same roof. It's a bit chaotic, but if you're lucky you might find something that looks more expensive than it really is.
Branch: Birger Jarlsgatan 18, Östermalm (611 80 40).

Made in Scandinavia
Döbelnsgatan 23, Norrmalm (411 44 38/www.formtanke.com). T-bana Rådmansgatan/bus 4, 42, 43, 46, 52. **Open** varies; call first. **Credit** AmEx, MC, V. **Map** p307 E6.
High-quality, well-designed home accessories, produced and made – as it says – in Scandinavia. Mainly stuff for use in the kitchen and bathroom, made in a wide range of materials, from wood to silver, bronze and brass.

Nordiska Galleriet
Nybrogatan 11, Östermalm (442 83 60/www.nordiskagalleriet.se). T-bana Östermalmstorg/bus 47, 55, 62, 69, 76. **Open** 10am-6pm Mon-Fri; 10am-3pm Sat. **Credit** AmEx, DC, MC, V. **Map** p303 F8.
In its large, fashionable facilities on Nybrogatan, Nordiska Galleriet sells furniture, lights and gifts from Scandinavian and international designers. Both past masters (Alvar Aalto, Frank Lloyd Wright) and contemporary names (Philippe Starck, Jonas Bohlin) are featured. Some of the chairs are truly worth sitting down in. Just round the corner is sister shop Sovrummet (Riddargatan 20; 661 86 15), which specialises in bedroom interiors.

Norrgavel
Birger Jarlsgatan 27, Östermalm (545 220 50/www.norrgavel.se). T-bana Östermalmstorg/bus 3, 43, 46, 55, 56. **Open** 10am-6pm Mon-Fri; 10am-3/4pm Sat; noon-4pm Sun (closed Sun May-Aug). **Credit** AmEx, DC, MC, V. **Map** p308 E8.
Functionalist furniture – with truly elegant beds, chairs and shelves – and a wealth of home accessories, inspired both by Japanese minimalism and 1950s Scandinavian design.

R.O.O.M.
Alströmergatan 20, Kungsholmen (692 50 00/www.room.se). T-bana Fridhemsplan/bus 3, 4, 94. **Open** *Summer* 10am-6pm Mon-Fri; 10am-4pm Sat. *Winter* 10am-6pm Mon-Fri; 10am-5pm Sat; noon-5pm Sun. **Credit** AmEx, DC, MC, V.
This is where young and trendy (and loaded) newlyweds come to sort out their domestic design dilemmas. There's quite pricey furniture designed and made by R.O.O.M.'s in-house team, plus accessories for the kitchen and bathroom, and a nice café (*see p148*).

Svenskt Tenn
Strandvägen 5, Östermalm (670 16 28/www.svenskttenn.se). T-bana Östermalmstorg/bus 47, 55, 62, 69, 76. **Open** 10am-6pm Mon-Fri; 10am-4pm Sat. **Credit** AmEx, DC, MC, V. **Map** p304 G9.
A Stockholm classic. Founded by artist and designer Estrid Ericson in 1924, Svenskt Tenn is best known for the furniture and textiles (particularly the colourful flower patterns) created by Josef Frank, who worked for the company for 30 years after joining in 1934. His designs are still the mainstay of the shop's products. It's not cheap, of course. *See also p35.*

Launderettes

Tvättomaten
Västmannagatan 61, Vasastaden (34 64 80/www.tvattomaten.com). T-bana Odenplan/bus 4, 40, 47, 53, 69. **Open** *Aug-June* 8.30am-6.30pm Mon-Fri; 9.30am-3pm Sat. *July* 8.30am-6.30pm Mon-Fri. **No credit cards. Map** p306 D4.
Because all apartment buildings have their own *tvättstuga* (laundry room), launderettes are rare in Stockholm. This is the only one in the city centre. A one-hour self-service wash costs about 67kr. Or let the staff deal with your dirty smalls: around 102kr if you want to pick it up the same day, 82kr for the next day. Tvättomaten also does dry-cleaning.

Music

Bashment
Bondegatan 6, Södermalm (no phone). T-bana Medborgarplatsen/bus 46, 55, 59, 66, 76. **Open** 10am-8pm Mon-Fri; 11am-8pm Sat; 11am-5pm Sun. **Credit** MC, V. **Map** p311 M8.
Bashment sells Jamaican reggae and dancehall in a laid-back manner. This is one of the few shops in Stockholm for obscure Afro-Caribbean music, and a good source of gig tickets too.

Mega Skivakademien
Sergels Torg, Norrmalm (56 61 57 00/www.mega.se). T-bana T-Centralen/bus 47, 52, 56, 59, 65. **Open** 10am-7pm Mon-Fri; 10am-5pm Sat; noon-4pm Sun. **Credit** AmEx, DC, MC, V. **Map** p303 G7.
Welcome to Northern Europe's biggest record store. It's on three floors; the basement is a bit too chart-oriented, but there's also a good selection of classical and jazz on the ground floor. There are videos, DVDs and magazines too.

Multi Kulti

St Paulsgatan 3, Södermalm (643 61 29/www.multi kulti.se). T-bana Slussen/bus 3, 46, 53, 59, 76. **Open** 11am-6.30pm Mon, Tue; 11am-7pm Wed-Fri; 11am-4pm Sat. **Credit** MC, V. **Map** p310 K7.

The smell of incense fills this tiny, classic shop for just about every style of world music you could mention. It also stocks a small range of literature and videos. Staff are committed and knowledgeable.

Nitty Gritty Records

St Eriksgatan 98, Vasastaden (33 32 80/ http://w1.833.telia.com/~u83303555). T-bana St Eriksplan/bus 3, 4, 42, 47, 72. **Open** 11am-6pm Mon-Wed, Fri; 11am-7pm Thur; 11am-3pm Sat. **Credit** AmEx, DC, MC, V. **Map** p306 D3.

A sweet little shop run by club promoter Robert Baum. You'll find an excellent selection of soul, R&B, funk, Latin and rare grooves – mainly new, but some second-hand stuff too.

Pet Sounds

Skånegatan 53, Södermalm (702 97 98/www.pet sounds.se). T-bana Medborgarplatsen/bus 46, 55, 59, 66, 76. **Open** 11am-7pm Mon-Fri; 11am-4pm Sat; noon-4pm Sun. **Credit** AmEx, MC, V. **Map** p311 M8.

Pet Sounds is the oldest and still the best indie shop in Stockholm. The enthusiasts here also stock a lot of '60s music and soundtracks, plus a well-assorted range of soul music.

Pitch DJ Store

Gamla Brogatan 27, Norrmalm (22 56 40/ www.pitch.nu). T-bana T-Centralen/bus 47, 52, 53, 59, 69. **Open** 11am-7pm Mon-Fri; 11am-4pm Sat. **Credit** AmEx, MC, V. **Map** p303 F6.

Where all the hip hop DJs of Stockholm hang out.

Snickars Records

Repslagargatan 11, Södermalm (643 13 44). T-bana Slussen/bus 3, 43, 55, 56, 59. **Open** noon-7pm Mon-Fri; noon-5pm Sat. **Credit** MC, V. **Map** p310 K7.

DJ and music producer Mika Snickars' shop is the best place for vinyl when it comes to new and retro house, garage and disco.

Second-hand

St Eriksgatan in Kungsholmen is *the* street for second-hand music. As well as the most wide-ranging shop, **Skivbörsen** (*see p173*), there

Glass with class

It's said that the distinctive, elegant style of Scandinavian glass and ceramic design comes from the harsh climate and extremes of light and dark. King Gustav Vasa founded the first glassworks in Stockholm in the mid 16th century, but the large amounts of fuel needed for the furnaces could only be found in the extensive forests in the south-east, in Småland. Known as the 'Kingdom of Crystal', this is where the country's glass industry has been centred for hundreds of years. Until the 20th century many factories and designers imitated foreign ideas, but from the 1920s experimentation and the development of new techniques made Sweden a world leader in cutting-edge design.

The Danish–Swedish design group Royal Scandinavia was founded in 1997 to protect and develop this long tradition. The Swedish element comprises glassware companies **Kosta Boda** and **Orrefors** and ceramic specialists **BodaNova** and **Höganäs**.

Kosta Boda (www.kostaboda.se) unites the three glassmaking villages of Kosta, Boda and Åfors. Kosta, founded in 1742, is the oldest surviving glassworks in Sweden. **Orrefors** (www.orrefors.se) has been working with art glass as well as crystal and utilitarian glassware for more than 100 years. Both companies' designers produce traditional and more innovative, modern designs. **BodaNova** (www.bodanova.se) creates simple but beautiful everyday implements to brighten up the kitchen. It's a young ('only' 30 years old), up-to-date brand, with an unpretentious and natural feel. **Hoganas** also produces modern kitchenware. Founded in 1909, its bestseller in the '90s was a simple ceramic jug on a black wooden plate. This, along with other beloved and functional everyday items, can be found in almost every Swedish home.

WHERE TO BUY IT

There are loads of shops in Stockholm that stock Royal Scandinavia's Swedish brands. Department stores **NK** and **Åhléns** (for both *see p152*) also have well-chosen selections of Swedish crystal and glassware, and ceramics from Höganäs, Gustavsberg and Rörstrand.

If you want to see how Swedish glass is traditionally made, visit the glassworks at **Skansen** (*see p84*).

Blås & Knåda

Hornsgatan 26, Södermalm (642 77 67/ www.blas-knada.com). T-bana Slussen or Mariatorget/bus 3, 43, 55, 59, 66. **Open** 11am-6pm Mon-Fri; 11am-4pm Sat; noon-4pm Sun. **Credit** DC, MC, V. **Map** p310 K7.

are plenty of other options, including **Record Palace** (No.56; 650 19 90); **55:ans Skivbörs** (No.59; 654 55 90); **The Beat Goes On** (No.67; 31 27 17); **Record Hunter** (No.70; 32 20 23); **Golden Oldies Shop** (No.96; 32 22 40); **Nitty Gritty Records** (*see p172*); **Masen's Rock Center** (No.100; 34 32 00); and nearby **Atlas** (Torsgatan 31; 34 06 17).

Mickes Serier, CD & Vinyl

Långholmsgatan 13, Södermalm (668 20 22). T-bana Hornstull/bus 4, 40, 66, 74. **Open** 11am-usually 9pm daily. **Credit** AmEx, MC, V. **Map** p301 L3.
Mickes has everything from second-hand ABBA albums to rarities that are not even for sale. Expect a cosy atmosphere and a lot of small talk.
Branch: Långholmsgatan 20 (668 10 23).

Skivbörsen

St Eriksgatan 71, Vasastaden (32 03 17). T-bana St Eriksplan/bus 3, 4, 42, 47, 72. **Open** 11am-6pm Fri; 11am-3pm Sat. **No credit cards**. **Map** p306 E3.
Second-hand CDs in all genres – though it's best for soul, funk, disco and reggae – as well as all kinds of vinyl in the basement.

Musical instruments

Halkan's Rockhouse

Götgatan 24, Södermalm (641 49 70/www.halkan.com). T-bana Slussen/bus 3, 43, 46, 55, 59. **Open** noon-6pm Mon-Fri; noon-3pm Sat. **Credit** (over 100kr only) AmEx, MC, V. **Map** p310 K8.
At the start of Götgatsbacken, near Slussen, Halkan's is the place to head if you're looking for old guitars or professional repairs. This is the first (and the best) in a row of instrument shops. Other good ones are Gamla Gitarrer (Götgatan 28; 643 10 83) for vintage guitars, and Estrad (Folkungagatan 54; 640 12 60) for keyboards and assorted studio equipment.

Opticians & eyewear

Stureoptikern

Grev Turegatan 9, Östermalm (611 55 00). T-bana Östermalmstorg/bus 1, 46, 55, 56, 62. **Open** 10am-7pm Mon-Fri; 10am-5pm Sat; noon-4pm Sun. **Credit** AmEx, DC, MC, V. **Map** p303 F8.
It's hard to find really nice sunglasses in Stockholm. Stureoptikern has by far the best range in town,

Fine glassware by **Kosta Boda**.

Gallery-cum-shop Blås & Knåda ('blow and knead') specialises in contemporary Swedish ceramics. Prices begin at 160kr for a teacup, but can go as high as 35,000kr for art-quality pieces. There's always some kind of show on, either work by one of Blås & Knåda's 45 members or by Swedish and international guest artists. The shop is situated in the beautiful setting of Hornsgatspuckeln.

Crystal Art Centre

Tegelbacken 4, Norrmalm (21 71 69/www.cac.se). T-bana T-Centralen/bus 3, 53, 62, 65. **Open** 9am-6pm Mon-Fri; 9am-2pm Sat. **Credit** AmEx, DC, MC, V. **Map** p303 H6.
Specialising in handmade crystal and Swedish designers since 1977.

Orrefors Kosta Boda

Birger Jarlsgatan 15, Östermalm (54 50 40 84). T-bana Östermalmstorg/bus 1, 46, 47, 55, 56. **Open** *May-Sept* 10am-6pm Mon-Fri; 10am-4pm Sat; noon-4pm Sun. *Oct-Apr* 10am-6pm Mon-Fri; 10am-4pm Sat. **Credit** AmEx, DC, MC, V. **Map** p303 F8.
Branch: Norrlandsgatan 18, Norrmalm (611 21 20).

Wasa Crystal

Tegelbacken 6, Norrmalm (20 28 00/www.wasacrystal.com). T-bana T-Centralen/bus 3, 53, 62, 65. **Open** 8am-6pm daily. **Credit** AmEx, DC, MC, V. **Map** p303 H6.
Located in the same building as the Sheraton Hotel, this boutique has a wide range of products from Kosta Boda, Orrefors and Strömbergshyttan, among others.
Branches: Västerlånggatan 31, Gamla Stan (10 15 94); Vasagatan 10C, Norrmalm (21 74 25); Kungsholmsgatan 31, Kungsholmen (652 19 00).

There's no shortage of shops for souvenirs big and small.

including Armani, Gucci, Helmut Lang and Hugo Boss. They also offer eye tests and consultations, contact lenses and glasses repairs.

Sex shops

Secrets

Katarina Bangata 17, Södermalm (640 92 10/ www.afroditesapotek.com). T-bana Medborgarplatsen or Skanstull/bus 3, 4, 55, 59, 66. **Open** noon-6.30pm Mon-Fri; noon-4pm Sat. **Credit** AmEx, MC, V. **Map** p311 M8.

A 'sensuality' shop for women and their lovers, run by 'Sweden's only erotic teacher and orgasm coach', Ylva Franzén. Vibrators, books, corsets, massage oils and games for lovers are some of the things you'll find in this cute passion cave. Orgasm classes are run a few times a year – so book early!

Souvenirs & crafts

As a tourist in Stockholm, all roads lead to the tacky shopping mecca of Västerlånggatan on Gamla Stan – avoid it if you're after the genuine article. The small shop inside the **tourist office** (*see p285*) has a limited range of typical Swedish souvenirs, including Pippi Longstocking books, the painted Dala horses that you see everywhere, assorted elks and mini Midsummer poles. The basement at department store **NK** (*see p152*) has a better selection, especially of Swedish glassware. For more info on Swedish glass and ceramics, *see p172* **Glass with class**.

Konsthantverkarna

Mäster Samuelsgatan 2, Östermalm (611 03 70/ www.konsthantverkarna.a.se). T-bana Östermalmstorg/bus 46, 47, 55, 69, 76. **Open** 10am-6pm Mon-Fri; 10am-4pm Sat. **Credit** AmEx, MC, V. **Map** p303 F8.

Founded 50 years ago, this co-operative of Swedish craftsmen has developed from a simple shop stocking handicrafts to a modern art-gallery-cum-shop. Most materials are represented – ceramics, glass, wood, silver, leather, textiles – and clothes. Artists from the co-operative or invited guests put on shows eight times every year.

Skansen Butik

Djurgårdsslätten 49-51, Djurgården (442 82 68/ www.skansen.se). Bus 44, 47. **Open** *Jan, Feb* 11am-4pm daily. *Mar, Apr, Sept-Dec* 11am-5pm daily. *June-Aug* 11am-7pm daily. **Credit** AmEx, DC, MC, V. **Map** p305 J11.

You don't have to pay the entrance fee if you just want to visit the shop at Skansen's front gate. As you might expect, it's got a fine array of traditional arts and crafts – wooden items, textiles, glassware and ceramics – as well as more modern designed products, specialist books and folk music CDs. If you visit the town quarter inside Skansen, you can have the satisfaction of buying items direct from the potter or glassblower as well as watching them being made in the old-fashioned way.

Svensk Slöjd

Nybrogatan 23, Östermalm (663 66 50/www.svensk slojd.se). T-bana Östermalmstorg/bus 46, 47, 55, 59, 62. **Open** 11am-6pm Mon-Fri; 11am-4pm Sat. **Credit** AmEx, DC, MC, V. **Map** p303 F8.

With its aim of broadening the audience for Swedish traditional crafts, the Association of Swedish Handicraft was founded in the late 19th century. Visit its new shop on Nybrogaten for exquisite work by 160 artisans, including glass, pottery, textiles, baskets, clothing and wooden objects, and Sami craft from the far north of the country. It's expensive, but well worth a look for a complete tour of characteristic Swedish craftsmanship. Bestsellers are traditional cardigans from Skåne in the south of Sweden, cute heart-shaped brooches, traditional candle-holders and embroidered scarves.

Sport

You can rent bikes all along Strandvägen; it will cost about 150kr a day for a mountain bike in fairly good shape. For specific shops, *see p220* **Cycling & rollerblading**.

Adidas Concept Store

Sveavägen 21-3, Norrmalm (53 48 08 30/www.adidas.se). T-bana Hötorget/bus 1, 43, 52, 56. **Open** 10am-7pm Mon-Fri; 10am-5pm Sat; noon-4pm Sun. **Credit** AmEx, DC, MC, V. **Map** p303 F6.

This relatively new store stocks quality ski wear (mostly Swedish brand Salomon) as well as clothes, shoes and equipment for golf, tennis and football. A brilliant place with friendly and helpful staff.

Fiskarnas Redskapshandel

St Paulsgatan 2-4, Södermalm (641 82 14/www.abfiskarnas.se). T-bana Slussen/bus 3, 46, 55, 59, 66. **Open** 9am-6pm Mon-Fri; 10am-2pm Sat. **Credit** AmEx, DC, MC, V. **Map** p310 K7.

You can fish bang in the middle of the city (popular spots include the bridges alongside the parliament building and along the eastern side of the Royal Palace). From angling to professional fly-fishing gear, Fiskarnas has the lot.

Friluftsbolaget

Sveavägen 62, Norrmalm (24 30 02/www.friluftsbolaget.se). T-bana Odenplan or Rådmansgatan/bus 42, 46, 52, 53, 72. **Open** 10am-6pm Mon-Fri; 10am-3pm Sat. **Credit** DC, MC, V. **Map** p307 E6.

Everything you need for that outdoors or camping weekend. Friluftsbolaget specialises in the Swedish brand Fjällräven, famous both for its outstanding quality and its timeless/70s cut.

Branch: Kungsgatan 26 (24 19 96).

Tickets

You can also book tickets for major events through **Biljett Direkt** (077 170 70 70/www.ticnet.se) and the **tourist office** (*see p285*).

Box Office

Norrmalmstorg, Norrmalm (10 88 00/www.boxoffice.se). T-bana Östermalmstorg or Kungsträdgården/bus 46, 47, 62, 69. **Open** *June-mid Sept* 10am-6pm Mon-Fri. *Mid Sept-May* 10am-6pm Mon-Fri; 10am-4pm Sat. **Credit** AmEx, DC, MC, V. **Map** p303 F8.

Tickets for opera and major theatre shows, concerts and sporting events, in both Stockholm and abroad. You have to visit the shop in person to buy tickets for Stockholm venues. Expect to pay 5% commission if you pay with a foreign credit card.

Toys

Kalikå (*see p157*) sells colourful finger puppets and plenty of artistic and learning-oriented toys. Maybe not a trendy kid's dream, but perfect for parents with a conscience. For the more usual branded plastic toys, there's a huge branch of **Toys'R'Us** (Tangentvägen 3; 710 39 00) in Kungens Kurva, near IKEA.

Brio Lekcenter

Fältöversen, Karlaplan 13, Östermalm (661 27 07). T-bana Karlaplan/bus 42, 44. **Open** 10am-7pm Mon-Fri; 10am-4pm Sat; noon-4pm Sun. **Credit** AmEx, DC, MC, V. **Map** p309 E10.

A favourite with middle-class parents, Swedish toy brand Brio's concept is that children learn while they play. In the small mall of Fältöversen, you'll find Brio's brilliant wooden toys and train sets, plus Barbie and other well-known brands.

Krabat & Co

Folkungagatan 79, Södermalm (640 32 20/www.krabat.se). T-bana Medborgarplatsen/bus 3, 46, 53, 66, 76. **Open** 10am-6pm Mon-Fri; 10am-3pm Sat. **Credit** AmEx, MC, V. **Map** p311 L9.

Who do you want to be? Krabat has great dressing-up outfits for wannabe knights, fairies, Indian chiefs, pirates, clowns and Robin Hoods. There are also authentic mini tools and kitchen equipment – the only difference from the real thing is the size.

Travel

Kilroy Travels

Kungsgatan 4, Norrmalm (0771 54 57 69/www.kilroytravels.com). T-bana Östermalmstorg or Hötorget/bus 1, 43, 46, 55, 56. **Open** *Shop* 10am-6pm Mon-Fri. *Phone enquiries* 9am-6pm Mon-Fri. **Credit** MC, V. **Map** p303 F7.

Cheap tickets for students and people aged under 26. Prepare for long queues. You can contact the branches on the same phone number.

Branches: Allhuset, Stockholm University, Frescati; Sveavägen 71, Norrmalm.

My Travel

Sveavägen 16, Norrmalm (0771 23 02 30/www.mytravel.se). T-bana T-Centralen/bus 43, 47, 52, 56, 59. **Open** 9am-6pm Mon-Fri; 10am-3pm Sat. **Credit** AmEx, DC, MC, V. **Map** p303 F7.

My Travel is a fusion of some of Sweden's leading charter holiday companies, and offers excursions to mostly European destinations.

Video rentals

To rent videos in Sweden you have to show ID and provide a local address and phone number (giving a hotel address is OK).

Casablanca

Sveavägen 88, Vasastaden (673 50 50). T-bana Rådmansgatan/bus 4, 43, 46, 52, 72. **Open** 11am-midnight Mon-Fri; noon-midnight Sat, Sun. **No credit cards. Map** p307 D6.

From Ingmar Bergman to the newest blockbuster, Casablanca has it all. Renting a video costs 19kr-40kr depending on how new the film is. For non-residents a deposit of 60kr-100kr is required.

Arts & Entertainment

Festivals & Events	**178**
Children	**184**
Clubs	**189**
Film	**194**
Galleries	**199**
Gay & Lesbian	**205**
Music	**210**
Sport & Fitness	**218**
Theatre & Dance	**229**

Features

A food for all seasons	180
Super Swedes: Astrid Lindgren	187
The best DJ bars	193
Welcome to Trollywood	197
Street art	202
Sex, indoors and out	209
Summer music	217
Super Swedes: Björn Borg	220
Bandying about	222
The big three	226

Festivals & Events

Marathons, markets and Midsummer maypoles.

Swedes love their festivals, and their sports, so there'll be something happening whenever you go to Stockholm. Not surprisingly, most celebrations take place in summer, when the long, dark winter is finally over and everyone can hold their face up to the sun and hear live music outdoors, enjoy sporting events or dance around the maypole at Midsummer. The bleak winter is, however, enlivened by traditional events such as Christmas, with its charming outdoor markets, and the lovely festival of light known as Luciadagen. For visitors, the best place to celebrate many of the traditional events is open-air museum **Skansen** (*see p84*).

For general information on seasonal events and festivals, a good bet is the **tourist office** (*see p285*), or for up-to-the-minute details of events happening during your visit, check out English-language mag *What's On Stockholm.* For info on the seasons, weather and dates of public holidays, *see p287.*

Spring

Påsk (Easter)

Date Mar/Apr.

For most Swedes, Easter's greatest significance is a coveted four days off (Good Friday through to Easter Monday), just the time for overhauling the boat, clearing the cobwebs off the summer cottage or tidying the garden. Many people take a skiing holiday. Eating painted eggs is a hallowed tradition at the Easter *smörgåsbord*, along with salmon prepared in many different ways. On Maundy Thursday (Skärtorsdag) or Easter Saturday, little girls dressed up and painted as witches go around begging sweets from their neighbours, in exchange for hand-drawn Easter cards. This custom recalls the old superstition that Easter was the time when the witches flew to the Devil on the mythical Blåkulla (Blue Hill).

Valborgsmässoafton (Walpurgis Night)

Date 30 Apr.

Custom has it that in pagan times Swedes lit bonfires on the last night of April to protect themselves against witches gathering that night to worship the Devil. Today, the celebration marks the end of winter and coming of spring, and usually involves a huge bonfire and choral singing – often by white-capped university graduates. Walpurgis Night is celebrated at numerous venues all over Stockholm (and Sweden, for that matter). For visitors, good spots include Evert Taubes Terrass on Riddarholmen, or Skansen, where fireworks add an extra sparkle to the evening's festivities.

Första Maj (May Day)

Date 1 May.

If you happen to be in Stockholm on May Day, you'll probably run into marchers waving banners at Sergels Torg and other large squares. Labour Day has been celebrated in various forms since the 1880s. In the early 20th century, it was a hugely popular festival in Djurgården with a royal procession, and an occasion for trips to the countryside. By the late 20th century, it had turned into a rally of industrial workers, but it's a much lower-key affair these days. Thanks to the cold northern climate, there's no maypole dancing – that is saved for later in the year, at Midsummer (*see p181*).

Tjejtrampet

Around Gärdet (450 26 10/www.tjejtrampet.com).
Date May.

It makes sense that the world's largest women's bicycle race should take place in bike-friendly Stockholm, with its numerous dedicated cycle paths. Tjejtrampet is now one of Sweden's classic athletic events, and celebrates its 14th anniversary in 2003. It's open to both elite athletes and casual cyclists. In 2002 some 4,000 women made it to the finishing line after cycling the 48km (29-mile) route. Everyone from teenage girls to grandmothers pedals alongside one another in a show of female unity and just for the joy of friendly physical competition.

Summer

Confidencen

Ulriksdals Slottsteater, Ulriksdals Slott, Solna (box office 85 60 10/www.confidencen.se). Pendeltåg train to Ulriksdal or T-bana Bergshamra then bus 503.
Box office *May-Sept* 11am-3pm Mon-Fri. Closed Sept-May. **Tickets** 150kr-300kr. **No credit cards.**
Map p237. **Date** May-mid Sept.

Built by Queen Lovisa Ulrika in 1753, Confidencen is the oldest rococo theatre in Sweden, located just a few miles north of the city. It was used by King Gustav III and the popular 18th-century troubadour Carl Michael Bellman. Performances are held every summer and for a few days over Christmas. The theatre presents a slightly lighter repertoire than Drottningholm (*see p180*), with opera productions by both the Kungliga Operan and Folkoperan, plus ballet, theatre and concerts. Ulriksdals Slott and the surrounding park are also well worth a visit; *see p246* **Palaces around Lake Mälaren**.

Midsummer fun and games at Skansen. *See p181.*

Nationaldag (National Day)

Date 6 June.

The Swedish flag flies from every official building and many private homes on National Day, which celebrates Gustav Vasa's election as King of Sweden on 6 June 1523 and the adoption of a new constitution on the same date in 1809. If you want a glimpse of the royal family in their traditional blue and yellow costumes, head for Skansen – where, since 1916, the King of Sweden has presented flags to representatives of various corporations in a big festive parade. Unlike neighbouring Norway, where National Day is one huge party, it's still a working day in less patriotic Sweden, so the flag presentation and ceremonial speeches are put off until the evening.

Stockholm Marathon

Starts and finishes at Stockholms Stadion, Lidingövägen 1, Hjorthagen (54 56 64 40/www.marathon.se). **Map** p308 C9. **Date** Sat in mid June.

The world-class Stockholm Marathon celebrates its 25th anniversary in 2003. Few cities can match the beauty of the route, which takes the 14,000 international runners along the lovely waterfronts of Strandvägen, Norrmälarstränd and Skeppsbron. The excellent organisation and views mean that it's considered one of the best marathons in the world. Much of the city centre is closed to cars during the race, so you'll have to make your way through the crowds by foot or public transport. For other running races, *see p221* **Jogging & running**.

Skärgårdbåtens Dag

Starts at Strömkajen, Norrmalm (662 89 02). T-bana Kungsträdgården/bus 46, 55, 65, 59, 76. **Map** p303 G8. **Date** 1st Wed in June.

If the idea of travelling on one of Stockholm's old-fashioned steamboats appeals, there's no better day to do it than Archipelago Boat Day. A parade of steam-driven vessels, whistles blowing, sets off in the early evening from Strömkajen for Vaxholm. If you don't want to go along for the ride, good viewpoints are Strömkajen, Skeppsholmen, Kastellholmen and Fåfängen. The boats arriving in Vaxholm are greeted by live music and an outdoor market; travellers have a couple of hours to explore Vaxholm before returning to Stockholm.

Slottsgala på Kungliga Ulriksdal

Ulriksdals Slottsteater, Solna (www.slottsgala.nu). Pendeltåg train to Ulriksdal or T-bana Bergshamra then bus 503. **Tickets** 300kr-895kr. **Map** p237. **Date** mid June.

A short annual festival set in the park of Ulriksdals Slott. The likes of Bryn Terfel and Montserrat Caballé sing classical hits to a dressed-up corporate audience. Some nights offer more popular show tunes and fireworks. Book tickets through Biljett Direkt (077 170 70 70/www.ticnet.se).

Drottningholms Slottsteater

Drottningholms Slott (box office 660 82 25/ www.drottningholmsslottsteater.dtm.se). T-bana Brommaplan then bus 301-323/theatre boat (mid June-mid Aug) from Klara Mälarstrand-City Hall jetty (Stadshusbron). **Box office** *Mar-Aug* 11am-noon, 2-3pm Mon-Fri. Closed Sept-May. **Tickets** 165kr-600kr. **Credit** AmEx, DC, MC, V. **Map** p237. **Date** June-mid Aug.

The court theatre at Drottningholm, designed by Carl Fredrik Adelcrantz in 1766, is a unique building, its original stage machinery and sets still in good working order. Dance, opera and concerts are presented in summer, with works by Haydn, Handel,

A food for all seasons

Most Swedes simply could not imagine sitting down to a Midsummer meal without pickled herring, new potatoes and the first crop of native strawberries, or a Christmas *Julbord* without sausages, meatballs and ham. Certain foods have become inextricably entwined with the celebration of certain holidays and the passing of the seasons, and the usually secular Swedes observe these food traditions with religious fervour: better to leave the country than turn your nose up at crayfish come August. Most of the following foods are eaten at home, but some are also available in restaurants and hotels.

Semla buns

When? January-March

What? These whipped-cream and almond-paste porous buns usually fill the windows of the city's bakeries right on the heels of Christmas. Once the customary dessert on Mondays or Tuesdays in Lent, they were traditionally served in a bowl of milk; now they are usually eaten with a cup of coffee. King Adolf Fredrik of Sweden gorged himself to death during Lent in 1771, partly on *semlor* and champagne.

Crayfish

When? August

What? Sweden's native *kräftor* were once the most sought-after crayfish in the world, but the devastation wreaked by a parasitic mould in the early 20th century means that nowadays most Swedes have to be content with importing this favourite delicacy. No matter – August is still the time for crayfish parties, preferably outside under a full moon. Don a party hat and a decorated bib, then dig in with gusto, under the traditional moon-face paper lanterns.

Surströmming

When? August

What? *Surströmming* is the one delicacy that non-Swedes have most trouble with. This fermented Baltic herring harks back to an ancient method of preserving fish: since salt was expensive, people used just enough salt to start the fish fermenting instead of rotting. These days the herring is put in tins and allowed to ferment for up to a year. The new 'vintage' is uncorked in early August, releasing a strange and, to many, foul stench. Accompanied by almond potatoes, *tunnbröd* ('thin bread') and onions, and washed down with beer, many Swedes can think of no finer treat. *Surströmming* parties are common in the north of the country, but many Stockholmers don't like to be left out either. Southern Sweden tends to have eel parties instead.

Ärtsoppa

When? Thursdays throughout the year, especially in autumn and winter

What? Split pea and pork soup, traditionally served on Thursdays and eaten with mustard, is a reminder of the time when a family had only one cooking pot and had to throw all

Gluck and Mozart. The music is played on authentic period instruments, and the ballets are reconstructed from the 18th century. *See also p239.*

Midsommar (Midsummer)

Date Fri & Sat closest to 24 June.

Midsummer is the Swedes' big summer festival, when they make the most of the long hours of daylight (even as far south as Stockholm it doesn't get completely dark). It's most likely descended from a prehistoric summer solstice festival of light and fertility. Many Stockholmers leave for the archipelago for the weekend, and the city pretty much closes down – shops, restaurants and museums are shut – but if you'd like to see some traditional celebrations, head for open-air folk museum Skansen. On both days there's dancing around the maypole, traditional games and folk dance displays. The festival wouldn't be complete without new potatoes boiled in dill, served with *matjes* herring.

the ingredients, meat and vegetables, in together. Along the way, it became traditional to follow the soup with pancakes and jam. On festive occasions, this national dish is accompanied by *punsch*, a sweet arak-like spirit.

Julbord

When? late November-Christmas
What? A traditional *Julbord* ('Christmas table') is typically eaten in three stages. You start with various types of herring and salmon, then move on to the meats (meatballs, sausages and ham), accompanied by 'Jansson's Temptation', an anchovy, potato and cream casserole. You polish it all off with a sweet berry-filled pastry. Later in the evening, rice porridge is eaten. Tradition has it that finding the hidden almond in the porridge means you're destined to marry within the year.

Brännvin

When? any time
What? Stockholmers use every possible excuse to drink a glass or more of *brännvin* (schnapps). It comes in numerous varieties, highly flavoured with native herbs and spices such as caraway, aniseed, coriander and fennel. The traditional way to drink *brännvin* is to fill the first glass to the brim, the second only halfway. Before downing the glasses, it's customary to sing a *snapsvisa* ('schnapps ditty'). Skål!

Stockholm Jazz Festival

Skeppsholmen (55 61 45 63/www.svd.se/jazz). Bus 65. **Map** p304 H9. **Date** 3rd wk in July.

Sweden's premier live music event takes place over six days in July, pulling in some top international artists in jazz, soul, blues, Latin and more. The site of the festival – the island of Skeppsholmen – couldn't be more picturesque. Some 30,000 spectators attend more than 40 concerts, and the island turns into one huge party, with restaurants overflowing and peddlers hawking festival merchandise.

Musik på Slottet

Kungliga Slottet, Slottsbacken, Gamla Stan (10 22 47/www.royalfestivals.se). T-bana Gamla Stan/bus 43, 46, 55, 59, 76. **Tickets** around 200kr. **Map** p303 H8. **Date** usually July-Sept.

Classical music, jazz and folk songs share centre stage at more than 25 evening concerts held in four beautiful rooms of the Royal Palace. Established artists and chamber ensembles, as well as up-and-coming young stars, make an appearance. Get your tickets from Biljett Direkt (077 170 70 70/www.ticnet.se) or Box Office (*see p175*).

Stockholm Pride Week

Tantolunden, Södermalm (www.stockholmpride.org). T-bana Zinkensdamm or Hornstull/bus 74, 94, 190, 191. **Map** p301 M4. **Date** July/Aug.

Stockholm Pride is the biggest Pride festival in the Nordic countries, with five days of partying, debates and entertainment. In 2002 30,000 gay, lesbian, bi and transgender people took to the streets to celebrate. The main venues, eating places and events are centred on the large open space of Tantolunden park in Södermalm, and there's also a flamboyant street parade on the Saturday.

Gröna Lunds Fyrverkeri Festivalen

Gröna Lund, Lilla Allmänna Gränd 9, Djurgården (58 75 01 00/www.gronalund.com). Bus 44, 47/tram 7/ferry from Slussen or Nybroplan. **Map** p304 J11. **Date** mid Aug.

Gröna Lund amusement park inherited the tradition of an annual fireworks festival from the now-defunct Stockholm Water Festival. During one week in mid August, firework displays are held every other day; it's become a world-class event with competitive pyrotechnics from China, Australia and the USA. The fireworks – set off from a pontoon in the water near Gröna Lund – start at 10.15pm and can be seen from all over the city. In addition to the park itself, good viewing points are the heights of Södermalm, along the water on Stadsgårdsleden and Skeppsbron, and the high ground of Skansen.

Kungliga Filharmonikerna på Gärdet

Next to the Sjöhistoriska Museet, Gärdet. Bus 69. **Map** p305 F13. **Date** 2nd or 3rd Sun in Aug.

It's easy to get a royal overdose during the summer music season in Stockholm. A popular and informal event is the free outdoor concert held by the Royal

Stockholm Philharmonic Orchestra in co-operation with *Dagens Nyheter* newspaper. Around 30,000 people gather with picnic baskets for an afternoon out in a fantastic setting by the canal.

Autumn

Stockholm Beer & Whisky Festival

Factory, Nacka Strand, Nacka (662 94 94/www.stockholmbeer.se). **Tickets** 150kr. **Minimum age** 20. **Date** Sept.

This festival, now in its 11th year, has earned a hallowed place as, it claims, one of the four best beer fests in the world, along with those in London, Denver and Antwerp. Thousands of beer, cider and whisky lovers visit the exhibition each year to sample the wares. Experts are on hand to teach you the right way to enjoy the beverages. Sounds like a bit of an excuse for a piss-up.

Lidingöloppet

Around Lidingö (765 26 15/www.lidingoloppet.se). **Date** late Sept-early Oct.

The world's biggest cross-country race has become a tradition for Swedes and runners from all over the world. The first Lidingöloppet was held in 1965. In 2001 more than half a million people took part, representing some 30 different countries. The main categories are 30km (18 miles) for men and 10km (6 miles) for women, but there are events for all ages and distances. All the races are held on the same weekend in the early autumn.

Stockholm Open

Kungliga Tennishallen, Lidingövägen 75, Hjorthagen (450 26 25/tickets 450 26 20/www.stockholmopen.se). T-bana Gärdet/bus 73, 291, 293. **Tickets** 70kr-440kr. **Credit** AmEx, DC, MC, V. **Map** p309 B11. **Date** Oct/Nov.

This prestigious tennis tournament was the brainchild of veteran tennis star Sven Davidson. In 1969 American colleagues asked him to arrange a competition in Sweden with tennis pros and amateurs from all over the world. The event was televised from the beginning, thus drawing a huge worldwide audience. Despite the nearly 40,000 spectators each year, the Stockholm Open has earned praise as one of the best-organised tournaments in Europe.

Stockholm International Film Festival

Various venues around Stockholm (www.filmfestivalen.se). **Date** mid Nov.

As the leading competitive film festival in northern Europe, the ten-day Stockholm Film Festival is aimed at launching young film-makers and broadening the audience for innovative quality films in Scandinavia. Celebrating its 14th anniversary in 2003, the festival screens 160 films from 40 countries, focusing on the Nordic countries, Asia and Latin America. There are also excellent retrospectives of past cinematic masters.

Stockholm International Horse Show

Globen, Arenavägen, Johanneshov (600 34 00/tickets 0771 31 00 00/www.stockholmhorseshow.com). T-bana Globen/bus 4, 150, 164. **Tickets** 145kr. **Date** late Nov/early Dec.

This international equestrian event covers everything from dressage and showjumping to a steeplechase with Shetland ponies. Nearly 70,000 people attend each year. There are special children's shows as well as a Christmas extravaganza, in deference to the season and the dire need, in Sweden's dark November, to find an occasion for glamorous and colourful displays of talent.

Winter

Christmas Markets

Date early-end Dec.

Skansen's Christmas market – one of the biggest in Sweden and dating back to 1903 – is held at weekends throughout December until Christmas Eve (the only day Skansen is closed). Look out for Swedish craft products, traditional Christmas ornaments made of straw, hand-dipped candles, sweets (including *polkagris*, oversized red and white striped sticks) and Christmas fare such as smoked sausage, eel, salmon, *pepparkakor* (gingersnaps), *glögg* (mulled wine) and saffron buns. Stortorget in Gamla Stan also holds a Christmas market, as does Rosendals Trädgård on Djurgården, with many tasty treats from its own gardens, such as lingonberry jam.

Nobeldagen

Date 10 Dec.

The year's Nobel Prize laureates are honoured in a ceremony at the Konserthuset, followed by a lavish banquet, attended by the royal family, in the Stadshuset's famous Blue Hall. Tickets for this glittering affair are coveted by Stockholmers, but they are usually granted only to a privileged few. The rest have to be content with watching the proceedings on TV and sighing over the fabulous menu, which is prepared by a top Stockholm chef who won the privilege in a competition. For more on the history and founder of the awards, *see p104* **Alfred Nobel & the Nobel Prizes**.

Advent

Date Dec.

You can tell Christmas is approaching when you start to spot the electric Advent candelabra and stars (made of straw, wood shavings or metal) hanging in the windows of homes, shops and offices. Every home has its Advent candlestick, usually a little box with four candleholders nestled in moss and lingonberry sprigs. Tradition has it that the first candle is lit on the first Sunday of Advent and allowed to burn down only one quarter, so that it won't burn out before the fourth candle is lit. The smell of baking Swedish gingersnaps (*pepparkakor*) also sweetens the long wait for Christmas.

At **Christmas**, don't miss the traditional markets, gingersnaps and mulled wine.

Luciadagen

Date 13 Dec.

Lucia Day is celebrated in the heart of the winter darkness. The Lutheran Swedes adopted the Sicilian St Lucia because her name is connected with *lux*, Latin for light. All over Sweden, girls dressed in white with red ribbons round their waist are led by a woman dressed as Lucia, with a crown of lit candles on her head. Stockholm's Lucia is crowned on the Solliden stage at Skansen at the first Christmas market in early December. On 13 December there are two ceremonies: at Skansen's Temperance Hall in traditional 1930s style with a children's choir, and at Solliden with Lucia and her maids arriving in procession, followed by traditional songs and fireworks. Visitors can also see Lucia processions at many churches, schools and even some hotels.

Jul

Date 24-26 Dec.

Christmas is Sweden's most important holiday. The main celebration is a private one, held on Christmas Eve (although many restaurants will be offering the traditional, overflowing *Julbord* – *see p180* **A food for all seasons**). A family member disguised as Father Christmas or the *Jultomten* (Christmas elf) arrives bearing gifts. (The Christmas goat, who used to hand out presents, remains the most typical Swedish Christmas decoration and is the oldest Christmas symbol the Swedes have.) Christmas Day itself is pretty quiet, reserved for recovering from the previous day's overeating and for visiting relatives and friends. Huge Christmas trees stand at Kungsträdgården and on Skeppsbron, and the festive window displays at department store NK (*see p152*) are always spectacular.

Nyårsafton (New Year's Eve)

Date 31 Dec.

New Year celebrations in Sweden are a raucous and public contrast to the quiet and private Christmas festivities. On New Year's Eve, crowds fill the streets, feasting on seafood at various restaurants, and moving from one bar to another. Visitors can join the crowds at Skansen, where New Year's Eve has been celebrated every year since 1895. At the stroke of midnight a well-known Swede recites Tennyson's 'Ring Out, Wild Bells', and streamers, party trumpets and general mayhem accompanies the sound of fireworks set off over the water.

Stockholm Furniture Fair

Sollentunamässan, Mässvägen 1, Älvsjö (www.stockholmfurniturefair.com). Pendeltåg train to Älvsjö. **Date** 2nd wk in Feb.

It's not surprising that a city obsessed with design should be the home of Scandinavia's premier interiors event. It's primarily a trade affair, but the general public are welcome on the last day. The city's hotels tend to be booked solid during the week of the fair, so book ahead. A new design fair, STHLM Form/Design, launches in January 2003.

Stockholm New Music Festival

Various venues in Stockholm including Nybrokajen 11, Konsersthuset, Berwaldhallen & Kulturhuset (www.rikskonserter.se). **Date** mid Feb.

This annual two-week festival for new music was set up by the Konserthuset, Berwaldhallen, Sveriges Radio and the Swedish Concert Institute, under the artistic leadership of composer Ivo Nilsson. For more information on ticket prices and so on, check the website nearer the time.

Stockholm Art Fair

Sollentunamässan, Sollentuna (www.sollfair.se). Pendeltåg train to Sollentuna. **Date** early Mar.

At the beginning of March, the Swedish art scene gets together for five intense days. Everyone's there – art students, artists, gallery owners, dealers, curators, critics and visitors – and events include seminars, talks and meetings, as well as the opportunity to just look at the art. It's true chaos, but organised chaos, and a lot of fun.

Children

Keep minds and bodies busy with an array of kid-centred attractions.

Stockholm has got to be one of the world's most child-friendly major cities. This is partly because of Sweden's healthy attitude towards kids; children are generally well taken care of and respected by society. Thanks to its very high taxes and large public sector, Sweden's much-admired social welfare policy includes a childcare system that is highly developed and heavily subsidised. All children from 18 months to school age are given a daycare spot if their parents work or study – much to the envy of parents from other countries.

Stockholm's excellent public transport system, with lifts and pram ramps in almost every metro station, makes getting around the city easy. Under-7s travel free on buses, the Tunnelbana and commuter trains, and bus travel is also free for one adult with a child in a pram or stroller. To keep restless, sightseeing-weary kids occupied, most museums and attractions have dedicated children's sections, usually with toys, hands-on displays or other special activities. There are often areas for eating packed lunches (handy if you're on a budget). Many restaurants offer high chairs, kids' menus and help with warming baby food. And you are positively encouraged to breastfeed in public.

If your family likes to spend time outdoors (as the Swedes do), the capital offers wide pavements, plenty of open green spaces and a beautiful location on the water – all bonuses in the warmer months. In winter, when the lakes are frozen, you'll see parents skating across the ice pushing prams. But if you're not that adventurous, or the winter cold and darkness get you down, there are plenty of indoor activities to keep youngsters amused.

The best place for children in Stockholm is the island of Djurgården,. As well as acres of grass to run around on, it contains most of the city's best kids' attractions; it's also mainly traffic-free (cars are banned at weekends) and there's ample opportunity for exploring on foot or by bike, bus or tram.

For a current list in English of museums, festivals and other events just for kids, pick up a copy of *What's On Stockholm* from the **tourist office** (*see p285*) or visit its website at www.stockholmtown.com. Also, **www.parentnetsweden.com** (in English) is packed with useful info, from doctors to sightseeing. If you're planning on visiting a lot of museums, consider investing in a **Stockholm Card** (*see p56* **Pick a card**).

Attractions

The **Aquaria Vattenmuseum** (*see p82*) on Djurgården is definitely worth a visit.

Fjärilshuset

Haga Trädgård, Hagaparken (730 39 81/ www.fjarilshuset.se). T-bana Odenplan then bus 515. **Open** *Apr-Sept* 10am-4pm Tue-Fri; 11am-

Gröna Lund. *See p185.*

5.30pm Sat, Sun. *Oct-Mar* 10am-3pm Tue-Fri; 11am-4.30pm Sat, Sun. **Admission** 60kr; 55kr concessions; 25kr 4-16s; free under-4s. **Free with SC**. **Credit** MC, V.
In a beautiful setting at the northern end of historic Hagaparken (*see p105*), the fantastic Butterfly House – all 850sq m/3,050sq ft of it – is the closest you'll get to a tropical rainforest in Stockholm. Mingle with free-flying exotic butterflies and birds, or check out the pond full of koi carp or the Asian garden. There's also a very child-friendly café and an area for eating packed lunches.

Gröna Lund

Allmänna Gränd, Djurgården (58 75 01 00/ www.tivoli.se/2000/eng/). Bus 44, 47/tram 7/ ferry from Slussen or Nybroplan. **Open** *early June-late Aug* noon-11pm Mon-Thur; noon-midnight Fri, Sat; noon-8pm/10pm Sun. *May-early June, late Aug-mid Sept* days & times vary; call for details. Closed mid Sept-Apr. **Admission** 50kr; free under-7s; multi-ride booklets 150kr-220kr. **Credit** AmEx, DC, MC, V. **Map** p304 J11.
Perched on the edge of Djurgården, with great views across the water, Gröna Lund ('the Green Grove') is Sweden's oldest amusement park. Built in 1883 and owned by the same family ever since, its historic buildings and well-preserved rides retain an old-world charm. You can even travel here by boat the way people did more than 100 years ago. Among the older (and tamer) favourites are carousels, bumper cars, Ferris wheels and a Fun House, while the newerfangled thrills include a rollercoaster and the free-fall 'power tower', Europe's highest at (gulp) 80m (264ft). You can buy multi-ride booklets or pay for each ride separately. Worried parents will find the park highly safety-conscious: leaflets in English provide detailed descriptions of each ride, and any age or height restrictions are clearly signposted. The park is a baby-friendly place, with pram ramps on all the stairs and a Happy Baby Centre – a secluded nursery with all the paraphernalia needed to feed and soothe tots. Fun for all the family.

Junibacken

Galärvarvsvägen, Djurgården (58 72 30 00/ www.junibacken.se). Bus 44, 47/tram 7/ferry from Slussen or Nybroplan. **Open** *June-Aug* 10am-5pm (23 June-10 Aug 10am-8pm) daily. *Sept-May* 10am-5pm Tue-Sun. **Admission** 95kr; 75kr concessions, 3-15s; free under-3s. **20kr discount with SC**. **Credit** AmEx, DC, MC, V. **Map** p304 G10.
No child will want to miss Junibacken, a mini indoor theme park dedicated to Pippi Longstocking and other characters created by Swedish author Astrid Lindgren. Take a train ride (ask for narration in English) that crosses miniature fictional landscapes, flies over rooftops and passes through quaint Swedish houses. In Pippi's house, Villa Villekulla, kids are welcome to dress up like Pippi, wreak havoc inside and slide down the roof. Stories by other writers feature too, and activities include face painting and storytelling. Adults seeking a bit of relaxation can take in the lovely views of the

Face painting fun at **Junibacken**.

water and shipyards. There's also a very good book/ gift shop. *See also p187* **Super Swedes: Astrid Lindgren**. Booking ia essential in high season.

Skansen & Skansen Akvariet

Djurgårdsslätten 49-51, Djurgården. Bus 44, 47/tram 7/ferry from Slussen or Nybroplan. **Map** p305 H-J12.
Skansen (442 80 00/www.skansen.se). **Open** *June-Aug* 10am-10pm daily. *May* 10am-8pm daily. *Sept* 10am-5pm daily. *Jan-Apr, Oct-Dec* 10am-4pm daily. **Admission** *May-Aug* 30kr-70kr; free-30kr 6-15s. *Sept-Dec* 30kr-60kr; 20kr 6-15s. Free under-6s. **Free with SC**. **Credit** AmEx, DC, MC, V.
Skansen Akvariet (660 10 82/www.skansen-akvariet.se). **Open** *Midsummer-early Aug* 10am-8pm daily. *Early Aug-Midsummer* 10am-4pm Mon-Fri; 10am-5pm Sat, Sun. **Admission** 60kr; 30kr 6-15s; free under-6s. **Free with SC**. **Credit** AmEx, MC, V.
Skansen is really a zoo, aquarium, amusement park, theatre and museum rolled into one. Young children might find the old buildings a bit dull, but the animals are always a hit. The regular zoo (feeding time 2pm daily) specialises in Nordic animals, among them brown bears and wolves, while the children's zoo, Lill-Skansen, houses Swedish farm animals. In the small aquarium (*akvariet*; separate entrance fee), kids can pet a snake or a ray. For a completely un-Disneylike experience, the charming Tivoli amusement park has rides dating back to the 19th century; there are even carousels for different-sized kids. Other diversions include guided pony rides, horse and carriage rides, and events for youngsters almost every day of the year. Some sights are only open in summer. *See also p84.*

Museums

The **Vasamuseet** (*see p86*) is a surefire hit for children over six who like (very) big boats.

Hobby och Leksaksmuseet

Mariatorget 1C, Södermalm (641 61 00). T-bana Mariatorget/bus 43, 55, 66. **Open** *Midsummer-mid Aug* 10am-4pm Mon-Fri; noon-4pm Sat, Sun. *Mid Aug-Midsummer* 10am-4pm Tue-Fri; noon-4pm Sat, Sun. **Admission** 45kr; 25kr 4-16s; free under-4s. **Free with SC**. **No credit cards**. **Map** p310 K6-7.

The children's zoo at **Skansen**. *See p185.*

The Hobby and Toy Museum contains five floors of old-fashioned toys and mechanical musical instruments. Since most of the objects are in display cases, they'll probably appeal more to nostalgic adults than children – though a Nintendo PlayStation provides some action. Of more interest is the theatre, where different troupes perform daily (usually 11am Mon-Fri; 1pm, 2pm Sat, Sun; Swedish only) for different age groups. Teater Bambino (www.teaterbambino.com) is popular with the pre-school set.

Musikmuseet

Sibyllegatan 2, Östermalm (519 554 90/www.stockholm.music.museum). T-bana Östermalmstorg/bus 47, 62, 69, 76. **Open** 11am-4pm Tue-Fri; noon-4pm Sat, Sun. **Guided tours** *Swedish* noon, 2pm 1st Sun of mth. *English* call to arrange. **Admission** 40kr; 20kr concessions, 7-18s; free under-7s. **Free with SC. Credit** MC, V. **Map** p303 F8.

A large part of the Music Museum is dedicated to fostering a love of music in children through song, play and dance. The Klåjnk room (loosely translated as 'Boing!') contains amazing instruments all painstakingly made for small fingers to manage, such as a pint-sized harp and an organ where you pull rather than press the keys. On Fridays (Oct-early Dec, Jan-May 11am-noon), informal music classes are offered on a drop-in basis. Trained musicians lead other activities (in Swedish) throughout the school year. You can bring your own food to the museum or visit the spacious café next door for lunch. *See also p97.*

Postmuseum

Lilla Nygatan 6, Gamla Stan (781 17 55/www.posten.se/museum). T-bana Gamla Stan/bus 3, 53. **Open** *June-Aug* 11am-4pm Tue-Sun. *Sept-May* 11am-4pm Tue, Thur-Sun; 11am-7pm Wed. **Admission** 50kr; 40kr concessions; 25kr 13-18s; free under-12s. **Free with SC. Credit** MC, V. **Map** p303 J7.

If you think kids would find a postal museum incredibly dull, think again – daily newspaper *Expressen* ranked Lilla Posten (Little Post Office) the number one children's play area in a museum. In a 17th-century vaulted cellar kids can create, stamp and post their own postcards, load a postal van with packages and deliver letters (to a talking postbox).

Tekniska Museet

Museivägen 7, Gärdet (450 56 00/www.tekniskamuseet.se). Bus 69. **Open** 10am-5pm Mon, Tue, Thur, Fri; 10am-8pm Wed; 11am-5pm Sat, Sun. **Tours** *Engine hall* adults 1pm Sat, Sun. *Mine* children 1pm Sat, Sun. *Miniature railway* 3pm Mon-Fri; noon, 3pm Sat, Sun. **Admission** (incl Telemuseum) 60kr; 40kr concessions; 30kr 6-19s; 120kr family; free under-6s. Free 5-8pm Wed. **Free with SC. Credit** MC, V. **Map** p305 G14.

The interactive Museum of Science and Technology is one of Sweden's largest science museums. Although it aims to be highly pedagogical, it's more like a fun house, and a great place for small babies and kids of all ages. The Minirama room will have babies cooing with special mirrors, blocks and assorted toys; in the Teknorama area, small kids can discover how machines work by using their own bodies (such as running in a huge wheel to generate electricity). For older children the main hall has aeroplanes suspended from the ceiling, steam-driven cars and a 1927 Harley-Davidson. Next door is the Telemuseum (admission included with Tekniska Museet). It's a bit dull, but at weekends kids get the chance to assemble old-fashioned dial phones and then test them out. *See also p100.*

Outdoors

Stockholm has no shortage of parks and open spaces. Djurgården is always a good option in nice weather if you have children in tow. The waterside café **Djurgårdsbrons Sjöcafe** (*see p220*), just across the bridge on Djurgården, doubles as a boat and bike rental company. You can hire paddleboats, rowing boats, canoes, kayaks, bicycles or rollerblades for a practical and fun way to explore the island and its waterways. The bikes come in different sizes, and some have child seats. Further into the island, at **Rosendals Trädgård**, you'll find a small but charming playground built from logs and natural materials. You can eat at the outdoor café (*see p144*) or bring along a picnic. Flowers, herbs, freshly baked bread and more are for sale at the shop.

The playground at **Humlegården** in Östermlam is graffiti-free, completely fenced in and has separate sections for different age groups, making it one of the city centre's most attractive and safe play areas. Part of Stockholm's publicly financed playground system, it contains a caretaker's building with toilets, changing tables and coffee and juice for sale. Tricycles, wagons and sandpit toys are provided for kids' use. It's recently been made handicapped-accessible. Further afield, there's glorious **Hagaparken**, whose delights include the **Fjärilshuset** (*see p184*).

Super Swedes: Astrid Lindgren

On 28 January 2002 nearly all of Sweden grieved over the death of Astrid Lindgren, its most famous and beloved children's author. She is best remembered for creating Pippi Longstocking, the original wild child who captured the hearts of generations of children around the world. Lindgren had enormous popular appeal and was an important public figure in Swedish life.

Lindgren was born Astrid Ericsson in 1907 in the small town of Vimmerby in southern Sweden. Like many Swedes of her generation, she grew up close to nature. She pointed to her happy childhood as the inspiration for most of her works, claiming that it superseded any later experiences. One turning point arrived when she was 19. Unmarried and pregnant, she was forced to leave her hometown for Stockholm, where she would live for more than 60 years.

After having her son, Lars, she married Sture Lindgren in 1931 and became a full-time homemaker to take care of Lars and later her daughter Karin. According to Lindgren, it was Karin who inspired the idea for Pippi, when she asked her mother to tell her a story when she was ill. In 1946 Lindgren became the children's books editor at Rabén & Sjögren, where she worked until her retirement. A prolific and multi-faceted author, she wrote some 80 books including children's and young adult fiction, detective novels, fairytales, TV and movie scripts, and fiction that blended a variety of genres.

Pippi Longstocking (1945) was condemned by some and praised by others when it first appeared. Fiercely independent, boisterous and rebellious, Pippi is an unconventional heroine who always challenges the status quo. She is anything but pretty, with red pigtails that stick straight out, freckles and dishevelled clothes. The richest and strongest girl in the world, she lives alone with a monkey and a horse, and throws great parties for her friends. A true humanitarian, Pippi saves children from danger, speaks up for the powerless and oppressed, and in her own way reveals the flaws in society.

Like Pippi, Lindgren herself was somewhat of a radical. In 1976, disillusioned with the governing Social Democratic party of which she was a member, she finally got fed up when they charged her 102 per cent tax on her income. She wrote a scathing letter to *Expressen*, disguised as a fairytale. The tax law was changed, and the incident contributed to the downfall of the Social Democratic government later that year. She was always a fierce and outspoken campaigner, fighting for environmental causes, animal rights, non-violence and a more child-centred educational system.

Children can play in Lindgren's imaginary world at **Junibacken** (*see p185*) and her books are widely available in bookshops. Other favourite characters to look out for are five-year-old Emil, the Lionheart Brothers and Ronja, the robber's daughter, a modern Pippi.

If you want to experience the Stockholm archipelago, but don't have time to explore it properly, tiny **Fjäderholmarna** island is just a 20-minute boat ride away. Kids can visit an aquarium, explore a wooden playground in the form of a ship, pet bunnies in the Trädgården garden and choose from extensive ice-cream options. You can also borrow life jackets for your kids if they want to play on the rocky shores. Boats to Fjäderholmarna are operated by **Strömma Kanal** (587 140 00/ www. strommakanalbolaget.com) from Nybrokajen, and **Stockholms Ström** (20 22 60/www.rss.a.se) from Slussen.

In winter, head for the outdoor miniature **ice skating rinks** (skates for hire) at Kungsträdgården and Medborgarplatsen (*see p222* **Ice skating**).

Swimming

If you're visiting Stockholm in the summer, you won't need a swimming pool – you can dive straight into the water around the city. *See p91* **Where to swim outdoors** for the best spots. If that sounds too chilly, the beautiful Jugendstil bath house **Centralbadet** (*see p168*) offers an alternative. A special baby pool is kept at a pleasantly warm 31°C (89°F), and older kids can use the rather small adult pool under supervision. For other options, *see p224* **Swimming**.

Vilda Vanadis

Vanadislunden, Sveavägen 142, Vasastaden (34 33 00). Bus 52, 40X, 515, 595. **Open** *May-Sept* 10am-6pm Mon-Sun. Closed Oct-Apr. **Admission** 50kr; free kids under 80cm/31.5in. **No credit cards.** **Map** p307 B5.

This outdoor adventure pool has got water slides, tube slides and a toddlers' pool, but is a bit uninspiring and run-down – and located beneath trees. However, it is currently being renovated and a new hotel added, with a dining room near the pool.

Theatre, film & music

Children's theatre is a pretty popular activity in Stockholm. There are regular performances (mostly in Swedish) at **Dramaten**, **Stockholms Stadsteatern**, **Dockteatern Tittut** and **Marionetteatern** (for all, *see chapter* **Theatre & Dance**), and the **Hobby och Leksaksmuseet** (*see p185*). **Teater Pero** (612 99 00/www.pero.se) and **Pygméteatern** (31 03 21/www.pygmeteatern.com) are also worth a visit.

If you're planning a trip to the cinema, remember that children's films are usually dubbed – though undubbed versions are sometimes shown too. There's also an **IMAX** (*see p198*), where you get earphones for an English translation of the films (mainly documentaries); under-5s are not admitted.

The **Konserthuset** (*see p215*), one of Stockholm's main venues for classical music, features a Family Saturday series where Stockholm's Royal Philharmonic plays to a boisterous crowd of toddlers and kids. Expect classical favourites like the *Nutcracker Suite*, popular Swedish music, singalongs and guest appearances by clowns, magicians and other characters.

Baby-bio

Sture, Birger Jarlsgatan 41, Norrmalm (678 85 48/ www.biosture.se). T-bana Östermalmstorg/bus 1, 43, 46, 55, 56. **Open** 11am every 2nd Fri Jan-June, Sept-Dec. **Tickets** 50kr; babies free. **Credit** MC, V. **Map** p307 E7.

The innovative concept of a 'baby cinema' was specially created for breastfeeding mothers and new parents who thought they'd never go to the movies again. Lock your pram outside the theatre and tow your baby and baby carrier with you (babies get their own seats inside). Dimmed lighting and sound, changing tables in the foyer and in the theatre itself, free nappies, microwaves for warming baby food, and an intermission where you can buy coffee and cakes all make for a unique breastfeeding/movie-watching experience. Fathers are welcome, although it's usually mainly mums. Current films are shown in their original language every other Friday.

Resources

Hemfrid i Sverige

55 59 15 00/www.hemfrid.se. **Open** 8am-5pm Mon-Fri. **No credit cards.**

This outfit offers an array of services for busy parents, including babysitting, house cleaning, laundry and cooking. Staff will even pick up your kids from daycare. Babysitting costs 290kr per hour; your hotel should be able to arrange it.

Rum för Barn

4th floor, Kulturhuset, Sergels Torg (switchboard 50 83 15 08/library 50 83 14 16/www.kulturhuset.stockholm.se). T-bana T-Centralen/bus 43, 47, 56, 59, 65. **Open** *Library* 11am-5pm Mon, Sat, Sun; 10am-6pm Tue-Fri. *Workshop* noon-4pm Mon, Sat, Sun; 1-4.30pm Tue-Fri. **Admission** library free; workshop 10kr. **No credit cards.** **Map** p303 G7.

The fourth floor of Kulturhuset (*see p71*), the city's main cultural centre, is dedicated to activities for children aged up to 12. There's an arts and crafts workshop, a children's library containing hundreds of books in English and other languages, and internet access just for kids. Daily events (in Swedish), such as film screenings, storytelling and poetry readings, are tailored to different age groups. Teens addicted to surfing can visit the Café Access cybercafé (*see p280*) in the basement.

Clubs

Stockholm's club scene may be small, but it's oh so stylish.

It was hardly a coincidence that made trend bible *Wallpaper** come out with a special Stockholm edition a few years ago (and editor Tyler Brûlé buy a black summer house in the archipelago): a more trend-conscious city is hard to find, and it doesn't take long until the latest buzz from Williamsburgh, Montmartre or Hoxton reaches the Swedish capital. Pick up a copy of *Bon* magazine, published here in Stockholm, and see for yourself.

The downside of this is that Stockholmers have their hands so full with what's happening in the rest of the world that they never stop to create anything genuinely their own, and they are a little stiff and nervous about saying or doing (or wearing, God forbid) anything wrong or un-hip (known in the rest of Sweden as 'the Stockholm syndrome'). The plus side is that you can go out dancing to good music every night of the week among good-looking, stylish and cool people, in a city that is actually quite small and about as far north as St Petersburg.

Clubs tend to come and go, almost none lasting longer than a couple of months, though the venues that house them – which are few in number and small in size – stay the same (as does the crowd). The lack of venues and regular turnover means no particular scene ever really gets a chance to establish itself, so there are fewer subscenes than in most other major cities. We've listed the best of the long-lasting venues below; many also have happening bars (*see chapter* **Bars** for details).

Stockholm's nightlife is concentrated in the inner city and, above all, split between Stureplan – the hub of Stockholm's glamorous VIP world of limousines and neon lights – and Södermalm – the alternative and hip district, which used to be more laid-back and bar-centred but over the past few years has been blessed with a couple of real dancefloor venues. The blocks around Skånegatan in east Söder are the hippest, where designers, artists, musicians and DJs hang out around the bars,

Über-hip **Berns Salonger**. *See p190.*

Arts & Entertainment

Legendary DJs play at Dr Alban's club **Stacy**. *See p191.*

cafés and record and clothes shops. In Söder the bars tend to close at 1am and the clubs at 3am; in Stureplan closing time is around 5am.

In Vasastaden and Kungsholmen you'll find the odd club, but mostly bars and restaurants in which to start the evening. In the suburbs there are sometimes hip hop and reggae clubs, and occasional (illegal) techno parties.

To find out what's on when, check the Friday editions of *Aftonbladet*, *Expressen* and *Dagens Nyheter*, or visit the websites run by the most popular club and party arrangers: **www.discosthlm.com** for dance stuff and **www.bomben.se** for indie, hip hop and electronica. Or pick up flyers at café **Svart Kaffe** (Södermannagatan 23; 462 95 00) or shops **Boutique Sportif** (Oxtorgsgatan 6; 411 12 13), **Pet Sounds** (*see p172*) and **Sneakersnstuff** (*see p161*).

The high price of alcohol means that people tend to go out pretty late, between 11pm and midnight, first having the Swedish speciality, *förfest* ('pre-party'), at someone's house. Note that party drugs are not that widespread, and the penalties for possession are strict.

On Fridays and Saturdays, there are always too many people everywhere, but many of the best clubs are open during the week. Still, there are almost always queues, so to be on the safe side, arrive early or have a plan B (or try to be on the guest list). Sometimes a flyer can give you priority in the queue. Around Stureplan your chances increase if you're good-looking, rich and a girl, and in the Söder clubs just try to look like you're with it. If you're English, talk loudly and you'll be all right. Or, even better, look Japanese.

Norrmalm

Berns Salonger

Berzelii Park (56 63 20 00/www.berns.se). T-bana Kungsträdgården/bus 46, 47, 55, 69, 76. **Open** *Bar Mid Aug-June* 11.30am-1am Mon, Tue; 11.30am-3am Wed, Thur; 11.30am-4am Fri, Sat; 11.30am-midnight Sun (*July-mid Aug* from 1pm Sat, Sun). **Minimum age** 23. **Credit** AmEx, DC, MC, V. **Map** p303 G8.

Under the guidance of Terence Conran, Berns Salonger has been redesigned as a mega entertainment palace on several floors. Since the historic interior had to stay intact, 19th-century elegance meets modern stylissimo. It still has the most beautiful ballroom in town, with a 20m-high (66ft) ceiling, balconies, cut-glass chandeliers, red velvet carpets outside and beautiful people inside, dancing to new house and garage or the latest club sounds from top DJs. There's a VIP room in the basement for those lucky ones considered hip enough. The best music is from Thursday to Saturday. The various bars are very popular (*see p131*) and the attached hotel is pretty cool too (*see p42*). In summer, the club in the basement moves to the terrace.

Daily News Café

Kungsträdgården (21 56 55). T-bana Kungsträdgården/bus 46, 47, 55, 59, 62. **Open** 10pm-3am Mon, Wed; 5pm-3am Thur; 9pm-3am Fri,

Sat. **Minimum age** 20. **Admission** 80kr-100kr. **Credit** AmEx, DC, MC, V. **Map** p303 G8.

Daily's was hotter than Spanish chilli in the 1980s, but after Stureplan took over from Kungsträdgården as the centre of the Stockholm universe, it – like the rest of the Kungsträdgården venues, such as Café Opera (*see p132*) – had some tough years. Daily's is the only one that has managed to get back on the right track. Located next to Sverigehuset, it's a large place (just try another room if the first disappoints), and perfect for a circle of friends with different musical tastes. Everyone from drag queens to club kids to office types out on a knees-up can enjoy themselves. Note that house club Monday Bar (on Monday nights) is likely to move to Sturecompagniet.

Fasching

Kungsgatan 63 (21 62 67/www.fasching.se). T-bana T-Centralen/bus 1, 47, 53, 69. **Open** 7pm-1am Mon-Thur; 7pm-4am Fri, Sat. **Minimum age** 20. **Admission** varies. **Credit** AmEx, DC, MC, V. **Map** p302 F6.

At legendary jazz club Fasching (*see p212*) there are concerts and jam sessions six nights a week, but on Friday and Saturday nights after midnight the roof really flies off. On Saturdays it's Soul!, a clubbing institution that's been running for almost ten years, providing the always packed dancefloor with the best in funk, rare groove, Latin and soul jazz from the past three decades. A mixture of top mods, jazz cats and party animals dance happily side by side, and if you don't move you're probably dead. There have been rumours about the club's temporary closure, so ring in advance to check it's up and running when you're in town.

Stacy

Regeringsgatan 61 (411 59 00). T-bana Hötorget/bus 1, 43, 47, 56, 59. **Open** 6pm-midnight Mon, Tue; 6pm-3am Wed-Sat. **Minimum age** Mon-Thur usually 20; Fri, Sat 25. **Admission** after 11.45pm Fri, Sat, club nights 100kr. **Credit** AmEx, DC, MC, V. **Map** p303 F7.

Dr Alban, anyone? The former Euro reggae star is now owner of this enormous restaurant and stylish nightclub, hosting clubs such as the legendary Swing-a-ling (dancehall) featuring Mikey Dodd, Micke Goulos and Michael Knight, and the very popular Keep it Moving (R&B and hip hop) with DJ Sleepy and Viet-Naam behind the decks. There are also lots of reggae and ragga concerts for a ghetto-fabulous, Crystal-sipping black crowd wearing Fubu and sneakers costing a fortune.

Södermalm

Aston

Mariatorget 3 (644 06 90/www.astonhotel.se). T-bana Mariatorget/bus 43, 55, 66. **Open** 10pm-3am Fri, Sat and sometimes other days. **Admission** 60kr-80kr. **Credit** MC, V. **Map** p310 K6.

In an old cinema lies one of Stockholm's best club venues, with two large dancefloors and one lounge area housed on three storeys. Clubs happen at least three nights a week, with hip hop, drum 'n' bass, house and indie for a (often very) young crowd wearing the latest in street fashions. The place consists almost entirely of dancefloors, so don't have any conversational ambitions – no one else does. Simply shake that ass, baby!

Mondo

Medborgarplatsen 8 (673 10 32). T-bana Medborgarplatsen/bus 55, 59, 66. **Open & admission** call for details. **Map** p310 L8.

This huge cultural centre – which Söder has been waiting years for – was due to open its doors at the time of going to press, with three stages, four dancefloors, five bars, a restaurant, café, gallery and cinema. There are to be at least four clubs a week (until 3am), with a music policy ranging from reggae to house. Try Fridays for underground disco, house and garage under the name of Club Guidelines, which once a month will fly in guest DJs such as Frankie Valentine and Marshall Jefferson. As if the hands-in-the-air crowd would notice any difference from the regular nights. *See also p213.*

Mosebacke Etablissement

Mosebacketorg 3 (55 60 98 90/www.mosebacke.se). T-bana Slussen/bus 3, 46, 53, 76. **Open** 4pm-1am Mon-Thur, Sun; 4pm-2am Fri, Sat. **Minimum age** varies. **Admission** 60kr-80kr. **Credit** AmEx, DC, MC, V. **Map** p310 K8.

Some of the best club nights in town are found at this classic jazz joint (*see p213*). On Fridays it's always Blacknuss, which still keeps the jazz vibe going but blends it with a twist of soul, disco and hip hop for a totally irresistible combination, often with live bands playing in the early hours. On Saturdays it's time for Raw Fusion, offering the freshest club sounds of underground hip hop and house mixed with some Latin, Brazilian and jazz dance flavours for a hip and initiated crowd. International top DJs play regularly, many of whom beg to come back to play again, and for free. There's a slightly older crowd than most places. The summer outdoor terrace bars (open 11am-1am daily) are also very popular (*see p136*).

Rangus Tangus

Götgatan 48 (640 28 68). T-bana Medborgarplatsen/bus 55, 59, 66. **Open** 5pm-1am Mon-Wed; 5pm-3am Fri, Sat. **Minimum age** 23. **Credit** AmEx, DC, MC, V. **Map** p310 L8.

In Medborgarplatsen, in the heart of Södermalm, lies this small but cool basement venue. Admission is always free, and there's always good music from the resident DJs, in the form of reggae, drum 'n' bass and electronica. It used to be the place where everyone would wind up, but now the competition is getting tougher, especially from across the square at Mondo (*see above*). The crowd consists of typical Söder types who for some strange reason can party all night and sleep all day. Upstairs is popular bar-restaurant Snaps (*see p137*).

Sturecompagniet: a beautiful club for the beautiful people.

Östermalm

Chiaro

Birger Jarlsgatan 24 (678 00 09). T-bana Östermalmstorg/bus 1, 46, 55, 56, 91. **Open** 11.30am-1am Mon-Wed; 11.30am-3am Thur; 11.30am-5am Fri; 7pm-5am Sat. **Minimum age** 25. **Admission** after 11pm Fri, Sat 120kr. **Credit** AmEx, DC, MC, V. **Map** p303 E8.

Restaurant Landbyska Verket, with its adjacent basement club Gilda's, was put in the plastic surgery clinic a few years ago and reappeared as Chiaro (say 'kiaro' loud to yourself and you've got it). The basement club (called Sinners on Friday and Saturday) boasts trendy sounds played by some of the city's most renowned DJs. The main floor is more traditionally nightclubby, filled with brats in pink shirts, Prada loafers and big Rolex watches ordering ice buckets of booze for 1,500kr. Still, never underestimate the entertainment in watching people spend a month's salary in one night. The restaurant's worth a visit too. There's dancing in the garden in summer.

Spy Bar

Birger Jarlsgatan 20 (54 50 37 01/www.thespybar.com). T-bana Östermalmstorg/bus 1, 46, 55, 56, 91. **Open** 10pm-5am Wed-Sat. **Minimum age** 25. **Admission** 120kr. **Credit** AmEx, DC, MC, V. **Map** p303 E8.

A favourite with current and former celebrities, Spy Bar is *the* most glamorous and extravagant club in Stockholm. The upstairs is a veritable catacomb of bars and VIP rooms adorned with plush carpets and chandeliers. Nicknamed Spyan ('the Puke'), Spy Bar is frequently mentioned in the national tabloids *Expressen* and *Aftonbladet* – always in the context of one scandal or another. To add to the mystique, the club has its own glossy magazine and distributes coveted VIP passes to the rich and famous. The rest of us are forced to stand in a circular horde and hope that the head bouncer (a celebrity in his own right) will be kind. Is it worth the fuss? If catching a glimpse of a former Swedish football star or pop singer is your idea of a perfect evening, then, yes, it is.

Sturecompagniet

Sturegatan 4 (611 78 00/www.sturecompagniet.se). T-bana Östermalmstorg/bus 1, 46, 55, 56, 91. **Open** 10pm-5am Wed-Sat. **Minimum age** 23. **Admission** after 10pm Fri, Sat 120kr. **Credit** AmEx, DC, MC, V. **Map** p303 F8.

At the weekend this really beautiful, three-storey, five-dancefloor party palace is Stockholm's most glamorous spot to be seen in, sipping on a Cosmo in your new Margiela outfit. Only for the happy (and good-looking) ones that manage to make it through the enormous queue, however. During the week, it's often the home of more alternative club nights, such as the pop-house-dancehall-hip-hop-electro-party Bomben XL, or the ghetto-fabulous reggae bash Club Studio One, with a very different crowd.

The best DJ bars

Since the early 1990s almost every bar in Stockholm has had a DJ spinning records in it. This is due to two facts. First, there are too few decent dancefloor venues. Second, there are too many DJs. The first fact results from legislation making it illegal to have people dancing if you haven't got a big enough (and approved) kitchen and the right to serve alcohol – which the rave commission sees to with a firmly fascistic hand. The second results from the trend that made the DJ beat stylist the coolest profession in the late '90s.

Club kids complain about this development, saying it corrupts real club culture and that the bar-clubs shouldn't be allowed to call themselves clubs. The restaurant owners are in favour of anything that brings in more customers. And the thirtysomethings still in streetwear think it's a great way to listen to good music without having to get all sweaty and knackered on the dancefloor. Well, make up your own mind. These are the best ones.

Bonden

Bondegatan 1 (641 86 79). T-bana Medborgarplatsen/bus 55, 59, 66. **Open** *Bar* 5pm-midnight Mon-Fri; 1pm-midnight Sat, Sun. *Kitchen* 5-11pm Mon-Fri; 1-11pm Sat, Sun. **Minimum age** 20. **Credit** AmEx, MC, V. **Map** p310 M8.

A small bar-club with different DJs every night. House, hip hop, soul and disco for a young, hip crowd in the heart of east Söder.

East

The best hip hop bar, with a predominantly black crowd, this is a Stureplan classic and the place to see how the Swedish rap stars look in the flesh. 'Oh, isn't he taller than that in real life?' *See p138.*

Fredsgatan 12

The DJ bar in summer, with very much the same crowd as Tranan (*see below*). It's a veritable institution for clubbers who want to end the evening with a swim in nearby Riddarfjärden. *See p132.*

Lokal

The best-looking bar in Kungsholmen plays a smooth blend of disco, house and garage for a trendy inner-city crowd. *See p139.*

Lydmar Hotel

The bar at the hip Lydmar Hotel has the likes of Adeva, Roy Ayers, De La Soul and many more playing live, and all the world's DJ stars at the decks. Often the place for secret weekday release parties. *See p138.*

Tranan

The original and archetypal DJ bar (*pictured*), where everyone in the world has played a few records and anyone can get on the minimal stage with an acoustic guitar. Otherwise, it's mostly disco, house and jazz from different DJs at the weekends. Plus some very cool photography exhibitions. *See p133.*

Film

There's a lot more to Swedish film than Ingmar Bergman. These days, some of it is even quite cheerful.

Sweden has a long and distinguished film-making history. Back in the silent era, Victor Sjöström and Mauritz Stiller were among the world's leading film directors, and movies such as Sjöström's *The Phantom Carriage* (1921) and Stiller's *The Treasure of Arne* (1919) are still shown today, and widely regarded as masterpieces. But the golden age of Sweden's film-making was brief, and Sjöström, Stiller and rising star Greta Garbo soon emigrated to Hollywood.

Not until the 1950s did Swedish film again attract the world's attention, when Alf Sjöberg's version of Strindberg's play, *Miss Julie* (1951), and Arne Mattsson's *One Summer of Happiness* (1952) stunned audiences in Venice and Berlin. Soon after, Ingmar Bergman won international acclaim with *Smiles of a Summer Night* (1955), and he remained in the spotlight as long as he continued making movies. Outside Sweden, he is still best known for his film work (even though his last feature film, *Fanny & Alexander*, was released as long ago as 1982). Nowadays Bergman is an honoured theatre director (often working at Stockholm's famous Kungliga Dramatiska Teatern – *see p230*), but he has recently started directing the follow-up to his internationally successful 1970s TV series *Scenes from a Marriage*.

Apart from the legendary Bergman, Swedish film wasn't very flourishing during the 1960s. It wasn't until the late '60s, following reform of the funding process, that a fresh generation of film-makers emerged. Directors such as Jan Troell, Bo Widerberg and Vilgot Sjöman became big names in a more and more politicised era of film-making.

Swedish film is often described as frozen, taciturn and deeply serious, largely due to the prominence of Ingmar Bergman (of whose films, perhaps, this is a fair description). Paradoxically, Sweden also has the largely undeserved reputation of being the birthplace of the modern pornographic film. Titles often cited as forerunners of the genre – *Do You Believe in Angels?* (1961), *Dear John* (1964) and *I Am Curious: Yellow* (1967) – were extremely daring for their time, but were far from being pure pornography. Perhaps Sweden did help pave the way for cinematic pornography, but the country hasn't ever contributed much in actual film production. Today, in fact, Swedish film is less serious, pretty wordy and not all that sensationally erotic.

Swedish film, past and present: Ingmar Bergman's *The Seventh Seal* (1956)...

A new, immigrant, generation of film-makers has begun to stand out internationally, and movies such as Reza Parsa's *Before the Storm*, Reza Bagher's *Wings of Glass* and Josef Fares' *Jalla! Jalla!* (all released in 2000) have been great successes. At the forefront of this new era of blossoming production were Lukas Moodysson and his excellent *Fucking Åmål* (1998). Moodysson's *Together* (2000) and Roy Andersson's *Songs from the Second Floor* (2000) also received international release – and praise. Swedish actors with an ongoing international career include Max von Sydow, Peter Stormare (both of whom starred in Steven Spielberg's 2002 sci-fi blockbuster *Minority Report*), Stellan Skarsgård, Lena Olin and Pernilla August.

THE INDUSTRY

Two companies, SF (Svensk Filmindustri; www.sf.se) and Sandrews (Sandrew Metronome; www.sandrew.se), completely dominate the film market in Sweden. Their huge 'vertically integrated' businesses cover production, distribution and exhibition, and take about 70 per cent of the total box office in Sweden. In Stockholm, they together run 19 of the city's 25 cinemas. SF is the biggest of the two, but Sandrews is the more creative when it comes to film choice – though both are pretty mainstream. Behind the two big players, Folkets Hus and Våra Gårdar are the largest cinema chains, with more than 200 cinemas up and down the country, sometimes housed in libraries and other temporary venues, but also often in conventional movie theatres.

TIMINGS AND TICKETS

Cinemas open one hour before their first screening, which is usually at around 11am or 5pm. All films are shown in their original language with Swedish subtitles. Only children's films are dubbed (look out for *Svenskt tal* or *sv tal* on the ad), though it's quite common to find an original-language showing too. Tickets cost 75kr-85kr, and many cinemas have reductions for children, pensioners, daytime screenings and so on. Listings and film information can be found in the daily papers.

The busiest days for cinema-going are Friday to Sunday, when you should book in advance. There are automated booking lines for the cinema chains – Sandrews: 10 13 00; SF: 56 26 00 00 – but they're in Swedish only. You can also buy tickets in any of each company's cinemas irrespective of where the film is being shown.

Adverts generally start five minutes before the listed film time, and the movie itself five to ten minutes after (art-house cinemas do not necessarily follow this rule). Films are usually classified as being suitable for 7-, 11- (though children younger than 7 or 11 are allowed in if accompanied by an adult) or 15-year-olds.

Cinemas

Note that art-house cinemas usually close for two to three weeks in June/July.

Astoria

Nybrogatan 15, Östermalm (660 00 25/www.sandrewmetronome.se). T-bana Östermalmstorg/bus 46, 47, 62, 69, 76. **Credit** MC, V. **Map** p303 F8.

... and Roy Andersson's *Songs from the Second Floor* (2000).

Art-house fave **Sture**.

A nice, modern, THX-classified single-screener, this is Stockholm's leading first-run cinema. Built in the late 1920s, it was restored in the '50s, which is still the style today. Blockbusters only.

Filmhuset

Borgvägen 1-5, Gärdet (665 11 00/www.sfi.se). Bus 56, 72, 76. **No credit cards. Map** p309 E12.

The Film House is located just on the border of Gärdet. A late-1960s concrete colossus designed by Peter Celsing (who was also responsible for the Kulturhuset), the building resembles a film camera and is full of witty architectural references to film-making. It houses the Swedish Film Institute, as well as the Department for Film Studies of the University of Stockholm, and the University College of Film, Radio, Television and Theatre. There's a cinema where SFI's Cinemateket film club screens films (40kr) on weekdays from August to May (members only; membership 80kr). You can also buy tickets for this cinema at Sture (*see below*). The book and video shop doesn't look much, but has several titles of interest to film fans.

Grand

Sveavägen 45, Norrmalm (411 24 00/www.sandrew metronome.se). T-bana Rådmansgatan/bus 43, 52. **Credit** MC, V. **Map** p307 E6.

Like the Victoria (*see p198*) and the Saga (*see below*), the Grand shows slightly more unusual films. It has four nice auditoriums and doors adorned with filmstars in intarsia. This is the cinema that Olof Palme visited just before he was shot.

Kvartersbion

Hornstulls Strand 3, Södermalm (669 19 95). T-bana Hornstull/bus 4, 40, 66. **No credit cards. Map** p301 L2.

Cinemas in Stockholm tend to be located either downtown or at the hip Medborgarplatsen in Söder. Kvartersbion is an exception. It's not only in the less trendy neighbourhood of Hornstull, but is completely free of all elements of luxury or modernity (it looks about the same as it did in the 1940s) and is run by one person. The programme is rather limited – mostly re-runs from Zita or Sture – but locals are very loyal to the place.

Röda Kvarn

Biblioteksgatan 5, Östermalm (56 26 00 00/www.sf.se). T-bana Östermalmstorg/bus 46, 47, 55, 59, 62. **Credit** MC, V. **Map** p303 F8.

Two-screen downtown cinema showing commercial and sometimes less commercial films. Screenings in the beautiful Röda Kvarn (a common cinema name: a direct translation of Moulin Rouge) are a pleasure – don't miss the spectacular colour show when the curtains are pulled back. The smaller Lilla Kvarn is nice too – but avoid the front row.

Saga

Kungsgatan 24, Norrmalm (56 26 00 00/www.sf.se). T-bana Hötorget/bus 1, 43, 46, 52, 56. **Credit** MC, V. **Map** p303 F7.

Similar to the Victoria (*see p198*) when it comes to the selection of films. But in a different area of the city, and with a much more glamorous look.

Skandia

Drottninggatan 82, Norrmalm (56 26 00 00/www.sf.se). T-bana Hötorget/bus 1, 47, 52, 53, 69. **Credit** MC, V. **Map** p303 F6.

This eccentric and internationally known cinema opened in 1923. The interiors were designed by world-famous architect Gunnar Asplund, and most are still intact. During the last few decades, Skandia has lived under a constant threat of being shut down and rebuilt. Daily screenings ceased in 1996 and today it's open only for 'singalongs' and short runs. If the cinema is open during your visit, don't miss it. The outer foyer doesn't look much (especially not since being occupied by a most inappropriate café), but the inner foyer is absolutely overwhelming.

Sture

Birger Jarlsgatan 41, Östermalm (678 85 48/www.biosture.se). T-bana Östermalmstorg/bus 1, 46, 55, 56. **Credit** MC, V. **Map** p307 E7.

Sture reopened in 2001 after being moved two blocks and expanded to three screens. It shows art-house films as well as more commercial fare – always carefully chosen. There are Cinemateket films twice a day, Filmögat (for young audiences) on Saturday afternoons, and Baby-bio screenings for parents with babies (*see p188*). Don't miss the curtain in cinema 1, made by one of Sweden's most famous contemporary artists, Ernst Billgren. It features a huge orange-red painting containing, among other

Welcome to Trollywood

This is the amazing rags-to-riches tale of three mavericks who put their heads together and took over the whole of Sweden's film production in just six years. And now they've set their sights on the rest of Europe. It's a story worthy of a film script in itself.

Until about six years ago, film production in Sweden took place only in Stockholm and was controlled by one of the two big players, either SF or Sandrews. And then a cheeky rival suddenly emerged: Film i Väst (www.filmivast.se) – better known as Trollywood – a regional production centre accommodating 11 production companies, among them internationally known Zentropa (Danish) and Memfis Film (Swedish). Almost every recent Swedish film success has been produced in Trollywood, located in Trollhättan, a small town 70 kilometres (43 miles) from Göteborg with barely 50,000 inhabitants.

Film i Väst was started back in 1992, but it was then only a meeting place for young people interested in film. The real turning point for the company came in 1996, when Peter Aalbæk Jensen (Zentropa) and Lars Jönsson (Memfis Film) came to town. They hit it off with Tomas Eskilsson, director of Film i Väst (although Aalbæk Jensen wondered what on earth Eskilsson, a former schoolteacher, could know about film production). In true pioneer spirit they decided to set the stakes high.

The chance of getting funding from the European Union, along with the regional government's realisation that the traditional motor and forestry industries were no longer worth investing in, made large-scale financing possible. Zentropa and Memfis Film decided to film their next movies in Trollhättan – which is why Moodysson's *Fucking Åmål* wasn't made in Stockholm and Lars Von Trier's *Dancer in the Dark* was shot in Sweden and not in Germany (as had been planned).

In the past few years, Film i Väst has co-produced several internationally renowned films, including *Together* (*pictured*) and *Jalla! Jalla!*, as well as *Before the Storm*, Ella Lemhagen's *Tsatsiki, Mum and the Policeman* (1999) and Colin Nutley's *Under the Sun* (1998). Films currently in the pipeline are Lars von Trier's *Dogville*, *It's All About Love* by Thomas Vinterberg, *Lilja 4-ever* by Moodysson and *Skagerrak* by Søren Kragh-Jacobsen (director of *Mifune*). Film i Väst is now Scandinavia's major regional film organisation, without which Swedish cinema would not be enjoying anything like the renaissance that it currently is. Its objective is to turn Trollywood into northern Europe's leading film producer.

Filmstaden Sergel: for the latest releases.

things, a pike, a flounder and a squirrel – after the 'proverb' saying, 'It's easier for a squirrel to catch a flounder in the sea than for a film consumer to find a cinema not showing Hollywood films.'

Victoria

Götgatan 67, Södermalm (642 01 00/www.sandrew metronome.se). T-bana Medborgarplatsen/bus 59, 66. **Credit** MC, V. **Map** p310 M8.

A modest five-screen cinema in Söder, showing the critics' favourites. There are rather odd Neptune fountains outside the toilets.

Zita

Birger Jarlsgatan 37, Östermalm (23 20 20/ www.folketsbio.se/zita). T-bana Östermalmstorg/ bus 1, 46, 55, 56. **No credit cards. Map** p307 E7.

The only cinema with its own bar, showing films from all over the world. It also screens films while you have lunch (they serve; you watch) – except in the summer. Run by pure idealists, and owned by the non-profit-making association Folkets Bio; Zita is its flagship in Sweden. Check out the old-fashioned elevator music in the loos.

Multiplexes

Other multiplexes are **BioPalatset** (644 31 00) and **Filmstaden Söder** (56 26 00 00), both located at Medborgarplatsen in Södermalm (T-bana Medborgarplatsen/bus 59, 66).

AMC (American Multi Cinema)

Heron City, Kungens Kurva (50 56 01 00/01/ www.amc.se). T-bana Skärholmen/bus 173, 707, 710, 737. **No credit cards.**

Eighteen screens and a total of 4,000 seats make AMC the largest cinema in Scandinavia. Located in a suburban area, opposite the world's largest IKEA and inside the multi-level entertainment centre Heron City, it really tries hard to attract a new audience. The stadium seating, wall-to-wall screens, retractable arm rests (to make 'love seats'), the latest technology and generous leg room indeed provide an extraordinary cinematic experience. But it hasn't really quite succeeded: Swedish people still prefer to spend hours and hours in the IKEA, and Heron City remains a mostly empty monument to an obscure American culture. In some ways, it's a pity. If you can stand the extremely loud surroundings and blipping slot machines for as long as it takes to reach the cinema on the top floor, the experience of watching a quality film in a cinema like this is worth it. One more obstacle must, however, be dealt with: the box office is on the ground floor, almost attached to enormous fountains. Having water cascading thunderously in your ear while trying to communicate through a tiny slit in a thick glass sheet makes buying a ticket very hard.

Filmstaden Sergel

Hötorget, Norrmalm (56 26 00 00/www.sf.se). T-bana Hötorget/bus 1, 52, 56. **Credit** MC, V. **Map** p303 F6.

Situated on lively Hötorget, this is the place to go to imbibe a bustling multiplex atmosphere. Fourteen screens and an average visitor's age of 15 implies a rather noisy and nasty milieu, but it works well for the type of films shown. As most tourists cross this square at least once a day, it's easy enough to buy your tickets in advance.

IMAX

Cosmonova

Naturhistorska Riksmuseet, Frescativägen 40, Norra Djurgården (51 95 51 30/www.nrm.se/cosmonova). T-bana Universitet/bus 40, 540. **Tickets** 75kr; 50kr 5-18s. No under-5s admitted. **Credit** AmEx, MC, V.

Located inside the Museum of Natural History, this IMAX cinema is a family paradise, but also worth a visit for any cinema buff. The films, usually documentaries, are worth seeing. A few tips for your visit: during the summer and school holidays, book in advance – and prepare to queue, even if you've booked ahead. Cosmonova's website, as well as the spoken information in the cinema and the screenings, are in Swedish only – so don't forget to buy an earphone for translation when buying your tickets.

Festivals

The most important festival in Sweden is the **Göteborg Film Festival** (www.filmfestival.org) in January/February, showing more than 500 films from all over the world. **Stockholm's International Film Festival** (*see p182*) takes place over ten packed days in November, but is unfortunately rather expensive (150kr for membership, 50kr per ticket). Uppsala, 80 kilometres (50 miles) north of Stockholm, holds a renowned **Short Film Festival** (www.short filmfestival.com) in October, which is well worth a visit. Other good festivals in Sweden include the official children's festival **BUFF** (www.buff.nu), in Malmö in March, and the **Umeå International Film Festival** (www. ff.umea.com) in September.

Galleries

The capital is the epicentre of the small but flourishing Swedish art scene.

Projekt Djurgårdsbrunn. *See p204.*

Ever since the 1990s, when a whole bunch of young and talented Swedes rushed into continental Europe, Swedish artists have made themselves heard and seen in the art world. The art scene in the capital, and Sweden in general, is now more international than in a long time, not only importing but also exporting some of the most interesting art around. This may well be thanks to the high standard of Swedish art schools, and to the work of organisations such as **Moderna Museet** (*see p73* **Breaking the mould**) and **IASPIS** (402 35 76/www.iaspis.com). The latter, the International Artists Studio Program, is an artist-in-residence programme set up in 1996 and funded by the Swedish government. Based at the **Konstakademien** (Royal Academy of Art), its main aim is to provide financial support for Swedish artists exhibiting abroad, but it also invites foreign artists to work in its 11 studios and exhibit in its gallery.

There is a rich variety of art spaces in Stockholm and its surroundings. In traditional Östermalm, where the major galleries settled in the early 1980s when the art-trading business was good, younger and trendier galleries are now emerging, revitalising and inspiring the area. Several of the galleries co-ordinate their exhibition openings on Thursdays and Saturdays. The avant-garde pack tend to stick to Södermalm, or the suburbs. The eastern part of Söder, in particular, is beginning to emerge as an area for cutting-edge, artist-run spaces, as well as art magazines and other outfits such as digital media workshop CRAC (Creative Room for Art and Computing; www.crac.org). Some of the most important galleries – such as **Magasin 3** and **Färgfabriken** (for both, *see p204*) – are not in the city centre at all, but in more outlying areas.

There is also a growing platform for electronic art and music. Organisations such as the **Nursery** (www.nursery.a.se) and the venerable **Fylkingen** (*see p232*) are making this slightly underground scene more accessible, inviting both Swedish and international artists to perform. Events are often a blend of VJs, concerts, performances, choreography and parties, and provide an important creative contribution to the Stockholm art world.

Free brochure *Konstguiden*, available at all major art spaces and galleries, provides comprehensive gallery listings; it's published twice a year, in autumn and spring. Also have a look at website **www.konsten.net** (Swedish only) for up-to-date exhibition reviews, or **www.come.to/artinsweden** and **www.artistfinder.com** for information about Swedish artists and links to galleries.

Note that many galleries open from noon onwards, and most are closed on Monday. Admission is free unless otherwise stated.

Norrmalm

The **Konstakademien** (*see p70*) also has an exhibition space.

The Life Gallery

Kammakargatan 33 (10 15 60/www.life-foundation.org). T-bana Rådmansgatan/bus 52. **Open** noon-6pm Wed-Fri; noon-4pm Sat. **Map** p307 E5.

The Life Foundation's aim is to spread information about HIV and AIDS, and it does so by organising different fundraising ventures, the Life Gallery being one of them. Besides its distinct purpose and

Iconic imagery by Andy Warhol at the lovely **Liljevalchs Konsthall.**

special financial arrangement (the gallery's profits go to the foundation), it functions much like any other gallery space. All disciplines are represented in exhibitions (about eight per year), as well as happenings and other events. The focus is on young emerging artists.

Wetterling Gallery

Kungsträdgården 3 (10 10 09/www.wetterling gallery.com). T-bana T-Centralen/bus 46, 55, 59, 62, 76. **Open** 11am-5.30pm Tue-Fri; 1-4pm Sat. Closed early June-early Sept. **Credit** AmEx, V. **Map** p303 G8.

Situated in the popular park Kungsträdgården, this large gallery exhibits youngish American and British artists (Gavin Turk, Julian Opie, Diti Almog, Karen Davie, Roy Kortick), as well as renowned Swedish and international artists from an older generation. It also hosts graduate shows from the Swedish art schools.

Vasastaden

Andréhn-Schiptjenko

Markvardsgatan 2 (612 00 75/www.andrehn-schiptjenko.com). T-bana Rådmansgatan/bus 4, 42, 43, 46, 53. **Open** 11am-5pm Tue-Fri; noon-5pm Sat. Closed Midsummer-end Aug. **No credit cards. Map** p307 C6.

Opened in 1991, Andréhn-Schiptjenko is one of the leading contemporary art galleries. Its portfolio includes international artists (Xavier Veilhan, Nina Saunders, Uta Barth, Abigail Lane), as well as new and established Swedish artists (Annika Larsson, Palle Torsson, Anna Kleberg, Carl Michael von Hausswolff). Internationally active, the gallery takes part in important art fairs around the world, successfully presenting what some critics in the 1990s referred to as the 'Swedish miracle' – the flow of talented young Swedish artists into Europe.

Galleri Enkehuset

Norrtullsgatan 45 (34 36 56/www.enkehuset.nu). T-bana Odenplan/bus 40, 46, 69. **Open** noon-5pm Wed-Sun. Closed mid June-mid Aug. **No credit cards. Map** p306 C4.

Housed on the first floor of an old building that was once a home for widows, Galleri Enkehuset has a large, high-ceilinged space at its disposal. The gallery is run by artists with a management board that is very open to suggestion, something that has created a special mix of installations, exhibitions and happenings. Galleri Enkehuset also works with different art schools throughout Sweden, exhibiting graduate shows in late spring or early autumn.

Galleri Thomas Ehrngren

Luntmakargatan 74 (645 42 75/www.thomas ehrngren.com). T-bana Rådmansgatan/bus 43, 52. **Open** noon-4pm Fri-Sun. Closed end July-mid Sept. **No credit cards. Map** p307 D6.

The place to see work by interesting young photographers from all over the world. Be warned: the discreet entrance can be easy to miss.

Djurgården

Liljevalchs Konsthall

Djurgårdsvägen 43 (50 83 13 30/www.liljevalchs.com). Bus 44, 47/ferry from Slussen or Nybroviken. **Open** *Sept-May* 11am-8pm Tue, Thur; 11am-5pm Wed, Fri-Sun. *June-Aug* 11am-5pm Tue-Sun. **Admission** 50kr; 30kr concessions; free under-18s. **Free with SC. Credit** DC, MC, V. **Map** p304 H11.

This beautiful 1916 building next to the aquarium is a fine example of Swedish neo-classicism. Originally built from a donation by businessman Carl Fredrik Liljevalch, it attracts a wide audience, from grandmothers to children. In its 12 exhibition rooms you can view themed and solo shows, by both

Swedish and international artists. A very popular event is the annual open exhibition, Vårsalongen, in which a jury selects work by both established artists and amateurs, resulting in a vivid blend of high art and kitsch. Also look out for the series of talks and discussions entitled Nyfiken på, running all year. Next to the building, connected by a nice garden, is the lovely restaurant-café Blå Porten (*see p144*). Altogether, Liljevalchs Konsthall is a unique place where contemporary art and architecture blend in an unusually successful way. *See also p80.*

Södermalm

Centrum för Fotografi

Götgatan 48 (640 20 95/www.centrumforfotografi.com). T-bana Medborgarplatsen/bus 59. **Open** noon-6pm Wed-Fri; noon-4pm Sat. Closed Midsummer-mid Aug. **No credit cards**. **Map** p310 L8.

CFF is an interest group working to spread information about photography and photographers. Its website has a digital gallery, where you can buy original photos by the group's members. It also runs a gallery space, used by the members and by invited international and Swedish artists. Also look out for talks, seminars and events.

ID:I Galleri

Tjärhovsgatan 19 (073 705 20 67/www.idigalleri.org). T-bana Medborgarplatsen/bus 59, 66. **Open** 1-5pm Thur-Sun. **Map** p311 L9.

One of the newest non-commercial venues in the city, ID:I is run by 19 artists who are each in charge of the space for three weeks, during which time they are free to exhibit, experiment or invite others to participate. United by the belief that government backing creates artistic restraints, they run the space with their own funds – and provide a meaningful input to the Stockholm art scene.

Index

St Paulsgatan 3 (640 94 92/www.indexfoundation.nu). T-bana Slussen/bus 59. **Open** noon-4pm Tue, Thur-Sun; noon-7pm Wed. Closed June-Aug. **No credit cards**. **Map** p3110 K7.

The Swedish Contemporary Art Foundation started out as a photography gallery, but has widened its exhibition practice to include video work and installations. Next to the desk of director Mats Stjernstedt is a small reading corner, where you can watch tapes from the gallery's 'videoteque'. Index presents Nordic newcomers and established international artists not previously shown in Sweden.

Konstakuten

Nackagatan 11 (641 77 90/www.konstakuten.com). Bus 46. **Open** (during exhibitions) noon-5pm Thur; noon-4pm Sat. **Map** p311 M11.

The Art Emergency Room is one of the most important artist-run spaces to have emerged in Stockholm in the past few years. Situated in the Hammarby harbour in south-east Söder, it's a vital part of an area that is becoming more and more significant for the avant-garde art scene. Showing mostly young newcomers from the Nordic countries and elsewhere in Europe, it offers a sure view of what's going on.

SOC.

Bondegatan 64 (640 98 07/www.soc.nu) Bus 46, 66. **Open** varies; call for details. **No credit cards**. **Map** p311 M10.

In everyday parlance SOC is the abbreviation for Socialen, the social welfare office – a place that artists and other cultural workers probably end up visiting a few times in their career. The seven members of this artist-run space in the heart of Södermalm want it to be 'a place for artistic and social experiment, a forum for discussions about art and society, and an exhibition space'. With a dynamic and flexible programming policy, they pretty much seem to have succeeded in their aims.

Östermalm

ALP Galleri Peter Bergman

Riddargatan 35 (661 61 10/www.alpgallery.com). T-bana Karlaplan/bus 47, 69, 76. **Open** noon-5pm Tue-Fri; noon-4pm Sat. Closed July, Aug. **No credit cards**. **Map** p304 G9.

The man who runs this gallery, Peter Bergman, a former student of art history and economics, has also worked in publicity and banking and been a graffiti artist. His gallery focuses on recently graduated and non-established Swedish artists. It's a good place to get a handle on the city's young art scene.

Lars Nilsson at **Magasin 3**. *See p204.*

Brändström & Stene@Milagro

1st floor, Nybrogatan 25 (660 41 53). T-bana Östermalmstorg/bus 47, 62, 69, 76. **Open** noon-4pm Sat, Sun. Closed Midsummer-mid Aug, 2wks over Christmas. **No credit cards. Map** p303 F8.

Within the space of three months in spring 2002, Brändström & Stene opened two galleries (*see also p204*). This gallery – the smaller of the two – is in a tidy second-floor apartment and shows younger and non-established artists.

Galerie Aronowitsch

Sturegatan 24 (663 80 87). T-bana Stadion/bus 1, 4, 42, 55. **Open** *Mid Aug-mid June* 11am-5pm Tue-Fri; noon-4pm Sat; 1-4pm Sun. Closed mid June-mid Aug. **No credit cards. Map** p308 E8.

Located on the first floor of an apartment building, this two-room gallery has a great location bang in the middle of Stockholm opposite Humlegården. Showing established artists from Sweden and abroad, it's a safe bet.

Galleri Charlotte Lund

Skeppargatan 70 (663 09 79). T-bana Karlaplan/bus 1, 42, 44. **Open** noon-6pm Tue-Fri; noon-5pm Sat. **No credit cards. Map** p308 E10.

Situated in the heart of Östermalm on Skeppargatan, where many of the city's galleries are located, this is one of the more reliable and interesting venues for high-quality art. The gallery's three rooms are in a first-floor apartment. You'll find established and upcoming, Swedish and international artists, working in a variety of media.

Galleri Flach

Skeppargatan 27 (661 13 99/www.galleriflach.com). T-bana Östermalmstorg/bus 56, 62. **Open** *Mid Jan-July, Sept-Christmas* 1-5.30pm Tue-Fri; noon-4pm Sat. Closed July, Aug, Christmas-mid Jan. **No credit cards. Map** p304 F9.

James Flach and his wife Eva-Lotta Holm Flach run this three-roomed space, where visitors can get see both Swedish and international artists, more or less established. Artists represented include Twan Janssen, Maria Hedlund and Andreas Eriksson.

Galleri Göran Engström

Karlaplan 9A (660 29 29/www.galleryengstroem.se). T-bana Karlaplan/bus 42, 44. **Open** *Aug-June* noon-5pm Tue-Fri; noon-4pm Sat; 1-4pm Sun. Closed July. **No credit cards. Map** p308 E10.

The area around Karlaplan and on Karlavägen heading towards the city centre – one of the city's smartest neighbourhoods – is also one of the most important gallery districts in Stockholm. Göran Engström's gallery, among the oldest art spaces in Stockholm, opened in the early 1970s and exhibits Swedish artists working with traditional techniques within painting or sculpture. His stable includes several of the most renowned contemporary Swedish artists, including Max Book, Martin Wickström and Ola Billgren (who died in November 2001). The gallery has expanded its portfolio to include younger artists such as Helena Mutanen and Sophi Vejrich.

Street art

Stockholm strikes most visitors as a remarkably clean city, free from litter, graffiti and other eyesores that blight most metropolises. The Swedish capital, sometimes referred to as Europe's Singapore, has earned its shining reputation through a fierce zero-tolerance policy against all forms of illegal painting, scribbling and flyposting, plus the clean-up efforts of an orange-dressed municipal army. Yet the city also boasts one of the most vibrant street art scenes in Europe; keep your eyes peeled as you wander around the city's streets and a whole new world will open up.

The police usually let the artists work free from interference. This is because a) the police have more important things to do, and b) the Swedish media has ruled street art, as opposed to graffiti, an accepted art form. Since most politicians don't want to be categorised as narrow-minded moralists, they focus their dislike on the 'destructive' graffiti culture.

Stockholm's two most active and internationally reputed artists work under the pseudonyms **Akay** (www.akayism.org) and **Bacteria**. Akay, once a leading graffiti artist, got tired of the scene and started to experiment with stencils and posters that could be put up much faster in the very heart of the city. Akay's black and white logo, a globe with an orbital ring spelling out 'AKAYISM' (*pictured*), comes with messages of a quasi political or religious

Galleri IngerMolin

Kommendörsgatan 24 (52 80 08 30). T-bana Stadion/bus 44, 56, 62. **Open** *Sept-mid June* noon-6pm Tue-Thur; noon-4pm Fri, Sat; 1-4pm Sun. Closed mid June-Aug. **No credit cards. Map** p308 E9.

For a long time Inger Molin has been working towards eliminating the line between 'art' and 'crafts'. Her gallery, which opened in 1998, shows crafts-oriented work, such as ceramics, textiles and glass, and is definitely worth a visit.

Galleri Lars Bohman

Karlavägen 16 (20 78 07/www.gallerilarsbohman.com). Bus 42. **Open** *Mid Jan-Midsummer, Sept-mid Dec* 11am-5.30pm Tue-Fri; noon-4pm Sat, Sun. Closed Midsummer-Aug, mid Dec-mid Jan. **No credit cards. Map** p307 D7.

As one of the city's most prominent galleries, Lars Bohman represents a rich range of contemporary artists, both Swedish and foreign, working in all

character. Bacteria, an art scholar influenced by the graffiti scene, has developed a distinctive style based on his fascination for the looks and life of microbes. The Bacteria project includes an infectious sticker campaign and larger postings of aubergine-shaped organisms. Akay and Bacteria often work together and their art is known to attentive urbanites in London, Berlin, Paris, Tokyo, New York and other cities.

Also look out for **Klister-Peters**' (Sticker Peter's) sad-looking deer (*pictured*) and other handmade screenprinted stickers, with sadly accusing slogans like 'doing what you're told', 'comfortably numb' and 'is there anybody out there'. **Big D** (www.bigd.nu) creates playful versions of Swedish and international logos and other interpretations of the urban surroundings.

Street art is perishable goods, which means that many of the big postings disappear almost immediately, while those on more concealed places can be around for months or even years. If you want to improve your odds of seeing the larger artworks, check the bridges that connect the central islands with each other and with the mainland. Smaller pieces – stickers, stencils and small posters – can be found everywhere, especially on the back of street signs, electrical boxes and traffic lights. Other popular places are cellar doors, windows, house walls and the Tunnelbana.

You can also visit http://lunattack.cjb.net (by Swedish street artist Luna) or the more general www.stadskonst.com (under reconstruction at the time of writing).

And if you ever see two people dressed in typical business suits pasting billboards, it might just be Akay and Bacteria in their sneaky disguises continuously changing the visual landscape of the Swedish capital.

kinds of media. The space comprises three rooms of different sizes, which slope slightly downwards towards the centre. In spring 2002 the gallery opened a small space just round the corner called **BB** (Rådmansgatan 23), in co-operation with artist Rikard Fåreus. BB shows only upcoming young Swedish artists in three-week-long exhibitions, and successfully serves as a flexible counterpoint to the main gallery.

Galleri Magnus Karlsson

Riddargatan 29 (660 43 53/www.gallerimagnus karlsson.com). T-bana Karlaplan or Östermalmstorg/ bus 47, 69, 76. **Open** noon-5pm Tue-Fri; noon-4pm Sat. Closed July, Aug. **No credit cards. Map** p304 F9.

Magnus Karlsson works primarily with Swedish painters, both emerging and more well known, such as Mamma Andersson and Jockum Nordstrom.

Roger Björkholmen Galleri

Karlavägen 24 (611 26 30/www.rogerbjorkholmen. com). Bus 42, 44. **Open** *Mid Aug-mid June* noon-5pm Tue-Fri; noon-4pm Sat. Closed mid June-mid Aug. **No credit cards. Map** p307 D7.

This small street-front gallery, which opened in 1992, shows important Swedish and international artists. You'll find photographic and video work, sculpture and painting. There's only room for a few pieces of art, which gives it an intimate atmosphere. Owner Roger Björkholmen was one of the organisers behind Stockholm's alternative art fair, the Stockholm Smart Show, from 1994 to 1997.

Schaper Sundberg Galleri

Skeppargatan 39 (660 96 20). T-bana Östermalmstorg/bus 56. **Open** *Mid Jan-Midsummer, mid Aug-Christmas* noon-5.30pm Tue-Fri; noon-5pm Sat. Closed Christmas-mid Jan, Midsummer-mid Aug. **No credit cards. Map** p304 F9.

A reliable gallery where you'll find a mix of artists from Sweden and abroad. Keep an eye out for work by recently graduated artists, as the gallery maintains an interest in new faces.

Zinc Gallery

Skeppargatan 86 (662 30 09/www.zincgallery.com). T-bana Karlaplan/bus 1, 4, 62, 72. **Open** noon-6pm Tue-Fri; noon-5pm Sat. Closed mid June-mid Aug. **Credit** AmEx, DC, MC, V. **Map** p308 D10.

With the director hailing from the US and the co-ordinator from England, Zinc Gallery sets out its international credentials from the very start. Artists include Swedes Bigert and Bergström, Jan Hietala and Monica Larsen Dennis, as well as non-Swedes Tracy Moffat, Brian Conley and Steinar Jakobsen.

Gärdet

Magasin 3 Stockholm Konsthall

Frihamnen (545 680 40/www.magasin3.com). Bus 1, 76. **Open** noon-7pm Thur; noon-5pm Fri-Sun. Closed June-Aug; 2wks over Christmas. **Admission** 25kr; free under-15s. **Credit** MC, V.

Magasin 3 opened in 1987, and is housed in an old warehouse in the port area ('*magasin*' means 'warehouse'). Whereas other institutions suffer from a lack of funds, Magasin 3 is one of the most busily expanding privately funded art spaces in Sweden. Showing three to four exhibitions a year, it focuses on young, established international and Swedish artists, with all medias represented. Recent shows have included Lars Nilsson, Jane and Louise Wilson, Ernesto Neto and Chris Burden. Exhibitions showing parts of the permanent collection are held continuously, and the huge space is used impressively flexibly.

Projekt Djurgårdsbrunn

Djurgårdsbrunnsvägen 68 (545 680 40/ www.magasin3.com). Bus 69. **Open** 10am-9pm daily.

In summer 2002 innovative Magasin 3 (*see above*) opened this new gallery. It's supposed to be an experimental and site-specific space, where invited artists, architects and theoreticians work in close relation to the surroundings and their history in an ongoing process. The opening exhibition was by Tony Oursler.

Further afield

Brändström & Stene

Mejerivägen 2, Liljeholmen (660 41 53). T-bana Liljeholmen/bus 133, 152. **Open** noon-6pm Thur, Fri; noon-4pm Sat, Sun. Closed Midsummer-mid Aug, 2wks over Christmas. **No credit cards.** **Map** p301 M2.

This space, opened in spring 2002, focuses on renowned Swedish and international artists. The inaugural exhibition was by Swedish artist Annica Karlsson Rixon. Opening a commercial gallery outside the city centre takes some courage, but considering the interesting artists the gallery represents it shouldn't pose too much of a problem.

Zinc Gallery: work by Bigert and Bergström.

Färgfabriken

Lövholmsbrinken 1, Liljeholmen (645 07 07/ www.fargfabriken.se). T-bana Liljeholmen/ bus 133, 152. **Open** usually noon-6pm Thur-Sun; call first to check. **Admission** 40kr; 30kr concessions; free under-18s. **Credit** AmEx, DC, MC, V. **Map** p301 L1.

The Centre for Contemporary Art and Architecture, located in the southern suburb of Liljeholmen, occupies an important position in the Stockholm art scene. Founded in 1995, Färgfabriken is supported by both private and public funds. The gallery is housed in an old factory building, which offers a large room as the main exhibition space, plus three smaller connecting rooms. A variety of projects – exhibitions, installations, talks, performances and meetings of various kinds – are facilitated by the big bar-café and reception on the ground floor. An opening night at Färgfabriken usually means party night. Recent projects have included an installation piece by artist and fashion photographer Jean-Pierre Kazhem and an exhibition by controversial Italian artist Maurizio Cattélan.

Tensta Konsthall

Taxingegränd 10, Tensta Centrum (36 07 63/www. tenstakonsthall.com). T-bana Tensta. **Open** noon-5pm Tue, Thur-Sun; noon-7pm Wed. **Admission** 20kr; 10kr 12-18s. **No credit cards.**

One of a number of interesting surburban exhibition spaces that has opened in the past ten years. Celia Prado and Gregor Wroblewski launched Tensta Konsthall in the mid 1990s, in Tensta Centrum, one of the most multicultural suburbs of Stockholm. Recent artists have included Danish artist Eva Koch, Shirin Neshat and Kutlug Ataman. With its socially engaged profile, Tensta Konsthall is a must. Don't be put off by the rather long T-bana trip: Tensta is well worth a visit not only for the exhibition hall but also for its great grocery stores and food markets.

Gay & Lesbian

Let it all hang out in free-thinking Stockholm.

Ever since the 1960s, liberal Sweden has had an open-minded attitude to homosexuality, as well as to swingers' parties in the suburbs and to teenage breasts on the screen. In recent years, legislation has been passed allowing people of the same sex to register their relationship officially (giving them the same legal rights as married couples), as well as (since summer 2002) to adopt children. Violence or discrimination against gays, dykes or trans people is uncommon (and if one is subjected to it, Sweden even has a 'homo-ombudsman'), especially in the major cities and most especially in Stockholm, where the largest gay community lives.

The drawback of all this, ironically, is that the exclusively gay and lesbian scene is relatively small. Many places are mixed, so the need for downright 'homosexual' (whatever that is) places is not as great as in more conservative countries – where the release when finally in a gay-only environment is also often greater. However, there is a growing scene in Stockholm, mostly because people started to realise the commercial potential of all that pink money spent by a pleasure- and culture-consuming gay community that just gets bigger and bigger every year.

Södermalm is, in all respects, Stockholm's most alternative district, the place where most underground parties and cultural and political events occur. It's a relaxed neighbourhood where nobody raises an eyebrow seeing girls kissing girls or boys holding hands – and it most deserves the somewhat dubious title of a gay ghetto. Most gay and lesbian bars and restaurants are clustered within walking distance of Gamla Stan and especially around Mariatorget and Hornsgatan on Söder, where you'll see lots of rainbow flags flying from the balconies. This is also the centre of the annual Pride festival (*see p181*) at the beginning of August.

As in most cities, the traditional gay and lesbian scenes are quite segregated, but the younger generation's clubs and the growing queer scene have loosened up old barriers and found new ways of defining themselves, listening to hip hop instead of the Swedish gay speciality, *Eurovision Song Contest* music. Such clubs are niched more by musical than sexual preferences.

Friendly, flirty **Mandus**. *See p206.*

Take your pick: pink drinks at **Torget** or simply hanging out in the sun.

To make sure you get to where you want, pick up the free magazine ***QX*** at gay and gay-friendly establishments; the magazine is only in Swedish, but its website, www.qx.se, has an English version. Or listen to **Stockholm Gay Radio** (88 MHz) or check out websites **Corky** (www.corky.nu) for lesbian life, **Sylvester** (http://sylvester.spray.se) for what's happening on the young, alternative gay scene, and **Sylvia** (http://sylvia.spray.se) for its lesbian counterpart. The websites are in Swedish only. For gay and lesbian healthcare and helplines, *see p278.*

Accommodation

Other popular hotels in Söder's gay quarter are **Aston** (Mariatorget 3; 604 06 90/fax 714 97 05/ www.astonhotel.se), with single rooms from 600kr and doubles from 755kr; and **Alexandra** (Magnus Ladulåsgatan 42; 84 03 20/fax 720 53 53), where singles cost 375kr and doubles 550kr. Budget alternatives are **Columbus Hotell** (*see p49*) and youth hostels **Långholmen** (*see p51*) and **Zinkensdamm** (*see p50*) – which all start from 200kr for a bed.

Pensionat Oden

Hornsgatan 66, Södermalm (796 96 00/fax 612 45 01/www.pensionat.nu). T-bana Mariatorget/bus 43, 55, 66. **Rates** single from 395kr; double from 550kr. **Credit** AmEx, MC, V. **Map** p310 K6.

One of Stockholm's three exclusively gay hotels, all under the same ownership (and with the same contact details). The newest one, in Norrmalm, is quite spiffy, with brightly lit wide corridors, a brand-new coat of paint and cheerful fabrics in the rooms; some of the doubles are extremely spacious. This one is in the middle of gay Söder, close to the bars and cruising, and has 22 rooms.

Branches: Kammakargatan 62, Norrmalm; Odengatan 38, Vasastaden.

Bars & restaurants

Babs

Birger Jarlsgatan 37, Östermalm (23 61 01). T-bana Östermalmstorg/bus 1, 43, 46, 55, 56. **Open** *Bar* 5pm-1am daily. *Kitchen* 5-11pm daily. **Credit** AmEx, MC, V. **Map** p306 E7.

Arty but friendly bar-restaurant in the same building as the Zita cinema (*see p198*), which attracts lots of lesbian cineastes dressed in black discussing Jeanette Winterson's latest novel – so don't interrupt them with a vulgar sexual come-on (or on second thoughts…). The food is great and the rum drinks are the best in town, as is the service. Now and then there are cool vernissage and première parties.

Mandus

Österlånggatan 7, Gamla Stan (20 60 55). T-bana Gamla Stan/bus 43, 46, 55, 59, 76. **Open** *Bar* 5pm-midnight daily. *Kitchen* 5-10.45pm daily. **Credit** AmEx, DC, MC, V. **Map** p303 H8.

The campily decorated Mandus is always packed (which isn't that strange considering the size of the place) and boasts a hysterical atmosphere. The staff are extremely flirtatious, and the food is absolutely delicious (trendy crossover with a Swedish touch). The crowd is a mix of cool gays and lesbians (and the odd misguided tourist). All these ingredients, together with its location amid the Old Town's alleyways, give you the strange feeling of being in Rome or Barcelona rather than Stockholm.

Side Track

Wollmar Yxkullsgatan 7, Södermalm (641 16 88/ www.sidetrack.nu). T-bana Mariatorget/bus 43, 55, 66. **Open** *Bar* 8pm-midnight Mon, Sun; 8pm-1am Tue-Sat. *Kitchen* 8-11pm daily. **Credit** AmEx, MC, V. **Map** p310 L7.

One of Stockholm's few real neighbourhood gay bars, located in the heart of the gay ghetto and open seven nights a week. On the rainbow flag outside is an erect penis in solid gold – logical enough, as the moustaches are many and the crowd is mostly 40-plus men, men and more men. The most popular drink is *stor stark* ('large, strong' beer) and the food is heavy and substantial (no sissy salads here). This is the kind of bar where people arrive alone but leave with someone else.

Torget

Mälartorget 13, Gamla Stan (20 55 60). T-bana Gamla Stan/bus 3, 46, 53, 55, 76. **Open** *Bar* 11am-1am daily. *Kitchen* 11am-10pm daily. **Credit** AmEx, DC, MC, V. **Map** p303 J7.

At this glamour bar you make a queen-like entrance through heavy, red velvet drapery and are greeted by a shower of red roses and sparkling cut-glass chandeliers. The carpets are covered with a pattern of enormous gold baroque mirrors, and video sequences of *Dynasty* and *The Sound of Music* are projected on the wall, along with Turkish Eurovision Song Contest contributions. Everyone drinks pink drinks and talks in a loud voice, and you get the feeling that the world is on the starting blocks for the party of its life.

Cafés

Anna på Kungsholmen

Drottningholmsvägen 9, Kungsholmen (652 11 19). T-bana Fridhemsplan/bus 3, 4, 40, 57, 62.
Open 10am-8pm Mon-Fri; 11am-6pm Sat, Sun.
No credit cards.
A small, cosy lesbian café on Kungsholmen with snacks and sandwiches, plus wine and beer on Monday nights, when it's women only.

Chokladkoppen

Stortorget 20, Gamla Stan (20 31 70). T-bana Gamla Stan/bus 3, 53, 55, 59, 76. **Open** 9am-11pm Mon-Thur, Sun; 9am-midnight Fri, Sat. **No credit cards.** **Map** p303 J7.
On the main square in Gamla Stan this very popular café attracts a young crowd. It's got superb ciabattas and cakes – and all the papers and magazines to read when you get bored of your date. It's also the place to pick up flyers or buy tickets to various parties and happenings. *See also p142.*

Djurgårdsterrassen

Sirishovsvägen 3, Djurgården (662 62 09). Bus 44, 47/tram 7/ferry from Slussen or Nybrokajen. **Open** *Bar/café Summer* 11am-late daily (depending on weather). *Kitchen Summer* 11am-10pm daily. Closed winter. **Credit** AmEx, DC, MC, V. **Map** p305 H13.
This beautiful, open-roofed café-bar-restaurant is perfect for a glass of wine on a summer evening, a coffee after a Sunday promenade, or for brunch and a gossip about who, what and where last night.

Clubs

In addition to the regular clubs below, keep an eye out for occasional special events. Queer party promoters **Kaos World** (www.kaos-world.com) sometimes run club nights of their own, but mostly organise decadent one-offs at secret(ish) locations. Their grand parties always include performances, happenings, several dancefloors, darkrooms and a crowd that is a spectacular show in itself – partying as an art form. **Doghouseboys** (www.doghouseboys.com) hosts the mixed Monday Bar, with a gay lounge, at **Daily's** (*see p190*) every Monday night. They also arrange huge techno and house parties with international DJs every now and then, always with a more or less gay angle.

Bitch Girl Club

Kolingsborg, Slussen, Södermalm (720 52 05/ www.bitchgirlclub.com). T-bana Slussen/bus 3, 46, 53, 76. **Open** 9pm-3am every other Sat. **Admission** varies. **Credit** MC, V. **Map** p310 K8.
Northern Europe's largest lesbian club (over 4,000 members) changes venues, so check the website or give them a ring to find out where they're at. Bitch attracts 500 dancing dykes of all ages to its two dancefloors, with music ranging from rock to house. Hostess Birgitta meets and greets you at the door and leads newcomers with a firm hand into a new and more beautiful world. Women only.

Häcktet. *See p208.*

Sunday night is gay night on party boat **Patricia**.

Häcktet

Restaurang Bysis, Hornsgatan 82, Södermalm (84 59 10). T-bana Mariatorget or Zinkensdamm/ bus 4, 43, 55, 66, 74. **Open** *Club* 7pm-1am Wed, Fri. *Bar* 11am-10pm Mon, Tue, Thur, Sun; 11am-1am Wed, Fri, Sat. *Kitchen* 11am-10pm daily. **Credit** AmEx, DC, MC, V. **Map** p310 K5.

This old rural-style manor house in the middle of Hornsgatan is popular with both sexes, but especially with lesbians, who love its farmyard, country feel and folksy hit music. Häcktet doesn't really attract the most glamorous lipstick lesbians, but it's a great place to find a warm and familiar atmosphere, with ordinary people of all ages and nationalities having fun. (Fun, remember? Dancing and laughing and looking silly.)

Lino Club

Restaurang Scorpio, Södra Riddarholmenshamnen 19, Riddarholmen (411 69 76). T-bana Gamla Stan/ bus 3, 53. **Open** 10pm-3am Sat. **Credit** AmEx, MC, V. **Map** p303 J6.

A non-trendy, classic gay club that plays 1970s disco classics, Euro hits and *schlager* music for not-so-young-anymore (mostly) men on two happy dancefloors every Saturday. Very popular and very gay – in the traditional way. It's the kind of familiar club that could be anywhere in the world – but sometimes it's good to know what you're getting. The management has just changed, as has the club's name – it was formerly called StarGayte.

Patricia

Stadsgårdskajen 152, Södermalm (743 05 70/ www.ladypatricia.se). T-bana Slussen/bus 3, 46, 53, 76. **Open** 5pm-1am Wed, Thur; 6pm-5am Fri, Sat; 6pm-3am Sun. **Minimum age** 20. **Admission** 80kr after 10pm Fri-Sun. **Credit** AmEx, DC, MC, V. **Map** p311 K8.

Every Sunday for the past ten years, until the sun rises over the Stadsgårdsfjärden, a variety of gays, lesbians and everything in between dance, drink and flirt at this three-level party boat (formerly a World War II British lightship) moored at Slussen. It's probably as close as you will ever get to feeling what it's like to be in the navy – and it's one of the few places that still has a drag show. A Stockholm must.

Regnbågsrummet

Sturecompagniet, Sturegatan 4, Östermalm (611 78 00/www.sturecompagniet.se). T-bana Östermalmstorg/ bus 1, 46, 55, 56, 91. **Open** 10pm-5am Fri, Sat. **Minimum age** 23. **Admission** 120kr. **Credit** AmEx, DC, MC, V. **Map** p303 F8.

The special VIP lounge at the glamour palace Sturecompagniet (*see p192*) is perhaps the trendiest gay place in town. Here the Östermalm brat fags with their model fag hags in their latest Prada outfits kiss the air, sip Martinis and dance to great house music from resident DJ Stefan Wendin. It can be quite difficult to get past the bouncers at Sturecompagniet, but just look your gayest and you should have no problems.

SLM

Wollmar Yxkullsgatan 18, Södermalm (643 31 00/ www.slm.a.se). T-bana Mariatorget/bus 43, 55, 66. **Open** 10pm-2am Wed, Fri, Sat. **Admission** membership 300kr per yr; non-Swedes just sign the guestbook and pay 50kr after 11pm Sat. **Credit** MC, V. **Map** p310 L6.

Scandinavian Leather Men is Stockholm's only leather bar. A heavy door (work those muscles, boy) and an iron stairway lead down to a labyrinth of darkrooms, bars and a dancefloor. To get in you'll have to respect the international dress code of skinhead, military, leather, denim or construction style. Expect a cool, raw atmosphere – SLM is not for the limp-wristed or the prudish. Men only.

TipTop

Sveavägen 57, Vasastaden (32 98 00). T-bana Rådmansgatan/bus 1, 43, 52, 56. **Open** 4pm-2am Mon, Tue; 4pm-3am Wed-Sat. **Admission** free-small fee sometimes. **Credit** AmEx, DC, MC, V. **Map** p307 D6.

Six nights a week there's action at TipTop, the largest and longest-running gay disco in town. With a lesbian lounge called 'Ladies Room', two dance-floors and four bars, this is where everyone tends to end up and where anything can happen (and does, every night). House, techno, electro and hits, depending on the night, for a mixture of guys and gals in different styles, and their friends. It's more mixed on Friday and Saturday, when the 'Oh-we're-so-crazy-we're-going-to-a-gay-club' crowd is on the prowl.

Shops

Also check out **Antikt, Gammalt & Nytt** (*see p160*). Camp doesn't get much higher than this; it's like walking into a Peter Greenaway film.

C.U.M.

Klara Norra Kyrkogata 21, Norrmalm (10 40 18). T-bana T-Centralen/bus 47, 52, 56, 59, 65. **Open** 11am-6pm Mon-Fri; noon-4pm Sat. **Credit** MC, V. **Map** p303 F6.

Where to buy hysterical clubwear in odd materials from even more hysterical shop assistants, and a tiny chihuahua called Fifi. Thumping techno and a throbbing stroboscope make you feel like you've taken too many Es, so bring along a friend to advise.

Läderverkstaden

Rosenlundsgatan 30, Södermalm (442 30 35). Bus 4, 43, 55, 56, 74. **Open** noon-6pm Mon-Fri. **Credit** MC, V. **Map** p310 L6.

A stone's throw from Stockholm's leather bar, this shop sells custom-made leather chaps, caps and underwear, various kinky armour stuff and sex toys for a good night out. Can also repair your clothes when you've had too much fun in them.

Maskeradaffären

Kocksgatan 56, Södermalm (642 02 50). Bus 3, 46, 53, 66, 76. **Open** noon-6pm Wed-Fri. **Credit** MC, V. **Map** p311 L9.

Leo from drag group Cunigunda runs this shop, truly a pop cultural treasure island. You can buy or rent old musical, opera and drag show outfits, latex nun dresses or any Madonna period uniform. Ideal if you're searching for a pair of high heels in size 13.

Revolt Shop

Nytorgsgatan 21, Södermalm (643 79 50). T-bana Medborgarplatsen/bus 3, 46, 53, 59, 66. **Open** 11am-6pm Mon-Thur; 11am-8pm Fri; noon-6pm Sat; 2-8pm Sun. **Credit** MC, V. **Map** p311 L9.

Stockholm's only exclusively gay sex shop, selling magazines, toys and films. It also has video cabins and a film lounge.

Other

Art cinema **Zita** (*see p198*) always has gay-, lesbian- and trans-related stuff in its repertoire, as well as photography exhibitions, lectures, seminars and the odd fun première party. During Pride Week it's the home of the small annual gay and lesbian film festival.

T.M.A. The Muscle Academy

Björngårdsgatan 1B, Södermalm (642 63 06). T-bana Mariatorget/bus 43, 55, 56, 59, 66. **Open** 1-10pm Mon-Fri; 4-10pm Sat, Sun. **Admission** day membership 80kr. **Credit** MC, V. **Map** p310 L7.

Stockholm's only exclusively gay gym is for serious training, not cruising (even if glances in the shower do occur) for all the muscle marys that hang around Wollmar Yxkullsgatan's bars. Men only.

Sex, indoors and out

When gay saunas were banned in the mid 1980s in a misguided attempt to stop the AIDS epidemic, the video clubs simply took over as the place to find sex indoors. They have all the same facilities as the saunas (except a sauna), with porn showing in small private rooms or big salons – although hardly anyone bothers about the films.

Video clubs worth a visit include **Basement** (Bondegatan 1; 643 79 10; open noon-6am Mon-Thur, Sun; noon-8am Fri, Sat), **Eros Video** (Hornsgatan 67; open 11am-6am daily) and **Revolt** (Nytorgsgatan 21; 643 79 50; open 11am-10pm Mon-Thur; 11am-8pm Fri; noon-6pm Sat; 2-7pm Sun) – all in Söder. In Norrmalm there's 24-hour **US Video** (Regeringsgatan 76; 10 42 53/www.usvideo.nu) and in Kungsholmen **Manhattan** (Hantverkargatan 49; open noon-6am daily).

In warm weather, outdoor cruising in parks is a popular leisure activity, a perfect combination of exercise and fresh air – and it's not especially dangerous. Check out these popular spots:

- **Skinnarviksberget** On Södermalm, parallel to Hornsgatan, at the level of Mariatorget, on top of the mountain.
- **Frescati** Take the T-bana to Universitetet, then turn left under the bridge. Walk towards the water and follow the beach promenade until suddenly everyone is naked and giving you the eye and the word 'GAY' is sprayed over the cliffs.
- **Långholmen** Take the T-bana to Hornstull, cross over the bridge on to Långholmen island and head west towards the cliffs and the beach. Ooh – it's almost like being in San Francisco.

Music

Stockholm rocks – in a rather subdued way – but the classical scene is vibrant.

Rock, Pop & Jazz

It gets rather tiresome listening to people complaining about the lack of good live music venues in Stockholm, but, sadly, it's true. There are huge arenas for megastars on world tours and small cellars or tiny pubs for jangling demo or cover bands, but very few good medium-sized venues for those in between. At the beginning of the 1990s, it was a different story, with legendary clubs such as Tantogården, Studion and Gino. Then came the IT boom and it seemed that everywhere was turned into offices for internet start-ups. These days, city-centre rents are sky-high, making it nigh on impossible to open any new venues.

And then there are the regulations. If you want to serve alcohol, you need to have an approved kitchen. Furthermore, neighbours moan about noise in the street, forcing clubs and live venues to close all the time – which is quite laughable considering Stockholm is a major city and living here should mean one wants a big-city life.

Still, there is no shortage of live acts playing in the capital. Despite its rather off-centre position geographically, all European and world tours include Stockholm – and no wonder. Sweden consumes enormous amounts of pop culture, and it's an important market for both the commercial teenie-bopper stuff and more underground music. If you can deal with diverse and sometimes ill-equipped venues, you should get the chance to see some great bands performing while you're here.

The small number of venues means they don't tend to specialise in one particular kind of music. One day there could be a pop nerd crowd jumping up and down to the latest indie hit, while the following night the same place is full of 50-year-old troubadour fans. Occasionally, there are more clubby gigs in places such as **Berns Salonger** (*see p190*), **Stacy** (*see p191*) and **Sturecompagniet** (*see p192*), and smaller (sometimes acoustic) ones in bars, especially around east Södermalm.

In summer, there are lots of outdoor concerts at **Stadion** (*see p226*), **Kungsträdgården** (*see*

Head to stylish **Göta Källare** for everything from hip hop to indie. *See p213.*

Legendary jazz club **Fasching**. *See p212.*

p71) and **Solliden**, a restaurant and outdoor stage in Skansen (*see p84*). Mid July brings the outdoor **Stockholm Jazz Festival** (*see p179*), which always pulls in top names from the soul, jazz and funk world, and **Accelerator – The Big One** (www.klubbacc.nu or www.luger.se). Held at cultural centre Münchenbryggeriet (*see p213*) in 2002, it draws the likes of Arab Strap, Magnetic Fields, the Doves and loads of well-known Swedish bands.

Stockholm has always had a good reputation for its home-grown jazz talent, but – with the exception of ABBA – hadn't had much of an impact on the pop/rock scene until the end of the 1990s. Then there was a small explosion of Swedish bands breaking internationally, including the likes of the Cardigans, Kent and, more recently, the Hives. The Cheiron studio, headed by Denniz Pop (now deceased) and Max Martin, has also helped to put Sweden on the musical map, by delivering a string of worldwide hits for megastars such as Britney Spears and the Backstreet Boys.

In the last few years there's also been a breakthrough of more rhythmical Swedish music, such as soul, reggae and, most of all, hip hop, often performed in Swedish. While most pop and rock bands usually come from smaller towns but move to Stockholm to be close to the record industry and the venues, these new stars almost exclusively spring from the suburbs of the capital, being second-generation immigrants from South America or Africa. Now they're part of the 'Swedish music wonder' that everyone brags about. Perhaps, if the politicians didn't brag so much but seriously tried to help musicians have venues where they could play or watch other bands to get inspiration, that wonder could grow even bigger in years to come.

INFORMATION AND TICKETS

To be sure you don't end up in the wrong place on the wrong day (or maybe you should try that some time), check the listings in the Friday editions of *Expressen*, *Aftonbladet* or *Dagens Nyheter*, or keep your eye out for fly posters (prohibited, but still the best and most common way of spreading the word).

For tickets to big concerts, try **Biljett Direkt** (077 170 70 70/www.ticnet.com) or record store **Mega** (*see p171*). For tickets to smaller events, try record shops such as **Pet Sounds** (*see p172*) and **Record Hunter** (St Eriksgatan 70; 32 30 23) for pop and rock gigs, **Sound Pollution** (Stora Nygatan 18; 10 66 60) for punk and nu metal, **Ablaze** (Östgötagatan 18; 714 00 70) for hip hop and reggae, and **Bashment** (*see p171*) for reggae.

Most places serve alcohol and therefore can have a lower age limit, usually 18 (we've noted if it's 19 or above). Venues that don't have a bar usually admit all ages.

Gamla Stan

Stampen Jazzpub

Stora Nygatan 5 (20 57 93/www.stampen.se). T-bana Gamla Stan/bus 3, 53, 55, 59, 76. **Open** 8pm-1am Mon-Wed; 8pm-2am Thur-Sat. **Admission** Tue-Thur 100kr; Fri, Sat 120kr. **Credit** AmEx, DC, MC, V. **Map** p303 H7.

Formerly a pawnshop, tiny Stampen is Stockholm's best-known jazz pub, dating back to 1968. It might have passed its heyday, but interesting live acts still appear (9pm-12.30am), not only swing, dixie and trad jazz, but also blues, rockabilly and country. The crowd is more mature these days (plenty of middle-aged tourists); the younger cats prefer the somewhat hipper Fasching (*see p212*). There's a dancefloor and another bar in the basement.

Norrmalm

Fasching

Kungsgatan 63 (21 62 67/www.fasching.se). T-bana T-Centralen/bus 1, 47, 53, 69. **Open** 7pm-1am Mon-Thur; 7pm-4am Fri, Sat. **Minimum age** 20. **Admission** varies. **Credit** AmEx, DC, MC, V. **Map** p302 F6.

Many of the greats have performed at this classic jazz club (capacity 600) – as the fading photos on the walls attest. Gigs and jam sessions are held nightly: you'll hear all forms of jazz, as well as Latin, Afro and Brazilian sounds and even some hip hop. The crowd is a happy mix of ages and nationalities, and always includes plenty of real-life musicians. All in all, a very cool and bohemian Manhattan-style vibe; the restaurant is worth a visit too. *See also p191.*

Glenn Miller Café

Brunnsgatan 21A (10 03 22). T-bana Hötorget/bus 1, 43, 52, 56. **Open** 5pm-midnight Mon-Thur; 5pm-1am Fri, Sat. **Credit** MC, V. **Map** p303 E7.

This simple jazz pub has live music on Mondays, Tuesdays and Saturdays. It's often packed with a mix of older fans and twentysomethings who are mates with the band. If you love trad jazz, and are not claustrophobic, this is your place. *See also p115.*

Nalen

Regeringsgatan 74 (453 34 00/www.nalen.com). T-bana Hötorget/bus 1, 43, 46, 56. **Box office** noon-4pm Mon-Fri. **Admission** free-250kr. **Credit** AmEx, DC, MC, V. **Map** p303 E7.

Nalen is a classic of the Stockholm music scene. Built in 1888, it was famous as a jazz mecca from the 1930s until the end of the '60s, when a church took over and got rid of all that sinful noise. Now it's back in business again, thoroughly but sensitively renovated. There are two auditoriums – Stora Salen (capacity 400) and Harlem Scenen (capacity 80) – plus a restaurant, a bar and a club room, Alcazar. All kinds of music, but almost exclusively Swedish.

Djurgården

Cirkus

Djurgårdslätten 43-5 (box office 660 10 20/ www.cirkus.se) Bus 47/tram 7/ferry from Nybroplan or Slussen. **Box office** 10am-6pm Mon, Tue; 10am-7.30pm Wed-Fri; noon-7pm Sat; 1-3pm Sun. **Tickets** 280kr-600kr. **Credit** AmEx, DC, MC, V. **Map** p305 J11.

In royal park Djurgården, next to Skansen's zoo and opposite Gröna Lund amusement park, lies Cirkus. A cylindrical wooden building built in 1892 to host large circus troupes, it's got seating for 1,700, a bar and a restaurant. It's an atmospheric place, but the fact that you're sitting – and quite far from the stage – can be a drawback. This is where bands like Suede and Oasis play when they're in town. The musical *Chess* is currently playing here.

Gröna Lundsteatern

Gröna Lund, Allmänna Gränd (58 75 01 00/ www.tivoli.se/2000/eng/). Bus 47/tram 7/ferry from Nybroplan or Slussen. **Tickets** 115kr. **Credit** AmEx, DC, MC, V. **Map** p304 J11.

In a listed building near the entrance to Gröna Lund is the intimate and charming Gröna Lundsteatern. Recently renovated, it has room for 230 (standing and seated) and a small bar. You'll find mainly Swedish pop and rock acts playing, usually once a

Experience that classic jazz vibe at tiny **Stampen**. *See p211.*

Kafé 44: no alcohol but plenty of punch.

week, but more often during the summer. You can buy tickets in person at the box office before the gig, or from Biljett Direkt. Bonus fascinating info: the Beatles played here once.

Södermalm

Göta Källare

Folkungagatan 45 (57 86 79 00/www.gotakallare.com). T-bana Medborgarplatsen/bus 55, 59, 66. **Open** concerts varies; nightclub 9pm-3am Fri, Sat. **Minimum age** varies; 18-25. **Tickets** 100kr-250kr. **Credit** AmEx, MC, V. **Map** p310 L8.

A funky-looking, medium-sized venue with a bar and dancefloor, this has become *the* place for international indie acts in the past few years. Recent gigs have included Coldplay and the feminist rockers Le Tigre, electronica acts such as Röyksopp and big-name Swedish bands, from pop to hip hop. It attracts alternative Södermalm types aged between 20 and 30. Note that the entrance is by the steps leading down to the T-bana station.

Kafé 44

Tjärhovsgatan 44 (644 53 12/www.kafe44.com). T-bana Medborgarplatsen/bus 3, 46, 53, 59, 66. **Open** concerts twice a wk. **Tickets** 40kr-100kr. **No credit cards**. **Map** p311 L9.

This hangout for Södermalm's anarchists hosts a lot of punk and hardcore concerts, as well as alternative hip hop. There's no lower age limit and no alcohol – but with the sort of bands that play here, you won't need a drink to get a kick. Try not to look too clean and well groomed if you don't want to stand out from the crowd.

Mondo

Medborgarplatsen 8 (673 10 32). T-bana Medborgarplatsen/bus 55, 59, 66. **Open & admission** call for details. **Map** p310 L8.

Håkan Waxegård, the man behind the successful Hultsfred and Lollipop festivals, has finally realised his dream of opening a commercially run cultural centre in the heart of Södermalm. Due to open as we went to press, Mondo promises eight to ten concerts a week of the most interesting acts in country, pop, rock, soul, hip hop and reggae. With three stages of different sizes (the largest with room for 900 people), five bars, four dancefloors, a cinema, a gallery and a café, this is what everyone in Söder has been waiting for. *See also p191.*

Mosebacke Etablissement

Mosebacketorg 3 (programme 55 60 98 90/www.mosebacke.se). T-bana Slussen/bus 3, 46, 53, 76. **Open** 4pm-1am Mon-Thur, Sun; 4pm-2am Fri, Sat. **Minimum age** varies. **Tickets** 80kr-250kr. **Credit** AmEx, DC, MC, V. **Map** p310 K8.

Many of Sweden's finest jazz artists have appeared over the years on Mosebacke's two stages – Stora Salen and the smaller, more intimate Cornelisrummet. Nowadays, there's still a lot of jazz performed here, but you'll also find pop, rock, salsa and reggae. It's been a well-known address since the time of 18th-century troubadour Carl Bellman, and playwright August Strindberg used to hang out here in the 19th century. There are also some popular bars (*see p136*) and great club nights (*see p191*) here. It's next door to Södra Teatern (*see below*).

Münchenbryggeriet

Söder Mälarstrand 29 (658 00 20/www.munchen-bryggeriet.se). T-bana Mariatorget/bus 43, 55, 66. **Open** varies. **Minimum age** varies; 18-20. **Tickets** 100kr-250kr. **Credit** AmEx, DC, MC, V. **Map** p303 K6.

This old brewery is now a popular concert hall and party venue for medium-sized acts of all kinds. One night the audience is packed with dreadlocked rastas praising Jah and raising their lighters to dancehall missionary Capleton, while the next lo-fi rockers in knitted caps queue for Elliot Smith. In summer, you might find gigs on the stage in the outside courtyard. It's also a good place to see the latest in dance and performance art.

Södra Teatern

Mosebacketorg 1-3 (55 69 72 30/www.sodrateatern.com). T-bana Slussen/bus 3, 46, 53, 76. **Box office** noon-6pm Mon-Fri; noon-4pm Sat. **Minimum age** varies; 18-20. **Tickets** 100kr-200kr. **Credit** AmEx, DC, MC, V. **Map** p310 K8.

This ever-popular cultural centre has always got something of interest happening. Built in 1859, the main auditorium, Stora Scenen (capacity 400), has red-velvet chairs for low-key pop and folk concerts, while the basement Kägelbanan (aka KGB, with a capacity of 700) hosts dance and singalong pop concerts – such as Accelerator on Fridays for the best in new Swedish indie pop. Otherwise, there's a lot of world music stuff, often with a political message. Spring 2002 saw some Hindu hip hop from Fun-Da-Mental, British-Jamaican dub poetry from Linton Kwesi Johnson, and Mexican punk rock from Los de Abajos, among others, as well as poetry readings and spoken-word performances. The crowd is as mixed as the acts. Touring theatre companies also perform here on occasion.

Östermalm

Lydmar Hotel

Sturegatan 10 (56 61 13 00/www.lydmar.se). T-bana Östermalmstorg/bus 1, 46, 55, 56. **Open** 11.30am-1am Mon-Thur; 11.30am-2am Fri; 1pm-2am Sat; 1pm-1am Sun. **Minimum age** 25. **Credit** AmEx, DC, MC, V. **Map** p308 E8.

The stylish bar (*see p138*) of this music-friendly hotel (*see p53*) hosts live gigs once a week and a small festival once a year in October: lots of acid jazz, funk and rare groove stuff, but also hip hop and organic house music. World stars such as Adeva, Roy Ayers and De La Soul have all stepped on to the intimate and sweaty stage for shows you'll never forget – but might miss, since they're often a totally word-of-mouth affair. Bands staying at the hotel but playing another venue sometimes make surprise appearances. DJs also play here regularly.

Elsewhere

Allhuset

Universitetsvägen 10, Frescati (16 20 00/www.su.se). T-bana Universitetet/bus 40. **Open** 11am-1am Mon-Thur; 11am-3am Fri. **Tickets** 50kr-200kr. **Credit** MC, V.

At this modern venue (capacity 500) on Stockholm University's campus, students wearing T-shirts adorned with their favourite band's name talk about music and drink cheap beer in a relaxed atmosphere. As well as Swedish bands, there's plenty of interesting international stuff; recent bookings have included American cult artist Daniel Johnson and British indie-poppers Spearmint.

Globen

Arenavägen, Johanneshov (box office 077 131 00 00/www.globen.se). T-bana Globen/bus 4, 150, 164. **Box office** *In person* 9am-6pm Mon; 9am-4pm Tue-Fri. *By phone* 9am-7pm Mon-Fri; 10am-4pm Sat; 10am-3pm Sun. **Tickets** 100kr-600kr. **Credit** AmEx, DC, MC, V.

Like it or not (and many don't), you can't deny that the golf ball-like Globen is Stockholm's most recognisable structure. It's also the world's largest spherical building. The arena is used for everything from sports events (*see p225*) to gala parties and, of course, concerts. It holds up to 16,000, so this is the place for the big elephants, from Bruce Springsteen to Destiny's Child. If you're seated high up in a corner, bring binoculars or simply watch the giant TV screens. The atmosphere, as ever with large stadiums, is practically non-existent.

Klubben

Fryshuset, Hammarby Fabriksväg 13, Södra Hammarbyhamnen (www.fryshuset.se). T-bana Gullmarsplan then bus 150/bus 74. **Open** concerts are held at least once a wk. **Tickets** 200kr-300kr. **No credit cards.**

Just a bit south of Södermalm lies Klubben, the key Stockholm venue for underground indie pop, rock, hardcore and hip hop. It's located in the Fryshuset youth centre, where lots of bands rehearse. Expect a young crowd and lots of headbanging and stage-diving. No bar and no age restrictions.

Classical Music & Opera

An amazing number of Stockholm's venues and orchestras sport the appellation '*kungliga*' (royal), since quite a few of Sweden's monarchs have devoted much time and money to the arts. These royalist institutions – some of them impressively old – have been kept alive during the past few decades by a social democratic cultural policy, which is probably why, despite the regal pomp, the classical music audience in Stockholm is relatively casual and diverse. It's possibly also why a city the size of Stockholm has two symphony orchestras that can compete with the best in Europe, two permanent opera houses and a healthy chamber music scene.

One of the main instigators of Stockholm's impressive classical music scene was King Gustav III (1746-92), who built the first opera house, the **Kungliga Operan** (*see p217*), in 1782. Unfortunately for him, he was later assassinated at a masked ball there – which inspired Verdi to write his opera *Un Ballo in Maschera* ('A Masked Ball'). The current opera house at Gustav Adolfs Torg is still the centre of the Swedish opera scene. Its orchestra, the famous Kungliga Hovkapellet (Royal Court Orchestra), was founded in the 16th century and is said to be the oldest continuously active orchestra in the world.

One could argue that the Stockholm music scene of today is more suggestive of socialism than royalism, with a high and even quality that won't disappoint anyone, but glamour, edginess and surprises are rare: it's not particularly sexy. The lack of stars at the Kungliga Operan is obvious, and its production of *Tosca*, which has run since the 1960s, has collected enough dust to start a nationwide epidemic of asthma. But once in a while, surprisingly vital productions and first performances, such as Sven David Sandström's *Staden*, in 1998, are staged. The orchestras also sometimes lack that extra lustre of glamour. But then again, how can you expect a local funding body to pay the fees of a star soloist? There are still enough great performers in the middle range of the market who do the job perfectly well, and the artistic quality is high.

Whereas Denmark has Nielsen, Norway Grieg and Finland Sibelius, Sweden has never had one of its composers enthroned in the

Konserthuset: a temple to classical music.

Classical Music Hall of Fame, but music by Swedish composers is frequently played in Stockholm. Look out for performances of music written by Wilhelm Stenhammar, Franz Berwald, Wilhelm Peterson-Berger, Hugo Alfvén, Allan Pettersson and Hilding Rosenberg. Among the frequently performed contemporary composers are Anders Hillborg, Jan and Sven-David Sandström (not related), Anders Eliasson and Daniel Börtz.

Musicians to keep an eye open for include trumpet player Håkan Hardenberger, trombonist Christian Lindberg and his brother, lutist Jacob Lindberg. Violinist Cecilia Zilliacus is one of the brightest instrumentalists of the new generation, and do not ever miss a gig with Swedish classical music's biggest name, mezzo soprano Anne Sofie von Otter.

THE SEASON

The concert season usually runs from August until June. During the summer months, the scene moves to the court theatres outside town and parks around town and is substituted by festivals and church concerts – *see p217* **Summer music**. The opera season runs from September to May.

INFORMATION AND TICKETS

The venues themselves and their websites are usually the most reliable source of information. Monthly English-language tourist magazine *What's On Stockholm* lists the main concerts, though the Friday entertainment section of daily *Dagens Nyheter* often provides better listings. Also check out the free daily paper *Metro*, distributed in the T-bana. Website **www.konsertguiden.nu** is a great search engine where you can search by genre and location for concerts all over the country – but you'd better brush up your Swedish language skills before trying.

You can buy tickets by phone or online from most venues. For the major venues, tickets are also sold by **Biljett Direkt** (077 170 70 70/ www.ticnet.se); the website is in English.

Main venues & ensembles

Berwaldhallen

Dag Hammarskjöldsväg 3, Östermalm (box office 784 18 00/www.berwaldhallen.se). Bus 56, 69, 76. **Box office** *Early Aug-Midsummer* noon-6pm Mon-Fri; also 2hrs before performance. Closed Midsummer-early Aug. **Tickets** 50kr-360kr. **Credit** AmEx, DC, MC, V. **Map** p305 F11.

The Berwaldhallen was built in 1979 to fill the need for a home for the Sveriges Radio Symfoniorkester (Swedish Radio Symphony Orchestra) and the Radiokören (Radio Choir). Named after Swedish composer Franz Berwald (1796-1868), the acclaimed modernist hall is built mainly underground. The Symfoniorkester, set up in 1967, has been led by conductors such as Sergiu Celibidache and Herbert Blomstedt, and enjoyed a particularly successful period under Esa-Pekka Salonen during the second half of the 1980s. The current conductor, Austrian Manfred Honeck, joined in 2000. The orchestra has a more contemporary touch than other Swedish orchestras, commissioning a significant amount of new music, from both Swedish and international composers. It also has a responsibility to perform a substantial amount of Swedish music. The Radiokören is considered to be one of the best choirs in the world, and has done several recordings with the Berliner Philharmonic and Claudio Abbado, who also invited them to his final concert with the orchestra in 2002. The choir's leader, Eric Ericson, was awarded the Polar Music Prize in 1997, a prize founded in 1992 with the ambition of becoming the Nobel Prize for music. The ceremony takes place every May at the Berwaldhallen.

Konserthuset

Hötorget, Norrmalm (box office 50 66 77 88/ www.konserthuset.se). T-bana Hötorget/bus 1, 43, 52, 56. **Box office** *Mid July-Midsummer* 11am-6pm Mon-Fri; 11am-3pm Sat. Closed 1mth from Midsummer. **Tickets** 60kr-400kr. **Credit** AmEx, DC, MC, V. **Map** p303 F7.

The Stockholm Concert Hall (*see also p72*) has been the home of the Kungliga Filharmonikerna (Royal Stockholm Philharmonic Orchestra) since its inauguration back in 1926. The vision of architect Ivar Tengbom was to 'raise a musical temple not far from the Arctic Circle'. The bright blue building is one of the foremost examples of early 20th-century Swedish neo-classical design, with contributions from all the major names of the 1920s. The Main Hall with its 1,800 seats has changed noticeably over the years; in the 1980s the organ was put in, thus eliminating some of the original atmosphere of a Greek temple. The remarkably beautiful chamber music hall, the Grünewald Hall (capacity 460), entirely decorated by painter Isaac Grünewald, has a warmer feeling, influenced by the Italian Renaissance.

The Kungliga Filharmonikerna, which celebrated its centenary in 2002, acquired an international reputation under the leadership of Antal Dorati and later with Gennady Rozhdestvensky and Paavo Berglund. Under its current chief conductor and artistic adviser, American Alan Gilbert, it has entered a new phase of development, heading for a place among Europe's top orchestras. The Konserthuset's repertoire is based in the classical and romantic periods, but it also hosts the internationally renowned annual Composer Festival in November, focusing on one or more living composers – such as, in 2002, Magnus Lindberg and Kaija Saariaho.

Nybrokajen 11

Nybrokajen 11, Norrmalm (box office 407 17 00/ www.nybrokajen11.rikskonserter.se). T-bana Kungsträdgården/bus 46, 55, 59, 62, 69, 72. **Box office** *Mid Aug-mid June* noon-5pm Mon-Fri. Closed mid June-mid Aug. **Tickets** 140kr-200kr. **Credit** MC, V. **Map** p303 G8.

The newest venue on the Stockholm classical music scene is Nybrokajen 11, which is named after its address opposite the Kungliga Dramatiska Teatern. The elegant former premises of the Royal Academy of Music have been nicely transformed into a permanent stage for the Rikskonserter (Swedish Concert Institute). The main hall (capacity 600) hosts mainly chamber music from all periods, with Swedish and international artists. Stallet, a converted stable, is an intimate venue especially for world music.

Other ensembles

Kroumata

54 54 15 80/www.kroumata.rikskonserter.se.

Kroumata was formed in 1978 and has since developed a huge cult status previously unheard of for a contemporary percussion ensemble. It commissions and performs works by Swedish and international composers, and has toured to more than 35 countries worldwide. Since 1997 Kroumata has had its own venue, Capitol (St Eriksgatan 82), a converted theatre that serves both as rehearsal studio and intimate concert hall for a few performances a year. Check the website for details.

Stockholm Sinfonietta

Riddarhuset, Riddarhustorget 10, Gamla Stan (www.sinfonietta.a.se). T-bana Gamla Stan/bus 3, 53. **Tickets** around 200kr. **Map** p303 H7.

The members of the Stockholm Sinfonietta came first from the Kungliga Filharmonikerna. It has worked with a host of venerable names, including conductors Sixten Ehrling and Okko Kamu and soloists Montserrat Caballé and Swedish cellist Frans Helmerson. The repertoire stretches from baroque to contemporary, and jazz soloists sometimes appear. The Sinfonietta possesses the sole right to perform at the marvellous Riddarhuset; check its website or the newspapers for concert details.

Stockholms Nya Kammarorkester (SNYKO)

Check press for concert details.

The Stockholm Chamber Music Orchestra, mostly known by its abbreviation SNYKO, is one of the most sought-after Scandinavian ensembles, with an international reputation for both its classical and contemporary repertoire. It was formed from members of the Sveriges Radio Symfoniorkester. The orchestra performs regularly in Stockholm and tours extensively, often with artistic advisor Esa-Pekka Salonen, who's been associated with the group since its founding in 1981.

Churches & other venues

Church music in Stockholm has a long history, and nowadays the programming, especially in the city-centre churches, is rich and ambitious. Check the daily papers to find out what's on when and where. Especially around Christmas you'll have more than you can handle of the usual passions and requiems.

One of the finest organs is to be found in the **Gustav Vasa Kyrka** (Vasastaden; *see p77*), which hosts the leading organ concert series in Stockholm. Other musical churches are **Storkyrkan** (on Gamla Stan; *see p64*), **Riddarholmskyrkan** (Riddarholmen; *see p66*), **Katarina Kyrka** (Södermalm; *see p90*), **St Jakobs Kyrka** (Norrmalm; *see p76*), **Engelbrektskyrkan** (Östermalmsgatan 20, Östermalm; 406 98 00) and **Hedvig Eleonora Kyrka** (Storgatan 2, Östermalm; 663 04 30).

Nalen

Regeringsgatan 74, Norrmalm (453 34 00/ www.nalen.com). T-bana Hötorget/bus 1, 43, 46, 56. **Box office** noon-4pm Mon-Fri. **Tickets** free-250kr. **Credit** MC, V. **Map** p303 E7.

Since the reopening of this legendary dance palace a few years ago, Nalen has become the sort of venue that Stockholm always lacked. Its different stages, bars and restaurants host rock, troubadours, salsa, electronica – and a classical chamber music series on Sundays, promoted by the Swedish Artists' and Musicians' Interest Organisation (SAMI).

Summer music

Even though the main city venues close down in June for a lengthy summer break, summer in Stockholm yields up some truly phenomenal musical experiences. Especially if opera in ancient settings is up your street. It all gets a bit royal to say the least, with productions in historic court theatres and palaces in and around the city. Summer seasons include those at **Drottningholms Slottsteater** (*see p180*) and **Confidencen** (*see p178*), with opera productions by both the Kungliga Operan and Folkoperan. Classical music festivals include **Musik på Slottet** (*see p181*), **Slottsgala på Kungliga Ulriksdal** (*see p180*) and **Kungliga Filharmonikerna på Gärdet** (*see p181*).

Contemporary & experimental

EMS (658 19 90/www.ems.rikskonserter.se) is the centre for electro-acoustic music in Sweden; it works closely with Fylkingen (*see below*) and is located in the same building, the former Munich Brewery. It provides studios for musicians, and promotes concerts and festivals.

For the **Stockholm New Music** festival in February, *see p183*.

Fylkingen

Münchenbryggeriet, Torkel Knutsonsgatan 2, Södermalm (84 54 43/www.fylkingen.se). T-bana Mariatorget/bus 4, 43, 55, 66. **Box office** 10am-5pm Mon-Fri. **Tickets** free-80kr. **No credit cards**. **Map** p302 K6.

This society for new music and intermedia art has a unique position in Swedish experimental music, having been the main forum for the artform since 1933. Undoubtedly, the golden era was the 1950s, which saw the first electro-acoustic music performances, and the '60s, when the likes of John Cage and Karlheinz Stockhhausen were frequent guests. Karl-Erik Welin (his reputation confirmed by his accidentally cutting into his leg while chainsawing a grand piano during a performance) was one of the big Swedish names at that time. This tradition (without the leg-cuttings, sadly) continues in Fylkingen's venue in a converted brewery in Södermalm. With the recent co-operation of independent arts organisation Nursery, a new audience again finds its way here. A lot of the music is available on Fylkingen's own record label. *See also p232.*

Opera

Folkoperan

Hornsgatan 72, Södermalm (box office 616 07 50/ www.folkoperan.se). T-bana Mariatorget/bus 1, 43, 55, 66, 74. **Box office** *Sept-May* noon-6pm Mon, Tue, Sat; noon-7pm Wed-Fri; noon-4pm Sun. Closed June-Aug. **Tickets** 250kr-390kr. **Credit** AmEx, DC, MC, V. **Map** p310 K6.

Folkoperan has been a healthy competitor to the institution of Kungliga Operan since its founding in 1976. The modern stagings of classic operas, all sung in Swedish, the unconventional and often controversial productions, and the intimacy of the auditorium are among Folkoperan's distinctive features. The company has toured Europe and the US with such productions as *Don Carlos*, *Carmen* and the newly written Swedish opera *Marie Antoinette* by Daniel Börtz. The opera house is currently in the middle of its own Wagner Ring Cycle, which is planned to be completed in 2005. Its bar-restaurant, called Folkoperan Bar & Kök, is popular not only with the opera audience but also with a trendy young crowd of Södermalm locals.

Kungliga Operan

Gustav Adolfs Torg, Norrmalm (box office 24 82 40/ www.operan.se). T-bana Kungsträdgården/bus 43, 46, 55, 59, 62, 76. **Box office** *Sept-May* noon-6pm Mon-Fri; noon-3pm Sat. Closed June-Aug. **Tickets** 40kr-460kr. **Credit** AmEx, DC, MC, V. **Map** p303 G7.

The old opera house, opened in 1782, was at the time considered to be one of the most modern in operation. But only 100 years later it was demolished to make way for the current opera house, which was completed in 1898. The Royal Opera has sent a string of great opera singers on to the international stage – among them Jenny Lind, Jussi Björling, Birgit Nilsson and Elisabeth Söderström – but, as is the case with Swedish footballers and hockey players, the most talented get picked up internationally at a young age and it's rare to have the opportunity to hear one of the Swedish stars back here at the Kungliga Operan. The building itself is an impressively ornate setting, with a golden foyer and a red and gold auditorium that can seat as many as 1,100. It's also the home of the Swedish Royal Ballet (*see p234*). In 1998 the Operan also took over the old Vasan theatre on Vasagatan, which is used as a complementary stage for operettas, ballet and smaller, more intimate, opera productions.

Sport & Fitness

Come snow or shine, Stockholmers love their sporting action.

Whether your interest in sport is as a participant or a spectator, there are plenty of alternatives in Sweden's capital. Stockholmers love to stay in shape, and public funding for sports is far more generous than in many countries.

There are big differences in the sports on offer in the different seasons. In summer, the city's parks fill up with rollerbladers, joggers, footballers and cyclists, while kayakers and swimmers take to the water. In winter, people stick to indoor facilities – watching ice hockey, playing badminton or training at the gym – or leave the city for skiing (both cross-country and downhill) or long-distance skating. The only sport that maintains interest all year round is football (*fotboll*), which is played during the summer but watched and gambled on during winter, when the other European football leagues play.

But what about tennis, the sport that has seen so many great Swedish players? The sad fact is that interest has diminished enormously, leaving the plentiful courts empty. Instead, golf – with stars such as women's tour dominant Annika Sörenstam and Jesper Parnevik, not to mention Tiger Woods' blonde-bombshell girlfriend Elin Nordegren – has boomed in the past decade, and there are dozens of great golf courses within an hour's drive of Stockholm.

Sweden has a law, *allemansrätten*, that encourages free access to the countryside. This, together with the plentiful lakes, long coastline and ubiquitous forest (covering half the country), provides good conditions for many sports and outdoor activities. Also noticeable is how the democratic tradition has shaped the whole sporting movement. The mottoes are 'sport for youth' and 'sport for all'. Almost all sports are practised within organisations, and little is improvised – Sweden is about as far from the street football of Brazil as you can get.

The growing interest in physical activity is reflected in a number of mass events, which are becoming more and more popular. These include such Swedish classics as **Vasaloppet** in March (a 90-kilometre/56-mile cross-country skiing race; www.vasaloppet.se), **Vätternrundan** (a 300-kilometre/186-mile bike ride around Lake Vättern in southern Sweden) and the **Stockholm Marathon**, considered one of the best marathons in the

Cycling is a great way to see the city. *See p220.*

Practise your double axels at the **Kunsträdgården ice rink**. *See p222.*

world, run in early June. Another spectacular event is the long-distance skating race **Vikingarännet** (*see p222* **Ice skating**).

For more information on the sports listed below, or any others, contact the **Swedish Sports Confederation** (605 60 00/www.svenskidrott.se) or the tourist office (*see p285*).

Participation sports/fitness

Badminton

Badmintonstadion

Hammarby Slussvägen 4, Södermalm (642 70 02/www.badmintonstadion.nu). T-bana Skanstull. **Open** 6am-11.30pm Mon-Thur; 6am-8.30pm Fri; 8.30am-5pm Sat; 9am-10pm Sun. **Rates** per court per hr 100kr-120kr; 65kr concessions. **Credit** MC, V. **Map** p311 O8.

Badminton is a popular recreational sport in Sweden, and this is the largest hall in the city.

Frescatihallen

Svante Arrhenius Vägen 4, Norra Djurgården (15 27 00/www.frescatihallen.com). T-bana Universitetet/ bus 40, 540. **Open** *Mid Aug-Midsummer* 7am-11pm Mon-Thur; 7am-9pm Fri; 8am-7pm Sat; 8am-10pm Sun. *Midsummer-mid Aug* 2-10pm Mon-Thur; 2-9pm Fri; noon-6pm Sat; noon-8pm Sun. **Rates** 100kr-110kr; 55kr-80kr concessions. **Credit** AmEx, DC, M, V.

Sundbybergs Rackethall

Örsvängen 10, Sundbyberg (628 20 29). T-bana Hallonbergen. **Open** *Winter* 7am-10pm Mon-Thur; 7am-9pm Fri; 8am-9pm Sat, Sun. *Summer* 7am-10pm Mon-Thur; 7am-7pm Fri; 8am-7pm Sat; 8am-10pm Sun. Closed July. **Rates** per court 60kr-90kr. **Credit** MC, V.

Billiards, snooker & pool

There are billiard clubs, which may have a bar, and then there are bars with pool or snooker tables. Almost all alternatives in the Stockholm region are in the latter category, but here are two clean billiard clubs with professional staff.

Jolo & Co

Västmannagatan 50, Vasastaden (31 50 60/www.jolo.se). T-bana Odenplan/bus 4, 40, 53, 69, 72. **Open** *Mid Aug-Midsummer* 11am-midnight Mon-Thur; 11am-1am Fri; 2pm-1am Sat. Closed Midsummer-mid Aug. **Rates** (1 per table must be a member: 12kr) 44kr per person per hr; 132kr groups per table per hr. **Credit** AmEx, MC, V. **Map** p306 D4.

Stockholms Biljardsalong

Gyldéngatan 2, Vasastaden (31 32 50/www.stockholmsbiljardsalong.nu). T-bana Odenplan/ bus 4, 42, 72. **Open** 4pm-midnight Mon, Sun; 4pm-2am Tue-Sat. **Rates** (1 per table must be a member: 24kr) 38kr per person per hr; 114kr groups per table per hr. **Credit** AmEx, MC, V. **Map** p307 D5.

Climbing

The most popular outdoor climbing is found at the rocks of **Häggsta**, 35 kilometres (22 miles) south of Stockholm outside Huddinge, where there are options for most levels. For more information check with the **Stockholm**

Super Swedes: Björn Borg

Probably no living Swede is more famous than former tennis player Björn Borg. Playing the game during its most entertaining period, he won Wimbledon five times in a row (1976-80), 37 out of 40 Davis Cup matches, two Master's trophies and six French Open titles. He invented the two-handed backhand and was the early master of baseline-topspin tactics. Tennis fans have never forgotten his battles with John McEnroe, Jimmy Connors and Ilie Nastase. Teenage girls around the globe swooned at his trademark long blond hair and striped headband. Nicknamed 'Ice Borg', he never expressed an emotion before a game was won. His patience was limitless, as was his stubbornness.

In his catastrophic comeback ten years after his retirement in 1983, he was so obstinate he insisted on using his old wooden racquets although the manufacturer had stopped producing them and the whole world was laughing at him.

Born in 1956, Borg grew up in Södertälje, a working-class town outside Stockholm, where you can still see the garage door that was his opponent during childhood – indefatigable, unlike his future antagonists. After living in Monaco during his career, Borg has been a famous figure in Stockholm in the past decade and one of the most gossiped about. He got married for the third time in 2002 and now, living at Strandvägen 9, the most fashionable street in the city, has said he is happier than ever.

Searching for an off-court niche, Borg failed as a businessman in the 1980s, but the clothing brand 'Björn Borg' lives on. You can buy underwear, shoes and shirts labelled with the tennis legend's name (www.bjornborg.net). A joke? Not at all. Although far from being a new Lacoste, the brand stands for high quality and good design.

Borg was recently named the greatest Swedish sportsman of the 20th century. One reason his popularity is undiminished is the impact of his legacy – think of Grand Slam winners such as Mats Wilander, Stefan Edberg and Anders Järryd (doubles giant in the '80s), who in their turn inspired Magnus Norman, Thomas Enquist and Thomas Johansson. Admittedly, there are no up-and-coming stars at present, but for the past 25 years Sweden has undoubtedly been the best tennis nation per head. Largely thanks to Björn Borg.

Climbing Club (www.utsidan.se/skk) or the **Swedish Climbing Association** (618 82 70). Or try one of the following indoor centres.

Karbin

Västberga Allé 60, Västberga (744 38 40/www.karbin.com). Bus 165 from Liljeholmen to Västberga Kyrkogårdsvägen. **Open** *Winter* noon-10pm Mon-Fri; noon-8pm Sat, Sun. *Summer* 4-10pm daily. **Rates** 80kr plus equipment. **Credit** AmEx, MC, V.

Located a few miles south of the city, with 430sq m (514sq yds) of indoor wall.

Klätterverket

Markusplatsen 17, Nacka (641 10 48/www.klatterverket.se). Bus 401-422 to Sickla station/Järnvägsstation Sickla. **Open** *Mid Aug-Midsummer* noon-10pm Mon-Fri; 10am-8pm Sat, Sun. *Midsummer-mid Aug* 3-9pm daily. **Rates** 80kr-130kr. **Credit** AmEx, DC, MC, V.

This is Sweden's biggest indoor climbing centre, with 1,000sq m (1,200sq yds) of wall.

Cycling & rollerblading

Stockholm is small enough to be discovered on your chosen set of wheels: rollerblades or bike. It's also a convenient way of getting about, as there are plenty of cycling paths and some really beautiful stretches. The island of **Djurgården** is a good place – lots of green space, no cars at weekends – or try the circuit around the bay of **Riddarfjärden** (across the demanding bridge Västerbron, along Söder Mälarstrand, Centralbron and Norr Mälarstrand).

Cykel och Mopeduthyrningen

Strandvägen, kajplats 24, Östermalm (660 79 59). Bus 47, 69, 76. **Open** *Summer* 9am-9pm daily; call for opening hours in winter. **Map** p304 G10.

Offers mopeds in addition to bikes and inline skates.

Servicedepån

Kungsholmsgatan 34, Kungsholmen (651 00 66). T-bana Rådhuset/bus 1, 40, 52. **Open** *Apr-Sept* 10am-6pm Mon-Sat. *Oct-Mar* 10am-6pm Mon-Fri. **Rates** 125kr 10am-6pm; 150kr 24hrs. **Credit** DC, MC, V. **Map** p302 G4.

Rents out normal bikes and tandems.

Djurgårdsbrons Sjöcafe

Galärvarvsvägen 2, Djurgården (660 57 57). Bus 44, 47. **Open** *Mar/Apr-Sept/Oct* 9am-9pm daily. **Rates** 60kr inlines and bikes per hr; 250kr bikes per day. **Credit** AmEx, DC, MC, V. **Map** p304 G10.

This is a handy place for renting both inlines and bikes, just over the bridge on Djurgården. It's also got a pleasant waterside café.

Fitness clubs

The number of fitness clubs in Stockholm continues to grow apace. The two most popular, with plentiful branches, are listed below, but for non-members these are rather expensive. For a one-time workout, many of the city's public swimming pools (*see p224* **Swimming**) have gym facilities, including Centralbadet, Eriksdalsbadet and Forsgrenska Badet. There are also plenty of small gyms dotted around the city: ask at your hotel or look in the Yellow Pages (under 'Gym'). Some fitness clubs have yoga classes, but yoga is far from as widespread as in, say, New York.

Friskis & Svettis

Mäster Samuelsgatan 20, Norrmalm (429 70 00/ www.sthlm.friskissvettis.se). T-bana Hötorget/ bus 43, 46, 55. **Open** 6.30am-9pm Mon-Thur; 6.30am-7pm Fri; 10am-12.30pm Sat; 3.30-6.30pm Sun. **Rates** 40kr members; 80kr non-members. **Credit** AmEx, DC, MC, V. **Map** p303 F7.

Less geared to the good-looking body than SATS (*see below*) and more to the health aspects. Therefore the average age of the rather more downbeat crowd is 45 rather than 30. The name means roughly 'healthy and sweaty'. The telephone number is the same for all branches.

Branches: Långholmsgatan 38, Södermalm; Ringvägen 111, Södermalm; St Eriksgatan 54 & 63, Kungsholmen; Tegeluddsvägen 31, Gärdet; Sveavägen 63, Vasastaden.

SATS Sports Club

Regeringsgatan 47, Norrmalm (791 22 30/ www.satssportsclub.com). T-bana Hötorget/bus 43, 47, 59, 69. **Open** 6.30am-10pm Mon-Fri; 10am-6pm Sat, Sun. **Rates** 200kr non-members. **Credit** AmEx, MC, V. **Map** p303 F7.

SATS has a dozen locations in Stockholm – we've listed the most central branches below (contact any of them for a complete list and updated information). All are well equipped and clean, with plenty of good classes. You will sweat along with a mix of successful young professionals, students (who are offered discounts for restricted membership) and some serious bodybuilders. The Regeringsgatan branch has an indoor climbing wall.

Branches: Kocksgatan 12-14, Södermalm (55 60 93 60); Åsögatan 117, Södermalm (640 70 30); Birger Jarlsgatan 6C, Östermalm (679 83 10); Odengatan 65, Vasastaden (31 12 14); St Eriksgatan, Kungsholmen (650 66 25); Sveavägen 20, Norrmalm (22 65 10).

Golf

Golf enthusiasts hardly have a shortage of facilities: there are some 50 courses within an hour's drive of Stockholm. But the game's increasing popularity has led to skyrocketing green fees, usually around 450kr-600kr. However, even if you will sometimes need to reserve a tee time, you are allowed to play at all courses, although some snobbish members who think they own the course may not make you feel welcome. Websites **www.golf.se** and **www.alltom golf.se** provide extensive information on golfing options – but only in Swedish.

For really great golf you should head north of Stockholm to **Ullna** (514 412 30/www.ullnagolf.se) or **Kungsängen** (584 507 30/ www.etc-sthlm.se), which hosted the Scandinavian Masters in 2002. The Värmdö courses **Fågelbro** (571 418 00/www.fagelbrogolf.se) and **Wermdö** (574 607 20/www.wgcc.nu) are located a half-hour drive south of the city. Also in the south is **Saltsjöbaden Golfklubb** (717 01 26/www.cyberstore.se/gks), which has steadily improved in recent years. Equally worth its price is **Stockholms GK** (544 907 15/www.sgk.nu) at Danderyd, situated north of the capital.

Ice skating

For a city surrounded by water, the choices are, not surprisingly, numerous: indoor and outdoor ice skating rinks, lakes or the frozen waters of the archipelago.

The most central outdoor skating rinks are in **Kungsträdgården** in Norrmalm and at **Medborgarplatsen** on Söder, where you can rent a pair of skates for a small fee and squeeze yourself on to the (very) small rinks. Popular with families, they're usually open from November to February. There are also plentiful ice hockey rinks, such as Zinkensdamm, which are open to the public a few hours every day. Call the tourist office (*see p285*) for a full list and updated information.

However, skating in the city cannot compete with lakes or the archipelago when it comes to experiencing nature. Tour or long-distance skating (*långfärdsskridskoåkning*) is a popular sport in Sweden, and Stockholm has perhaps the best conditions in the world for it. The Baltic Sea around Stockholm does not freeze every year, but when it does skating there is a very special experience. The smallest lakes may freeze in November, but the main season usually lasts from December to March. Be careful to make sure you have up-to-date information on ice quality and weather reports.

The golden rule is never to skate alone: it's best to join a group with a guide. The **Stockholm Ice Skate Sailing & Touring Club** (768 23 78/www.sssk.se) is the largest skating organisation outside the Netherlands, with about 11,000 members, and is famous for its excursions. Before becoming a member you have to pass a beginner's course; contact the club for more details. Website **Isplanket** (Ice Billboard; www.isplanket.com) has information in English.

For a real challenge, try the 80-kilometre (50-mile) **Vikingarännet** ('the Viking Run'; 556 312 45/www.vikingarannet.com) skating race from Uppsala to Stockholm. It's held when there's enough ice, usually in February.

Östermalms Idrottsplats

Fiskartorpsvägen, Hjorthagen (508 283 51). T-bana Stadion/bus 55, 77, 291, 293. **Open** varies; call for details. **Map** p308 B/C9.

This place usually has a 'natural' ice rink/lane from December to the end of February, and is open to the public when there are no matches. It's ideal for practising long-distance skating.

Zinkensdamms Idrottsplats

Ringvägen 12-14, Södermalm (668 93 31). T-bana Zinkensdamm/bus 4, 66, 76. **Open** *Nov-mid/end Feb* 8am-2pm Tue-Thur; 8am-11pm Sat; 1-4pm Sun. **Admission** free. **Map** p301 L5.

Next to the bandy field for Zinkensdamms IP, which is also open to the public. Bring your hockey (or bandy) stick and ask if you can join any of the spontaneous games that are usually in progress.

Bandying about

Sweden's third-biggest sport – after football and ice hockey – is bandy. Little known outside Scandinavia and Russia (although it originated in Britain), bandy re-established itself in Stockholm in the late 1990s when Hammarby IF became one of the nation's best teams. Bandy fans must admit that its offspring, ice hockey, is far more popular, but, as the saying goes, 'Bandy is culture', while ice hockey is transforming itself into just another attraction in the McWorld Theme Park.

The skating is like hockey, the strategy is like football and the shooting is something like golf. To understand bandy, look first at ice hockey. Then increase the number of players on a team from six to 11, remove most of their pads, get rid of much of the rough stuff, replace the puck with an orange, vinyl-covered sphere slightly larger than a racquetball, spread the players out on an outdoor rink roughly the size of a football field and with a 15-centimetre (six-inch) barrier round the edge, and put a goalie without a stick in a goal slightly smaller than a football goal.

Bandy's rules are almost identical to football, except that you hit rather than kick the ball. As with soccer, much of the

Jogging & running

Stockholm is great for jogging, both on the cycle paths, such as around **Riddarfjärden**, and in the numerous parks. The parks are definitely safe in daytime, but are poorly lit otherwise. Try **Långholmen**, **Djurgården** or beautiful **Hagaparken**.

There are several annual races. The **Stockholm Marathon** in June (*see p179*) is one of the best marathons in the world, attracting both top-class runners and numerous visiting amateurs, who together with the locals mingle in a festive atmosphere in central Stockholm. Exclusively for women, and very popular, is **Tjejmilen** ('Girls' Own Run'), in late August or early September, a ten-kilometre/six-mile street race on Djurgården (545 664 40/www.tjejmilen.se). Another street race, this time on Södermalm, is the carnival-like action takes place a long way from the net. The sticks are short and curved, resembling those used in field hockey. With only limited substitutions allowed, players skate for miles during the two 45-minute halves. It's played from November to March, so is sometimes called 'winter soccer'.

The result is a fast, fluid, complex game with greater speed and far more skating than ice hockey, and with more goals and more entertaining corners than soccer. However, the small ball and the speed make it difficult to watch. (Watching it on TV is even worse.) This doesn't mean it isn't fun to go to a match. It's free from hooligans, but rich in traditional skills and interest.

Bandy was being played in north-east England in the mid 1800s, but is older than that, being the English cousin of Irish hurley and Scottish shinty. Even Shakespeare mentions bandy, in *Romeo and Juliet*. Bandy was introduced to Sweden in 1894 by a player from Bury-on-Fen in England.

Hammarby's rink **Zinkensdamm** (*see p222*) is in west Södermalm, convenient for a traditional bandy Sunday afternoon or a weekday evening match. Fans usually warm up at nearby pub Zinken), but it is more traditional to carry your own 'bandy briefcase', usually an old brown bag containing a thermos filled with *kaffekask*, a mix of spirits and coffee. Guaranteed to make you feel warm and happy while stamping in the slush on a rickety wooden stand munching a hot dog. As an alternative to spirits, try *glögg*, a sort of mulled wine.

The forerunner of ice hockey is currently only played well in Sweden, Finland and Russia, but a few more countries are trying – with the modest objective of keeping the score low enough to fit on the scoreboard. One newish member of the bandy world is the USA, after a Swedish bandy team played a demonstration game in 1979 and sparked some interest. But it has stayed in Minnesota, the American area with most people of Scandinavian descent.

ten-kilometre **Midnattsloppet** ('Midnight Race'; 649 71 71/www.midnattsloppet.com), which takes place in August.

Kayaking & canoeing

Since Stockholm is probably the best city in the world for kayaking and canoeing, you should not miss this combination of a demanding workout and beautiful sightseeing. There are even competitions in kayaking in Strommen, the current between the Kungliga Slottet and the Riksdagshuset. **Djurgårdsbrons Sjöcafe** (*see p220*) rents out kayaks and canoes, as well as pedal boats and rowing boats. Reliable canoeing outfits are **Svima Sport** in Solna (Ekelundsvägen 26, 730 22 10/www.svima.se) and **Brunnsvikens Kanotcentral**, north of the city by Brunnsviken lake (Hagavägen 5, Frescati, 15 50 60/www.bkk.se).

For trips in the archipelago or around enormous Lake Mälaren a good start is to contact the tourist office (*see p285*). Agencies include **Kajakboden Aquarius** in Tyresö (Varvsvägen 9, Tyresö Strand, 770 09 50/ www.kajakboden.com), **Kayak support** in Bromma (Nockeby backe 20, 87 73 77/ www.kayak.se), **Archipelago Ljusterö Kajakcenter** on the island of Ljusterö (542 432 07) and **Skärgårdsgumman** on Utö (501 576 68).

Sailing & boats

Most outfits focus on corporate sailing tours, but those listed below offer smaller boats that can be rented without a skipper for a few thousand kronor per day. Rates vary depending on the type of boat you want. For nautical charts, books and other equipment, try well-stocked **Nautiska Magasinet** on Gamla Stan (Slussplan 5; 677 00 00).

Blue Water Cruising Club

717 68 00/www.bluewatercc.com. **Open** 9am-6pm Mon-Fri; answerphone Sat, Sun. **Credit** AmEx, DC, MC, V.

Segelfartygsrederiet

702 02 02/www.segelfartygsrederiet.se. **Open** *Phone enquiries* 9am-6pm daily.

Tvillingarnas Båtuthyrning

Strandvägskajen 27, Östermalm (663 37 39/ www.tvillingarnas.com). Bus 44, 47, 69, 76. **Open** *Apr-Oct* 9am-7pm daily. Closed Nov-May. **Credit** DC, MC, V. **Map** p304 G10.

This central rental agency, located just before the bridge to Djurgården, has a popular restaurant and hires out little sailing boats and a dozen motorboats, ranging from small ones to 40ft launches.

Skiing

Skiing, cross-country as well as downhill, is a real mass-participation sport in Sweden. The country has had several successful sportsmen and women in the two disciplines, among them Gunde Svan, Thomas Wassberg and Pär Elofsson in cross-country, and Ingemar Stenmark, Pernilla Wiberg and Anja Pärson in downhill.

Stockholm is relatively close to good downhill skiing. **Flottsbro** (449 95 80/www.flottsbro.com) is located 40 kilometres (25 miles) south of the city and is all right for a day trip but not very demanding. A four-hour drive by car will take you to some real ski slopes in **Sälen** (0280 187 00/www.salen.se/www.skistar.com/salen) in the region of Dalarna. The best downhill skiing in the country is found in **Åre** (0647 177 00/www.skistar.com/are), which is close enough by plane for a weekend trip.

Stockholm Marathon. *See p222.*

Cheaper alternatives are the numerous day trips, which usually take place only at the weekend. These start around 7am and after three hours in a bus you get six hours of skiing, for an all-in price of around 300kr. **Romme** (0243 23 53 00/www.rommealpin.se) is best for slalom, and **Kungsberget** (0290 622 10/ www.kungsberget.se) has a big half-pipe for snowboarders. Website **www.skiinfo.se** (in various languages) offers all the information you'll need, including snow reports and accommodation options.

The most likely place to find enough snow for cross-country skiing in the Stockholm area is at **Rudan** (606 89 75), a few miles south of the city close to Haninge.

Swimming

Stockholm's swimming pools vary from modern swimming baths that contain everything one can think of plus a bit more, to beautiful Roman-inspired bathing temples. In the latter category are **Centralbadet** and **Sturebadet** (for both, *see p168*): both have weights and machines and, for a little extra, you can also get a massage. If you're into serious swimming, try **Eriksdalsbadet** or **Forsgrenska Badet**, both of which also have weights and machines. Suitable in summer for kids is the outdoor pool **Vilda Vanadis**. Of course, in summer you can also swim in the waters around the city (*see p91* **Where to swim outdoors**).

Eriksdalsbadet

Hammarby Slussväg 20, Södermalm (50 84 02 50/ www.eriksdalsbadet.com). T-bana Skanstull. **Open** *Late Aug-late May* 6.30am-9pm Mon-Thur; 6.30am-8pm Fri; 9am-5pm Sat; 9am-6pm Sun. *Late May-late Aug* 6.30am-8pm Mon-Fri; call for details Sat, Sun. **Admission** 65kr; 45kr concessions; 30kr 4-17s; free under-4s. **Credit** AmEx, DC, MC, V. **Map** p311 O8.

Recently opened, this is the main arena for Swedish swimming competitions. It also has adventure pools for children and an outdoor pool.

Forsgrenska Badet

Medborgarplatsen 2-4, Södermalm (50 84 03 20). T-bana Medborgarplatsen/bus 59, 66. **Open** *Sept-May* noon-9pm Mon; 6.30am-9pm Tue-Sun. Closed June-Aug. **Admission** 50kr; 30kr students; 15kr 7-19s; free under-7s. **Credit** MC, V. **Map** p310 L8.

Liljeholmsbadet

Bergsunds Strand 2, Södermalm (668 67 80). T-bana Hornstull/bus 4, 40. **Open** *Sept-mid June* 7am-7pm Mon, Fri; 7am-4pm Tue, Wed; 7am-5pm Thur; 8am-2pm Sat. Closed mid June-Aug. **Admission** 50kr; 30kr concessions. **No credit cards**. **Map** p301 K2.

A swimming pool in the old style, but bohemian rather than classy, located on a pontoon moored in western Södermalm. Mondays is for women only; Fridays is men only.

Vilda Vanadis

Vanadislunden, Sveavägen 142, Vasastaden (34 33 00). Bus 52, 40X, 515, 595. **Open** *May-Sept* 10am-6pm daily. Closed Oct-Apr. **Admission** 50kr; free kids under 80cm/31.5in. **No credit cards**. **Map** p307 B5.

An outdoor adventure pool with water slides that is currently being renovated. A new hotel is to be added, with a dining room near the pool.

Tennis

Eriksdal

Hammarby Slussväg 8, Södermalm (640 78 64/ www.hellas.a.se). T-bana Skanstull. **Open** *Courts* 7am-11pm Mon-Thur; 7am-9pm Fri; 9am-6pm Sat; 9am-11pm Sun. *Reception* 9am-4pm Mon-Fri. **Rates** 110kr-160kr per court. **No credit cards**. **Map** p311 O8.

Outdoor courts in southern Södermalm.

Haga Tennis

Hagaparken, Hagalund (33 70 77). Bus 52, 69. **Open** *May-mid Sept* 11am-7pm Mon-Fri; 11am-6pm Sat, Sun. Closed mid Sept-Apr. **Rates** 100kr-110kr per court. **Credit** DC, MC, V.

This is a great summer option, located in beautiful Hagaparken north of Norrtull.

Kungliga Tennishallen

Lidingövägen 75, Hjorthagen (459 15 00/www. kungl.tennishallen.com). Bus 73. **Open** 7am-11pm Mon-Thur; 7am-9pm Fri; 8am-8pm Sat; 8am-10pm Sun. **Rates** 235kr-255kr per hr. **Credit** AmEx, DC, MC, V. **Map** p309 B11.

The Stockholm Open tournament is played at the Royal Tennis Hall, which is also open to the public.

Tennisstadion

Fiskartorpsvägen 20, Hjorthagen (545 252 54). Bus 55, 73. **Open** *Mid Aug-Midsummer* 8am-11pm Mon-Fri; 8am-8pm Sat; 8am-10pm Sun. *Midsummer-mid Aug* 8am-9pm Mon-Fri; 9am-5pm Sat, Sun. **Rates** 180kr-215kr. **Credit** MC, V. **Map** p308 B9.

A good place for both indoor and outdoor tennis.

Ten-pin bowling

All the bowling centres below rent out shoes and have cafeterias. They also feature occasional 'disco bowling', with DJs, loud music, bars and late hours; call for details.

Birka Bowling

Birkagatan 16-18, Vasastaden (30 50 10). T-bana St Eriksplan/bus 3, 4, 72, 507. **Open** 11am-11pm Mon-Sat; 11am-10pm Sun. **Rates** 50kr per person. **Credit** AmEx, MC, V. **Map** p306 D3.

Kungsholmens Bowling

St Göransgatan 64, Kungsholmen (651 55 16). T-bana Fridhemsplan/bus 1, 49, 57, 74. **Open** *Winter* noon-11pm Mon-Sat; noon-8pm Sun. *Summer* call for details. **Rates** 220kr-270kr per lane per hr. **Credit** MC, V.

Kayaking in Djurgårdsbrunnsviken. *See p223.*

Svea Bowlinghall

Sveavägen 118, Vasastaden (441 85 50/www.svea bowlinghall.se). Bus 52, 40. **Open** noon-midnight Mon-Sat; noon-7pm Sun. **Rates** 300kr-400kr per lane per hr. **Credit** AmEx, DC, MC, V. **Map** p307 C5.

Södra Bowlinghallen

Hornsgatan 54, Södermalm (642 25 00/www. bowlinghallen.com). T-bana Mariatorget/bus 4, 43, 53, 66. **Open** *Winter* noon-midnight daily. *Summer* 4-10pm daily. **Rates** 170kr-220kr per lane per hr. **Credit** AmEx, DC, MC, V. **Map** p310 K6.

Spectator sports

All the daily papers carry massive amounts of sports analysis and provide listings of the day's events and TV coverage, concentrating on football and ice hockey. The drawback, though, is that everything is written in Swedish. A good way to get information is to ask ticket brokers, who sell tickets to all big events (expect a service fee of 5-30kr). The biggest ticket broker is **Biljett Direkt** (077 170 70 70/www.ticnet.se). Alternatives are **Derbybutiken** (Mäster Samuelsgatan 46, 21 03 03), **the** ticket office at **Globen** (Globentorget 2077, 131 00 00), **Boxoffice** (*see p175*) or the **tourist office** (*see p285*). For details of Stockholm's three main sports teams, *see p226* **The big three**.

Major stadiums

Globen

Arenavägen, Johanneshov (600 34 00/725 10 00/ box office 077 131 00 00/www.globearenas.se). T-bana Globen/bus 4, 150, 164. **Box office** *In person Mid Aug-mid May* 9am-6pm Mon-Fri; 9am-4pm Sat. *Mid May-mid Aug* 9am-6pm Mon; 9am-4pm Tue-Fri. *By phone* (tickets collected from a Globen distributor; ask for nearest) 9am-7pm Mon-Fri; 10am-4pm Sat; 10am-3pm Sun. **Credit** (in person only) AmEx, DC, MC, V.

The most famous sports hall in Stockholm is the futuristic Globen – the huge white sphere south of Söder that you can see from all over the city. It hosts major competitions in tennis, ice hockey, handball, showjumping and floorball (Sweden's fastest-growing sport), as well as concerts and other big events. With a capacity of just under 14,000, it is also the home arena of ice hockey teams Djurgården and AIK. Next door are **Söderstadion** (T-bana Globen or Gullmarsplan), Hammarby football team's home ground; and **Hovet**, used for ice hockey, handball derbies and concerts.

Råsunda Stadion

Solnavägen 51, Solna (box office 735 09 35). T-bana Solna Centrum/bus 505. **Box office** 9am-4.30pm Mon-Thur; 9am-3pm Fri. **Credit** MC, V.

A short T-bana ride from the city centre, this is the national football stadium and home ground for AIK. Built in 1937, it has a capacity of just over 37,000. You can buy tickets for most Råsunda events at Globen (*see p225*) or try Biljett Direkt.

Stockholms Stadion

Lidingövägen 1, Hjorthagen (50 82 83 62). T-bana Stadion/bus 4, 72, 73. **Map** p308 C8/9.

The historic Stockholm Olympic Stadium, usually known as the Stadion, was built for the 1912 Olympic Games and is also the home ground of Djurgården IF's football team. Some 83 world

The big three

Stockholm has no Man United, a name synonymous with football and football alone. Instead, three local teams – **Hammarby**, **Djurgården** and **AIK** – dominate all big sports in the city and have made Stockholm the nation's capital for football and ice hockey. If you're thinking of watching a game of football or ice hockey, you should definitely look for a derby match – they're always party-like affairs, with a great atmosphere and much prestige at stake. Football derbies are played at **Råsunda** (*see p226*), the national stadium and AIK's home ground; ice hockey derbies are played in **Globen** (*see p225*).

All three teams are among the best football sides. AIK won the championship (Allsvenskan) in 1998 and Hammarby in 2001. In ice hockey, Hammarby has won eight championships (Elitserien) overall, but the last one was 50 years ago and, despite big efforts in recent years, the team now plays in the second league. Djurgården won the ice hockey title in 1999. Hammarby and Djurgården also play in the premier handball league. In bandy, Hammarby has one of Sweden's most prominent men's teams, while AIK dominates the women's league.

All three teams were founded in the 1890s and have strong traditions. A survey of the original membership lists shows that more than half of AIK's supporters were clerks, engineers or businessmen. Only ten per cent were labourers. About half of Djurgården's members were labourers, while Hammarby's consisted only of labourers. In some ways these class divisions are still noticeable.

The teams also have clear affiliations to certain neighbourhoods, especially Hammarby, which is strongly connected to Södermalm (known as 'Bajenland', a reference to Hammarby's nickname, Bajen). In general, AIK's fans mostly come from the north-west part of Stockholm, whereas Djurgården supporters are from the wealthy northern suburbs and classy Östermalm.

If you're brought up supporting a club, you stay with it forever. And it is very rare for a player to switch from one Stockholm club to another. Although there have been riots between AIK and Djurgården fans over the years, Stockholmers are more like the 'ice-cold Swede' stereotype when it comes to discussing the latest results – keen, but keeping their voices down.

AIK

735 96 00/www.aik.se.
Founded 1891.
Colours black and yellow.
Stadiums *football* Råsunda; *ice hockey* Globen.
Famous players Börje Salming (ice hockey, Toronto Maple Leafs), Johan Mjällby (football, Celtic), Anders Limpar (football, formerly Arsenal).
Supporters' pubs before games *football* Caffrey's (Solnavägen 104, T-bana Råsunda) and Dick Turpin (Solnavägen 55, T-bana Råsunda); *ice hockey* Röda Kvarn (Arenavägen 33, T-bana Globen).
The only Swedish club that has won titles in the big four team sports: bandy, football, ice hockey and handball. These days it has strong teams in football and women's bandy.

Djurgården

Football: 545 158 00/www.dif.se.
Ice hockey: 556 108 00/www.skategate.com.
Handball: www.difhf.nu.
Founded 1891.
Colours light and dark blue.
Stadiums *football* Stockholms Stadion; *ice hockey* Globen; *handball* Eriksdalshallen.

Arts & Entertainment

records have been set here, far more than at any other stadium in the world. Architecturally, it's well preserved, but the old-fashioned facilities result in some practical difficulties. For tickets, contact Biljett Direkt or other ticket outlets.

Athletics

The biggest annual sporting event in Sweden is the track and field meet **DN Galan** (14 12 41/ www.dngalan.com), held in July at the fabulous **Stadion** (*see above*). Swedes nowadays keep their fingers crossed primarily for the high-jumper Kajsa Bergqvist and the triple-jumper Christian Olsson. The **Stockholm Marathon** (*see p179*) is also a great event.

Bandy

An exotic experience for a sports-keen foreigner would be to watch a bandy match (*see p222* **Bandying about**). Since Hammarby joined the top league in the mid 1990s, great bandy is again being played in Stockholm; its home rink is **Zinkensdamms Idrottsplats** (*see p222*). The season is from November to March.

It's only a game, lads. **AIK** battle it out with **Djurgården**.

Famous players Mats Sundin (ice hockey, Toronto Maple Leafs), Tommy Salo (ice hockey, Edmonton Oilers, formerly New York Islanders).
Supporters' pubs before games *football* Esplanad (Karlavägen 36, T-bana Stadion), Lagom (Sturegatan 19, T-bana Stadion or Östermalmstorg); *football/ice hockey* Östra Station/Järnvägsrestaurangen (Valhallavägen 77, T-bana Tekniska högskolan).
Djurgården has been strongest in ice hockey during the past decade, last winning the championship in 1999, but it now has a good football team too.

Hammarby

462 88 25/462 88 10/www.hammarby-if.se/ www.hammarbyfotboll.se.
Founded 1897.
Colours white and green.
Stadiums *football* Söderstadion; *bandy* Zinkensdamm; *ice hockey* Johanneshov; *handball* Eriksdalshallen.
Famous players Ronnie Hellström (football, formerly Kaiserslautern), Lennart 'Nacka' Skoglund (football, formerly Inter).
Supporters' pubs before games *all sports* almost anywhere you can think of in Södermalm, but the most traditional spot is undoubtedly Kvarnen (Tjärhovsgatan 4, T-bana Medborgarplatsen – *see p136*) and there is also the 'official' restaurant Hammarby Bar & Kök (corner of Ringvägen and Hornsgatan, T-bana Zinkensdamm/bus 4); *bandy* Zinkens krog (Ringvägen 14, T-bana Zinkensdamm/bus 4).
Hammarby is involved in most sports overall, including boxing, athletics, skiing, rowing and floorball – though the focus is on football, especially after the rather unexpected championship title win in 2001. Bohemian Hammarby is traditionally famous for its cavalier playing style, and its fans' preference for a beer and a chat rather than a scrap has made the club very popular.

Take a dip in **Centralbadet**, one of Stockolm's loveliest pools. *See p224.*

Football

Stockholm has three teams in Sweden's premier league Allsvenskan – Hammarby, Djurgården and AIK. Hammarby's stadium **Söderstadion**, next to Globen (*see p225*), is small (capacity 11,500), but the fans create a great atmosphere. Djurgården and AIK play their home matches at bigger arenas, at **Stockholms Stadion** and **Råsunda** respectively (for both, *see p226*), and are seldom sold out. The exception are the derbies, which are always played at Råsunda. The season runs from April to November.

Handball

Handball arouses enormous interest in Sweden because of the success of the national team – it's also an excellent spectator sport. Since Hammarby and Djurgården joined the premier league in 2002, there are now three good Stockholm teams (the third is IFK Tumba). Both city teams play in **Eriksdalshallen** in southern Söder (Ringvägen 68-70, 50 84 64 90) except when they play against each other, when they play in the much bigger **Hovet** (next to **Globen**; *see p225*). Handball is played from September to April.

Horse racing & showjumping

The **Stockholm International Horse Show** (*see p182*) in November/December offers a three-day show with everything relating to horses – dressage, four-in-hand driving and showjumping. For trotting (*trav* in Swedish; in which horses pull a small two-wheeled vehicle and driver), go to **Solvalla** in Sundbyberg (635 90 00/www.solvalla.se). It hosts the prestigious two-million-kronor race Elitloppet on the last weekend of May. For horse racing, **Täby Galopp** (756 02 30/ www.tabygalopp.se), 20 kilometres (12 miles) from Stockholm, is the premier track in Scandinavia. Racing takes place throughout the year, which allows a variety of events, from dirt racing until May to the top flat and jump races during the summer and autumn. Ring for the dates of the major races.

Ice hockey

Ishockey is the most popular sport in winter, and elite teams Djurgården and AIK draw big crowds to the national sports hall **Globen** (*see p225*). As with football matches, try to attend a derby as they're usually the most exciting games. The season is from September to April.

Tennis

The flagship event is the **Stockholm Open** (*see p182*) in October/November, although it was much more popular 15 years ago when Stefan Edberg and Mats Wilander both attracted other great players and big crowds. It is played in **Kungliga Tennishallen** (*see p225*) and rather easy to get tickets to.

Theatre & Dance

The performing arts scene is strong – though a knowledge of Swedish will help.

Theatre

It is said that Stockholm has more theatres per capita than any other European city. But quantity, as we all know, is not always the same thing as quality. When it comes to well-crafted, well-acted, well-written plays, Sweden's capital is among the elite in Europe, but if you're looking for innovative directing, risk-taking or concept-based theatre, the Stockholm scene is still learning. The heroes of Swedish theatre are, of course, Ingmar Bergman – still going strong in his 80s – and August Strindberg. Sweden's national author, Strindberg started his own theatre in the 1900s (now reborn as Strindbergs Intima Teatern). and his plays are still performed regularly in the capital (*see also p78* **Super Swedes: August Strindberg**).

Stockholm is undoubtedly the capital of Scandinavian theatre, but it lacks an international outlook. There are only two regular stages for foreign touring productions: Kilen in the **Kulturhuset** (*see p230*), which presents both local and international groups, and **Södra Teatern** (*see p213*), which puts on more concerts than plays.

Most of Stockholm's theatres are in the centre of the city, but there are also some in the suburbs. The two main institutions are **Kungliga Dramatiska Teatern** (known as Dramaten – *see p230*) and **Stockholms Stadsteatern** (*see p231*). Dramaten has a national agenda, while the Stadsteatern has a more local outlook. Still, the outcome is very similar: both tend to shape a certain safe repertoire, with large-scale classics or musicals on their main stages and more contemporary 'experimental' work on the smaller stages.

Stockholm also has a large number of fringe groups, which produce everything from really bad amateur theatre to the most interesting theatre in the city (the best are listed below). It's a jungle out there…

The musical is an immensely popular theatre form; you'll find classic English originals translated and produced in Swedish, such as *West Side Story* and *Phantom of the Opera*, as well as home-grown fare, such as *Garbo the Musical*, which opened in autumn 2002. Private producers dominate this commercial genre, but in the past five years the large institutions have (with government funding) started to compete with the private sector. Stockholm has some really good artists in the musical genre.

Sweden is also world-famous for its children's theatre. Some of the country's best artists, such as Staffan Westerberg and Suzanne Osten, make their most important work for kids. Take a look at what's happening at Stadsteatern's **Unga Klara** or check out some master puppetry at **Dockteatern Tittut** (*see p231*).

OTHER LANGUAGES

Almost all productions are in Swedish. In some theatres this doesn't really matter because the visual language is so intense. You'll find splendid physical theatre (**Teater Salieri** – *see p233*) and mime-based theatre (**Teater Tre**; 669 00 60/www.teatertre.se), a Spanish-speaking theatre (**Aliasteatern** – *see p231*), the (very conventional) **English Theatre Company** (*see p231*) and, uniquely, even a group that performs in sign language (**Tyst Teater**, part of Riksteatern; www.riksteatern.se). Touring productions in various languages also appear quite regularly.

Stockholm is also home to one of the world's most interesting nouveau cirque groups, **Circus Cirkör** (53 19 98 30/www.cirkor.nu), which has a large production centre and school in the southern suburb of Norsborg. Co-productions have included *Romeo and Juliet* (with Dramaten), *Trix* (with Orionteatern) and, most recently, *Virus 02* (with Stadsteatern). Its work is beyond language, and always spectacular.

THEATRE IN SUMMER

In summer, the performance scene transforms as many venues close and new ones open, often outdoors. From June until August, cafés (including **Lasse i Parken** – *see p145*), parks and old castles are the places to see theatre. The biggest is **Parkteatern**, which presents theatre and dance, home-grown and international, in parks all over the city, including Djurgården and Humlegården. And it's free. Bring a blanket and a picnic and get to the park in good time before the show. The magnificent 18th-century theatre at **Drottningholms Slott** is also open in summer, and well worth a visit. Come August, the city is once again bombarded with flyers and theatre posters.

You'll find European classics at **Dramaten**, such as this 2002 production of Ibsen's

INFORMATION AND TICKETS

You usually have to call or visit the box office at the venue to book a ticket. Tickets are often available within the week or even for the same day, but if it's a big hit you'll need to book weeks in advance. For the large institutions and productions, you can also book tickets via **Biljett Direkt** (077 170 70 70/www.ticnet.se; MC, V accepted) or go in person to **Box Office** (*see p175*) or the **tourist office** (*see p285*).

For up-to-date listings, check *På Stan*, the Friday supplement of *Dagens Nyheter* (www.dn.se/pastan), website www.alltom stockholm.se (both in Swedish) or the tourist office's monthly *Teater Guide* (in English).

Most theatres are closed on Mondays.

Major venues

Large commercial theatres showing Broadway-style hits, musicals and comedies (in Swedish) include **Göta Lejon** (Götgatan 55; box office 642 40 20), **Maxim Teatern** (Karlaplan 4; box office 663 40 23), **Intiman** (Odengatan 81; box office 30 12 50) and **China Teatern** (Berzelii Park 9; box office 56 63 23 50). **Cirkus** (*see p212*) on Djurgården also presents large-scale commercial shows; it's currently showing *Chess*, with music by Benny Andersson and Björn Ulvaeus (of ABBA fame).

Also check out **Södra Teatern** (*see p213*) in Södermalm; it's mainly a music venue, but occasionally there are visiting theatre shows.

Kungliga Dramatiska Teatern

Nybroplan, Östermalm (box office 667 06 80/ www.dramaten.se). T-bana Östermalmstorg or Kungsträdgården/bus 47, 55, 62, 69, 76, 91. **Box office** *Sept-July* noon-6pm Mon-Fri; noon-3pm Sat, Sun. Closed Aug. **Tickets** 120kr-280kr. **Credit** AmEx, DC, MC, V. **Map** p303 F8.

Dramaten is Sweden's number one theatre, the home of Ingmar Bergman and some of the country's best actors. Beret-clad Bergman has been the driving force behind Dramaten since the early 1960s, directing a colossal number of productions, the latest (February 2002) being Ibsen's *Ghosts*. The theatre's repertoire is conventional and European – with a Swedish touch – and you are guaranteed to find well-produced work. Look out for what goes on at its new experimental stage, Elverket (Linnégatan 69). Unsold tickets are available at a 35% discount an hour before curtain-up. The Jugendstil building is glorious. *See also p96.*

Kulturhuset

Sergels Torg, Norrmalm (box office 50 62 02 00/ www.kulturhuset.stockholm.se). T-bana T-Centralen/ bus 47, 52, 56, 59, 69. **Box office** *Winter* noon-7pm Tue-Fri; noon-6pm Sat; noon-4pm Sun. *Summer* noon-3pm Tue-Sat. **Tickets** 100kr-185kr. **Credit** AmEx, DC, MC, V. **Map** p303 G7.

The Kulturhuset is one of the most beautiful modern buildings in Stockholm, designed by architect Peter Celsing in the 1960s. This is truly a 'House of Culture': there's a gallery, cafés, a lovely roof terrace, Stockholm's best art book shop and so on. There are two stages in the building: Kilen and Hörsalen. The Kulturhuset don't produce any work but has a lot of guest performances: dance, performance art and

Ghosts, directed by Ingmar Bergman.

theatre, both local and international. If Peter Brook or Jan Fabre come to town this is where they'd play.

Oscarsteatern

Kungsgatan 63, Norrmalm (box office 20 50 00/ www.oscarsteatern.se). T-bana T-Centralen/bus 47, 53, 69. **Box office** *late July-late June* 11am-8.30pm Wed-Fri; noon-8.30pm Sat; noon-4pm Sun. Closed late June-late July. **Tickets** approx 395kr-495kr. **Credit** MC, V. **Map** p302 F6.

A large-scale private venue, managed by the queen of commercial theatre, Vicky von der Lancken. The place to see comedies or musicals, West End-style. *Garbo the Musical* opened here in autumn 2002.

Stockholms Stadsteatern

Sergels Torg, Norrmalm (box office 50 62 02 00/ www.stadsteatern.stockholm.se). T-bana T-Centralen/ bus 47, 52, 56, 59. **Box office** *Winter* noon-7pm Tue-Fri; noon-6pm Sat; noon-4pm Sun. *Summer* noon-3pm Tue-Sat. **Tickets** 45kr-210kr. **Credit** AmEx, DC, MC, V. **Map** p303 G7.

With six stages and a summer programme with Parkteatern, this is one of Scandinavia's largest theatrical institutions. It shares an entrance with the Kulturhuset. It has a pretty lame standard repertoire, but makes well-crafted theatre. Keep an eye on what is playing at Backstage/Lilla Scenen and Unga Klara – these are the stages for experimental work aimed at attracting a new theatre audience. In the past decade Stadsteatern has made a name for itself by inviting such prominent directors as Frank Castorf and Robert Wilson to put on massive shows. The (free) Parkteatern productions are very often high quality, and include international groups, both theatre and dance.

Smaller venues & groups

Aliasteatern

Hälsingegatan 3, Vasastaden (box office 32 82 90/ www.aliasteatern.se). T-bana St Eriksplan/bus 3, 4, 47. **Box office** *Aug-June* noon-6pm Mon-Fri. Closed July. **Tickets** 60kr-250kr. **No credit cards**. **Map** p306 D4.

The home of Teatro Popular Latinoamericano, Stockholm's only Spanish-speaking theatre company, which has been producing work since the 1970s. Lately, it has done some productions in Swedish.

Dockteatern Tittut

Lundagatan 33, Södermalm (box office 720 75 99/ www.dockteatern-tittut.com). T-bana Zinkensdamm/ bus 4, 66. **Box office** *Sept-May* 9am-5pm Mon-Fri. Closed June-Aug. **Tickets** 60kr. **No credit cards**. **Map** p301 K4.

This puppet theatre group in Söder has performed high-quality theatre for children (aged from two) for the past 25 years. Kids love it, and adults have a ball too. Performances are held at 9.30am and 10.45am weekdays, and at 1pm and 3pm at the weekend.

The English Theatre Company

Information 660 11 59/www.englishtheatre.se. **Tickets** 220kr-300kr. **Credit** varies.

Stockholm's only English-speaking theatre company makes that fact its livelihood. It presents a conventional repertoire, ranging from the plays of Oscar Wilde to an annual production of *A Christmas Carol*. Performances are usually at Vasan (aka Vasateatern, Vasagatan 19-21; box office 10 23 63). Check the website (in English, of course) for the current schedule.

Fylkingen

Münchenbryggeriet, Torkel Knutsonsgatan 2, Södermalm (84 54 43/www.fylkingen.se). T-bana Mariatorget/bus 4, 43, 55, 66. **Box office** 10am-5pm Mon-Fri. **Tickets** free-80kr. **No credit cards**. **Map** p302 K6.

Founded way back in 1933, Fylkingen is the place to go if you're into new music (*see p217*) and intermedia art. It's always been committed to new and experimental forms: happenings, musical-theatre and text-sound compositions were prominent in the 1960s; in recent years, more and more performance art and dance have been presented. The venue (the one-time Munich Brewery) is hard to find, but in the world of performance and art music, this is mecca.

Intercult

Box office 644 10 23/www.intercult.se. **Box office** 9am-5pm Mon-Fri. **Tickets** 100kr-220kr. **Credit** varies, depending on where performance is held.

Intercult is more a production outfit than a theatre, and one of Stockholm's few internationally focused performing arts producers. Set up in 1992, it spotlights the Balkans and the Baltic countries, arranging large-scale co-productions and gatherings on cultural policy, as well as guest performances. It's a very political forum, and very high quality.

Judiska Teatern

Djurgårdsbrunnsvägen 59, Gärdet (box office 667 90 13/information 660 02 71/www.judiska teatern.org). Bus 69. **Box office** *Oct-May* 6-7pm Wed, Thur; 2-7pm Fri; 5-6pm Sat; 3-4pm Sun. Closed June-Sept. **Tickets** 90kr-180kr. **Credit** DC, MC, V.

The Jewish Theatre is not as focused on religion as the name might suggest. Actors perform finely crafted poetic theatre – mainly new work – in a beautiful old building with a super-modern interior. Well worth a visit.

Marionetteatern

Brunnsgatan 6-8, Norrmalm (box office 411 71 12/ www.marionetteatern.com). T-bana Östermalmstorg/ bus 1, 46, 55, 56. **Box office** *Sept-Midsummer* usually 9am-5pm Mon-Fri. Closed Midsummer-Aug. **Tickets** 130kr; 65kr children. **No credit cards**. **Map** p303 E7.

Puppet master Michael Meschke's lifelong devotion to puppetry gave birth to this legendary fringe group in the 1950s. Today, a new generation has taken over, but the Marionette Theatre still produces high-quality work (mainly for kids). The adjacent puppet museum contains more than 4,000 puppets from all over the world.

Moment

Gubbängstorget 117, Gubbängen (box office 50 85 01 28/www.moment.org.se). T-bana Gubbängen. **Tickets** 160kr. **No credit cards**.

This fairly new constellation of young artists has created their own culture house in an old cinema called City, about 20 minutes from the centre of Stockholm in the suburb of Gubbängen. They produce some of the most interesting contemporary work in town – keep an eye out for young director Andreas Boonstra. You can book tickets via an answerphone. The centre also presents films and concerts, and has a café.

In Maria Blom's Head at the **Stadsteatern**. *See p231*.

Arts & Entertainment

Orionteatern

Katarina Bangata 77, Södermalm (information 640 29 70/box office 643 88 80/643 37 16/ www.orionteatern.se). T-bana Skanstull/bus 3, 59, 76. **Box office** *Sept-Midsummer* noon-5pm Tue-Sun (later on performance days). Closed Midsummer-Aug. **Tickets** 100kr-230kr. **Credit** DC, MC, V. **Map** p311 N10.

The Orion Theatre, Stockholm's largest avant-garde theatre company, was formed in 1983, and is one of Sweden's most interesting and innovative groups. It has collaborated with the likes of the Peking Opera from Shanghai, Theatre de Complicité from London and Le Cirque Invisible from Paris. The building, once a huge factory, makes for an unusual theatre space. A smaller stage called Vinden has recently opened, where young groups perform.

Stockholms Improvisationsteater

Sigtunagatan 12, Vasastaden (box office 30 62 42/ www.impro.a.se). T-bana Odenplan or St Eriksplan/ bus 3, 4, 42, 47, 507. **Box office** *mid Jan-June, Aug-mid Dec* 9am-5pm Mon-Fri. Closed July, mid Dec-mid Jan. **Tickets** 60kr-160kr. **No credit cards. Map** p306 D4.

To stand on a stage trying to give the impression that you are someone other than you really are is difficult enough. But try standing there without a clue about what you will say next. This group has been working with improvised theatre since the 1980s, and they're really good at it – but you'll need to speak Swedish to get the most out of it. Performances are at 7pm Thursdays, and 7pm and 9.30pm on Fridays and Saturdays.

Teater Brunnsgatan Fyra

Brunnsgatan 4, Norrmalm (box office 10 70 50). T-bana Östermalmstorg/bus 1, 46, 56. **Box office** *Aug-June* 5-7pm Tue-Sat; 2-4pm Sun. Closed July. **Tickets** 150kr-200kr. **No credit cards. Map** p303 E7.

One of Sweden's best, and best-known, poets and dramatists, Kristina Lugn, took over this small theatre when its creator, Allan Edwall, died. Its modest appearance is not to be mistaken for modest work; some of Sweden's most prominent actors and dramatists can be found down in this stone cellar, among them Staffan Göthe, Lena Endre and Staffan Westerberg. You will need to understand Swedish.

Teater Galeasen

Slupskjulsvägen 32, Skeppsholmen (box office 611 00 30/611 09 20/www.galeasen.se). Bus 65. **Box office** *Mid Jan-June, Aug-mid Dec* 10am-4pm (10am-8pm on performance nights). Closed July, mid Dec-mid Jan. **Tickets** 150kr-200kr. **Credit** V. **Map** p304 H9.

In the 1980s and early '90s this was the hip spot for theatre-goers. Gallons of red wine were consumed in the name of art. Nowadays, things have changed and members of that generation are household names and work in film or at Stadsteatern or Dramaten. But the work at Galeasen – new Swedish and foreign drama – is still high-quality stuff.

Teater Giljotin

Torsgatan 41, Vasastaden (box office 30 30 00/ www.teatergiljotin.com). T-bana St Eriksplan/bus 3, 4, 72, 77, 507. **Box office** 9am-5pm Mon-Fri. **Tickets** 100kr-200kr. **No credit cards. Map** p306 D3.

Led by director Kia Berglund and musician Richard Borggård, this outfit deserves its reputation as one of Sweden's finest. It produces very well-directed – and often new – Nordic plays.

Teater Salieri

Box office 644 35 58/www.salieri.nu.

Since the late 1990s, Teater Salieri has been one of the most talked-about new groups. Led by director/ dramatist Kajsa Isakson, the company presents, if not the best, then certainly the most breathtaking political theatre in town. It doesn't have a venue of its own, but usually performs at KGB, at Södra Teatern (*see p213*). Phone or check the website for more information.

Teater Scenario

Odengatan 62, Vasastaden (box office 643 71 82/ www.teaterscenario.com). T-bana Odenplan/bus 4, 40, 42, 46, 53, 72. **Box office** *mid Aug-mid June* 9am-4pm Mon-Fri or via answerphone. Closed mid June-mid Aug. **Tickets** 80kr-150kr. **No credit cards. Map** p307 D5.

A small theatre company featuring a new generation of exciting dramatists, notably Daniela Kullman and Dennis Magnusson. In Swedish.

Teater Tribunalen

Hornsgatan 92, Södermalm (box office 84 94 33/ http://w1.872.telia.com/~u87202722). T-bana Zinkensdamm or Mariatorget/bus 4, 43, 55, 66. **Box office** *Early Aug-May* 2hrs before performance. Closed June-early Aug. **Tickets** 100kr-160kr. **No credit cards. Map** p310 K5.

Angry, political, radical theatre with an ideological inheritance from the 1970s, and loved by the critics. Brecht and Fassbinder are the house gods. Check the website for the current schedule.

Dance

When it comes to dance the tables are turned. The local dance scene is not especially vibrant and the number of venues is limited – but the international outlook is superb.

Stockholm has a prestigious dance history: it's home to one of the oldest ballet companies in the world, the **Kungliga Balett** (Royal Ballet), founded in 1733. In terms of modern dance, Sweden boasts world-class dancers and some really good choreographers, but only one with a worldwide reputation: Mats Ek. Artistic leader of the Cullberg Ballet for many years, he is now freelance and creates large-scale shows all over the world. Dance-theatre is a growing scene. Look out for Birgitta Egerbladh, who creates humorous pieces using both actors and

The **Kungliga Operan**, home of the Swedish Royal Ballet.

dancers; Philippe Blanchard (and his company Adekwhat), who produces very good, very aggressive, performance-based work; young star choreographer Jens Östberg, who turns more and more towards theatre; and Clara Diesen, who choreographs moods in a similar style to acclaimed English company DV8. Mats Ek often does dance-theatre pieces around town; if one is on, don't miss it.

Other choreographers to watch for are veteran Margaretha Åsberg, one of the modernist greats in Swedish dance history; Christina Caprioli, the queen of postmodern dance; and Kenneth Kvarnström, one of the many Finland-Swedes that has enlightened the Swedish dance scene. Örjan Andersson also provides hope for a bright future, along with new talents Anna Koch and Helena Franzén.

Foreign (and some Swedish) companies appear at **Dansens Hus** (*see below*), the city's foremost dance venue. The smaller **Moderna Dansteatern** (*see below*) mostly presents Swedish work but occasionally has guest performances. Almost none of the Stockholm dance companies has a theatre of their own, so they perform wherever they can. For dance listings, check the daily papers or magazine *Danstidningen* (www.danstidningen.se).

Venues

Dance performances are also held at the **Kulturhuset** (*see p230*) and **Fylkingen** (*see p232*). In summer, you can see ballet in the glorious surroundings of the 18th-century court theatres **Confidencen** (*see p178*) and **Drottningholms Slottsteater** (*see p180*).

Dansens Hus

12-14 Barnhusgatan, Norrmalm (box office 50 89 90 90/www.dansenshus.se). T-bana Hötorget or T-Centralen/bus 1, 47, 53, 69. **Box office** *Mid Aug-Midsummer* noon-6pm Mon-Sat (mid-end Aug noon-6pm Mon-Fri). Closed Midsummer-mid Aug. **Tickets** 160kr-270kr. **Credit** AmEx, DC, MC, V. **Map** p303 E6.

The 'House of Dance' has kept Swedish audiences up to date when it comes to new choreography and dance. This is where the Cullberg Ballet performs when it's in town, along with greats such as Pina Bausch or Anne Teresa de Keersmaeker's company Rosas. There is one large auditorium and the smaller Blå Lådan ('Blue Box').

Kungliga Operan

Gustav Adolfs Torg, Norrmalm (box office 24 82 40/ www.operan.se). T-bana Kungsträdgården/bus 43, 46, 55, 59, 62, 76. **Box office** *Sept-May* noon-6pm Mon-Fri; noon-3pm Sat. Closed June-Aug. **Tickets** 40kr-460kr. **Credit** AmEx, DC, MC, V. **Map** p303 G7.

The Royal Opera is also the home of Sweden's finest classical company, the Royal Ballet. The repertoire tends to the conventional and classical, with some modern work. The dancers are superb. And the interior is completely over the top, especially the Golden Room. Operan also runs Vasan, which it rents out to guest productions. *See also p217.*

Moderna Dansteatern

Slupskjulsvägen 32, Skeppsholmen (box office 611 32 33/www.mdt.a.se). Bus 65. **Tickets** 150kr. **No credit cards. Map** p304 H9.

The small Modern Dance Theatre is the home for all Sweden's freelance choreographers. Under the direction of Margaretha Åsberg, it has single-handedly provided a space for postmodern dance. More recently, performance art has also found a refuge here. It may be closed from May to August.

Trips Out of Town

Introduction **238**
Day Trips **239**
Central Archipelago **251**
Southern Archipelago **259**
Northern Archipelago **265**
The Baltic & Beyond **267**

Features

Vikings ahoy 240
Palaces around Lake Mälaren 246
Rowing madams 253
Free for all 257
Strindberg's isle 262
Ferry cross the Baltic 268
The big chill 270

Maps

Trips Out of Town 236

Trips Out of Town

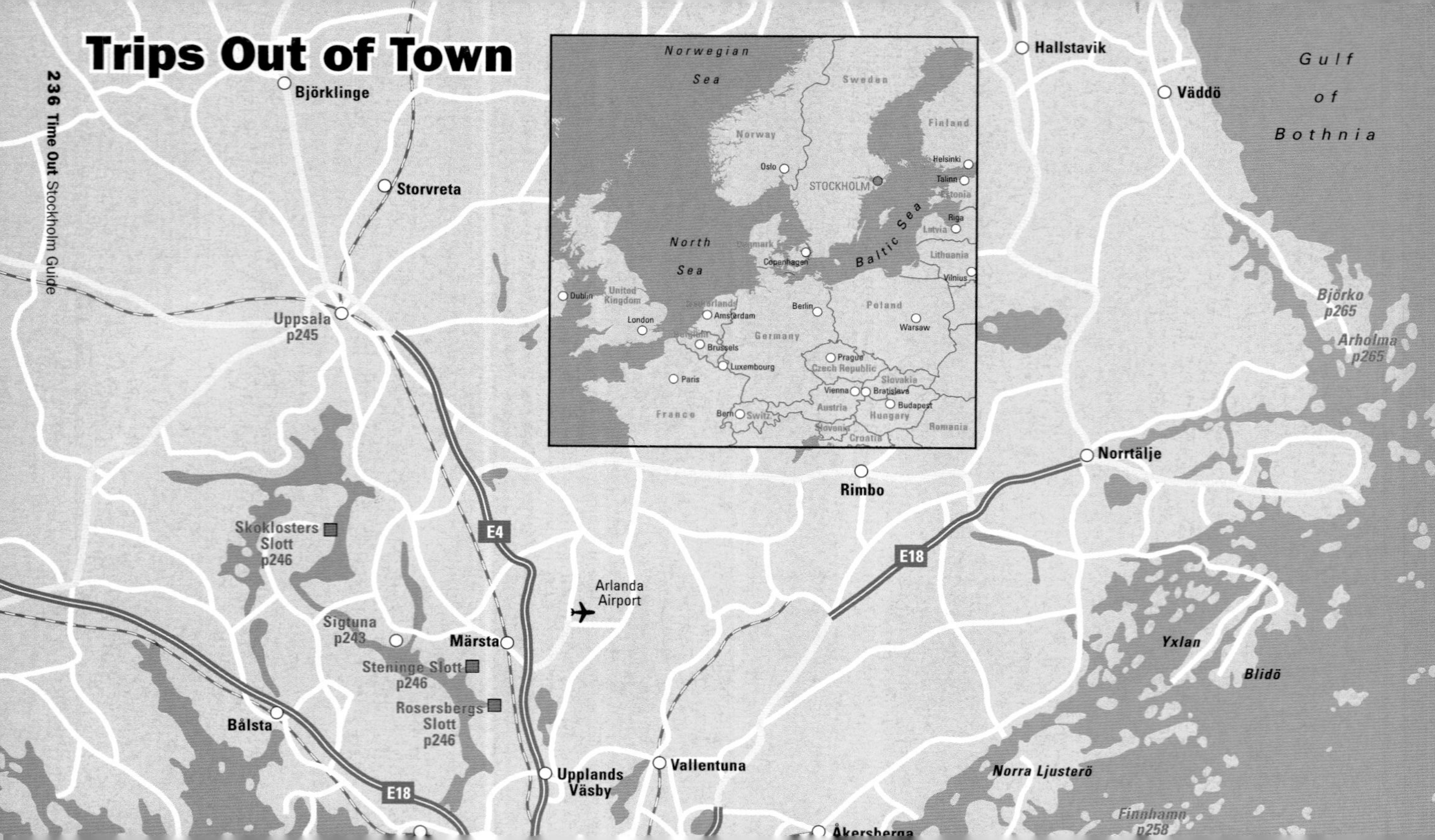

Selaön
Lake Mälaren
Adelsön
Färingsö
Bromma Airport
Ulriksdals Slott p246
Vaxholm p253
Gällnö p255
Sollenkroka
Vindö
Lidingö
Fjäderholmarna p251
Birka p240
Drottningholms Slott p239
Munsön
STOCKHOLM
Boo
Gustavsberg
Runmarö
Sandhamn p259
Ekerö
Mariefred p242
Tyresö
E4/E20
E20
Tumba
Södertälje
Nämdö p260
Handen
Smådalarö
Dalarö
Kymmendö p262
Västerhaninge
Järna
Årsta Havsbad
Ornö
BALTIC SEA
Gnesta
Fjärdlång p261
E4
Muskö
Tullgarns Slott p246
Vagnhärad
Utö p263
Ränö
Ålö
Nynäshamn
Nåttarö
Järflotta
0
20 km
0
10 miles
© Copyright Time Out Group 2003

Introduction

Water, water everywhere – and some ornate palaces and historic towns.

Lovely though Stockholm is, it would be a great shame to not to head outside the city at all during your visit. There are some fantastic places within easy reach, many of them perfect for day trips. The region's rich history means the area to the west is stuffed with castles and palaces, the grandest being the royal family's home of **Drottningholm** – an hour's trip by boat from the city centre. **Mariefred** boasts Gustav Vasa's fortress of **Grippsholms Slott**, while other palaces occupy scenic positions along the shores of Lake Mälaren. North of Stockholm lies the former Viking stronghold of **Sigtuna**, one of the oldest towns in Sweden, and beyond that is charming and historic **Uppsala**, dominated by its university and grand cathedral. You can also explore Viking remains on the island of **Birka**. All these places are featured in the **Day Trips** chapter.

A few miles east of the capital begins the amazing Stockholm archipelago, comprising a staggering 24,000 islands covering about 140 kilometres (90 miles) from north to south. Only 150 of the islands are inhabited, but many Stockholmers have summer houses in the archipelago and visitor numbers swell in the warmer months, especially July. The landscape varies tremendously, from the more populated, thickly wooded inner archipelago to the bare, flat rocks of the central and outer islands. We've highlighted certain islands within three sections: the **Central Archipelago** (nearest to Stockholm, and best for day trips or if you have only a spare day or so), and the remoter and less populous **Southern Archipelago** and **Northern Archipelago**.

The easiest way to get around is by ferry, of course – we've listed the main companies below. If you want to visit a lot of islands, Waxholmsbolaget's 16-day **Batluffarkortet** (Archipelago Pass; 385kr) allows unlimited travel on its ferries (and travel for 20kr per trip on Strömma Kanalbolaget and Cinderella Båtarna boats). It's also available from the Stockholm tourist office (*see p285*). The tourist office produces a useful free brochure to accommodation in the archipelago, covering hotels, B&Bs, youth hostels and camping.

The archipelago is best visited from mid June to mid August – during the rest of the year many hotels, restaurants and other facilities are closed, ferries are few and far between, and some islands pretty much shut down to visitors. The archipelago often gets more sunshine than the mainland, but it's still a good idea to pack a raincoat and sweater. Sunscreen, mosquito repellent and tweezers (in case of ticks) are also recommended. Shops and restaurants can be a rarity on the smaller and remoter places, so you might also need to take your own food.

Skärgårdsstiftelsen (Archipelago Foundation; 440 56 00/www.skargardsstiftelsen.se), set up in 1959 to preserve the archipelago's landscape and wildlife and to encourage public use, owns about 15 per cent of the islands' land. Its website offers plenty of info; other useful sites are www.dess.se, www.archipelago.nu and www.skargardshandlarna.com (Swedish only).

Further into the Baltic lie other attractions, notably the large island of **Gotland** to the south, once a prosperous Viking settlement and now a hugely popular summer resort. On the other side of the Baltic Sea are Finland and the Baltic states; if you've got time, you can take a weekend ferry to **Helsinki** or **Tallinn**.

Remember that many destinations have their high season during the sweet but short Swedish summer, and opening hours may be limited at other times. We've given transport and eating options for all destinations, and accommodation choices for places where you might want to spend the night. Room prices quoted are for a standard double room, unless otherwise stated.

Ferry companies

Cinderella Båtarna

58 71 40 50/www.cinderellabatarna.com. **Leave from** Strandvägen, Ostermalm. **Map** p304 G9.
Cinderella's three boats go to many of the most popular archipelago islands.

Strömma Kanalbolaget

58 71 40 00/ www.strommakanalbolaget.com. **Leave from** Strandvägen, Ostermalm. **Map** p304 G9.
Run by the same company as Cinderella Båtarna, its ferries serve the key islands in the archipelago and many destinations around Lake Mälaren.

Waxholmsbolaget

679 58 30/457 00 01/www.waxholmsbolaget.se. **Leave from** Opposite the Grand Hôtel, Strömkajen, Norrmalm. **Map** p303 G-H8.
In operation since 1896, Waxholmsbolaget services the whole archipelago. It has three classic steamers, eight new fast ferries and seven year-round vessels.

Day Trips

Explore historic towns, Viking ruins, castles and palaces galore.

Drottningholm

The palatial estate of Drottningholm lies ten kilometres (six miles) west of downtown Stockholm on the sparsely populated island of Lovön. Drottningholm Palace has been the royal family's permanent residence since 1981, and receives more than 100,000 visitors a year. Trees planted 300 years ago frame the statues and fountains of the beautiful French formal garden behind the palace. A functioning theatre from 1766 stands next door, and the exotic Kina Slott is hidden at the park's western end. The well-preserved grounds and excellent examples of 17th- and 18th-century architecture led UNESCO to add the entire site to its World Heritage List in 1991.

Built at the height of Sweden's power in Europe during the mid 17th century, **Drottningholms Slott** was designed to impress – and it still does. The wealthy dowager Queen Hedvig Eleonora financed the initial construction of the palace, which lasted from 1662 to 1686. Even before her time, Drottningholm had been associated with royal women – the name means 'Queen's Island'. The royal architect Nicodemus Tessin the Elder modelled the waterfront residence on the Palace of Versailles. Two wings topped with octagonal domes extend north and south from the grand apartments of the central building. Highlights include the monumental staircase, Ehrenstrahl drawing room and Hedvig Eleonora's state bedchamber. After Tessin's death in 1681, his son, Tessin the Younger, took over the project; Karl XI's gallery dates from this period.

The palace's second period of growth began after Lovisa Ulrika married Crown Prince Adolf Fredrik in 1744. She added a second storey above the wings and decorated its rooms with rococo furnishings and paintings. Her extensive library of books and natural specimens was visited by the famous botanist Carl von Linné (also known as Linnaeus) and other leading scientists of the 18th century.

Since Lovisa Ulrika was also a great lover of the arts, she commissioned architect Carl Fredrik Adelcrantz to build **Drottningholms Slottsteater**. The theatre still has its original stage sets and hand-driven machinery, and is the world's oldest working theatre – concerts, ballets and operas are held in the summer (for details, *see p180*). Simple sound effects include a wooden box filled with stones used to create thunder. The tour of the theatre also includes the **Teatermuseum**, located in the same courtyard as the theatre itself. It focuses on 18th-century theatre, displaying drawings, paintings, costumes and stage models. In the gift shop diagonally across from here you can buy, among other things, books, miniature models of Swedish chairs, and apple juice from Drottningholm's orchards.

The royal family currently lives in the palace's southern wing, although Princess Victoria now has a separate house on the estate. Armed soldiers dressed in camouflage ensure that their residences stay closed to the public, and at times certain sections of the garden may be taped off. The family attends Christmas mass in the Palace Chapel, housed beneath the dome of the northern wing.

Behind the palace is the long rectangular French baroque garden, laid out in five stages separated by lateral paths. Its bronze statues are copies of early 17th-century works by the Dutch sculptor Adriaen de Vries. To protect

Drottningholms Slott: home to the royals.

Vikings ahoy

If you liked the Viking collection at the **Historiska Museet** (*see p96*), you might want to visit the excavated ruins of the real Viking city from where many of the artefacts originated. Located 25 kilometres (15 miles) west of central Stockholm on the green island of Björkö, **Birka** was founded around AD 700, making it one of Sweden's oldest settlements. Archaeological evidence from Birka has revealed that the Vikings were not the barbarians of popular culture, but rather had a strong hierarchical class system and a wealth of carefully crafted products. A king who lived on the nearby island of Adelsön governed the city's roughly 1,000 permanent inhabitants, mainly farmers, craftsmen and professional soldiers. Arabic coins and east European pearls found among the ruins testify to the international importance of Birka's harbour and the nautical skills of the Vikings. For unknown reasons – perhaps due to the spread of Christianity or the development of nearby **Sigtuna** (*see p243*) – the Vikings abandoned Birka around 960.

Amateur archaeologists and treasure hunters had been poking at the island's ruins since the early 1600s, but it wasn't until the 1870s that a concerted effort was made to catalogue the finds and protect the site. The island is now partly owned by the state and inhabited by about a dozen people, mostly farmers and employees of Sweden's cultural heritage board.

Stepping off from the steamboats that bring visitors to Birka in summer, you'll see little evidence of the former city aside from the fields dotted with hundreds of burial mounds. But the **Birkamuseet** (*pictured*; 56 05 14 45/ www.raa.se/birka; open daily May-3rd wk Sept), located next to the dock on the western shore, contains magnificent finds from the excavations plus detailed models of how the city once looked, including townspeople practising their crafts and ships anchored at the old harbour. Outside the museum you can watch people in Viking costumes perform traditional handicrafts – and try them out yourself. On the guided tour you get to visit archaeologists at work, the recently excavated field of Svarta Jorden (Black Earth) and the ruins of an old fort on a hill. After the tour, you can explore the grave fields more thoroughly on your own, or hike through the forested areas on the south of the island.

The best way to get to Birka is by steamboat with **Strömma Kanalbolaget** (58 71 40 00/www.strommakanalbolaget.com, 10am daily May-3rd wk Sept, 225kr), which leaves from Stadshubron near the Stadshuset. Or take the 1880 steamer *Edjern* with **Museiföreningen Ångfartyget Ejdern** (55 01 88 99/http://ejdern.start.at, 180kr), which runs every few days from mid May to mid September from Borgmästaruddena near Central Station. The price with both companies includes the cost of the museum and guided tour. Unless you bring a picnic lunch, the only food available on Birka is at **Restaurang Särimner** near the museum (56 05 10 31, 8am-6.30pm Midsummer-Aug, noon-3.30pm May-Midsummer, Sept, main courses 65kr-130kr). It serves lunch specials, sandwiches and meat pies.

If Birka piques your curiosity, two very entertaining novels about the Vikings are Michael Crichton's *Eaters of the Dead* (based on an actual travel log from 922) and Frans G Bengtsson's Swedish classic *The Long Ships*.

the original statues from weathering they were moved across the street to the **Museum de Vries**, which opened in 2001. The statues – spoils of war from Denmark's Fredriksborg Palace and Prague – are arranged in the former royal stable in the same pattern as those in the garden. Ring ahead to check that the museum is open in 2003/4, as lack of visitor interest may reduce the number of tours.

North of the baroque garden lies the lake-studded extensive **English Park**, so named because it followed the English style of naturalistic landscaping and planting that was fashionable at the time. It was added by Gustav III after he took over the palace in 1777. He also thoughtfully planned a memorial for himself – never finished – on one of the islands in the lakes north of the theatre.

The **Kina Slott** stands near the end of the garden down a tree-lined avenue. As a surprise for Lovisa Ulrika's 33rd birthday in 1753, Adolf Fredrik had a Chinese-inspired wooden pavilion built here. Ten years later it was replaced by this rococo pleasure palace, also designed by CF Adelcrantz. Little was known about China at the time and the country was considered an exotic paradise. Wall paintings inside the pavilion's two curved wings show Chinese people playing cards and relaxing under trees. The royal family used to come here during the day to escape work, to read books and take naps. The pavilion has recently been repainted in its original red colour with yellow trim and light-green roofs; guided tours are available.

Adelcrantz also designed the nearby **Vakttältet**, a Turkish tent-style structure painted with blue and white stripes. Built as a barracks for Gustav III's dragoons, it's now a musty-smelling exhibit that shows the guards' kitchen and waiting area. Across from the Kina Slott lies the small **Confidencen** pavilion. When the family wanted to dine in private, they sat in the top room and servants hoisted up a fully set table from below. Down the road behind the palace is the former studio of the 20th-century Swedish artist **Evert Lundqvist** (402 62 70, open for guided tours in Swedish 4pm Sun May-Aug, 50kr).

The rest of Lovön is dotted with private homes and old red barns. The waterworks on its western shore produces 40 per cent of Stockholm's drinking water, direct from Lake Mälaren. Kärsön, the island across the bridge from Drottningholm, has an 18-hole Frisbee golf course and a swimming area on its northern tip.

Drottningholms Slott

Slott 402 62 80/www.royalcourt.se. Slottsteater 55 69 31 00/www.drottningholmsslottsteater.dtm.se. Museum de Vries 402 62 80/81. Kina Slott & Vakttältet 402 62 70. **Open** *Slott May-Aug* 10am-4.30pm daily. *Sept* noon-3.30pm daily. *Oct-Apr* noon-1.30pm Sat, Sun. *Slottsteater* (guided tours only) *May* noon-4.30pm daily. *June-Aug* 11am-4.30pm daily. *Sept* 1-3.30pm daily. Closed Oct-Apr. *Museum de Vries* (guided tours only) *May-Aug* 2pm daily. *Sept* 3pm Sun. Closed Oct-Apr. *Kina Slott May-Aug* 11am-4.30pm daily. *Sept* noon-3.30pm daily. Closed Oct-Apr. *Vakttältet Mid June-mid Aug* noon-4pm daily. Closed mid Aug-mid June. **Admission** *Slott* 60kr; *Slott & Kina Slott* 90kr; *Slott, Kina Slott & Museum de Vries* 130kr. *Slottsteater* 60kr. *Museum de Vries* 50kr. *Kina Slott* 50kr. *Vakttältet* free. **Free with SC. Map** p237.
There are regular guided tours around the palace in Swedish, English and German.

Where to eat

First-class restaurant **Drottningholms Wärdshus** (759 03 08/www.drottningholms wardshus.se, main courses 165kr-295kr, closed dinner Mon, closed Jan) occupies an 1850 building across the street from the estate, near the jetty. Enjoy dishes such as pepper-marinated tenderloin of beef, stuffed corn-fed chicken and steamed char with vermouth sauce; there's also a bar, conference facilities and tables in the garden in summer.

Drottningholmspaviljongen (759 04 25/ www.drottningholmspaviljongen.com, main courses 85kr-185kr, closed Mon-Fri Nov, Dec, closed Jan) offers sandwiches as well as steak, wiener schnitzel and grilled fish. Located in an early 20th-century villa near the palace's waterfront, it has outdoor seating in the summer and children's specials.

Drottningholm's only café, **Kina Slotts Servering** (759 03 96, closed dinner, closed Mon-Fri Apr, Oct, closed Nov-Mar), is located in an old building with an open fireplace and slanted roof near the Kina Slott. It sells fresh waffles, assorted pastries and sandwiches.

Prices at the restaurants and café are on the high side, so taking a picnic to eat on the lawns is a good option.

Getting there

By metro/bus

T-bana to Brommaplan, then bus 177, 178, 301-323.

By boat

The nicest way to get to Drottningholm by far. Between May and early Sept you can travel by steamboat from Stadshusbron near the Stadshuset on Kungsholmen (70kr single, 100kr return); the journey takes 1hr. The most frequent service is between early June and mid Aug, when there are also guided boat tours in English (180kr) at 11am and 1pm. Contact Strömma Kanalbolaget (58 71 40 00/www.strommakanalbolaget.com) for more information and prices.

The magnificent 16th-century fortress of **Gripsholms Slott**, in Mariefred.

By car

From Kungsholmen take Drottningholmsvägen west towards Vällingby, then at Brommaplan follow the signs to Drottningholm. It's about a 15mins drive.

By bicycle

There is a well-signposted bike path from outside the Stadshuset in Stockholm to Drottningholm; it takes about 50mins at a normal pace.

Mariefred

The small town of Mariefred, with about 5,000 inhabitants, lies 70 kilometres (43 miles) south-west of Stockholm on the shores of beautiful Lake Mälaren. You can travel here in summer by bus, train and steamboat to visit the town's main sight, **Gripsholms Slott** (*see p243*), originally built as a fortress for King Gustav Vasa in 1537. Arriving by boat, you get a fine view of the magnificent castle. The town itself is charming, with two-storey buildings painted white, yellow and red, and laid out according to a late 17th-century streetplan.

Gripsholms Slott lies a couple of hundred metres south of the town on an island just big enough for its four round brick towers and two courtyards. It's named after Lord High Chancellor Bo Jonsson Grip, who built the first fortress on the site in the 1380s. King Erik XIV, Gustav Vasa's son, used the castle to imprison his brother Johan and his wife for six years. In the 17th century, Queen Hedvig Eleonora was sent here after her husband's death to prevent her from meddling in the country's politics. Gustav III finally took some pride in the castle in the late 18th century and built a theatre in one of the towers; today it's one of the best-preserved theatres from that time in Europe. The castle's three floors are full of furniture and artwork from more than 400 years. The Swedish national collection of portraits is also displayed here, including famous paintings of Gustav Vasa and the present royal family.

The **tourist office** (*see p243*) in the Rådhuset on the town square provides a free leaflet describing a short walking tour of the town's historic buildings. **Mariefreds Kyrka**, a white church with a tall black spire not far from the tourist office, was built in 1624 and restored in 1697 after a fire. At **Callanderska Gården** (Klostergatan 5, open 1-4pm daily in summer), next to the church, a turn-of-the-20th-century house has been preserved with its original furnishings and décor. The ground-floor shops along pedestrianised **Storgatan**, which leads down to the water, sell fabrics, glassware, linen clothes and local handicrafts.

Other sights include **Grafikens Hus** (0159 231 60/www.grafikenshus.se, closed Mon, admission 50kr), which lies down the road from the castle in a red and white building, the former Royal Barn. Drawings, prints and paintings for sale are exhibited, and you might also see artists using its printmaking workshop. The artwork is high quality but not worth the admission fee, unless you're planning on buying something. Behind the building, on a hill overgrown with trees, stand the stone ruins of **Kärnbo Kyrka** – Mariefred's first church, from the 1100s. Look for the Viking rune stone built into one of the walls near the entrance.

Rides on a 100-year-old steam train are offered by **Museijärnvägen** (0159 210 06/ www.oslj.nu), situated in the yellow railway station near the main road into town. You can also use this train to arrive in Mariefred from Läggesta station.

Gripsholms Slott

Mariefred (0159 101 94/www.royalcourt.se). **Open** *Mid May-mid Sept* 10am-4pm daily. *Mid Sept-mid Dec, Jan-mid May* noon-3pm Sat, Sun. Closed 21 Dec-1 Jan. **Admission** 60kr; 30kr concessions; free under-7s; tour 10kr. **Free with SC. Credit** AmEx, MC, V. **Map** p237.
Tours in English are at 1pm during the summer.

Where to eat

The formal dining room and veranda of **Gripsholms Värdshus & Hotel** (Kyrkogatan 1, 0159 347 50/www.gripsholms-vardshus.se, main courses 250kr, closed 1st wk Jan) serves fresh fish, grilled steaks and wonderful concoctions of beetroot and goat's cheese. **Strandrestaurangen** (0159 133 88/ www.strandrestaurangen.com, mains 78kr-150kr, closed dinner Mon-Fri, Sun Sept-May, closed 2wks over Christmas), located at the end of Storgatan, serves traditional Swedish fare in an old house overlooking the water. **Konditori Fredman** (0159 121 10), the café and bakery across from the Rådhuset, has lunch specials of meat pies, pizza and other lighter dishes. If you come in summer, there are also plenty of kiosks selling hot dogs, waffles and ice-cream.

If you're driving from Stockholm, you may want to stop off at **Taxinge Slottscafé** (0159 701 14/www.taxingeslott.se, closed Christmas and New Year). This castle café located a few kilometres east of Mariefred claims to have northern Europe's largest dessert table, with 50 kinds of cakes, cookies and pastries – hence its nickname, Kakslottet ('cookie castle').

Where to stay

You can see Mariefred in a day but, if you want to stay overnight, the nicest accommodation is at Sweden's oldest inn, **Gripsholms Värdshus & Hotel** (*see above*; rates 1,760kr-2,190kr). Established in 1609, it's one block south of the town square. The foundations of Mariefred's 15th-century monastery were discovered during renovations of the inn in 1987; timbers and other artefacts pulled from the excavation site were used to decorate the beautiful two-storey hotel. Many rooms have views of the water and castle.

Less expensive and only a few blocks from town, the **Röda Korsets Idé- och Utbildningscenter** (Red Cross Education Center, 0159 367 00/www.redcross.se/gripsholm) has a hotel (rates 800kr) on its lovely campus that is open year-round and a summer youth hostel in the student dorms (190kr-235kr per bed, closed mid Aug-mid June).

In addition to camping spots (110kr), **Mariefreds Camping** (0159 132 50, closed mid Sept-mid Apr), located a kilometre east of town near the water, also has cottages and rooms (250kr with shared bathroom) for rent, as well as a lovely swimming area.

Tourist information

Mariefred Turistbyrå

Rådhuset, Rådhustorget (0159 296 99/ www.imariefred.com). **Open** *May-Aug* 9.30am-6.30pm daily. *Sept-Apr* 9am-5pm Mon-Fri.

Getting there

By train

In summer, you can catch an express train from the Central Station to Läggesta station, where you continue to Mariefred by bus or on a vintage steam train. It runs daily end June-mid Aug, at weekends mid June-Sept. The Museijärnvägen (0159 210 06/ www.oslj.nu) offers a round-trip package (express train, steam train, steamboat) in the high season (mid June-mid Aug Tue-Sun; mid May-mid June, mid Aug-mid Sept Sat, Sun). It costs around 230kr. A non-express train service runs in winter.

By boat

Gripsholms-Mariefreds Ångfartygs (669 88 50/www. gmaa.se) provides a steamboat service (180kr round trip) to and from Mariefred on the *Mariefred*, built in 1903. It departs Klara Mälarstrand near the Stadshuset at 10am, arriving in Mariefred at 1.30pm; the return boat leaves at 4.30pm, arriving in Stockholm at 8pm. The steamboat runs 2nd wk June-Aug Tue-Sun; mid May-1st wk June, 1st week Sept Sat, Sun. There's no service during the rest of the year.

By car

Head south from Stockholm on the E4/E20 to Södertälje, then follow the E20 west towards Göteborg. After about 30km (19 miles) exit on to highway 223 towards Mariefred and follow the signs to the town centre and castle. The whole trip takes about 40mins.

Sigtuna

A thousand years ago Sigtuna was the most important town in Sweden. Founded around 980 by King Erik Segersäll, who built a royal hall in the middle of the town where the first Swedish coins were minted, it was a major trading port during Viking times. Later it became the centre of activity for Christian missionaries. A group of Estonian pirates changed everything in 1187 when they raided the town and burned it down. After the founding of Stockholm in the mid 13th century, and King Gustav Vasa's later Reformation, when he demolished numerous churches and monasteries, Sigtuna fell into ruin. Nearly all that is left from its great period are the remains of three 12th-century granite churches (from an original seven) bordering the town centre, and a large collection of artefacts on display in the Sigtuna Museum.

Most of the buildings in Sigtuna today were built in the 18th and 19th centuries. Old wooden houses painted red and yellow crowd the town's narrow pedestrian street, **Stora Gatan** – also Sweden's oldest street. Here you'll find shops selling antiques, handicrafts and clothes, as well as restaurants with beautiful views of the water. The **Rådhus** in the central square was built in 1744 and is said to be the smallest town hall in Sweden. A key to the hall used to be stored in a hidden compartment to the left of the door, so people would have a place to sleep if the weather suddenly turned cold.

The **Sigtuna Museum** (*see below*) is built on the site of a former king's residence and has an excellent exhibition on the Vikings. It also runs the **Rådhus** and **Lundströmska Gården**, a middle-class house kept as it was in 1900. Stop by the **tourist office** (*see below*) on Stora Gatan – the building with a carved dragon head over the door – to book a tour of the town or one of its historic buildings.

Off the main street, you can take a rather melancholy stroll through the church ruins and cemeteries of St Lars, St Per and St Olof. The red-brick church of St Mary, which looks quite new compared to the others, was actually built by the Dominicans in the 13th century. Down by the water on Strandvägen, at **Café Våfflan** (592 508 00) you can rent boats and bicycles. There's also a miniature golf course and paths for walking and cycling.

Summer is the ideal time to visit Sigtuna (when it hosts a concert series), but seeing the frozen Lake Mälaren during the winter is also breathtaking. On your way to or from the town, you might want to visit the palaces of **Rosersberg** and **Steninge** (*see p246* **Palaces around Lake Mälaren**).

Sigtuna Museum

Stora Gatan 55 (597 838 70/http://195.190.203.17/museer). **Open** *Museum, Rådhus, Lundströmska Gården June-Aug* noon-4pm daily. *Sept-May* noon-4pm Tue-Sun. **Admission** *Museum* 40kr; 20kr concessions; free under-16s. *Rådhus* free. *Lundströmska Gården* 10kr; 5kr concessions; free under-16s. **Credit** AmEx, MC, V.

Where to eat

For a good meal in a charming 18th-century pub, head two blocks west from the town square to **Amandas Krog** (Långgränd 7, 592 500 24, main courses 125kr-180kr). You can order a lunch special of fish, meat or pasta, or something fancier such as crayfish soup or grilled venison. The **Båthuset Krog & Bar** on Kallbadhusviken (592 567 80, main courses 180kr-220kr, closed lunch & Mon) is located out on the water from Strandpromenaden, down the hill from the city centre. A wooden dock leads to the restaurant, which is decorated with lanterns, fishing nets and marine-themed paintings, and serves hearty portions of fresh mussels and cod. For one of the best waterfront views in town, sit on the terrace at the **Sigtuna Stadshotell**'s restaurant (*see below*). Traditional Swedish *husmanskost* is served for lunch, while for dinner specialities such as grilled beef with roasted garlic sauce are laid down on the linen-covered tables. Main courses cost 145kr-265kr.

If you've got a sweet tooth, duck into **Tant Bruns Kaffestuga** (Laurentii Gränd 3, 592 509 34). This low-ceilinged café named after a character in a popular children's book is famous for its desserts and its life-size doll out front.

Where to stay

Founded in 1909, the **Sigtuna Stadshotell** (Stora Nygatan 3, 592 501 00/www.sigtuna stadshotell.se, rates 1,550kr-2,150kr, closed 4wks July-Aug) lies near the western end of the town's main pedestrian street. Its 27 smart rooms, furnished with Scandinavian classics, have recently been renovated and updated with the latest IT technology. Sigtuna's proximity to Arlanda Airport has made it a popular location for conference hotels, including **Stora Brännbo Kursgård** (Stora Brännbovägen 2-6, 592 575 00/www.stora.brannbo.se, rates 65kr-1,200kr, closed weekends Sept-May). This environmentally friendly hotel north-west of the town square has 100 plainly furnished rooms and a large dining hall. Open from May to September, **Rävsta Camping** (592 527 00) is situated about three kilometres (two miles) to the east of Sigtuna's town centre in a nature reserve.

Tourist information

Sigtuna Turism

Stora Gatan 33 (592 500 20/http://sal.sigtuna.se/turism). **Open** *June-Aug* 10am-6pm Mon-Sat; 11am-5pm Sun. *Sept-May* 10am-5pm Mon-Fri; noon-4pm Sat, Sun.

Another useful website (in English) is http://195.190.203.17/turism.

Getting there

By train & bus

Take the Pendeltåg train (www.sl.se) or the Uppsala train (www.tim-trafik.se) to Märsta. The Uppsala train (55kr single) is faster – but make sure the train passes by Märsta and not Arlanda. From Märsta, change to bus 570 or 575 to Sigtuna bus station, near the town centre. From Stockholm Central Station the trip takes about 1hr.

By boat

In summer, Strömma Kanalbolaget (587 140 00/ www.strommakanalbolaget.com) offers day-long steamboat cruises (550kr-660kr) from Stockholm to Uppsala, and vice versa, that stop off in Sigtuna for about 1hr.

By car

Head north on the E4 for about 30km (18 miles) then exit on to the 263 and follow the signs to Sigtuna. Drive about 10km (6 miles) west until you come to a roundabout, where you turn towards Sigtuna Centrum. The entire journey takes about 50mins.

Uppsala

At the northern tip of Lake Mälaren, about 70 kilometres (40 miles) north of Stockholm, lies the historic university city of Uppsala – Sweden's equivalent of Oxford and Cambridge. With 190,000 residents – including 30,000 students, who guarantee a lively atmosphere – it's one of Sweden's most charming cities, its ancient buildings, old-fashioned cafés and beautiful parks providing plenty of interest for visitors. The magnificent Domkyrkan, Scandinavia's largest cathedral, stands on a ridge to the west of the downtown area beside a 16th-century brick castle. The small Fyrisån river runs along a man-made stone channel through the centre of town. One block to the east is a pedestrian shopping street and the bustling main square of Stora Torget. The former home and garden of the famous botanist Carl Linnaeus (whose face adorns the 100kr note) are located nearby, along with several other university museums.

Lakeside restaurants and 12th-century ruins in the ancient town of **Sigtuna**. *See p243.*

Uppsala was founded slightly to the north of its present location; it moved southwards in the 13th century as construction began on the **Domkyrkan** (*see p249*), today the city's most striking landmark by far. This red-brick Gothic cathedral was built on a cross plan and completed in 1435. The building is as tall as it is long, with two western towers rising up a neck-craning 118.7 metres (389 feet). More than half a million people visit the cathedral each year, and it's really Uppsala's best attraction. Inside there's an enormous vaulted ceiling, a floor covered with gravestones, and Sweden's largest baroque pulpit, designed by Tessin the Younger. It's also the last resting place of some famous dead Swedes. Linnaeus and the philosopher Emanuel Swedenborg are buried here, and Gustav Vasa is entombed beneath a monument depicting him and his two queens. The **Skattkammaren** (Treasury) is situated in the northern tower; it displays medieval tapestries and treasures, along with the bloodied clothes of members of the Sture family who were murdered by King Erik XIV in 1567.

The buildings of Uppsala University, which was founded in 1477, are scattered throughout the city. Across from the cathedral stands the **Gustavianum** (*see p249*), formerly the

Palaces around Lake Mälaren

During Sweden's century-long Age of Greatness, beginning in the early 17th century, many of the nobility, generals and businessmen growing wealthy from the country's wars built palatial estates in the countryside around Stockholm, especially along the shores of Lake Mälaren. Today, many of these palaces are open to the public – usually only in summer – offering guided tours of their stately, antique-laden interiors, magnificent gardens and special events. Since sailing on Lake Mälaren and the Baltic Sea was the main means of transport, most of the grand entrances to these show-off homes face the water.

The closest to Stockholm is **Ulriksdals Slott**, about seven kilometres (four miles) to the north of the city centre on the shore of Edsviken, an inlet of the Baltic Sea. The palace was built in 1640 for Jacob de la Gardie, who led the Swedish forces that captured Moscow in 1610. Summertime performances are given at **Confidencen** (*see p178*), the country's oldest rococo theatre, and the palace's Orangery Museum – a converted greenhouse – exhibits Swedish sculptures from the 18th and 19th centuries.

Rosersbergs Slott stands 20 kilometres (13 miles) north of Stockholm between Upplands Väsby and Sigtuna. This white baroque palace was built in the 1630s on a small hill above Lake Mälaren. King Karl XIV Johan vacationed here in the summer in the early 1800s, and the palace still has many well-preserved furnishings from the period. A few kilometres north along the shore lies the much livelier **Steninge Slott** (*pictured*). Royal architect Nicodemus Tessin the Younger designed this bright yellow palace and its two wings in 1680, with a central staircase modelled after the one at Drottningholms Slott (*see p239*). The cultural centre that opened in the former stables behind the palace in 1999 has a large selection of discounted handmade glassware, an upstairs gallery and a cafeteria-style restaurant. You can also test your skill at glass blowing or have a swim at the nearby sandy beach.

An even grander palace, **Skoklosters Slott**, lies 15 kilometres (nine miles) north-west across the same inlet. The four round corner towers of this palace, with a white-plastered stone façade, are a perfect background for the jousting tournaments held in July. Count Carl Gustav Wrangel, the governor of Swedish-occupied northern Germany who commissioned the palace in 1654, only spent two weeks of his life in the castle. A guided tour shows the ornately decorated rooms, a 17th-century armoury and the scaffolding left standing in the incomplete ballroom after the count's death in 1676. A church from 1225 is located nearby, along with old racing cars and automobile oddities in the **Skokloster Motormuseum**.

About 45 kilometres (28 miles) south of Stockholm on the Baltic Sea is the early 18th-century **Tullgarns Slott**. Gustav III's youngest brother lived here in the 1770s, although most of the interior decor was changed a century later when Crown Prince Gustav began using the palace as a summer residence. An English-style park and ponds surround the estate, which also contains a design shop, an excellent restaurant and a lovely greenhouse. In summer, you can feast on wild hogs cooked over an open fire or watch outdoor concerts and drama.

university's main building and now a museum. Beneath its copper onion dome are exhibits on the history of science and the university, an old anatomical theatre, some Nordic, classical and Egyptian antiquities, and the curiosities of the Augsburg Art Cabinet. It's worth a look.

At the top of the main street, Drottninggatan, the very striking early 19th-century university library, called **Carolina Rediviva** (Dag Hammarskjöldsväg 1, 018 471 39 00/www.ub.uu.se/hum/carol.cfm), looks down on the town centre. The library contains five million volumes and the famous Silver Bible, written in silver and gold letters around AD 520 (the bible is open for viewing 9am-8pm Mon-Fri, 10am-5pm Sat). For science lovers, the university also has museums on biology, evolution, medicine and even psychiatry; there's more information on http://info.uu.se/popvet.nsf.

The **Upplandsmuseet** (St Erikstorg 10, 018 16 91 00/www.uppmus.se, open noon-5pm Tue-Sun, admission 30kr) – one of the city's few non-university museums – is housed in a former watermill near the river and exhibits cultural and historical objects dating from Viking to modern times. Up the hill from the cathedral is the huge, earth-red **Uppsala Slott** (*see p249*), built by Gustav Vasa in the late

For more information on these and other palaces in the region, visit www.royalcourt.se or www.malarslott.nu.

Rosersbergs Slott

59 03 50 39/www.royalcourt.se. Strömma Kanalbolaget ferry from Stadshusbron/Pendeltåg train to Rosersberg then 2km walk. **Open** (guided tours only) *Mid May-Aug* 11am-3pm daily. Closed Sept-mid May. **Admission** 50kr; 25kr 7-18s; free under-7s. **No credit cards. Map** p236.

Skoklosters Slott

018 38 60 77/www.lsh.se/skokloster. Strömma Kanalbolaget ferry from the Stadshusbron/train to Bålsta then bus 894. **Open** (guided tours only) *Apr, Oct* 1pm Mon-Fri; noon-3pm Sat, Sun. *May* noon-3pm daily. *June-Aug* 11am-4pm daily. *Sept* 1-3pm Mon-Fri; noon-3pm Sat, Sun. Closed Nov-Mar. **Admission** 65kr; 50kr concessions; 20kr 7-18s; free under 7s. **Credit** DC, MC, V. **Map** p236.

Steninge Slott

59 25 95 00/www.steningeslott.com. Train to Märsta then taxi. **Open** *Castle* (guided tours only) *Jan-Aug* noon, 2pm Sat, Sun. *Sept-early Dec* 2pm Sat, Sun. *Cultural Centre* 10am-5pm Mon-Sat; 11am-5pm Sun. **Admission** 40kr; 25kr concessions; 20kr 6-18s; free under-6s. **Credit** AmEx, DC, MC, V. **Map** p236.

Tullgarns Slott

55 17 20 11/www.royalcourt.se. Train to Södertälje Hamn then bus 702 then 2km walk. **Open** (guided tours on the hr) *Mid May-Aug* 11am-4pm daily. *Sept* noon-3pm Sat, Sun. Closed Oct-mid May. **Admission** 50kr; 25kr 7-18s; free under-7s. **Map** p237.

Ulriksdals Slott

402 61 30/www.royalcourt.se. T-bana Bergshamra or train to Ulriksdal then bus 503. **Open** (guided tours only) *June-Aug* noon-3pm Tue-Sun. Closed Sept-May. **Admission** 50kr; 25kr concessions, 7-18s; free under-7s. **Credit** MC, V. **Map** p237.

Uppsala's **Domkyrkan**. *See p246.*

1540s as a fortress. His sons later added on to the building, although much of it was destroyed in the city fire of 1702. Formerly the county's administrative headquarters, it now houses an art gallery and the mayor's residence and is not as spectacular as you might wish. A guided tour goes through its apartments and grand ballroom, and helps you sort out the rivalries within the Vasa family. Wax models in the Vasavinjetter portray scenes from the 16th century. The castle's freestanding bell tower, Gunillaklockan, has become a symbol of Uppsala; it strikes daily at 6am and 9pm.

To the north-east, down a steep hill, you come to an oval-shaped duck pond that borders the city park, Stadsträdgården. The university's grand **Botaniska Trädgården** (Villavägen 8, 018 471 28 38/www.botan.uu.se) behind the castle includes a tropical greenhouse, a baroque formal garden and 11,000 species of plants.

To see where the university's first botanical garden stood, visit the **Linnéträdgården** (*see p249*), situated one block north of pedestrianised Gågatan. Carl Linnaeus (1707-78) – also known as Carl von Linné in Sweden – restored the garden in 1741 soon after becoming a professor at the university. One of Sweden's most famous scientists, Linnaeus developed a method of classifying and naming plants that was adopted by botanists around the world. His attempts at growing coffee, cacao and bananas here – to make Sweden more economically independent – were thwarted (unsurprisingly) by the Swedish winter. He lived in the small house on the corner of the property, now the **Linnémuseet** (*see p249*). It has a permanent exhibition on his life and work (much of which was carried out in the house), and you can see the original furnishings, his writing room and doctor's medical kit.

Linnaeus also had a country residence ten kilometres (6.2 miles) south-east of the city at **Hammarby** (018 32 60 94/www.hammarby.uu.se, open May-Sept 8am-8pm daily), where he stored his extensive collections and cultivated an idyllic meadow. The last week of July is Linnaeus Week in Uppsala, when 18th-century costumed characters roam the streets and there are lectures and botanical walks.

When you get tired of sightseeing, there are several opportunities for relaxing, shopping and entertainment. The city's six-block-long pedestrian shopping street, Gågatan, has two indoor malls and several restaurants and pubs. The huge window of the pool at the **Centralbadet** (St Persgatan 4, 018 10 16 60, admission 35kr) looks out across the river to the two towers of the cathedral. For a bit more splash with your swimming, head for the adventure pool and slides at **Fyrishov** (Idrottsgatan 2, 018 27 49 50/www.fyrishov.se, admission 75kr-90kr). You can also stay the night here (*see p250*).

Gamla Uppsala (Old Uppsala), two kilometres to the north of Uppsala, is the site of the original settlement. Between AD 500 and 1,000 Sweden's pagan kings ruled from this site, which was also a busy marketplace and point of departure for expeditions. As you might expect from pagans, they gathered here every nine years to sacrifice humans and animals over a period of nine days. Visiting the area today, you'll see the grass-covered, sixth-century burial mounds of three kings and a stone church built on the site of a heathen temple. The **Gamla Uppsala Historiskt Centrum** (*see p249*) opened in 2000 with exhibits about Viking history and myths. Catch bus 2 from Stora Torget to get there.

If you're going to be in the area for a few days, a couple of castles outside the city are also well worth a visit. The medieval 15th-century fortress of **Wiks Slott** (018 56 10 00/www.wiksslott.com), 20 kilometres (12.5 miles) to the south-west, is highly recommended. It's one of Sweden's most well-preserved houses from the time. Guided tours (60kr) are offered daily from Midsummer to mid August, at 1pm and 3pm. A 45-minute drive to the north is **Örbyhus Slott** (0295 614 00, open for guided tours mid May-early Sept) – where Erik XIV was poisoned with pea soup – and the old ironworks villages of Uppland County.

Domkyrkan

Domkyrkoplan (018 18 72 01/www.uppsala domkyrka.nu). **Open** *Cathedral* 8am-6pm daily. *Treasury May-Sept* 10am-5pm Mon-Sat; 12.30-5pm Sun. *Oct-Apr* 11am-3pm Tue-Sat; 12.30-3pm Sun. **Admission** *Cathedral* free. *Treasury* 30kr; free under-16s.

Gamla Uppsala Historiskt Centrum

Disavägen (018 23 93 00/www.raa.se/gamlauppsala). **Open** *June-Aug* 11am-5pm daily. *Sept-May* noon-3pm Sun. **Admission** 50kr; 30kr concessions, 7-18s; free under-7s.

Gustavianum

Akademigatan 3 (018 471 57 06/www.gustavianum. uu.se). **Open** 11am-4/5pm Tue-Sun. **Admission** 40kr; 30kr concessions; free under-12s.

Linnéträdgården & Linnémuseet

Svarbäcksgatan 27 (Garden 018 10 94 90/ www.linnaeus.uu.se/Museum 018 13 65 40/ http://info.uu. se/popvet.nsf/sida/linne). **Open** *Garden May-Sept* 9am-7/9pm daily. Closed Oct-Apr. *Museum June-mid Sept* noon-4pm Tue-Sun. Closed mid Sept-May. **Admission** *Garden* 20kr. *Museum* 25kr.

Uppsala Slott

018 27 24 85. **Open** *Castle* (guided tours only) *June-Aug Swedish* 12.15pm, 2pm, *English* 1pm, 3pm daily. Closed Sept-May. *Art gallery* noon-4pm Wed-Fri; 11am-5pm Sat, Sun; noon-8pm 1st Wed of the mth. *Vasavinjetter May-Aug* noon-4pm daily; 11am-5pm Sat, Sun. Closed Sept-Apr. **Admission** 80kr guided tour, art gallery, Vasavinjetter.

Where to eat

Whether you're after sushi, Greek, Thai or standard meat and potatoes dishes, there are plenty of options. The city's finest dining is found at **Domträppkällaren** (St Eriksgränd 15, 018 13 09 55/www.domtrappkallaren.se, main courses 110kr-290kr, closed lunch Sat & all Sun), which serves Swedish and French cuisine in a 13th-century vault near the steps to the cathedral. Some of the rooms were once used to imprison disobedient students. If you want the atmosphere but not the high prices, opt for the Swedish *husmanskost* specials.

One block east lies **Hambergs Fisk** (Fyristorg 8, 018 71 00 50, main courses 135kr-450kr, closed Mon, Sun & July), specialising in seafood from all regions of the world. The simply decorated dining room looks out on Fyristorg square and a bridge over the river. To watch the pedestrian traffic at Stora Torget while you eat, visit **Restaurang Rådhussalongen** (Stora Torget 6-8, 018 69 50 70, main courses 98kr-192kr). It occupies part of the old town hall, and is also a popular nightclub and bar in the evenings.

For excellent vegetarian food, try **Fröjas Sal Vegetarisk Restaurang** opposite the bus station (Bäverns Gränd 24, 018 10 13 10,

The **River Fyrisån** flows through the old university town of Uppsala. *See p245.*

main courses 65kr-80kr, closed Sun, closed Sat June-Aug, closed 2wks from Christmas). One of Uppsala's most famous old-fashioned cafés is **Ofvandahls Hovkonditori** (Sysslomansgatan 5, 018 13 42 04, closed Sun July), founded in the late 19th century.

You can also fill up on pastries and marzipan sweets at the **Güntherska Hovkonditoriet** (Östra Ågatan 31, 018 13 07 57), located by the river near the main square.

In Gamla Uppsala, **Restaurang Odinsborg** (018 32 35 25/www.odinsborg.com, main courses 92kr-120kr, closed Mon-Fri Oct, Nov) serves meals and snacks in a late 19th-century rustic-style building.

Where to stay

Since Uppsala is located less than 30 minutes away from Arlanda Airport, there are several accommodation options. The **Radisson SAS Hotel Gillet** (Dragarbrunnsgatan 23, 018 68 18 00/www.radissonsas.com, rates 1,740kr) lies one block east of Uppsala's main shopping street in a recently renovated 1806 building. It's got a pool and sauna, as well as a restaurant and bar, and serves a generous breakfast buffet.

All the rooms at the **First Hotel Linné** (Skolgatan 45, 018 10 20 00/www.firsthotels.se, rates 1,453kr, closed 2wks Dec/Jan) have views of Linnaeus's botanical garden next door. More than 200 wines are available by the glass at the hotel's cosy restaurant and wine bar, and there's a sauna and solarium for the dark winter days. Three blocks south-west of the train station, the scenically located **Grand Hotell Hörnan** (Bangårdsgatan 1, 018 13 93 80/ www.grandhotellhornan.com/hornan.html, rates 1,100kr-1,350kr) has been partially renovated to its original early 20th-century style. Its spacious, high-ceilinged rooms have nice views overlooking the Fyrisån river, the cathedral and Uppsala Slott.

Cheaper options include youth hostel **Vandraren STF** (Vattholmavägen 16C, 018 10 43 00/www.vandraren.com, rates 185kr-225kr, closed mid Aug-mid June), a short walk or bus ride north of downtown. All the clean, newly renovated rooms have bathrooms. If you prefer sleeping outdoors, a 15-minute walk north-west of the town centre brings you to the year-round **Fyrishovs Camping** (Idrottsgatan 2, 018 27 49 60/www.fyrishov.se, rates tent/ caravan 115kr-195kr). It has tent sites and cottages in a grassy area near to the indoor swimming pools, as well as a miniature golf course and canoe rentals.

Sunday afternoon in Uppsala.

Tourist information

Uppsala Tourism

Fyristorg 8 (018 27 48 00/fax 018 13 28 95/ http://res.till.uppland.nu). **Open** 10am-6pm Mon-Fri; 10am-3pm Sat.
Also try www.its.uu.se/sightsandsounds (in English).

Getting there

By train

Trains for Uppsala depart from the northern section of the Central Station at 10 and 40mins past the hour, more frequently during commuting hours. A one-way ticket costs 70kr (105kr first class). Call Trafik i Mälardalen (TiM; 0771 846 846) for more information, or check out the website of Tåg Plus (www.sam trafiken.se) for timetables. Depending on the day's schedule, trains stop during the 40mins trip in Knivsta, Arlanda or Märsta. Once in Uppsala, you can walk to most of the major sites but there is also an excellent bus system.

By bus

Swebus Express (www.swebusexpress.se) bus 899 departs at 25 and 55mins past the hour from Stockholm's City terminal. It leaves Uppsala bus station at 20 and 50mins past the hour. The journey takes 70mins and the cost is 50kr one way.

By car

Follow the E4 north from Stockholm for about 50mins. The highway passes through the eastern half of Uppsala, from where you follow the signs to Uppsala Centrum to the west.

Central Archipelago

For an easy-to-reach introduction to archipelago life.

The islands that fall within the Central Archipelago (Mellersta Skärgården) are all easily accessible from Stockholm. Nearest to the city – perfect for a half-day trip if you're really short of time – are the **Fjäderholmarna** islands, while historic **Vaxholm** is one of the most bustling of the archipelago's settlements. Further out are the quieter retreats of **Gällnö** and **Stora Kalholmen**, historic **Möja** and the very popular island group of **Finnhamn**.

Fjäderholmarna

The four small islands that make up the Fjäderholmarna are the closest archipelago islands to Stockholm – a mere six kilometres (four miles) east of downtown. Only 25 minutes away by boat, they're the perfect place to get a glimpse of the archipelago without having to take a long boat ride or spend the night. They're also well set up for kids.

Ferries drop visitors off at the main island of **Stora Fjärderholmen** (which is often what people mean when they say Fjäderholmarna). A paved walking path circles the island, passing the restaurants, small museums and handicraft boutiques on the northern and eastern shores and the forested area and flat rocks to the west. Private homes occupy **Ängsholmen** island, and the smaller islands of **Libertas** and **Rövarns Holme** provide sanctuary for birds – but there's no way to get to the other islands unless you have your own boat.

If you do have a boat, you can spend the night in Stora Fjärderholmen's guest harbour, which is run by the Shell petrol station (716 39 10, open May-mid Aug, 95kr per night). There is no other accommodation on any of the islands, and camping is not allowed.

Sailors and archipelago residents regularly visited the islands as early as the 1600s. The first tavern was built on Stora Fjärderholmen around 1700, and sailors stopped there to eat, drink or play cards before heading on to Stockholm. In the 1800s the tavern was turned into a restaurant, and a new boathouse tavern was added on the southern shore. In the mid 1850s Ängsholmen had a run of bad luck: it was first used by the city as a sewage dump, then as a place to quarantine sick immigrants. The Swedish military occupied the islands from World War I to the mid '80s, and burned down most of the historic buildings. Once the islands were reopened to the public, they became a popular tourist destination and are now part of Ekoparken, the National City Park.

Picturesque **Stora Fjärderholmen.**

The ferries from Stockholm dock on the northern shore next to the guest harbour and the **Östersjöakvariet** (718 40 55, open daily May-early Sept, admission 40kr), an aquarium. Housed in a cave dug out by the military to store ammunition, it features Baltic Sea fish in five large tanks illustrating different areas of the archipelago. A few reptiles crawl around behind glass, and the gift shop sells marine paraphernalia and local handicrafts.

The **Spiritum Museum** (Vodka Museum; 55 67 88 20/www.spiritum.se, open 10.30am-5.30pm daily May-Sept, admission 40kr) opened in 2002 in the cave next door to the aquarium and focuses on the island's 'Vodka War' of the 1880s. When the city authorities wouldn't let Lars Olsson Smith sell his distilled vodka, made using a new technique, he arranged for a partner to distribute it at the island's tavern. Free boat rides were offered from Stockholm

Getting up steam for the **Fjäderholmarna**. *See p251.*

and the venture was an enormous success – until the city refused to renew the firm's liquor licence. Smith's distillation method is still used by Sweden's famous Absolut Vodka company. Inside the museum are stacks of vodka bottles, explanatory text in Swedish and – the highlight – Smith's silver toothbrush, behind glass.

Rowing boats of all kinds, black with tar, are exhibited in front of the **Allmogebåtar Museum** (Boat Museum; 612 20 97) on the eastern side of the island. Note the extra thick walls of the building, which was previously used to store torpedo ammunition. Nearby there's an outdoor theatre and a playground that resembles a ship sunk into the sand.

Further round, on the southern shore, a small street contains an art gallery and studios where artists make pottery, linen goods and wooden handicrafts. At **Åtta Glas** (716 11 24, open 10.30am-5.30pm daily May-Sept) you can see glass being blown or book a time to try it for yourself, then buy the products. At the top of the hill in the middle of the island is a garden (open 11am-5pm daily) with a picnic area and a small petting zoo.

Guided tours of Stora Fjärderholmen with **We Fix Fjäderholmarna** (715 80 65) start in front of the Systrarna Degens Glasstuga (*see below*), near the dock. Tours are at 11.30am and 1.30pm daily mid June-early Aug, weekends only earlier and later in the season. Tours are available in English on request.

Where to eat

As you step off the ferry, the **Rökeriet** (716 50 88/www.rokeriet.nu, open 10.30am-midnight daily May-mid Sept, main courses 90kr-230kr), built to look like old fishing huts, lies to your left along the water's edge. At the café counter you can order smoked salmon, charred herring or potato salad. The indoor restaurant, adorned with fishing nets, has a beautiful view over the neighbouring islands. On a nearby eastern spur, **Fjäderholmarnas Krog** (718 33 55/www.fjaderholmarna.com, open 11.30am-midnight daily May-early Sept, Dec for Julbord, main courses 110kr-345kr), has a more modern look. It serves dishes such as whole-fried lemon sole, steamed halibut and grilled steak. The bar offers 20 different kinds of aquavit.

For something lighter, try a vegetarian or chicken wrap at **Systrarna Degens Glasstuga** behind the Rökeriet (716 78 01, open 11am-6pm daily May-Sept, mains 50kr-60kr). It specialises in ice-cream and smoothies. Along the southern shore is **Fjäderholmarnas Magasin** (718 08 50/www.fjaderholmarna.com, open 11am-1.30pm daily May-Sept), where you can order typical Swedish lunch specials (from 70kr) from the counter and sit in the large hall or on the patio with a view of Nacka Strand.

Tourist information

The island doesn't have its own tourist office, but information is available from the **Östersjöakvariet** (718 01 00; *see p251*). You can usually pick up a free brochure with a map on board the ferry, which has everything you need to know about the island. Or try website www.fjaderholmarna.nu (Swedish only).

Getting there

By boat

Strömma Kanalbolaget ferries (*see p238*) depart every hour from Nybrokajen (May-mid Aug 10am-midnight daily; mid Aug-Sept 5.30pm-midnight Fri-Sun). **Fjäderholmslinjen** boats (21 55 00/www.rss.

a.se/fjaderholmslinjen) depart hourly from Slussen 10am-10pm daily May-early Sept. **Cinderella Båtarna** boats (*see p238*) run from Strandvägen May-end Sept (every half-hour 10am-midnight at peak times, less often in the early/late season). Or there are the less frequent **Waxholmsbolaget** boats (*see p238*) from Stromkajen (Easter-Christmas outward 10am, 5.30pm Tue-Thur; returning 7.25am, 6pm Mon-Thur). Return fare 60kr-75kr. Departures are less frequent the rest of the year.

Vaxholm

Vaxholm is by far the most populated and easily accessible island in the archipelago. It lies about 17 kilometres (11 miles) north-east of Stockholm and is connected to the mainland by highway 274. The island is overrun in the summer with both Stockholmers and tourists, coming for its many waterfront restaurants, handicraft shops and art galleries. Ferries from Stockholm dock at Vaxholm's historic downtown, located on the island's south-east corner. The town has a lively, beach-side feel and frequent outdoor events in the summer. Booths selling everything from used books to wooden figurines line the wharf. On the main street of Hamngatan, to the north, you'll find all the conveniences of a small town, including an early 20th-century cinema.

Gustav Vasa founded the city of Vaxholm in the 1540s after winning Sweden's war with Denmark. The city supplied food and water to the newly constructed fortress and tower located on a small island to the east. Several additions were made to the fortress in the 1800s, and today it contains the **Vaxholms Fästnings Museum** (541 721 57/open noon-4pm daily mid June-Aug, admission 50kr). Exhibits focus on the defensive history of Stockholm, the castle's former role as a prison, and the nearby Ytterby mine. The museum, which has a summer café, has been closed for renovations but will reopen in June 2003. You can get to the fortress in a few minutes by boat (30kr return) from Vaxholm wharf; they leave roughly every half-hour when the museum is open.

People began building summer houses on Vaxholm in the 1850s when a daily steamboat service from Stockholm started running. Many of these small wooden homes, painted yellow and red, are tucked into the town's pretty, narrow streets and along the north-eastern shore. A 19th-century fisherman's house in the Norrhamn area, north of downtown, has been preserved at the **Hembygdsgården Museum** (Trädgårdsgatan 19, 541 317 20, open 11am-4pm Sat, Sun May-Aug, admission free). You see how the family might have lived, as well as objects related to fishing, hunting and boating. The museum's outdoor café (open daily May-mid Sept) is beautiful, situated on a grassy peninsula next to a popular swimming spot.

West of Hamngatan lies the neo-classical **Vaxholm Kyrka** (541 300 03, open 10am-3pm daily July, Aug, admission free) designed in the 1760s by Carl Fredrik Adelcrantz, who also built several churches in Stockholm. It took more than 40 years to build because of an embezzlement scandal on the church board. It hosts evening concerts in summer. The city's old **Rådhuset** (Town Hall; due to reopen in summer 2003) puts on temporary art shows in summer, and every year the harbour hosts

Rowing madams

During the 18th century, before Stockholm developed the system of roads and bridges it has today, working-class women known as the *roddarmadammer* ('rowing madams') transported passengers around the city and to the closer islands of the Central Archipelago. These hard-working women sat at the front of open rowing boats, in all weathers, ferrying people and goods from Gamla Stan over to Djurgården, and from Skeppsbron to the Fjäderholmarna, Lidingö and Vaxholm.

With scarves wrapped round their heads and often a cigarette between their lips, the rowing madams were notorious for their excessive cursing and hard drinking. Considering their low wages, heavy loads and the fact that few of them owned the boats they rowed, the woman had good reason to swear. In the early 1800s the city authorities attempted to curb their rough language and drunkenness with new regulations for boat traffic.

Competition came from the north in the 1820s when women from Dalarna county, dressed in their beautiful folk costumes, descended on the city to operate their own boats. Although people tended to prefer the charming *dalkullor* over the very sharp-tongued rowing madams, both were soon competing with the steamboats and horse-drawn carriages that arrived in the late 1830s. For the following two decades the women rowed side by side with the steamboats, but by the end of the century almost all of their boats had stopped operating. The rowing madams had their last hurrah in the 1880s when LO Smith hired them to row passengers to the Fjäderholmarna, where he was selling, somewhat appropriately, cheap vodka.

a steamboat festival, **Skärgårdbåtens Dag** (*see p180*), on the first Wednesday in June.

The rest of Vaxholm has been more recently developed, but if you have a bike or car you may want to visit **Eriksö Friluftsområde** (541 301 01), on the island's western tip, which has a park, swimming area, miniature golf course and campsite (*see below*). Further to the south-west, on the mainland, stands the 17th-century castle of **Bogesunds Slott** (info from nearby youth hostel on 541 322 40). It's usually open for guided tours May-June, Aug-Sept.

Where to eat

There are a wide variety of restaurants and cuisines to choose from along the wharf, including seafood, Italian and Chinese. For fine dining and a grand view of the water, visit the restaurant at **Waxholms Hotell** (Hamngatan 2, 541 301 50/www.waxholmshotell.se, main courses 108kr-300kr, closed dinner Sun), serving dishes such as rack of lamb with roasted veg or fillet of roe deer with lingonberry sauce. The hotel's nightclub is also busy on Friday and Saturday evenings. For some more down-to-earth fare, have a seat on the outdoor patio of the popular restaurant and pub **Hamnkrogen** (Söderhamnen 10, 541 320 39, main courses 80kr-180kr). If pizza and hamburgers are your thing, they can be found in abundance around the downtown area.

Where to stay

Since Vaxholm is generally a destination for day-trippers, there aren't many places to stay. The sole hotel, **Waxholms Hotell** (*see above*; rates 1,080kr-1,500kr, closed Christmas-1st wk Jan), built in 1901, has light, tastefully decorated rooms and satellite TV. Rates include breakfast. There are also various B&Bs (around 250kr per person per night), which you can book through the Vaxholm tourist office (*see below*).

Vaxholms Camping (541 301 01, closed Oct-Apr) lies at the western end of the island, and a youth hostel, **Bogesunds Vandrarhem** (541 322 40, members 150kr, non-members 195kr, closed Christmas), is located next to Bogesunds Slott on the mainland to the south-east.

Tourist information

Vaxholms Turistbyrå & VisitVaxholm AB

Söderhamnsplan (541 314 80/www.visitvaxholm.se). **Open** *May-Sept* 10am-5pm Mon-Fri; 10am-4pm Sat, Sun. *Oct-Apr* 10am-3pm Mon-Fri; 10am-2pm Sat, Sun.

Stop by the tourist office, currently located in a kiosk by the wharf (but due to return to the Rådhuset in summer 2003), for maps, fishing licences and an events schedule. Also, website www.vaxholm.se (in English, German and Swedish) is pretty useful for general information on facilities and attractions.

Getting there

By metro & bus

T-bana Tekniska Högskolan, then bus 670 to Vaxholm. The whole journey takes about 1hr.

By boat

Waxholmsbolaget boats (*see p238*) from Stromkajen are the best option: they run several times a day all year. **Cinderella Båtarna** boats (*see p238*) from Strandvägen are less frequent, running one to three times a day every day May-Aug, at weekends only Sept-Nov. The old-fashioned **Strömma Kanalbolaget**

The fortress on **Vaxholm**. *See p253.*

Trips Out of Town

steamboat (*see p238*) runs two to three times a day daily June-late Aug, only at weekends Feb-May, late Aug-late Nov. The single fare is 70kr. The journey takes around 60-90mins.

By car

Head north on the E18 for 15km (9 miles) then exit at the Arninge Trafikplats on to highway 274. Follow the signs to Vaxholm, which will lead you through Stockholmsvägen and Kungsgatan to the central downtown area.

Gällnö

For more than 500 years people have farmed and fished on the X-shaped island of Gällnö, which is located 15 kilometres (nine miles) east of Vaxholm and one kilometre north of Vindö. The well-preserved village of **Gällnöby** stands near Hemfladen harbour on the western shore, surrounded by woods and fields. Along the curved peninsula to the north lie a youth hostel, camping spots and beaches of flat rocks and sand. Few summer houses have been built on Gällnö, and pine forests and two working farms cover most of the island. A 10,000-year-old cave, carved out by glaciers, is located in the north, below the Torsviken inlet.

The island's early farmers struggled with meagre harvests and suffered invasions by both the Danes and Russians. The Danes stopped at Gällnö in 1612 on their way to plunder Vaxholm; the Russians made a more thorough job of it in 1719, burning down a farm and destroying all the island's crops. The oven they built to bake coarse bread can still be found halfway between Gällnöby and Gällnönäs, a smaller village on the eastern side. In 1977, Skärgårdsstiftelsen (*see p238*) bought parts of the island to avoid private exploitation. Today it runs the old Gustavsberg farm, which is north of Gällnöby, administers a nature reserve and leases out other fields for cultivation.

Ferries dock at two points along the island's elongated southern shore, first at **Gällnö** on the south-western shore, then at **Gällnönäs** to the east. From the Gällnö dock, visitors can walk about one kilometre north to Gällnöby, where most of the island's 30 permanent residents live. The shop at Gällnö (*see below*) runs a very small photo exhibition about the history of the island. There's also a freshwater pump, public telephone and post office. A gravel road winds through the village, which is made up of red wooden houses with shingle roofs, some built as long ago as 1815.

If you want to explore the neighbouring island of **Karklö**, a rowing boat is available on the northern Brännholmen peninsula. After rowing across to Karklö, you must attach the two boats together then row back over to Brännholmen, leave one boat and row over to Karklö again. This rather complicated (and tiring) method means that there are always boats on both shores.

Where to eat

The waterfront store, **Gällnö Handelsbod** (571 663 10, open 10am-5pm Mon-Fri, 11am-2pm Sat, Sun mid June-mid Aug, weekends only April-mid June & end Aug), sells basic supplies and fresh bread. It also has a café that's open the same hours. No other food is available on the island, aside from wild blueberries, so it's wise to stock up before you arrive.

Where to stay

Gällnö Vandrarhem (571 661 17, rates 150kr-195kr, closed Oct-April if the weather is bad) lies in the middle of a field, a short walk just north of Gällnöby. Opened in 1981 in a former schoolhouse, the youth hostel also acts as the island's tourist information centre (*see below*). The hostel has 35 beds, a sauna and no TV. You must book in advance. In winter it's possible to rent one of the hostel's four-bed cottages for 1,100kr for two nights (which is the minimum stay). Gällnö's **campsite** lies about 1.5 kilometres (one mile) further north, by a sandy beach on Torsviken.

Tourist information

There's no tourist office, but the youth hostel, **Gällnö Vandrarhem** (*see above*), provides information on cottage rentals, B&Bs and local events. They will also help you find a guide or arrange a boat taxi.

Värmdö Turistbyrå

Farstavikens Gästhamn, Odelbergs Väg, Gustavsberg, Värmdö (570 345 67/www.varmdo.se/turism).
Open 9am-6pm daily.
If the youth hostel on Gällnö is closed, there is a tourist office on the nearby island of Värmdö.

Getting there

By boat

Waxholmsbolaget boats (*see p238*; 160kr return) run year round from Strömkajen to Gällnö's two docks, arriving in 2hrs. From May to mid Sept only **Cinderella Båtarna** ferries (*see p238*; 200kr return) leave Strandvägen twice a day, taking 90mins.

By car/bus & boat

Drive east on highway 222, or take bus 434 from Slussen, to Sollenkroka on the island of Vindö (80mins). From there you can board one of the **Waxholmsbolaget** boats (*see p238*), or book a private boat taxi for the short trip.

Möja

Hiking and bicycle trails crisscross the pine forests and beautiful meadows of this large island situated 45 kilometres (28 miles) east of Stockholm. Just under 300 people live on Möja throughout the year, but its population more than triples in the summer. The island's services and businesses are centred on the village of **Berg** to the south-east. Here you'll find a restaurant, bakery, grocery store and post office, as well as a very small museum. Summer houses and guest harbours border the five-kilometre-long (three-mile) road to the north, which ends at **Långvik** village, where there's a youth hostel. Since there are few cars on the island, the best way to get around is on foot or by bicycle, although locals seem to prefer mopeds. Come for the nature and history but not the swimming, since buildings and plant life block access to most of the shores.

Fishermen have been living on Möja since the 13th century, but Viking artefacts found here indicate that it could have been inhabited much earlier. When the water froze over in the winter, the fishermen used to take their catch to Stockholm by horse and sleigh. The island's residents endured more than most during the Russian archipelago invasion of 1719, when every building on the island was burned down, with the exception of the church. Have a look for the ovens the Russians built around the western harbour of Hamn.

When Stockholmers began building summer houses on Möja in the early 1900s, the island became known for its strawberries. The climate and landscape allowed the strawberries to ripen slowly, and by the 1940s there were as many as 500,000 strawberry plants growing here. Since then fishing and agriculture have declined and today tourism is the main industry.

The ferries arriving from Stockholm make several stops around the island, although most of Möja's main attractions lie in or near the well-preserved old village of Berg. Next to the Möja Krog restaurant (*see below*) stand two 18th-century cottages containing the **Möja Hembygdsmuseum** (755 99 42/www.hembygd.se/stockholm/moja, open noon-3pm Wed, Thur, Sat July-1st wk Aug, but closed Thur 1st wk Aug), with some exhibits dealing with the island's cultural history.

Across Kyrkviken harbour lies **Möja Kyrka** (571 640 05), which was built in 1768 and has free concerts and singalongs in July. For more secular entertainment, visit the **Dansbanan** (571 649 55), north-west of the village, home to occasional discos and a beer tent. A great view can be had of Möja and the archipelago from the rocky hill to the north-east of the village. At the very top you'll find a reconstructed beacon of the kind used to signal between islands in the past.

Halfway up the road to the north of Berg lies the small village of **Ramsmora**, which boasts the very popular Wikströms Fisk restaurant (*see below*) and its accompanying shop. **Långvik** village lies on the island's north-west corner. Its **Skärgårdsgalleriet** (571 642 03/www.skargardsgalleriet.se) sells handicrafts, books and art. A road runs north-west from Berg to the village of **Hamn**, situated in the middle of the western coast. Along the way, at **Saltvik**, is one of the island's few sandy beaches. The western side of Möja is less developed, with pine forests often running right down to the water. Bicycles can be rented in Berg near the harbour (571 643 09) or in Långvik at the youth hostel (*see below*).

Where to eat

Möja Krog (Bergs Brygga, 571 641 85, main courses 78kr-250kr) sits near the ferry harbour in Berg. Located in an old yellow house, it's known for its beautiful view, grilled fish and live music in the summer. It's often closed out of season (mid August to mid June), so phone ahead to check the opening hours. **Wikströms Fisk** (571 641 70/www.wikstromsfisk.nu, main courses 75kr-150kr, closed Oct-Nov), located in Ramsmora, is run by one of the few full-time fishermen remaining on the island. Fresh fish such as salmon and herring are served on the outdoor patio or in the wooden tavern behind it. The busy Wikström family also operates a shop on the same premises, selling fresh, smoked and pickled fish.

Grocery chain **Konsum** runs two shops on the island, in Berg and Långvik (both 571 640 13, open summer 9am-6pm Mon-Sat, 11am-3pm Sun, winter 2-5pm Mon, Tue, Thur, 9am-noon Wed, 9am-noon, 2-5pm Fri, 10am-2pm Sat). At both you can load up on food and supplies, and order alcohol from Systembolaget. There's also a **bakery** in Berg for those with a sweet tooth.

Where to stay

The small youth hostel **Möja Gästhem** (571 647 20, rates 130kr per person, closed Oct-Apr) in Långvik has 18 beds and a kitchen for guests. It can also recommend B&Bs and cottages in the area. Cottages and room rentals can also be arranged through **Erpemo HB** (571 646 46/649 69, rates 250kr per person). The **Wikström family**, who run Wikströms Fisk (*see above*), also have a few cottages for rent. There are no official campsites on the island, so when you set up your tent be sure to obey the public access laws (*see p257* **Free for all**).

Tourist information

The Möja tourist office is currently closed due to lack of funds, but you could try the website at www.moja.nu (Swedish only) or ring the Värmdö tourist office (*see p255*).

Getting there

By boat

By far the best way to get to Möja is by ferry with **Waxholmsbolaget** (*see p238*) from Stromkajen or **Cinderella Båtarna** (*see p238*) from Strandvägen. Boats depart twice a day and take 2-3hrs.

By car/bus & boat

For less time on the boat, take bus 434 from Slussen, or drive east on highway 222, to Sollenkroka on the island of Vindö (80mins). From there you can board one of the above ferries to Möja or take a private boat taxi, such as **Arne Östermans Båtvarv** (0733 756 756). It's about 25mins from Sollenkroka to Möja.

Stora Kalholmen

The secluded little islands of **Stora** and **Lilla Kalholmen**, connected to one another by a foot bridge, lie three kilometres (two miles) north-west of Möja and just east of Träskö-Storö. Aside from two cottages, the youth hostel on Stora Kalholmen's northern shore is the only building. There is no electricity and all fresh water is pumped by hand – it's definitely a place for those who like an outdoorsy, back-to-basics experience. Skärgårdsstiftelsen (*see p238*) purchased the islands in 1962 and turned them into a nature reserve; a marker set on the northern shore of Stora Kalholmen was created in memory of the organisation's founder.

You can walk around Stora Kalholmen in 45 minutes, but you might want to take it more slowly to enjoy the pine forest and views along the way. The cove between the two islands is a popular swimming area and guest harbour. At the wood-burning, waterfront sauna you can experience an archipelago tradition: heating up inside the sauna then leaping into the cold water. If you'd rather not get too wet, canoe rentals are available from the hostel to explore the channels and neighbouring islands. The youth hostel, painted red and white, stands on a hill above the water near the ferry dock. Built in 1914, it was originally the summer residence of the personal physician of King Gustaf V.

Where to stay

With its bunk beds and cottages, the **Stora Kalholmen Vandrarhem** (542 460 23) can accommodate up to 22 people. It's only open mid June-late Aug (except for group bookings)

Free for all

Sweden has a long tradition, dating back to medieval times, of allowing public access to state and privately owned land. Today, these rights, collectively known as *allemansrätten*, also include rules about hiking, camping, lighting fires and berry picking, among many other things. The rules can get rather complicated – defining what you can't do rather than what you can do – but if you follow the basic guidelines of 'do not disturb or destroy', you should be OK. Different laws can apply for different areas, such as national parks and nature reserves, and it is up to the individual to find out the specific regulations.

You can walk where you like, as long as you don't damage nature, cross cultivated fields or come too close to people's homes. Cyclists are usually given the same freedom (though there may be restrictions in nature reserves). The owners of private roads may restrict motorised vehicles but cannot ban pedestrians or cyclists. Note that hiking rights do not extend to golf courses.

You can camp on private property at a reasonable distance from buildings for 24 hours, without asking the landowner for permission – although it's usually a good idea to do so. In nature reserves you can camp for two days on the same spot, after which you need permission from the warden. If a nature reserve has an official campsite, you may have to camp there.

Campfires are allowed, except during dry spells, when they may be banned. You can use fallen branches and twigs for fires, but can't cut limbs from living trees or bushes. Avoid lighting fires on flat rocks, since this can crack them. Always put out any fire before you leave. You are allowed to pick wild berries, mushrooms and flowers, but do not touch people's private gardens. Certain flowers are protected, so do be careful what you pick.

You can swim or boat where you like – but not from private docks. Fishing with a rod and reel is allowed from the shore (generally without a licence), but not with nets or from boats. Dogs must be kept on a lead between 1 March and 20 August when in the countryside, and at all times on nature reserves. Take your rubbish with you, close gates and, unless you're a wild fox or badger, leave birds' eggs alone.

and you should book well in advance if you're planning a weekend visit. Guests can borrow kerosene lamps to read by at night, or sit by the open fire. Although there's a little kiosk at the youth hostel, there is no restaurant on the island so you'll have to bring your own food.

Getting there

By boat

Cinderella Båtarna boats (*see p238*) leave from Strandvägen twice a day every day June-Sept, and only at weekends Oct-Nov. The single fare costs 115kr. **Waxholmsbolaget** boats (*see p238*) from Stromkajen run daily June-Aug, less often the rest of the year. The journey takes about 2hrs 20mins.

Finnhamn

The island group of Finnhamn, 45 kilometres (28 miles) north-east of central Stockholm and just under five kilometres (three miles) north-west of Möja, comprises **Stora Jolpan**, **Lilla Jolpan**, **Idholmen** and several smaller islands. With as many as 200,000 visitors each year, it's one of the most visited areas in the archipelago. The ferry dock and a restaurant can be found on the northern tip of Stora Jolpan, and further south on a hill stands an old youth hostel. A land bridge connects this island to Idholmen to the west, which has cottages for rent, meadows dotted with wildflowers in the spring, and an organic farm. The islands are well known for their excellent swimming areas, either in the sea or in natural harbours.

During the last Ice Age, glaciers descended upon the islands from the north, flattening out the rocks on their north shores and leaving the area to the south relatively steep and rugged. Finnhamn was named after the Finns who anchored in its harbours while waiting for winds to take them to Stockholm. In 1915 a coal merchant had a summer house built here by the famous architect Ernst Stenhammar (who also designed Stockholm's Grand Hôtel). A yellow building with a shingle roof, it's now the youth hostel. In 1943 the city of Stockholm purchased the island group to prevent it from becoming exploited. Skärgårdsstiftelsen (*see p238*) took control of Finnhamn in 1998, and it became a nature reserve back in 2000.

Almost all the businesses on the island are run by one couple, who live in a cottage on Idholmen. At the youth hostel you can rent rowing boats or book a time for the sauna on the dock near the north-west corner of Stora Jolpan. The large farm on Idholmen shut down in the 1940s, but a recently opened organic farm sells eggs, produce and preserves. The area is great for fishing and hiking, and if you want to explore the smaller neighbouring islands to the west, there's a boat you can borrow moored on Idholmen's shore.

Where to eat

The **Café-Krogen** restaurant-bar on Stora Jolpan (542 464 04, main courses 85kr-205kr, closed lunch Fri, closed early Nov-Easter) has a rustic wooden interior and views of the water. It's open to all on weekends, but only for groups on weekdays – but individual visitors can still usually join in, or eat sandwiches on the patio. At the weekends there's often live music. If you don't want to haul in all your own supplies, the **Sommarbutik** behind the restaurant (542 462 07, open 10am-6pm daily June-Aug) stocks just about everything you might need, including charcoal for the barbecuing areas around the island. Visitors can rent the **Sliphuset** building for private parties (542 460 02); it's got wooden benches, a gravel floor and kerosene lamps.

Where to stay

The 80-bed youth hostel, **Vandrarhemmet Utsikten** (542 462 12/www.finnhamn.nu, 250kr per person per night, closed mid Dec-mid Jan), has a spectacular view of the water. The nearby **Sommargården** is open for group bookings in summer. There's also a small kiosk and TV room; the buffet breakfast costs 45kr. Through the youth hostel you can also rent one of the 36 **cottages** on Idholmen, which have kitchens and outdoor picnic tables (600kr per night for a two-bed cottage, 700kr for a four-bed). A few apartments are available for those who want a little more civilisation, and camping spots for those who don't.

Tourist information

Österåker Turism

Storängstorget 8, Åkersberga (540 815 10/www.finnhamn.nu). **Open** *May-late June, mid Aug-Sept* 10am-6pm Mon; 10am-4pm Tue-Fri; 10am-1pm Sat. *Late June-mid Aug* 9am-5pm Mon-Fri; 9am-2pm Sat. *Oct-Apr* 10am-6pm Mon; 10am-4.30pm Tue-Fri; 10am-1pm Sat.
Based in Akersberga on the mainland, but you can call for information on Finnhamn.

Getting there

By boat

Cinderella Båtarna boats (*see p238*) leave twice a day mid May-mid Aug from Strandvägen, reaching Finnhamn in about 2hrs (single 115kr, return 230kr). The less modern **Waxholmsbolaget** boats (*see p238*) may take as long as 3hrs. Boats run less frequently the rest of the year.

Southern Archipelago

Explore islands large and small, bustling and tranquil.

Lovely **Utö**. *See p263.*

A few large islands dominate the Southern Archipelago (Södra Skärgården), including, far away in the south, **Utö**, one of the few islands that is open to visitors all year round. Closer to Stockholm are the sailing mecca of **Sandhamn** and the nature reserves of **Nämdö** and **Fjärdlång**. Tiny **Kymmendö** was once a retreat for the writer August Strindberg.

Sandhamn

For those who want to see the archipelago's beauty without losing the refinements of the big city, Sandhamn is the place. The island (officially named Sandön, but known as Sandhamn) boasts a newly rebuilt hotel and conference centre, various restaurants and bars, as well as a long sandy beach. Sandhamn lies 48 kilometres (30 miles) east of Stockholm and is the sailing capital of the east coast. The **Kungliga Svenska Segel Sällskapet** (www.ksss.se; Royal Swedish Yacht Club) was established here a century ago, and the famous international sailing race, Gotland Runt, starts and finishes at Sandhamn at the end of June, when more than 500 boats are anchored in its harbours. Although pine forests cover most of the island, Sandhamn village dates back to the 1600s and has a few shops and a small museum.

Unlike other islands in the archipelago that relied on fishing and agriculture, Sandhamn developed as a toll and pilot station. The early buildings in the village centred on these services, such as **Sandhamns Värdshus**, a restaurant (*see p260*) built in 1672 by the boat pilots. When the Russians briefly occupied the island in 1719, many of its original structures were destroyed. The restaurant was moved in 1752 when architect Carl Hårleman designed the new Tullhuset (toll house) in its place. In the late 19th century, steamboats travelling to the island brought summer residents who built many of the small, red cottages still seen today on the village's narrow streets. Sandhamn is one of the most popular archipelago islands, with more than 100,000 visitors each year.

Many of the island's points of interest are a near the ferry dock. The **Hembygdsmuseum** (0708 53 13 90, open usually noon-3pm daily Midsummer-Aug) stands by the water in a small, red 18th-century storehouse, containing equipment from the toll station and an exhibit on alcohol smuggling. The **Tullhuset** is nearby; it operated until 1965 but is now leased out to private residents. In the 1870s August Strindberg lived with his wife in the building, now called **Strindbergsgården**, situated along the walkway overlooking the harbour.

On the hill above the village stand a 1935 chapel and a cement tower built as a lookout station in 1962. Below the tower is a giant cave that was carved out during the last Ice Age. Although there are beaches at **Fläskberget** to the west of the village, and at **Dansberget** to the east, you should really take the 20-minute walk through the forest to the beautiful sandy beach of **Trouville** on Sandhamn's southern shore. Bicycles can be rented at the **Viamare Sea Club** (574 504 00/www.viamareseaclub.com), which also has an outdoor pool (open 11am-6/8pm daily June-mid Aug), a bar and café (both open June-Aug).

Where to eat

With an additional 2,400 residents over the summer, Sandhamn has enough restaurants to satisfy most tastes and budgets. An upmarket choice is **Seglarrestaurangen**, the restaurant in the Sandhamn Hotell & Konferens (574 504 21/www.sandhamn.com, main courses 95kr-219kr, closed dinner Sun, closed mid Dec-early Jan). Housed in an old sailing clubhouse built in 1897, it has views of the harbour, a beautiful veranda and seating for up to 400. The historic **Sandhamns Värdshus** (571 530 51/www.sandhamns-vardshus.se, main courses 175kr-220kr) serves fish and wild game in a cosy environment, and also has a pub and outdoor seating. An even livelier time can be had at **Dykarbaren** (571 535 54/www.dykarbaren.se) a popular bar with a restaurant upstairs.

For lighter meals, try **Strindbergsgården** (571 530 54), which has a café and a barbecue in the garden. Sandhamn also has a bakery near that dock that's been operating since the late 19th century, and two groceries that are open year round.

Where to stay

The **Sandhamn Hotell & Konferens** (*see above*; 574 504 00, rates 1,590kr), overlooking the guest harbour, was rebuilt in 1999 as a modern conference centre with 84 luxurious rooms, a sauna and an indoor pool. There's also an elegant restaurant and bar (*see above*), and live concerts on the dock in the summer. You can also rent B&B accommodation (880kr for two people) in the village through **Sandhamns Värdshus** (*see above*). Cottages are also available at a similar price from the **Hembygdsmuseum** (*see p259*).

Tourist information

Contact **Sandhamns Turistinformation** on 571 530 00.

Getting there

By boat

Boats operated by **Sandhamnspilen** (765 04 70/www.sandhamn.com) travel direct from Strandvägen to Sandhamn once or twice a day every day Midsummer-mid Aug, only at weekends during spring and autumn. Single is 110kr; the trip takes about 2hrs. **Waxholmsbolaget** (*see p238*) and **Cinderella Båtarna** boats (*see p238*) leave twice a day from Stockholm in summer.

By bus & boat

Waxholmsbolaget and **Cinderella Båtarna** boats leave more frequently from Stavsnäs throughout the year, from where it's a 30mins hop to the island. To get to Stavsnäs, catch bus 433 or 434 from Slussen. **Sandhamns Båttaxi/Expressbåtarna** (571 535 55) is another quick alternative from Stavsnäs (single fare 55kr), with regular crossings daily in summer, Fri-Sun only in spring and autumn.

Nämdö

Gravel trails for cyclists and hikers cross the beautiful meadows and fields of this car-free island, 38 kilometres (27 miles) south-east of Stockholm. Pristine pine forests cover Nämdö's hilly western half, home to elk, deer and foxes. Most of the island's buildings line the eastern shore, including the main village of **Sand**. Near the ferry dock you'll find a school, arts and crafts store, museum and library. An excellent view of the archipelago can be had from the island's highest point, **Nämdö Böte**, located in the north-east corner, 42 metres (138 feet) above sea level. The main reason to visit is to enjoy nature; there are also a few swimming spots, and two small lakes dot each end of the eight-kilometre (five-mile) long island.

Sand hosts the island's annual Nämdödagen (Nämdö Day) celebrations at the end of July, with musical performances and a flea market. The **Hembygdsmuseum** (571 590 47, open noon-3pm daily Midsummer-mid Aug), a branch of the Skärgårdmuseet in Stavsnäs, is situated in an 19th-century schoolhouse and displays handicrafts, artwork and old photos. On Saturdays in summer there is also a market on Sand's dock selling fresh produce and fish.

The island's church, **Nämdö Kyrka** (571 544 00), was built nearby in 1876 and hosts concerts in the summer. At the time the church was constructed the island's population was at its peak, with around 300 inhabitants. Farm closures and the decline of the fishing industry in the 20th century means it now has only 35 permanent residents.

Fishing on **Utö**. *See p263.*

The village of **Solvik**, further north, has a popular restaurant, its own ferry dock and year-round grocery store **Guns Livs** (*see below*), which also rents out bikes. Skärgårdsstiftelsen owns the northern half of Nämdö, where it runs an organic farm, **Östanviks Gård** (*see below*). You can take a guided tour of the farm, which is also the starting point for a six-kilometre (four-mile) nature trail. The store and farm also act as Nämdö's tourist information centres. Some of the island's oldest structures stand around the village of **Gamla Östanvik** north of Solvik. This area was rebuilt after Russians destroyed most of Nämdö's buildings in 1719.

Where to eat

In an old farm shop behind the dock in Solvik, **Nämdö Hamnkrog** (571 561 57/ www.ldc.se/krogar/mellan/namdokro.htm, closed Oct-Apr) serves cocktails, beer, sandwiches and hot meals of pasta, fish and Wiener schnitzel. The restaurant has seating outside for 130, and live music on Saturdays. **Guns Livs** in Solvik (571 563 79/www. algonet.se/~nautica/16.namdo/16.html) offers a wide range of food for picnics, and customers can also order alcohol or pick up pharmacy items. Further north, **Östanviks Gård** (571 564 18/www.ostanviksgard.se) sells fresh produce and meat, such as lamb sausage. At the old school in Sand, where the museum is located, a garden café is open in summer.

Where to stay

Guns Livs (*see above*) has cottages with ovens, fridges and running water (closed Dec-Mar). Some are located on grass lawns near the shore and others in meadows or surrounded by trees. The year-round cottages at **Östanviks Gård** (*see above*) have similar facilities, as well as bunk or double beds. **Wästerängs Gård** (571 565 43/21/www.namdo.nu/portal/hem/ vang/vang.shtml) rents simple, comfortable cottages around the island (closed Oct-May). Rates are 175kr-300kr per person per night.

Camping is allowed on the island, as long as tents are away from buildings and cultivated fields. Two good spots are near the dock at Östanviks Gård and on the eastern beach of Långvik harbour in the north.

Tourist information

Guns Livs and **Östanviks Gård** (for both, *see above*) provide info for visitors. Also check out www.namdo.nu (Swedish only).

Getting there

By train/bus/car & boat

Waxholmsbolaget boats (*see p238*) leave from Strömkajen in spring and summer; journey takes 2-25hrs. Boats also leave, year round, from **Saltsjöbaden** (single fare 60kr) and **Stavsnäs** (50kr); trip takes 1-1.5hrs. To get to Saltsjöbaden, take the train from Slussen or drive via highway 222 through Nacka, then follow the exit towards Saltsjöbaden. To get to Stavsnäs, catch bus 533 or 434 from Slussen, or drive east on highway 222 for about 1hr. From Stavsnäs, you can also travel with **Stavsnäs Båttaxi** (571 501 00), which stops at some of the smaller docks on Nämdö.

Fjärdlång

Fjärdlång, three kilometres (two miles) east of Ornö, is a popular retreat for kayakers and boat owners. They can paddle around the island's narrow inlets and neighbouring islands or anchor at its several secluded natural harbours. The island, three-and-a-half kilometres (two miles) long, is a nature reserve known for its many varieties of birds, managed by the local municipality, Haninge Kommun, and Skärgårdsstiftelsen. Along the shore, smooth flat rocks dip down into the water. Trails wind through the lush pine and deciduous forests, leading to the highest point on the island in the north near **Mörkviken** harbour. Here you're 36 metres (120 feet) above sea level and have a spectacular view of the archipelago. A Boy Scout camp lies nearby, and in the south-west by the ferry dock there's a well-known youth hostel, **Fjärdlångs Vandrarhem** (*see p262*), where you can rent kayaks and boats.

At the beginning of the 20th century, archipelago farmers began selling their land to well-off businessmen from Stockholm, who were more interested in recreation than

Strindberg's isle

The island of **Kymmendö**, 33 kilometres (21 miles) south-east of Stockholm, became famous in 1887 when August Strindberg wrote a very thinly disguised novel about its residents. Strindberg had lived on the island for a total of seven summers, beginning in 1871, and rented a house from the family whose descendants still own the island today. In the book, *Hemsöborna* ('The People of Hemsö'), a widow marries a farmer who does not get on with his new stepson. The widow has a miscarriage, catches pneumonia while chasing her husband and a young woman through the forest, and dies leaving everything to the stepson. The people of Kymmendö were not happy, and Strindberg was never allowed back on the island.

Today, the Wahlström family run 15 companies on the tiny island, including a restaurant, farm, petrol station, shop and boat builder's yard. The main attraction is Strindberg's small cottage. The island is a mix of pine, birch and oak trees, and rich green fields grazed by sheep and horses.

Day-trippers arrive on the south-west shore, where the restaurant **Carlssons Backficka** (open noon-6/9pm May-mid Aug) and other facilities are located, all operated by **Kymendö Service** (501 542 65). You can swim from the flat rocks along the shore or at the sandy beach near the dock. One of the Wahlström daughters gives walking tours (in Swedish) of Kymmendö (spelled with one 'm' by locals); book on 501 541 62.

After *Hemsöborna* was published, Strindberg said that he longed to return to the island and it was the only place on earth he loved. Nevertheless, he didn't quite learn his lesson. He later wrote books about other islands, from which he was also subsequently banned.

In summer, you can get to Kymmendö from Stockholm with **Waxholmsbolaget** (June-Aug) or **Strömma Kanalbolaget** (July-1st wk Aug – for both, *see p238*); the trip takes 2-3hrs. The rest of the year, take a train to Haninge Centrum and switch to bus 839 to Dalarö, or drive south on highway 73 to Handen, then highway 227 east. From Dalarö, it's a short boat ride with Waxholmsbolaget or **Dalarö Kustfart** (501 507 00/www.dalarokustfart.se).

agriculture. Once such man was the wealthy financier Ernest Thiel, who purchased Fjärdlång in 1909. Thiel started his career working in the office of Enskilda Banken, but by the mid 1880s he had grown rich by arranging state bonds and speculating on stocks. Other businessmen avoided him after the scandal caused when he divorced his wife and married his maid. He found a new group of friends among Sweden's most prominent writers and artists, including Carl Larsson, Bruno Liljefors and Anders Zorn, who frequently visited him on the island.

Thiel built a large summer house on Fjärdlång in 1917, today used as the youth hostel. After a series of bad speculations, he was forced to sell his home on Djurgården to the state (now the Thielska Galleriet – *see p85*), as well as parts of the island.

Where to eat

There is no restaurant on the island, but the hostel (*see below*) does run a kiosk (closed end Sept-Apr and weekdays when quiet) with a strictly limited range of food. You should make sure you have enough supplies before you arrive on the island.

Where to stay

The grand **Fjärdlångs Vandrarhem** (501 560 92/www.stfturist.se, rates 110kr-155kr, closed end Sept-May) offers hostel accommodation in a red-painted, two-storey building standing on a round stone hill. The hostel also offers cottages for rent called **Långstugan** (May-mid June 250kr per night, mid June-Aug only weekly rent at 1,250kr per week, closed Sept-Apr), by the waterfront, and **Fågelhuset** (1,800kr per week, closed Sept-May), on the cliffs. The hostel is also the office for the guest harbour, and gives out information on camping.

Tourist information

During the summer, the **youth hostel** (*see above*) can help you out with most queries. **Haninge Kommun** (606 75 50/www.haninge.se), may be able to help out of season.

Getting there

By boat

Waxholmsbolaget boats (*see p238*) run from Strömkajen mid Apr-Nov only and take about 2.5hrs; single fare is 95kr. To travel via Dalarö (single 55kr), see the info for Kymmendö (*see left* **Strindberg's isle**), which is on the same ferry route.

Utö

It takes up to three hours to get to Utö, one of the largest and most interesting of the islands in the archipelago. About 15 kilometres (nine miles) long and three kilometres (two miles) at its widest, it falls into two sections, the northern portion containing the main harbour, **Gruvbryggan** – where the ferries from Stockholm stop first – and most of the island's facilities, including a hotel and restaurant that are open all year round. The north part of Utö is also a nature reserve, popular with birdwatchers and fishermen, while the southern section is a military shooting range (don't be alarmed if you hear the sound of distant gunfire). Off limits for most of the year (though you can still cycle or drive through on the road), it's fully open between June and August. Ferries from Stockholm also call at **Spränga** midway along the island and on the southern tip of the adjoining island of **Ålö**, which lies just to the south of Utö and is connected to it by road.

Utö is busiest in summer, when Stockholmers flock to their holiday homes, and boats bustle about the marina (one of the largest in the archipelago), but it never seems to get too crowded. Pretty red wooden cabins nestle among the birch and pine trees, and there's plenty of natural and human history to uncover. You can cycle through shady woods and fields filled with wildflowers, scramble along rocky foreshores, swim off sandy beaches, fish, play tennis or beach volleyball, or just hang out.

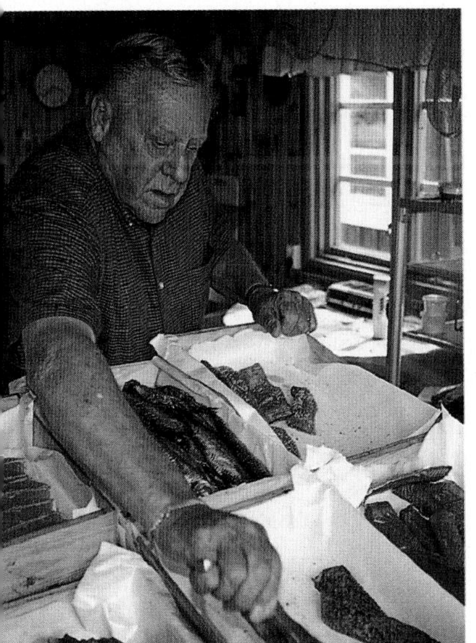

Fresh fish for sale by Utö's marina.

Utö has been inhabited since pre-Viking times; burial grounds at Skogsby on the southern half of the island reveal there was a permanent settlement between 550 and 1050, and by the 12th century iron ore was being mined. The geological uniqueness of Utö is what drew these early prospectors – it's one of very few places in the world to contain the iron mineral holmquistite – and mining continued uninterrupted for more than 700 years, until 1879. The mine was one of the earliest and certainly one of the most important in Sweden. When mining was no longer profitable, Utö was bought by industrial magnate 'Plank Anders' Andersson, who set up a sawmill and timber yard. At the end of the 19th century, the island became the property of merchant EW Lewin, who promoted it as a fashionable summer resort for the Stockholm elite. Famous visitors included artists Hanna and Georg Pauli, Einar Jolin and Anders Zorn, and authors Gustav Hellstrom and Hasse Z (who wrote a minor classic set on the island). The locals were not made so welcome: when Lewin needed accommodation for his visitors, the former miners were forced to vacate their homes in **Lurgatan** (today used as holiday cottages).

The marina by the main harbour provides services and supplies for visiting sailors, and there's also a tourist office (*see p264*), shop, post office, bakery and restaurant nearby. A five-minute walk uphill is **Utö Värdshus** (*see p264*), the island's only hotel. The main building, housed in the mine's 18th-century office, contains the reception, bar and fine restaurant (*see p264*); accommodation is in various buildings nearby.

Behind the hotel are the **old mine pits**, now filled with water and rocks (the latter were thrown in by the Russian army in 1719 in an attempt to destroy the mine). The pits are still an impressive sight, though it's hard to imagine the harsh life of the 18th-century mine workers. The deepest mine, Nyköppingsgruvans, is a staggering 215 metres (705 feet) deep; every morning a priest stood at the top to bless each miner before they started their descent – by ladder – to the bottom of the shaft.

The small **Gruvmuseet** (Mining Museum; open 1-3pm daily mid June-mid Aug, admission 10kr) is housed in an old wooden barn (the former fire station) beside the hotel. At the top of the nearby hill is the wooden **Kvarnen** (windmill; open 11am-3pm daily mid June-mid Aug, weekends only Sept, admission 10kr), built in 1791 and in operation until 1927. The old grinding machinery is still inside and there's a fantastic view from the top.

The fine restaurant at **Utö Värdshus**.

Nowadays, about 230 people live on Utö year-round, mainly in the centre of the island at **Spränga**, where there are also 3,000 summer houses. It's also the site of the island's school and impressively large stone church, built in 1850 and containing the oldest working church organ in Sweden.

Utö is ideal for swimming. Among the best beaches are the lovely sandy stretches on the southern coast at **Storasand**, and at **Storsand** on the southern edge of Ålö. Families should head for **Barnesbad**, a child-friendly beach 1.5 kilometres (one mile) north of Gruvbryggan harbour. At the harbour you can also play tennis, beach volleyball, miniature golf, football and boules. The best way to get around Utö is by bicycle, which you can rent at Gruvbryggan in the high season. Alternatively, hire a kayak or rowing boat to explore the coast; guides are also available if you need tuition.

Where to eat

Gourmet cooking is on offer at the newly redecorated **Utö Värdshus** restaurant (50 42 03 00/www.uto-vardshus.se, main courses 200kr-250kr), voted best restaurant in the archipelago in 2001 and 2002. Specialising in Swedish ingredients, it's renowned for its fish (shrimp and pike sausages, perch, halibut, salmon), much of it caught locally. Above is an old-fashioned clubhouse with a pool table, and below an atmospheric cellar bar, **Bakfickan** (open 10pm-3am Wed-Sun June-Aug).

In summer, you can also eat **Seglarbaren** restaurant (50 42 03 00, open 10am-10pm daily Midsummer-Aug, main courses 70kr-150kr) on the waterfront by the main harbour. The island's bakery, **Utö Bagerie** (50 15 70 79, open daily June-Aug, Fri-Sun May, Sept), also near the harbour, sells great pastries and a mean *caffè latte* as well as its own special sailors' bread, Utölimpia, a dense, aromatic bread that stays fresh for three weeks if stored in a cool, dark place. The adjoining restaurant, **Dannekrogen** (same phone), is a homely place with red and white checked tablecloths. You can pick up picnic supplies at the shop opposite.

Other summer-only eating options include pizza parlour **Pizzastugan** at Spränga (50 15 73 50, open 3-9pm daily mid June-mid Aug), and **Båtshaket** (50 15 74 63, open noon-6/9pm mid June-Aug), a shack next to the landing stage on Ålö that sells fantastically fresh fish.

Where to stay

Utö Värdshus (*see above*; rates from 795kr) offers a variety of accommodation in a scattered collection of historic buildings. These include 30 red-painted wooden **cottages**; the 18th-century **Stenhotellet** (with both double rooms and bunk beds); and the **Kvarnvillan,** just below the windmill, with eight en suite double rooms and views across the harbour. Busy with conference and business guests throughout the year, the hotel fills with tourists in summer, so it's best to book ahead for July and August.

Just up from Gruvbryggan is the **STF/HI Youth Hostel** (50 42 03 15, 245kr per person per night, closed Oct-Apr). It's got space for 44 in two- or four-bed rooms. You can also rent cottages through the tourist office (*see below*) – most are located around Spränga and are small and basic; some have a kitchen, shower, toilet and electricity. Camping is available near the harbour; get details from the marina office.

Tourist information

Utö Turistbyrå

Gruvbryggan (50 15 74 10/www.utoturistbyra.se). **Open** usually 10am-4/5pm daily.

Getting there

By boat

Waxholmsbolaget boats (*see p238*) run from Strömkajen several times a day May-Aug (single 95kr). The journey takes 2.5-3hrs. Boats also stop at the next-door island of Alö, so if you phone ahead you can arrange for a bike to be waiting there and cycle from the south to the north of Utö.

By train, bus & boat

You can also get to Utö by a faster but more complicated route. From Central Station take a Pendeltåg train to Västerhaninge, then bus 846 to Årsta Havsbad (SL passes are valid on the train and bus), then boat (50kr one way) to Utö. The whole journey takes about 1.5hrs to Gruvbryggan, and another 15mins to Spranga. This is the only option in winter, when boats don't run from Stockholm.

Northern Archipelago

Head north for farms, pine forests and rocky shores.

The Northern Archipelago (Norra Skärgården) hugs close to the mainland. On its northern edge is the large and lively island of **Björkö** (which is connected to the mainland by road) and its smaller neighbour, **Arholma**.

Björkö

Located over 80 kilometres (50 miles) north-east of Stockholm, Björkö is the northernmost island in the archipelago. A small strip of land to the north-west connects it to the mainland. Pine forests interspersed with fields dominate the landscape, and narrow harbours cut its jagged shoreline. It is one of the few active farming communities in the archipelago, and cattle and horses can be seen grazing almost everywhere. Two inlets from the north and south nearly divide the 13-kilometre (eight-mile) long island in half. Most of Björkö's amenities, such as its early 20th-century church, seafaring museum and youth hostel, lie on or east of this divide. The ferries from Stockholm and Arholma arrive in **Simpnäs**, on the eastern shore.

Björkö's shipbuilding industry grew in the 18th century as trade increased with Stockholm. The Crimean and Franco-Prussian Wars during the 19th century were boom years for the island, and almost every tree was cut down to make ships. As motors replaced sails, production declined and tourism became the new moneyspinner. The men made rich by the island's small shipping companies built themselves grand homes on farms around the island. A few of these residences still stand, at **Kulla**, **Blekunge** and Simpnäs; the house at Skeppsmyra on the southern shore is now the hostel **Lyckhem Vandrarhem** (*see below*). You can learn more about the island's shipping history at the **Sjömannaförenings Museum** in Simpnäs (0176 940 54/910 05, open 11am-2pm Sat, Sun Midsummer-end Aug, admission free).

On top of a hill in the middle of the island is **Björkö-Arholma Kyrka** (0176 524 10/ www.svenskakyrkan.se/vaddo, closed Oct-Apr except for Sun service). This wooden church, decorated with paintings by the well-known artist Harald Lindberg, was built in 1914 after residents complained of having to row several kilometres to Sunday services on Vätö island. Hikers can explore the beautiful flora and fauna of the island by walking the trail that follows the eastern shore. For something a little faster, check with the youth hostel about renting a bicycle (45kr per day) or canoe or boat (150kr per day). Rowing boats and canoes (20kr/75kr per hour/day) are also available from the **Björkögården** hostel (*see below*) on the western shore. In **Bofjärden**, the harbour north-west of Simpnäs, there are smooth, flat rocks from which you can swim.

Where to eat

Aside from the pub (open 7-11pm daily May-Aug), café and shop (both open 2-6pm May-Aug) at the **Skeppsmyra Lyckhem Vandrarhem** (*see below*), there is only one other place to eat on the island. This is the summer-only **Simpnäs Hamncafé** (0176 917 98/http://home. swipnet.se/simpnascafe), by the harbour in Simpnäs, which serves pastries and sandwiches, and has exhibitions and evening concerts during the summer.

Where to stay

The **Skeppsmyra Lyckhem Vandrarhem** (0176 940 27/www.lyckhemhb.se, rates 150kr-195kr, closed Sept-Apr), on the southern shore, is a two-storey yellow house built in the 1850s. Situated on an expansive green lawn, the hostel has 80 beds, a sauna, washing machines and a TV room. The building has recently been remodelled to include conference facilities. You must book in advance. There's also a café, small shop and a pub, as well as nearby walking trails. Newly renovated cottages (4,200kr per week) are available for rent, and there's also a campsite (100kr per day per tent) with a kitchen and showers. The hostel staff will help you plan excursions or find a guide.

On the western shore lies **Björkögården** (0176 910 55/www.kgh.nu/indexb.html, rates 170kr per person), a private youth hostel with cottages (closed Nov-end Apr, 300kr-340kr per night), a campsite and a wonderful area for swimming.

Arholma

The island of Arholma lies less than a kilometre east of Björkö and is the last stop in the archipelago before the Finnish island of Åland.

A large portion of Arholma, which is just five kilometres long and two kilometres wide (three miles by just over one mile), has been designated a nature reserve. The ferries dock on the western shore, next to a grocery shop, dancehall, lovely church and a windmill. Skärgårdsstiftelsen owns a quarter of the island and manages two old farms and a newly built guest harbour. An archipelago police headquarters also recently opened on the island, adding 15 people to Arholma's 80 permanent residents.

Before the 18th century, hunting, fishing and agriculture were the mainstays of the island's economy. But as on Björkö, the people of Arholma learned to be skilled shipbuilders, and in the 19th century several farmers became comparatively wealthy from the trade. Many of the splendid homes these men built were turned into boarding houses at the start of the 20th century. Around the harbour of **Österhamn**, on the eastern side of the island, stand several old boathouses. Many of them are no longer at sea level since the land around Stockholm is continually rising. Another reminder of the island's seafaring past is **Arholma Båk** (0176 561 67/660 12/www.algonet.se/~arholma1/torn.htm, open 1-5pm Mon-Thur, Sat, Sun Midsummer-early Aug, admission 10kr), standing on a hill south of the ferry dock. This red and white circular tower, built in 1768 and used to signal to ships, exhibits local artwork and handicrafts for sale.

Near the ferry dock, the charming dancehall, **Arholma Dansbana** (0176 560 87, closed mid Aug-Midsummer) was built in the 1940s and has live music on Saturdays in July, as well as occasional dance courses. The nearby **Arholma Handel** shop (*see below*) also acts as a post office and petrol station, and has bicycles for rent.

Where to eat

For ready-made food, your best bet is the organically prepared dishes at **Café Sol & Vind** (0176 560 87, open 11am-6pm daily Midsummer-mid Aug) at the Arholma Dansbana. At **Arholma Handel** (0176 560 12), by the ferry dock, you can buy groceries and order alcohol from Systembolaget.

Where to stay

Arholma Vandrarhem (0176 560 18/www.algonet.se/~arholma1/vandra.html, phones answered 9-10am, 5-7pm daily, rates 110kr-155kr) is located at the Bull August Farm just south of the church on the western shore. The hostel comprises three red buildings with shingle roofs, all clean and decently furnished.

There are a total of 34 beds, although only half are used in the off-season. A washing machine is available, and staff will help arrange boat or fishing trips. There's also a campsite on a promontory at the island's north-west corner.

Tourist information

Queries can be answered either by the Roslagen district tourist office at **Norrtälje** or the **Väddö** office (0176 520 50/www.vaddo.nu), both on the mainland. Also check out Arholma's two websites – www.algonet.se/~arholma1 and www.algonet.se/~tnh/ar – both in Swedish only.

Norrtälje Turistbyrå

Danskes Gränd 4-6, Norrtälje (0176 719 90/www.roslagen.nu/engelska/index.html). **Open** *Midsummer-Aug* 9.30am-7pm Mon-Fri; 9.30am-5pm Sat; 11am-5pm Sun. *Sept-mid May* 9.30am-5pm Mon-Fri. *Mid May-Midsummer* 9.30am-5pm Mon-Fri; 10am-3pm Sat.

Getting there

By boat

Waxholmsbolaget ferries (*see p238*) from Strömkajen run to Björkö and Arholma once daily mid June-mid Aug, taking approximately 3hrs 45mins. **Passbåt** ferries (0176 561 16/www.algonet.se/~tnh/ar/passbat.html) make the 20mins trip (30kr) between Arholma and Björkö five to six times a day in the week, twice on Saturdays and four times on Sundays.

By car & bus

Since Björkö is connected to the mainland, you can also reach it by both car and bus. Catch bus 640 from Stockholm's Tekniska Högskolan T-bana station to Norrtälje, then bus 636 to Björkö. Or head north on the E18 for about 55km (34 miles) until you reach Norrtälje. From there, head north on highway 283 to Väddö, from where you follow the signs south-east to Björkö. There are frequent boats between Björkö and Arholma (*see above*).

The Baltic & Beyond

Discover what else the Baltic region has to offer.

Out in the middle of the Baltic Sea about 160 kilometres (100 miles) south-east of Stockholm lies the island of **Gotland**. With its many sandy beaches, medieval architecture and sunny weather, it is one of Sweden's most popular summer destinations. Every year more than 400,000 visitors arrive on this island of 58,000 inhabitants, on the ferries and planes that leave daily from Stockholm. Or you could take a short cruise to **Tallinn** or **Helsinki** (*see p268* **Ferry cross the Baltic**). Further afield still, in the frozen north of Sweden, lies the famous **Icehotel** (*see p270* **The big chill**).

Gotland

The island of Gotland is 125 kilometres (80 miles) long and 53 kilometres (33 miles) at its widest point. **Visby**, its largest city, is located on the north-western shore and surrounded by a 13th-century wall. With a car, you can reach anywhere on Gotland from Visby in under two hours. Driving or cycling around the island you'll see unusual rock formations, fields of wild roses, medieval church ruins and lots of sheep. You can also visit some of the smaller isles off Gotland, such as Stora and Lilla Karlsö.

People first lived on Gotland about 8,000 years ago, relying on fishing and hunting. Hundreds of Bronze Age grave sites are dotted around the island. At the time of the Roman Empire, the Gotlanders started sailing around the Baltic, trading fur, weapons and slaves. In the ninth century Gotland Vikings plundered the fortunes of Russia, the Black Sea and the Mediterranean. By the 1200s, the island – then an autonomous republic – was the largest and very richest trading post in the region; gold and silver treasure from this period has been found buried all over the island. Civil war broke out in 1288 between Visby, heavily populated by Germans, and the rest of the island. When Denmark attacked in the year 1361, the newly independent residents of Visby sat safely behind the city walls as the farmers outside were killed. Danish occupation marked the end of Gotland's greatness. Ownership of the island alternated between Denmark and Sweden for years before it finally became part of Sweden in 1679.

A 13th-century gate and the striking Domkyrka in medieval **Visby**. *See p268.*

Today, Visby is one of the best-preserved medieval cities in Europe. Its narrow streets lined with 13th- and 14th-century buildings are still protected by the defensive wall, which is 3.5 kilometres (two miles) long and has 50 towers. To see some of the amazing artefacts found on the island, visit the state-run museum **Gotlands Fornsal** (Strandgatan 12-14, 0498 29 27 00/www.got mus.i.se, open 10am-5pm daily mid May-mid Sept, noon-4pm Tue-Sun mid Sept-mid May, admission 60kr), located a few blocks east of the docks. It contains silver Viking hoards, re-created interiors from different periods and the Fenomenalen science centre for kids. The **Gotlands Naturmuseum** (Museum of Natural History) is also in the same building; nearby is the **Gotlands Konstmuseum** (The Museum of Art; St Hansgatan 21, 0498 29 27 75). Both have the same hours and admission as the Historical Museum.

The ruins of a dozen medieval churches stand around the city, the most impressive being **St Nicolai** (0498 20 33 20, closed except for concerts). The magnificent **Visby Domkyrka** (Västra Kyrkogatan 5, 0498 20 68 00/www.visby domkyrkoforsamling.nu, open 8am-5pm daily mid Aug-mid June, 8am-9pm daily mid June-mid Aug, admission free), is also worth a look. Visby's oldest structure, the 12th-century tower of **Kruttornet** (0498 29 27 00, open daily in summer), stands along the western section of wall next to the shore. One block north is the entrance to the beautiful **Botaniska Trädgård** (Botanical Garden; 0498 27 10 17/www.dbw.nu). **Kapitelhusgården** (Drottensgatan 8, 0498 24 76 37/www.gotmus.i.se, open noon-6pm Tue-Sat Midsummer-early Aug, noon-11pm daily early Aug-mid Aug, admission 50kr) is a courtyard in the centre of town with a herb garden where you can try medieval handicrafts. People pack

Ferry cross the Baltic

If you're the kind of person who likes to pack as many countries as possible into your holidays, consider taking a short cruise from Stockholm to **Helsinki** or **Tallinn**. Ships generally leave Stockholm in the evening and arrive the next morning. During the boat trip, passengers can shop at the tax-free stores, dine in the restaurants, tour the many bars or dance in the discos – it's almost a rite of passage for young Swedes. Some ships even have saunas and jacuzzis. When you arrive – having slept or not – you get a full day to explore the city before the ship leaves again that evening. In the off-season a package deal, including a round-trip ticket and buffet dinner, can cost as little as 300kr.

The red and white **Viking Line boats** (452 40 00/www.vikingline.se) are known for their sloppy drunken youths and live entertainment by some B-class popstars, particularly on the weekend cruises. If you know what to expect, and enjoy a party atmosphere, you should have a good time. The cabins can be a little rundown, but are usually cheap. The classier and pricier **Silja Line** (22 21 40/www.silja.se) is more popular with young families and people who have already sown most of their wild oats. Long shopping promenades with high glass ceilings run down the centre of the ship, and the entertainment is more family-oriented. The **Tallink** ships (667 00 01/www.tallink.se) – the only ones that travel directly to Tallinn – have pubs with live music, a few tax-free shops and a show by Estonian dancers followed by a disco.

Harbouring dreams of **Helsinki**...

Helsinki, the capital of Finland, is one of the trendiest cities in northern Europe; don't miss its Museum of Contemporary Art (KIASMA). Tallinn is the capital of Estonia and boasts a fortified medieval old town, several museums, and a truly great exchange rate. For more information on what to do when you land, contact the **Helsinki Tourist Office** (+358 9 169 37 57/www.hel.fi/tourism/index.html) or the **Tallinn Tourist Information Centre** (+372 645 7777/www.tallinn.ee).

When booking your ticket, check the local newspapers for special deals. Prices vary depending on the size of the cabin, how many people share it and where it's located on the boat. To get the absolutely cheapest price, you will probably end up below the car deck sharing a room with three strangers, while the sounds of the engine and ice scraping against

Visby's streets for one week in August when the island hosts **Medeltids Veckan** (0498 29 10 70/www.medeltidsveckan.com), a medieval festival with markets, pageants and jousting.

The flat countryside outside Visby is perfect for bike riding, or you could rent a car (ask at the tourist office; *see p270*). North of Visby, the **Lummelundagrottan** caves (0498 27 30 90/www.lummelundagrottan.se, open 9am-4pm daily May-end June, mid-end Aug, 9am-6pm daily end June-mid Aug, 10am-2pm daily end Aug-mid Sept, admission 60kr) were created by underground currents. On the way, stop at **Krusmyntagården** (Krusmyntavägen 4, Brissund, 0498 29 69 04/www.krusmynta.se, open 9am-6/8pm daily June-Aug, admission 25kr), which has a lovely herb garden and restaurant. Nearby is a swimming area.

The beautiful ruins of a 12th-century monastery stand in the centre of Gotland at

... or up-and-coming **Tallinn**?

the hull make sleep nigh on impossible. Cabins above the water are better: they don't cost much more and are quieter.

Silja and Viking Line ships depart every day, and Tallink every other day. Silja's terminal is at Värtahamnen just north of Ladugårdsgärdet, Viking Line's is on the northern shore of Södermalm, and Tallink's is at Frihamnen, just south of Värtahamnen (for more details, *see p273*). Remember: on the journey back, if a group of Finns gets hold of the karaoke machine you're in for a long and painful night.

Roma Kungsgård (0498 501 23/www.roma kungsgard.nu, open 10am-4pm Sat, Sun mid May-mid June, Sept, 10am-6pm daily mid June-Aug, admission 20kr). South of Visby, at Tofta, is a re-created Viking village, **Vikingabyn** (0498 29 71 00/www.vikingabyn.se, open 10am-5pm daily mid June-mid Aug, admission 60kr).

Offshore further to the south are the two small islands of **Stora Karlsö** and **Lilla Karlsö**, the latter a bird sanctuary. There's a restaurant (*see below*) and hostel (*see p270*) on Stora Karlsö (boat booking and times 0498 24 05 00/www.stora.karlso.com, May-Aug only), and its rocky shores and trails are popular with nature fans. The boat timings make it possible to get to the island and return in one day.

Off the north-east corner of Gotland is **Fårö**, which has camping, beaches and ancient ruins (and is the home of Ingmar Bergman). Before you catch the ferry (free), visit open-air museum **Bungemuseet** (0498 22 10 18/www.guteinfo.com/bungemuseet, open 10am-4/6pm daily mid May-Aug, admission 60kr) in Fårösund. A bit like a mini Skansen, it's got buildings dating from the Middle Ages to the 1800s and costumed employees demonstrating traditional handicrafts. From Fårösund you can also take a two-hour ferry trip, leaving three times a week, to the isolated island of **Gotska Sandön** (0498 24 04 50/www.gotskasandon.com), which has sandy beaches and small cottages for rent.

Where to eat

Anything the visitor could want to chew on, within reason, can be found in Visby. Several critics claim the island's best food is served at cosy **Donners Brunn** (Donnersplats, 0498 27 10 90/www.donnersbrunn.nu, main courses 185kr-240kr, closed lunch & Sun). **Värdhuset Lindgården** (Strandgatan 26, 0498 21 87 00/www.lindgarden.com, main courses 100kr-225kr, closed lunch, closed Sun Sept-Apr) is situated in a historic house with a beautiful garden. Its extensive menu includes Gotland specialities, such as pickled salmon and boiled, breaded lamb with mustard. **Bakfickan** (0498 27 18 07/www. bakfickan-visby.nu/bakfickan .html, main courses 118kr-200kr), on the main square, Stora Torget, has excellent seafood.

There's also a restaurant and pub/café on the island of **Stora Karlsö (**0498 24 10 19, closed Oct-Apr), handy for both lunch and dinner.

Where to stay

The classy **Strand Hotel** (0498 25 88 00/www.strandhotel.net, rates 1,340kr) lies in the centre of Visby's activity at Strandgatan 34. Since the city does not allow structures higher than three storeys, the hotel has stretched out its 110 rooms in three separate buildings. It has a sauna, pool, bar and library. **Hotell Gute** (Mellangatan 29, 0498 20 22 60/www.hotellgute.se, rates 795kr-975kr), with 28 rooms, is more family-oriented. A prison built at the harbour in 1857 is now a youth hostel, **Visby Fängelse Vandrarhem** (0498 20 60 50/http://gotland.net/visbyfangelse, rates 200kr-330kr), which is very close to the attractions but sadly not at all cosy. Camping (85kr-145kr) and some wooden cabins (350kr-890kr) are also available within walking distance of Visby at **Norderstrands Camping** (0498 21 21 57/www.norderstrandscamping.se, closed mid Sept-mid Apr).

Book ahead if you want to stay at the youth hostel on the nature lover's paradise of **Stora Karlsö** (0498 24 05 00/www.stora.karlso.com, rates 145kr-195kr, closed Oct-Apr).

Getting there

By boat

Destination Gotland (0498 20 10 20/www.destinationgotland.se) runs ferries (3-5hrs) between Visby and Nynäshamn, which is 40km (25 miles) south of Stockholm at the end of the Pendeltåg train line. The same company also runs ferries (2.5-4hrs) between Gotland and Oskarshamn, a town on the mainland 110km (68 miles) south-west of Visby.

By air

Flights (40mins) to Visby leave several times a day from Arlanda, Bromma, Nyköping and Norrköping airports. Check with **Gotlandsflyg** (0498 22 22 22/www.gotlandsflyg.se) or **Skyways** (50 90 50 50/www.skyways.se) for schedules and rates.

Package tours

Tours to Gotland, including transport and accommodation, are organised by **Gotland City** (406 15 00/www.gotlandcity.se), **Gotlands Resor** (0498 20 12 60/www.gotlandsresor.se) and **Gotlands Turistservice** (0498 20 33 00/www.gtsab.se).

Tourist information

Also check out websites http://gotland.net and www.gotlandsattraktioner.com.

Gotlands Konferens & Turistservice

Östervåg 3A, Visby (0498 20 33 00/www.gotlandsturistservice.com). **Open** *In person* 9.30am-6pm Mon-Fri; 10am-2pm Sat. *By phone Summer* 8am-8pm daily. *Winter* 8am-6pm Mon-Fri; 11am-4pm Sun.

Gotlands Turistförening

Hamngatan 4, Visby (0498 20 17 00/fwww.gotland.com). **Open** *Mid June-mid Aug* 8am-7pm Mon-Fri; 8am-6pm Sat, Sun. *May-mid June, mid Aug-Sept* 8am-5pm Mon-Fri; 10am-4pm Sat, Sun. *Oct-Apr* 8am-noon, 12.30-4pm Mon-Fri.

The big chill

In Stockholm over winter? Not cold enough for you? Then head north to the super-cool **Icehotel** (980 668 00/www.icehotel.com), which lies about 200 kilometres (125 miles) above the Arctic Circle, close to the village of Jukkasjärvi in northern Lapland. Each December the hotel is freshly constructed out of ice and snow, only to melt again by late April or early May. Artists and craftsmen carve absolutely everything out of the ice, from the windows to the chairs, to create a giant ice sculpture filled with a strange light and incredibly delicate detailing.

Most visitors spend only one night in one of the ice bedrooms, which cost from 1,960kr (a double room) to 5,590kr (for a deluxe suite with details carved by a guest artist). There, in temperatures of -4 to -9°C (24-16°F), you sleep on an ice bed, in a special sleeping bag, to be woken by a hot drink followed by a sauna. If you want to stay longer, try the Aurora Cabins (1,045kr per person), with skylights in the bedrooms for watching the Northern Lights.

If you want to get married somewhere really inaccessible for your family and friends, you can tie the knot in the hotel's beautiful Ice Church. Naomi Campbell has been known to hang out at the Absolut Icebar, where the decor is as stylish as anything in Stockholm. Winter activities, which all cost extra, include dogsled tours to see local Sami camps, massages or swimming in an icy river – the last one for masochists only. It's also possible to stay at the Icehotel in summer, when igloos (1,000kr) are built inside a giant freezer, and activities include hiking and fishing.

There are daily 90-minute flights with SAS (0770 727 727/www.sas.se) from Arlanda Airport to Kiruna, which is 12 kilometres (eight miles) from the Icehotel. Winter flights cost about 1,000kr-3,700kr. Arrange with the hotel for transfer from Kiruna by snowmobile or more traditional transport. The hotel recommends that you don't bring children as the cold can be too much for them. Also pack plenty of warm clothes, including thermal underwear, though the hotel does supply specially warm outer garments.

If this all sounds a bit too extravagant, you can get a taste of the frozen north in Stockholm at the **Icebar** (*see p132*), which is also built entirely out of ice.

Directory

Getting Around 272
Resources A-Z 276
Vocabulary 289
Further Reference 290
Index 292
Advertisers' Index 298

Features

Tourist offices 285
Average climate 287

Directory

Getting Around

Stockholm is a compact city and much of it is easy to explore on foot – in fact, walking is often the best way to get around. There's also an efficient Tunnelbana (metro) system and a comprehensive network of buses. Cyclists are well catered for with bike lanes, and bikes are great for exploring the likes of Djurgården. A car is usually more of a liability: parking is limited and expensive – and the public transport system will get you to most places outside the city.

Arriving & leaving

By air

Four airports serve Stockholm: Arlanda, Bromma, Skavsta and Västerås.

Arlanda Airport

Flight information 797 61 00/ other enquiries 797 60 00/ www.lfv.se/site/airports/arlanda.
Stockholm's main airport, the largest in Scandinavia, is 45km (28 miles) north of the city centre and serves over 18 million passengers a year. International flights arrive and depart from terminals 2 and 5. Domestic flights depart from terminals 3 and 4.

It's a light, spacious, well-designed place, and facilities are good. For currency exchange there is Forex (terminal 2), X-Change (terminal 5) and SEB exchange (terminal 5), as well as Handelsbanken and SEB banks in the Sky City shopping and eating area (which connects terminal 5 with 3 and 4). All terminals contain cafés and bars (open 10am-10pm Mon-Fri, Sun; 10am-6pm Sat), but head to Sky City for more serious eating. There are shops throughout the airport, selling glassware and souvenirs, books and newspapers and the usual travel items (open 7am-7.30pm Mon-Fri; 8am-6pm Sat; 8am-7.30pm Sun). You'll also find a branch of the state-run alcohol shop Systembolaget (open 10am-8pm Mon-Fri; 10am-2pm Sat) and a pharmacy (open 7am-7.30pm Mon-Fri; 8am-7.30pm Sat, Sun). Conference and business facilities are also available, along with a hair salon, dry-cleaner, storage boxes, playgrounds, a chapel and a photo booth.

The fastest way to get into Stockholm is on the super new, bright yellow **Arlanda Express** train service (020 22 22 24/www.arlanda express.com), which arrives at its own terminal next to Central Station (the main station for trains and the Tunnelbana). Trains depart 4-6 times an hour – from Arlanda 5.05am-00.05am daily, and from Central Station 5.05am-11.35pm daily. Journey time is 20mins; single fare is 160kr (80kr under-18s; one under-18 free with each full-price paying passenger). You can buy tickets over the counter, from yellow automatic ticket booths at Arlanda or Central Station or on the train (30kr supplement). The booths take all major credit cards.

Alternatively, **Flygbussarna airport buses** (600 10 00/www. flygbussarna.se) leave about every 10mins from all terminals to Cityterminalen (the main bus station next to Central Station). Buses run from Arlanda 6.45am-11.45pm daily, and from Cityterminalen 4am-10pm daily. Journey takes around 40mins; single fare is 80kr (four under-18s free with each full-price paying passenger). There are also plenty of **taxis** at the airport. The usual fixed rate to the city is 350kr, but do ask the driver first since there are many different taxi firms and they set their own prices.

Bromma Airport

797 68 74/www.lfv.se/site/airports/ bromma/index.asp.
Stockholm city airport, Bromma, located 8km (5 miles) west of the city centre, has around a million passengers per year. Its location makes it very popular, but only five airlines operate from it. The airport has a simple café and restaurant (open 6.30am-8.30pm Mon-Fri; 8.30am-7pm Sat; noon-8pm Sun) as well as a kiosk and flight shop.

You can get into the city centre on **Flygbussarna airport buses**, but their schedules change according to the flight times. Single fare is 60kr; the journey takes about 15mins to Cityterminalen. A **taxi** into town usually costs around 170kr.

Skavsta Airport

0155 28 04 00/www.skavsta-air.se.
Skavsta also serves Stockholm even though it's 100km (62 miles) to the south. It's the airport of choice for the budget airlines, such as Ryanair. Airport facilities include a Forex exchange bureau, restaurant, café, bar, playground and a small tax-free shop. **Flygbussarna airport buses** (single 100kr) take 60mins to reach the centre of Stockholm, and depart from Skavsta 20mins after each arriving flight and from Cityterminalen about 90mins before a departing flight. If you can't find a **taxi** at the airport, you can order one, but the trip to Stockholm will set you back about 1,200kr.

Västerås Airport

021 80 56 10/www.vasteras flygplats.se.
Ryanair flies into Västerås, located 110km (68 miles) from Stockholm. Facilities include a café (open 6am-6pm Mon-Fri; when there are flights Sat, Sun), bar, tax-free shop and car hire. The **airport bus** (single 100kr; journey 75mins) leaves 20mins after an arriving flight for Cityterminalen in Stockholm; it returns about 2hrs before departing flights. There are **trains** every hour to the city (but you'll have to take a bus or taxi to the train station first). A **taxi** ride to Stockholm will cost around 1,300kr.

Airlines

Air France 51 99 99 90/ www.airfrance.com
Austrian Airlines 665 64 80/ www.aua.com
British Airways 0200 77 00 98/ www.britishairways.com
Finnair 020 78 11 00/ www.finnair.com
KLM 59 36 24 30/www.klm.com
Lufthansa 611 22 88/ www.lufthansa.com
Malmö Aviation 020 55 00 10/ www.malmoaviation.se
Ryanair 0900 20 20 240/ www.ryanair.com
SAS 020 72 77 27/www.sas.se
Spanair 020 72 75 55/ www.spanair.com
United 020 79 54 02/www.ual.com

By train

The major rail travel company in Sweden is **SJ** (www.sj.se). It was formed in 2000 from a branch of the old Swedish State Railways. International, domestic and commuter trains arrive and depart from Stockholm's main train station, **Central Station**. Just below the station, and linked to it, is T-Centralen, the main station for the Tunnelbana system, and there is always a long queue of taxis outside.

SJ

Central Station, Vasagatan, Norrmalm (0771 75 75 75). T-bana T-Centralen/bus 3, 47, 53, 62, 65. **Open** *Domestic tickets* 6am-10pm Mon-Fri; 8am-10pm Sat, Sun. *International tickets* 9am-6pm Mon-Fri. **Map** p303 G6.
To book tickets from abroad, call +46 (0)498 20 33 80 or visit www.sweden booking.com.

By bus

Most long-distance coaches (national and international) stop at **Cityterminalen**, Stockholm's main bus station, situated next to Central Station. This is also where the airport buses arrive and depart. T-Centralen is just an escalator ride away, and there are plenty of taxis outside the terminal.

Eurolines

Cityterminalen, Klarabergsgatan, Norrmalm (440 85 70/www.eurolines.se). T-bana T-Centralen/bus 3, 47, 53, 62, 65. **Open** 9am-5.30pm Mon-Fri. **Map** p303 G6.
Operates buses to most major European cities.

Swebus Express

Cityterminalen, Klarabergsgatan, Norrmalm (0200 21 82 18/www.swebusexpress.se). T-bana T-Centralen/bus 3, 47, 53, 62, 65. **Open** 8am-8pm Mon-Fri; 9am-6pm Sat, Sun. **Map** p303 G6.
One of the larger Swedish bus companies that covers many of Sweden's major cities, along with Oslo and Copenhagen. Tickets can be purchased at Cityterminalen or on the bus; it doesn't take reservations because it always guarantees its passengers a seat.

By car

Stockholm's highway links with Europe have been made easier thanks to the Öresund toll (275kr) bridge between Sweden and Denmark, which opened in 2000. It's 615 kilometres (382 miles) from Stockholm to Malmö; 475 kilometres (295 miles) to Göteborg. Driving in Sweden is relatively safe – Swedish roads are in great condition and there are no tolls.

By sea

If you arrive in Stockholm by boat, then you have most likely come from Finland or Estonia. These are the main companies:

Birka Cruises

Södermalmstorg 2, Södermalm (702 72 30/www.birka.se). T-bana Slussen/bus 46, 53, 76, 96. **Open** 10am-6pm Mon-Fri; 10am-5pm Sat; 10am-2pm Sun. **Map** p303 K8.
Daily cruises in summer to Gotland, Finland, Tallin, Riga and Poland. The boat terminal, Stadsgårdskajen, is right next to Slussen.

Silja Line

Kungsgatan 2, Norrmalm (22 21 40/www.silja.se). T-bana Östermalmstorg/bus 55, 56, 91. **Open** 9am-6pm Mon-Fri; 11am-3pm Sat. **Map** p303 F8.
Ferries to/from Finland. Boats dock at Värtahamnen just north of the city centre. The terminal has parking, luggage lockers, an ATM, a kiosk and a café. There are taxis at the terminal and Silja Line has its own bus connection to Cityterminalen (single 20kr). Signs tell you how to walk the 5-10mins to the nearest T-bana station, Gärdet (as well as from Gärdet to the terminal).

Tallink

Frihamnen, Ladugårdsgärdet (666 60 01/www.tallink.net/www.tallink.se). Bus 1, 72, 76. **Open** 8am-8pm Mon-Fri; 9am-5.30pm Sat, Sun.
Ferries to/from Estonia. Boats dock at the Frihamnen terminal, just north of the city centre. There is parking available as well as taxis. Tallink also runs its own bus service between the terminal and Cityterminalen (single 20kr).

Viking Line

Cityterminalen, Klarabergsgatan, Norrmalm (452 40 00/75/www.vikingline.se). T-bana T-Centralen/bus 3, 47, 53, 62, 65. **Open** 8am-7pm Mon-Sat; noon-7pm Sun. **Map** p303 G6.
Ferries to/from Finland, and from Helsinki to Tallinn. Boats dock at Vikingterminalen on Södermalm. The terminal has parking, luggage lockers, a café and kiosk. There are plenty of taxis at the terminal but many people prefer to walk the 10mins to Slussen. Viking Line also has its own direct bus link to Slussen and Cityterminalen (single 30kr).

Public transport

The Tunnelbana (often abbreviated to T-bana) metro system is generally the quickest, cheapest and most convenient way of getting around the city, although there is also a very efficient and comprehensive bus network. Buses operate around the clock and cover some areas that cannot be reached by the metro or the commuter trains. Both the Tunnelbana and city buses are operated by Statens Lokaltrafik, known as **SL** (600 10 00/www.sl.se).

SL Center

Sergels Torg, T-Centralen, Norrmalm. T-bana T-Centralen/bus 47, 52, 56, 59, 65. **Open** 7am-6pm Mon-Fri; 10am-5pm Sat, Sun. **Map** p303 G7.
This information centre in the entrance hall to T-Centralen can answer any questions you might have about public transport. You can also pick up maps and timetables.
Branches: Central Station, bottom floor (open 6.30am-11.15pm Mon-Sat; 7am-11.15pm Sun); Slussen, by Saltsjöbanan (open 7am-6pm Mon-Fri; 10am-5pm Sat); Fridhemsplan (open 7am-6.30pm Mon-Fri; 10am-5pm Sat); Tekniska Högskolan (open 7am-6.30pm Mon-Fri; 10am-5pm Sat).

Fares & tickets

Single tickets on the bus or T-bana cost 20kr-60kr depending on how far you're travelling, and are valid for 1hr from when the trip started. However, it is cheaper to buy multi-ticket coupons or travel cards, which are available from Pressbyrån kiosks and at SL Centers. Coupons are available in sets of ten (60kr) or 20 (110kr). A 24hr pass with unlimited travel costs 80kr; 150kr for 72hrs. You can also get a 30-day unlimited travel pass (500kr), and the new weekend pass (220kr), which allows unlimited travel over four consecutive weekends. There is also the very useful **Stockholm Card**, which includes unlimited travel on public transport, free admission to over 70 museums and sights, sightseeing by boat and more (for more details, *see p56* **Pick a card**).

Tunnelbana

The three metro lines are identified by colour – red, green or blue – on maps and station signs. All three lines intersect at T-Centralen. At interchanges, lines are indicated by the names of the stations at the end of the line, so you should know which direction you're heading when changing between lines. The T-bana runs from around 5am-midnight Mon-Thur, Sun; 5.30am-3am Fri, Sat.

Buses

Bus stops are easy to spot and often have see-through shelters to protect waiting passengers from wind, rain and snow. The city has many one-way streets, so buses often do not follow exactly the same route in both directions, but run along parallel streets.

Most bus routes operate between 5am and midnight daily. You board at the front, and get off through the middle or rear doors. Only single tickets can be bought on board; if you have pre-paid tickets, get them stamped by the driver. Travel passes should also be shown to the driver.

Night buses

There are plenty of night bus routes that serve the city centre as well as the suburbs. Most night buses run from midnight until 5am, when the regular buses take over. The main stations for night buses are Slussen, T-Centralen, Odenplan, Fridhemsplan and Gullmarsplan.

Ferries

Many different ferry companies operate around the waterways of Stockholm. Some routes are used daily by people who commute to and from work, others are designed for sightseeing or excursions into the archipelago (*see also* **Trips Out of Town**). SL travel passes are not valid on the archipelago ferries.

Cinderella Båtarna

58 71 40 50/www.cinderellabatarna.com. **Credit** AmEx, DC, MC, V.
Ferries to Vaxholm, Grinda, Möja, Sandhamn and more. Boats depart from Nybrokajen on Strandvägen. Tickets can be purchased on board.

Djurgårdsfärjan

Year-round ferry service operated by Waxholmsbolaget (*see below*) within Stockholm harbour. It goes to/from Slussen to Djurgården (stopping at Allmänna Gränd, next to Gröna Lund), Skeppsholmen and Nybroplan. From May-Aug the ferry also stops at the Vasamuseet.
Buy tickets in ticket booths before boarding; single 25kr. SL travel passes are valid.

Strömma Kanalbolaget

58 71 40 00/www.strommakanalbolaget.com. **Credit** MC, V.
Departs from Stadshusbron (next to the Stadhuset) to Birka and Drottningholm, and from Strandvägen to Fjäderholmarna, Vaxholm and Sandhamn. Tickets can be purchased on the boat (cash only) or in the ticket booths next to the departure points.

Waxholmsbolaget

614 64 65/www.waxholmsbolaget.se. **Credit** MC, V.
Covers the whole archipelago, from Arholma in the north to Landsort in the south. Boats depart from Strömkajen outside the Grand Hôtel, opposite the Royal Palace. Tickets can be purchased on the boat. The useful website (in English) includes timetables that you can download.

Local trains

For trips into the suburbs and surrounding towns, there are (as well as buses) commuter trains run by SL. The same tickets may be used on these trains as on the T-bana. The main commuter train station is Central Station, and trains will take you to as far north as Bålsta and Kungsängen and as far south as Södertälje, Nynäshamn and Gnesta.

Maps

Central street maps are included at the back of this guide, starting on *p301*; there's also a Tunnelbana system map on *p316*. The tourist office has various free street maps that are of quite good quality; the best is the large *Greater Stockholm Map*, which marks museums and sights. Bus and Tunnelbana timetables (with maps at the back) can be picked up for free at SL Centers (*see p273*) and ticket booths (though don't expect the booths to have all the timetables to hand). SL Centers also sell a very good transport map (35kr). T-bana maps are clearly displayed on the platforms and inside carriages.

Taxis

Taxis are easy to find in Stockholm. They can be ordered by phone, online or hailed on the street. There are taxi ranks by main squares and the railway and bus stations. You'll also find plenty of cabs outside nightclubs and concert venues at closing time, as well as at ferry terminals when a ferry arrives. Taxis can be hailed on the street when the light on the roof is lit. Cab companies are required by law to have some baby/child seats, but it's best to call the company first to request one, since not all cabs carry them.

Fares

Taxi fares (starting at around 30kr) are quite steep; current rates and supplements should be displayed inside each cab. Rates are lower on weekdays and higher on weekends and in the evening, but there's more traffic during the day so the ride will take longer. Rates for the different cab companies can be found on their websites. All the larger taxi firms take credit cards. Don't expect drivers to carry a lot of change.

Taxi companies

The firms listed below take bookings 24hrs a day. All operators speak English, but make sure you have a specific street address or the name of a bar or restaurant where you can wait or they will not send a taxi.

Flygtaxi (airport taxis) 020 97 97 97/www.flygtaxi.se
Taxi Kurir 30 00 00/ www.taxikurir.se
Taxi Stockholm 15 00 00/ www.taxistockholm.se
Top Cab 33 33 33

Driving

Driving in Stockholm can be a hassle. There's a lot of traffic during office hours, free parking is difficult to find and petrol is expensive. Within the city limits a car is rarely a time-efficient form of transport, and it's only out in the country that one becomes an asset. If you do choose to drive, remember the following:

- Tourists can drive in Sweden with a valid licence from most other countries. An international driving licence or EU photo licence can be useful as a translation/credibility aid.
- Keep your driving licence, vehicle registration and insurance documents with you at all times.
- It is compulsory to wear seat belts in the front and back seats and to carry warning triangles, spares (tyre, bulbs, fanbelt) and tools to fit them.
- Third party motor insurance is compulsory.
- Children have to sit in special car seats until around age four (depends on the child's height) and after that on special cushions until age seven.
- The speed limit is 50kmph (31mph) in towns, 90kmph (56mph) on most highways and 110kmph (68mph) on motorways. Swedes keep to speed limits more than most Europeans.
- The legal alcohol limit for drivers is low at 0.02 per cent. Penalties for exceeding the limit are severe.
- You must use dipped headlights during the day.
- A new law means you must stop for pedestrians at designated pedestrian crossings that do not have traffic lights.
- You must stop at traffic lights when the light turns yellow.

Breakdown services

If your car breaks down, look up *Bilreparationer* in the Yellow Pages. If it's a rental car, contact the rental firm.

Motormännens Riksförbund

Problems 020 21 11 11. **Open** 9am-4pm Mon-Fri. *Office: Sveavägen 159, Norrmalm 690 38 00/www.motormannen.se). Bus 40, 46, 52, 515, 595.* **Open** 8.30am-5pm Mon-Fri. **Map** p307 B5.
The Swedish equivalent to the British AA, with reciprocal arrangements with most European motoring organisations. Call the toll-free number if you have a problem.

Fuel

Petrol stations (*bensinstation*) sell unleaded fuel (*blyfri* 95 or 98), leaded (just called 96 or 98) and diesel (*diesel*). Unleaded petrol pumps are colour-coded green, leaded is red and diesel black.

Jet

Norra Stationsgatan 59-61, Vasastaden. **Open** 24hrs daily. **Map** p306 B4.
Lower prices than most.

OKQ8

Katarinavägen 16, Södermalm (668 01 80/www.okq8.se). **Open** 24hrs daily. **Map** p311 K8.

Preem

Norr Mälarstrand 32, Kungsholmen (652 68 60/www.preem.se). **Open** 24hrs daily. **Map** p302 H4.

Statoil

Birger Jarlsgatan 120, Norrmalm (15 51 71/www.statoil.se). **Open** 7am-midnight Mon-Fri; 8am-midnight Sat, Sun. **Map** p307 B6.

Parking

Parking is not easy in central Stockholm. If you have parked illegally or not paid the right fee, you'll get a hefty fine from parking attendants employed by Stockholm city, security firm Securitas or the police. Parking is allowed on most streets but you'll have to pay, at least on weekdays. *Parkering Förbjuden* means parking prohibited, and it's illegal to park closer than ten metres (33 feet) to a pedestrian crossing. Car parks (*parkings*), signalled by a white 'P' on a blue sign, charge 20kr-50kr per hour in the city centre.

Your car will be towed only if it is left in a spot that hinders traffic or is dangerous to people's safety. Most of the time you'll just get a fat fine. If your car is towed, call 508 287 83/4/5. You'll have to pick it up at Finspångsgatan 1, Lunda (about 18 kilometres/ 11 miles from the city centre) and pay a fine of 1,500kr.

Vehicle hire

Car hire is relatively pricey, but it's a competitive market so shop around. The key is to check carefully what's included: ideally, you want unlimited mileage, tax and full insurance cover. You have to be 25 years of age to rent a car in Sweden, and you will need a credit card. Larger companies often advertise special offers on their websites.

Avis

Vasagatan 10B, Norrmalm (20 20 60/020 78 82 00/www.avis-se.com). T-bana T-Centralen/bus 3, 47, 53, 62, 65. **Open** 6am-6pm Mon-Fri; 9am-2pm Sat, Sun. **Credit** AmEx, DC, MC, V. **Map** p303 G6.
Branches: Ringvägen 90, Södermalm (644 99 80); Arlanda Airport (797 99 70); Bromma Airport (28 87 00).

Europcar

Tegelbacken 6, Norrmalm (21 06 50/ 020 78 11 80/www.europcar.se). T-bana T-Centralen/bus 3, 47, 53, 62, 65. **Open** 7am-6pm Mon-Fri; 10am-2pm Sat; noon-4pm Sun. **Credit** AmEx, DC, MC, V. **Map** p303 H6.
Branches: Hamngatan 17, Norrmalm (611 45 60); Fiskartorpsvägen, Östermalm (20 44 63); Arlanda Airport (59 36 09 40); Bromma Airport (80 08 07).

Hertz

Vasagatan 26, Norrmalm (24 07 20/ 020 21 12 11/www.hertz.nu). T-bana T-Centralen/bus 3, 47, 53, 62, 65. **Open** 7.30am-6pm Mon-Fri; 9am-3pm Sat, Sun. **Credit** AmEx, DC, MC, V. **Map** p303 G6.
Branches: Arlanda Airport (797 99 00); Bromma Airport (797 99 14).

Cycling

For good places to cycle and bike rental places, *see p220*.

Resources A-Z

Addresses

Addresses are always written with the building number after the street name. As in the UK, but not in the US, the first floor is the floor above street level. The floor at street level is called *bottenvåning* and is abbreviated to 'BV' in elevators.

Age restrictions

In Sweden, you have to be 18 to drink in a bar or buy low-alcohol beer in a grocery store, but 20 to buy alcohol at the state-owned monopolistic off-licence Systembolaget (*see also p166* **How to buy alcohol**).

You can smoke or drive at 18 and have sex at 15. At 15 a person is considered to become *byxmyndig*, which, loosely translated, means they are 'in charge of their pants'. Boys, in particular, often receive condoms on their 15th birthday.

Business services

Stockholm is known as a great city for doing business – except in July, when most people take a month's vacation and it's difficult to find anything but an answering machine to take your call. The city is widely recognised as receptive and sophisticated and is often used as a test market for new products.

Plenty of conventions take place in Stockholm, so many hotels cater mainly to business travellers (hence higher rates Sun-Fri) and there are a great number of places that can be hired for conferences and meetings. The city is also within easy reach of Arlanda Airport and, last but not least, it is very beautiful.

Conventions & conferences

There are two main trade fair/conference centres just on the edge of Stockholm: **Stockholmsmässan**, Mässvägen 1, Älvsjö (749 41 00/fax 99 20 44/www.stofair.se); and **Sollentunamässan**, Box 174, Sollentuna (50 66 50 00/fax 50 66 52 25/www.massan.com). The website **www.fairlink.se** provides useful information about trade fairs in all the Nordic countries.

Many bureaus can assist organisations and individuals in holding events in the city – look up *Konferansarrangörer* (conference organisers) in the Yellow Pages. It's often also possible to contact the place where you want to hold a conference and have them arrange it all for you – look under *Konferanslokaler* (conference venues) in the phone book.

Amica (02 01 12 22 22/www.amica.se) organises conferences of any size, while **Svenska Kursgårdar** (07 71 50 55 00/fax 59 41 11 88/www.svenska-kursgardar.se) offers 80 different conference locations in the city.

Note that hotels are often booked up during fairs and conferences. Below are dates in 2003 for major events; dates in subsequent years are likely to be similar:

Pet Fair 3-6 Jan
Stockholm Design 15-18 Jan
Formex 16-19 Jan
Stockholm Art Fair 21-23 Jan
Stockholm Furniture Fair 5-9 Feb
Stockholm International Antiques Fair 23-26 Jan
Lighting 2003 5-9 Feb
Health Fair 14-16 Feb
Stockholm International Boat Show 28 Feb-9 Mar
GastroNord 17-23 Mar
Stockholm Motor Show 5-13 Apr
Swedish Cardiovascular Meeting 7-8 May
Vård.expo 14-16 May
Home Improvement Fair Sept
Networks Telecom Sept
Sectech 28-29 Oct
Swedental Oct
Bio Tech Forum Nov
Scandinavian Sail & Motorboat Show 6-9 Nov
Travel Fair 7-9 Nov
Med.xpo 26-28 Nov

Couriers

Try looking in the Yellow Pages under *Budservice* for couriers. Prices vary but a small package sent within Stockholm on the same day costs around 200kr with the following international companies:

DHL

690 02 00/toll-free 020 345 345/fax 33 34 40/www.dhl.se. **Open** 24hrs daily. **Credit** AmEx, DC, MC, V.

TNT

625 58 00/toll-free 020 960 960/fax 625 58 70/www.tnt.com. **Open** 8am-6pm Mon-Fri. **Credit** AmEx, MC, V.

UPS

611 70 71/toll-free 020 788 799/fax 611 70 95/www.ups.com. **Open** 8am-7pm Mon-Fri; 9am-1pm Sat. **Credit** AmEx, MC, V.

Office & computer services

Megabyte System Svenska

Drottninggatan 94, Norrmalm (55 51 11 11/fax 55 51 11 99/www.mega byte.se). T-bana Hötorget/bus 1, 47, 52, 53, 69. **Open** 10am-6pm Mon-Fri. **Credit** AmEx, MC, V. **Map** p307 E6.
The latest products from Hewlett-Packard for sale, as well as software, components and servicing.

Mycom

Drottninggatan 63, Normalm (55 54 12 00/fax 55 54 12 50/ www.mycom.se). T-bana Hötorget/ bus 1, 47, 53, 69. **Open** 10am-7pm Mon-Fri; 10am-5pm Sat; noon-5pm Sun. **Credit** AmEx, MC, V. **Map** p303 F6.

An excellent shop with all kinds of computer equipment for sale, including laptops, scanners and software.

New Sec

Regeringsgatan 65, Norrmalm (454 40 00/fax 404 40 01/ www.newsec. se). T-bana Hötorget/ bus 1, 43, 56. **Open** 8.15am-noon, 1-4.15pm Mon-Thur; 8.15am-noon, 1-4pm Fri. **Map** p303 F7.

A leading commercial property estate agent with offices for lease within the whole greater Stockholm district.

Office Space

Byängsgränd 14, Årsta (681 00 04/ fax 681 04 45/www.office space.se). T-bana Enskede Gård. **Open** 8.30am-4.30pm Mon-Fri.

Offices at quite low rents in the city area for small or medium-sized businesses.

Translation services

Abcom

Kungstensgatan 59, Vasastaden (020 92 19 21/fax 30 60 94/www. abcom.se). T-bana Odenplan or Rådmansgatan/bus 40, 47, 53, 69. **Open** 8am-5pm Mon-Fri. **No credit cards**: bank transfers only. **Map** p303 E5.

A language-services provider that translates documents quickly and professionally for corporate Sweden.

SpråkCentrum

Stureplan 4, Östermalm (50 62 09 50/fax 50 62 09 99/www.sprak centrum.se). T-bana Östermalmstorg/ bus 1, 46, 55, 56. **Open** 8.30am-5pm Mon-Thur; 8.30am-4pm Fri. **No credit cards** (bank transfers only). **Map** p303 F8.

This is one of Sweden's oldest translation agencies. The staff translate to and from a huge number of languages and within every field, for both companies and individuals.

Useful organisations

Ministry of Foreign Affairs

405 10 00/www.utrikes. regeringen.se.

National Institute of Economic Research

453 59 00/www.konj.se.

National Tax Board

764 80 00/www.rsv.se.

Statistics Sweden

50 69 48 01/www.scb.se.

Sveriges Riksbank

787 00 00/www.riksbank.com.

Economic and financial data.

Swedish Stock Exchange

405 60 00/www.stockholmsborsen.se.

Customs

Items imported in excess of Sweden's duty-paid allowance will be liable for the Swedish selective purchase tax, which is quite steep (for example, 196kr per 1 litre of spirits, 1,760kr for 20 cigarettes). You must be aged 18 to bring in tobacco products and 20 to bring in alcohol.

Visitors arriving from the EU can take the following into Sweden without incurring customs duty, provided tax has already been paid in another EU country:

- 400 cigarettes or 200 small cigars or 100 cigars or 550 grams (19.4 ounces) of loose tobacco;
- 2 litres of spirits (over 22 per cent alcohol), 6 litres of fortified wine or alcoholic drinks containing less than 22 per cent alcohol, 26 litres of wine and 32 litres of beer.

Allowances for residents of non-EU countries entering from outside the EU with goods purchased in non EU-countries are:

- 200 cigarettes or 100 small cigars or 50 cigars or 250 grams (8.82 ounces) of tobacco;
- 1 litre of spirits (over 22 per cent alcohol) or 2 litres of any other alcoholic drink with less than 22 per cent alcohol;
- 2 litres of wine and 32 litres of beer;
- 50 grams (1.76 ounces) of perfume.

Check **Swedish Customs** website (www.tullverket.se) for more detailed info.

Disabled visitors

Recent legislation demands that all public buildings have to be accessible to the disabled and visually impaired; the goal for completion of the required renovations is 2005. However, facilities in Stockholm are already very good compared to many other European cities, so it is not usually a problem for disabled visitors to get around the capital.

The streets are in good condition and have wide pavements with ramped curbs for wheelchairs and prams. Wheelchair-adapted toilets can be found in larger restaurants, shopping centres, department stores and in some public and private buildings. Allergy sufferers will also find many hotels have allergy-free rooms.

The public transport system is quite wheelchair-accessible, especially the Tunnelbana, which has plenty of elevators, and most buses can 'kneel' at bus stops – though a common complaint is the quite wide gap between local commuter trains and the platform.

Most taxis are large enough to take wheelchairs, but do check when you order the cab. Try **Taxi Stockhom** (15 00 00).

De Handikappades Riksförbund

Katrinebergsvägen 6, Liljeholmen, 100 74 Stockholm (685 80 00/fax 645 65 41/www.dhr.se). T-bana Liljeholmen/bus 133, 143, 152. **Open** *Aug-June* 8.30am-noon, 1-4pm Mon-Fri. Closed July. **Map** p303 M2.

Supplies information on facilities for the mobility-impaired in Stockholm. The website has an English version.

Drugs

Approach with caution – drugs, including cannabis, are nothing like as widely accepted in Sweden as in some other parts of Europe. Possession of any drug, including medicine that you do not have a prescription for, is illegal, and you can be fined for even the very smallest amount.

The number of party-drug users has increased in the past ten years, and a special undercover police squad works to catch drug users at nightclubs and parties. Many clubs, including even several of the 'in' places, have taken a stand against drugs by not letting in anyone they suspect of using.

Electricity

Sweden, in common with most of Europe, has 220-volt AC, 50Hz current and uses two-pin continental plugs. The 220V current works fine with British-bought 240V products with a plug adaptor (available at Arlanda Airport and department stores). With US 110V equipment you will also need to have a current transformer.

Embassies & consulates

Many foreign embassies – including those of the UK, US, Japan and Norway – are clustered in Diplomatstaden, an enclave of villas on the edge of Ladugårdsgärdet. You'll find a full list of embassies in the phone book under *Ambassader*. There's also a list on the tourist office website (*see p285*). There is no New Zealand consulate or embassy in Stockholm: the New Zealand representative in the Hague (00 31 703 658 037) takes care of 'Swedish business'.

Australian Embassy

Sergels Torg 12, Norrmalm (613 29 00/fax 24 74 14/www.austemb.se). T-bana T-Centralen/bus 47, 52, 56, 59, 65. **Open** 8.30am-12.30pm, 1.30-4.30pm Mon-Fri. **Map** p303 G7.

British Embassy

Skarpögatan 6-8, Östermalm (671 30 00/fax 662 99 89/www.britishembassy.com). Bus 69. **Open** *Information* 10am-noon Mon, Wed, Fri. *Visas* 9.30am-noon Mon-Fri. *Consulate* 9.30am-noon, 2-4pm Mon-Fri. **Map** p305 F12.

Canadian Embassy

Tegelbacken 4, Norrmalm (453 30 00/information 453 30 44/fax 453 30 16/www.canadaemb.se). T-bana T-Centralen/bus 3, 53, 62, 65. **Open** 8.30am-noon, 1-5pm Mon-Fri. **Map** p303 H6.

Irish Embassy

Östermalmsgatan 97, Östermalm (661 80 05/fax 660 13 53/irish.embassy@swipnet.se). T-bana Karlaplan/bus 4, 42, 44, 72. **Open** 10am-noon, 2.30-4pm Mon-Fri. **Map** p308 E10.

US Embassy

Dag Hammarskjöldsväg 31, Östermalm (783 53 00/fax 660 58 79/www.usemb.se). Bus 56, 69, 76. **Open** 8.30am-4pm Mon-Fri. **Map** p305 F12.

Emergencies

To contact the police, ambulance or fire service in an emergency, call **112** (free of charge, including from public pay phones). For emergency rooms at hospitals, *see p279* **Accident & emergency**. For central police stations, *see p283* **Police & security**.

Gay & lesbian

Organisations

Gaystudenterna

Universitetet, Nobelhuset, Frescati (674 62 13/16 55 03/www.sus.su.se/gaystudenterna). T-bana Universitetet. **Open** *Office* 3-4.30pm Mon.

This largeish group of gay activist students (non-students are also welcome) works for gay awareness in education, as well as having fun outside the classroom. They arrange parties, film screenings, seminars, debates and a pub night on the first Wednesday of the month at Café Bojan (T-bana Universitetet; there's a sign right outside the T-bana exit), which is aways packed with people you never get to see anywhere else. Times for all events vary, so call first or look at the website.

RFSL

Sveavägen 57-9, Vasastaden (457 13 22/www.rfsl.se). T-bana Rådmansgatan/bus 43, 52. **Open** *Phone enquiries* 9am-4pm Mon-Fri. **Map** p307 D6.

The National Association for Sexual Equality, Sweden's nationwide organisation for gay, lesbian and trans rights, has its main office in a large building on Sveavägen. Hundreds of sub-minority groups – for foreigners, disabled, bisexuals, teenagers, seniors, parents of homosexuals, homosexual parents and so on – share the space with counsellors, the monthly *Kom ut!* magazine's editorial staff, a radio station and a library. The great website (Swedish only) provides all you need to know.

Healthcare

For an HIV-positive support group, *see p279* **AIDS/HIV**.

Lesbisk Hälsomottagning

Södersjukhuset, Ringvägen 52, Södermalm (616 11 44). Bus 3, 4, 55, 74. **Open** *Phone enquiries* 10-11am Tue; 3-4pm Thur. **Map** p310 N6.

Free gynaecological healthcare for lesbians only. Call first to make an appointment.

Venhälsan

Södersjukhuset, Ringvägen 52, Södermalm (616 25 00/www.hiv.nu). Bus 3, 4, 55, 74. **Open** 5.30-8.30pm Tue-Thur. **Map** p310 N6.

Free healthcare for both bi- and homosexual men. Located on the fifth floor; take elevator D.

Health

Don't go straight to an emergency room unless it really is an acute emergency. Instead, for advice on minor illnesses or prescription drugs, ring the 24-hour **Healthcare Information Service** (528 528 00/32 01 00/www.telefonakuten.se) Stay on the line if the automatic answering service kicks in and you will be connected to a nurse, who can provide up-to-date information (in English) about the city's hospitals, assign patients to a suitable hospital or doctor and also answer questions about illnesses.

For any information on prescription medicines, call the **Läkemedelsupplysningen** (medicine information office, open 24 hours) toll-free on 020 66 77 66. English is spoken.

Accident & emergency

The following hospitals have 24-hour emergency rooms:

St Görans Sjukhus

Sanktgöransplan 1, Kungsholmen (587 010 00). T-bana Fridhemsplan/ bus 57, 59, 74.

Södersjukhuset

Ringvägen 52, Södermalm (616 10 00). Bus 3. **Map** p310 N6.

AIDS/HIV

The escalation of HIV/AIDS has been quite slow in Sweden compared with many other countries, but about 30 new cases per month are still reported. The **AIDS Helpline** (020 78 44 40) can direct you to the closest hospital for tests, treatment and information.

Noaks Ark

Drottninggatan 61, Norrmalm (700 46 00/www.noaksark.redcross.se). T-bana Hötorget or T-Centralen/ bus 1, 47, 52, 56, 59. **Open** *June-Sept* 9am-4pm Mon-Fri. *Oct-May* 9am-5pm Mon-Fri. **Map** p303 F6.

The Red Cross's HIV and AIDS help organisation arranges parties and happenings, and runs the Life Gallery exhibition space (*see p199*) and a café. There's an English version of the website.

Posithiva Gruppen

Magnus Ladulåsgatan 8, Södermalm (720 19 60/www.posithivagruppen. se). Bus 3, 4, 43, 55, 74. **Open** 6pm-midnight Mon-Thur; 6pm-2am Fri; 8pm-2am Sat. **Map** p310 M6.

Support group for HIV-positive bi- and homosexual men. Soup nights, theme nights, relatives' night, pub nights and parties.

Alternative medicine

Alternative medicine, especially massage, is very common in Sweden – who hasn't heard of Swedish massage? The use of other complementary treatments, such as homeopathy and acupuncture, is also rapidly increasing. Acupuncture is even practised on women in labour at the hospitals.

AAA Kliniken

Odengatan 62, Vasastaden (31 21 00). T-bana Odenplan/bus 4, 42, 46, 72. **Open** *Phone enquiries* 8am-8pm Mon-Fri. **No credit cards. Map** p307 D5.

A clinic offering acupuncture, massage and chiropractic treatments. Always ring in advance for an appointment.

Björn Lundberg

Rådmansgatan 88, Vasastaden (765 04 31). T-bana Rådmansgatan/ bus 40, 47, 53, 69. **Open** *Phone enquiries* 9am-5pm Mon-Fri. **Credit** AmEx, DC, MC, V. **Map** p307 E5.

Help with allergies, asthma, skin problems, headaches and infertility. It costs 450kr for the first visit, 350kr for subsequent visits. Always ring for an appointment.

Family planning

Condoms can be found in grocery stores, pharmacies, Pressbyrån, 7-Eleven and in vending machines at some bars and clubs. The contraceptive pill requires a doctor's prescription. Abortions are legal until week 18, after which time there has to be a serious medical reason; non-residents may have trouble getting treatment at any time.

Mama Mia

Karlavägen 58-60, Östermalm (20 90 02/www.mamamia.se). T-bana Stadion/bus 42, 44, 55, 56, 62. **Open** usually 9am-6pm Mon-Fri. **Map** p308 E9.

Family planning and postnatal care. Call in advance for an appointment.

Dentists

Dentists can be found in the Yellow Pages under *Tandläkare*. No appointment is needed for any emergency dental care. Try visiting the **Emergency Dental Clinic** at St Eriks Sjukhus, Polhelmsgatan 46, Kungsholmen (545 512 20/28); open 7.45am-9pm daily. Rates vary greatly depending on the treatment, but start at 490kr; if you arrive after 7pm, prices increase by 50 per cent.

Afta Akuttandvård

Sergels Torg 12, Norrmalm (20 20 25). T-bana T-Centralen/bus 47, 52, 56, 59, 65. **Open** *Drop-in patients* 8am-6pm Mon-Fri; 9am-3pm Sat, Sun. **Map** p303 G7.

Akut Tandvård

Kungsgatan 29, Norrmalm (10 92 93). T-bana Hötorget/bus 1, 43, 52, 56. **Open** 8am-11pm daily. **Map** p303 F7.

Doctors

Call beforehand to set up an appointment with these general practitioners. A visit to a doctor costs 120kr with the E111 form, 500kr without.

Husläkarjouren

Sabbatsbergs Sjukhus, Olivecronas Väg 2, Vasastaden (672 39 90). T-bana Odenplan/bus 4, 40, 47, 53, 72. **Open** *Phone enquiries* 4.30-10pm Mon-Fri; 8am-8pm Sat, Sun. **Map** p306 E4.

Overnight GP. Call first to make an appointment.

Södermalms Husläkare

Wollmar Yxkullsgatan 25, Södermalm (616 61 00). T-bana Mariatorget/bus 43, 55, 66, 74. **Open** 8am-8pm Mon-Fri. **Map** p310 L6.

Stureplans Husläkarmottagning

Riddargatan 1, Östermalm (58 75 36 00). T-bana Östermalmstorg/bus 46, 55, 62. **Open** 8am-5pm Mon-Fri. **Map** p303 F8.

Insurance

EU nationals are entitled to some free medical and hospital treatment in Sweden if they have a filled-in E111 form and passport or some other form of identification. Not all treatment is covered, however, so it's advisable to also take out separate medical insurance.

Non-EU nationals should take out insurance as a matter of course.

Opticians

See p173.

Pharmacies

Pharmacies (*apotek*), identified by a green and white J-shaped sign, can be found all over the city. Most are open 10am-6pm Mon-Fri, and closed at the weekend. For two pharmacies with extended opening hours, *see p168.*

Helplines

Alcoholics Anonymous

720 38 42. **Open** 11am-1pm, 6-8pm daily.

Children's Helpline (BRIS)

0200 230 230. **Open** 24hrs daily.

Medications Hotline

33 12 31. **Open** 24hrs daily.

Narcotics Anonymous

Helpline 411 44 17/answering service with information about meetings 411 44 18. **Open** 6-8pm Mon; or leave a message on the answerphone and a cousellor will call back within 24hrs.

Poison Information

33 12 31. **Open** 24hrs daily.

ID

Swedes do have national identity cards, but people tend to use their driver's licence as ID. It is a good idea to carry some form of identification when you go to bars and clubs if you're under 25 or look like you could be – bartenders and bouncers will often ask for proof. Also, ID will be needed if you want to pay the lower price sometimes offered at musems for people aged under 25 or over 65.

Internet

Stockholm is a world-leader in e-commerce, new media and software development, and has the highest internet use per capita in the world. For information on the Inform@fon internet phones, *see p286* **Public phones**.

Internet service providers

The best solution for a short-term visitor is to find an internet café, as setting up an internet subscription can be quite time-consuming for anything less than a stay of several months. Most hotels, even the ones that do not provide internet outlets in every room, can usually help travellers.

If you're staying for a long time and your business hasn't set you up with internet access, try the main phone company **Telia** (90 200/www.telia.com in English or www.telia.se in Swedish).

Internet cafés

There are quite a few cybercafés in the city centre, including the following. You can also surf the net at libraries and many hotels.

Café Access

Basement, Kulturhuset, Sergels Torg, Norrmalm (50 83 14 89/ www.kulturhuset.stockholm.se). T-bana T-Centralen/bus 47, 52, 59, 65. **Open** 11am-6pm Mon; 10am-7pm Tue-Fri; 10am-5pm Sat; 11am-4pm Sun. **No credit cards. Map** p303 G7.

Has 27 computers, costing 20kr per half-hour.

Café Zenit

Sveavägen 20, Norrmalm (698 57 40). T-bana Hötorget/bus 1, 43, 52, 56. **Open** *Aug-June* 10am-6pm Mon-Fri; 11am-5pm Sat; noon-5pm Sun. Closed July. **No credit cards. Map** p303 F7.

If you eat at the café, you can use one of the four computers for free.

ICE

Vasagatan 42, Norrmalm (24 88 00/www.ice.se). T-bana T-Centralen/ bus 1, 47, 53, 69. **Open** noon-midnight Mon-Thur, Sun; noon-3am Fri, Sat. **No credit cards. Map** p302 F6.

Has 40 terminals at 50kr per hour.

Internet Café

3rd floor, PUB, Hötorget 13-15, Norrmalm (24 57 59). T-bana Hötorget/bus 1, 52, 56. **Open** 10am-7pm Mon-Fri; 10am-5pm Sat; noon-5pm Sun. **No credit cards. Map** p303 F6.

Ten computers at 30kr per half-hour.

M@trix

Hötorget T-bana station, Norrmalm (20 02 93/www.matrix-se.com). T-bana Hötorget/bus 1, 43, 52, 56. **Open** 10am-midnight Mon-Thur, Sun; 10am-3am Fri, Sat. **Credit** AmEx, DC, MC, V. **Map** p303 F7.

Forty terminals at 50kr per hour, with a minimum cost of 12.50kr.

Nine

Odengatan 44, Vasastaden (612 67 97). T-bana Rådmansgatan/bus 4, 42, 53, 72. **Open** 10am-1am Mon-Fri; 11am-1am Sat, Sun. **No credit cards. Map** p307 C6.

Three floors with 40 computers at 0.75kr per minute.

Left luggage

There are left-luggage lockers in Arlanda Airport, and at the bus, train and ferry terminals.

Arlanda Airport

Lockers **Rates** 20kr-30kr per 24hrs. *Manual left-luggage storage* **Open** 6am-10pm Mon-Fri; 6am-6pm Sat, Sun. **Rates** 280kr per wk for a suitcase.

Central Station

Open 5am-12.30am. **Rates** 25kr-35kr per 24hrs.

Silja Line Terminal

Open 8am-8.15pm daily.

Viking Line Terminal

Open 6.15am-8.15pm daily. Lockers can be used for a maximum of 24hrs.

Legal help

Information about legal help can be got from the police, trade unions or legal advisers. Lawyers' offices are found in the Yellow Pages under *Advokater*. They are not obliged to help you but most will at least recommend what you should do or where you should call – which depends quite a lot on the kind of legal help you are in need of.

Libraries

Stockholm's libraries are open to anyone for reference, but if you want to take a book out, you will need ID and an address in Sweden (a hotel address will not do).

Kungliga Biblioteket

Humlegården, Östermalm (463 40 00/www.kb.se). T-bana Östermalmstorg/bus 42, 44, 46, 55, 56. **Open** 9am-6pm Mon-Thur; 9am-5pm Fri; 11am-3pm Sat. **Map** p308 E8.
The national library is mainly for research. It has all publications that refer to or are published in Sweden.

Stockholms Stadsbiblioteket

Sveavägen 73, Vasastaden (50 83 11 00/www.ssb.stockholm.se). T-bana Odenplan/bus 4, 40, 42, 46, 53, 69, 72. **Open** 10am-8.30pm Mon-Thur; 10am-6pm Fri; noon-4pm Sat, Sun. **Map** p307 D5.
The main library is known to most Stockholmers for its architecture, but it also has books in many different languages. Newspapers, magazines and computer terminals can be found in the building next door called Annexet. *See also p28* **Super Swedes: Gunnar Asplund**.

Utrikespolitiska Biblioteket

Lilla Nygatan 23, Gamla Stan (696 05 27/www.ui.se). T-bana Gamla Stan/bus 3, 53. **Open** 10am-4.30pm Mon-Thur; 10am-4pm Fri. **Map** p303 J7.
A library specialising in international politics.

Lost property

The two main public transport companies have lost-and-found centres.

SL

Klara Östra Kyrkogata 4, Norrmalm (412 69 60). T-bana T-Centralen/bus 42, 47, 59, 62, 65. **Open** noon-7pm Mon-Fri; noon-4pm Sat. **Map** p303 G6.
For objects lost on the Tunnelbana, city buses and commuter trains.

SJ

Central Station, Vasagatan, Norrmalm (762 25 50). T-bana T-Centralen/bus 42, 47, 59, 62, 65. **Open** 10am-6pm Mon-Fri. **Map** p303 G6.
For long-distance trains.

Media

Newspapers

The two main daily papers are **Dagens Nyheter** (738 10 00/www.dn.se), which is fairly middle of the road politically, and the more right-leaning **Svenska Dagbladet** (13 50 00/www.svd.se). If you take public transport in the morning, you're more likely to see people reading **Metro** (402 20 30/www.metro.se/metro), a free daily paper distributed at T-bana and train stations. **Aftonbladet** (725 20 00/www.aftonbladet.se) and **Expressen** (738 30 00/www.expressen.se) are two popular evening tabloids that give readers the latest scandals and gossip, as well as weekly TV guides.

On Fridays *Aftonbladet* publishes **Puls** (*Pulse*), its entertainment listings for the week; *DN*'s equivalent is **På Stan** (*On the Town*). You can pick both up for free on Fridays at the tourist office (*see p285*). If you can navigate the Swedish, *DN*'s *På Stan* website has an excellent search engine and calendar to help you find events. *Expressen* has recently come out with its pocket-format **Guiden** (*The Guide*), available on Fridays and throughout the weekend. The monthly **Nöjesguiden** (www.nojesguiden.se) features stories about the Stockholm scene and events listings. It's available free from shops, cafés and newsstands.

For Swedish news in English, **SR Radio Sweden International** lists brief summaries on its website (http://www.sr.se/rs/red/ind_eng.html).

Magazines

For the latest in lifestyle trends and fashion, buy English-language glossy **Stockholm New** (www.stockholmnew.com), but it's published rather sporadically. The house-proud Swedes can choose from several magazines on interior design, of which **Sköna Hem**, **Elle Interiör** and **Lantliv** are among the most popular. Swedish **Cosmopolitan** has recently arrived on the scene, although **Amelia**, **Damernas Värld** and **Vecko-Revyn** are the main contenders for female readership. Men's magazines **Café** and **Slitz** focus on music, fashion and celebrity interviews. **Sonic** and **Groove** have the low-down on the Swedish music scene, and independently published **ETC** offers up left-wing political criticism. **Situation Sthlm**, about the city's street life and politics, is typically sold in T-bana stations by homeless people.

Architecture and design magazines include **Forum**, **Arkitektur** and **FORM**. Sweden's biggest art magazine is **Konstperspektiv** (www.konstperspektiv.nu), while **Paletten** (www.natverkstan.net/paletten) takes a theoretical approach to contemporary art. English-language art mags are **nu** (www.nordic artreview.nu); quarterly **Merge** (www.mergemag.com), which covers film, art, design, music and architecture; and **Site**, also published quarterly, which deals with art, film, philosophy and architecture.

International newsstands

Most of the major foreign newspapers and magazines, especially English-language ones, can be found in the city.

Interpress

NK department store, Hamngatan 18-20, Norrmalm (762 87 80). T-bana Kungsträdgården or Östermalmstorg/bus 43, 47, 55, 59, 69. **Open** 10am-7pm Mon-Fri; 10am-5pm Sat; noon-5pm Sun (June, July noon-4pm Sun). **Credit** AmEx, DC, MC, V. **Map** p303 F7.

Press Stop

Götgatan 31, Södermalm (644 35 10/www.press-stop.se. T-bana Medborgarplatsen or Slussen/bus 43, 55, 59, 66. **Open** 10am-6.30pm Mon-Fri; 10am-5pm Sat; 11am-5pm Sun. **Credit** AmEx, MC, V. **Map** p310 L8.

This branch of Press Stop – in the same complex as DesignTorget (*see p165*) and a popular branch of Wayne's Coffee (*see p148*) – services Söder's cultural elite with magazines specialising in art, architecture and design. Among the 2,500 titles, there's also a decent selection of international magazines and newspapers.

Branches: Drottninggatan 35, Norrmalm (411 11 93); Gallerian, Hamngatan 37, Norrmalm (723 01 91); Kungsgatan 14, Norrmalm (21 91 03).

Pressbyrån

www.pressbyran.se.

This chain has 320 kiosks throughout Sweden that sell international magazines and newspapers as well as sweets, cigarettes, batteries and the like. Kiosks can be found at most Tunnelbana and train stations.

Radio

E-FM

107.5 Mhz

Soul and dance classics from the 1970s and '80s.

Lugna Favoriter

104.7 Mhz

Old and new slow songs.

Mix Megapol

104.3 Mhz

Old and new pop and rock hits.

NRJ

105.1 Mhz

The latest hits.

Radio Sweden

89.6 Mhz

Check the schedule (www.sr.se/rs) for English programming, which generally includes sports and political topics.

Rockklassiker

106.7 Mhz

Rock classics.

Sveriges Radio P2

93.8/96.2 Mhz

Classical, jazz and opera.

Vinyl

107 Mhz

Golden oldies.

Television

The state channels of **SVT 1** and **SVT 2** were the first to broadcast in Sweden and still attract the majority of viewers. Their commercial-free programmes are varied to appeal to audiences of all ages.

Deregulation during the mid 1980s ended the state's television broadcasting monopoly and allowed for the creation of several private channels. The most successful of these today is the terrestrial **TV4**, with news, soap operas, sitcoms and game shows. Similar programming can be found on **TV3** and **Kanal 5**, which are broadcast from abroad and – much to the chagrin of the government – do not always obey Swedish broadcasting regulations. Hip youths with carefully dishevelled hair present the entertainment programming at popular **ZTV**.

Luckily for visitors, foreign-made programmes and films are shown in their original language with Swedish subtitles.

Money

The Swedish *krona* (plural *kronor*, abbreviated to kr or SEK) is divided into 100 *öre*. It comes in coins of 50 *öre*, 1kr, 5kr and 10kr, and notes of 20kr, 50kr, 100kr, 500kr and 1,000kr. At the time of going to press £1 = 14.38kr; US$1 = 9.46kr; €1 = 9.18kr.

Sweden is currently outside the European Monetary Union (EMU), whose members – now using the euro – are Belgium, Greece, Germany, Spain, France, Italy, Ireland, Austria, Luxembourg, the Netherlands, Portugal and Finland. As in the UK, there are many discussions in Sweden about the possibility of joining the EMU, but the earliest this could happen now is 2005. However, euros are accepted in many shops, restaurants and hotels, at least in areas with a lot of tourists.

ATMs/cash machines

There are two types of ATM: **Bankomat** (the joint system of the business banks) and **Uttag** (which belongs to Foreningssparbanken). With major credit cards you can withdraw cash from most ATMs, which provide instructions in different languages at the push of a button. Don't forget that a commission will be charged. You'll find ATMs all over the city, in department stores, shopping centres and at banks.

Banks & bureaux de change

You can change money in the city at banks, many hotels and specialist bureaux de change, such as **Forex** and **X-change**; the bureaux de change tend to be the best option because they often provide a more favourable exchange rate and have numerous offices in the city centre. There are exchange offices in the tourist office, Central Station (inside the main entrance hall and on the underground train level) and at Arlanda Airport (Terminals 2 and 5).

Banks are usually open 9am-3.30pm Mon-Fri, and some stay open until 6pm at least once a week. All banks are closed at weekends and on public holidays, as well as the day before a public holiday.

Forex

Stockholm Information Service tourist office, Sverigehuset, Hamngatan 27, Norrmalm (20 03 89/www.forex.se). T-bana Kungsträdgården/bus 46, 47, 55, 59, 62, 76. **Open** 8am-7pm Mon-Fri; 9am-5pm Sat, Sun. **Map** p303 G7.

Branches: NK, Hamngatan 18-20, Norrmalm (762 83 40); Central Station, Norrmalm (411 67 34); Cityterminalen, Normalm (21 42 80);

Vasagatan 14, Norrmalm (10 49 90); Arlanda Airport, Terminal 2 (59 36 22 71).

X-change

Kungsgatan 30, Norrmalm (50 61 07 00/www.x-change.se). T-bana Hötorget/bus 1, 52, 56. **Open** 8am-7pm Mon-Fri; 9am-4pm Sat. **Map** p303 F7.

The other branches are also open on Sundays.

Branches: PUB, Hötorget 13-15, Norrmalm (10 30 00); Arlanda Airport, Arrivals Hall, Terminal 5 (797 85 57).

Credit cards

Major credit and debit cards are widely accepted by hotels, shops, restaurants and many other services (including Tunnelbana ticket machines, and pay-and-display parking machines in the street). If you pay by credit card in a shop, you will often be asked for photo ID. Banks will advance cash against a credit card, but prefer you to use an ATM.

Note that Systembolaget (the state-run alcohol shops) only accepts cash or Swedish debit cards.

For **lost or stolen credit cards**, phone one of the following 24-hour numbers:

American Express

During business hours 429 56 00/ after business hours 429 54 29.

Diners Club

14 68 78.

MasterCard

020 79 13 24.

Visa

020 79 31 46.

Swedish MasterCard and Visa members should contact the bank that issued the credit card.

Money transfers

Local banks do not do money transfers unless you are a customer of the bank. **Forex** (*see p282*; fee from US$20) and **Western Union** are your best bets for money transfers to and from Sweden, and have branches all over Stockholm.

Western Union

020 74 17 42. **Open** 8am-8pm Mon-Fri; 8am-5pm Sat; 10am-4pm Sun.

Call the toll-free number to find your nearest branch. Transferring up to 5,300kr costs 390kr.

Tax

The sales tax for most commodities is 25 per cent. There is a 12 per cent sales tax on food and hotel bills, and 6 per cent sales tax on books, movie/concert tickets and transport (taxis, flights, trains). The sales tax is included in the bill, and it always says on your receipt how much of what you paid was tax.

Non-EU residents can reclaim tax on purchases above 200kr in shops displaying a 'Tax-Free Shopping' sticker. All you have to do is ask for a tax-free receipt when paying for an item. When you leave the EU, show your purchases, receipts and passport to customs officials and have your Global Refund cheques stamped. The refund can be collected from any Global Refund office or credited to, for example, your own bank account. For more information, call Global Refund (0410 48 450/www.globalrefund.com).

Travellers' cheques

Travellers' cheques are accepted as payment in the more touristy areas, but do not expect to be able to use them in smaller shops or restaurants. It's probably better to exchange your travellers' cheques at a bank since they exchange any currency and usually offer the best rates. All major brands are accepted these days, except for Eurocheques.

Opening hours

Normal opening hours for shops are 10am-6pm Mon-Fri, 10am-5pm Sat, noon-4pm Sun, but some smaller shops are shut earlier on Saturdays and are closed on Sundays. All shops are closed on public holidays (*see p287* **When to go**) except for some grocery stores that are open every day of the year.

Restaurant opening hours vary greatly. They are usually open by 11am if they serve lunch; otherwise they'll open some time in the afternoon. Closing time is often around midnight unless the restaurant has a bar area, in which case they may stay open until 1am or even later.

Office hours are generally 8.30am-5pm Mon-Fri. For bank opening hours, *see p282* **Banks & bureaux de change**. For post office opening hours, *see p284* **Postal services**.

Police & security

The police are not that common a sight in Stockholm, but can always be spotted at concerts or any special event. They speak English and are known to be friendly and helpful. If you are the victim of a crime, you should always call the police on **112**.

Stockholm is considered a very safe city, so the chance of something bad happening to you is small. However, it's always wise to take the usual city precautions: don't openly flaunt money or jewellery, do keep a close eye on your surroundings, and be careful in quiet or badly lit areas late at night.

Pickpocketing does occur in crowded places. Mugging is very rare and there are no particular areas that are considered dangerous, but it's not recommended to walk in dimly lit areas such as parks at night.

Women of all ages do walk around and use public transport to get home in the middle of the night – but take the usual precautions.

Police HQ

Norra Agnegatan 33-7, Kungsholmen (401 00 00). T-bana Rådhuset/bus 3, 40, 52, 62. **Map** p302 G4.
This is the main police station for Stockholm. City-centre stations are also found at Bryggargatan 19, Tulegatan 4, Sergels Torg (at the entrance to the underground station), the Central Station and Södermannagatan 5.

Postal services

Most post offices are open 10am-6pm Mon-Fri, 10am-2pm Sat; they have a yellow sign containing a blue crown and horn symbol. You can also buy stamps at tobacco kiosks, Pressbyrån kiosks (*see p282*) and the tourist office (*see p285*).

Letters and postcards weighing up to 20g cost 5kr within Sweden; 8kr to the rest of Europe; 10kr to the rest of the world.

Mail sent to other European countries generally arrives in 2-3 days, and to the USA in about 4-5 days. The yellow post boxes are for national and international mail, while the blue boxes are for mail within the Stockholm area (postcodes starting with 1). For the express delivery of packages, *see p276* **Couriers**.

Posten

Central Station, Vasagatan, Norrmalm (020 23 22 21/www.posten.se). T-bana T-Centralen/bus 1, 47, 52, 53, 59, 69. **Open** 7am-10pm Mon-Fri; 10am-7pm Sat, Sun. **Map** p303 G6.
This large post office is in a handy place, at the Central Station, and has long opening hours.

Poste Restante

Letters sent Poste Restante can be sent to any post office and there is no extra charge. Items will be kept for a month, and you'll need some form of ID to collect them. To find the address of the nearest post office (*Postkontor*) to you, try looking up *Posten* in the Yellow Pages.

Queuing

Swedes, like the British, have a highly developed queuing culture. People just love standing in line, and queue-jumpers will be met with angry glares. In many shops you'll find a ticket machine near the door; even if there's no one else in the shop, don't expect to get served instantly – you'll have to take a ticket and wait for your number to come up. And woe betide if you miss your slot: you'll probably have to get another ticket and start all over again.

Religion

Most Swedes are nominally members of the Church of Sweden, which is Evangelical Lutheran, but less than ten per cent of the population attends church regularly. In January 2000, church and state were officially separated. Many other Christian sects are represented in Stockholm, and 50,000 Muslims and around 10,000 Jews live in or near the city.

The service and opening times listed below often change in summer, so call ahead to double-check.

Immanuelskyrkan (Evangelical)

Kungstensgatan 17, Vasastaden (58 75 03 31). T-bana Rådmansgatan/bus 42, 43, 46, 52. **Services** *English* 11am Sun. **Map** p307 D6.

Katolska Kyrkan (Catholic)

Folkungagatan 46B, Södermalm (640 15 55). T-bana Medborgarplatsen/bus 59, 66. **Open** *Winter* 7.30am-6pm daily. *Summer* 7.30am-noon, 2-6pm daily. **Services** 5pm, 8pm Mon-Fri; 9am, 5pm Sat; 10am, 11am Sun. **Map** p310 M8.

St Jacob (Ecumenical Church of Stockholm)

Västra Trädgårdsgatan 2, Norrmalm (723 30 00). T-bana Kungsträdgården/bus 46, 55, 59, 62, 76. **Open** 24hrs daily. **Services** *English* 6pm Sun. **Map** p303 G7.

Stockholms Moské (Muslim)

Kapellgränd, Södermalm (50 91 09 00). T-bana Medborgarplatsen/bus 59, 66. **Open** 10am-6pm daily. **Map** p311 L8.

Stora Synagogan (Jewish)

Wahrendorffsgatan 3, Norrmalm (58 78 58 00). T-bana Kungsträdgården/bus 46, 55, 59, 62, 76. **Tours** 10am, noon, 2pm Mon-Fri, Sun. **Services** 9am-midnight Sat (bring a passport in order to be let in). **Map** p303 G8.
The Great Synagogue is conservative/liberal rather than orthodox.

Storkyrkan (Protestant)

Trånsgrund 1, Gamla Stan (723 30 16). T-bana Gamla Stan/bus 43, 46, 55, 59, 76. **Services** 11am Sat, Sun. **Map** p303 J8.
Stockholm's 700-year-old cathedral; *see also p64.*

Smoking

Norway may soon become the first country in the world to ban smoking in public, and apparently Sweden is considering similar measures – though it's not likely to happen any time soon. The city streets are very clean and you'll be frowned upon if you throw your cigarette butt on to the pavement, but you will still see quite a lot of people smoking. You can't smoke in most public places, including bus stop cubicles and all Tunnelbana stations. Most hotels offer non-smoking rooms and from January 2003 restaurants must have a non-smoking area by law, though it will probably take a while before all restaurants abide.

Study

Many students come from abroad to study in Sweden, and a lot of Swedes take the opportunity to study in a foreign country. To find educational institutions look up *Utbildning* in the Yellow Pages.

Tourist offices

Stockholm Information Service

Sverigehuset (Sweden House), Hamngatan 27, Norrmalm (789 24 90/fax 789 24 91/ www.stockholmtown.se). T-bana Kungsträdgården/bus 45, 47, 55, 56, 62. **Open** 9am-6pm Mon-Fri; 10am-3pm Sat, Sun. **Map** p303 G7.

This is the main tourist office in Stockholm, with huge amounts of useful info, plus free books and maps and the free monthly magazine *What's On Stockholm* (in English). Make this your first stop before you head anywhere else. Staff can also answer almost any question you have and provide great advice on what to do or where to go. You can also buy the Stockholm Card (in person or online – *see p56* **Pick a card**) and theatre and concert tickets, and there's a small gift shop, a Forex exchange bureau and, upstairs, a highly recommended bookshop, **Sverigebokhandeln** (*see p151*). The website – in eight languages – is excellent and well worth scouring before you visit.

Hotellcentralen

Concourse, Central Station, Vasagatan, Norrmalm (789 24 56/90/hotels@ stoinfo.se). T-bana T-Centralen/bus 1, 47, 53, 69. **Open** *June-Aug* 8am-8pm daily. *Sept-May* 9am-6pm daily. **Map** p303 G6.

The tourist office's hotel-booking centre can find and book hotels in all price brackets. If you ring them to arrange a hotel booking, it's free; if you visit, it costs 50kr (20kr for youth hostels). Staff can only make same-day bookings for hostels. You will also find loads of free information, about the city as well as its accommodation.

Outside Sweden

Swedish Travel & Tourism Council

11 Montagu Place, London W1H 2AL, UK (00800 3080 3080/fax 020 7724 5872/ www.visit-sweden.com). **Open** *Phone enquiries* 9am-7pm Mon-Fri.

The Swedish tourism council has an excellent website with all the information you could possibly need in a variety of languages, and also tailored for visitors from particular countries. There are plenty of useful links and telephone numbers.

US office: 655 Third Avenue, New York, PO Box 4649 Grand Central Station (+1 212 885 9700).

Universities & colleges

Berghs School of Communication

PO Box 1380, 111 93 Stockholm (58 75 50 00/fax 58 75 50 10/ www.berghs-soc.com).

Offers programmes in journalism, media, advertising and PR.

Handelshögskolan

PO Box 6501, 113 83 Stockholm (736 90 00/fax 31 81 86/www.hhs.se).

Stockholm's School of Economics, the city's main business school, was founded in 1909 and is the oldest private Swedish institution of university standing. The school co-operates with business institutions around the globe and has an exchange programme with 155 places each year.

Konstfack

PO Box 24115, 10 451 Stockholm (450 41 18/international office 450 41 13/fax 450 41 92/ www.konstfack.se).

The University College of Arts, Crafts and Design on Valhallavägen opened way back in 1844 and has almost 2,000 applicants every year – only 100 are admitted. The school takes part in Erasmus, Socrates and Nordplus exchange programmes and has about 30 exchange students per year. In summer 2003 it's due to move to new premises in the old Ericsson factory in the suburb of Telefonplan.

Kungliga Tekniska Högskolan

100 44 Stockholm (790 60 00/fax 790 81 92/international@admin. kth.se/www.kth.se).

The Institute of Technology has just turned 175 years old and has 18,000 students. It provides one-third of Sweden's technical research and has established exchanges all over the world through such programmes as Socrates, Erasmus and Nordtech.

Stockholms Filmskola

Hornsagata 65, 118 49 Stockholm, 616 00 35/fax 616 00 34/ info@stockholmsfilmskola.a.se.

A private school offering pre-university foundation courses (lasting 1.5 years) in film studies.

Stockholms Musikpedagogiska Institut

PO Box 26164, 100 41 Stockholm (611 05 02/52 61/www.smi.se).

A small, independent college in Östermalm that offers education in music and related arts at undergrad and postgrad levels.

Stockholms Universitet

106 91 Stockholm (switchboard 16 20 00/international office 16 28 45/fax 16 13 97/gunnar.arrhed@ sb.su.se/www.su.se).

Stockholm University – located north of the city centre, with its own T-bana stop, Universitetet – has about 34,000 undergraduate students and 2,200 postgraduate students. Opened in 1878, it has an international graduate programme and such exchange programmes as Socrates, Erasmus, Nordplus and Nordlys.

Telephones

International & local dialling codes

To make an international call from Stockholm, dial 00 and then the country code, followed by the area code (omitting the initial 0, if there is one) and the number. The international code for the UK is 44; it's 1 for the US and Canada; 353 for the Irish Republic; 61 for Australia; and 64 for New Zealand.

To call Stockholm from abroad, dial 00, then 46 for Sweden, then 8 for Stockholm, then the number. Stockholm phone numbers vary in the number of digits they contain. The area code for Stockholm (including the archipelago) is 08, but you don't need to dial it if you're within the area. All phone numbers in this guide are given as dialled from within Stockholm.

Swedish mobile phone numbers begin with 07. Numbers beginning 020 are always toll-free lines.

Operator services

All operators in Sweden speak English or will be happy to connect you to someone who does.

National directory enquiries *118 118*
International directory enquiries *118 119*
National and international operator *90 200*
Telephone charges/faults helpline *90 200*
Telegrams *020 0021*
Time *90 510*
Wake-up calls *90 180*
Or dial *55* and then the time at which you want to be woken, in four figures according to the 24hr clock (eg 0730), then dial #. To delete the command, press #55#.

Public phones

Public phones, operated by semi-state-owned phone company **Telia**, are not as widespread as they used to be because of the rise in the use of mobile phones. They accept either credit cards or pre-paid phonecards (the few coin-operated phones that still exist can be found at railway stations and airports), which are available in 30, 60 or 100 units and can be bought at most newsagents, tobacconists and Pressbyrån (*see p282*). One unit buys one minute of a local call; long-distance calls cost two units per minute.

Instructions are given in English. You can make reverse-charge (collect) calls from all public phones, and also call the emergency services (on 112) for free.

You'll also find the newfangled 'Inform@fon' at the airport and some train stations, shopping centres and financial institutions. It looks like a normal payphone (and can be used as such), but can do almost everything except walk the dog – send and receive emails and faxes, connect to the internet, carry out banking transactions. The hard of hearing can write messages using the keyboard. You pay for this multimedia kiosk with a credit card or normal phonecard.

Mobile phones

Stockholm, home of telecom giant Ericsson, has embraced the mobile phone revolution with wide-open arms. Almost everyone owns a mobile phone (whether they know how to use it is another matter).

You'll see signs telling you to turn off your phone at, for example, pharmacies and banks, and most restaurants prefer you to switch off or at least turn down the ringing tone.

Sweden is on the worldwide GSM network, so compatible mobile phones should work without any problem.

Komab

Norrlandsgatan 15, Norrmalm (412 11 00/www.komab.se). T-bana Östermalmstorg/bus 46, 47, 55, 59, 69. **Open** 9.30am-6pm Mon-Fri; 10am-3pm Sat. **Credit** MC, V. **Map** p303 F8.
Low prices on mobile phones – cheaper, in fact, than the price of renting one for a week.

Time

Stockholm is one hour ahead of GMT, six hours ahead of US Eastern Standard Time and nine ahead of Pacific Standard Time. So, when it's 6pm in Sweden, it's 5pm in London and noon in New York. Summer time operates in Sweden from late March to late October, with the same changeover days as the UK.

Tipping

There are no fixed rules about tipping in Sweden because the service charge is always included. In restaurants, most people leave 5-15 per cent, depending on how fancy the restaurant is and how satisfied they were. Rounding up the bill is usually sufficient when you pay a bartender (at the bar) or a taxi driver. Tip hotel porters 20kr or so if they carry your luggage to or from your room, and give more if they've lugged lots of horrifically heavy bags.

Toilets

Public toilets (*toalett*; often small, green booths) are usually found near or in parks. They cost 5kr and are clean.

Handy ones that are always open include: the corner of Humlegårdsgatan and Sturegatan, on the park side (Östermalm); in the Kungsträdgården park (Norrmalm); and the corner of

Average climate

Month	Max temp	Min temp	Rainfall
Jan	0°C/32°F	-5°C/22°F	39mm/1.5in
Feb	0°C/32°F	-5°C/22°F	27mm/1.1in
Mar	3°C/38°F	-3°C/26°F	26mm/1in
Apr	8°C/48°F	1°C/33°F	30mm/1.2in
May	15°C/59°F	6°C/44°F	30mm/1.2in
June	21°C/70°F	11°C/52°F	45mm/1.8in
July	22°C/71°F	13°C/56°F	72mm/2.8in
Aug	20°C/68°F	13°C/56°F	66mm/2.6in
Sept	15°C/59°F	9°C/50°F	55mm/2.2in
Oct	10°C/50°F	5°C/43°F	50mm/2in
Nov	4°C/40°F	0°C/32°F	53mm/2.1in
Dec	1°C/33°F	-3°C/26°F	46mm/1.8in

Odengatan and Sigtunagatan, on the park side (Vasastaden).

You can also pop into a restaurant or café and use its facilities as long as a) you ask first, and b) it's not a very touristy area, where toilets tend to be reserved for customers. Non-guests can use toilets in fast-food restaurants, but some charge 5kr – as do department stores. There are public toilets and showers at Sergels Torg, by the entrance to the T-Centralen T-bana station (open 7.15am-10.30pm daily; toilets 5kr; shower with towel 20kr).

Visas & passports

Sweden is one of the European Union countries covered by the Schengen agreement, meaning many shared visa regulations and reduced border controls (with the exception of the UK and Ireland, the Schengen zone now takes in the entire EU, and also extends to Norway and Iceland). To travel to Schengen countries, British and Irish citizens need full passports; most EU nationals need carry only their national identity card. Passports, but not visas, are needed by US, Canadian, Australian and New Zealand citizens for stays of up to three months. Citizens of South Africa and many other countries do need visas, obtainable from Swedish consulates and embassies abroad (or in other Schengen countries that you are planning to visit).

EU citizens intending to work, study or live long-term in Sweden are required to obtain a residency card after arrival; non-EU nationals have a different procedure and should get a special visa in their home country before entering Sweden.

Visa requirements can change, so always check the latest information with your country's Swedish embassy.

Weights & measures

Sweden uses the metric system. Decimal points are indicated by commas, while thousands are defined by full stops. Throughout this guide, we have listed measurements in both metric and imperial.

When to go

You'll have a very different experience of Stockholm depending on whether you arrive in winter or summer, but all seasons have their charm. Most tourists choose to visit Stockholm between May and September, which is when most sights and attractions have extended opening hours. But the Midsummer weekend (nearest 24 June) is not a great time to visit because this is the big summer holiday weekend, when many people leave town and much of the city is closed.

July, with its very long days and short nights, is the main holiday month for Stockholmers, and many restaurants, bars and some shops close for some or all of the month. Another problem is that mosquitoes can be a big nuisance outside the city between June and late September, especially at dusk and out in the archipelago.

Winter (November-March) brings short days and cold temperatures – some of the waterways freeze over, though snow is something of a rarity. When it does fall, the city looks stunning, especially on clear crisp sunny days, which are relatively common.

Public holidays

On public holidays, virtually all shops, banks and offices, and many restaurants and bars, are closed. Banks are also closed the day before a public holiday. Public transport runs a limited service on Christmas and New Year's Day. When a holiday falls on a Tuesday or Thursday, some people also take off the intervening day before or after the weekend.

Annual public holidays are:

Nyårsdagen
(New Year's Day) 1 Jan.

Trettondedagsafton
(Eve of Epiphany) 5 Jan.

Trettondedag Jul
(Epiphany) 6 Jan.

Skärtorsdagen
(Maundy Thursday) 17 Apr 2003, 8 Apr 2004.

Långfredagen
(Good Friday) 18 Apr 2003, 9 Apr 2004.

Påskdagen
(Easter Sunday) 20 Apr 2003, 11 Apr 2004.

Annandag Påsk
(Easter Monday) 21 Apr 2003, 12 Apr 2004.

Valborgsmässoafton
(Walpurgis Night) 30 Apr.

Första Maj
(May Day) 1 May.

Krist Himmelfärds Dag
(Ascension) 29 May 2003, 20 May 2004.

Pingstdagen
(Whit Sunday) 8 June 2003, 30 May 2004.

Annandag Pingst
(Whit Monday) 9 June 2003, 31 May 2004.

Midsommarafton
(Midsummer's Eve) 3rd Fri in June.

Midsommardagen
(Midsummer's Day) 3rd Sat in June.

Nationaldagen
(National Day) 6 June.

Alla Helgons Dag
(All Saints' Day) Sat between 31 Oct and 6 Nov.

Julafton
(Christmas Eve) 24 Dec.

Juldagen
(Christmas Day) 25 Dec.

Annandag Jul
(Boxing Day) 26 Dec.

Women

Great measures have been taken in Sweden to guarantee equal opportunities for men and women, but the goal is not yet reached even though Sweden has come very far compared with many other European countries. Today, women in Sweden can combine having a family and working thanks to the state-sponsored childcare programme; almost 80 per cent of all women work and around 75 per cent of children aged one to six use the state childcare system. Swedish women still earn less than men, however, partly because of the professions they choose and the fact that many mothers work part-time.

It is very unlikely that female visitors will face any kind of harassment, and Stockholm is a very safe city to walk around, though the normal precautions are always recommended (*see p283* **Police & security**).

Kvinnoforum (562 288 00/ www.kvinnoforum.se) works to enhance the empowerment of women in all aspects of life, while **KvinnorKan** (723 07 02/www.kvinnorkan.se) is a foundation that demonstrates and encourages women's knowledge.

Working in Stockholm

The current unemployment rate in Stockholm is around five per cent. Most people speak English very well and a great number of companies use English as a working language. If you want to work in Stockholm, but you're not yet in the country, the best way to find a job is to register at some of the many online recruiting companies, such as **Jobfinder** (www.jobfinder.se), **Jobline** (www.jobline.se), **Stepstone** (www.stepstone.se), **Topjobs** (www.topjobs.se) and **Wideeyes** (www.wideeyes.se).

The European Employment Services network, **EURES** (http://europa.eu.int/jobs/eures), provides a database of job vacancies throughout the EU and contains useful information about working conditions.

If you're already living in Sweden, most people start looking for a job by going to the state employment agency, **Arbetsförmedlingen**; it has a lot of information in one place and offers free guidance.

Arbetsförmedlingen
Kungstensgatan 45, 113 99 Stockholm (58 60 60 00/www.ams.se). T-bana Odenplan or Rådmansgatan/bus 40, 47, 53, 69. **Open** *Phone enquiries* 7.30am-5pm Mon-Fri. *Office* 8am-4.30pm Mon-Fri. **Map** p307 D6.

Work permits

All EU nationals can obtain a work permit in Sweden; non-EU citizens must apply for a work permit abroad and hand in the application to a Swedish embassy or consular representative. The rules for obtaining work permits vary for different jobs.

EU citizens can stay in Sweden for three months, but then have to apply for a residence permit (which can take a month to process, so it's best to apply as soon as you arrive). Non-EU citizens must apply for a residence permit from outside Sweden. You'll need to produce a valid ID card or passport and other documents depending on your status (employee, job-seeker, self-employed, student, etc). Contact the **National Immigration Authority** (Migrationsverket), which is at 601 70 Norrköping (011 15 60 00/011 10 81 55/www.migrationsverket.se).

Useful organisations

The EU has a website (**http://citizens.eu.int**) providing you with general information on your rights and useful telephone numbers and addresses in your home country. It also holds specific information on tax, the rules governing recognition of your diplomas, your rights on access to employment, rights of residence and social security, the national education system and a route map for job applicants in the EU.

Vocabulary

It will only take a few minutes in Stockholm to realise that just about everyone speaks strikingly good English and is happy to oblige you by using it. However, as anywhere else, any attempts you make to learn a few basic phrases will be met with pleasure – or hilarity (Swedish is notoriously difficult to pronounce and a slight difference in stress can sometimes change the meaning embarrassingly).

Vowels

Vowels are long when at the end of a word or followed by one consonant, and short when followed by two consonants.

å – when long as in **tore**
ä – as in **pet**
ö – as in **fur**
y – as in **ewe**
ej – as in **late**

Consonants

g (before e, i, y, ä and ö), j, lj,dj and gj – as in **yet**
k (before e, i, y, ä and ö), sj, skj, stj, tj and rs – all more or less like **sh**, with subtle differences
qu – as **kv** (though q is hardly ever used in Swedish)
z – as in **so**

Alphabetical order

Swedish alphabetical order lists å, ä and ö, in that order, after z.

Useful words & phrases

yes *ja* (yah); **no** *nej* (nay); **please/ thank you** *tack;* **hello** *hej* (hay); **goodbye** *hej då* (hay daw); **excuse me** *ursäkta* (ewr-shekta); **I'm sorry** *förlat* (furr-lawt); **do you speak English?** *talar du engelska?* (tah-lar dew engelska?); **how are you?** *hur mår du?* (hewr mawr dew?)

Sightseeing

entrance *ingång* (in-gawng); **exit** *utgång* (ewt-gawng); **open** *öppen* (ur-pen); **closed** *stängd* (staingd); **toilet (women/men)** *toalett* (too-a-let) *(kvinnor/män);* **where** *var*; **when** *när* (nair); **near** *nära* (naira); **far** *långt* (lawngt); **(city) square** *torg* (tohrj); **church** *kyrka* (chewr-ka); **art gallery** *konstgalleri;* **town hall** *stadshus;* **street/road** *gata/väg;* **palace** *slott;* **metro** *tunnelbana;* **ticket to...** *biljett till...* (bill-yet till); **how much is this/that?** *hur mycket kostar den/det?* (hewr mewkeh costar den/det?); **which way to...?** *hur kommer jag till...?* (hewr comer yah til...?)

Accommodation

hotel *hotell;* **youth hostel** *vandrarhem;* **I have a reservation** *jag har beställt ett rum* (yah har bes-telt ett room); **double room** *dubbelrum;* **single room** *enkelrum;* **double bed** *dubbelsäng;* **twin beds** *två sängar;* **with a bath** *med bad;* **with a shower** *med dusch*

Days of the week

Monday *måndag;* **Tuesday** *tisdag;* **Wednesday** *onsdag;* **Thursday** *torsdag;* **Friday** *fredag;* **Saturday** *lördag;* **Sunday** *söndag*

Numbers

0 *noll;* **1** *ett;* **2** *två* (tvaw); **3** *tre* (trea); **4** *fyra* (few-ra); **5** *fem;* **6** *sex;* **7** *sju* (shew); **8** *åtta* (otta); **9** *nio* (nee-oo); **10** *tio* (tee-oo); **11** *elva;* **12** *tolv;* **13** *tretton;* **14** *fjorton* (fyoor-ton); **15** *femton;* **16** *sexton;* **17** *sjutton* (shew-ton); **18** *arton;* **19** *nitton;* **20** *tjugo* (chew-goo); **21** *tjugoett* (chew-goo-ett); **30** *trettio* (tretti); **40** *fyrtio* (fur-ti); **50** *femtio* (fem-ti); **60** *sextio* (sex-ti); **70** *sjuttio* (shew-ti); **80** *åttio* (otti); **90** *nittio* (nitti); **100** *hundra* (hewndra); **1,000** *tusen* (tews-sen); **1,000,000** *miljon* (milly-oon)

Eating out

have you got a table for...? *har ni ett bord för...?* (hahr nee ett boord furr...?); **bill** *notan* (noo-tan); **menu** *meny* (men-ew); **wine list** *vinlista* (veen-lista); **breakfast** *frukost* (frew-cost); **lunch** *lunch* (lewnch); **dinner** *middag* (mid-daag); **main course** *huvudrätt* (hew-vew-dret); **starter** *förrätt* (fur-et); **bottle** *flaska;* **glass** *glas;* **restaurant** *restaurang;* **cake shop** *konditori;* **bakery** *bageri;* **bar-restaurant** *krog*

Basic foods & extras

ägg egg; **bröd** bread; **gräddfil** sour cream; **ost** cheese; **pommes frites** chips/fries; **potatis** potatoes; **ris** rice; **senap** mustard; **smör** butter; **smörgås** sandwich; **socker** sugar; **sylt** jam

Swedish specialities (*husmanskost*)

ärtsoppa split pea and pork soup; **black & white** steak and mashed potato; **fisksoppa** fish soup; **Janssons frestelse** gratin of anchovies and potatoes; **kåldolmar** stuffed cabbage rolls; **köttbullar** meatballs; **lufsa** pork dumpling with smoked salmon; **potatissallad** potato salad; **pytt i panna** fried meat and potatoes with a fried egg and pickled beetroots; **rimmad oxbringa** lightly salted brisket of beef; **sillbricka** an assortment of herring dishes; **smörgåsbord** typical self-service buffet, starting with herring, followed by cold dishes, then hot dishes, then dessert

Fruit & veg (*frukt & grönsaker*)

apelsin orange; **ärtor** peas; **bönor** beans; **citron** lemon; **hallon** raspberry; **hjortron** cloudberry; **jordgubbar** strawberries; **kål** cabbage; **lingon** lingonberry; **lök** onion; **morötter** carrots; **nötter** nuts; **persika** peach; **smultron** wild strawberries; **svamp** mushrooms; **vindruvor** grapes; **vitlök** garlic

Meat & game (*kott & vilt*)

älg elk; **biff** beef; **fläsk** pork; **kalvkött** veal; **korv** sausage; **kyckling** chicken; **lammkött** lamb; **rådjur** roe deer; **ren** reindeer; **skinka** ham

Fish (*fisk*)

ål eel; **blåmusslor** mussels; **forell** trout; **gös** pike-perch; **hummer** lobster; **kräftor** crayfish; **lax** salmon; **räkor** prawns; **sjötunga** sole; **strömming/sill (inlagd/ sotare)** herring (pickled/blackened); **surströmming** fermented Baltic herring; **torsk** cod

Cakes & desserts (*bakverk & desserter*)

dammsugare cake made with green marzipan and chocolate; **glass** ice cream; **kaka/tårta** cake (*kaka* can also mean cookie); **lussekatt** saffron bun with raisins; **ostkaka** Swedish cheesecake; **pepparkakor** gingerbread biscuits; **plättar** miniature pancakes served with jam and cream; **semla** whipped cream and almond-paste buns

Drinks (*drycker*)

brännvin schnapps; **varm choklad** hot chocolate; **fruktjuice** fruit juice; **glögg** fortified mulled wine; **kaffe** coffee; **mineral-vatten** mineral water; **mjölk** milk; **öl** beer; **punsch** sweet arak-like spirit; **rödvin** red wine; **te** tea; **vitt vin** white wine.

Further Reference

Books

For books about Sweden written in English, and translations of classic Swedish novels and plays, visit **Sverigebokhandeln** (*see p151*) above the tourist office, and department store **NK's** (*see p152*) book section.

Architecture, art & design

Caldenby, Claes & Hultin, Olof: *Architecture in Sweden 1995-9* (2000) With text in both English and Swedish.
Cargill, Katrin: *Creating the Look: Swedish Style* (1996) A practical guide to achieving the Swedish interior design look.
Davis, Courtney: *A Treasury of Viking Design* (2000) Scandinavian Viking design in ceramics, textiles, woodwork and so on.
Fiell, Charlotte: *Scandinavian Design* (2002) In-depth illustrated guide focusing on 200 designers and design companies.
Hakan, Groth & Schulenburg, Fritz van der: *Neoclassicism in the North: Swedish Furniture and Interiors 1770-1850* (1999) Excellent photographs trace the evolution of the neo-classical style in Sweden.
Helgeson, Susanne: *Swedish Design* (2002) A survey of more than 30 Swedish designers of all sorts of products, ranging from glass to furniture. It also offers a good insight into Swedish design philosophies.
Hultin, Olof, Johansson, Bengt Oh, Mårtelius, Johan & Waern, Rasmus: *The Complete Guide to Architecture in Stockholm* (1998) Written by experts, this guide introduces the reader to 400 of the most notable buildings in the Stockholm area.
Larsson, Carl & Karin (eds): *Carl and Karin Larsson: Creators of the Swedish Style* (1998) Numerous essays by experts.
Liljedahl, Agneta: *Stockholm Designer's Guide* (1998) Covers architecture, design, galleries, museums, shopping and restaurants.
Ostergard, Derek E & Stritzler-Levine, Nina: *The Brilliance of Swedish Glass 1918-1939* (1996) Illustrated essays that put Swedish glass production into a wider perspective.
Sjöberg, Lars & Ursula: *The Swedish Room* (1994) Illustrated guide to interior design through different periods and regions.
Stoeltie, Barbara, Stoeltie, René & Taschen, Angelika: *Country Houses of Sweden* (2001) Coffeetable book with lovely photographs of Swedish country houses from a variety of periods.

Biographies

Linnea, Sharon: *Raoul Wallenberg: The Man who Stopped Death* (1993) Biography of the famous Swedish diplomat who saved the lives of 100,000 Hungarian Jews during World War II and then mysteriously disappeared.
Lovejoy, Joe: *Sven-Goran Eriksson* (2002) For football lovers only.
Martinus, Eivor: *Strindberg and Love* (2001) In-depth biography of the troubled dramatist.
Palm, Carl Magnus: *From Abba to Mama Mia: The Official Book* (2000) The first book published with the co-operation of the band, with loads of good photos.

Fiction

Bengtsson, Frans G: *The Long Ships* (1945) Truly a Swedish classic, this novel enchants its readers with the many adventures of a fictional Viking named Orm.
Boye, Karin: *Kallocain* (1940) A bleak vision of a future totalitarian world state.
Johnson, Eyvind: *Dreams of Roses and Fire* (1949) Novel by the winner of the 1974 Nobel Prize for Literature.
Lagerlöf, Selma: *The Wonderful Adventures of Nils* (1906) One of Sweden's best-loved modern folk tales, written to teach Swedish schoolchildren about the geography of their country. Tiny Nils explores the Swedish landscape on the back of a wild goose and lives through many hair-raising experiences.
Lindgren, Astrid: *Pippi Longstocking* (1945) One of Lindgren's fantastic series of children's books about the girl who does exactly as she pleases.
Moberg, Wilhelm: *The Emigrants* (1949) Moving story about what it was like to emigrate from Sweden to the United States in the 19th century, later made into a film (*see p291*).
Strindberg, August: *Miss Julie and Other Plays* (1998) Contains some of the dramatist's key plays: *Miss Julie, The Father, A Dream Play, Ghost Sonata* and *The Dance of Death.*

History, politics & society

Berlin, Peter: *The Xenophobe's Guide to the Swedes* (1999) A hilarious book explaining the complex rules that govern Swedish social interaction.
Daun, Ake: *Swedish Mentality* (1996) Focuses on the development of Swedish culture and society.
Erling, Matz: *Glorious Vasa: The Magnificent Ship and 17th-century Sweden* (2001) Fascinating book that provides a great insight into what life was like in 17th-century Stockholm.
Ericson, Lars: *Stockholms historia under 750 år* (2001) The history of Stockholm, written to celebrate the city's 750th birthday. In Swedish.
Hadenius, Stig: *Swedish Politics during the 20th Century* (1999) Authoritative treatment of all the dramatic political changes that took place between 1900 and 1999.
Hargittai, Istvan & Watson, James: *The Road to Stockholm: Nobel Prizes, Science and Scientists* (2002) Discusses the selection process for the scientific laureates and the ingredients for scientific discovery and recognition.
Malmborg, Mikael Af: *Neutrality and State-building in Sweden* (2001) The history and future of Swedish neutrality.
Nordstrom, Byron J: *The History of Sweden* (2002) Swedish history from prehistoric times to the present.
Swahn, Jan Öjvind: *Maypoles, Crayfish and Lucia: Swedish Holidays and Traditions* (1997) A guide to Swedish customs and festivals published by the Swedish Institute.

Music

Classical

Hugo Alfvén (1872-1960) Composer of the ballet *Bergakungen* ('Mountain King'), five symphonies and numerous songs.
Franz Berwald (1796-1868) Wrote operas, chamber music and four symphonies.
Daniel Börtz (born 1943) Composer whose contemporary chamber music and solo pieces reflect earlier periods.
Anders Eliasson (born 1947) Composer of complex orchestral works, most notably *Canto del Vagabondo.*
Håkan Hardenberger (born 1961) Internationally renowned trumpeter.

Anders Hillborg (born 1952) Writes everything from chamber music to film scores; most famous for his *Celestial Mechanics* for solo strings.
Christian Lindberg (1958) International trombone virtuoso.
Wilhelm Peterson-Berger (1867-1942) Composer of operas and piano miniatures with a strong folk influence.
Allan Pettersson (1911-80) Composer most renowned for his *Symphony No.7*.
Hilding Rosenberg (1892-1985) Wrote numerous string quartets.
Wilhelm Stenhammar (1871-1927) Composed chamber music, operas and orchestral pieces.
Jan Sandström (born 1954) Renowned for his *Motorbike Concerto* for trombone and orchestra.
Sven-David Sandström (born 1942) Composer of complex orchestral works, ballets and percussion pieces.
Anne Sofie von Otter (born 1955) The world-famous mezzo-soprano.

Pop & rock

ABBA Their phenomenally successful albums include *Waterloo* (1974) and *Super Trouper* (1980).
Ace of Base 1990s dance band responsible for 'All That She Wants'.
The Cardigans Pop band formed in 1992, with *Life* probably their most well-known album.
Europe Remembered for the terrible 1986 hit 'The Final Countdown'.
The Hives Fivesome playing, in their words, 'punk rock music avec kaboom'; albums include *Your New Favourite Band* and *Barely Legal*.
Roxette Worryingly successful '80s-style pop duo most famous for 'It Must Have Been Love' and 'Joyride'.

Film

Before the Storm (Reza Parsa, 2000) Excellent thriller with interweaving stories examining the conflict between violence and ethics.
The Best Intentions (Bille August, 1992) The story of Ingmar Bergman's parents, written by Bergman himself.
Elvira Madigan (Bo Widerberg, 1967) Beautiful-looking film about a doomed love affair.
The Emigrants (Jan Troell, 1970) First of two films – the second is *The New Land* – dealing movingly with 19th-century Swedish emigrants to America.
Fanny and Alexander (Ingmar Bergman, 1982) A family saga seen through the eyes of a small boy, revisiting the typical Bergman themes of religious doubt and apocalypse.
The Father (Alf Sjöberg, 1969) Film version of Strindberg's play about a battle between husband and wife, descending into madness and death.
Fucking Åmål (US title *Show me Love*, Lukas Moodysson, 1998) All-girl twist to the high-school romance genre, which won multiple awards.
House of Angels (Colin Nutley, 1992) Prejudice and conflict in rural Sweden.
I am Curious: Yellow (Vilgot Sjöman, 1967) Sexually frank but morally involved tale mixing reportage and fiction.
Lilja 4-ever (Lukas Moodysson, 2002) Moodysson's latest offering, darker than usual but very popular in Sweden.
My Life as a Dog (Lasse Hallström, 1985) A witty and touching story of a young boy in 1950s rural Sweden.
Persona (Ingmar Bergman, 1966) An actress refuses to speak, perhaps due to the impossibility of true communication, while her nurse chatters away about her sex life.
The Seventh Seal (Ingmar Bergman, 1956) Unforgettably striking medieval allegory, with plague sweeping through an apocalyptic Sweden and Max von Sydow's knight playing a lengthy game of chess with Death.
Songs from the Second Floor (Roy Andersson, 2000) Loosely connected vignettes deal with traffic jams and redundancy in a surreal black comedy.
Together (Lukas Moodysson, 2000) Excellent comedy about life and love in a '70s commune.
The Treasure of Arne (often called *Herr Arnes Pengar*, Mauritz Stiller, 1919) Bravura premonition-laden drama set in 16th-century Sweden.
Tsatsiki, Mum and the Policeman (Ella Lemhagen, 1999) Engaging story of a young Stockholmer who longs to meet his Greek father.
Under the Sun (Colin Nutley, 1998) Sweet and satisfying film based around an unconventional love story.
Wild Strawberries (Ingmar Bergman, 1957) Warm story of a dried-up academic who relives and rediscovers his youth.
Wings of Glass (Reza Bagher, 2000) Emotionally involving film about a Swedish-Iranian family's conflict between their Muslim roots and Swedish environment.

Websites

Throughout the guide we've listed any websites that are relevant or useful. Here are some others of interest.

Bed & Breakfast Agency
www.bba.nu
Easy-to-use site offering B&Bs in the Stockholm area in a variety of price ranges.
Bed and Breakfast Center
www.bed-and-breakfast.se
Book B&B accommodation in the greater Stockholm area.
City of Stockholm
www.stockholm.se/english
Official information on the city's government, services and history, with some useful links.
Destination Stockholm
www.destination-stockholm.se
Offers discounted accommodation, plus restaurant reviews, virtual walks and loads of other useful city information. In multiple languages.
Ingmar Bergman
www.geocities.com/the_magic_works_of_i_b
A tribute site to the great man, with information on his cinema and theatre careers, plus a filmography and photographs.
Nobel Prizes
www.nobel.se
Everything you ever wanted to know about the Nobel Prizes, their history and the winners.
Restaurant Reviews
www.alltomstockholm.se/E/F/STOSE/0000/01/63/1.html
Recommends restaurants throughout Stockholm.
Royal Family
www.ritva.com
Unofficial and quite amusing fan site about the Swedish royal family.
Scandinavian Design
www.scandinaviandesign.com
The products and personalities of Nordic design, plus information on museums, magazines and design schools.
Stockholm Guide
www.stockholmtown.com
Official tourist office site with loads of good information on events, activities and attractions in the city and archipelago.
Stockholm Map
www.map.stockholm.se/kartago
A zoom-in, zoom-out map of the city, with instructions in Swedish.
Sweden
www.sverigeturism.se/smorgasbord
The world's largest source of information on all things Swedish, with sections on famous people, the weather, culture and history.
Swedish Institute
www.si.se
You can get hold of books, films and further information about Sweden and Swedes in general, plus find out about studying in Sweden.
Swedish Recipes
www.santesson.com/recept/swelist.htm
All your favourite Swedish recipes, with easy-to-follow instructions.

Index

Note: numbers in **bold** indicate key information on a topic; *italics* indicate photographs.

In Swedish alphabetical listings, the letters å, ä and ö appear at the end of the alphabet, after z. For ease of use, however, we have listed these as if they were standard a and o.

Aalbæk Jensen, Peter 197
ABBA 98, 106, 290, 291
accident & emergency 279
accommodation
by price
budget/youth hostels 45, 47, 50-52
deluxe 41-43, 49, 52, 54
expensive 43-45, 45-46, 49, 53-54
moderate 45, 46-47, 49-50, 54
boat hotels 50-53
camping 54
chain hotels 47
gay 206
Hotellcentralen (booking service) 40, **285**
addresses 276
Adelcrantz, Carl Fredrik 25, 90, 241
Adelcrantz, Göran Josuae 25, 76
Adolf Fredrik, King 25, 60, 239, 241
Adolf Fredriks Kyrka 72
Advent 182
Af Chapman (ship) **50**, *50*, 87
age restrictions 276
Åhléns 72, **152**
Ahnborg, Erik 96
AIDS/HIV 279
AIK **226**, 228
airlines 272
airports 272
Albrecht of Mecklenburg, Duke 9
alcohol 130, 166-167
Alfvén, Hugo 215, 290
allemansrätten 218, **257**
Almgren, Knut August 89
Almgren Sideväveri Museum, KA 89
Älmhult 34, 35
Ålo 263
alternative medicine 279
amusement/theme parks
Gröna Lund 80, *81*, 99, **185**, *185*
Junibacken 80, **185**, *185*, 187
Vilda Vanadis 77, **188**
see also zoos & aquariums
Anckarström, Johan Jacob 15
Anderberg, Axel 107
Andersson, Melker 113, 115
Andersson, Örjan 234
Andersson, 'Plank Anders' 263
Andersson, Roy 195, 291
antiques & second-hand shops 169
Aquaria Vattenmuseum 80, **82**
archipelago 238, **251-266**
Arholma 265-266
Arkitekturmuseet 31, 70, **87**
Arlanda Airport 272
left luggage 280
Arlanda Express 70
Armémuseum 59, 95, **96**, *97*
art *see also* galleries
fair 183
street art 202-203
Arvfurstens Palats 71
Åsberg, Margaretha 234
Asplund, Gunnar **28-29**, 34, 77
athletics 227
ATMs 282
auctions 151
August, Pernilla 195

badminton 219
Båge 30
Bagher, Reza 195, 291
bags, gloves & hats 159-160
bakeries & pâtisseries 162
Ballo in Maschera, Un 15, 214
balloon flights, hot-air 57
Baltic region 267-270
bandy **222-223**, 227
banks 282
bars 130-139
best 130
bars 193
gay 206
Batluffarkortet 238
beaches 103, 107, 256, 260, 264
Before the Storm 195, 197, 291
Bellman, Carl Michael 14, 19, 88, **89**, **92**, 178
Bellmanhuset 88, **89**
Bellmanmuseet 91, **92**
Berg 256
Bergianska Trädgården 106
Berglund, Paavo 216
Bergman, Ingmar 97, **194**, 230, 269, 291
Bergman, Ingrid 105
Bernadotte, Marshal *see* Karl IV Johan, King
Berns Salonger 73, 79, *112*, **113**, 116, **131**, 210, **210**
Berwald, Franz 215, 290
Berwaldhallen 96, **215**
Berzelii Park 73
Biblioteksgatan 94, 149
bicycles *see* cycling
billiards 219
Biologiska Museet 80, **82**
Birger Jarl **7**, *8*, 19, 23, 58, 65, 68
Birger Jarl Hotel *37*, 38, **45**
Birger Jarls Torg 65
Birger Jarls Torn 66
Birger Jarlsgatan 94
Birger, King 9
Birka 7, 238, **240**
Birkamuseet 240, *240*
Björkö 265
Björkö (1790), Battle of *12*
Björkvist, Karin 37
Blå Tornet 76
Blockmakarens House 93
Blom, Fredrik 25, 26, 84, 87
Blue Hall 104, *104*
boat
arriving by 273
festival (Skärgårdbåtens Dag) 180
hotels 50-53
'rowing madams' 253
tours & trips 57, 188
see also ferries
Boberg, Ferdinand 27, 83, 85
Bofill, Ricardo 30
Bogesunds Slott 254
Bohlin, Jonas 33, **37**, 38, 46, 117
Bondeska Palatset 24, **63**
books
reference 290
shops 151-152
Borg, Björn 220
Borgström, Hans 100
Börsen 14, 25, 69
Börtz, Daniel 215, 290
Bosse, Harriet 78
Botaniska Trädgården, Uppsala 248
bowling, ten-pin 225
Boy, Willem 76
brännvin (schnapps) 181
Branting, Hjalmar 16
Brask, Bishop Hans 66
breakdown services 275
Brolin, Tomas 127
Bromma Airport 272
Bromma Kyrka 23
Brunkeberg, Battle of 10
budget fashion 153-154
BUFF 198
bureaux de change 282
buses 273-274
business services 276

c

cafés 140-148
best 143
gay 207
internet 280
cameras 153
camping 54
canoeing 223
Caprioli, Christina 234
Cardigans, The 210, 291
Carl XVI Gustav, King **19**, 105
Carl Eldhs Ateljémuseum 105
Carolina Rediviva, Uppsala 247
car 274
arriving by 273
hire 275
cash machines 282
castles and palaces
Bogesunds Slott 254
Drottningholms Slott 13, 19, 25, *25*, 69, 89, **239-241**, *239*
Gripsholms Slott 242-243, 238, *242*
Haga Slott 25, 105
Karlsbergs Slott 25
Kastellet 26
Kina Slott 25
Kungsliga Slottet 13, 19, 25, 56, 57, **58-61**, *59*, 69
Rosendals Slott 25, 81, **83**
Rosersbergs Slott 244, **246-247**
Skoklosters Slott 246-247
Steninge Slott 244, **246-247**, *247*
Tre Kronor castle 8, 13, 23, 24, 58, 59, 60 66, 103
Tullgarns Slott 246-247
Ulriksdals Slott 25, 178, **246**, 247
Wiks Slott 248
Catenacci, Stefan 113
Celsing, Peter 29, 71
Celsius, Anders 14
cemetery, pet 98
Central Station 26, 70, **273**
left luggage 280
Centralbadet 27, 72, **168**, *168*, 188, 224, *228*
Changing the Guard *59*
Cheiron studio 211
children 184-188
fashion shops 157-158
see also amusement/theme parks *and* zoos and aquariums
chocolate shops 162
Christian II 'the Tyrant' of Denmark, King **11-12**, 19, 66
Christina, Queen 12-13
Christopher of Bavaria, King 10
churches
services in 284
venues for music 216
Adolf Fredriks Kyrka 72
Bromma Kyrka 23
Engelbrektskyrkan **95**, 216
Finnska Kirkan **63**, 69
Gustav Vasa Kyrka **77**, 216
Hedvig Eleonora Kyrka **95**, 216
Högalidskyrkan 89
Katarina Kyrka 25, 89, *89*, **90**, 92, 216
Kungsholms Kyrka 101
Maria Magdalena Kyrka 88, **90**
Riddarholmskyrkan 8, 23, *24*, 65, **66**, 216
St Clara Kyrka 70, **76**
St Jacobs Kyrka 71, **76**, 216
Skeppsholmskyrkan 87
Skogskapellet 29
Solnakyrka 23
Storkyrkan 8, 10, 11, 23, 59, **64**, *65*, 216
Tyska Kyrkan 25, *58*, 63, **64-65**

Uppsala Domkyrkan 245, **246**, *248*, 249
Christmas 182, **183**, *183*
markets 84, **182**
cinemas 195-198
circus 229
Cirkus 80, **212**
City (Norrmalm) 70
City Hall *see* Stadshuset
Cityterminalen 273
Clason, Isak Gustav 26, 82, 95
classical music 214-217, 290-291
climate 287
climbing 219
clothes *see* fashion
clubs 189-193
DJ bars 193
gay 207-209
coffee 140
coffee & tea shops 162
colleges 285
complementary health shops 166
computer services 276
Confidencen **178**, 217, 234
consulates 278
contemporary & experimental music 217
conventions & conferences 276
cosmetics & perfume 167
couriers 276
Court House *see* Rådhuset
crafts 174
credit cards 283
customs 277
cycling 178, *218*, **220**, 275

Dahlgren, Mathias 113, **121**, *121*
dance 233-234
Dancer in the Dark 197
Danderydsgatan 28
Dansens Hus 72, **234**
Dansmuseet 71, **73**
delicatessens 162
dentists 279
department stores 152
Derkert, Siri 37
design 32-38
Design Torget 165, *165*
designer fashion 155-157
Desprez, Louis Jean 25, 59
dialling codes 286
Diesen, Clara 234
Diplomatstaden 28
disabled visitors 277
Djurgården 56, 57, **80-87**, 98, 186, 222
acccommodation 49
cafés 144
galleries 200-201
restaurants 120
rock, pop & jazz 212-213
sports teams 98, **226**, 228
swimming 91
Djurgårdenstaden 81
Djurgårdensvägen 80
Djurgårdsbrunnskanalen 81
Djurgårdsbrunnsviken *225*
doctors 279
Dogville 197
Dorati, Antal 216
Döteber, Christian Julius 24
Dream Play, A 79
drinking 130, 166-167
Drottninggatan **72**, 149
Drottningholm 59, 238, **239-242**, *239*
Drottningholms Slott 13, 19, 25, *25*, 69, 89, **239-241**, *239*
Drottningholms Slottsteater **180**, 217, 229, 234, 239
drugs 277
dynamite 104

Easter 178
Eckert, Fritz 97
Edelsvärd, Adolf Wilhelm 26
Egerbladh, Birgitta 233
Ek, Mats 233
Ekholmsnäsbacken 107
Ekoparken 80, 98, 251
Ekotemplet 25, 105
Ekström, Yngve 33
Eldh, Carl 103, **105**
electricity 278
electronic goods 153
Eliasson, Anders 215, 290
Elliott, David 73
embassies 278
emergencies 278
EMS 217
Engelbrektskyrkan **95**, 216
Ericson, Eric 215
Ericson, Estrid 35
Ericsson, LM 100
Erik Eriksson, King 7
Erik Jedvardsson, King 7
Erik Segersäll, King 243
Erik VII of Pomerania, King 9
Erik XIV, King 12, 242, 246
Eriks Gondolen 88, 90, 99, **123**, 123, 135, *135*
Eriksson, Gustav *see* Gustav Vasa, King
Eriksson, Liss 69
Eriksson, Sven-Göran 290
Erlander, Tage 18
Eskilsson, Tomas 197
Essen, Baroness Siri von 78
Etnografiska Museet 98
Eugen, Prince 80, 81, 83
Evert Taubes Terrass 65

Fågelöuddebadet 107
family planning 279
Fanny & Alexander 194, 291
Fares, Josef 195
Fårö 269
Fasching 211, **212**
fashion shops 153-159
fashion accessories shops 159-161
Father, The 78, 291
ferries 238, 273, 274
festivals & events 178-183
classical music/opera 180, 181, 183
dance/ballet 180
film 182
fireworks 181
gay 181
jazz 87, **181**
theatre 178
fetish shops 158
fika 140
film 194-198, 290
for children 188
cinemas 195-198
festivals 182, 198
Film i Väst 197
Filmstaden 72
Finngrundet (ship) 82
Finnhamn 251, **258**
Finnish Embassy 31
Finnska Kirkan **63**, 69
fitness clubs 221
Fjäderholmarna 98, 188, **251-252**, *252*
Fjällgatan 88, 92
Fjärdlång 261
Fjärilshuset 105, *106*, **184**, 186
Fleminggatan 101
florists 160
Folkoperan 217
food & drink shops 162-165
cookies and cakes 140
seasonal 180-181
Swedish, traditional 118-119
football 228
Forseth, Einar 72, 103
Första Maj (May Day) 178
Försvarshögskolan 98
Frank, Josef 35
Franzén, Anders 85
Fredhäll 91
Frescati 106
gay cruising 209
Frithiof, Pontus 111
Fucking Åmål 195, 197, 291
fuel 275
Funkis 28
furniture & home accessories 170-171
Fylkingen 217, **232**, 234

Galärparken 80
Gallerian 71, **152**
galleries, art 199-204
Carl Eldhs Ateljémuseum 105
Millesgården 107
Moderna Museet 31, **73**, **87**, *87*, 199
National Museum 26, 38, *38*, 72, **75**, *76*
Prins Eugens Waldemarsudde 73, 81, **83**
Thielska Galleriet 27, 81, **85**, 262
Gällnö 251, **255**
Gällnöby 255
Gamla Stan 56, **58-65**
accommodation 41-42
bars 131
cafés 140-142
gay scene 205
restaurants 111
rock, pop & jazz 211
shopping 149
Gamla Uppsala 248
Gamla Uppsala Historiskt Centrum **248**, 249
Garbo, Greta 194
gardens *see* parks and gardens
Gärdet 56, 57, **98-100**
accommodation 54
galleries 204
Gardie, Jacob de la 246
gay & lesbian 205-209
healthcare 278
organisations 278
Stockholm Pride Week **181**, 205
Ghost Sonata 79
gifts 165
Gilbert, Alan 216
Gjörwell, Carl Christopher 25
glass shops 172-173
Globen 30, *30*, 89, **214**, **225**, 226, 228
golf 221
Gondolen *see* Eriks Gondolen
Göransson, Peter 11
Göta Canal 14
Götar, the 6
Göteborg Film Festival 198
Götgatan *88*, 149
Gotland 238, **267-270**, *267*
Gotland Runt 259
Gotska Sandön 269
Grand Hôtel 16, 40, *42*, **43**, 73
Gråsten, Viola 37
Great Northern War **13**, 19
Grev Turegatan 94
Grillska Huset 24
Grip, Bo Jonsson **9**, 242
Gripsholms Slott 242-243, 238, *242*
Gröna Lund 80, *81*, 99, **185**, *185*
Gröna Lunds Fyrverkeri Festivalen 181
Grut, Torben 98
Gruvbryggan 263
Gullberg, Elsa 34
Gullichsen, Kristian 31
Gustafsson, Emilia 93
Gustav II, King 66
Gustav II Adolf, King **12**, 60-61, 65, 66, 71, 86, 103
Gustav III, King 12, *13*, 19, **14-15**, 25, 59, 60, 61, 65, 70, 71, 75, 105, 142, 178, 214, 241
Gustav III's Antikmuseum 59, **60**
Gustav III's Paviljong 25, 105
Gustav IV Adolf, King 14
Gustav V, King 66, 257
Gustav Vasa, King 10, **11-12**, 19, 23, 60, 66, 67, 70, 71, 82, 90, 179, 238, 242, 244, 247, 253
Gustav Vasa Kyrka **77**, 216
Gustavianum, Uppsala **246**, 249
Gyllenstierna, Kristina 66
gyms 221
gay 209

h

Haga 105
Haga Forum 105
Haga Slott 25, 105
Hagaparken 24, 57, 105, *106*, 186, 222
Hahn, Birgitta 36
hair salons 168
Håkansson, Ingela 36
Hallberg, Katja 33
Hallman, Per Olof 27
Hallwyl, Count and Countess Walther and Wilhelmina von 97
Hallwylska Palatset 95, **96**
Hammarby 248

Hammarby (sports team) **227**, 228
Hammarskjöld, Dag 18
Hamn 256
Hamngatan 71
handball 228
Handelshögskolan 77
Hardenberger, Håkan 215, 291
Hårleman, Carl 25, 76
Hazelius, Artur 16, 19, 27, 82, **83**, 84
health 278
health & beauty shops 167-169
health food shops 165
Hedqvist, Paul 101
Hedqvist, Tom 36, 46
Hedvig Eleonora, Queen 239, 242
Hedvig Eleonora Kyrka **95**, 216
Helgeandsholmen 56
helplines 280
Helsinki 238, 256, **268**, *268*
Hemsöborna 262
Hildemark, Ove
Hillborg, Anders 215, 291
hire, vehicle 275
Historiska Museet 7, 94, **96**
history 6-19
Hives, The 210, 291
Hobby och Leksaksmuseet 185
Högalidskyrkan 89
Höglund, Erik 33
Högvakten 59
holidays, public 287
Honeck, Manfred 215
horse racing 228
Horthagen 98
hostels, youth/budget 45, 47, 50, 51
Hotellcentralen 40, 285
hotels *see* accommodation
Hötorget 72, *75*
Hötorgshallen 72, 163, *163*
Hötorgshusen 29
housing 31, 21
Humlegården 95, 186
Hultén, Pontus 73
Hultin, Olof 30

IASPIS 199
ice hockey 228
ice skating 188, *219*, **222**
Icehotel 267, **270**
ID 280
Idholmen 258
IKEA **34-35**, **170**
IMAX 188, **198**
immigration 22
insurance, health 279
interiors shops 169-171
international food shops 165
internet 280
It's All About Love 197

Jalla! Jalla! **195**, 197
Järnpojken 69
jazz festivals 87, **181**
jewellery 160
jogging 222
Johan III, King **12**, 76, 90
Johansson, Aron 26, 67
Jolpan, Stora & Lilla 258
Jönsson, Lars 197
Judiska Museet 77, **78**
Jukkasjärvi 270
Jul (Christmas) 182, **183**, *183*
Julbord 181
Junibacken 80, **185**, *185*, 187

k

Kåkbrinken 68
Kaknästornet **98**, 99, *100*
Kalholmen, Stora & Lilla 251, **257-258**
Kalmar Union **9-12**, 19, 66
Kamprad, Ingvar 34
Kandell, John 33
Kappen, Ulf 111
Karklö 255
Karl Knutsson, King 80
Karl IV Johan, King 14
Karl IX, King **12**, 76
Karl X Gustav, King 13
Karl XI, King **13**, 24, 60, 80
Karl XII, King **13**, 25, 71, 140
Karl XIII, King **14**, 71
Karl XIV Johan, King **25**, 60, 68, 71, 81, 84, 246
Karl XV, King 14
Karlaplan 96
Karlavägen 95
Karlsbergs Slott 25
Karlshäll 91
Karlsö, Store & Lilla 269
Karolinska Sjukhuset 105
Kastellet 26
Kastellholmen 87
Katarina Kyrka 25, 89, *89*, **90**, 92, 216
Katarinahissen 88, **90**, *123*
kayaking 223, *225*
Kiljekvist, Fredrik 27
Killa Skinnarviksgränd 88
Kina Slott, Drottningholm 25, **241**
Klarabergsviadukten 73
Klemming, Wilhelm 27
Knutsson, Torgil 9
Konradsberg Sjukhus 26
Konserthuset 34, 72, 188, **215**, *215*
Konstakademien (Royal Academy) 70, 199
Köpmansgatan 69
Koppartälten 25, 105
Kosta Boda 172
Kragh-Jacobsen, Søren 197
krog 130
Kronobageriet 95
Kronobergsparken 101
Kulturhuset 29, 71, *72*, 229, **230**, 234
Kungens Kurva 35, **170**
Kungliga Balett 233
Kungliga Biblioteket 95, **281**
Kungliga Dramatiska Teatern 27, 94, **96**, 229, **230**, *230*
Kungliga Filharmonikerna 72, **216**
Kungliga Filharmonikerna på Gärdet **181**, 217
Kungliga Hovkapellet 214
Kungliga Hovstallet 95, **97**
Kungliga Konsthögskolan 87
Kungliga Musikhögskolan 98
Kungliga Myntkabinettet 59
Kungliga Operan 14, 71, 214, **217**, **234**, *234*
Kungliga Slottet 13, 19, 25, 56, 57, **58-61**, *59*, 69
Kungliga Svenska Segel Sällskapet 259
Kungsberget 224
Kungsholmen 56, **101-104**
  bars 139
  cafés 147-148
  restaurants 128-129
  shopping 149
  swimming 91
Kungsholms Kyrka 101
Kungsträdgården *70*, **71**
  skating 222
Kvarnström, Kenneth 234
Kymmendö 262

l

Ladugårdsgärdet 57, 98
Lallerstedt, Erik 61
Långholmen 56, 57, 222
  accommodation 51-52
  gay cruising 209
  swimming
Långholmens Fängelsemuseum 91, **93**
language 289
Långvik 256
Lapland 270
Lärkstaden 28
Larsen, Henning 31
Larsson, Carl 33, 76, 97, 262
launderettes 171
left luggage 280
legal help 280
Lejonslätten 80
Leksaks Palatset 77
Lemhagen, Ella 197, 291
Lewerentz, Sigurd 29
Lewin, EW 263
Libertas 251
libraries 281
Lidingö 57, 98, **107**
Lidingöloppet 182
Lilja 4-ever 197, 291
Liljefors, Bruno 262
Liljekvist, Fredrik 97
Liljevalch, Carl Fredrik 80
Liljevalchs Konsthall 80, **200**
Lilla Jolpan 258
Lilla Karlsö 269
Lilla Nygatan 63, 68
Lilla Värtan 98
Lindberg, Christian 215, 291
Lindberg, Harald 265
Lindberg, Jacob 215
Lindberg, Stig 33
Lindgren, Astrid 145, 185, **187**, *187*, 290
Lindhagen, Albert 95
Lindhagen, Claes 16
Lindros, Bengt 100
Lindström, Sune 96
lingerie shops 158-159
Lingström, Christer 116, **129**
Linnaeus 14, 239, 245, 246, 248
Linné, Carl von *see* Linnaeus
Linnémuseet, Uppsala **248**, 249
Linnéträdgården, Uppsala **248**, 249
Livrustkammaren 59, **60**, *61*
lost property 281
Lovisa Ulrika, Queen 60, 178, 239, 240
Luciadagen 183
Lugn, Kristina 233
Lundberg, Theodor 97
Lundqvist, Evert 241
Lutter-am-Barenburg (1626), Battle of 12
Lydmar Hotel 40, **53**, *53*, 94, **125**, 138, **214**

Magasin 3 73
magazines 281
Magnus Ladulås, King **8**, 66
Mälaren, Lake 6, 8, 58, 65, 242
  palaces around 246-247
Mälarpromenaden 103
malls 152
Malmsten, Carl 34, 103
Månsson Mandelgren, Nils 37
maps 274
Marathon, Stockholm **179**, 218
Maré, Rolf de 75
Margaret I of Denmark, Queen **9**, 19
Maria Magdalena Kyrka 88, **90**
Marieberg 101
Mariefred 238, **243-244**
markets 72, *75*, 95, **163**
  Christmas 84
  food 163
Mårten Trotzigs Gränd 63
Martin, Max 211
Mäster Mikaels Gata 89, 92
Master Olof 19, 78
Mäster Samuelsgatan 94
Mathsson, Bruno 33, **36**, *36*
Mattsson, Arne 194
May Day 178
Medborgarplatsen 31, 88, 222
Medelhavsmuseet 71, **75**
media 281-282
Medicinhistoriska Museet 105
Memfis Film 197
Midsommar (Midsummer) *179*, 180, **181**
Milles, Carl 11, 57, 72, 80, 82, 83, 97, **107**
Millesgården 107
Million Programme 30, **31**, 90
mines 263
Minority Report 195
Miss Julie 78, 194
mobile phones 286
Moderna Museet 31, **73**, **87**, *87*, 199
Möja 256-257
Mondo 88, **213**
Moneo, Rafael 31
money 282-283
  transfers 283
Monteliusvägen 88
Moodysson, Lucas 195, 197, 291
Mosebacke Etablissement 89, **213**
Museet Tre Kronor 23, 59, **60**
Museifartygen 82
Museum de Vries, Drottningholm 241
'Museum Park' 98
museums
  antiquities Gustav III's Antikmuseum 59, **60**; Medelhavsmuseet 71, **75**; Östasiatiska Museet 87
  archaeology Historiska Museet 7, 94, **96**
  architecture Arkitekturmuseet 31, 70, **87**
  astronomy Observatorie Museet 77, **78**
  children Hobby och Leksaksmuseet 185

coins Kungliga Myntkabinettet 59
cultural history Nordiska Museet *11*, 16, 26, 38, 79, 80, **82**, *82*, 83
customs Tullmuseet 101, **103**
dance Dansmuseet 71, **73**
drink Spiritum Museum, Stora Fjäderholmarnen 251; Systembolagets Museet 71, **77**; Vin & Sprithistoriska Museet 77, **79**
ethnography Etnografiska Museet 98
history Museet Tre Kronor 23, 59, **60**; Stockholm Stadsmuseum 88, **90**; Stockholms Medeltidsmuseet 23, **67**
Jewish life Judiska Museet 77, **78**
literature Bellmanhuset 88, **89;** Bellmanmuseet 91, **92**; Strindbergsmuseet 72, **76**, 77, 79
maritime Museifartygen 82; Sjöhistoriska Museet 98, **100**; Vasamuseet 57, 80, **85**, *85*, **86**, *86*
military/police Armémuseum 59, 95, **96**, *97*; Livrustkammaren 59, **60**, *61*; Polishistoriska Museet 101, **103**
miscellaneous Hallwylska Palatset 95, **96**
music Musikmuseet 95, **97**, 186
natural history Biologiska Museet 80, **82**; Naturhistoriska Riksmuseet 106, **107**
Nobel Prizes Nobelmuseet 61, **63**, *63*, 69, 104
post Postmuseum 63, **64**, 186
prison Långholmens Fängelsemuseum 91, **93**
royalty Kungliga Hovstallet 95, **97**
science/technology/ medicine KA Almgren Sideväveri Museum 89; Medicinhistoriska Museet 105; Tekniska Museet 98, 186, **100**
telecommunications Telemuseum 98, **100**
toys Leksaks Palatset 77
transport Spårvägsmuseet 89, **90**
music 210-217, 290-291
  for children 188
  jazz festivals 87, **181**
  shops 171-173
  summer 217
  tickets & information 211
Musik på Slottet **181**, 217
Musikmuseet 95, **97**, 186

Nalen 216
Nämdö 260
Narvavägen 95
National Museum 26, 38, *38*, 72, **75**, *76*
Nationaldag 11, 179
Naturhistoriska Riksmuseet 106, **107**
New Year's Eve 183
newspapers 101, **281**
nightlife 189-193
Nittve, Lars 73
NK 71, *71*, *150*, **152**
Nobel, Alfred 16, 64, **104**
  Nobel Prizes 16, 61, 63, 72, 103, **104**, 105, **182**
  Nobeldagen 182
  Nobelmuseet 61, **63**, *63*, 69, 104
Nordegren, Elin 218
Nordiska Museet *11*, 16, 26, 38, 79, 80, **82**, *82*, 83
Norr Mälarstrand 103
Norra Djurgården 98
Norrmalm 56, **70-76**
  accommodation 42-45
  bars 131-132
  cafés 142-143
  clubs 190-191
  galleries 199-200
  restaurants 113-116
  rock, pop & jazz 212
  shopping 149
Notke, Bernt 64
Nutley, Colin 197, 291
Nyårsafton (New Year's Eve) 183
Nybrokajen 11 216
Nybroviken 94, *95*

Observatorie Museet 77, **78**
Observatorielunden 77
Observatoriet 25
Odengatan 77, 149
Odenplan 77
office services 276
Öhrström, Edvin 71
Olin, Lena 195
Olof Skotkonung, King **7**, 19
Olsson, Christian 127
Olsson, Jan Olof 17
Olympic Games 1912 98
One Summer of Happiness 194
opening hours 149, **283**
opera 214-217
Operakällaren **113**, 116
opticians & eyewear 173
Orrefors 172, 173
Oscar I, King 14
Oscarteatern 231
Östasiatiska Museet 87
Ostberg, Jens 234
Östberg, Ragnar 28, 93, 100, 103, 105
Österlånggatan 14, 26, 63
Östermalm 56, 57, **94-98**
  accommodation 52-54
  bars 138-139
  cafés 146-147
  clubs 192
  galleries 201-204
  restaurants 125-128
  rock, pop & jazz 214
Östermalms Läroverket 28
Östermalms Saluhall 26, 95, *95*, **163**
Östermalms Torg 95
Östersjöakvariet 251
Otter, Anne Sofie von 215, 291
Oxenstierna, Axel 12
Oxenstierna family 10
Oxenstiernska Palatset 25

palaces *see* castles and palaces
Palme, Olof **15**, **18**, 19, 72
Palmsted, Erik 25
Parhelion Painting *9*, 64
parking 275
parks and gardens
  Bergianska Trädgården 106
  Berzelii Park 73
  Hagaparken 24, 57, **105**, *106*, 186, 222
  Humlegården 95, 186
  Kronobergsparken 101
  Kungsträdgården *70*, **71**
    skating 222
  Ladugårdsgärdet 57
  Observatorielunden 77
  Rålambshovparken 103
  Rosendals Trädgård 81,**144**, 186
  Tantolundaen 89
  Tegnérlunden 77
  Vasaparken 77
  Vita Bergen 89
Parkteatern 229
Parnevik, Jesper 218
Parsa, Reza 195, 291
Påsk (Easter) 178
passports 287
Patent och Registreringsverket 28
Persson, Göran 20
Persson, Sigurd 33
Petersenska Huset 24
Peterson-Berger, Wilhelm 215, 291
Pettersson, Allan 215, 291
Pettersson, Christer 15
Phantom Carriage, The 194
pharmacies 168, **280**
phones 286
Piper, Fredrik Magnus 25
Pippi Longstocking 145, **185**, **187**
police & security 283
Polishistoriska Museet 101, **103**
Poltava (1709), Battle of 13
Pop, Denniz 211
pornography 194
postal services 284
poste restante 284
Postmuseum 63, **64**, 186
Prästgatan 63, 68
Prins Eugens Waldemarsudde 73, 81, **83**
PUB 72, **152**
public holidays 287
public transport 273-274

q

queuing 284

Rådhuset 27, 101
radio 282
Radiokören 215
Rålambshovparken 103
Ramsmora 256
Råsunda Stadion **226**, 228
Red Room, The 78
Reimersholme 57, 91
Reissur, Mikael 92, 93
religion 284
Renstiernas Gata 93
Representationsvåningarna 59, **60**
resources A-Z 276-288
  for children 188
restaurants
  best 116
  gay 206
  in Drottningholm 241
  in Mariefred 243
  in Sigtuna 244
  in Uppsala 249-250
  by cuisine
    American/French 111
    Asian 116, 120, 125, 128
    Central European 120
    contemporary 111, 113, 117, 121, 125, 128, 129
    Mediterranean 115, 118, 123, 127
    Middle Eastern 118, 123, 127, 129
    Swedish, traditional 111, 115, 119, 120, 123, 127, 129
  see also individual areas
Riddarfjärden 222
Riddarholmen 56, **65-66**
Riddarholmskyrkan 8, 23, *24*, 65, **66**, 216
Riddarhuset 24, **63**
Rikdagshuset 26, **67**
Riksdag 14
Rödabergsområdet 28
roddarmadammer 253
rollerblading 220
Romme 224
Rörstrandsgatan 77
Rosenbad 71
Rosendals Slott 25, 81, **83**
Rosendals Trädgård 81,**144**, 186
Rosenberg, Hilding 215, 291
Rosersbergs Slott 244, **246-247**
Rövarns Holme 251
rowing madams 253
Royal Academy 199
Royal Apartments 59, **60**
Royal Palace, *see* Kungliga Slottet
Royal Swedish Academy of Science 106
Royal University College of Fine Arts *see* Kungliga Konsthögskolan
Rozhdestvensky, Gennady 216
Rudan 224
running 222
  Stockholm Marathon **179**, 218, 222, *224*, 227

sailing 223
St Clara Kyrka 70, **76**
St Erik (ship) 82
St Eriksgatan 7, 101, 149
St Eriksplan 7, 77
St Jacobs Kyrka 71, **76**, 216
St Lucia 183
Salénhuset 30
Salonen, Esa-Pekka 215, 216
Sampe, Astrid 33
Sand 260
Sandell, Thomas **37**, 38, 46, 117
Sandhamn 259-260
Sandön *see* Sandhamn
Sandrews 195, 197
Sandström, Jan 215, 291
Sandström, Sven-David 215, 291
Sason, Sixten 33

Index

Schantzska Huset 24, 69
Scheelegatan 101
Scholander, Fredrik Wilhelm 26
second-hand & vintage fashion shops 159
Sergel, Johan Tobias 15, 72
Sergels Torg *26*, 29, **71**, 149
Seven Years War 13
Seventh Seal, The 194, 291
sex, gay 209
sex shops 174
SF (Svenska Filmindustri) 195, 197
shoes 160-161
shops & services 101, **149-175**
gay 209
showjumping 228
sightseeing 55-107
introduction 56-57
best sights 57
Sigtuna 238, 240, **243**, 243-245, *245*
Simpnäs 265
Sista Styverns Trappor 93
SJ 273
Sjöberg, Alf 194, 291
Sjöhistoriska Museet 98, **100**
Sjöman, Vilgot 194, 291
Sjöström, Victor 194
Skandia cinema 28
Skansen 16, 19, 27, 57, 81, 83, **84**, *84*, 99, 178, *178*, **185**, *186*
Skansen Akvariet 81, **84**, **185**
Skärgården *see* archipelago
Skärgårdsstiftelsen 238
Skarsgård, Stellan 195
Skattkammaren 59, **60**
Skattkammaren, Uppsala 246
Skavsta Airport 272
Skeppsholmen 56, 57, **87**
Skeppsholmskyrkan 87
skiing 224
Skinnarviksberget, gay cruising in 209
Skogskapellet 29
Skogskrematoriet 29
Skogskyrkogården
Skoklosters Slott 246-247
Skulpturens Hus 73
SL Center 273
Slottsbacken 59
Slottsgala på Kungliga Ulriksdal **180**, 217
Slussen 88
Smedsuddsbadet 91, 103
Smiles of a Summer Night 194
Smith, Lars Olsson 251, 253
smoking 284
smuggling 103
snooker 219
Social Democrats 16-18, 20-22
Söder cliffs 99
Söder Malarstrand 88
Söderhallarna 163
Södermalm 56, 57, **88-90**
accommodation 49-51
bars 135-138
cafés 144-146
clubs 191
galleries 201
gay scene 205
restaurants 120-124
rock, pop & jazz 213
shopping 149
Söderstadion 228
Södra Teatern 88, **213**, 229
Solna Kyrkogard 105
Solnakyrka 23
Songs from the Second Floor 195, *195*, 291
Sörenstam, Annika 218
souvenirs 174
Spårvägsmuseet 89, **90**
spas 168
Spiritum Museum, Stora Fjäderholmarnen 251
sport shops 175
Spränga 263, 264
stadiums, major 225
Stadsbiblioteket 28, 77, **281**
Stadshuset 28, 34, 57, 91, 99, 99, 101, *102*, **103**
'Starvation Island' 101
Stenbock, Fredrik 65
Stenbockska Palatset 65
Stenhammar, Ernst 258
Stenhammar, Wilhelm 215, 291
Steninge Slott 244, **246-247**, *247*
Stiernhielm, George 13
Stigbergsgatan 93
Stiller, Mauritz 194, 291
Stockholm Art Fair 183
Stockholm Beer & Whisky Festival 182
Stockholm Bloodbath 10, 11, 19, 61, **66-67**, *67*, 69, 90
Stockholm Card 56
Stockholm Exhibition 80
Stockholm Fair 1930 28, 34
Stockholm Furniture Fair 32, **183**
Stockholm Information Service 56, **285**
Stockholm International Film Festival **182**, 198
Stockholm International Horse Show **182**, 228
Stockholm Jazz Festival 87, **181**, 211
Stockholm Marathon **179**, 218
Stockholm New Music Festival **183**, 217
Stockholm Open (tennis) 182
Stockholm Philharmonic Orchestra 182
Stockholm Pride Week 181
Stockholm Sinfonietta 63, **216**
Stockholm University 106
Stockholms Stadsmuseum 23, 88, **90**
Stockholms Medeltidsmuseet 23, **67**
Stockholms Nya Kammarorkester (SNYKO) 216
Stockholms Stadion 98, **226**, 228
Stockholms Stadsteatern 229, **231**, *232*
Stora Fjäderholmen 251, *251*
Stora Jolpan 258
Stora Kalholmen 251, **257-258**
Stora Karlsö 269
Stora Nygatan 63, 68
Storkyrkan 8, 10, 11, 23, 59, **64**, *65*, 216
Stormare, Peter 195
Stortoget **61**, 63, 69
Strandvägen 95
street art 202-203
Streiff 60, *61*
Strindberg, August 16, 19, 47, 66, 72, 77, **78-79**, 105, 194, 259, **262**, 290
Strindbergsgården, Sandhamn 259
Strindbergsmuseet 72, **76**, 77, 79
strömming 110, **118**
study 284
Stüler, Friedrich August 26, 75
Sture the Elder, Sten 9, **10**, 64
Sture the Younger, Sten 10, 66
Sturebadet 94
Sturegallerian 94, 152
Stureplan **94**, *94*, 130, 149
Sundberg, Johan Ludvig 142
supermarkets 165
Svampen 94
Svear, the 6
Sveavägen 77
Svensk Form 87
Svenskt Tenn *32*, **35**, 36, 46, 95, **171**
Sveriges Radio Symfoniorkester 215
Swedenborg, Emanuel 14, 79, 246
'Swedish Grace' 28
Swedish Radio Symphony Orchestra & Radio Choir 96
Swedish Sports Confederation 219
Swedish Travel & Tourism Council 285
swimming 188, 224
outdoors 91
see also beaches
Sydow, Max von 195
Synagogan 26
Systembolaget 71, 77, **166**, *167*
Systembolagets Museet 71, **77**

t

Tallinn 238, 267, **268**, *269*
Tantolunden 89
tattoos & piercing 169
Taube, Evert 65, *65*
Taube, Jesper 115
tax 283
tax refunds 149
taxis 274
T-Centralen 70
Teatermuseum, Drottningholm 239
Tegnérlunden 77
Tekniska Museet 98, 186, **100**
Telemuseum 98, **100**
telephones 286
television 282
10-Swedish Designers *35*, 36, **166**
Tengbom, Anders 72
Tengbom, Ivar 72, 77
tennis 220, **225**, **228**
Björn Borg 220
Stockholm Open 182, 228
ten-pin bowling 225
Tessin the Elder, Nicodemus 13, 19, 24, 63, 65, 70, 90, 239
Tessin the Younger, Nicodemus 13, 19, 25, 58, 60, 64, 69, 87, 90, 239, 246
Tessin, Carl Gustav 13, 25, 75
Tessingparken 29
theatre 229-233
for children 188
in old theatres 178, 180
puppet 232
Theselius, Nils 37
Thiel, Ernest 85, 262
Thielska Galleriet 27, 81, **85**, 262
'Third Way' 18
Thirty Years War **12**, 19
tickets
classical music & opera 215
film 195
theatre 230
public transport 273
rock, pop & jazz 211
time 286
Timmermansordern 27
tipping **110**, **286**
Tjejtrampet 178
Together 195, 197, *197*, 291
toilets 286
Törnqvist, Albert 26
tourist offices 56, 71, **285**
tours, guided 57
toys 175
trains 273-274
träldom 9
translation services 277
transport, public 273-274
travel agencies 175
travellers' cheques 283
Tre Kronor (castle) 8, 13, 23, 24, 58, 59, 60 66, 103
Treasure of Arne, The 194, 291
Trier, Lars von 197
trips, day 239-250
Troell, Jan 194
Trolle, Archbishop Gustav 11, 66
Trollywood 197
Tsatsiki, Mum and the Policeman 197, 291
Tullgarns Slott 246-247
Tullmuseet 101, **103**
Tunnelbana 17, 30, 90, **273-274**
Tyska Kyrkan 25, *58*, 63, **64-65**

u

Uhl, Frieda 78
Ulriksdals Slott 25, 178, **246**, 247
Ulvaeus, Björn 106
Umeå International Film Festival 198
Under the Sun 197, 291
universities 285
Upplandsgatan 149
Upplandsmuseet, Uppsala 247
Uppsala 7, 8, 10, 19, 238, **245-250**, *248, 249, 250*
Uppsala Domkyrkan 245, **246**, *248*, 249
Uppsala Slott **247**, 249
Utö 259, *259*, *260*, *263*, **263-264**

Vakttältet, Drottningholm 241
Valborgsmässoafton (Walpurgis Night) 65, 178
våldgästning 8
Valhallavägen 95
Valleé, Jean de la 24, 25, 63, 90
Valleé, Simon de la 24, 63
Vällingby 30
värma 131
Vasa (ship) *see* Vasamuseet
Vasa, King Gustav *see* Gustav Vasa, King
Vasaloppet 11, **218**
Vasamuseet 57, 80, **85**, *85*, **86**, *86*

Vasaparken 77
Vasastaden 56, 57, **77-79**
accommodation 45-47
bars 133-135
cafés 143-144
galleries 200
restaurants 116-119
shopping 149
Västerås Airport 272
Västerbron 101
Västerlånggatan 63
Västermalmsgallerian 101, 153
Vätternrundan 218
Vaxholm 251, **253-255**, *254*
video clubs, gay 209
video rentals 175
viewpoints, the best 99
Vikingarännet 219, **222**
Vikings **7**, **240**, 267, 269
Vilda Vanadis 77, **188**
Vin & Sprithistoriska Museet 77, **79**
Vingboons, Justus 63
Vinterberg, Tomas 197
visas 287
Visby 267, *267*
Vita Bergen 89
vocabulary 289
Volvo 71
Vreeswijk, Cornelis 61
Vreeswijkmuseet 61
Vries, Adriaen de 239

Wahlman, Lars Israel 95
Waldemarsudde 91
walking 257
Wallenberg, Raoul **17**, 291
Walpurgis Night 65, **178**
weather 287
websites 291
weights & measures 287
Westman, Carl 27, 101
when to go 287
Widerberg, Bo 194, 291
Wiks Slott 248
Wilhelm, Heinrich 63
Wings of Glass 195, 291
women 288
working in Stockholm 288
World War I 16
World War II *16*, 17
Wrangel, Count Carl Gustav 65, 246
Wrangelska Palatset **65**, 66
Wretman, Tore 113

Zentropa 197
Zilliacus, Cecilia 215
zoos & aquariums
Aquaria Vattenmuseum 80, **82**
Östersjöakvariet 251
Skansen 16, 19, 27, 57, 81, 83, **84**, *84*, 99, 178, *178*, **185**, *186*
Skansen Akvariet 81, **84**, **185**
Zorn, Anders 262, 263

Accommodation

Af Chapman (boat hotel) **50**, *50*, 87
Berns Hotel 40, **42**
Birger Jarl 40, **45**, *46*
campsites 54
Choice Hotels Scandinavia 47
City Backpackers Inn 45
Clas på Hörnet 46
Columbus Hotell 49
Ersta Konferens & Hotell 50
First Hotel Amarenten 47
First Hotel Reisen **41**, 47
First Hotels 47
Grand Hôtel 40, *42*, **43**, 73
Gustaf Af Klint (boat hotel) 52
Hasseludden Konferens & Yasuragi 54
Hilton Stockholm Slussen 49
Hostel Bed & Breakfast 47
Hotel Diplomat 40, **52**
Hotel Gustav Vasa 46
Hotel J 54
Hotel Tegnérlunden 47
Hotel Oden 47
Hotel Tre Små Rum 50, *51*
Hotell August Strindberg 46
Hotell Bema 46
Lady Hamilton Hotel 41
Långholmen Hotel *49*, 51
Lighthouse Hotel (boat hotel) 52
Log Inn Hotel (boat hotel) 50, **52**
Lord Nelson Hotel 41
Lydmar Hotel 40, *43*, **53**, *53*, 94
Mälardrottningen (boat hotel) 50, **53**, 66
Nordic Light 40, *43*, **43**
Nordic Sea 40, **43**
Pensionat Oden 45, **206**
Queen's Hotel 45
Radisson SAS Hotels 47
Radisson SAS Royal Viking Hotel 47
Radisson SAS Strand Hotel **43**, 47
Rica City Hotel Gamla Stan **42**, 47, 63
Rica City Hotels 47
Röda Båten Mälaren, Den (boat hotel) 51
Scandic Hotel Anglais 47
Scandic Hotel Continental 47
Scandic Hotel Hasselbacken 47, **49**
Scandic Hotel Sergel Plaza **45**, 47
Scandic Hotels 47
Victory Hotel *41*, **42**, 63
Villa Källhagen 54
Zinkensdamm Vandrarhem & Hotel 51

Restaurants

Babs Kök & Bar 116, **125**, **206**
Bakfickan 115, *115*
Berns Salonger 73, 78, *112*, **113**, 116
Bistro Ruby & Grill Ruby 111
Bistro de Wasahof, Le 119
Bon Lloc **113**, 116, **121**
Brasserie Godot 94, **127**
Broncos Bar 116, **119**
Cave de Roi 129
Crêperie Fyra Knop 123
Divino 127
Edsbacka Krog 116, **129**
Elverket 125
Eriks Gondolen 88, 99, **123**, *123*
Eyubi 118
Fjäderholmarnas Krog 129
Folkhemmet 121
Franska Matsalen **113**, 116
Fredsgatan 12 113
Glenn Miller Café **115**, 116, 212
Grand National 115
Gyldene Freden, Den **111**, 116
Halv Grek Plus Turk 127
Hong Kong 128
Ho's 120
Humlehof 120
Koh Phangan 120
Koreana 116
Lao Wai 116
Letizia 115
Lilla Pakistan 116
Lydmar Hotel 94, **125**
Malaysia 116
Matkultur 121
Mandus **111**, 116, **206**
Merhaba 123
Miyako 125
Moldau 120
Mooncake 116
Narknoi 117
Operabaren 115
Operakällaren 71, **113**, 116, 118
Östgötakällaren 124
PA & Co 94, *124*, 125
Papphanssons Soppor 116, **128**
Pelikan 116, **124**
Perssons 129
Pontus in the Green House **111**, *111*, 116
Prinsen 127
Rabarber 119
Restaurangen™ **115**, 116
Riche 125
Rolks Kök 117
Roppongi 128
Sahara 123
Salzer 128
Scudetto, Lo 123
South of Siberia 117
Spisa Hus Helena 129
Storstad 117
Sturehof 94, **127**, *128*
Sushi Bar Sone 120
Tamrab Thai 120
Tranan *117*, 118
Undici 125
Värdshuset Ulla Winbladh 118, **120**
Vassa Eggen 116, **127**

Bars

Akkurat 135
Bagpipers Inn, The 133
Berns Salonger 73, 130, **131**, **190**
Bonden 193
Café Opera *131*, 132
Cliff Barnes 133
Dovas 130, **139**
East 94, 130, **138**, 193
Engelen 131
Fenix 135
Folkhemmet 135
Fredsgatan 12 130, **132**, 193
Gondolen 88, 99, 130, **135**, *135*
Gotchå 133
Guldapan 136
Habana, La 133
Halv Trappa Plus Gård 94, 130, **138**, *139*
Icebar 132, *132*
Johnny's 130, **139**
Kvarnen 88, 130, **136**, *136*
Laroy 94, 130, **138**
Lokal **139**, 193
Loft, The 132
London New York 136
Lydmar Hotel 94, **138**, 193, 214
Medusa 131
Mosebacke Etablissement 89, 130, **136**, *137*, **191**, **213**
Musslan Bar 133
O-baren 130, **139**
O'Learys 137, *138*
Paus 133
Pelikan 130, **137**
Side Track 206
Sky Bar 99
Snaps 137
Spy Bar 94, 130, **192**
Stampen Jazzpub 131, **211**
Storstad 130, **133**
Tonic 137
Torget 206, *206*
Tranan 130, **133**, 193
WC 137

Cafés

Anna på Kungsholmen 207
Atrium 142
Blå Porten 80, **144**
Blooms Bageri 144
Café Julia 147
Café Kåkbrinken 142
Café Kanel 147
Café Panorama 72, 99, **142**, 143
Café Restaurant Austria 146
Café dello Sport 145
Chokladkoppen *141*, **142**, **207**
Cinnamon 145
Coffee Cup 140
Creem 143
Djurgårdsterrassen 207
Gateau 143, **146**
Glasbruket Café & Galleri 145
Gli Angelini 147
Grillska Husets Konditori 140
Kafe Kompott 143
Kaffekoppen 142
Lasse i Parken 145
Lisas Café & Hembageri 145
Muffin Bakery *146*, 148
113 50 Café & Deli 143
Piccolino **142**, 143
Ritorno 143
Robert's Coffee 140
R.O.O.M. 148
Rosendals Trädgård 81, 143, **144**, *145*, 186
Saturnas 143, **146**
Sirap 143
Soda 145
Sosta 143, *144*
Spårvagn 142
Stockholms Glass & Pastahus 147
String 145
Sturekatten 147
Sundberg's Konditori 142
Thelins 101, 143, *147*, **148**
Tilt 147
Tintarella di Luna 142
Valand 143, **144**
Vete-Katten 142
Viva Espresso 146
Wayne's Coffee 140, **148**, *148*
Wienerkonditoriet 147

Advertisers' Index

Please refer to relevant sections for addresses and telephone numbers

Grand Hôtel **IFC**

In Context

Forex **4**

Accommodation

Berns Hotel **44**
HotelConnect **48**
Destination Stockholm **48**

Sightseeing

Naturhistoriska Riksmuseet **62**
Skansen **74**

Eat, Drink, Shop

Sophies **108**

Restaurants

Grands Veranda **114**
Calle P **122**
Foam **126**

Bars

Berns **134**

Shops & Services

Ordning & Reda **164**
Time Out City Guides **176**

Destination Stockholm **IBC**

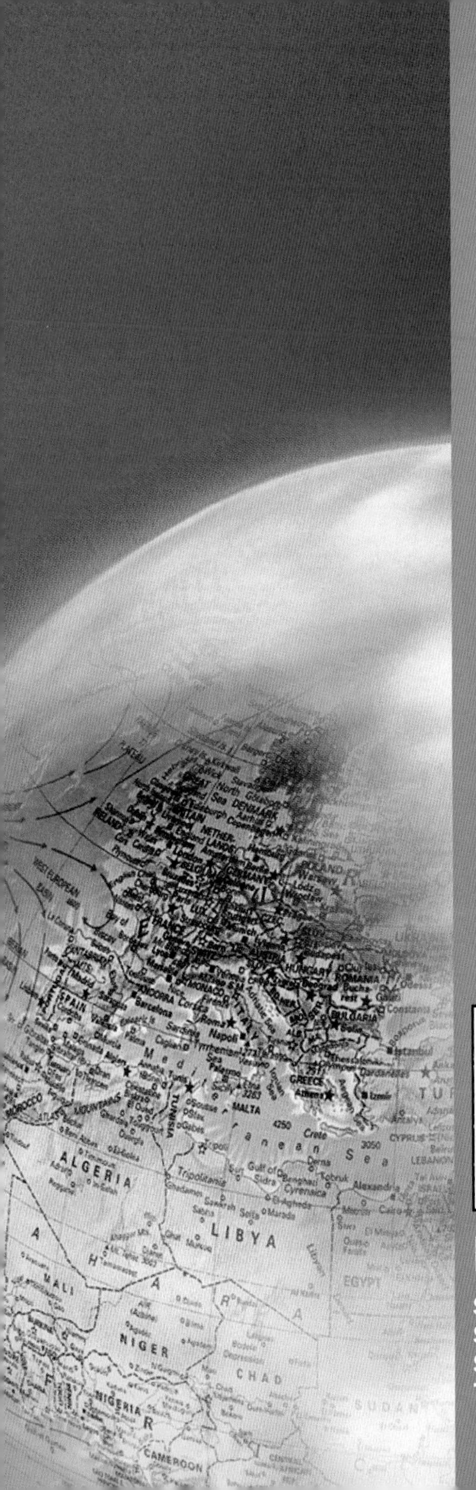

Place of interest and/or entertainment	
Railway station	
Park	
College/hospital	
Area name	GAMLA STAN
Tunnelbana station	T
Tourist information	i

Maps

Stockholm Overview 300
Stockholm street maps 301
Street Index 312
Tunnelbana map 316

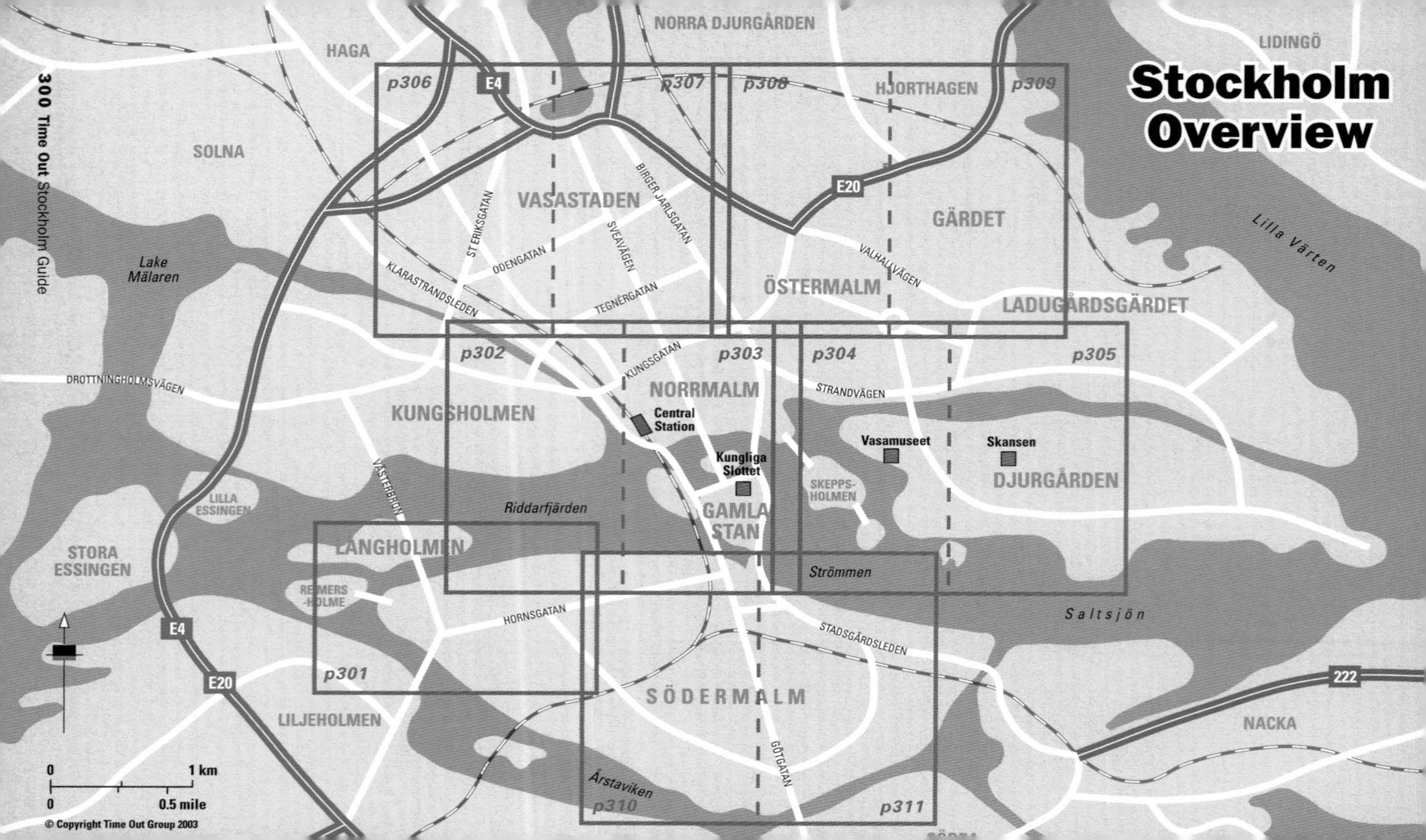

Stockholm Overview
NORRA DJURGÅRDEN
HAGA
LIDINGÖ
SOLNA
p306
E4
p307
p308
HJORTHAGEN
p309
VASASTADEN
BIRGER JARLSGATAN
ST ERIKSGATAN
SVEAVÄGEN
ODENGATAN
KLARASTRANDSLEDEN
TEGNÉRGATAN
E20
GÄRDET
Lilla Värten
VALHALLVÄGEN
ÖSTERMALM
LADUGÅRDSGÄRDET
Lake Mälaren
p302
KUNGSGATAN
p303
p304
p305
DROTTNINGHOLMSVÄGEN
NORRMALM
STRANDVÄGEN
KUNGSHOLMEN
Central Station
Vasamuseet
Skansen
Kungliga Slottet
VÄSTERBRON
SKEPPS-HOLMEN
DJURGÅRDEN
LILLA ESSINGEN
Riddarfjärden
GAMLA STAN
STORA ESSINGEN
LÅNGHOLMEN
Strömmen
REIMERS-HOLME
Saltsjön
HORNSGATAN
E4
STADSGÅRDSLEDEN
E20
p301
222
SÖDERMALM
LILJEHOLMEN
NACKA
GÖTGATAN
0 1 km
0 0.5 mile
Årstaviken
p310
p311

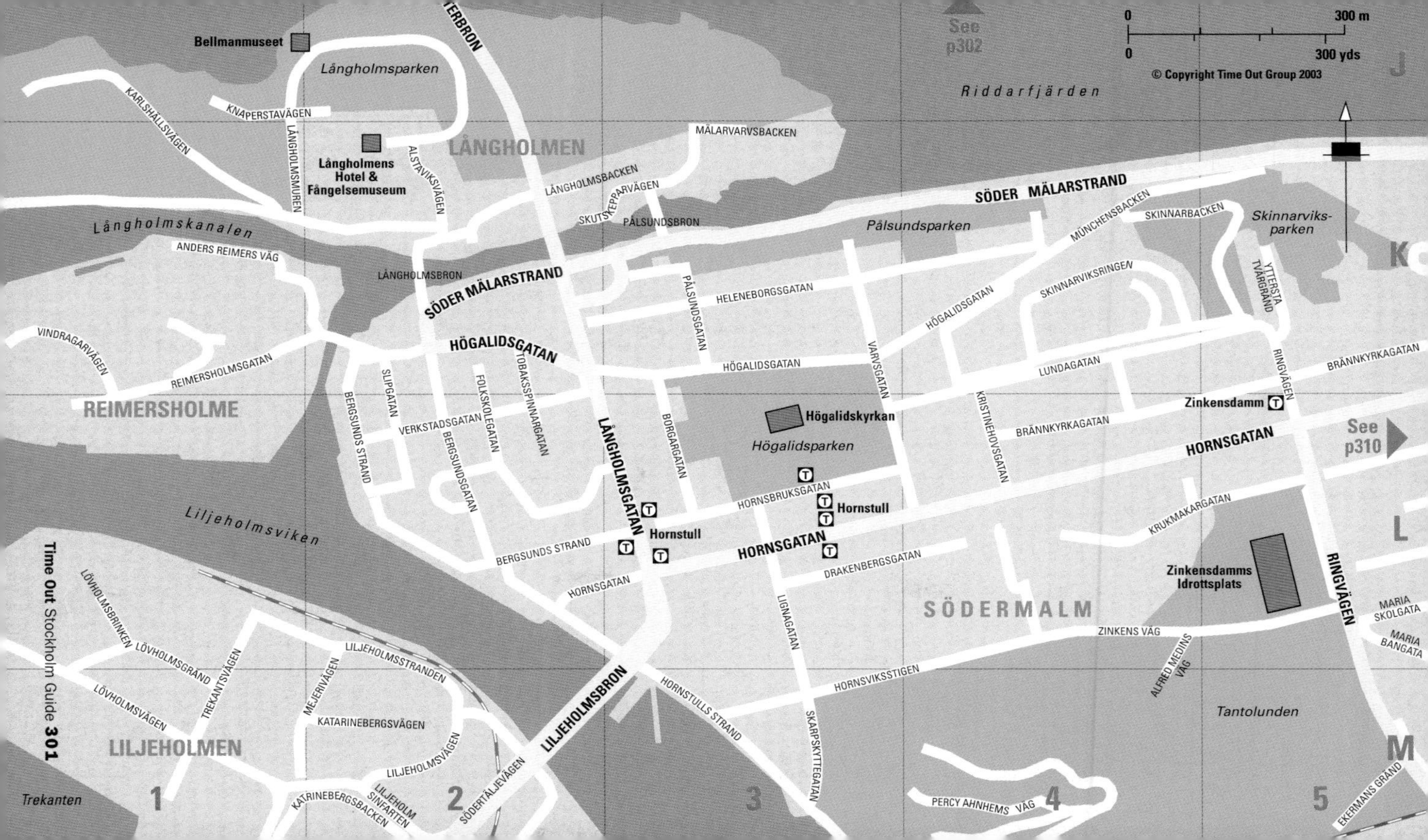

Bellmanmuseet
Långholmsparken
KARLSHÄLLSVÄGEN
KNAPERSTAVÄGEN
LÅNGHOLMSMUREN
Långholmens Hotel & Fängelsemuseum
ALSTAVIKSVÄGEN
LÅNGHOLMEN
TERBRON
See p302
0
300 m
0
300 yds
© Copyright Time Out Group 2003
J
Riddarfjärden
MÄLARVARVSBACKEN
LÅNGHOLMSBACKEN
SKUTSKEPPARVÄGEN
PÅLSUNDSBRON
SÖDER MÄLARSTRAND
Pålsundsparken
MÜNCHENSBACKEN
SKINNARBACKEN
Skinnarviksparken
K
Långholmskanalen
ANDERS REIMERS VÄG
LÅNGHOLMSBRON
SÖDER MÄLARSTRAND
PÅLSUNDSGATAN
HELENEBORGSGATAN
HÖGALIDSGATAN
SKINNARVIKSRINGEN
YTTERSTA TVÄRGRÄND
VINDRAGARVÄGEN
REIMERSHOLMSGATAN
HÖGALIDSGATAN
HÖGALIDSGATAN
VARVSGATAN
LUNDAGATAN
RINGVÄGEN
BRÄNNKYRKAGATAN
REIMERSHOLME
BERGSUNDS STRAND
SLIPGATAN
VERKSTADSGATAN
BERGSUNDSGATAN
FOLKSKOLEGATAN
TOBAKSSPINNARGATAN
LÅNGHOLMSGATAN
BORGARGATAN
Högalidskyrkan
Högalidsparken
KRISTINEHOVSGATAN
BRÄNNKYRKAGATAN
Zinkensdamm
See p310
HORNSGATAN
HORNSBRUKSGATAN
Hornstull
Hornstull
Liljeholmsviken
BERGSUNDS STRAND
HORNSGATAN
DRAKENBERGSGATAN
KRUKMAKARGATAN
L
Zinkensdamms Idrottsplats
RINGVÄGEN
HORNSGATAN
SÖDERMALM
MARIA SKOLGATA
MARIA BANGATA
ZINKENS VÄG
LIGNAGATAN
ALFRED MEDINS VÄG
LÖVHOLMSBRINKEN
LÖVHOLMSGRÄND
TREKANTSVÄGEN
LÖVHOLMSVÄGEN
MEJERIVÄGEN
LILJEHOLMSSTRANDEN
KATARINEBERGSVÄGEN
LILJEHOLMSVÄGEN
LILJEHOLMSBRON
HORNSTULLS STRAND
HORNSVIKSSTIGEN
Tantolunden
LILJEHOLMEN
SKARPSKYTTEGATAN
M
Trekanten
1
KATARINEBERGSBACKEN
LILJEHOLM SINFARTEN
2
SÖDERTÄLJEVÄGEN
3
PERCY AHNHEMS VÄG
4
5
EKERMANS GRÄND

KLARASTRANDSLEDEN
TORSGATAN
See p306
Sabbatsbergs Sjukhus
TEGNÉRGATAN
See p307
WALLINGATAN
Barnhusviken
KUNGSHOLMS STRAND
ÅNGSTRÖMSGATAN
HALLMANS GATA
POLHEMS TVÄRGRÄND
GRUBBENSRINGEN
GRUBBENS GATA
FLEMINGGATAN
PARKGATAN
KUNGSHOLMEN
BARNHUSBRON
SCHEELEGATAN
PIPERSGATAN
NORRA BANTORGET
VASAGATAN
KUNGSGATAN
Kronobergsparken
Polishistoriska Museet
Rådhuset
KUNGSHOLMSGATAN
BERGSGATAN
HANTVERKARGATAN
COLDINUTRAPPAN
KUNGSKLIPPAN
Kungsholms Kyrka
World Trade Center Stockholm
KLARABERGSVIADUKTEN
Klara Sjö
GARVARGATAN
KUNGSHOLMS TORG
NORR MÄLARSTRAND
STADSHUSBRON
Stadshuset
RAGNAR ÖSTBERGS PLAN
Ferries to Drottningholm, Birka & Mariefred
Riddarfjärden
300 m
300 yds
© Copyright Time Out Group 2003
SÖDER MÄLARSTRAND
See p301
Pålsundsparken
SÖDERMALM
Skinnarviksparken

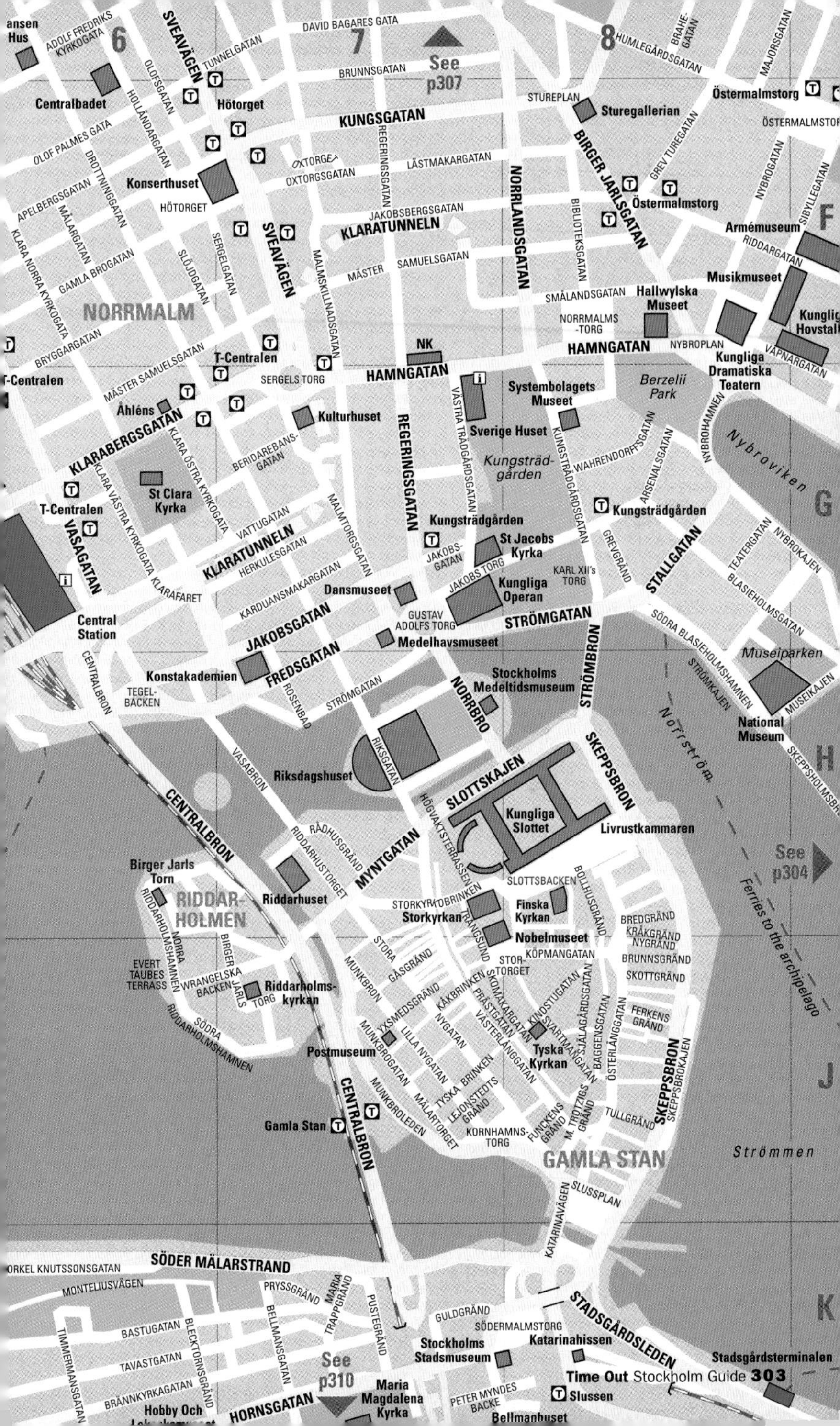
NORRMALM
RIDDARHOLMEN
GAMLA STAN
Kungsträdgården
Berzelii Park
Museiparken
Nybroviken
Norrström
Strömmen
Ferries to the archipelago
Kungliga Slottet
Riksdagshuset
Central Station
Konserthuset
Kulturhuset
Sverige Huset
Kungliga Operan
National Museum
Storkyrkan
Riddarhuset
Riddarholmskyrkan
Tyska Kyrkan
Nobelmuseet
Stockholms Stadsmuseum
Katarinahissen
Stadsgårdsterminalen
Slussen
See p307
See p304
See p310

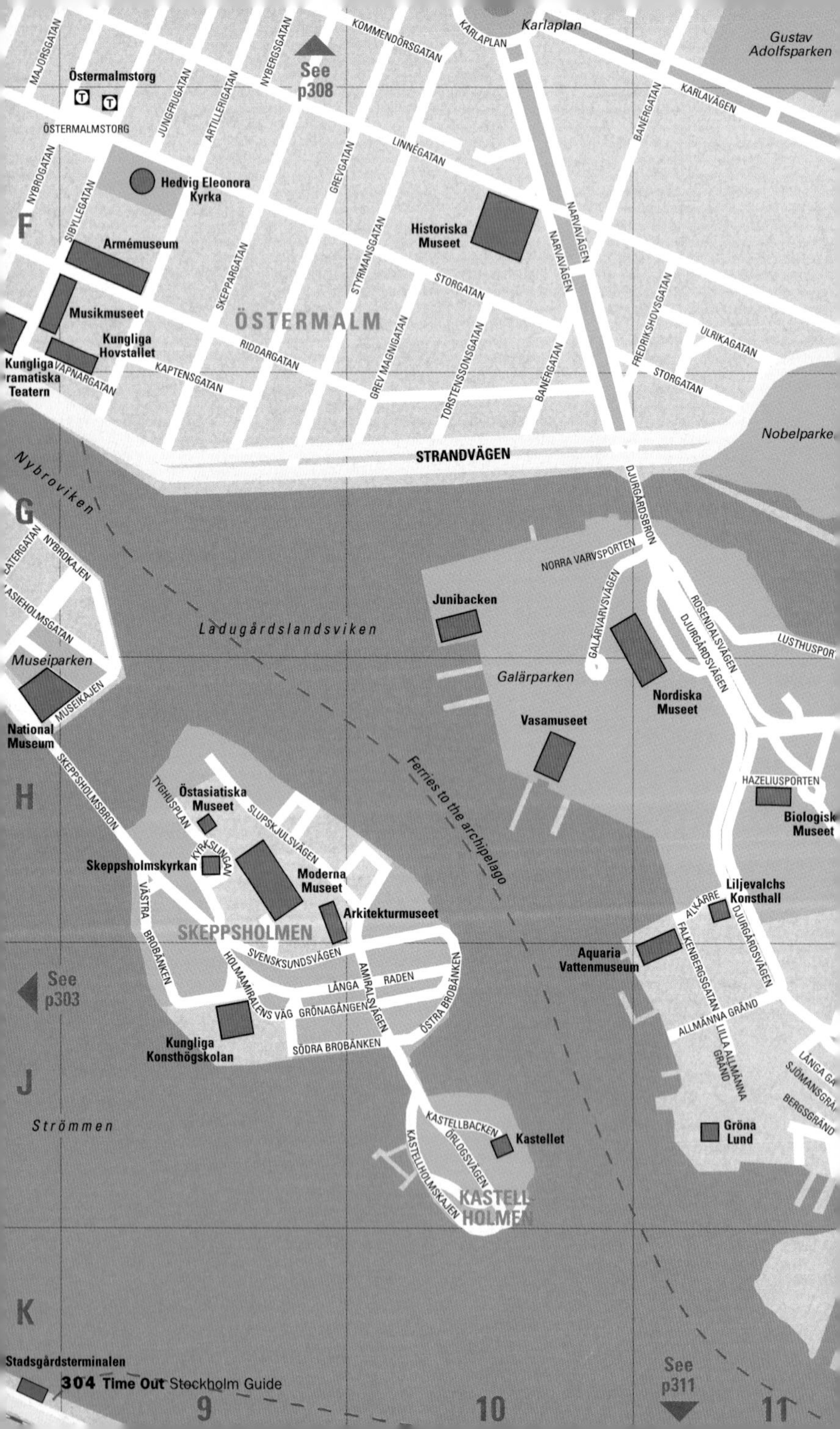

Karlaplan
KARLAPLAN
Gustav Adolfsparken
KOMMENDÖRSGATAN
See p308
MAJORSGATAN
NYBERGSGATAN
Östermalmstorg
ÖSTERMALMSTORG
JUNGFRUGATAN
ARTILLERIGATAN
KARLAVÄGEN
BANÉRGATAN
LINNÉGATAN
NYBROGATAN
Hedvig Eleonora Kyrka
SIBYLLEGATAN
GREVGATAN
F
Armémuseum
Historiska Museet
NARVAVÄGEN
STYRMANSGATAN
SKEPPARGATAN
STORGATAN
FREDRIKSHOVSGATAN
Musikmuseet
ÖSTERMALM
ULRIKAGATAN
Kungliga Hovstallet
GREV MAGNIGATAN
TORSTENSSONSGATAN
RIDDARGATAN
Kungliga Dramatiska Teatern
VAPNARGATAN
KAPTENSGATAN
STORGATAN
Nobelparken
STRANDVÄGEN
Nybroviken
DJURGÅRDSBRON
G
NYBROKAJEN
NORRA VARVSPORTEN
ASIEHOLMSGATAN
Ladugårdslandsviken
Junibacken
GALÄRVARVSVÄGEN
ROSENDALSVÄGEN
DJURGÅRDSVÄGEN
LUSTHUSPORTEN
Museiparken
Galärparken
Nordiska Museet
MUSEIKAJEN
National Museum
Vasamuseet
SKEPPSHOLMSBRON
Ferries to the archipelago
TYGHUSPLAN
Östasiatiska Museet
SLUPSKJULSVÄGEN
HAZELIUSPORTEN
H
Biologiska Museet
KYRKSLINGAN
Skeppsholmskyrkan
Moderna Museet
Liljevalchs Konsthall
ALKÄRRET
VÄSTRA BROBÄNKEN
Arkitekturmuseet
SKEPPSHOLMEN
Aquaria Vattenmuseum
FALKENBERGSGATAN
DJURGÅRDSVÄGEN
SVENSKSUNDSVÄGEN
HOLMAMIRALENS VÄG
AMIRALSVÄGEN
LÅNGA RADEN
ÖSTRA BROBÄNKEN
See p303
GRÖNAGÅNGEN
ALLMÄNNA GRÄND
Kungliga Konsthögskolan
SÖDRA BROBÄNKEN
LILLA ALLMÄNNA GRÄND
LÅNGA GATAN
SJÖMANSGRÄND
J
BERGSGRÄND
Strömmen
KASTELLBACKEN
Kastellet
Gröna Lund
ÖRLOGSVÄGEN
KASTELLHOLMSKAJEN
KASTELLHOLMEN
K
Stadsgårdsterminalen
See p311
9
10
11

See p309
LADUGÅRDSGÄRDET
0
300 m
0
300 yds
© Copyright Time Out Group 2003
Gärdet
F
TAPTOGATAN
VALHALLAVÄGEN
TV-huset
OXENSTIERNSGATAN
GÄRDESGATAN
SKARPÖGATAN
British Embassy
Radiohuset
US Embassy
Berwaldhallen
DAG HAMMARSKJÖLDS VÄG
DJURGÅRDSBRUNNSVÄGEN
LABORATORIEGATAN
NOBELGATAN
Sjöhistoriska Museet
Telemuseum & Tekniska Museet
MUSEIVÄGEN
Etnografiska Museet
Djurgårdsbrunnsviken
G
ROSENDALSVÄGEN
ROSENDALSTERRASSEN
Rosendals Slott
Skansen
H
Rosendals Trädgård
ORANGERIVÄGEN
VALMUNDSVÄGEN
DJURGÅRDEN
SIRISHOVSVÄGEN
Cirkus
Skansen Akvariet
SINGELBACKEN
SOLLIDSBACKEN
DJURGÅRDSVÄGEN
J
BECKHOLMSVÄGEN
BERGSJÖLUNDSVÄGEN
NORDENSKIÖLDS-GATAN
RYSSVIKSVÄGEN
PRINS EUGENS VÄG
BECKHOLMSBRON
BECK-HOLMEN
Waldemarsviken
K
Prins Eugens Waldermarsudde
12
13
14

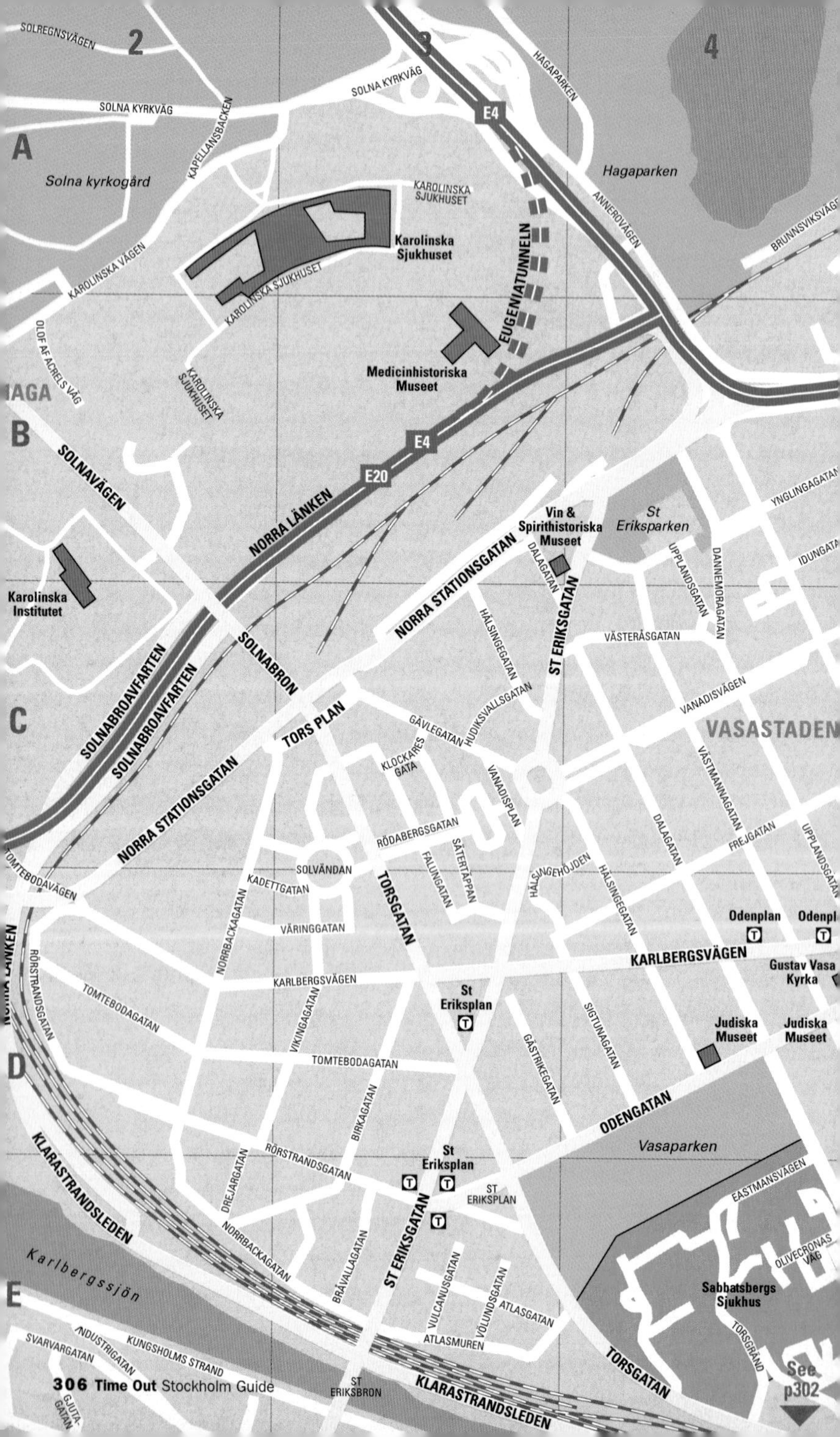
SOLREGNSVÄGEN
2
3
4
SOLNA KYRKVÄG
SOLNA KYRKVÄG
HAGAPARKEN
E4
A
KAPELLANSBACKEN
Solna kyrkogård
Hagaparken
KAROLINSKA SJUKHUSET
Karolinska Sjukhuset
ANNEROVÄGEN
BRUNNSVIKSVÄGEN
KAROLINSKA VÄGEN
KAROLINSKA SJUKHUSET
EUGENIATUNNELN
OLOF AF ACRELS VÄG
KAROLINSKA SJUKHUSET
Medicinhistoriska Museet
HAGA
B
E4
E20
SOLNAVÄGEN
NORRA LÄNKEN
YNGLINGAGATAN
St Eriksparken
Vin & Spirithistoriska Museet
DALAGATAN
IDUNGATAN
NORRA STATIONSGATAN
UPPLANDSGATAN
DANNEMORAGATAN
Karolinska Institutet
ST ERIKSGATAN
HÄLSINGEGATAN
VÄSTERÅSGATAN
SOLNABRON
SOLNABROAVFARTEN
SOLNABROAVFARTEN
HUDIKSVALLSGATAN
VANADISVÄGEN
C
TORS PLAN
GÄVLEGATAN
VASASTADEN
KLOCKARES GATA
VANADISPLAN
NORRA STATIONSGATAN
VÄSTMANNAGATAN
RÖDABERGSGATAN
SÄTERTÄPPAN
FALUNGATAN
DALAGATAN
FREJGATAN
UPPLANDSGATAN
TOMTEBODAVÄGEN
SOLVÄNDAN
KADETTGATAN
TORSGATAN
HÄLSINGEHÖJDEN
HÄLSINGEGATAN
VÄRINGGATAN
NORRBACKAGATAN
Odenplan
Odenpl
NORRA LÄNKEN
KARLBERGSVÄGEN
KARLBERGSVÄGEN
Gustav Vasa Kyrka
RÖRSTRANDSGATAN
TOMTEBODAGATAN
St Eriksplan
VIKINGAGATAN
SIGTUNAGATAN
Judiska Museet
Judiska Museet
D
TOMTEBODAGATAN
GÄSTRIKEGATAN
BIRKAGATAN
ODENGATAN
KLARASTRANDSLEDEN
Vasaparken
RÖRSTRANDSGATAN
DREJARGATAN
St Eriksplan
ST ERIKSPLAN
EASTMANSVÄGEN
NORRBACKAGATAN
Karlbergssjön
BRAVALLAGATAN
ST ERIKSGATAN
VULCANUSGATAN
VÖLUNDSGATAN
ATLASGATAN
OLIVECRONAS VÄG
Sabbatsbergs Sjukhus
E
INDUSTRIGATAN
SVARVARGATAN
KUNGSHOLMS STRAND
ATLASMUREN
TORSGRÄND
TORSGATAN
ST ERIKSBRON
KLARASTRANDSLEDEN
GJUTA-GATAN
See p302

5
6
7
A
B
C
D
E
0
300 m
0
300 yds
© Copyright Time Out Group 2003
Roslagsvägen
Valhallavägen
Cedersdalsgatan
Brunnsviksvägen
Bellevuevägen
Carl Eldhs Ateljémuseum
Vanadislunden
Vilda Vanadis
Sveavägen
Hagagatan
Vanadisvägen
Ingemarsgatan
Roslagsgatan
Birger Jarlsgatan
Frejgatan
Surbrunnsgatan
Tekniska Högskolan
Odengatan
Tulegatan
Döbelnsgatan
Verdandigatan
Tyrgatan
Friggagatan
Östermalmsgatan
Bragevägen
Engelbrekts Kyrkogata
Engelbrektskyrkan
Uggleviksgata
Karlavägen
Kungstensgatan
Rådmansgatan
Eriksbergsgatan
Runebergs Plan
Runebergsgatan
Eriksbergsgatan
Engelbrektsgatan
Rimbogatan
Jarlaplan
Markvardsgatan
Rehnsgatan
Leksaks Palatset
Stadsbiblioteket
Norrtullsgatan
Sandåsgatan
Observatorielunden
Observatorie Museet
Rådmansgatan
Handelshögskolan
Upplandsgatan
Vegagatan
Observatoriegatan
Kungstensgatan
Teknologgatan
Drottninggatan
Holländargatan
Saltmätargatan
Luntmakargatan
Tegnérgatan
Rosengatan
Kammakargatan
Johannes Kyrka
Regeringsgatan
Johannesgatan
Jutas Backe
Snickarbacken
Smala Gränd
Tegnérlunden
Strindbergs-museet
Adolf Fredriks Kyrka
Adolf Fredriks Kyrkogata
Olofsgata
Dansen Hus
Centralbadet
Wallingatan
Tunnelgatan
Brunnsgatan
Tegnérgatan
Ruddammsbacken
Brunbärsvägen
Ruddammsvägen
Bigarråvägen
Körsbärsvägen
Drottning Kristinas Väg
Brinellvägen
Uggleängsvägen
Lögebodavägen
See p308
See p302
See p303

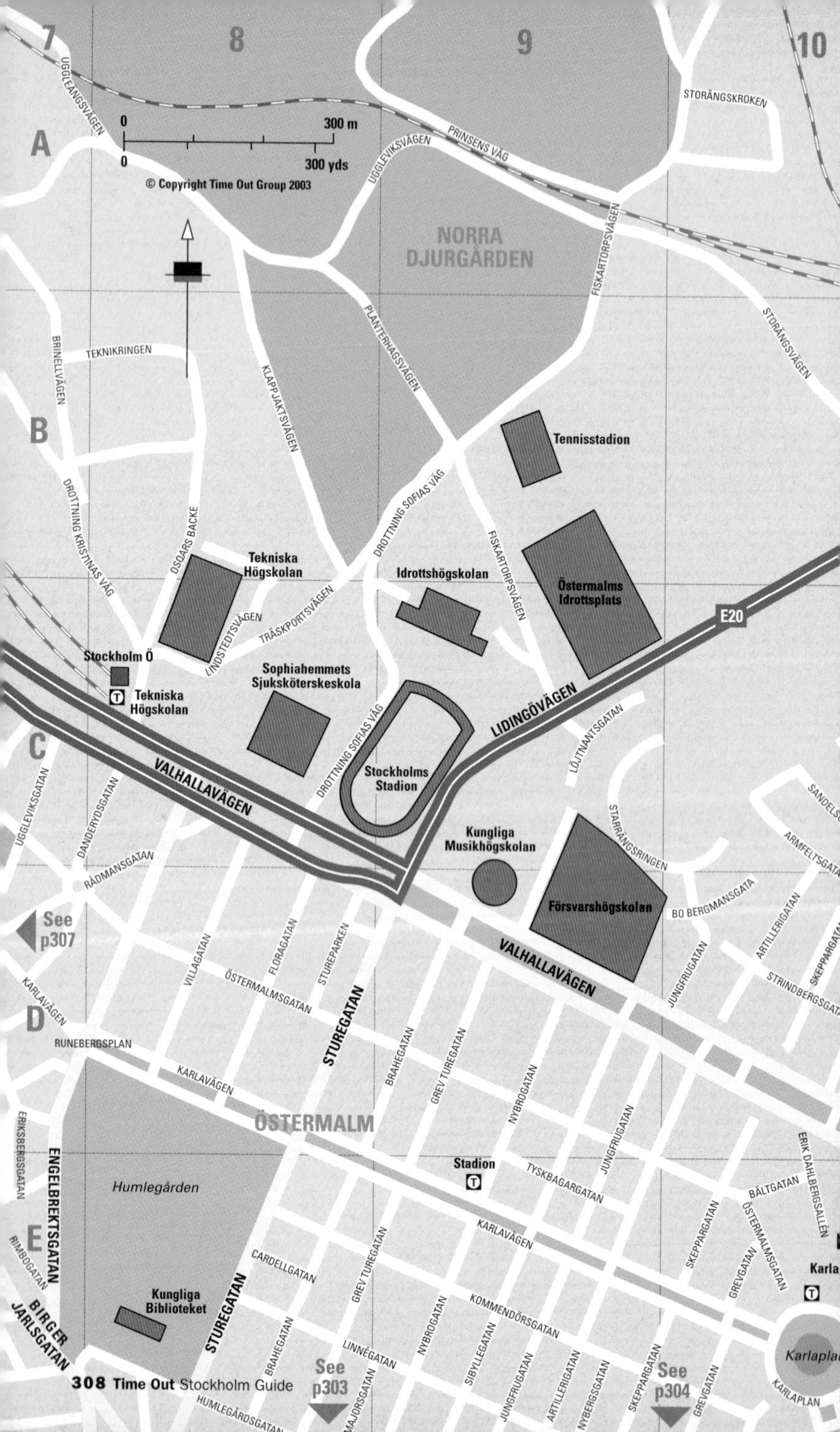

See p307
See p303
See p304

11
12
13
A
B
C
D
E
WENSTRÖMSVÄGEN
AHLSELLVÄGEN
ÄLVKARLEÖVÄGEN
UNTRAVÄGEN
TROLLHÄTTEVÄGEN
MOTALAVÄGEN
KRÅNGEDEVÄGEN
LANFORSVÄGEN
PORJUSVÄGEN
SKOGVAKTARGATAN
ARTEMISGATAN
KOLARGATAN
JÄGMÄSTARGATAN
HJORTHAGEN
MIDSKOGSGRÄND
LIDINGÖVÄGEN
NORRA HAMNVÄGEN
HAMNPIRSVÄGEN
YTTRE HAMNPIRSKAJEN
Kungliga Tennishallen
Silja Line Terminalen
Ferry to Helsinki
E20
TEGELUDDSVÄGEN
SÖDRA BASSÄNGKAJEN
FÖRSTA BASSÄNGVÄGEN
ANDRA BASSÄNGVÄGEN
HANGÖVÄGEN
TREDJE BASSÄNGVÄGEN
FJÄRDE BASSÄNGVÄGEN
SÖDRA HAMNVÄGEN
STUDENTBACKEN
TROPPSTIGEN
SMEDSBACKSGATAN
Gärdet
ERIK DAHLBERGSGATAN
PATRULLSTIGEN
LIVRYTTARSTIGEN
FURUSUNDSGATAN
VÄRTAVÄGEN
SANDHAMNSPLAN
MALMVÄGEN
LAGERHUSGRÄND
RINDÖGATAN
KAMPEMENTSGATAN
SANDHAMNSGATAN
ÖRESUNDSGATAN
GILLÖGAGATAN
BRANTINGSGATAN
RÖKUBBSGATAN
ASKRIKEGATAN
BLANCHEGATAN
Tessinparken
GÄRDET
ÖSTHAMMARSGATAN
KALLSKÄRSGATAN
ÄNGSKÄRSGATAN
DE GEERSGATAN
STORSKÄRSGATAN
HEDINSGATAN
SEHLSTEDTSGATAN
Danshögskolan
STRINDBERGSGATAN
Karlaplan
BANÉRGATAN
Filmhuset
BORGVÄGEN
VALHALLAVÄGEN
LINDARÄNGSVÄGEN
Konstfack
GREVE VON ESSENS VÄG
LÜTZENGATAN
TYSTAGATAN
WITTSTOCKSGATAN
RIGAGATAN
LADUGÅRDSGÄRDET
Gustav Adolfsparken
See p305
TV-huset
TAPTOGATAN

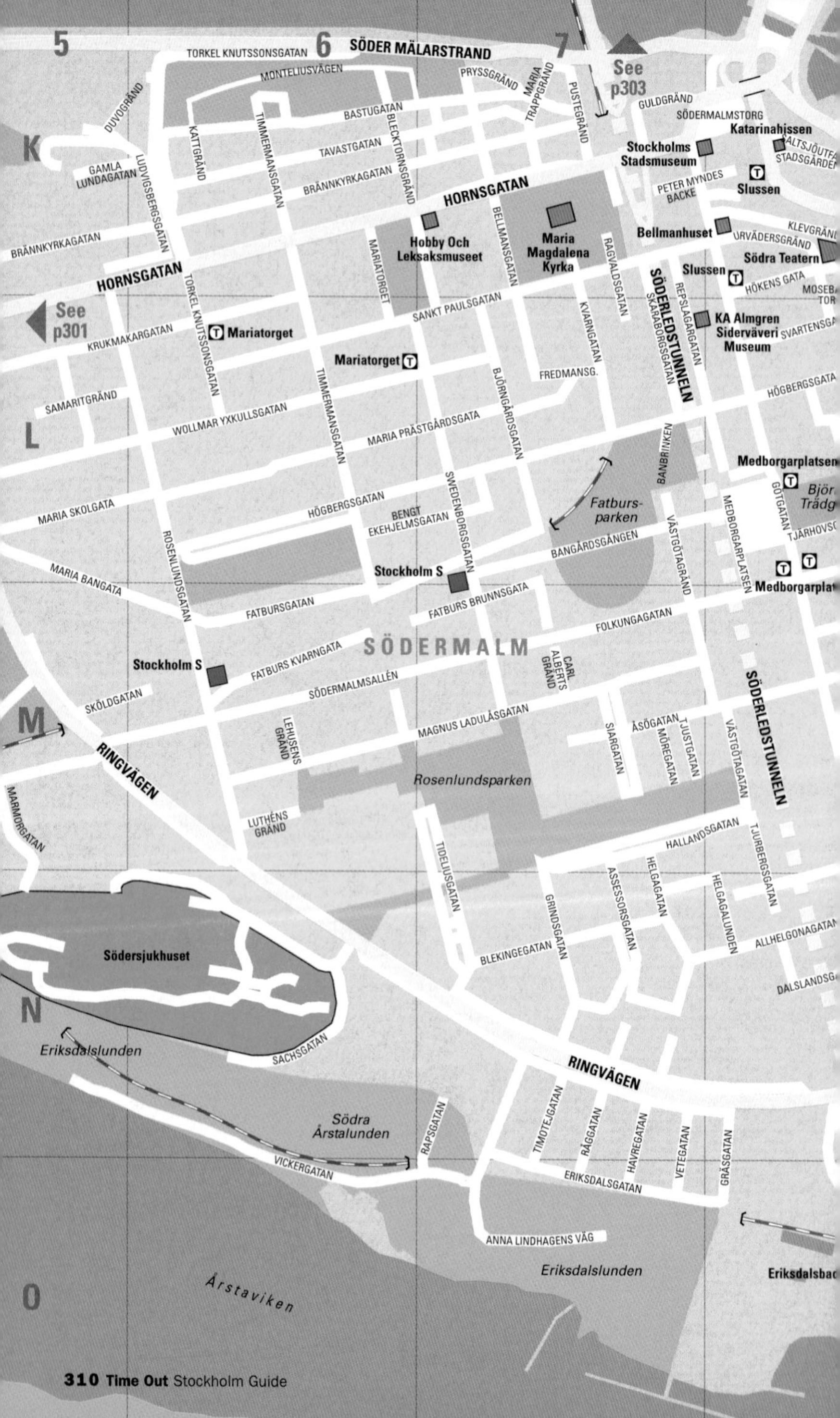

5
6
7
K
L
M
N
O
SÖDER MÄLARSTRAND
TORKEL KNUTSSONSGATAN
MONTELIUSVÄGEN
PRYSSGRÄND
MARIA TRAPPGRÄND
PUSTEGRÄND
See p303
GULDGRÄND
SÖDERMALMSTORG
Katarinahissen
Stockholms Stadsmuseum
Slussen
PETER MYNDES BACKE
DUVOGRÄND
KATTGRÄND
TIMMERMANSGATAN
BASTUGATAN
BLECKTORNSGRÄND
TAVASTGATAN
GAMLA LUNDAGATAN
LUDVIGSBERGSGATAN
BRÄNNKYRKAGATAN
HORNSGATAN
BELLMANSGATAN
Hobby Och Leksaksmuseet
Maria Magdalena Kyrka
RAGVALDSGATAN
Bellmanhuset
URVÄDERSGRÄND
KLEVGRÄND
Södra Teatern
HÖKENS GATA
SÖDERLEDSTUNNELN
SKARABORGSGATAN
REPSLAGARGATAN
KA Almgren Sidenväveri Museum
SVARTENSGATAN
MARIATORGET
SANKT PAULSGATAN
KVARNGATAN
See p301
KRUKMAKARGATAN
Mariatorget
FREDMANSG.
HÖGBERGSGATAN
SAMARITGRÄND
WOLLMAR YXKULLSGATAN
MARIA PRÄSTGÅRDSGATA
BJÖRNGÅRDSGATAN
BANBRINKEN
Medborgarplatsen
GÖTGATAN
SWEDENBORGSGATAN
Fatburs-parken
MARIA SKOLGATA
BENGT EKEHJELMSGATAN
BANGÅRDSGÅNGEN
VÄSTGÖTAGRÄND
MEDBORGARPLATSEN
ROSENLUNDSGATAN
MARIA BANGATA
Stockholm S
FATBURSGATAN
FATBURS BRUNNSGATA
FOLKUNGAGATAN
SÖDERMALM
FATBURS KVARNGATA
CARL ALBERTS GRÄND
SKÖLDGATAN
SÖDERMALMSALLÉN
MAGNUS LADULÅSGATAN
LEHUSENS GRÄND
SIARGATAN
ÅSÖGATAN
MÖREGATAN
TJUSTGATAN
VÄSTGÖTAGATAN
RINGVÄGEN
Rosenlundsparken
MARMORGATAN
LUTHÉNS GRÄND
TIDELIUSGATAN
HALLANDSGATAN
TJURBERGSGATAN
ASSESSORSGATAN
HELGAGATAN
GRINDSGATAN
HELGAGALUNDEN
ALLHELGONAGATAN
Södersjukhuset
BLEKINGEGATAN
DALSLANDSGATAN
Eriksdalslunden
SACHSGATAN
TIMOTEJGATAN
RÅGGATAN
HAVREGATAN
VETEGATAN
GRÄSGATAN
Södra Årstalunden
RAPSGATAN
VICKERGATAN
ERIKSDALSGATAN
ANNA LINDHAGENS VÄG
Eriksdalslunden
Årstaviken

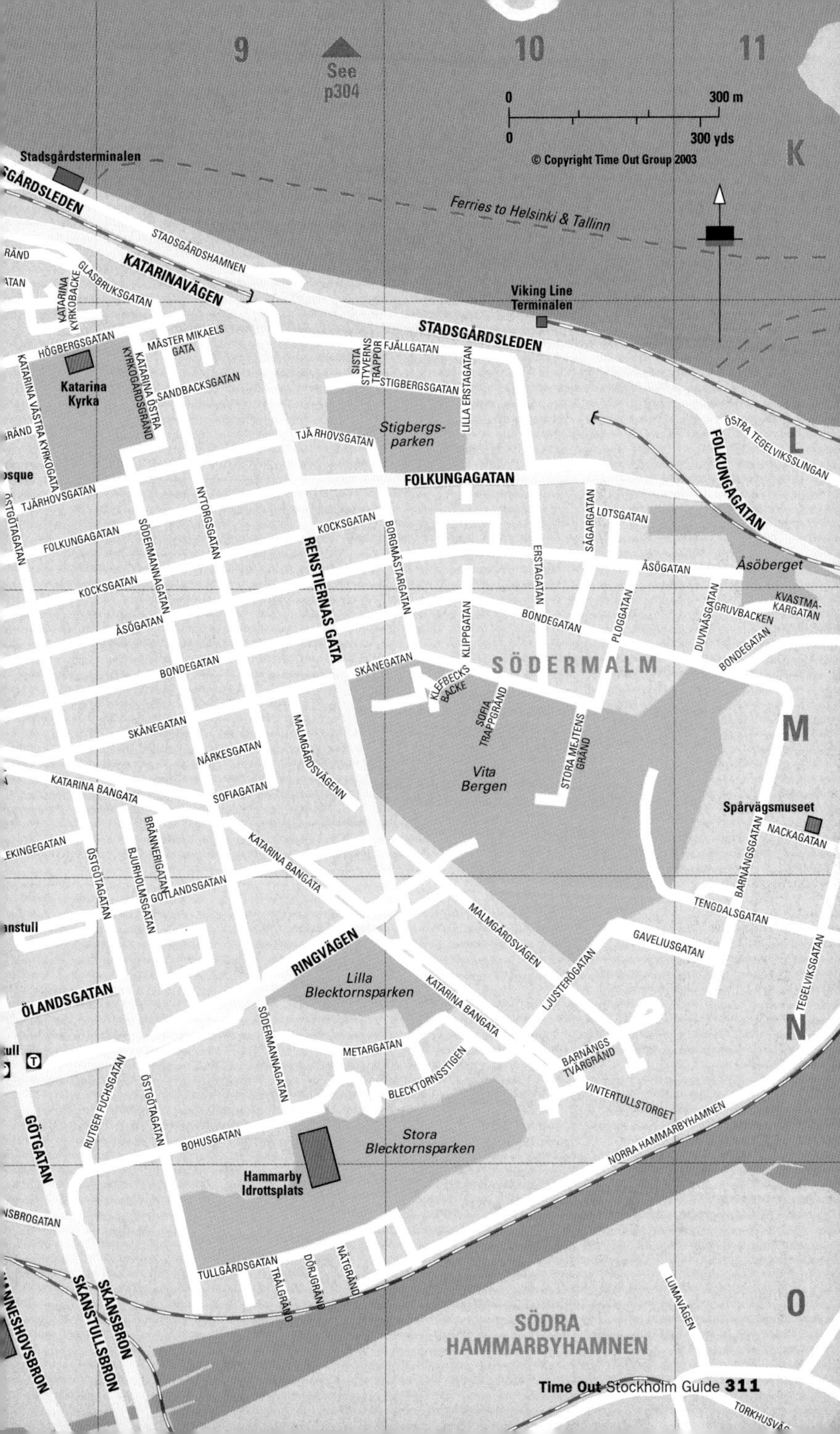
9
10
11
See p304
0
300 m
0
300 yds
© Copyright Time Out Group 2003
K
L
M
N
O
Stadsgårdsterminalen
Ferries to Helsinki & Tallinn
Viking Line Terminalen
STADSGÅRDSLEDEN
STADSGÅRDSHAMNEN
KATARINAVÄGEN
GLASBRUKSGATAN
KATARINA KYRKOBACKE
HÖGBERGSGATAN
MÄSTER MIKAELS GATA
KATARINA ÖSTRA KYRKOGÅRDSGRÄND
SANDBACKSGATAN
Katarina Kyrka
KATARINA VÄSTRA KYRKOGATA
FJÄLLGATAN
SISTA STYVERNS TRAPPOR
STIGBERGSGATAN
LILLA ERSTAGATAN
Stigbergs-parken
TJÄRHOVSGATAN
FOLKUNGAGATAN
ÖSTRA TEGELVIKSSLINGAN
LOTSGATAN
SÅGARGATAN
KOCKSGATAN
NYTORGSGATAN
SÖDERMANNAGATAN
RENSTIERNAS GATA
BORGMÄSTARGATAN
ERSTAGATAN
ÅSÖGATAN
Åsöberget
KVASTMA-KARGATAN
GRUVBACKEN
DUVNÄSGATAN
PLOGGATAN
BONDEGATAN
KLIPPGATAN
SKÅNEGATAN
SÖDERMALM
KLEFBECKS BACKE
SOFIA TRAPPGRÄND
STORA MEJTENS GRÄND
NÄRKESGATAN
MALMGÅRDSVÄGEN
Vita Bergen
SOFIAGATAN
KATARINA BANGATA
Spårvägsmuseet
NACKAGATAN
BARNÄNGSGATAN
BRÄNNERIGATAN
BJURHOLMSGATAN
ÖSTGÖTAGATAN
GOTLANDSGATAN
TENGDALSGATAN
GAVELIUSGATAN
TEGELVIKSGATAN
RINGVÄGEN
ÖLANDSGATAN
Lilla Blecktornsparken
LJUSTERÖGATAN
BARNÄNGS TVÄRGRÄND
METARGATAN
BLECKTORNSSTIGEN
VINTERTULLSTORGET
NORRA HAMMARBYHAMNEN
RUTGER FUCHSGATAN
GÖTGATAN
BOHUSGATAN
Stora Blecktornsparken
Hammarby Idrottsplats
TULLGÅRDSGATAN
TRÅLGRÄND
DÖRJGRÄND
NÄTGRÄND
SKANSBRON
SKANSTULLSBRON
SÖDRA HAMMARBYHAMNEN
LUMAVÄGEN
TORKHUSVÄG

Street Index

In Swedish alphabetical listings, the letters å, ä and ö fall at the end of the alphabet. For ease of use, however, we have listed these as if they were standard a and o.

Adolf Fredriks Kyrkogata – p303 E6, p307 E6
Ahlsellvägen – p309 A11
Alfred Medins Väg – p301 L4
Alkärret – p304 H11
Allhelgonagatan – p310 N8
Allmänna Gränd – p304 J11
Alstaviksvägen – p301 K2
Älvkarleövägen – p309 A10-11
Amiralsvägen – p304 J10
Anders Reimers Väg – p301 K1
Andra Bassängvägen – p309 B13
Ängskärsgatan – p309 D11
Anna Lindhagens Väg – p310 07
Annerovägen – p306 A3-4
Ångströmsgatan – p302 F3
Apelbergsgatan – p303 F6
Armfeltsgatan – p308 C10/D10
Arsenalsgatan – p303 G8
Artemisgatan – p309 A11-12
Artillerigatan – p304 F9/E9, p308 E9/D10
Askrikegatan – p309 C11
Åsögatan – p310 M7-8, p311 M8-9/L9-11
Assessorsgatan – p310 N7
Atlasgatan – p306 E3
Atlasmuren – p306 E3

Baggensgatan – p303 J8
Bältgatan – p308 E10
Banbrinken – p310 L7
Banérgatan – p304 G10/F10-11/E11, p309 E11/D11
Bangårdsgången – p310 L7
Barnängs Tvärgränd – p311 N10
Barnängsgatan – p311 N11/M11
Barnhusbron – p302 F4
Barnhusgatan – p302 F6
Bastugatan – p303 K6-7, p310 K6-7
Beckholmsbron – p305 J12
Beckholmsvägen – p304 J11, p305 J11
Bellevuevägen – p307 A5
Bellmansgatan – p303 K7, p310 K7/L7
Bengt Ekehjelmsgatan – p310 L6-7
Bergsgatan – p302 G3-5
Bergsgränd – p304 J11
Bergsjölundsvägen – p305 J14
Bergsunds Strand – p301 L2
Bergsundsgatan – p301 L2
Beridarebansgatan – p303 G7
Biblioteksgatan – p303 F8
Bigaråvägen – p307 A7
Birger Jarls Torg – p303 J7
Birger Jarlsgatan – p303 F8, p307 B6/C6-7/D7/E7, p308 E7-8
Birkagatan – p306 D3
Björngårdsgatan – p310 L7
Bjurholmsgatan – p311 M9/N9
Blanchegatan – p309 C11/D11
Blasieholmsgatan – p303 G8-9, p304 G8-9
Blecktornsgränd – p303 K6, p310 K6
Blecktornsstigen – p311 N10
Blekholmsgatan – p302 G5
Blekingegatan – p310 N7, p311 M8
Bo Bergmansgata – p308 D10
Bohusgatan – p311 N9
Bollhusgränd – p303 H8
Bondegatan – p311 M8-11
Borgargatan – p301 L3
Borgmästargatan – p311 L10/M10
Borgvägen – p309 E12
Bragevägen – p307 C7
Brahegatan – p303 E8, p308 E8/D8-9
Brännerigatan – p311 M9/N9
Brännkyrkagatan – p301 K5/L4, p303 K6-7, p310 K5-K7
Brantingsgatan – p309 C11
Bråvallagatan – p306 E3
Bredgränd – p303 H8
Brinellvägen – p307 A7/B7, p308 A7/B7
Brunbärsvägen – p307 A6
Brunnsgatan – p303 E7, p307 E7
Brunnsgränd – p303 J8
Brunnsviksvägen – p306 A4
Bryggargatan – p303 F6
Cardellgatan – p308 E8
Carl Alberts Gränd – p310 M7
Carl Gustaf Lindstedts Gata – p302 F4
Cedersdalsgatan – p307 B5-6
Celsiusgatan – p302 G3/F3
Centralbron – p303 H6-7/J7
Coldinutrappan – p302 G4

Dag Hammarskjölds Väg – p305 F12
Dalagatan – p306 C4/D4, p307 E5
Dalslandsgatan – p310 N8
Danderydsgatan – p308 A7-8
Dannemoragatan – p306 B4/C4
David Bagares Gata – p303 E7
De Geersgatan – p309 D11
Djurgårdsbron – p304 G11
Djurgårdsbrunnsvägen – p305 F13-14
Djurgårdsvägen – p304 G11/H11, p305 J14
Döbelnsgatan – p307 C6/D6/E6-7
Dörjgränd – p311 09
Drakenbergsgatan – p301 L3-4
Drejargatan – p306 E2
Drottning Kristinas Väg – p307 A6-7/B7, p308 B7/C8
Drottning Sofias Väg – p308 C8-9/B9
Drottninggatan – p303 F6, p307 D5-6
Duvnäsgatan – p311 M11
Duvogränd – p302 K5, p310 K5

Eastmansvägen – p306 E4
Ekermans Gränd – p301 M5
Engelbrekts Kyrkogata – p307 C7
Engelbrektsgatan – p307 D7/E7, p308 D7/E7
Erik Dahlbergsallén – p308 D10/E10
Erik Dahlbergsgatan – p309 B10/C10/D10
Eriksbergsgatan – p307 D7/E7, p307 D7/E7, p308 D7/E7
Eriksdalsgatan – p310 07
Erstagatan – p311 L10/M10
Eugeniatunneln – p306 B3/A3
Evert Taubes Terrass – p303 J6

Falkenbergsgatan – p304 H11/J11
Falungatan – p306 C3/D3
Fatburs Brunnsgata – p310 M7
Fatburs Kvarngata – p310 M6
Fatbursgatan – p310 M6
Ferkens Gränd – p303 J8
Fiskargatan – p311 K8
Fiskartorpsvägen – p308 C9/B9/A9
Fjällgatan – p311 L9-10
Fjärde Bassängvägen – p309 C13/B13
Fleminggatan – p302 F3-4/G4-5
Floragatan – p308 D8
Folkskolegatan – p301 K2/L2
Folkungagatan – p310 M7-8, p311 L8-11
Första Bassängvägen – p309 B13
Fredmansgatan – p310 L7
Fredrikshovsgatan – p304 F11
Fredsgatan – p303 H7/G7
Frejgatan – p306 C4/D4, p307 C5-6/B6
Friggagatan – p307 C7
Funckens Gränd – p303 J8
Furusundsgatan – p309 C11

Galärvarvsvägen – p304 G10
Gambrinusgatan – p302 G3
Gamla Brogatan – p303 F6
Gamla Lundagatan – p302 K5, p310 K5
Gärdesgatan – p305 F12
Garvar Lundins Gränd – p302 H4
Garvargatan – p302 H4
Gåsgränd – p303 J7
Gästrikegatan – p306 D3-4
Gaveliusgatan – p311 N10-11
Gävlegatan – p306 C3
Gederdalsgatan – p307 B5
Gillögagatan – p309 C11
Gjutagatan – p306 E2
Glasbruksgatan – p311 K8-9

Götgatan – p310 K8-M8, p311 N8/O9
Gotlandsgatan – p311 N9/M9
Gräsgatan – p310 N8/O8
Grev Magnigatan – p304 G10/F10
Grev Turegatan – p303 F8, p308 E8/-9/D9
Greve Von Essens Väg – p309 E12-13
Grevgatan – p304 F9/E9, p308 E10
Grevgränd – p303 G8
Grindsgatan – p310 N7
Grönagången – p304 J9-10
Grubbens Gata – p302 F3
Grubbensringen – p302 F4
Gruvbacken – p311 M11
Guldgränd – p303 K7, p310 K7
Gustav Adolfs Torg – p303 G7

Hagagatan – p307 B5/C5
Hagaparken – p306 A3-4
Hallandsgatan – p310 M7-8
Hallmans Gata – p302 F3-4
Hälsingegatan – p306 C3-4/D4
Hälsingehöjden – p306 D3/C4
Hamngatan – p303 G7/F8
Hamnpirsvägen – p309 A12-13
Hangövägen – p309 B12-13
Hantverkargatan – p302 G3-4/H4-5
Havregatan – p310 N7/O7
Hazeliusbacken – p304 H11/J11
Hazeliusporten – p304 H11
Hedinsgatan – p309 D10/11
Heimdalsgatan – p306 C4
Heimdalsgatan – p307 C5
Heleneborgsgatan – p301 K3-4, p302 K3-4
Helgagalunden – p310 N8
Helgagatan – p310 M7/N7
Herkulesgatan – p303 G7
Hjärnegatan – p302 G4
Högalidsgatan – p301 K2-K4, p302 K4
Högbergsgatan – p310 L6-8
Högvaktsterrassen – p303 H7
Hökens Gata – p310 K8
Holländargatan – p303 E6/F6, p307 E6
Holmamiralens Väg – p304 J9
Hornsbruksgatan – p301 L3
Hornsgatan – p301 L2-L5, p303 K7
Hornsgatan – p310 K5-7
Hornstulls Strand – p301 M3
Hornsviksstigen – p301 L4/K3
Hötorget – p303 F6
Hudiksvallsgatan – p306 C3
Humlegårdsgatan – p303 E8/F8, p308 E8

Idungatan – p306 B4
Industrigatan – p306 E2
Inedalsgatan – p302 F3
Ingemarsgatan – p307 B6
Ivan Oljelunds Gränd – p302 F4

Jägmästargatan – p309 A11
Jakob Westinsgatan – p302 H4
Jakobs Torg – p303 G7-8
Jakobsbergsgatan – p303 F7-8
Jakobsgatan – p303 G7
Jarlaplan – p307 C6
Johannesgatan – p307 E7
Johanneshovsbron – p311 O8
John Ericssonsgatan – p302 H3/G3
Jungfrugatan – p304 F9/E9, p308 E9/D9
Jutas Backe – p307 E7

Kadettgatan – p306 D2-3
Kåkbrinken – p303 J7
Kallskärsgatan – p309 D10
Kammakargatan – p302 E5, p307 E5-7
Kampementsgatan – p309 C12
Kapellansbacken – p306 A2
Kapellgränd – p311 L8
Kaplansbacken – p302 H5/G5
Kaptensgatan – p304 F9/G10
Karduansmakargatan – p303 G7
Karl XIIs Torg – p303 G8
Karlaplan – p304 E10, p308 E10
Karlavägen – p304 E11/F11, p307 C7/D7, p308 D8/E9-10, p309 E10-11
Karlbergsvägen – p306 D2-4
Karlshällsvägen – p301 J1/K1
Karolinska Sjukhuset – p306 A2-3/B2
Karolinska Vägen – p306 A2
Kastellbacken – p304 J10
Kastellholmskajen – p304 J10
Katarina Bangata – p311 M8-9/N9-10
Katarina Kyrkobacke – p311 K8/K8
Katarina Östra Kyrkogårdsgränd – p311 L9
Katarina Västra Kyrkogata – p311 L8
Katarinavägen – p303 K8/J8, p311 K8-9
Katarinebergsvägen – p301 M2
Katrinebergsbacken – p301 M1-2
Kattgränd – p310 K6
Kindstugatan – p303 J8
Klappjaktsvägen – p308 B8
Klara Norra Kyrkogata – p303 F6/G6
Klara Östra Kyrkogata – p303 G6
Klara Västra Kyrkogata – p303 G6
Klarabergsgatan – p303 G6
Klarabergskopplet – p302 G5-6/H6
Klarabergsviadukten – p302 G5-6
Klarafaret – p303 G6
Klarasjörampen – p302 G5/H6
Klarastrandsleden – p302 E3/F4-5/G5, p306 D2/E2-3
Klaratunneln – p303 G6-7/F7
Klefbecks Backe – p311 M10
Klevgränd – p310 K8, p311 K8
Klippgatan – p311 M10
Klockares Gata – p306 C3
Knaperstavägen – p301 J1
Kocksgatan – p311 M8/L9
Kolargatan – p309 A11-12
Kommendörsgatan – p304 E10, p308 E8-10
Köpmangatan – p303 J8
Kornhamnstorg – p303 J7-8
Körsbärsvägen – p307 B6-7
Kråkgränd – p303 H8/J8
Krångedevägen – p309 A10-11
Kristinehovsgatan – p301 L4
Kronobergsgatan – p302 F3
Krukmakargatan – p301 L4-5, p310 L5-6
Kungsbro Strand – p302 G5
Kungsgatan – p302 G4-5/F5, p303 F7
Kungsholms Hamnplan – p302 H4
Kungsholms Kyrkoplan – p302 G5
Kungsholms Strand – p302 E3/F3, p306 E2-3
Kungsholms Torg – p302 H4
Kungsholmsgatan – p302 G3-5
Kungsklippan – p302 G4-5
Kungstensgatan – p307 E5/D5-7
Kungsträdgårdsgatan – p303 G8
Kvarngatan – p310 L7
Kvastmakargatan – p311 M11
Kyrkslingan – p304 H9

Laboratoriegatan – p305 G12
Lagerhusgränd – p309 C13
Långa Gatan – p304 J11
Långa Raden – p304 J9-10
Långholmsbacken – p301 K2
Långholmsbron – p301 K2
Långholmsgatan – p301 K2/L3
Långholmsmuren – p301 K1
Lästmakargatan – p303 F7
Lehusens Gränd – p310 M6
Lejonstedts Gränd – p303 J7
Lidingövägen – p308 C9-10, p309 B10-12/A12
Lignagatan – p301 L3
Liljeholm Sinfarten – p301 M2
Liljeholmsbron – p301 M2-3
Liljeholmsstranden – p301 L2/M2
Liljeholmsvägen – p301 M2
Lilla Allmänna Gränd – p304 J11
Lilla Erstagatan – p311 L10
Lilla Nygatan – p303 J7
Lindarängsvägen – p309 E12-13
Lindstedtsvägen – p308 C8
Linnégatan – p304 E9/F9-11, p308 E8-9
Livryttarstigen – p309 C11/B11
Ljusterögatan – p311 N10
Lögebodavägen – p307 A5
Löjtnantsgatan – p308 C9
Lotsgatan – p311 L10
Lövholmsbrinken – p301 L1
Lövholmsgränd – p301 L1/M1
Lövholmsvägen – p301 M1

Ludvigsbergsgatan – p310 K6
Lumavägen – p311 O11
Lundagatan – p301 K4
Luntmakargatan – p307 D6/E6-7
Lusthusporten – p304 G11
Luthéns Gränd – p310 M6
Lützengatan – p309 E10

Martin Trotzigs Gränd – p303 J8
Magnus Ladulåsgatan – p310 M6-7
Majorsgatan – p303 E8, p304 E8, p308 E8
Målargatan – p303 F6
Mälartorget – p303 J7
Mälarvarvsbacken – p301 K3, p302 K3
Malmgårdsvägen – p311 M9-10/N10
Malmskillnadsgatan – p303 F7
Malmtorgsgatan – p303 G7
Malmvägen – p309 C13
Maria Bangata – p301 L5, p310 L5/M5-6
Maria Prästgårdsgata – p310 L6-7
Maria Sandels Gränd – p302 F4
Maria Skolgata – p301 L5, p310 L5
Maria Trappgränd – p303 K7, p310 K7
Mariatorget – p310 K6/L6
Markvardsgatan – p307 D6/C6
Marmorgatan – p310 M5
Mäster Mikaels Gata – p311 L9
Mäster Samuelsgatan – p303 G6//F6-8
Medborgarplatsen – p310 L8
Mejerivägen – p301 M1-2
Metargatan – p311 N9-10
Midskogsgränd – p309 A11
Monteliusvägen – p303 K6, p310 K6
Möregatan – p310 M7
Mosebacketorg – p310 K8/L8
Motalavägen – p309 A10-11
Münchensbacken – p301 K4, p302 K4
Munkbrogatan – p303 J7
Munkbroleden – p303 J7
Munkbron – p303 J7
Museikajen – p303 H9, p304 H9
Museivägen – p305 G14/F14
Myntgatan – p303 H7

Nackagatan – p311 M11
Närkesgatan – p311 M9
Narvavägen – p304 E10/F10/G10
Nätgränd – p311 O9
Nobelgatan – p305 G12
Nordenskiöldsgatan – p304 J11, p305 J11
Norr Mälarstrand – p302 H3-5
Norra Agnegatan – p302 G4
Norra Bantorget – p302 F5
Norra Hammarbyhamnen – p311 O10/N10-11
Norra Hamnvägen – p309 B12/A12
Norra Länken – p306 D2/C2/B2-4
Norra Riddarholmshamnen – p303 H6/J6
Norra Stationsgatan – p306 B3-4/C2-3
Norra Varvsporten – p304 G10
Norrbackagatan – p306 C1/D1/E1-3
Norrbro – p303 H7
Norrlandsgatan – p303 F8
Norrmalmstorg – p303 F8
Norrtullsgatan – p307 C5/D5
Nybergsgatan – p304 E9, p308 E9
Nybrogatan – p303 F8, p304 F8, p308 E9/D9
Nybrohamnen – p303 G8
Nybrokajen – p303 G8-9, p304 G8-9
Nybroplan – p303 F8
Nygränd – p303 J8
Nytorgsgatan – p311 L9/M9

Observatoriegatan – p307 E5/D5
Odengatan – p306 D4, p307 D5/C6-7
Olaus Petrigatan – p308 C10, p309 C10
Ölandsgatan – p311 N8-9
Olivecronas Väg – p306 E4
Olof AF Acrels Väg – p306 B2
Olof Palmes Gata – p303 F6
Olofsgatan – p303 E6/F6, p307 E6
Orangerivägen – p305 H13
Öresundsgatan – p309 C13
Örlogsvägen – p304 J10
Osqars Backe – p308 C8/B8
Österlånggatan – p303 J8
Östermalmsgatan – p307 C7, p308 D7-9/E10
Östermalmstorg – p303 F9, p304 F9
Östgötagatan – p311 L8/M8/N9/O9
Östhammarsgatan – p309 D13-C13
Östra Brobänken – p304
Östra Tegelviksslingan – p311 L11
Oxenstiernsgatan – p305 F11-12
Oxtorget – p303 F7
Oxtorgsgatan – p303 F7

Pålsundsbron – p301 K3
Pålsundsgatan – p301 K3
Parkgatan – p302 F3
Parmmätargatan – p302 H4/G4
Patrullstigen – p309 C11
Percy Ahnhems Väg – p301 M4
Peter Myndes Backe – p303 K7-8, p310 K7-8
Pilgatan – p302 H3/G3
Pipersgatan – p302 G4/F4
Planterhagsvägen – p308 A8/B8-9
Ploggatan – p311 M10
Polhems Tvärgränd – p302 F3
Polhemsgatan – p302 H3/G3/F3
Porjusvägen – p309 A11
Prästgatan – p303 J7-8
Prins Eugens Väg – p305 J13-14
Prinsens Väg – p308 A8-9
Pryssgränd – p303 K7, p310 K7
Pustegränd – p303 K7, p310 K7

Rådhusgränd – p303 H7
Rådmansgatan – p307 E5-6/D6-7, p308 D8/C8
Råggatan – p310 N7
Ragnar Östbergs Plan – p302 H5
Ragvaldsgatan – p310 K7/L7
Rapsgatan – p310 N7
Regeringsgatan – p303 E7/F7/G7, p307 D7/E7
Rehnsgatan – p307 D6
Reimersholmsgatan – p301 K1
Renstiernas Gata – p311 L9/M9
Repslagargatan – p310 K7/L7-8
Riddargatan – p303 F8-9, p304 F9/G9-10
Riddarhustorget – p303 H7
Rigagatan – p309 E11
Riksgatan – p303 H7
Rimbogatan – p307 E7, p308 E7
Rindögatan – p309 C11
Ringvägen – p301 K5/L5/M5, p310 M5-6/N6-8, p311 N8-9
Rödabergsgatan – p306 C3
Rökubbsgatan – p309 C13
Rörstrandsgatan – p306 D2/E3
Rosenbad – p303 H7
Rosendalsterrassen – p305 H13
Rosendalsvägen – p304 G11/H11, p305 G12
Rosengatan – p307 E6
Rosenlundsgatan – p310 L6/M6
Roslagsgatan – p307 B6/C6
Roslagsvägen – p307 A5-6
Ruddammsbacken – p307 A6
Ruddammsvägen – p307 A6-7/B7
Runebergsgatan – p307 D7
Runebergsplan – p307 D7, p308 D7-8
Rutger Fuchsgatan – p311 N8-9
Ryssviksvägen – p305 J13

Sachsgatan – p310 N6
Sågargatan – p311 L10
Saltmätargatan – p307 D6/E6
Saltsjöutfarten – p310 K8
Samaritgränd – p310 L5
Samuel Owens Gata – p302 H5
Sandåsgatan – p307 D5
Sandbacksgatan – p311 L9
Sandelsgatan – p308 C10
Sandhamnsgatan – p309 C12-13/D13
Sandhamnsplan – p309 C12
Sankt Paulsgatan – p310 L6-7/K7
Sätertäppan – p306 C3/D3
Scheelegatan – p302 G4/F4
Sehlstedtsgatan – p309 D13
Serafimergränd – p302 H5
Sergelgatan – p303 F6-7
Sergels Torg – p303 G7
Siargatan – p310 M7
Sibyllegatan – p303 F8-9, p304 F9
Sibyllegatan – p308 E9/D9
Sigtunagatan – p306 D4
Singelbacken – p305 J12-13
Sirishovsvägen – p305 J13-H13
Sista Styverns Trappor – p311 L9

Själagårdsgatan – p303 J8
Sjömansgränd – p304 J11
Skånegatan – p311 M8-10
Skansbrogatan – p311 O8
Skansbron – p311 O9
Skanstullsbron – p311 O8-9
Skaraborgsgatan – p310 K7/L7
Skarpögatan – p305 F12
Skarpskyttegatan – p301 M3
Skeppargatan – p304 F9/E9, p308 E9-10
Skeppsbrokajen – p303 J8
Skeppsbron – p303 H8/J8
Skeppsholmsbron – p303 H8-9, p304 H8-9
Skillinggränd – p302 H5
Skinnarbacken – p301 K4-5, p302 K4-5
Skinnarviksringen – p301 K4, p302 K4
Skogvaktargatan – p309 A11-12
Sköldgatan – p310 M5-6
Skomakargatan – p303 J7-8
Skottgränd – p303 J8
Skutskepparvägen – p301 K2-3
Slipgatan – p301 K2/L2
Slöjdgatan – p303 F6-7
Slottsbacken – p303 H8
Slottskajen – p303 H7-8
Slupskjulsvägen – p304 H9
Slussplan – p303 J8
Smålandsgatan – p303 F8
Smedsbacksgatan – p309 B11/C11
Snickarbacken – p307 E7
Söder Mälarstrand – p301 K2-K5, p302 K3-6, p303 K6-8, p310 K5-7
Söderledstunneln – p310 K7/L7-8/M8/N8
Södermalmsallén – p310 M6-7
Södermalmstorg – p303 K7-8, p310 K7-8
Södermannagatan – p311 L9/M9/N9
Södertäljevägen – p301 M2
Södra Agnegatan – p302 H4/G4
Södra Bassängkajen – p309 B12-13
Södra Blasieholmshamnen – p303 G8/H8
Södra Brobänken – p304 J9-10
Södra Hamnvägen – p309 B12-13/C13
Södra Riddarholmshamnen – p303 J6-7
Sofia Trappgränd – p311 M10
Sofiagatan – p311 M9
Sollidsbacken – p305 J12
Solna Kyrkväg – p306 A2-3
Solnabroavfarten – p306 C2
Solnabron – p306 C2-3
Solnavägen – p306 B2
Solregnsvägen – p306 A2
Solvändan – p306 C3/D3
St Eriksbron – p302 E3, p306 E3
St Eriksgatan – p306 E3/D3/C3
St Eriksplan – p306 E3
Stadsgården – p310 K8
Stadsgårdshamnen – p311 K9
Stadsgårdsleden – p303 K8, p310 K8, p311 K8-9/L10
Stadshusbron – p302 H6, p303 H6
Stallgatan – p303 G8
Starrängsringen – p308 C9-10
Stigbergsgatan – p311 L9-10
Stora Mejtens Gränd – p311 M10
Stora Nygatan – p303 J7
Storängskroken – p308 A10
Storängsvägen – p308 A9-10/B10
Storgatan – p304 F9-10/G11
Storkyrkobrinken – p303 H7
Storskärsgatan – p309 D11
Stortorget – p303 J7/8
Strandvägen – p304 G9-11
Strindbergsgatan – p308 D10
Strindbergsgatan – p309 D1-11
Strömbron – p303 H8/G8
Strömgatan – p303 H7/G8
Studentbacken – p309 B11
Sturegatan – p308 E8/D8
Stureparken – p308 D8
Stureplan – p303 F8
Styrmansgatan – p304 G9/F9-10/E10
Surbrunnsgatan – p307 C5-7
Svartensgatan – p310 L8
Svartmangatan – p303 J8
Svarvargatan – p306 E2
Sveavägen – p303 E6/F7, p307 B5/C5/D6/E6
Svensksundsvägen – p304 J9
Swedenborgsgatan – p310 L7/M7

Taptogatan – p305 E11-12, p309 E11-12
Tavastgatan – p303 K6, p310 K6-7, p303 G8
Teatergatan – p304 G8
Tegelbacken – p303 H6
Tegeluddsvägen – p309 B11-12/C12-13/D13
Tegelviksgatan – p311 N11
Tegnérgatan – p302 E5, p307 E5-6/D6-7
Tegnérlunden – p307 E5
Teknikringen – p308 B7-8
Teknologgatan – p307 E5
Tengdalsgatan – p311 N11
Terminalslingan – p302 G5
Tideliusgatan – p310 M7/N7
Timmermansgatan – p303 K6, p310 K6/L6
Timotejgatan – p310 N7
Tjärhovsgatan – p310 L8, p311 L8-9
Tjurbergsgatan – p310 M8/N8
Tjustgatan – p310 M7
Tobaksspinnargatan – p301 K2/L2
Tomtebodagatan – p306 D2-3
Torkel Knutssonsgatan – p303 K6, p310 K6/L6
Torkhusvägen – p311 O11
Tors Plan – p306 C3
Torsgatan – p302 E4/F5, p306 C3/D3/E3-4
Torsgränd – p306 E4
Torstenssonsgatan – p304 G10/F10
Trålgränd – p311 O9
Trångsund – p303 J7
Träskportsvägen – p308 C8/B8
Tredje Bassängvägen – p309 C13/B13
Trekantsvägen – p301 L1/M1
Trollhättevägen – p309 A10
Troppstigen – p309 B11
Tulegatan – p307 C6/D6
Tullgårdsgatan – p311 O9
Tullgränd – p303 J8
Tunnelgatan – p303 E6-7, p307 E7
Tyghusplan – p304 H9
Tyrgatan – p307 C7
Tyska Brinken – p303 J7
Tyskbagargatan – p308 E9
Tystagatan – p309 E10-11

Uggleängsvägen – p307 A7, p308 A7-8
Uggleviksgatan – p307 C7/D7, p308 A8-9
Uggleviksvägen – p308 C7
Ulrikagatan – p304 F11
Untravägen – p309 A10-11
Upplandsgatan – p306 B4/C4/D4, p307 D5/E5
Urvädersgränd – p310 K8

Valhallavägen – p305 E12/F12, p307 B6-7/C7, p308 C7-8/D9-10, p309 E11-13
Valmundsvägen – p305 H14
Vanadisplan – p306 C3
Vanadisvägen – p306 C4, p307 C5/B5
Väpnargatan – p303 F8/G9, p304 G9
Väringgatan – p306 D2-3
Värtavägen – p309 E10/D11/C11-12/B12
Varvsgatan – p301 K3/L3
Vasabron – p303 H7
Vasagatan – p302 F6, p303 G6
Vasaplan – p302 G6
Västeråsgatan – p306 C4
Västerbron – p301 J2
Västerlånggatan – p303 J7-8
Västgötagatan – p310 M8
Västgötagränd – p310 L7/M7
Västmannagatan – p306 C4/D4, p307 D5/E5
Västra Brobänken – p304 H9/J9
Västra Trädgårdsgatan – p303 G7
Vattugatan – p303 G7
Vegagatan – p307 D5
Verdandigatan – p307 C7
Verkstadsgatan – p301 L2
Vetegatan – p310 N7/O7
Vickergatan – p310 N6/O6
Vidargatan – p307 C5
Vikingagatan – p306 D2-3
Villagatan – p308 D8
Vindragarvägen – p301 K1
Vintertullstorget – p311 N10
Völundsgatan – p306 E3
Vulcanusgatan – p306 E3

Wahrendorffsgatan – p303 G8
Wallingatan – p302 E6/F5, p307 E6
Wargentinsgatan – p302 G4/F4
Wenströmsvägen – p309 A11
Wittstocksgatan – p309 E11
Wollmar Yxkullsgatan – p310 L5-L7
Wrangelskabacken – p303 J6-7

Ynglingagatan – p306 B4
Yttersta Tvärgränd – p301 K5, p302 K5
Yttre Hamnpirskajen – p309 B13/A13
Yxsmedsgränd – p303 J7

Zinkens Väg – p301 L4-5

Stockholm
Tunnelbana • Metro • U-Bahn

- Hässelby-Farsta/Hagsätra/Skarpnäck
- Mörby centrum/Ropsten-Fruängen/Norsborg
- Akalla/Hjulsta-Kungsträdgården

Hjulsta
Tensta
Rinkeby
Rissne
Duvbo
Sundbybergs centrum
Vreten
Huvudsta
Akalla
Husby
Kista
Hallonbergen
Näckrosen
Solna centrum
Västra skogen
Stadshagen
S:t Eriksplan
Odenplan
Rådmans-gatan
Hö-torget
Mörby centrum
Danderyds sjukhus
Bergshamra
Universitetet
Tekniska högskolan
Stadion
Ropsten
Gärdet
Karlaplan
Östermalmstorg
T-CENTRALEN/Centralstation
Kungsträdgården
Gamla stan
Slussen
Medborgarplatsen
Skanstull
Gullmarsplan
Skärmarbrink
Hammarbyhöjden
Björkhagen
Kärrtorp
Bagarmossen
Skarpnäck
Blåsut
Sandsborg
Skogskyrkogården
Tallkrogen
Gubbängen
Hökarängen
Farsta
Farsta strand
Globen
Enskede gård
Sockenplan
Svedmyra
Stureby
Bandhagen
Högdalen
Rågsved
Hagsätra
Hässelby strand
Hässelby gård
Johannelund
Vällingby
Råcksta
Blackeberg
Islandstorget
Ängbyplan
Åkeshov
Brommaplan
Abrahamsberg
Stora mossen
Alvik
Kristineberg
Thorildsplan
Fridhemsplan
Rådhuset
Liljeholmen
Hornstull
Zinkens-damm
Mariatorget
Mälarhöjden
Bredäng
Sätra
Skärholmen
Vårberg
Vårby gård
Masmo
Fittja
Alby
Hallunda
Norsborg
Axelsberg
Örnsberg
Aspudden
Midsommar-kransen
Telefonplan
Hägerstensåsen
Västertorp
Fruängen

Stockholm Please let us know what you think

Visit Time Out's website at **www.timeout.com**
or email your comments to **guides@timeout.com**

(FIRST EDITION)

About this guide...

1. How useful did you find the following sections?

	Very	Fairly	Not very
In Context	❑	❑	❑
Accommodation	❑	❑	❑
Sightseeing	❑	❑	❑
Eat, Drink, Shop	❑	❑	❑
Arts & Entertainment	❑	❑	❑
Trips Out of Town	❑	❑	❑
Directory	❑	❑	❑
Maps	❑	❑	❑

2. Did you travel to Stockholm...?

Alone ❑ With children ❑
As part of a group ❑ On vacation ❑
On business ❑ To study ❑
With a partner ❑ I live here ❑

3. How long was your trip to Stockholm? (write in)

days

4. Where did you book your trip?

Time Out Classifieds ❑
On the Internet ❑
With a travel agent ❑
Other (write in) ❑

5. Where did you first hear about this guide?

Advertising in *Time Out* magazine ❑
On the Internet ❑
From a travel agent ❑
Other (write in)

6. Is there anything you'd like us to cover in greater depth?

7. Are there any places that should/should not* be included in the guide? (*delete as necessary)

8. How many other people have used this guide?

none❑ 1❑ 2❑ 3❑ 4❑ 5+❑

9. What city or country would you like to visit next? (write in)

About other Time Out publications...

10. Have you ever bought/used *Time Out* magazine?

Yes ❑ No ❑

11. Have you ever bought/used any other Time Out City Guides?

Yes ❑ No ❑

If yes, which ones?

12. Have you ever bought/used other Time Out publications?

Yes ❑ No ❑

If yes, which ones?

About you...

13. Title (Mr, Ms etc):

First name:

Surname:

Address:

Postcode:

Email:

Nationality:

14. Date of birth: ❑❑/❑❑/❑❑

15. Sex: male ❑ female ❑

16. Are you...?

Single ❑
Married/Living with partner ❑

17. What is your occupation?

18. At the moment do you earn...?

under £15,000 ❑
over £15,000 and up to £19,999 ❑
over £20,000 and up to £24,999 ❑
over £25,000 and up to £39,999 ❑
over £40,000 and up to £49,999 ❑
over £50,000 ❑

❑ Please tick here if you'd like to hear about offers and discounts from Time Out and relevant companies.

Time Out Guides
FREEPOST 20 (WC3187)
LONDON
W1E 0DQ